G000143899

EUROPE'S
NEW SECURITY
CHALLENGES

EUROPE'S NEW SECURITY CHALLENGES

edited by
Heinz Gärtner
Adrian Hyde-Price
Erich Reiter

LYNNE
RIENNER
PUBLISHERS

BOULDER
LONDON

Published in the United States of America in 2001 by
Lynne Rienner Publishers, Inc.
1800 30th Street, Boulder, Colorado 80301
www.rienner.com

and in the United Kingdom by
Lynne Rienner Publishers, Inc.
3 Henrietta Street, Covent Garden, London WC2E 8LU

Library of Congress Cataloging-in-Publication Data
Europe's new security challenges / edited by Heinz Gärtner, Adrian Hyde-Price, and Erich
Reiter.
   p. cm.
  Includes bibliographical references and index.
  ISBN 1-55587-905-5 (hc. : alk. paper) — ISBN 1-55587-930-6 (pbk. : alk. paper)
  1. National security—Europe. 2. Europe—Defenses. I. Gärtner, Heinz. II. Hyde-Price,
Adrian G. V. III. Reiter, Erich, 1944–

UA646.E9447 2000
355'.03304—dc21

                                        00-042550

British Cataloguing in Publication Data
A Cataloguing in Publication record for this book
is available from the British Library.

Printed and bound in the United States of America

The paper used in this publication meets the requirements
of the American National Standard for Permanence of
Paper for Printed Library Materials Z39.48-1984.

5 4 3 2 1

Contents

PART 5: THE ROLE OF MAJOR POWERS

Preface

The book is the result of a cooperative venture undertaken by the Bureau for Military Scientific Studies, the Austrian Institute for International Affairs, and the Austrian Defense Academy. It is focused around two major concerns. The first is the empirical concern with the nature of, and policy responses to, the new security agenda in Europe and the wider international system. The second is an intellectual and theoretical concern with the future development of security studies as an academic discipline. A primary motive for publishing the book was our conviction that security studies urgently needs to further develop—or even perhaps fundamentally rethink—its conceptual and analytical tools. Such a conceptual retooling of security studies has become necessary because of four historic developments: the end of Cold War bipolarity; global political and economic transformations; the European integration process, institutionally embodied in the European Union; and the new challenges facing European security institutions such as the North Atlantic Treaty Organization (NATO) and the Organization for Security and Cooperation in Europe (OSCE).

The contributors to this volume come from across the Euro-Atlantic community and include policymakers and advisers as well as academics. This mix ensured that the book's agenda remained focused on the need for theoretically informed, empirically grounded, and policy-relevant studies of contemporary security. The academic authors are drawn from several disciplines and subdisciplines, including international relations, area studies, political economy, history, strategic studies, and political sociology. This interdisciplinary approach lends an innovative perspective that is reflected in the willingness of many contributors to move beyond the dichotomies and disciplinary boundaries that traditionally dominate academic and policy thinking.

The authors were able to meet to discuss the contours of post–Cold War European security and present their individual analyses on two occasions in Vienna. The first was a workshop at the Austrian Defense Academy on 3–4

April 1998. The second was a panel at the Third Pan-European International
Relations Conference and Joint Meeting with the International Studies
Association on 16–19 September 1998. The authors were then able to rethink
and revise their contributions, particularly in light of Operation Allied Force
in Spring 1999.

We want to thank the three organizing institutes for their generous support and, in particular, Otmar Höll and Ernest König. In addition, the editors
thank the Bureau for Military Scientific Studies for its financial support and
the Austrian Institute for International Affairs for its administrative support.
We are also very grateful for the research assistance of Thomas Pankratz and
the administrative support of Angelika Theurl.

—*The Editors*

1

Introduction

HEINZ GÄRTNER AND ADRIAN HYDE-PRICE

One of the central controversies among academics and policymakers is the nature and significance of security in the post–Cold War world. For much of the Cold War the concept of security was largely defined in military terms. Thus the main focus of investigation for academics and policymakers tended to be the military capabilities required by states to address perceived outside threats. More recently, however, the idea of security has been broadened to include politics, economics, society, the environment, as well as aspects of the military. The state-centrism of traditional security studies has also been questioned: much of the debate now revolves around the question, Security for whom? and more attention has been paid to security risks facing individuals and minority groups (especially national and ethnic minorities). The purpose of this volume is to explore the new post–Cold War security agenda and to examine future security challenges facing Europe and the international system. It will also assess the relevance and utility of different actors and instruments for tackling these new security challenges and examine the options for the future institutional development of European security.

TRADITIONAL UNDERSTANDINGS OF SECURITY

For much of the Cold War and before, security was primarily defined in military terms and concerned primarily with the national security of the territorial state. In the absence of a legitimate international authority—in other words, in an anarchical international system—states were seen as responsible for their own security. The only reliable means perceived to guarantee security was military power. For smaller states, this necessitated alliances with or security guarantees from larger powers or groups of states. For the great powers, the balance of power was seen as a key mechanism for providing security in a multipolar international system, with power being defined in terms of military capabilities.[1] In this context, security was defined as the absence of threat or the capability to deter threat.

Along with the balance of power, a key concept of traditional security thinking has been the security dilemma. Robert Jervis defines this as a situation in which "the means by which a state tries to increase its security decrease the security of others."[2] The existence of a security dilemma, it is argued, means that when states arm themselves (even for self-defense) they weaken the security of neighbors by shifting the military balance in their favor. Neighbors will therefore feel compelled to increase their military capabilities to restore equilibrium.

Therefore traditional security thinking has located security at the intersection of threats and capabilities. When threats exceed capabilities, it is argued, states become inviting victims; when capabilities exceed threats, a classic security dilemma ensues. Capabilities are resources actors use to pursue desired outcomes. Security is a universally desired outcome, and capabilities are used to deter threats (with counterthreats) or to defeat those who try to carry out such threats.

Traditional security thinking dominated the Cold War. Increasing military capability was the primary strategy adopted to achieve security. The result, however, was a steadily growing security dilemma. With the end of the Cold War, there is much greater awareness that states should seek to balance threats and capabilities rather than try to exceed the military strength of potential adversaries. As Daniel Nelson points out (see Chapter 17), this wider perspective of security challenges should allow states to achieve security by threat abatement instead of capacity enhancement.

The Cold War concept of security held that if the probability of defeat in war for a state is zero, then that state is perfectly secure regardless of the probability of war. Even if a state is constantly under attack and would be wiped out if defeated, if a state is powerful enough to fend off all comers it enjoys perfect security. Hence traditional Cold War concepts of security emphasized that lowering one's probability of defeat by increasing one's military power made for greater security. The lower the probabilities of war and defeat, the higher the level of security. In the more benign security environment since the end of the Cold War, major war between the great powers is much less likely. Hence military buildups offer less of a security boost than they did in the more threatening Cold War environment in which war was more likely and could have led to the physical annihilation of the losers.

Increases in military power can increase security by lowering the possibility of defeat, but this can also be accomplished by lowering the probability of war through strategies of international reassurance and cooperation. Indeed, spiral theorists often argue that military preparations, although lowering the probability of defeat, may raise the probability of war by provoking the other side—hence nullifying their security effects.[3]

With the demise of the East-West conflict, much of the discussion on a future European security architecture has stressed the need to go beyond the traditional Cold War focus on military power and national territorial defense. The dominant concern has been to develop new structures and relations that avoid realpolitik approaches to security and reduce the possibilities for the emergence of new security dilemmas. Debates on new European security arrangements have therefore tended to stress the need for any new system to promote cooperation among members; facilitate communication and provide information; develop common principles, norms, and rules; constrain aggressive behavior; and provide a basis for collective action, conflict prevention, crisis management, and the peaceful resolution of disputes.[4]

Given these concerns, the security debate has moved away from its preoccupation with realist approaches to international relations and focused more on other approaches developed in the postwar period. One such approach is liberal institutionalism. Advocates of this approach accept many of the central tenets of realism, particularly the anarchical nature of the international system and the prevalence of power politics. Nevertheless, they believe that international institutions can facilitate cooperation between states, thereby modifying the operation of the security dilemma. They also contend that institutions can have an interactive effect, which means that their impact on outcomes varies depending on the nature of power and interests.[5]

Another more fundamental challenge to realist thinking was defined by Karl Deutsch and his colleagues. Their work on the concept of a security community has proven very influential and has recently been developed by several scholars, including Emanuel Adler and Michael Barnett.[6] According to Deutsch,

> A *security community* is a group of people that has become "integrated." By integration we mean the attainment, within a territory, of a "sense of community" and of institutions and practices strong and widespread enough to assure . . . dependable expectations of "peaceful change" among its population. By sense of community we mean a belief . . . that common social problems must and can be resolved by processes of peaceful change [that is, the] assurance that members will not fight each other physically, but will settle their disputes in some other way.[7]

A *security community* involves not only the absence of war but, more important, the absence of the military option in the interactions of states within the security community. In *pluralistic security communities*[8] such conditions can hold even among a set of independent, nonamalgamated states. The conditions for these security communities are: compatible values for the member states; that states must be relevant to each other and mutually responsive (criteria can be assessed by the level of communication, consultation, and transaction); and shared identity.

These conditions should provide enough assurance for states not to fight each other. Institutional structures should be added, and of course political differences among the member states are possible. Pluralistic security communities need not have formal intergovernmental machinery, though at a minimum all offer easy access to one another's decisionmaking processes, and typically they have mechanisms for routine consultation. For such security communities, no strategic ties or formal alliances are necessary. This model of a pluralistic security community suggests that national sovereignty over security and defense need not pose any obstacle to the emergence of an integrated community.

At the same time, security communities will have global connections and are affected by security risks and challenges in the wider international system: "Rightly understood, the self-interest of the West-centric states and peoples advises them to cope with conflict beyond their immediate borders if for no other reason than their long-term security, material welfare, and open, democratic ways of life depend on the progressive development of a global security community."[9]

COMPREHENSIVE SECURITY

One of the key themes to emerge from the post–Cold War debate on the nature of security has been the need to go beyond traditional understandings of security. Traditional approaches to security, particularly those grounded in the realist school, are increasingly seen as inadequate to deal with the new security agenda. The nature of international security is undergoing dramatic developments. It is becoming much more complex, which in turn necessitates a more conceptually sophisticated set of analytical tools.

Above all it is necessary to develop a broader and more comprehensive approach to security. Future security challenges will not primarily concern territorial defense. Although states will continue to pay attention to territorial defense, other security challenges are likely to demand greater attention in the future. Human rights, environmental degradation, political stability and democracy, social issues, cultural and religious identity, and immigration are issues that are becoming ever more important for security and conflict prevention. The concept of *societal security* has been proposed as a means to understand the importance of political identity for security, particularly ethnonational identity. Indeed, in much of Europe the threats to societal identity have become as important—if not more so—than traditional military concerns.

In the contemporary international system, threats and vulnerabilities can emerge in many different areas. The nonmilitary dimension of security has always been important, but it is increasingly so now that the East-West conflict has ended. However, this raises difficulties for academics and analysts of security. The key problem is to define clear criteria for specifying what is, and what is not, a security problem.[10] If this is not done, then an expanded definition of security will lose its intellectual coherence.[11] The increasing importance of the nonmilitary dimension of security poses a serious obstacle to security studies remaining an analytically rigorous discipline.

Yet the array of military, political, societal, economic, and ecological risks and challenges does not constitute a static agenda for national security. Indeed, the dramatic changes in priority among them are the driving force behind the shift from the narrow military agenda of strategic studies to the broader one of international security studies. Military threats still retain a central theoretical role in much security thinking, and so long as international politics remains an "anarchical society"[12] it will remain of vital interest and importance for many states. But increasingly, especially for the most developed states in the global system, their importance is declining relative to nonmilitary risks and challenges. This is particularly so given that worries about military security have traditionally masked underlying issues in politics and society.[13]

During the Cold War, the military dimension dominated all the other dimensions of security. Bipolarity, the balance of power, deterrence, and compellence were regarded by decisionmakers on both sides of the Iron Curtain as more important security concerns than cultural identity, the legitimacy of political systems, and economic and ecological survival. With the end of the Cold War, however, other risks and challenges have come to the fore, along with some new existential threats. Some of these reflect several dimensions of security.

Some of the most challenging security issues today are proliferation of weapons of mass destruction, humanitarian crises, and the disruption of world energy supplies. Many contemporary security problems affect U.S. as well as European interests: social tensions; religious extremism in North Africa and the Maghreb; arms exports to the Middle East (which account for nearly half of total world exports); rogue states (such as North Korea or Iraq); ethnic hatred in the Balkans; nationalist and religious rivalries in the Transcaucasus region and elsewhere; and so on.[14] Future wars could grow out of any number of explosive factors: economic difficulties, water shortages, religious fanaticism, mass migration. The Mediterranean is a particularly sensitive region. It supports the world's busiest shipping lanes (including oil and commercial goods); therefore a major conflict there—triggered by conflicts over territory, ethnic or religious conflicts, or political unrest—would have serious consequences for the health and stability of the global economic and political system.

Tackling this changing security agenda necessitates new instruments and strategies. In the *military* sector, new crisis management instruments are required, including traditional peacekeeping, humanitarian intervention, and disaster relief, along with peace-enforcement and peace-support operations. Many of these instruments will be employed for the defense of common interests rather than for the protection of vital national interests against outside threats. At the same time, the prevention of conflicts, crisis management, peacekeeping, and peace-support operations require more rapid, efficient, and collective responses than in the past. This in turn means that traditional military strategies will be less and less relevant to managing the new security agenda.

In the *political* sector, the existence of the state itself may be threatened. The contemporary security agenda is more and more concerned with intrastate, rather than interstate, conflict. This has emerged as a major issue in the post–Cold War world and is a theme that is extensively explored in this volume. The main security threat to many states is not externally derived; rather it comes from anarchy within states. Today ethnonational tensions no longer tend to generate major interstate conflicts—as was the case with, for example, the wars of German and Italian unification and in the interwar period in Europe. Instead, ethnonational tensions tend to threaten the internal coherence of states or are used by ethnically defined state elites against minority groups within their borders. Nationalism can emerge when state boundaries do not coincide with national boundaries. Hence the main enemy of the principle of ethnicity and nationalism appears to be the state, which is seen as the major obstacle to achieving a homogeneous nation. As a consequence, conflicts emerge over borders, territories (most of the time both sides claim historical rights), and minorities (within or outside of the respective state). Many conflicts have therefore shifted from interstate to intrastate levels. A key security problem has thus become the threat posed by ethnonationalism to democratic statehood.

This theme has been examined by several scholars. Among them, Barry Buzan has distinguished between weak and strong states. States in which society and government are at odds are weak states; states that are coherent in sociopolitical terms are strong. "Reducing contradictions between the states and societal security is thus a precondition for successful 'national' security policy."[15] In a similar vein, K. J. Holsti has argued that war has not declined in our time; rather, its locus has changed. We live in an age of internal wars;

wars within states—as opposed to wars between states—now present the greatest threat to international stability. This fact, Holsti asserts, means that most of our traditional thinking about how to deal with the problem of war is irrelevant. He terms such internal conflicts *wars of the third kind* in order to distinguish them from the limited interstate wars of the eighteenth century and the total wars of the first half of the twentieth century. Wars of the third kind are usually long wars of attrition and fought with a vicious mixture of guerrilla tactics and terrorism. They obliterate the distinction between combatants and noncombatants, devastate communities, produce high casualty rates and waves of refugees, and exacerbate seemingly irreconcilable differences. They are not fought over territory per se but over issues of statehood and relations among communities within states. Holsti maintains that such wars will continue to persist in weak states; that most recently formed states are weak states; and that such states are weak because they have been formed out of such wars. Holsti's cure for the problem is to construct internally strong states. He equates internal strength with a state's capacity to obtain domestic political legitimacy.[16]

As regards the societal sector, certain collective identities, such as nationality and ethnicity, can come into conflict with stability in the political sector. If a society is dominated by divisive ethnic and national cleavages, then the gap between society and the state will widen and the state will be weakened, particularly if the state itself is not ethnically homogeneous. If national identities remain, what becomes of the state?[17] Will it become less significant within a European federation?

Perhaps the key to domestic political legitimacy and stability—and therefore to international security as well—is civic rather than ethnic nationalism. Only with a society based on strong political identity (i.e., citizenship),[18] and not on ethnic origin, can society and state be reconciled. Ethnonational identity should not be conceptualized as part of statehood (as suggested by the notion of societal security). To defend democratic forms of statehood it is necessary to denationalize and de-ethnicize the concept of the state. The state should be defined on civic grounds rather than by reference to the ethnically based nation. It should not matter that the boundaries of states and nations do not coincide. Indeed, there is no convincing reason why people who speak the same language or belong to the same ethnic group should belong to the same state—as the separate existence of Austria and Germany illustrates. If nations are "imagined communities" (to use Benedict Anderson's phrase), if they are an instrument to forge political loyalty rather than an enduring characteristic of human nature, then it should be possible to separate nationhood from the concept of the state. Nationality and ethnic identity could then become a private matter, like religion. Indeed, the parallel to religion is instructive. For centuries, religion was tied to the state; eventually, however, the secular state has come to prevail, at least in Western societies, and religious belief has become a matter of personal conscience.

A POSTMODERN WORLD?

A crucial issue facing international security studies is the implications of the globalization process for the future security agenda. What happens, for example, if globalization results in the steady dissolution of states, as many postmodernists predict? This question has been widely discussed and debated by a variety of academics. Hedley Bull, for example, wrote of the possibility of a neomedieval international system emerging as a replacement to the Westphalian state's system, characterized by "overlapping authority and multiple loyalties." In such a system, he suggested, states would come to share their authority with "other associations."[19] For Bull, such a neomedieval order would tend to be less stable than the existing state system. Barry Buzan, in contrast, argues that the international society of states does not contradict world society, which is based on individuals, nonstate organizations, and the population as a whole as functionally differentiated actors with shared identities. Buzan argues that they are symbiotic and complementary.[20]

The theme of the changing character of international relations and, by implication, of international security is addressed by a broad range of scholars. Andrew Moravcsik, for example, sees individuals and privately constituted groups as fundamental actors in world politics; governments constitute a subset of domestic social actors.[21] For Mark Zacher, the decay of the Westphalian system of sovereignty and state autonomy is directly related to the increasing level of cooperation among states: states, he argues, "are becoming increasingly enmeshed in a network of collaborative arrangements or regimes."[22] Charles Kegley argues that this process requires the active moral commitment of states to cooperative arrangements: "The voluntary sacrifice of sovereignty for collaborative problem-solving . . . requires states to conceive morally of transnational co-operation as compatible with their national interests."[23] James Rosenau goes one step farther and envisages a multicentric world emerging that "is in sharp contrast to that which prevails in the state-centric world."[24] The number of essential actors would increase to "hundreds of thousands."[25] The state system would eventually give way to a twofold process of "globalization" and "localization," which Rosenau dubs *fragmegration* (from *fragmentation* and *integration*):

> While different sources underlie the operation of fragmegrative dynamics in the political, social, and economic realms, they all contribute to the same major outcome: in each realm the close links between territoriality and the

state are breaking down and thereby posing the question of what constitutes the boundaries of communities.[26]

For Hans-Henrik Holm and Georg Sørensen, the intensification of economic, political, social, and cultural relations across borders is resulting in a process of "uneven globalization." However, they stress the active role played by the state in this process.[27] Michael Zürn, in contrast, looks at the other side of the coin and speaks of "uneven denationalization." For Zürn, this results from the weakening of the state through globalization and the presence or emergence of "strong societies."[28] Robert Cox sees in these developments greater opportunities for social movements:

> Moreover, the changes taking place in states [diminished importance] give new opportunities for self-expression by nationalities that have no state of their own, in movements for separation or autonomy; and the same tendencies encourage ethnicities and religiously defined groups that straddle state boundaries to express their identities in global politics. . . . Social movements like environmentalism, feminism, and the peace movement transcend territorial boundaries. Transnational co-operation among indigenous peoples enhances their force within particular states.[29]

If statehood is dissolved by globalization and the emergence of a postmodern form of nonterritorial politics, however, it is by no means clear that this would provide more global security, order, or justice. The disappearance of the state may not lead to the emergence of a society of overlapping, and more or less equal, authorities and actors with shared identities and common interests. On the contrary, it could lead to new forms of hierarchy and hegemony. If the boundaries of the territorial state are dissolved through fragmegration processes, they may well be replaced by borders based on ethnicity, nationalism, cultural divisions, and language. The weakening of existing state structures might therefore lead to a proliferation of national identities based on ethnicity, rather than to equal rights for all individuals or societal collectivities. In much of Europe and the developed world today, democracy has flourished within the framework of the territorial state: its demise might therefore lead to demise of democratic political structures as well.

In conclusion, therefore, the deepening of the processes associated with globalization poses important questions for the future of international security. Some suggest that the existence of strong states—that is, democratic states with effective governmental and administrative structures enjoying widespread domestic political legitimacy and based on social market economies—is essential for tackling many of the transnational and nontraditional security problems that dominate the contemporary international agenda. Others have argued that globalization makes both possible and necessary the emergence of new forms of so-called cosmopolitan democracy.[30] What is certainly true is that globalization and the transformation of statehood that it entails will have far-reaching—and as yet only partially explored—consequences for European and international security.

AIMS AND OBJECTIVES

This edited volume focuses on two major concerns: first, an empirical and analytical concern with the nature of, and policy responses to, the new security agenda; second, an intellectual and theoretical concern with the future development of security studies as an academic discipline. A key motive for publishing this book was the conviction that security studies urgently needs to further develop—if not to fundamentally rethink—its conceptual and analytical tools. Such a conceptual retooling of security studies has become necessary because of three historic developments: the end of Cold War bipolarity; the broadening and deepening of the European integration process, institutionally embodied in the European Union; and the uneven impact of the deep-seated and far-reaching processes of globalization and regionalization. Taken together, these three historic developments are reshaping the structural dynamics of the global system, with profound implications for international security.

The strength of this volume, we believe, is the diversity and breadth of knowledge of its contributors. The authors come from across the Euro-Atlantic community and include policymakers and advisers alongside academics. Two meetings were held to discuss the individual chapters, and the mix of academics and policymakers helped ensure that the book as a whole provides a theoretically informed, empirically grounded, and policy-relevant approach to the study of security. The academics come from a variety of disciplines and scholarly backgrounds—including international relations, area studies, political economy, history, strategic studies, and political sociology—providing a multidisciplinary perspective on security.

ACADEMIC AND ANALYTICAL CONCERNS

The conceptual starting point for the book is the new range of security problems and issues dominating the international security agenda. Many of these are nonmilitary in character and derive from intrastate tensions. This has proved a significant challenge to orthodox postwar security analyses, which have traditionally focused almost exclusively on the problem of interstate war. Consequently, many of the chapters of this book take as a point of reference the notion of comprehensive security. Although considerable work needs to be done in order to flesh out and define this concept, it does provide a point of departure for the debate contained in this book. Above all, it reflects a widely shared belief that the traditional state-centric and military-focused concept of security is no longer adequate for addressing the new range of security risks and challenges.

The changed post–Cold War security agenda has thus raised serious questions about traditional ways of conceptualizing security. Much academic analysis has tended to be channeled along disciplinary boundaries: this is particularly inappropriate given the multiplicity and multidimensionality of the new security challenges. At the same time, much intellectual thinking is patterned by binary opposites: this is certainly the case for traditional security studies, which has tended to think in terms of war versus peace, conflict versus cooperation, hard versus soft security, state versus society, and so on. This book, however, seeks to avoid dichotomous thinking. Instead, many of the chapters adopt a more nuanced approach and seek to explore the areas of ambiguity and complexity between war and peace, for example, or between hard and soft security.

OVERVIEW OF THE BOOK

The central theme of this book is the need for conceptual retooling and fresh thinking among the security studies community. Thus many authors are concerned with exploring the new security agenda in terms of the new constellation of risks and challenges that constitute it, as well as in terms of the broader range of instruments and institutional structures available to policymakers. Most of our contributors also seek to go beyond a traditional realist focus on the military dimension of state security.

In order to provide a clearer guide to the themes and issues explored in these pages, this book is structured into five parts. Part 1 deals with conceptual issues in the contemporary security studies debate. Part 2 focuses on European security. The central theme here is Europe's changing institutional architecture, in particular the enlargement and evolving role of NATO and the EU. Although these two Euro-Atlantic organizations are clearly the best-resourced and most influential multilateral bodies in Europe, an important role in Europe's security architecture is also played by the Organization for Security and Cooperation in Europe (OSCE). The contribution and potentiality of the OSCE is often overlooked in discussions on European security, given the attention given to NATO and the EU. Consequently, Part 3 is devoted specifically to exploring the nature and impact of the OSCE on Europe. Part 4 addresses regional security issues, from the problems of security management and peace operations in a regional context to the specific regional security concerns of the Baltic Sea area and Central Asia. Part 5 considers the role of the major powers in global security. Despite the emergence of multilateral structures and the impact of globalization on patterns of complex inter-dependence, global security is still very much affected by the policies and preferences of major international actors. In Part 5, particular attention is paid to the United States, Russia, and China.

Part 1, on the conceptual framework of security studies, begins with Chapter 2 by Adrian Hyde-Price. It takes the metaphor of the Jabberwock (a mythical creature from a poem by Lewis Carroll) as its starting point for a series of reflections on the demands facing contemporary security studies. Hyde-Price calls for a third way for security studies that avoids both the limitations of traditional realist approaches to national security and the dangers of indiscriminate broadening of the concept of security. He argues that the central task facing security studies in the twenty-first century is delineating the boundaries of a broadened concept of security. He also suggests that security studies is concerned with both the causes of violent conflict and the conditions of peace, and it must therefore engage with the agendas of Clausewitz, Metternich, and Kant.

These conceptual reflections are followed by Walter C. Clemens Jr. (Chapter 3). Complexity theory modifies Darwin's emphasis on natural selection as the key to evolution and portrays fitness "as an ability to cope with complexity, a capacity to survive challenges and make the most of opportunity." Clemens argues that despite the utility of complexity theory for thinking about European security, it is rather general and cannot prescribe how to strengthen the system or forecast how it will evolve. He therefore suggests that it should be linked to other approaches to international relations, in particular the insights of Immanuel Kant on shaping the conditions for peace; the model of complex interdependence; and analysis of value-creating versus value-claiming in European affairs.

These two chapters address the task of rethinking conceptual approaches to the study of European security. Chapter 4 by David Robertson focuses on a more specific conceptual question: how to conceptualize the role of ground forces—particularly infantry—in the context of a changed security agenda. Robertson develops a post-Clausewitzian approach to military theory. His concern is to explore the role of soldiers in military operations other than war. His central argument is that ground forces, despite the revolution in military affairs, will continue to have an important role—perhaps an ever greater role—in addressing many of the new security concerns in the post–Cold War world. Nonetheless, he argues, soldiers will operate under very different political, societal, and technological conditions than in the past. In light of the Kosovo campaign, Robertson's arguments provide an important corrective to those who argue that airpower alone provides a viable instrument of military crisis management.

Jan Willem Honig in Chapter 5 is concerned with the nature and significance of the new security agenda facing Western democracies. He begins with an overview of some of the recent literature seeking to understand the new types of conflicts that have emerged after the end of the Cold War. A growing consensus is that conflict is moving beyond the control of the state. Honig also notes that much of this new literature emphasizes the sociocultural dimensions of war and conflict rather than focusing on the specific dynamics of the international system. Honig's approach is to eschew developing a grand theory of new conflicts, offering instead a more empirical and pragmatic approach that includes some practical responses to contemporary conflicts. His argument is premised on two assumptions: first, that force in contemporary conflicts is a means to an end, rather than simply an irrational and primordial act; and second, that the West needs to respond to all types of conflict by developing a concept of limited war. The bulk of Chapter 5 consists of a clear exposition and analysis of different types of conflict, from interstate wars and rogue-state wars, to terrorism and ethnic conflict. He concludes that none of the conflicts in the post–Cold War world poses a fundamental security risk to the West. The greatest challenge to the West is ethnic conflict, where domestic pressure to undertake humanitarian interventions can be expected to grow. Honig stresses that in dealing with ethnic conflict the West needs to avoid the trap of moral absolutism and to recognize that effective intervention demands political flexibility and compromise with unsavory regimes. On the military side, he suggests, Western military establishments will have to learn to achieve limited objectives with limited force, rather than relying on doctrines of overwhelming force.

Chapters 6–9 in Part 2 address various aspects of European security. In Chapter 6, Alpo Rusi considers the global role of the European Union in the international system. He argues that the EU is a new kind of actor in world politics—primarily a civilian power, but one that is increasingly obliged to assume a more political role as a result of its forthcoming enlargement and the creation of the euro. In particular, he emphasizes the importance of the euro as a factor that will strengthen the EU's collective identity as an economic actor in global affairs. In this way, he suggests, the development of the EU will contribute to the emergence of a new system of international order based on emergent trading areas, rather than nation-states as such. He also argues that the EU will be a global actor in the following areas: environmental protection, development policy, the Common Foreign and Security Policy (CFSP), and the liberalization of trade and investment regimes.

In Chapter 7, Heinz Gärtner addresses an issue that has become central to the European security agenda over recent years—namely, how best to organize and conduct European crisis-management and peacekeeping operations. Crisis management, he notes, has become the cornerstone of the post–Cold War system of international security. Gärtner's primary concern is to propose a new framework for organizing crisis-management operations that avoids the problems inherent in old Cold War or realist-based security arrangements.

These, he notes, were based on collective defense. A new European security framework, he suggests, must aim to facilitate communication; provide information; develop common principles, norms, and rules; constrain aggressive behavior; and provide a basis for joint actions and conflict prevention, management, and resolution. After reviewing the development of NATO and the EU/WEU (that is, the European Union/Western European Union) in the 1990s, including the Partnership for Peace (PfP) program, the creation of the Euro-Atlantic Partnership Council (EAPC), the definition of the WEU's so-called Petersberg tasks, and the emergence of the Common European Security and Defense Policy within the EU in 1999, he proposes a new common command structure for crisis management. This command structure, he suggests, should deal exclusively with non–Article V operations and would be based both in NATO and the Western European Union (WEU). In effect, it would involve a merger of Petersberg tasks and the PfP. These new command structures would draw on Combined Joint Task Forces assets and could involve both the United States and Europe. The advantages of such command structures, he argues, would be that they would leave NATO and the WEU to concentrate on collective defense; they would allow European neutral and non-aligned states to participate in crisis management on an equal basis; they would be nonthreatening to Russia; and they would provide a mechanism through which the new democracies of Central and Eastern Europe could participate in European security. Such command structures, designed to facilitate multinational cooperation in non–Article V crisis management operations, Gärtner argues, would provide an inclusive security framework capable of addressing the new security agenda of the twenty-first century.

Peter Schmidt in Chapter 8 addresses Europe's security architecture from another perspective. His concern is to assess how well Europe's main security organizations—NATO and the EU/WEU—have coped with the new demands they faced in the 1990s. His particular interest is how the process of institutional enlargement and adaptation upon which these two security providers have embarked will affect the transatlantic relationship. Both NATO and the EU have embarked on a process of opening up to new members from Central and Eastern Europe and have sought to redefine their functions and roles. One growing problem he identifies is the need to coordinate relations between different security organizations. As the experience in the former Yugoslavia has underlined, an important task facing policymakers is ensuring that Europe's many security organizations are interlocking, not interblocking. Schmidt's concern is not to scrutinize in detail the reform efforts of the major institutions but rather to look at the potential problems facing them in the future, particularly in terms of transatlantic relations. In terms of the EU/CFSP/WEU triangle, he posits several future problems: the structural difficulties in acting cohesively, especially in the context of Eastern enlargement; the need for financial restructuring; the continuing uncertainty surrounding the relationship among the EU, the WEU, and the CFSP, particularly given divergences in membership between the EU and the WEU; and the need for the EU/WEU to use NATO assets for future operations. In terms of NATO, he draws attention to four problems: a second round of enlargement; uncertainties surrounding NATO's role and purpose; institutional overload; and the relationship between the Alliance and the EU/WEU. He concludes with a discussion of the need for flexibility in European security and defense cooperation in order to facilitate coalitions of the willing.

In Chapter 9, Heiko Borchert addresses two questions: Where do we stand? and Where should we go? His central argument is that a European security architecture comprising the transatlantic community and the countries of Central and Eastern Europe (including Russia and Ukraine) has to be multilateral in character. Multilateralism provides a way of overcoming the security dilemma and facilitating international cooperation based on expectations of diverse reciprocity. Borchert argues that a durable multilateral security structure must be based on four pillars: democratic peace, institutions, supranational integration, and leadership. His main conclusions are threefold: first, that Europe's security organizations tend to work on the basis of identical core values, such as openness, transparency, reciprocity, and the peaceful resolution of conflicts; second, that Europe's security organizations make a twofold contribution to security and stability—they strengthen the four pillars of multilateralism and influence member states' policies; and third, that a pressing requirement for European security and stability in the future is improved coordination between different policy sectors (i.e., political, economic, military) and functional organizations (OSCE, NATO, EU, WEU). This is particularly important in the context of the dual enlargement of NATO and the EU and will require qualitative shifts in the manner in which governments approach international politics.

Although NATO and the EU are undoubtedly Europe's primary security organizations, there are certain issues and aspects of European security for which they are not well suited and for which other organizations are better equipped. In this respect, the OSCE is an important, but often undervalued, element of Europe's security architecture. Part 3 thus consists of three chapters on the OSCE, beginning with P. Terrence Hopmann's chapter on the OSCE's role in conflict management (Chapter 10). Many of Europe's contemporary security problems, Hopmann notes, derive not from military confrontation between rival states and alliance systems but from ethnonational conflict and the violent disintegration of multinational communist states, namely, the Soviet Union and Yugoslavia. Indeed, the security agenda in Eurasia is dominated by ethnonational conflicts and tensions. Hopmann's concern is to evaluate the explanatory power of realist, liberal, and cognitivist approaches to international relations in the face of the new security agenda in Eurasia, applying these theoretical approaches to an analysis of the OSCE's role in conflict management. Conflict management, Hopmann argues, consists of four distinct categories of activities: conflict prevention through democratization, aimed at promoting the political conditions conducive to the peaceful resolution of disputes; preventive diplomacy, including activities to strengthen the human dimension and intervention by OSCE officials in crisis situations that threaten to escalate to violence; third-party conflict resolution, which usually takes place in the wake of violence; and postconflict security building, which involves rebuilding infrastructure and constructing new political and societal institutions. He argues that the OSCE is particularly well suited to address many of the new security problems in Eurasia and that its potential for conflict management has not been recognized by either security studies analysts or policymakers. The strengths of the OSCE are its promotion of democracy and its flexibility. Nonetheless, he notes that it has been less successful in ending conflicts once they have erupted into violence. He concludes by suggesting that the role of the OSCE can be strengthened by defining a clearer division of labor with other international organizations and by more concerted efforts on the part of political leaders to develop its potential for conflict management.

Walter Kemp in Chapter 11 is concerned with the relationship between political will and public relations in respect to the OSCE. His concern is to understand and explain the reasons for the OSCE's relatively low profile. Is the apparent modesty of the OSCE an excuse, a strategy, or an inherent characteristic? Kemp argues that there are several reasons why the work of the OSCE remains little known beyond a specialized community of academics and policymakers. The first is that promoting comprehensive security is a subtle, long-term, and multifaceted process. Successful preventive diplomacy is often slow and apparently uneventful—Kemp compares it to watching concrete harden. In addition, successful OSCE activities are not always very newsworthy. Telling Humpty-Dumpty to get off a wall in order to prevent an accident is not something that generates much public or media interest. Second, the OSCE is often engaged in obscure and apparently distant lands, which only become newsworthy when violent conflict emerges (as in Nagorno-Karabakh, Kosovo, and Chechnya). Third, compared to the EU, NATO, and the UN, the OSCE is a relatively underresourced organization. Consequently, it has not been able to devote many resources to media promotion and public relations. Fourth, the nature of diplomacy and conflict prevention is that it often works best away from the glare of publicity. The largely unsung achievements of the High Commissioner on National Minorities (HCNM) and the OSCE Missions are due in no small measure to the fact that they have promoted dialogue behind the scenes. This means than many of the successes of the OSCE go unrecognized, whereas its failures receive much greater media attention. Kemp concludes by posing two questions: Should the OSCE's profile be raised? If so, how? His answer is that the impact of the

OSCE on European security would be greater if the organization had a higher profile. This would strengthen its legitimacy and its ability to prevent conflicts and facilitate cooperation. The key to achieving this, he concludes, is better information about the OSCE and a more proactive approach by the organization in informing the press and the public.

Wolfgang Zellner, in Chapter 12, provides a detailed analysis of one of the most important and interesting institutions created within the OSCE since the end of the Cold War: the HCNM. The new security agenda that emerged in the 1990s following the demise of the East-West conflict was dominated by ethnonational conflicts, notably in the Caucasus and the Balkans. The OSCE was one of the first international organizations to create instruments specifically designed to address these new security concerns. Its most important instrument in this regard was the HCNM, created by the Helsinki Summit in 1992. The mandate of the HCNM was to "provide 'early warning' and, as appropriate, 'early action,' at the earliest possible stage in regard to tensions involving national minority issues which have not yet developed beyond an early warning stage, but . . . have the potential to develop into conflict within the Conference on Security and Cooperation in Europe area, affecting peace, stability or relations between participating States." The office of HCNM has been filled since 1992 by Max van der Stoel, a much-respected former Dutch diplomat. Zellner's analysis focuses on four issues. First, he considers the High Commissioner's own views on how to fulfill his mandate, examining his understanding of ethnopolitical categories, the nature of conflict prevention, and the appropriate instruments. Second, he examines the content and tendency of the HCNM's recommendations, focusing on Hungarian minorities in Romania and Slovakia; Russian minorities in Estonia, Latvia, and Ukraine; and the Albanian minority in Macedonia. Third, Zellner evaluates the effectiveness of the High Commissioner's activities. Finally, he outlines a series of recommendations for strengthening the institution of the HCNM.

Part 4 addresses the issue of regional security and comprises four chapters. The assumption underpinning all four is that in the postbipolar international system regional patterns of international relations are growing in importance. Consequently, security analysts need to pay closer attention to the specific regional dynamics of security relations. In Chapter 13, Kari Möttölä's concern is security management in regional contexts, particularly Europe. The concern of security management is an important one that provides a useful conceptual framework within which to understand the changing nature of security relationships in post–Cold War Europe. Möttölä argues that whereas during the Cold War the dominant structural feature of European security was bipolarity, today its dominant feature is regionality. He also argues that post–Cold War European security is not based on collective security but rather on an ad hoc and ambiguous—but nonetheless pragmatic—model of cooperative security. Within this system of cooperative security there remains some competition for influence and status in the construction and management of a cooperative security order. An example of this is the competition between Russia and NATO over Kosovo and Chechnya.

Pertti Joenniemi, in Chapter 14, is a perfect complement to Möttölä. Joenniemi begins by noting that in contemporary Europe security relations are increasingly characterized in terms of cooperative security and are concerned with the political management of security risks and challenges. At the same time, he notes that European security is more and more a function of regionally specific dynamics and developments. A new regionalism has emerged in Europe in which regions have their own logic and emerging subjectivity. Regions are thus evolving as sites of multiple identities and patterns of authority. In this context, the role and function of arms control is undergoing significant change. Traditionally, arms control was embedded in the logic of power politics and the balance of power. Today, however, arms control is linked to other concerns, such as insecurity from below or stabilizing the democratic peace. Arms control agreements have also been developed to cope with specific regional concerns, that is, the arms control dimension of the Dayton Accords. Joenniemi's concern is to explore these multiple logics of arms control by focusing on the Baltic Sea region. He considers the policies and perspectives of the key players, particularly the United States, Russia, the so-called Nordic neutrals, and the three Baltic republics. He concludes by arguing that although regionalism and region building only have a subsidiary role to play in producing security for states at the moment, trends in the contemporary European security system are likely to encourage the development of a spatially new type of arms control. His analysis of the role of arms controls in the Baltic Sea region also provides a fascinating case study illustrating the manner in which different arms control logics are generating a rich mix of old and new, hard security and soft.

In Chapter 15, Erich Reiter provides a timely reminder that while developments in regions such as the Baltic Sea or Mitteleuropa may offer evidence of the emergence of new and more cooperative forms of security management, elsewhere the security environment is much less benign and sanguine. Reiter's focus is Central Asia, his concern to explore the geopolitical implications of developments in this region for European security. He begins by noting that despite the changes that have swept the international system since the late 1980s there is still considerable conceptual inertia and thus a tendency to think in traditional geopolitical categories. Reiter's objective is to encourage new thinking and stimulate the search for new scenarios. He does this by engaging in a mind game drawn from his perception of past and current developments in Central Asia. He begins by suggesting that rather than the East-West conflict simply having ended it may rather have shrunk to a more geographically focused area because of the relative weakness of Russia compared to the former Soviet Union. This reduced geopolitical conflict is now focused on Eastern Europe and the region of Central Asia and the Caspian Sea. At the same time, in Central Asia the old East-West confrontation has expanded to include new actors, above all China but also Turkey, Iraq, Iran, and Afghanistan. Central Asia and the Caspian Sea region is of particular geopolitical importance because of its oil and gas resources, which, coupled with the perceived power vacuum in the region, have created a new set of geopolitical rivalries and ambitions. Reiter considers the traditional perspectives of geopolitical thinkers and assesses the current patterns of bilateral relations that crisscross what is perceived to constitute the geographical center of the "world island." He also explores the linkages between NATO enlargement and geopolitical rivalries in Central Asia, as well as the impact on European security of wider constellations of relations between the great powers outside of the continent. Reiter concludes by noting that the European integration process—with its aspiration to create a Common Foreign and Security Policy and a European Security and Defense Identity—is an important development that will "completely change geopolitics in the Eurasian-African world."

In Chapter 16, Erwin Schmidl addresses an issue that increasingly occupies a central place in discussions on international and European security—the role and significance of peace operations. After the Kosovo war, this is a major theme in security debates. Schmidl's chapter provides a valuable reminder that peace operations were not invented by the UN in 1948 or in 1956 after the Suez crisis. Rather, they developed in the course of the late nineteenth century as one element of deepening international cooperation between the European powers after the Napoleonic Wars. Schmidl distinguishes peace operations from other types of military interventions or war by five criteria: an international mandate or authorization; a multinational force structure; the goal of preserving the status quo or effecting the transition to a new status enjoying international support; acting in the interests of the population concerned; and adhering to the principle of minimum damage or measured force. According to these criteria, the first peace operations were those in Crete (1897–1908) and Albania (1913–1914), followed by several missions carried out under the aegis of the League of Nations in the interwar years (notably the Saarland operation of 1934–1935). Schmidl discusses the ambiguities and difficulties involved in defining the term *peace operations* and argues that talk of a new era of international security management in which the major powers will act to protect the welfare of others without reference to their own national interests is premature. He provides convincing evidence for this view by drawing on postwar experiences of peace operations and argues that there are now three different models for international interventions: the UN approach, involving traditional instruments of peacekeeping; the lead-nation type of multinational intervention; and operations led by regional organizations (such as the Economic Community of West African States in Liberia or Sierra Leone). He concludes by arguing that a century after the

Crete operation there are still fundamental questions surrounding peace operations that remain unresolved and goes on to suggest some ways in which they can be improved in the future.

Part 5 focuses on the role of the major powers. In Chapter 17, Daniel Nelson argues that states—particularly the largest and most powerful—retain a principal role in human affairs not because of their vitality and intrinsic merit but simply because there is yet no clear successor. Nonetheless, states aren't what they used to be, he contends. States now operate in the context of postinternational dynamics that are making borders more permeable, institutions less effective, and political power more diffuse. State institutions continue to function, but with "less efficiency, fewer resources, and reduced legitimacy." However, states remain the "principal organizational unit of human society and a key plane on which global peace and prosperity depend." This is particularly the case for the great powers—the United States, China, Russia, Japan, and the EU.

Nelson's overview of great-power relations in the contemporary international security system is followed by two chapters focusing on two of the most important but enigmatic states in global politics: Russia and China. Gerhard Mangott's chapter on Russia (Chapter 18) provides a detailed and closely argued analysis of a former superpower in a process of decay and decline. He develops the argument that Russia suffers from multifaceted weaknesses and constraints that prohibit it from playing a decisive and influential role in international affairs. Russia has lost both its internal and external empire, and the geopolitical space once occupied by the Soviet Union is now deeply penetrated by external actors, including Western powers, Turkey, Iran, Pakistan, India, China, and Japan. The parameters for Russian foreign, security, and defense policies have been substantially altered, and Russian leaders have been left in considerable geopolitical confusion. Russia is still searching for an inclusive, integrative, postimperial identity, whereas Russia itself is still in a political transition period and is facing serious economic and financial problems. This means that Russia lacks the economic and financial means to pursue confrontational foreign policies. Mangott suggests that Russian foreign policy faces three geopolitical options: reintegration of the post-Soviet space; antihegemonial coalitions and counteralliances; and Western orientation. He concludes by suggesting that Russia, on a purely rational-choice calculation, has no alternative but to cooperate with Western countries. Russia lacks the means and resources to pursue a strategy of confrontation and has no powerful allies with which to conduct an aggressive anti-Western campaign. Most important, Russia remains dependent on Western assistance in modernizing its moribund economic, financial, and social structures. The most likely perspective is thus of a continuation of pragmatic cooperation with the West. Nevertheless, he warns, Russia will for some time remain a "tumbling actor in the international arena, struggling hard to remain [in] a position considered dignified for a power reminiscent of a glorious past."

The final chapter of the book (Chapter 19, by Kay Möller) notes that since the mid-1990s China has been regarded as an emerging new international player. Broadly speaking, the outside view of China is of an authoritarian, but strong and unitary, actor. U.S. policy has been premised on the idea that China's historical opposition to cooperation and interdependence might be diluted through a process of cognitive learning. The United States has thus sought to develop a policy based on constructive engagement. In asking whether China is a great power, a partner, or a chaotic actor, Möller examines China's foreign policy perceptions and policies since the early 1990s. He considers the possibilities for sustained economic growth along with prospects for domestic political stability. He also examines possible alternative power configurations involving China and other global great powers. Möller concludes by arguing that China is not a great power with a global reach. Indeed, it is not even a power with major global interests. Rather, it is a traditional regional player that has increased its foreign policy leeway since the reforms of Deng Xiaoping and the end of the Cold War. However, with economic reform reaching its limits and growth slowing, China's evolution into a dominant regional player, let alone a global actor, becomes increasingly doubtful. Political fragmentation, accompanied by deepening power struggles at all levels and China's cross-border projection, is at least as likely. In this context, he argues, attempts to engage China bilaterally or multilaterally may not be very fruitful. With the return of power politics in East Asia, and growing political and economic problems within China, the prospects for peace and stability in the region are at best uncertain. In this context, he argues, a careful diplomatic balancing act is required, involving a carrot-and-stick strategy centered on the very region where Beijing locates its vital interests. As Möller notes, "carrots and sticks are a feature of any diplomacy, not least of the Chinese variety."

This edited volume provides a thorough and coherent study of contemporary security studies. Although its focus is on the challenges facing the European security system, the issues it addresses are of interest to all concerned with global peace and cooperation. The end of the twentieth century—a "century of extremes," as it has become known[31]—provides an appropriate occasion to reflect on the problems and prospects facing the international community in the post–Cold War era. The editors hope that this volume will provide suitable food for thought for all those interested in the problems of international peace and security in the twenty-first century.

NOTES

1. Michael Sheehan (1996) *The Balance of Power* (London: Routledge).

2. Robert Jervis (1978) "Cooperation Under the Security Dilemma," *World Politics* 30 (January): 76.

3. Andrew Kydd (1997) "Sheep in Sheep's Clothing: Why Security Seekers Do Not Fight Each Other," *Security Studies* 7, no. 1 (Autumn): 114–154.

4. Robert O. Keohane, Joseph S. Nye, and Stanley Hoffmann (eds.) (1993) *After the Cold War: International Relations and State Strategies in Europe, 1989–1991* (Cambridge: Harvard University Press), p. 2.

5. Robert O. Keohane and Lisa L. Martin (1995) "The Promise of Institutionalist Theory," *International Security* 20, no. 1 (Summer): 42.

6. Emanuel Adler and Michael Barnett (eds.) (1998) *Security Communities* (Cambridge: Cambridge University Press).

7. Karl Deutsch et al. (1957) *Political Community and the North Atlantic Area* (Princeton: Princeton University Press), p. 5.

8. Karl Deutsch (1968) *Die Analyse Internationaler Beziehungen* (Frankfurt am Main: Fischer), pp. 272–288.

9. Edward A. Kolodziej and Roger E. Kanet (eds.) (1996) *Coping with Conflict After the Cold War* (Baltimore: Johns Hopkins University Press), p. 390.

10. Barry Buzan, Ole Wæver, and Jaap de Wilde (1998) *Security: A New Framework for Analysis* (Boulder: Lynne Rienner).

11. Stephan Walt (1991) "The Renaissance of Security Studies," *International Security Studies Quarterly* 35, no. 2 (June): 211–237.

12. Hedley Bull (1977) *The Anarchical Society: A Study of Order in World Politics* (London: Macmillan).

13. Barry Buzan (1991) *People, States, and Fear: An Agenda for International Security Studies in the Post–Cold War Era*, 2nd ed. (New York: Harvester-Wheatsheaf), pp. 116–134.

14. David C. Gombert and F. Stephen Larrabee (1997) *America and Europe: A Partnership for a New Era* (Cambridge: Cambridge University Press), p. 237.

15. Barry Buzan (1993) "Societal Security, the State, and Internationalization," in O. Wæver et al. (1993) *Identity, Migration, and the New Security Agenda in Europe* (London: Pinter), p. 57. For the Third World, see K. J. Holtsi (1993) "Armed Conflicts in the Third World: Assessing Analytical Approaches and Anomalies," paper presented at the annual meeting of the International Studies Association, Acapulco, Mexico, March 23–27, 1993.

16. Holsti's state-level prescription for the prevention of intrastate conflict has interesting parallels with a traditional state-level prescription for the prevention of interstate war offered three decades ago by American realist Henry Kissinger. In his work *A World Restored* (Boston: Houghton Mifflin, 1964), Kissinger argued that the key to interstate peace lay in a shared belief by the major powers that the existing international order was legitimate. Holsti's argument follows the same logic, although he substitutes the domestic state for the international system and constituent communities for the major powers. That does not invalidate his argument. Kissinger's notion of legitimacy was based on the degree to which the most powerful members of the system accepted the principles upon which the order of the system was based. Eighteenth-century Europe found itself in a general war when one of its most powerful members, Napoleonic France, did not accept the legitimating principle of an order based on dynastic state regimes. Holsti makes a similar argument at the state level when he emphasizes the importance of "the principle on which the 'right to rule' is based."

17. See Gidon Gottlieb (1993) *Nation Against State: A New Approach to Ethnic Conflicts and the Decline of Sovereignty* (New York: Council on Foreign Relations).

18. On definitions of citizenship, see Rainer Bauböck (1994) "Changing Boundaries of Citizenship: The Inclusion of Immigrants in Democratic Polities," paper prepared for the annual convention of the American Political Science Association, New York, September 1–3, 1994.

19. Bull (1977), pp. 254–255 and 264–276.

20. Barry Buzan (1993) "From International System to International Society: Structural Realism and Regime Theory Meet the English School," *International Organisation* 47, no. 3 (Summer): 327–352.

21. Andrew Moravcsik (1992) *Liberalism and International Relations Theory* (Centre for International Affairs Working Paper, no. 6, July), p. 10.

22. Mark W. Zacher (1992) "The Decaying Pillars of the Westphalian Temple: Implications for International Order and Governance," in James N. Rosenau and Ernst-Otto Czempiel (eds.) (1992) *Governance Without Government: Order and Change in World Politics* (Cambridge: Cambridge University Press), p. 100.

23. Charles Kegely Jr. (1993) "Cold War Myths and the New International Realities: Reconsidering Theoretical Premises," *Österreichische Zeitschrift für Politikwissenschaft* 22, no. 2 (1993), pp. 149ff.

24. James N. Rosenau (1990) *Turbulence in World Politics: A Theory of Change and Continuity* (New York: Harvester-Wheatsheaf), p. 271.

25. Ibid., p. 250.

26. James N. Rosenau (1994) "New Dimensions of Security: The Interaction of Globalization and Localizing Dynamics," *Security Dialogue* 25, no. 3 (September): 255–281.

27. Hans-Henrik Holm and Georg Sørensen (eds.) (1995) *Whose World Order? Uneven Globalisation and the End of the Cold War* (Boulder: Westview).

28. In the context of the argument being presented here, Zürn means "destateiza-tion." See his chapter, "The Challenge of Globalisation and Individualisation: A View from Europe," in Holm and Sørensen (1995) *Whose World Order?* pp. 137–164.

29. Robert W. Cox (1992) "Towards a Post-Hegemonic Conceptualisation of World Order: Reflections on the Relevance of Ibn Khaldun," in Rosenau and Czempiel (eds.) (1992) *Governance Without Government*, p. 144.

30. These issues are clearly debated by Barry Buzan and David Held in Barry Buzan and David Held (1998) "Realism Versus Cosmopolitanism" *Review of International Studies* 24, no. 3 (July): 387–398.

31. Eric Hobsbawn (1994) *Age of Extremes: The Short Twentieth Century, 1914–1991* (London: Michael Joseph).

PART 1

Conceptual
Framework

2

"Beware the Jabberwock!": Security Studies in the Twenty-First Century

ADRIAN HYDE-PRICE

> *'Twas brillig, and the slithy toves*
> *Did gyre and gimble in the wabe;*
> *All mimsy were the borogroves,*
> *And the mome raths outgrabe.*
> *"Beware the Jabberwock, my son!*
> *The jaws that bite, the claws that catch!*
> *Beware the Jubjub bird, and shun*
> *The frumious Bandersnatch!"*
> —Lewis Carroll, "Jabberwocky"

In his magnificent nonsense poem "Jabberwocky," Lewis Carroll invented a new vocabulary to conjure up a strange world of mystery and foreboding centered on the fearsome Jabberwock. The Jabberwock provides an apt metaphor for these reflections on contemporary security. In the post–Cold War world, many security risks and challenges lack the physicality and directness of the East-West conflict, with its clear and present dangers. Instead, the new security agenda is increasingly composed of more intangible and diffuse risks and challenges. These often involve unfocused fears, perceptions of insecurity, and feelings of unease and cannot always be precisely specified. It is in this respect that the metaphor of the Jabberwock is so pertinent to security in what is best termed the *late modern era*.[1]

My aim in this chapter is to contribute to the collective task of retooling security studies so that it is able to address the challenges of a changing global system. I do so by offering a series of reflections on the nature of security in the twenty-first century. The perspective developed here is grounded on two assumptions. The first is that the concept of security needs to be broadened beyond its traditional preoccupation with national security and military threats; the second is that it is essential to preserve a distinctive analytical focus for security studies. Security studies must therefore find a third way between traditional security studies and an unrestrained sort of broadening. In contrast to more traditional approaches that limit their concern to the use and management of coercive power, the central argument outlined here is that security studies must examine both the causes of war and the conditions of peace.

Security has two dimensions: avoiding war (its negative dimension) and building peace (its positive dimension). At the same time, security studies must develop a more comprehensive approach to the study of conflict—from coercive power to peacebuilding—which requires a clear analytical and conceptual focus. Security studies cannot—and should not—attempt to address all aspects of human injustice, poverty, suffering, misery, and underdevelopment. Issues such as poverty, immigration, and environmental degradation are not intrinsically security issues. They become a concern for security studies only when they threaten to provoke conflict and insecurity. The core concern of security studies is thus conflict (particularly, although not exclusively, violent conflict) between organized political communities—that is, managing conflict and creating the conditions that prevent its occurrence.

This chapter is structured into three sections. The first outlines the development of academic thinking on issues of war and peace. It explores the trajectories of the contemporary security debate and examines the main points of contention. The first section ends by arguing that the most pressing intellectual and analytical task of security studies is to define the boundaries of a broadened concept of security. The second section provides a critical analysis of some of the most interesting and influential attempts to rethink the nature of post–Cold War security. The third section offers some reflections on the nature of security studies, focusing in particular on the changing structural dynamics of European security. I conclude by arguing that there are three aspects to contemporary security studies: the agendas of Clausewitz, Metternich, and Kant.

A BRIEF HISTORY OF SECURITY STUDIES

Security Studies and
International Relations Theory

Consideration of the issues of war and peace has played a constitutive role in the development of international relations as a discipline. Indeed, the establishment of international relations as a distinctive discipline in the early twentieth century was itself a response to the traumas of World War I. Although as an academic discipline international relations is relatively new, it has drawn sustenance from a long intellectual heritage that can be traced back through Machiavelli and Kant to Thucydides. Today, concerns about war and peace remain—rightly—at the heart of contemporary international relations. As sociologist Michael Mann has made clear, "What we outsiders *really* want from international relations is substantive theory on its most important issue of all: the question of war and peace."[2] Not surprisingly, therefore, many of the most engaging and controversial debates in contemporary international relations revolve around the contested concept of security. These debates and controversies reflect the diverse response of the international relations discipline to the changing dynamics of global politics. Some argue that the world has changed so much that a major paradigm shift in our understanding of security is also required. Others, however, remain convinced that traditional concepts retain their utility and that writers such as Thucydides are as relevant today as they were at the time of the Peloponnesian Wars. Many engaged in the study of security would therefore be forgiven for feeling that they are, in the concluding words of Matthew Arnold's poem "Dover Beach," "here as on a darkling plain/Swept with confused alarms of struggle and flight/Where ignorant armies clash by night."

Security thus remains one of the essentially contested concepts that abound in the social sciences.[3] Even before the demise of the Cold War, traditional state-centric and military-focused approaches to security studies were being questioned by a growing number of scholars and practitioners.[4] With the end of the East-West conflict, a major debate has unfolded on the meaning and character of security.[5] This debate has ranged from the epistemological and ontological foundations of security to its appropriate referent object and the composition of the security agenda. Despite a spirited rear-guard action by those who have celebrated the renaissance of security studies in its traditional form,[6] mainstream opinion in the security studies community has shifted toward a broadened concept of security. This reflects the fact that with the end of the "short twentieth century,"[7] it has become hard to deny that the nature of global politics—particularly in Europe—has changed substantially since the time of Bismarck, Castlereagh, and Woodrow Wilson.[8] For this reason, therefore, few security analysts rest content with a traditional realist approach to international politics.

As efforts have intensified to retool security studies in the age of late modernity, an interesting development has occurred. Whereas international relations as a discipline once grew from reflections on international security, contemporary security studies seeks to rejuvenate itself by opening up to new intellectual currents in international relations theory. Indeed, security studies is now engaged in appropriating conceptual and theoretical tools developed more broadly in the social sciences and beyond. In addition to feminism and critical theory, security studies has looked to social and cognitive psychology, contemporary historiography, and international political economy. Thus there is good reason to believe that contemporary security studies in the early twenty-first century stands on the verge of a major paradigm shift. What is beyond doubt is that the end of the Cold War has had a profound impact on security studies. "The old certainties," one commentator has noted, "were suddenly swept away by events in ways in which the 1980s critics could never have achieved. . . . The sparks struck by the revolutionary events across central Europe blew into the groves of academe, igniting a conflagration. Familiar shibboleths of international security studies burned on a bonfire of the certainties."[9]

Conceptualizing Security: Three Approaches

Amid the confused alarms of struggle and flight within contemporary security studies, three approaches stand out as especially important and influential: realism, liberal institutionalism, and critical security studies.

Traditional thinking about security has been deeply colored by the realist paradigm, which has dominated the discipline of international relations since roughly 1950. As a theory of international politics, realism emphasizes the centrality of structural anarchy and power politics in the international system. Its point of departure is a sharp delineation between the domestic and international spheres. Within the domestic sphere—defined by the boundaries of the sovereign state—it is possible to pursue justice, community, democracy, and social progress. Outside of the state—in the absence of a central authority—anarchy prevails. In this harsh and unforgiving self-help system, the struggle for survival is the primary concern of all states. For realists, therefore, sovereignty is a key organizing principle of the international system; states must remain the referent object of security; and security is primarily to be gained through power politics and military force. The security dilemma constitutes the central and inescapable feature of international life.[10] Moreover, in a multipolar system states can most effectively find security through alliances and the effective operation of the balance of power.

Traditional realism was increasingly challenged from the early 1970s onward by neoliberal institutionalism, or simply liberal institutionalism. This accepted many realist assumptions (notably the anarchic nature of the international system) but rejected its conclusions. In particular, liberal institutionalists stressed the potential for international cooperation, especially through multilateralism and institutional integration. Their focus on the emergence of complex interdependence also led them to highlight the importance of the economic and political dimensions of the international system, and thus to move away from realism's concentration on power politics and military force. Associated with this was a recognition of the growing role of nonstate actors in the international system.[11] These intellectual moves led to a new concept of power that differed significantly from that of structural realists.[12] Liberal institutionalists distinguished between hard and soft power. They argued that in a system characterized by complex interdependence military (i.e., hard) power was of declining utility relative to economic, political, and social (i.e., soft) forms of power.[13] These insights had an important impact on academic thinking about security and stimulated a rethinking of many of the traditional realist assumptions about security. They also encouraged a growing emphasis on the importance of the nonmilitary dimensions of security and accelerated an associated shift from strategic studies to security studies.

The liberal-institutionalist approach has been remarkably influential in security studies, particularly in Europe. Its influence is reflected in the very rich debate on multilateralism and democratic peace theory, both of which are among the most interesting debates in contemporary international relations. However, liberal institutionalism has drawn increasing criticism for its failure to break more radically with realist assumptions about the international system. Robert Keohane, for example, an influential figure in the liberal-institutionalist camp, has acknowledged his approach "borrows as much from realism as from liberalism."[14] The convergence between many of the leading U.S. neorealists and neoliberal institutionalists created a focused and productive debate[15] but also generated dissatisfaction with this "neo-neo" synthesis— also termed *neoutilitarianism* by John Ruggie.[16] Dissatisfaction with the theoretical limitations of neoutilitarianism contributed to the emergence in the mid-1980s of a third influential approach to international relations: post-Marxist critical theory.[17]

Broadly speaking, critical theory denies the existence of a firebreak between theory and practice and frames its research with the explicit intention of furthering the interests of marginalized and excluded groups. Critical theory has spawned the third main approach to security: critical security studies.[18] This is a broad church, embracing elements of post-Marxism, feminism, peace studies, and postmodernism, although it is not identical with any one of them. It is methodologically, epistemologically, and conceptually diffuse but shares a common rejection of many of the ontological assumptions common to both realism and liberal institutionalism.[19] In particular, critical security studies tends to emphasize the constructed nature of security relations. Broadly speaking, critical security studies rejects the notion of anarchy as a defining feature of international relations; replaces the state by either societal groups or individuals as the referent object of security; emphasizes the role of both nonstate actors and the nonmilitary dimension of security; and identifies security with wider social, economic, environmental, and political goals, loosely defined as *emancipation*.[20] This approach also tends to problematize the notions of interests and identities by breaking with more rationalist or utilitarian concepts of interests as materially determined and endogenously given.

Clearly, this is a highly schematic presentation of what is actually a very rich and broad-ranging debate. Most writers cannot be so easily pigeonholed, and the three approaches overlap considerably. Moreover, each of these three approaches is characterized by tremendous diversity. Realism, for example, is "not a single theory but a family of interpretations."[21] Realist thinking is much more sophisticated than its critics acknowledge, particularly when one looks beyond the parsimonious theorizing of Ken Waltz and engages with the richer tradition of Hans Morgenthau, Reinhold Niebuhr, and Arnold Wolfers. Feminism, too, is a broad church, and many feminists have contributed enormously to perspectives and approaches other than critical security studies.[22] Similarly, critical theory, as defined above, is characterized by considerable diversity. Indeed, in many respects it owes its sense of cohesion to its significant other—realism. John Ruggie quotes Mark Neufield to the effect that "the debate with the camp of constructivism may prove to be as vigorous as that between [them] and their positivist critics."[23]

Nonetheless, despite the diversity of contemporary security studies, this threefold schematic division offers a useful heuristic tool for understanding the main issues in the security debate. Much of this debate has revolved around four questions, the two most important of which are, What is the referent object of security? and, What is the nature of the threat? The two supplementary questions are: Who provides security? and, With what instruments can security be provided?[24]

Four Areas of Controversy

One issue that has generated considerable debate in security studies is the question of the referent object of security—in other words, who or what is to be secured? Traditionally, international security studies have focused on the state and national security. Liberals, however, tend to operate on the basis of a methodological individualism that privileges individual citizens as the referent object of security. Others, rejecting such methodological individualism, point to societal groups, nongovernmental organizations, or other collective agents.[25] The result of this debate has been to question the assumption that security simply equals national security. This has encouraged analysts to specify from the start what their preferred level of analysis is and why they have chosen this level rather than another.

The second area of debate concerns the nature of the threat. This question has generated considerable controversy. As early as 1983, Richard Ullman suggested that traditional concepts of security were "excessively narrow" and "excessively military." He argued that our understanding of security should be broadened to include economic and development factors. Similar arguments were made by Barry Buzan in his seminal text, *People, States, and Fear* (the first edition of which was also published in 1983). One of the pivotal questions in this debate has been whether environmental problems constitute a legitimate concern for security studies. For some proponents of a broadened security concept, virtually any environmental problem—however long-term its impact or unintentional its cause—constitutes a security problem.[26] Others have suggested that only those environmental issues that threaten to generate violent conflict between organized political communities should be classed as security problems. Norman Myers, for example, argues that although not all environmental problems will lead to conflict, there is nonetheless a causal link between the two that will tend to increase unless current environmental policies change.[27] T. Homer-Dixon makes a similar case. As a consequence of pollution, climate change, and resource depletion, he suggests, three sets of environmental challenges to security are likely to emerge. First: interstate conflicts over both nonrenewable and renewable resource scarcities. Second: large-scale population movements caused by environmental stress that could induce conflicts fueled by rival group identities. And third: environmental scarcity could increase economic deprivation and disrupt social institutions, thereby precipitating civil strife and insurgency.[28] In contrast, Marc Levy has argued that although environmental factors have contributed to regional conflicts, they are rarely the sole cause. Indeed, there are so many other intervening variables that it is difficult to see the unique contribution environmental factors make to conflict situations.[29] A more radical critique of the broadening of security to include environmental issues has come from Daniel Deudney. He has argued that linking environmental issues to national security, thereby "militarizing" it, would generate considerable conceptual and policy confusion.[30]

For some critical theorists, insecurity comes not only from specific agents (terrorists or enemy armies) or policies (nuclear deterrence or pollution). Instead, it derives from what they term *structural violence*. It comes, in other words, from deeply embedded socioeconomic inequalities that degrade the life expectancy and opportunities of oppressed groups.[31] This perception has been articulated in some official UN publications. The Commission on Environment and Development,[32] for example, has emphasized the complex casual interrelationship of problems of poverty, conflict, and environmental degradation. "Poverty, injustice, environmental degradation, and conflict interact in complex and potent ways," it argues. "The immediate cause of any mass movement of refugees may appear to be political upheaval and military violence. But the underlying causes often include the deterioration of the natural resource base and its capacity to support the population."

Other scholars have argued that the existence of a threat is the defining feature of a security problem.[33] Issues such as environmental degradation can be seen as security problems if they share the same characteristics of threats—"in particular the singular appropriateness of worst case assumptions (the core of military analysis of uncertainty) when dealing with phenomena whose potential downside was simultaneously uncertain and great." Gwyn Prins therefore speaks of "threats without enemies" and argues that the existence of a threat is the defining criterion for inclusion in security analysis. Others, however, have argued that the existence of a threat is not enough to define an issue as a security problem. Rather, as Deudney has argued,[34] intentionality is the essential factor: "Threats of violence are highly intentional: organizations are mobilized, weapons procured, and wars waged with relatively definite aims in mind. In contrast, environmental degradation is largely unintentional, the side effect of many other activities." Finally, some commentators have stressed the temporal dimension as an important consideration when assessing the nature of the threat. Some of those advocating a broadening of the security agenda to include issues such as environmental degradation argue that to constitute a threat an issue must develop within a narrow temporal frame. Ullman, for example, has argued that threats should be understood as events that threaten "drastically and over a relatively brief span of time to degrade the quality of life for the inhabitants of a state."[35]

Although the debate has primarily revolved around the questions of the referent object and the nature of the threat, two other questions have also fueled significant controversies: Who provides security and with what instruments? Again, traditional security studies has adopted a realist approach and focused on the state and the military instrument. However, some analysts maintain that security threats are increasingly global in nature (e.g., AIDS and pollution) and that states are less and less able to deal with them. In addition, it has been suggested that many of the new issues on the contemporary security agenda cannot be addressed through traditional military instruments—in the words of Gwyn Prins and Robbie Stamp, "You can't shoot an ozone hole."[36] The contemporary security debate is thus broad-ranging and diverse. It is not only concerned with the complexities of the contemporary security agenda; it is also increasingly bound up with methodological and epistemological debates at the heart of the social sciences more generally, in particular the levels-of-analysis question and the agent-structure problem.

The Problem of Boundaries and Focus

Within security studies, there has been a steady trend since the early 1980s onward toward a broadening of the concept of security to embrace nonmilitary concerns, as well as a widening of the referent object to include societal collectivities beyond the state. This reflects increasing dissatisfaction with the traditional analytical preoccupation with states as the providers of military security. Although this conceptual broadening and widening is a necessary and overdue development, it is not unproblematic.

The central problem facing contemporary security studies is where the boundaries of security as a subdiscipline lie. What are the boundaries between security policy and public policy? When is environmental or ecological degradation a security problem rather than an issue of acute political and economic concern? Some have suggested that security studies, in the words of seventeenth-century mathematician Blaise Pascal, should be conceived as a "fearful sphere whose centre is everywhere and whose circumference is nowhere." Writing from a feminist perspective, Jill Steans has argued that rethinking security "involves thinking about militarism and patriarchy, maldevelopment and environmental degradation. It involves thinking about the relationship between poverty, debt and population growth. It involves thinking about resources and how they are distributed."[37] The problem with this all-encompassing approach is that security, if it is defined so broadly that it embraces all aspects of human existence, ends up being about everything and nothing. An indiscriminate broadening and widening of the concept of security will inevitably rob it of any analytical utility. Security studies will simply dissolve into international relations, if not into the social sciences and humanities more generally. To retain its analytical utility, and to give security studies as a subdiscipline some coherence, the concept of security needs a clear focus and distinct boundaries.

This case—as one might expect—has been made most forcefully by defenders of a more traditional approach to security. The traditional state-centric, military-focused approach to security was restated by Joseph Nye and Sean Lynn-Jones in the dying days of the Cold War: "The central questions are concerned with international violence," they argued. "A subject that is only remotely related to central political problems of threat perception and management among sovereign states would be regarded as peripheral."[38] In an influential article celebrating the renaissance of traditional security studies, Stephen Walt developed this line of thought at greater length.[39] He argued that if the loss of a rain forest or pollution or disease were to be viewed as a security issue, then "defining the field in this way would destroy its intellectual coherence." Consequently, he argued, security studies should be defined as the exploration of "the conditions that make the use of force more likely, the ways that the use of force affects individuals, states and societies, and the specific policies that states adopt in order to prepare or engage in war." Similarly, Lawrence Freedman has argued that broadening the concept of security too far risks loosing its focus and generating an agenda that would be "off-puttingly vague." The "defense of the nation against infectious disease," he points out, "is an altogether different problem than defense against ballistic missile attack." Thus while acknowledging that a certain amount of retooling is required so that security studies can address issues like ethnic conflict or disputes over freshwater resources, he advocates retaining a defining role for force in security studies.[40]

It is therefore apparent that security studies faces a major dilemma:

> On the one hand, it is clear that the traditional definition of security that has dominated the Western literature on the subject is inadequate to explain the

multifaceted and multidimensional nature of the problem of international
security as faced by the majority of members in the international system. On
the other, the often indiscriminate broadening of the definition of security
threatens to make the concept so elastic as to render it useless as an analytical tool.[41]

This dilemma lies at the very heart of contemporary security studies. A broad
consensus has emerged among both practitioners and academics that the concept of security needs to broadened and widened. However, attempts to broad-
en the concept so that it includes virtually all aspects of the human condition
open the door for realists to reassert a more narrowly focused agenda. What is
required is an approach that steers a third way between excessive broadening
and traditionalist retrenchment.

   This third way involves a two-step approach to defining security. First,
conflict between discrete political communities—particularly, although not
exclusively, large-scale organized violence—should remain the primary focus
of security studies. This focus is essential in order to retain the analytical
focus of security studies and makes sense given the continuing prevalence of
war and conflict in many parts of the globe. However, security is not simply
about the use or management of coercive power in international society, as
realists argue. Security studies is also about the conditions that make the use
of force *less* likely. To focus exclusively on "the conditions that make the use
of force more likely," as Walt suggests, would be to limit the analytical utility of security studies in the late modern world. This takes us to security's second defining feature: security studies is about the causes of war *and* the conditions for peace. Limiting security studies to a consideration of force and
coercion in global politics would exclude it from some of the most important
and interesting debates in contemporary international security: the relationship between democracy and peace,[42] security and integration,[43] and stable
peace theory,[44] for example. Security studies thus has two aspects, negative
and positive: the causes of war, as well as the conditions of peace. As I shall
argue below, this twofold definition offers a promising point of departure for
a theoretical retooling of security studies in the twenty-first century.

THE DIFFICULTIES OF RETHINKING SECURITY

Before outlining in greater detail a third way for security studies, it would be
useful to briefly consider some of the most interesting and innovative attempts
to rethink the nature of security. These are security as emancipation, societal
security, and so-called securitization. These three examples are worthy of consideration not only because of their intrinsic merit but also because they illus-

trate many of the problems inherent in seeking to move beyond traditional security studies.

Security as Emancipation

One of the main concerns of critical security studies has been to embed the concept of security in broader societal and political concerns. A prime example of this perspective is Ken Booth's 1991 essay on security as emancipation. He argues that security involves the emancipation of human beings from oppression and exploitation. This echoes Marxist arguments that class society causes war and that only by a proletarian revolution abolishing the capitalist mode of production is an enduring peace possible. Booth's argument also draws on ideas of structural violence associated with peace studies. In Booth's 1991 version, emancipation replaces proletarian revolution, and various inequalities and injustices replace class oppression; nonetheless, the general structure and thrust of the argument remains the same

The problem with this argument is that Booth never adequately defines *emancipation*. Emancipation, as understood by Che Guevara, would be very different from that of General Augusto Pinochet. To replace an essentially contested concept by one that is even more ill-defined does not advance security studies very far. Moreover, even if Booth and successive generations of Marxists are correct—that only by abolishing all injustice, inequality, and oppression can an enduring peace order be created—what do we do in the meantime? How can we reduce conflict and insecurity in a world still characterized by various forms of injustice? Can a stable peace be fostered between neighboring countries or communities enjoying very different degrees of social justice and prosperity (i.e., Germany and Poland, or Russia and Finland)? Are peaceful relations between states with very different political systems, cultural attributes, and religious persuasions possible? These and related questions are—or should be—of fundamental concern to security studies. The central intellectual task facing contemporary security studies is thus to identify sources of insecurity and conflict; to specify ways of reducing the risk of insecurity in an imperfect world; and to suggest strategies and structures for moving toward a stable peace order. Unfortunately, Booth's eschatological conception of security is of limited utility in addressing these questions.

Societal Security

One intriguing attempt to broaden and widen the concept of security has come from the so-called Copenhagen school.[45] Its adherents suggest that alongside threats to the state there are also threats to society: hence they have coined the term *societal security*. Whereas state security has sovereignty as its ultimate criterion, threats to society involve concerns about identity. "Survival for a society," they argue, "is a question of identity, because this is the way a society talks about existential threats: if this happens, we will no longer be able to live as 'us.'"[46] The writings of the Copenhagen school on societal security represent a valuable attempt to address some significant weaknesses in existing theories of security. Few problems of contemporary security can be fully comprehended without reference to questions of collective identity and political affiliation. The Copenhagen school has thus helped foster a conceptual focus on the problem of ethnonational conflict and drawn attention to the all-too-frequent lack of fit between states and societal collectivities in the modern world.

However, their notion of societal security is not without its problems. Its central tenet is its tendency to assume that society and identity are categories taken as given rather than intersubjectively constituted. In addition, the distinction between society and societal groups is not clear; neither is it clear how societies articulate and express their identity: through political parties or movements (such as Solidarity in communist Poland), or through organizational structures with the attributes of states (as with the Serbs and Croats in Bosnia)? The concept of societal security is undertheorized and ambiguous on these points, and therefore it is difficult to operationalize. Moreover, as Bill McSweeney has argued,[47] the concept of identity employed by the Copenhagen school is deeply problematical and fails to provide an adequate understanding of the reflexive relationship between identity and interests. Thus even though the concept of societal security has served a valuable purpose in encouraging debate on an important issue of contemporary security studies,[48] its analytical utility is limited in light of its failure to address several core epistemological and substantive questions.

Securitization

Another conceptual innovation from the Copenhagen school—one associated in particular with Ole Wæver[49]—is the notion of securitization. This concept has been presented as the solution to the problems involved in broadening the definition of *security* without thereby robbing it of its analytical utility. Wæver and his colleagues start from the assumption that security is not a concept with a fixed meaning or a determinate social condition. Security, in other words, cannot be objectively defined. Rather, they argue that it constitutes a distinctive form of politics. To *securitize* an issue means to take it out of the normal realm of political discourse and to signal a need for it to be addressed urgently and with exceptional means. Moreover, security is not just any threat or problem. Rather, security issues are "existential threats to a referent object by a securitizing actor who thereby generates endorsement of emergency measures beyond rules that would otherwise bind."[50]

Securitization thus focuses almost exclusively on the discursive domain and eschews any attempt to determine empirically what constitutes *security concerns*. It does not aspire to comment on the reality behind a securitization discourse or on the appropriate instruments for tackling security problems. Instead, it suggests that security studies—or what Wæver calls *securitization studies*—should focus on the discursive moves whereby issues are securitized. The Copenhagen school thus emphasizes the need to understand the "speech acts" that accomplish a process of securitization. Their focus is on the linguistic and conceptual dynamics involved, even though they recognize the importance of the institutional setting within which securitization takes place.

The concept of securitization offers some important insights for security studies. However, it is too epistemologically restricted to contribute to a significant retooling of security studies. On the positive side, it draws attention to the way in which security agendas are constructed by politicians and other political actors. It also indicates the utility of discourse analysis as an additional tool of analysis for security studies. However, at best, securitization studies can constitute one aspect of security studies. It cannot provide the foundations for a paradigm shift in the subdiscipline. Its greatest weakness is its epistemological hypochondria,[51] that is, its tendency to reify epistemological problems and push sound observations about knowledge claims to their logical absurdity. Although it is important to understand the discursive moves involved in perceptions of security in, say, the Middle East, it is also necessary to make some assessment of nondiscursive factors like the military balance or access to freshwater supplies. For the Copenhagen school, however, these nondiscursive factors are relegated to second place. They are considered only to the extent that they facilitate or impede the speech act.[52] In this way, the Copenhagen school is in danger of cutting security studies off from serious empirical research and setting it adrift on a sea of floating signifiers.

CHARTING A THIRD WAY FOR SECURITY STUDIES

Having outlined the historical evolution of security studies and considered some of the most innovative—albeit flawed—attempts to rethink the nature of security, the task remaining is to specify the building-blocks of a third way in security studies in the age of the Jabberwock. This third way must aim to go beyond the narrow approach of traditional realism while avoiding the dangers of an indiscriminate broadening of the concept of security. Developing a full-fledged theory of security is beyond the scope of this chapter. Instead, the more limited aim is to propose a series of conceptual building-blocks in the form of eight theses.

The Core Concern of Security Studies Is
Conflict in the International System

Any academic discipline requires a specific focus that delineates its subject matter and range of analytical tools. Economics, for example, focuses on the market and the efficient use of scarce resources. Politics focuses on the processes whereby competing social interests interact within specific forms of government and governance. International relations focuses on the interaction of distinct political communities in the global system. The focus of security studies, I would suggest, is threats to the values and way of life of political communities associated with conflict, particularly violent conflict. A political community's way of life and values can be affected by external cultural influences (rock and roll music or Hollywood movies), disease, or environmental pollution. However, these become the concern of security studies only if they threaten to generate conflict and violence. Thus the Hungarian-Slovak dispute over the Danube dams became a security problem when it threatened to generate conflict between the two states.[53] British pollution of the North Sea, in contrast, has not become a security issue despite its adverse impact on Norway. Without this conceptual focus on conflict, security studies would, like a sugar lump in a cup of Earl Grey tea, dissolve into the wider social sciences.

Security Studies Is Concerned with the
Causes of War and the Conditions for Peace

Although its core concern is conflict in the international system, this does not mean that security studies is exclusively focused on the use and management of coercive force. There are two aspects to security: negative and positive.[54] Security involves preventing war through military preparations to deter armed aggression from within and without and, more positively, fostering conditions conducive to building a legitimate and enduring peace order.

Hence security has a broad agenda and several dimensions: military, political, economic, social, and ecological-environmental. In certain times and places, the security agenda will be dominated by concerns about the balance of power, alliances, and military postures (as was the case in Europe in the late 1930s or as it has been in the Middle East for much of the postwar period). At other times, however, security is concerned primarily with shaping the conditions for peace. This was the case with postwar Western Europe and is increasingly also the case with the wider Europe after the end of the Cold War (with the exception of parts of the Balkans and the Caucasus). In this context, security studies is primarily concerned with the nonmilitary dimensions of security, that is, the political, economic, social, and cultural preconditions for shaping a stable peace and fostering the emergence of a security community.

The Texture of International Society

All concepts of security are embedded in specific theoretical understandings of the nature of the international system. Traditional approaches to security, for example, are explicable only in the context of their realist assumptions about the anarchic nature of international relations and the intractability of the security dilemma. These assumptions, however, are less and less relevant when it comes to understanding the more complex and diffuse nature of security risks and challenges in the modern world. To return to our opening metaphor: the nature of the Jabberwock cannot be comprehended with the conceptual lenses and parsimonious theories of traditional realism.

Instead, security studies needs to be situated in the context of an understanding of the international system that acknowledges its socially textured nature. "International relations," John Ruggie notes, "like all social relations, exhibit *some* degree of institutionalization: at minimum, a mutual intelligibility of behavior together with the communicative mechanisms and organizational routines which make that possible."[55] Although no world government exists, a plethora of ordering principles and forms of governance has developed in the international system. These are nested in thickening webs of social, economic, and cultural exchanges; within epistemic communities; and in international regimes. They are also nourished by shared norms, values, and principles, which generate regular patterns of behavior. They have been institutionalized in a network of multilateral organizations, most notably in Europe, where the fabric of international society is particularly rich and intricately woven.

If security studies is to be able to offer insights into the complexities of preventing war and building peace in an age without a clear and present danger, it needs to be embedded within a more sophisticated theory of international relations than that offered by realism. The bleak and parsimonious theories of neorealism—with their assumptions of an anarchical international system in which rational, utility-maximizing states clash in a never-ending struggle for power and survival—have little to tell us about the dynamics of international security in contemporary Europe.[56] A better starting point is offered by the English school, with its emphasis on the elements of society in international politics. The great strength of the English school is its recognition of the importance of history and culture to the development of international society, along with its analysis of the complex institutionalization of international politics. The new institutionalist literature is also of interest in this regard.[57] This approach, which has been influential in economics and sociology, conceives of institutions—broadly defined—as structures that generate routinized patterns of behavior and forms of governance. Organizations (with formal decisionmaking mechanisms) operate within a context of broader forms of institutionalization and draw much of their strength and effectiveness from these wider networks of institutions.[58] The new institutionalist approach would suggest, for example, that the effectiveness of the European Union derives not simply from its formal decisionmaking capacities and powers of compliance but rather from the wider forms of governance and accepted codes of behavior between member states upon which these formal structures rest.

Regional Differentiation in Contemporary Security Studies

Neorealist approaches to security studies have often aspired to develop general theories of security with universal and global relevance. However, it is increasingly apparent in the post–Cold War era that most conflicts in the world have specific regional origins and dynamics. This reflects the fact that the fabric of international society is of uneven texture and richness. Consequently, states define their interests and goals in different ways and have different conceptions of what resources are most appropriate for the conduct of their foreign and security policies. As Joseph Nye has argued, "The games of world politics are being played by different actors with different piles of chips at different card tables."[59] This generates very different patterns of security relations between regionally based groups of states. This phenomenon was already apparent in the Cold War, but it is even more marked today given the trend toward growing regional differentiation within the international system.

The importance of a regional perspective for security studies has been recognized by several writers. Barry Buzan, for example, has proposed a regionally focused security complex theory.[60] He defines a *regional security complex* as "a set of states whose major security perceptions and concerns are so interlinked that their national security problems cannot reasonably be analyzed or resolved apart from one another."[61] Similarly, Amitav Acharya, a writer on Third World security, has argued that we need a "greater regionalization of our understanding of the sources of conflict and the requirements of international order, with the Third World serving as a central conceptual and empirical focus."[62] He has also argued that understanding regional conflicts and security in the post–Cold War period "requires conceptual tools and methodology beyond what is provided by orthodox notions of security developed during the Cold War."[63]

The process of regional security differentiation is affected by a variety of systemic and unit-level factors. At the level of the international system, five factors are crucial: the existence of multilateral structures and international organizations; the existence of extensive forms of governance and patterned behavior; respect for international law; the pervasiveness of socioeconomic interdependence; and acceptance of international norms, values, and principles. At the unit level, two factors are particularly pertinent: the nature of statehood (strong or weak states) and the character of the domestic political system (democratic or authoritarian). These factors have had a very different impact on different parts of the global system, giving rise to several distinctive security zones or regions. In much of the developed industrial world (North America and Western Europe), a zone of stable peace has emerged within which war—even the threat of war—no longer plays a role in interstate relations.[64] In this zone of stable peace, postmodern states have emerged that no longer regard territory as the key to national power and for whom welfare not warfare is the overriding concern. In areas such as the Middle East, Eastern Europe, the Balkans, and Asia, by way of contrast, interstate relations are still characterized by balance-of-power issues and more traditional power politics. In parts of Africa, the Caucasus, and Central Asia (notably Afghanistan and Tajikistan), security concerns are focused on the prevalence of weak states, bitter societal conflicts, and the threat of anarchy, or warlordism. Thus contemporary security studies must increasingly focus on regional security dynamics rather than seeking to develop parsimonious and ahistorical theories that purport to explain security issues in all areas of global international society.

Europe: Back to the Future or Beyond the Balance of Power?

The primary concern of this book is the European regional security system. The dynamics of this regional security complex pose some particularly interesting puzzles for academics and policymakers. Modern Europe is not only very different from other regions in the wider global system; it is also very different from the Europe of the nineteenth and early twentieth centuries. "Back to the Future"[65] might be a catchy title for a journal article, but it does not help us understand the nature of twenty-first-century European security. The Europe of Castlereagh, Bismarck, and Stresemann has passed into history. With globalization, interdependence, democratization, and integration, change has taken place in Europe at the level of the *longue durée* (long duration), not simply at the level of events and personalities. Consequently, faced with a new security agenda and the transformed political, economic, and strategic landscape in Europe, we cannot rely on the traditional tools of realist-inspired security studies. These were developed to explain a world that no longer exists. Conceptual rethinking and retooling is thus needed, if not a more profound paradigm change.

A major task for academics and analysts is identifying the elements of continuity and change in contemporary Europe. Clearly the events of 1989–1991 have spelled the end of the Europe of Yalta—a Europe characterized by bipolar antagonism. The end of the Cold War has also been followed by the unraveling of much of the Europe of Versailles—in other words, of the territorial settlement that followed World War I and that led to the creation of Czechoslovakia, Yugoslavia, and the Soviet Union, all of which have now disappeared. The more problematical question is whether the Europe of Westphalia is also disappearing—the system of European order based on sovereign territorial states. There are certainly indications that the pillars of this Westphalian system have been significantly eroded in Europe, even if they have not been fully overturned. To begin with, the European integration process has resulted in a development that realists must find astonishing—a significant pooling of sovereignty in multilateral structures.[66] Second, the Kosovo war has suggested that states no longer enjoy sovereignty if they commit gross violations of human rights. This severely qualifies the operation of the Westphalian system.

If, as a growing number of academics and policymakers now believe, the events of 1989–1991 mark a watershed so profound that they signify the end of the Westphalian system in Europe, then a paradigm shift in our understanding of European security is inevitable. A major concern for studies of European security must therefore be to analyze the extent and significance of the changes associated with the end of the short twentieth century.[67] This involves reconsidering the central tenets of both realism and liberal institutionalism concerning the anarchical nature of global politics and the primacy of the state. It also involves considering the significance for security studies of the gradual demise of the security dilemma in much of Western and Central Europe, as well as the consequent decline of the balance of power as the dominant ordering principle of the European security system.[68]

Building a Stable Peace in Post–Cold War Europe

With the end of the Cold War, it is ever more clear that the security agenda in Europe is primarily concerned with forging the conditions for a stable and enduring peace order, rather than simply preventing war. This latter task is still on the agenda in the Balkans and around the fringes of the former Soviet Union, but it no longer occupies much of the attention of security policy elites in Western and Central Europe. This is because of the emergence of a pluralistic security community,[69] or stable peace,[70] in the transatlantic area in which war—even the threat of war—no longer plays a role in interstate relations. These concepts, both of which point to a similar development, provide useful lenses for analyzing the changing European security agenda.

The emergence of a security community in Western Europe has been the result of a complex, multidimensional process. However, at its heart is the crucial nexus of democracy, integration, and markets. These three elements all contribute to a process of deepening societal integration—building what Karl Deutsch called a *sense of community*, or "we-feeling." The consolidation of stable liberal democracies founded on the rule of law and respect for human rights; the development of institutionalized forms of multilateral cooperation (above all, EU and NATO) along with associated forms of multilevel governance; and the emergence of complex interdependence between market economies—these three factors have been crucial to the development of a zone of stable peace in Western Europe. The central task facing Europe today is to extend this security community steadily eastward into the former communist lands of Central and Eastern Europe. Thus an important analytical concern for contemporary security studies is to examine the modalities and implications of an eastward extension of the transatlantic security community. Here again, the crucial nexus for investigation will be the interrelationship between democracy, integration, and markets.[71]

The task in most of contemporary Europe, most notably Central Europe, is therefore not managing the military balance or deterring threats to national security. Rather, it is developing *trust* and *integration* between peoples. This can emerge only through the creation of webs of interaction between distinct political communities based on transnational exchanges, communications flows, shared normative frameworks, and common interests. A central object of study in European security is thus the relationship between security and integration, which in turn involves considering a wide range of economic, political, cultural, and societal factors. A broad concept of security is therefore essential in order to study the fabric of European international society within which a security community develops.

The Renaissance of Strategy

One paradoxical consequence of the end of the Cold War has been the renaissance of strategy. Despite the greatly improved military security environment in Europe (with the exception of parts of the Balkans and the Caucasus), the classic concern of strategy—the use of military force for political purposes (the agenda of Clausewitz)—is now a major concern for the foreign and security policy elites in much of Europe. This is evident in the United Kingdom from the establishment, in September 1993, of the Inspectorate General of Doctrine and Training by the British Army to explore the nature and implications of conflict in the twenty-first century.

The renaissance of strategy is paradoxical because the dramatic events of 1989–1991 diffused the East-West military confrontation in Europe and ended the risk of large-scale continental war between two nuclear-armed alliances.

The likelihood of large-scale war in Europe is now less than ever before in history, and there are now few direct military threats to European security. Yet new nonmilitary risks and challenges have proliferated. In the words of one commentator, "The dragon is dead, but the woods are still full of dangerous snakes."[72] For European armed forces, this development has had unexpected consequences. During the Cold War, the armed forces of NATO and the Warsaw Pact were locked in a nuclear stalemate: their primary purpose was deterrence and defense, and their training primarily involved preparing to fight a large-scale conventional and nuclear war in Central Europe. Given the sensitivity of the East-West conflict, deploying military forces for other purposes was strictly limited. Today, however, military forces in European countries are being called upon to conduct a wide range of military operations other than war. These range from rescue missions and humanitarian aid, through peace-support operations, to more conventional forms of military action (such as the Gulf War). This is already having far-reaching consequences for training, procurement, organization, and deployment. In this context, the traditional concern of strategy—the use of military forces for political purposes—is very much back on the agenda. As a subset of security studies, therefore, strategic studies—the agenda of Clausewitz—has become very much a growth area and is certainly having to engage with a much richer and more analytically challenging set of concerns than it faced during the nuclear stalemate.

In the post–Cold War era, three issues stand out as vital areas of future research. First: the use of military force for political purposes in the context of a transformed security agenda and an increasingly complex international society. In particular, the issue of humanitarian intervention: Is there a right to humanitarian intervention? If so, then by whom and on the basis of what moral or political authority? This set of questions was posed anew by the experience of the Kosovo war. Second: the role and purpose of nuclear weapons in the twenty-first century. Traditional deterrence theory is less applicable to the sort of multipolar environment that has emerged in South Asia (where India, Pakistan, and China all have nuclear weapons). At the same time, the issue of proliferation—both of weapons of mass destruction and of ballistic missile systems—needs to be comprehensively addressed, particular given debates in the United States on missile defense. Third: security studies needs to address the implications of the changing character of war and the proliferation of new actors. As K. J. Holsti has argued, war has not declined in our time, but its locus has changed. Most wars today are civil wars, fought using guerrilla tactics and terrorism, and generating enormous civilian causalities. Whereas many conflicts in the pre-1945 period were fought by territorially defined nation-states numbering millions of civilians, future conflicts are more likely to be conducted by smaller, less cohesive, and less powerful political entities—similar in many respects to the character of warfare prior to the 1648 Treaty of Westphalia. Holsti therefore speaks of the emergence of "wars of the third kind." As the Carnegie Commission Report notes:[73] "In the post–Cold War era, most violent conflict can be characterised as internal wars fought with conventional weapons, with far greater casualties among civilians than soldiers." The transformation of warfare at the end of the twentieth century thus constitutes a third key area of research for contemporary strategic studies.

Epistemological Realism and Social Constructivism

If security studies is to retool itself to face the challenges of security in the modern age, it must open up to new thinking elsewhere in international relations and the wider social sciences. One such area is concerned with epistemological and methodological approaches to knowledge claims. The central debate here is between positivists, who accord ontological priority to material factors, and postpositivists, who privilege ideational factors. In keeping with the third way for security studies outlined above, I would suggest that security studies should adopt a third approach between these two dichotomous positions. Here the work of what in studies of social science epistemology is termed *realism* is of greatest utility. The realist model of social science should not be confused with realism in international relations theory. Epistemological realism in the social sciences has been developed as an alternative to more conventional positivist approaches. It is defined by its attempt to preserve an objective, "scientific" attitude toward social analysis while recognizing the importance of actors' meanings and incorporating them in research.[74] In this way, it seeks to combine the strengths of humanism with a scientific attitude. A key aspect of the realist project "is a concern with causality and the identification of causal mechanisms in social phenomena in a manner quite unlike the traditional positivist search for causal generalizations."[75]

In the domain of international relations theory, epistemological realism is best represented by social constructivism. Social constructivism, which builds on the work of the English school,[76] seeks to offer a third way between positivism and postpositivism. As Emanuel Adler has argued, constructivism

> seizes the middle ground because it is interested in understanding how the *material*, subjective and intersubjective worlds interact in the social construction of reality, and because, rather than focusing exclusively on how structures constitute agents' identities and interests, it also seeks to explain how *individual agents* socially construct these structures in the first place.[77]

Constructivist approaches to security studies question traditional realist assumptions about the materially given and endogenously derived character of interests. They stress that security cannot be objectively defined without reference to intersubjective perceptions any more than can individual or state interests. Perceptions of security and insecurity cannot be divorced from the values, beliefs, and identity of the person or thing concerned. At the same time, however, security is not simply subjectively defined; it is not simply "all in the mind." As Thomas Risse-Kappen has argued, ideas "do not float freely."[78] The task for security studies is thus to combine analysis of material structures with investigation of the perceptions and assumptions of the relevant actors. Thus, for example, Poland's sense of insecurity in the face of Nazi Germany in the late 1930s cannot be analyzed simply at the level of discourse. Hitler's demonization of Poland and the Polish people is only one aspect of a security analysis of interwar Poland; another important factor to consider must be the operational capabilities of the Wehrmacht, particularly the potency of its Panzer divisions and the doctrine of blitzkrieg.

Security must therefore be seen in terms of a reflexive interaction between subjective perceptions and material structures, between what is observed and what is imagined. Security is not a given any more than a state's interests or national identity are givens. Security, like interests and identities, is constructed. Facts do not simply speak for themselves. They require evaluation and analysis. In this sense, they are socially constructed. An operationalizable concept of security must acknowledge the constructed nature of social reality. This does not mean that security studies must reject a materialist ontology as some critical theorists and most postpositivists do. Rather, it involves recognizing that the material is mediated through human subjectivity. Interests—including security interests—are not exogenously given by the nature of the international system or the mode of production but are intersubjectively constituted through a process of reciprocal interaction.

CONCLUSION

Security has long been an essentially contested concept. There is no indication that its contested nature is likely to change in the foreseeable future; indeed, over the last two decades it has become ever more subject to contestation. At the same time, security studies remains at the heart of contemporary international relations. Whereas in the past international relations as a discipline developed from a study of the core concerns of what has become security studies—that is, the causes of war and the conditions of peace—today security studies needs to renew and retool itself by feeding off broader debates, not just in international relations but in the wider social sciences and humanities. For this reason, security studies should be seen as an integrative field of research, drawing not just from international relations and political science but also from history, political economy, sociology, and philosophy.

Security studies is thus, above all, a bridging discipline, bridging the domestic and the international, military strategy and political economy, policy studies and normative theory.

Security studies will also remain characterized by a diversity of methodological approaches, epistemological and ontological assumptions, and normative and empirical concerns. This is not a weakness but reflects the vibrancy of the subdiscipline as the short twentieth century draws to a close. Security studies should therefore continue to provide an intellectual space within which a diversity of different approaches, perspectives, and schools of thought can develop and engage with each other's competing perspectives. This broad and inclusive approach to security studies is essential given the breadth of contemporary security concerns. Contemporary security studies is a broad field not only because of the diversity of competing theoretical perspectives but also because it contains three distinct agendas of issues. These are, first, the use of military force for political purposes (the agenda of Clausewitz); second, identifying and managing security threats, risks, and challenges through diplomacy and statecraft (the agenda of Metternich); and third, exploring the conditions of peace (the agenda of Kant).

Despite—or rather because—security studies encompasses the agendas of Clausewitz, Metternich, and Kant, it requires a clear focal point and distinct boundaries. These boundaries may be blurred in places, but without them security studies risks losing its intellectual coherence and relevance to policy. The central task facing security studies in the early twenty-first century is thus to define the boundaries of a broadened concept of comprehensive security with which to address the challenges of a changing security environment. Only if security studies is successful in this collective endeavor will it continue to provide one of the most exciting and intellectually stimulating areas of contemporary academic inquiry and to provide the analytical tools required by policymakers and the wider public as they confront an increasingly complex security agenda.

NOTES

1. Nicolaus Greenwood Onuf (1997) *The Republican Legacy in International Thought* (Cambridge: Cambridge University Press), pp. 133 and 169.

2. M. Mann (1996) "Authoritarian and Liberal Militarism: A Contribution from Comparative and Historical Sociology," in Ken Booth, Steve Smith, and Marysia Zalewski (eds.) (1996) *International Theory: Positivism and Beyond* (Cambridge: Cambridge University Press), pp. 221–239, esp. 221.

3. W. Gallie (1962) "Essentially Contested Concepts," in Max Black (ed.) *The Importance of Language* (Englewood Cliffs, N.J.: Prentice Hall), pp. 121–246.

4. R. Ullman (1983) "Redefining Security," *International Security* 8, no. 1 (Summer): 129–153.

5. R. Lipschutz (ed.) (1995) *On Security* (New York: Columbia University Press); M. Clarke (ed.) (1995) *New Perspectives in Security* (London: Brassey's, for the Centre for Defence Studies); S. Lynn-Jones and S. Miller (eds.) (1995) *Global Dangers: Changing Dimensions of International Security* (London: MIT Press).

6. S. Walt (1991) "The Renaissance of Security Studies," *International Studies Quarterly* 35, no. 2 (June): 211–239.

7. E. Hobsbawn (1994) *Age of Extremes: The Short Twentieth Century, 1914–1991* (London: Michael Joseph).

8. J. Mueller (1995) *Quiet Cataclysm: Reflections on the Recent Transformation of World Politics* (New York: HarperCollins); T. Knutsen (1999) *The Rise and Fall of World Orders* (Manchester: Manchester University Press), pp. 264–269.

9. G. Prins (1998) "The Four-Stroke Cycle in Security Studies," *International Affairs* 74, no. 4 (October): 781–808, esp. 794–795.

10. R. Jervis (1981) "The Spiral of International Insecurity," in M. Smith, M. Shackleton, and R. Little (eds.) *Perspectives on World Politics* (Milton Keynes: Open University Press); N. Wheeler and K. Booth (1992) "The Security Dilemma," in John Baylis and Nick Rengger, *Dilemmas in World Politics* (Oxford: Clarendon).

11. R. Keohane and J. Nye, eds. (1972) *Transnational Relations and World Politics* (Cambridge: Harvard University Press).

12. R. Baumann, V. Rittberger, and W. Wagner (1999) "Neorealistische Aussenpolitiktheorie und Prognosen über die deutsche Aussenpolitik nach der Vereinigung," in *Zeitschrift für Internationale Beziehungen* 6, no. 2 (December): 245–286, esp. 255–256.

13. R. Keohane and J. Nye, eds. (1977) *Power and Interdependence* (Boston: Little, Brown).

14. R. Keohane (1993) "Institutionalist Theory and the Realist Challenge After the Cold War," in David Baldwin (1993) *Neorealism and Neoliberalism: The Contemporary Debate* (New York: Columbia University Press), pp. 269–300, esp. 272.

15. D. Baldwin, ed. (1993) *Neorealism and Neoliberalism: The Contemporary Debate* (New York: Columbia University Press), p. 3.

16. John G. Ruggie (1998) *Constructing the World Polity: Essays on International Institutionalization* (London: Routledge), pp. 9–16.

17. M. Hoffman (1987) "Critical Theory and the Inter-Paradigm Debate," *Millennium: Journal of International Studies* 16: 231–249.

18. K. Krause and M. Williams, eds. (1997) *Critical Security Studies: Concepts and Cases* (London: UCL).

19. "Whatever the differences between these 'critical' perspectives may be, they tend in common to focus upon the ways in which definitions of security and understandings of what is being secured, how, and from whom or what, need to be seen as socially constructed realms of practice embedded in broader social and political structures and dynamics," quoted in Krause and Williams (1997), p. 288.

20. Ken Booth defines the task of critical security studies as "broadening and deepening" conceptions of security to reveal Cold War security studies as an "Anglo-American, statist, masculinist and militarised ideology," and "not one that is calculated to deliver a more secure world by the middle of the next century." Ken Booth and Steve Smith (1995) *International Relations Theory Today* (Cambridge: Polity), p. 335.

21. Benjamin Frankel, ed. (1996) *Roots of Realism* (Ilford, U.K.: Frank Cass), p. xxiii.

22. C. Enloe (1987) "Feminist Thinking About War, Militarism, and Peace," in B. Hess and M. Ferree (eds.) *Analysing Gender: A Handbook of Social Science*

Researach (London: Sage); Jill Steans (1998) *Gender and International Relations* (Cambridge: Polity).

23. John G. Ruggie (1998) *Constructing the World Polity: Essays on International Institutionalization* (London: Routledge), p. 36.

24. T. Terriff et al. (1999) *Security Studies Today* (Cambridge: Polity).

25. J. A. Tickner (1995) "Re-visioning Security," in Booth and Smith (1995), pp. 175–197.

26. Gwyn Prins and Robbie Stamp (1991) *Top Guns and Toxic Whales: The Enviroment and Global Security* (London: Earthscan).

27. Norman Myers (1993) *Ultimate Security: The Enviromental Basis of Political Stability* (New York: W. W. Norton).

28. T. Homer-Dixon (1991) "On the Threshold: Environmental Changes as Causes of Acute Conflict," *International Security* 16, no. 2 (Fall): 76–116.

29. M. Levy (1995) "Is the Environment a National Security Issue?" *International Security* 20, no. 2 (Fall): 35–62.

30. D. Deudney (1990) "The Case Against Linking Environmental Degradation and National Security," *Millennium* 19, no. 3 (Winter): 461–476.

31. Jill Steans (1998) *Gender and International Relations* (Cambridge: Polity), p. 127.

32. UN Commission on Environment and Development (New York: UN, 1987), pp. 290–291.

33. G. Prins (1998) "The Four-Stroke Cycle in Security Studies," *International Affairs* 74, no. 4 (October): 781–808, esp. 793.

34. D. Deudney (1991) "Enviroment and Security: Muddled Thinking," in *Bulletin of Atmomic Scientists* (April): 24.

35. R. Ullman (1983) "Redefining Security," *International Security* 8, no. 1 (Summer): 129–153.

36. Prins and Stamp (1991).

37. Jill Steans (1998) *Gender and International Relations* (Cambridge: Polity), p. 129.

38. Joseph Nye and S. Lynn-Jones (1988) "International Security Studies," *International Security* 12, no. 4: 6–7.

39. S. Walt (1991) "The Renaissance of Security Studies," *International Studies Quarterly* 35, no. 2 (June): 211–239, esp. 211–213.

40. Lawrence Freedman (1998) "International Security: Changing Targets," *Foreign Policy* (Special Edition, "Frontiers of Knowledge"), no. 110 (Spring): 52–53.

41. Mohammed Ayoob (1997) "Defining Security: A Subaltern Realist Perspective," in Krause and Williams (1997), pp. 121–148, esp. 121.

42. M. Doyle (1983) "Kant, Liberal Legacies, and Foreign Affairs," Parts 1 and 2, *Philosophy and Public Affairs* 12, nos. 3–4 (Summer and Autumn): 205–254, 323–353.

43. K. Deutsch (1957) *Political Community and the North Atlantic Area* (Princeton: Princeton University Press); E. Adler and M. Barnett, eds. (1998) *Security Communities* (Cambridge: Cambridge University Press).

44. K. Boulding (1978) *Stable Peace* (Austin: University of Texas Press).

45. O. Wæver et al. (1993) *Identity, Migration, and the New Security Agenda in Europe*; Jeff Huysmans (1998) "Revisiting Copenhagen: Or on the Creative Development of a Security Studies Agenda in Europe," *European Journal of International Relations* 4, no. 4 (December): 479–505.

46. O. Wæver et al. (1993), p. 25.

47. B. McSweeney (1999) *Security, Identity, and Interests: A Sociology of International Relations* (Cambridge: Cambridge University Press).

48. B. McSweeney (1996) "Identity and Security: Buzan and the Copenhagen School," *Review of International Studies* 22, no. 1 (June): 81–93; Barry Buzan and O. Wæver (1997) "Slippery? Contradictory? Sociologically Untenable? The Copenhagen School Replies," *Review of International Studies* 23, no. 2 (April): 241–250; B. McSweeney (1998) "Durkheim and the Copenhagen School: A Response to Buzan and Wæver," *Review of International Studies* 24, no. 1 (January): 137–140; M. Williams (1998) "Modernity, Identity and Security: A Comment on the 'Copenhagen Controversy,'" *Review of International Studies* 24, no. 3 (April): 435–439.

49. O. Wæver (1995) "Securitization and Desecuritization," in Lipschutz (1995) *On Security*, pp. 46–86.

50. B. Buzan et al. (1998) *Security: A New Framework for Analysis* (Boulder: Lynne Rienner), p. 5.

51. F. Halliday (1996) "The Future of International Relations: Fears and Hopes," in Smith, Booth, and Zalewski (1996), pp. 318–327, esp. 320.

52. B. Buzan et al. (1998) *Security*, pp. 26, 32.

53. As the dispute over the Gabcikovo-Nagymaros hydroelectric dam project worsened in 1992, the federal minister of environment of the then Czechoslovakian government issued dark warnings that a failure to resolve the controversy could result in "armed conflict" between the two sides. Tensions were particularly strong because the project involved diverting the flow of the Danube River, which delineated the border between the two sides. For details, see Adrian Hyde-Price (1996) *The International Politics of East-Central Europe* (Manchester: Manchester University Press), pp. 95–97.

54. "More recent theorizing about security has attempted to shift attention away from the negative connotations of security towards a more positive aspect. This is reflected in the widely preferred terminology of common or cooperative security which emphasizes a shift away from the mere absence of violence between states and towards meeting basic human needs and rights, broadly conceived." I. Clark (1997) *Globalization and Fragmentation* (Oxford: Oxford University Press), p. 180.

55. John G. Ruggie (1998) *Constructing the World Polity: Essays on International Institutionalization* (London: Routledge), p. 2.

56. Classicial realism is much richer than neorealism in this regard. As Ruggie (1998, p. 5) notes, the classical realists, in contrast to the neorealists, also recognized the socially textured character of international politics. "Nothwithstanding Morgenthau's emphasis on power as the driving force, he saw the world of international politics in socially textured terms"; for example, he recognized how shared values and universal standards of action could affect the operation of the balance of power, and acknowledged a role—albeit limited—for law and organizations.

57. J. G. March and J. P. Olsen (1989) *Rediscovering Institutions* (New York: Free); P. DiMaggio and W. Powell (eds.) (1991) *The New Institutionalism in Organizational Analysis* (Chicago: University of Chicago Press).

58. "Formal organizations may represent the concrete locus at which the other forms of institutionalization can be most clearly aggregate and transformed into more conventional manifestations of power. . . . Organizations are not powerful in themselves, but only in so far as they are constituted within the other elements so far described. Only so far as they can generate, maintain and deploy the social capital upon which they are based—and can continue to do so in ways which accord with the desires of their members—can they maintain themselves as powerful and socially

effective actors." Williams (1997) "The Institutions of Security," *Cooperation and Conflict* 23, no. 3: 287–300, 299–300.

59. J. Nye (1990) *Bound to Lead: The Changing Nature of American Power* (New York: Basic), p. 182.

60. Buzan (1993), pp. 105–115.

61. Buzan et al. (1998) *Security*, p. 12.

62. A. Acharya (1997) "The Periphery as the Core: The Third World and Security Studies," in Krause and Williams (1997), pp. 299–328, esp. 319.

63. Ibid., p. 317.

64. Conflicts of interest and persistent rivalries have not been abolished in this zone of peace and continue to provide the dynamics of international relations in contemporary Europe. However, they are pursued without recourse to military threats, often through multilateral settings, and certainly within an established normative framework underpinned by a dense institutional matrix. As Chris Donnelly, NATO's special adviser for Central and East European affairs, has written, "There is no longer any fear, in either East or West, of a general high-intensity war. We all need to recognise that we have been viewing the world with a hefty residue of Cold War mentality, about Russia, about NATO, and so on. Now is the time to turn the corner and build security in Europe on a brand new basis" (Donnelly 1996: 23).

65. J. Mearsheimer (1990) "Back to the Future: Instability in Europe After the Cold War," *International Security* 15: 5–57.

66. W. Wallace (1999) "Europe After the Cold War: Interstate Order or Post-Sovereign Regional System?" *Review of International Studies* (Special Issue) 25 (December): 201–224.

67. Hobsbawn (1994) *Age of Extremes*.

68. Robert Cooper, a member of the British diplomatic service (although writing in a personal capacity), has declared that "what happened in 1989 was not just the end of the Cold War, but also the end of the balance-of-power system in Europe." Robert Cooper (1996) *The Post-Modern State and World Order* (London: Demos), p. 7. Similarly, U.S. Secretary of State Madeleine Albright has argued that "today in Bosnia, virtually every nation in Europe is working together to bring stability to a region where conflict earlier this century tore the continent apart. This reflects a sharp departure from the spheres of influence or balance of power diplomacy of the past, and an explicit rejection of the politics based on ethnic identification." Madeleine Albright (January 9, 1997), USIS Official Text (U.S. Embassy, London).

69. K. Deutsch (1957) *Political Community and the North Atlantic Area* (Princeton: Princeton University).

70. K. Boulding (1978) *Stable Peace* (Austin: University of Texas).

71. This is evident from the debate on EU enlargement. In Sweden, for example, it has been argued that "enlargement is essential because accession to the EU will enhance security, not only for the new member states but also for the present ones. It will open markets, generate trade and investment and underpin economic growth and development. It will secure and promote a good environment" (Sven-Olof Petterson, deputy undersecretary of state, Swedish Foreign Ministry). Similarly, Gunnar Lund (Swedish undersecretary of state and permanent representative to the EU Inter-Governmental Conference) has argued that "for us, such enlargement would strengthen the possibilities of peace in our immediate vicinity and through it increase security levels in the region." See G. Lindström (1997) *Sweden's Security Policy* (Paris: WEU Institute), p. 33.

72. J. Mueller (1994), *Quiet Cataclysm*, p. 536.

73. Carnegie Commision Report (1997), p. 25.

74. R. Bhaskar (1979) *The Possibility of Naturalism* (Brighton, U.K.: Harvester); R. Keat and J. Urry (1975) *Social Theory as Science* (London: Routledge).

75. D. Layder (1993) *New Strategies in Social Research* (Cambridge: Polity), p. 54.

76. T. Dunne (1995) "The Social Construction of International Society," *European Journal of International Relations* 1, no. 3 (September): 367–389.

77. E. Adler (1997) "Seizing the Middle Ground: Constructivism in World Politics," *European Journal of International Relations* 3, no. 3 (September): 319–363, esp. 322.

78. T. Risse–Kappen (1994) "Ideas Do Not Float Freely: Transnational Relations, Domestic Structures, and the End of the Cold War," *International Organization* (Spring).

3

Complexity Theory and European Security: What Capacity to Describe, Prescribe, or Forecast?

Walter C. Clemens Jr.

Proponents of complexity theory hope to develop a general theory able to explain many different types of phenomena—social as well as biological and physical. If complexity theory fulfills this goal, it should also improve our understanding of international relations.[1] How well does it perform this function?

This chapter reviews the capacity of complexity theory to describe, guide, and predict the nature of European security. I argue that complexity theory helps us to describe and understand Europe's evolving security system but that this theory—partly because it is so general—cannot forecast how the system will evolve or recommend ways to improve it. I also argue, however, that prevailing international relations theories that stress material power or ideational factors do little or no better. A broader understanding of European security could gain from linking complexity theory with insights from Immanuel Kant's vision of the conditions for peace, from the model of complex interdependence, and from policy analysis of value-creating for mutual gain versus value-claiming for zero-sum gain.[2]

I begin by attempting to define complexity theory and tracing its ties to other forms of systems theory. Second, I apply complexity theory to illustrate its strengths and weaknesses for explaining, prescribing, and predicting Europe's ability to deal with issues of military, economic, and cultural security. These applications, we shall see, point to several paradoxes. For example, the theory cannot anticipate whether a unified Europe will bolster or undermine Europeans' capacity for defense; neither can it say whether closer unity will nurture or throttle Europeans' capacity for innovation. Complexity theory cannot say whether Europeans concerned with fitness should give priority to Europe as a whole or to its parts. The concept of fitness does not help to say where Europe should begin and end. Neorealism and most other theories of international relations, however, suffer from similar limitations.

Despite the limitations of complexity theory, I argue that this theory, especially when tied to other disciplines concerned with evolution, can enlarge our vision and complement other approaches to the study of international relations and European security. Not just rugged individualism but a capacity for self-organization, we may see, is a weighty factor in survival and prosperity.

WHAT IS COMPLEXITY THEORY?

Developed by scholars from various disciplines, complexity theory integrates concepts from many fields to produce a new slant on evolution. Let us summarize some key propositions of complexity theory, particularly as articulated by Stuart Kauffman and other scholars—from Nobel physics laureate Murray Gell-Mann to Nobel economics laureate Kenneth Arrow—who have interacted at the Santa Fe Institute.[3]

Fitness

Complexity theory modifies Darwin's emphasis on natural selection as the key to evolution. It portrays fitness as an ability to cope with complexity, a capacity to survive challenges and make the most of opportunity. Fitness is found between rigid order and chaos; not in a crystal, where every atom resides in an ordered hierarchy, or in gases, where molecules move at random.

Self-organization—"Order for Free"

Complexity theory notes that evolution is shaped not only by Darwinian selection but also by spontaneous self-organization. This need not imply a Creator or Grand Watchmaker. Evolution often gives rise to emergent properties, holistic phenomena richer and larger than the sum of their parts, for example, their chemical ingredients. Thus an infant's brain can learn more rules than are contained in its genes.

An agent-based system is one in which independent agents, each following a few rules, self-organize to form an emergent phenomenon without central direction from above. Thus many species interlock in a coral reef and provide one another protection from predators, temperature extremes, and strong currents. Without planning, they cooperate for mutual gain. Like the coral reef, every durable ecosystem is an emergent phenomenon.

Complexity theory borrows and incorporates concepts from many disciplines. One is self-organized criticality. Balanced between order and chaos, a fit being is like a sand pile that, if one more grain of sand is added, may collapse in an avalanche. This fragile equilibrium is called *self-organized criticality*. Avalanches follow a bell curve—many small avalanches and some large ones.

Another imported concept is that of punctuated equilibrium. Evolution is often marked by surges of speciation and avalanches of extinction.[4] Species often develop quickly, endure with little change for a long time, and then die out suddenly—not gradually. Thanks to mutation and self-organization, members of the species find their niche and hang on to it.[5] When their environment changes, they must adapt or disappear. The complexity theory notion of fitness helps account for punctuated equilibrium.

Coevolution

No individual or species evolves alone. Each coevolves with others and with their shared environment.[6] A change in any one element can alter the fitness of multiple actors. This idea is implicit in Darwinism, in systems and chaos theory, and in much international relations analysis.

Complexity theory depicts coevolution by means of fitness landscapes. The relative and changing fitness of each organism or species can be portrayed as a peak rising from a valley floor—peaks that rise and fall as a consequence of coevolution. As in an arms race, the peaks of a predator and its prey may increase and decline with changes in their offensive and defensive capabilities. If attackers increase their speed or lethal weapons, the fitness peak of the prey will decline. If individuals among the prey population acquire characteristics that reduce their vulnerability, their peak will rise.

Common Patterns of Coevolution

Complexity theory carries forward in some ways the work of Petr Kropotkin nearly a century ago. He, too, studied the evolution of all life forms, summarized in his book *Mutual Aid*. Like Kropotkin, complexity theory denies that rugged individualism is the sole key to survival; cooperation—spontaneous or deliberate—can also promote survival. Many societies decline when their members fail to pool their strengths for the common good.[7] One reason to study complexity theory is that, if true, it might permit scholars to understand more than one organism or system without having to know the details of each one's structure and logic. Complexity theory searches for commonalities in biological evolution, technological evolution, and societal evolution.[8]

SYSTEMS THINKING IN
INTERNATIONAL RELATIONS

If valid, complexity theory should help us understand the place of international relations in the great chain of being. Complexity theory could help international relations scholars to transcend the simplistic visions of most realists and idealists.[9] It could reinforce calls for a new paradigm, perhaps one rooted in the interdependence of multiple international relations actors—their shared vulnerability and capacity to hurt or help one another.[10]

From ancient thinkers such as Plato to today's long-cycle theorists, philosophers and historians have searched for systemic patterns within political and economic networks.[11] Complexity theory offers another step in the quest for a general systems theory—holistic and dynamic. Systems thinking steps past linear thinking and instructs us to look at how parts interact to shape a whole. It alerts us to the prospect of nonlinear behavior, multiplier and threshold effects, positive and negative feedback, unforeseen and unintended consequences. It warns that actions intended to advance a certain goal may trigger system effects that render that goal less attainable.

Today's systems theorists are sometimes overconfident in their ability to perceive the whole. Such hubris can also infect international relations theory. Certainly students of world affairs need to see the forest, but they must also know the trees, the bushes, and other parts of the whole. They must trace not only structure but actual behavior.[12]

Complexity theory shares with other forms of systems theory a capacity to transcend a narrow focus on material factors of power or on ideational factors. Carried to an extreme, however, all such approaches tend to be highly deterministic, ignoring the differences between individual units in the system. Systems theorists also tend to minimize the effects of subjective elements such as self-identity and conscious decisions to pursue one goal rather than another, using certain tactics and not others.[13]

IS COMPLEXITY THEORY RELEVANT
TO EUROPEAN SECURITY?

Complexity Theory's Power to Describe

Complexity theory, as noted earlier, aspires to explain diverse phenomena. It integrates many concepts that help us to describe key issues of European security and diagnose its problems:

- The concept of fitness tied to coevolution reminds us that European security must be evaluated in tandem with the security of other actors, beginning with Russia, and trends in their shared environment. Westerners often seem oblivious to Moscow's perception of actions that extend NATO to Russia's doorstep. They forget what they once esteemed—Mikhail Gorbachev's insight that for security to be genuine it must be mutual.[14]

- The idea that optimal fitness is found between rigid order and chaos also illuminates Europe's deep assets. Europe has shed much of the rigid order that undermined its fitness in the past while reducing or transcending chaos. Today Europe has shown it can cope with many, though not all, complex challenges.

- The concept of emergent property gives insight into European integration. Since the late 1940s an emergent property of European unity has taken shape—laws, customs, and institutions plus an expectation that Europeans will cooperate to address their problems. This emergent phenomenon has been cultivated by functionalist and neofunctionalist leaders who saw opportunity as well as challenge in the dynamics of technology and economics.

- The notion of punctuated equilibrium also helps explain the movement toward European integration. The concept helps us understand why there have been surges toward European unity followed by long periods of stability.[15] Some commentators have erroneously declared that "Europe is going nowhere" when, in fact, the forces of change were consolidating, ready to be punctuated by more rapid change. Commentators would often have been more accurate if they had said merely that "European unity has stalled." Periods of equilibrium, of course, need not be followed by closer integration; fragmentation is also possible, as happened to the Association of Southeast Asian Nations when buffeted by economic chaos starting in 1997.

- Defining fitness as the ability to cope with complexity helps us to compare the European Union with other international governmental organizations (IGOs) striving to tap the energies of still sovereign states. Despite its growing pains, the EU is far more fit than the Commonwealth of Independent States (CIS), endangered by fears of excessive order as well as by near anarchy among its members. The lesser parties to the CIS worry that the erstwhile hegemon, Russia, may bully them. By contrast, the Organization for Security and Cooperation in Europe (OSCE) is weak because it has too many members and too little central power.

- Complexity theory stimulates us to think about the landscape of fitness. The fitness peaks of individual European states rise and fall relative to one another. The internal fitness of Europe certainly gained relative to Russia in the 1990s, but it may have declined relative to the United States.

The Power to Prescribe

Although complexity theory helps us to understand recent trends, it has little capacity to prescribe ways to enhance Europe's fitness. It holds that self-organization, like the invisible hand of Adam Smith, arises spontaneously from nature. If this is so, proactive policy guidance and rules are unnecessary. They could even be counterproductive.

What if we relax this assumption and concede that optimal fitness, for human societies, may require active political intervention? Such a theoretical modification would resemble the way that neoliberal economists impose on Adam Smith's trust in an invisible hand. Even if we allow an important role for human intervention, complexity theory does not spell out policy content. Fitness for whom? is one underlying question. We may assume that each actor wishes to enhance its own fitness (however defined), but Europe consists of many parts. Which should have priority—the whole or its parts? If the latter, *which* parts—business interests or labor? Germany or Portugal?

A second basic problem is to identify and prioritize security threats. The definition of *security*, of course, has many dimensions—military, economic, cultural, environmental. But complexity theory cannot say whether the most pressing dangers come from within or from outside Europe. If the greatest menace is internal, which problems are most pressing? Should Europeans worry more about environmental degradation, social disorder, unemployment, lagging competitiveness, unwanted immigration, or falling birthrates? If Europe's greatest threats are from outside, do they come from renewed Russian military pressure or from Balkan-type conflicts on the periphery?

Both internal and external threats exist, but their salience varies across Europe. Germany, for example, is more attuned to threats from Russia than is Spain. Also, some threats are latent but can quickly become actual. Complexity theory offers no way to explain whether Europeans should seek to uplift their quality-of-life rankings on the UN Human Development Index or beef up their military prowess.

The bottom line is that complexity theory cannot state whether policy should seek the fitness of the whole or some parts. Neither can it say which security threats should take priority. Despite its devotion to emergent properties, complexity theory cannot say whether enlightened actors will pursue self-reliance or collective action when facing diverse threats. In short, there is no clear route to fitness. Let us begin with military threats from outside.

Military security. Assume that Europeans give priority to security from external military threats. If a resurgent Russia should again menace Europe, complexity theory's devotion to emergent properties might imply that Europeans should strengthen their collective military ability. But this recommendation could be wrong, for a united Europe might be weaker than the sum of its parts.

Europe might better resist an external threat if it consisted of many distinct homelands, heavily armed like Sweden and Switzerland. A unified Europe might well suffer from a smug overconfidence or from the parasitic logic of collective action: Europe as a whole might invest fewer resources in defense than would a single state relying on its own resources. A nuclear ultimatum from Moscow might conceivably bring a unified Europe to its knees; a Europe of strongly armed individual states might be more difficult to subdue.

If Europeans worry about the spread of Balkans-type wars, should they unite to extinguish those fires without depending on the United States? The answer could depend on many factors. But if the danger of Balkan escalation is minimal, the EU states might as well wait for Washington to take the lead. In that way the Europeans could spend fewer resources than would be needed if they attempted to do the job without U.S. arms and diplomacy.

So far the EU and the Western European Union have demonstrated very little ability to deal with military threats. Europe may be better off without a WEU than with one that occasions false hopes. Neither is it clear that European security would gain if Europeans pooled their strengths to become a third superpower. Bipolarity or unipolarity might be more stable than tripolarity—especially if one pole is weaker than the others.

Economic security. What if the main threat to Europe is thought to be economic stagnation? Complexity theory cannot tell Europeans whether they should continue to give high priority to social welfare or do more to enhance industrial competitiveness. If welfare gets priority, local policies may be best suited to the task. But if Europeans want to strengthen their industry, complexity theory cannot say whether more or less integration is optimal. Some planners will say that a more integrated Europe could better tap disparate strengths, bolster critical industries, and promote their exports to foreign markets. But the merits of a Japanese-style industrial and trade policy are unclear. Honda succeeded in making world-class autos against the advice of Japan's central policy planners. The United States, with far less industrial or trade policy than Japan or Europe, set the pace in high-technology research and development in the 1990s.

Whose economic fitness should have priority? Should any European country subsidize its farmers? Switzerland does so to keep them in business and to uphold the country's self-reliance. But these subsidies increase the cost of food for most Swiss. Subsidies also distort trade within Europe and globally, overriding complementary strengths. What is good for some Swiss may be bad for Europe as a whole; it may also be bad for most Swiss—unless a global crisis limits food imports.

There is an apparent contradiction in Kauffman's writing about the relative merits of individualism and unity. Kauffman's analysis of "patches" suggests that reducing tensions between parts may promote the health of the whole. But Kauffman's more general thesis is that diversity begets more diversity and growth—in economics and in other spheres.[16]

Contrary to the patch thesis, a whole whose parts are all pointing in the same direction could be weaker than one whose parts are not integrated. In peacetime, economic integration based on complementary specialization and trade can be beneficial, but in times of crisis the units with local self-sufficiency could have better survival prospects. Even in peace, local self-sufficiency can be a plus. The interdependent Soviet city concentrated on producing tractors or TV monitors had less capacity for innovation and growth than a European city such as London with many products. London, of course, has long been linked to the entire world, but its diversity generates strength in times of stability and of crisis.

A resolution to the problem may be that Kauffman's patch analysis deals with what is present; his broader thesis concerns what could be created. A whole with few tensions is likely to be less creative than one alive with thesis and antithesis—compare, for example, Japan with the United States. But creativity requires a blend of order and freedom. The Soviet Union was even more heterogeneous than the United States, but the Soviet system failed to tap the potential of diversity; instead it repressed diversity through top-down directives. The fitness of the United States is more at risk from the other extreme—centrifugal cultural chaos.

Cultural security. What if the most salient threat to Europe is thought to be cultural—the homogenizing forces of McDonald's and MTV? Cultural diversity may hold some inherent advantage akin to biodiversity or genetic diversity in humans.[17] Surely there are special forms of wisdom, beauty, and other values in the many cultures at risk from homogenization. The pressures for McWorld expediency may push Europeans to march in lockstep toward American or EuroEnglish, thus eroding other languages.[18] But many Catalans, Scots, and other minorities believe that their cultural autonomy will be better served by pan-European institutions than by the nation-state in which they are a minority.

Still, if Europeans are more closely wedded to their local cultures than to European culture, if most prefer a local language that few others know (Catalan, Danish, Finnish), then European unity may be a distant dream. Many analysts see the common tongue and shared cultural aspirations of most Americans as a source of U.S. fitness. If a growing percentage of Americans regards English as its second language, U.S. fitness will probably suffer.

On these topics, complexity theory can articulate neither an appropriate strategy nor tactics. It cannot say whether fitness will be better served promoting cultural diversity or by cultivating a common tongue and culture.

Multiple conflicting priorities. We could ignore minority interests and assert that the basic criterion for policy should be the well-being of the largest number of Europeans. Even then, complexity theory cannot say what policy is appropriate except to avoid the poles of rigid order and of chaos. The capacity to deal with complexity may lie between these poles—but *where?* Is overall fitness best promoted at the local, regional, pan-European, transatlantic, or global level? Should Western Europeans—for their own good or the good of Europe—admit Eastern Europeans to the EU? For policy guidance, should Europeans look to the governments of their distinct homelands, to bureaucrats in Brussels, or to bankers in Frankfurt? For defense, should Europeans cultivate the Western European Union or NATO or the OSCE? Should they integrate national aerospace companies to compete with a few merged U.S. giants or try to maintain national vitality? For example, should British Aerospace align closer with Airbus Industrie or with Lockheed or go it alone? For environmental fitness, should Europeans follow the lead of their governments, IGOs, or transnational Green movements? Should Europeans try to perfect the EU, a transatlantic union, or the United Nations? Complexity theory does not say whose fitness should be promoted or how.

Some tasks can probably be done more effectively at one level than another. We can speculate that an integrating Europe will be better able to cope with terrorism and environmental threats than a continent of self-centered homelands influenced by the logic of collective action. Europe's industrial competitiveness—for example, in defense and aerospace—probably requires large markets and limits on the number of producers.

But more unity is not necessarily better for all forms of fitness. Border controls may be stricter when state sovereignty is kept strong. (If common borders prevail, the costs of lax controls are shared like a collective good.) On many issues it is difficult even to speculate: Would Germany and Greece be better able to generate jobs by unilateral actions or by cooperation in an integrating Europe? Time frames are important: Long-term gains might require short- and medium-term sacrifices; social scientists may think of long-term horizons, but politicians focus on the next elections and CEOs on quarterly balance sheets.

Realism and neorealism also give little guidance on how to juggle multiple priorities. An arch realpolitiker might say that power maximization should be the criterion—either for single states or for Europe as a superstate. But this answer is almost as general as the recommendation to pursue fitness. And it may not be politically feasible, because many goals—welfare, cultural, environmental—compete with power maximization.

The Power to Predict

Complexity theory has little ability to predict the future of European security. Kauffman tells us that self-organization generates "order for free." But if this quality is available to all humans, we must wonder: Why are large hunks of humanity entombed in rigid order while others suffer from virtual anarchy?

In retrospect we see that certain regions have lost fitness while others have gained. Chinese, Islamic, Aztec, Incan, and other civilizations have declined relative to the West since 1500. Centers of fitness and creativity have been concentrated in Western Europe and North America, joined in the last century by Japan and, intermittently, by Russia.

Chinese and Islamic civilizations suffered from too much order or too much chaos. Since all humans have approximately the same genetic endowment, differential fitness must be partly explained by culture and luck. Geography is important but rarely decisive. (North America is rich in resources, Japan poor; Europe is between America and Japan; the Soviet Union, however, had a wider resource base even than the United States.) The key to the riddle lies elsewhere. Culture has been the matrix. The distinct cultures of the West and of Japan have permitted and encouraged autonomous economic and other activities; in the West they also encouraged democracy— probably the least-bad form of government.[19]

Looking back we divine that freedom to innovate helped Westerners become more fit. But in 1500 the content of an optimal fitness policy was not clear. The Ottomans, for example, took Constantinople in 1453 and besieged the disorganized Europeans for more than two centuries before they were driven back from Vienna in 1683; the undemocratic Russian Empire was a major actor in nineteenth-century politics; the totalitarian dictatorships of Mussolini, Stalin, Hitler, and Japan looked quite formidable for many years. Only in retrospect do we know that authoritarians started and lost most major wars of the twentieth century.[20]

Complexity theory expects punctuated equilibrium but cannot predict whether Europe will surge toward greater unity or remain at a given level for long periods. Complexity theory implies that freedom to innovate is a vital ingredient in fitness. But complexity theory cannot anticipate whether a unified Europe will nurture or throttle innovation.

COMPLEXITY PLUS OTHER THEORIES

Though deficient in some respects, complexity theory may gain from and enrich other theories relevant to European security. More than two centuries ago Immanuel Kant forecast that the synergy of representative government, a spirit of trade, the growth of law and international organization, and hospitality to diverse cultures would generate peace. Without using the term, Kant portrayed *peace* as an emergent property. Kant's prognosis has spurred a liberal peace theory with much prescriptive and predictive power.[21] But the sample size for the theory and its relatively brief historical basis may be too narrow to form solid inferences. The theory may omit other variables that could explain the same outcome, such as simple satisfaction with the status quo.[22] Finally, the theory does not tell status quo countries how to cope with aggressive revisionists except to push them toward democracy—seldom an option for urgent problems.

The model of complex interdependence developed by Robert Keohane and Joseph Nye overlaps with complexity theory and with Kantian synergy.[23] Interdependence, these authors say, amounts to mutual vulnerability. But when states are linked by *complex* interdependence, the threat of force is almost excluded from their interactions. Such states have many issues on their shared agenda, but none is so important that it overwhelms all others and justifies a resort to arms. These states do not just have summit meetings; their societies interact on many levels—governmental, economic, scientific, and cultural. U.S. ties with Canada and Australia approach this model; so do those linking Western Europeans. Washington and Moscow have long been dependent on the other's strategic restraint; in other realms, however, Russia depends far more on the United States than vice versa.[24]

Complexity theory and the model of complex interdependence took shape nearly at the same time, but complexity theory is cast as a general theory whereas the Keohane-Nye model focuses on international relations. Like Kant's vision, complex interdependence spells out conditions that, if realized, conduce to peace. Like complexity theory, however, complex interdependence does not say how to save local values while promoting broader ones. Neither does it say how to balance the needs of internal fitness against the demands of external security.[25]

The failure of complexity theory to deal adequately with the whole-versus-parts problem could be met, at least partially, by constructivism's assertion that each entity's interests are a product of its identity—its self-portrait. Both identities and interests, it says, are generated by social practices.[26] Giving priority to these variables could help to overcome the excessive determinism of complexity theory. Attention to these variables reminds us of the deep question: Fitness for what—that is, for what values and for whom?

Complexity theory also harmonizes with a paradigm of global interdependence and a predictive-prescriptive policy based on the distinction between creating values for mutual gain and claiming values (exploiting others) for private gain. As the world becomes more closely entwined, and international relations become more complex, policies oriented toward mutual gain (conditioned on reciprocity) have the best prospects of enhancing mutual security and other concerns shared by diverse actors.[27]

Exploitative policies conduce to low fitness by way of anarchy or by rigid dictatorship, for each generates sterility and tends over time to backfire. Mutual gain policies harmonize with self-organization; democracy, creativity; and fitness with the ability to cope with complexity.[28]

CONCLUSION

Our theories respond to mounting complexity and interdependence in the real world. Complexity theory alerts us to many dimensions of fitness, but it is too general to prescribe or predict. Still, complexity theory adds to our understanding of multiple actors in world affairs who share a capacity to hurt or help one another. As Maxim Litvinov put it in the 1930s, peace is indivisible. European security requires world security; one without the other is unthinkable.

Perhaps the conclusion is that the study of security issues and international relations generally could benefit from more positive linkage with other streams of knowledge. Edward O. Wilson, for one, calls for consilience—a jumping together—by natural and social science, ethics, and the arts. Long a student of insect communities, Wilson urges social scientists to follow more closely the discoveries and insights that arise from biology.[29] This kind of consilience would surely push international relations specialists to consider complexity theory as it tries to update Darwin's vision of evolution.

NOTES

1. For background, see *International Studies Quarterly* (Special Issue, Evolutionary Paradigms in the Social Sciences) 40, no. 3 (September 1996); for applications and an extensive bibliography, see Joshua M. Epstein and Robert Axtell (1996) *Growing Artificial Societies: Social Science from the Bottom Up* (Cambridge: MIT Press); and Robert Jervis (1997) *System Effects: Complexity in Political and Social Life* (Princeton: Princeton University Press).

2. These questions are addressed to small and to large countries in Walter C. Clemens Jr. (forthcoming) *The Baltic Transformed: Complexity Theory and European Security*, and (2000) *America and the World, 1898–2025: Achievements, Failures, Alternative Futures* (New York: St. Martin's).

3. Research on complexity at the Santa Fe Institute is summarized in Roger Lewin (1992) *Complexity: Life at the Edge of Chaos* (New York: Macmillan). Stuart Kauffman's major works are (1993) *The Origins of Order: Self-Organization and Selection in Evolution* (New York: Oxford University Press), and (1995) *At Home in the Universe: The Search for Laws of Self-Organization and Complexity* (New York: Oxford University Press). For a skeptical view of complexity theory, see John Horgan (1996) *The End of Science: Facing the Limits of Knowledge in the Twilight of the Scientific Age* (Reading, Mass.: Addison-Wesley), chaps. 5–9. For a more balanced appraisal, see the "Edge of Chaos" and many relevant entries in Ian Marshall and Danah Zohar (1997) *Who's Afraid of Schrödinger's Cat: All the Science Ideas You Need to Keep up with the New Thinking* (New York: Morrow).

The Santa Fe Institute, founded in 1984, publishes the journal *Complexity*. Recent institute working papers include Martin Shubik, "Game Theory, Complexity, and Simplicity, Part I: A Tutorial" (98–04–027); and Melisa Savage and Manor Askenazi, "Arborscapes: A Swarm-based Multi-agent Ecological Disturbance Model" (98–06–056).

Complexity theory has stimulated many essays by political scientist Robert M. Axelrod, who has worked at the Santa Fe Institute. Axelrod's focus, however, has been on solving complex problems by a variety of methods rather than on applying complexity theory as developed by Kauffman et al. See Robert M. Axelrod (1997b) *The Complexity of Cooperation: Agent-Based Models of Competition and Cooperation* (Princeton: Princeton University Press), and his paper, "Advancing the Art of Simulation in the Social Sciences," prepared for the International Conference on Computer Simulation and the Social Sciences, Cortona, Italy, September 22–25, 1997. For an application of complexity theory by a former student of Axelrod, see Lars-Erik Cederman (1997) *Emergent Actors in World Politics: How States and Nations Develop and Dissolve* (Princeton: Princeton University Press). The utility and limitations of complexity theory were assessed also by Hayward R. Alker and Simon Fraser (1996) "On Historical Complexity: 'Naturalistic' Modeling Approaches from the Santa Fe Institute," paper delivered at the American Political Science Association annual meeting, San Francisco, August 31, 1996; see also Hayward R. Alker (1996) *Rediscoveries and Reformulations: Humanistic Methodologies for International Studies* (Cambridge: Cambridge University Press).

4. See Stephen Jay Gould (1989) *Wonderful Life: The Burgess Shale and Nature of History* (New York: W. W. Norton).

5. Punctuated equilibrium arises because the entire universe is expanding. Ours is a nonequilibrium universe with multitudes of free energy. Like the universe, the earth's biosphere is a nonequilibrium system, shaped by the flux of solar radiation. The order we perceive in life reflects both low-energy equilibrium forms and dissipative structures—living whirlpools that import and export matter and energy.

6. Kauffman places all life in the context of coevolution. See also Charles J. Lumsden and Edward O. Wilson (1981) *Genes, Mind, and Culture: The Coevolutionary Process* (Cambridge: Harvard University Press); Martin A. Nowak et al. (1995) "The Arithmetics of Mutual Help," *Scientific American* 272, no. 6 (June): 76–81.

7. Kropotkin's book *Mutual Aid* (1902) sought to rebut Thomas H. Huxley (1888) *The Struggle for Existence*. Both works are republished in Kropotkin (1955) *Mutual Aid: A Factor of Evolution* (Boston: Extending Horizons); see also Petr Kropotkin (1924) *Ethics, Origin, and Development* (New York: Dial).

8. This kind of quest has engaged many Russian thinkers: Kropotkin, cited above; Vladimir Vernadsky, Andrei D. Sakharov, and others. Despite party pressures to praise the insights of Marxism, the quest also engaged some Soviet scholars who endeavored in the late 1970s and early 1980s to develop an interdisciplinary approach to the study of global problems known as *globalistika*. See Kendall E. Bailes (1990) *Science and Russian Culture in an Age of Revolutions: V. I. Vernadsky and His Scientific School, 1863–1945* (Bloomington: Indiana University Press); and Walter C. Clemens Jr. (1990) *Can Russia Change? The USSR Confronts Global Interdependence* (Boston: Unwin Hyman), chaps. 5 and 6.

9. For a critique of neostructuralism's emphasis on the power hierarchy of the international system, see Jack Snyder and Robert Jervis (eds.) (1993) *Coping with Complexity in the International System* (Boulder: Westview); see also Jervis (1997), *System Effects*.

10. Walter C. Clemens Jr. (1998) *Dynamics of International Relations: Conflict and Mutual Gain in an Era of Global Interdependence* (Lanham, Md.: Rowman and Littlefield).

11. For an analysis of civilizations, see Arnold J. Toynbee (1934–1961) *A Study of History*, 12 vols. (New York: Oxford University Press); see also the works of sys-

tems theorists such as Ludwig von Bertalanffy, Ervin Laszlo, and Jay W. Forrester (1971), which was adapted in several Club of Rome studies of the global problematique; see also the book of international relations specialists Nazli Choucri and Robert C. North (1975) *Nations in Conflict* (San Francisco: Freeman).

12. Walter C. Clemens Jr. (1972–1973) "Ecology and International Relations," *International Journal* (Special Issue, Earth Politics) 28, no. 1 (Winter): 1–27.

13. As a result, complexity theory would tend to dismiss the weight of cultural clashes and how an actor identifies itself. On the importance of these variables, see Michael C. Desch (1998) "Cultural Clash: Assessing the Importance of Ideas in Security Studies," *International Security* 23, no. 1 (Summer): 141–170, and Ted Hopf (1998) "The Promise of Constructivism in International Relations Theory," *International Security* 23, no. 1 (Summer): 171–200.

14. For documentation, see chapter 7 in Clemens (1990) *Can Russia Change?*

15. See Daniel Lerner and Morton Gorden (1969) *Euratlantica: Changing Perspectives of the European Elites* (Cambridge: MIT Press).

16. Compare *At Home in the Universe*, pp. 247–252, 265–271, and 289 ff.

17. A heterogeneous population with great diversity of genes is probably more disease-resistant than a relatively homogeneous population. Europeans whose ancestors endured and survived the Black Plague may have genetic structures that protect them against HIV infection better than Africans and others never exposed to the plague. Europeans in Spain and elsewhere remote from the Black Plague may have less protection than other Europeans who faced it directly. Descendants of survivors who have two copies of the gene, one from each parent, are immune to most forms of HIV infection. Those with one copy may be infected with HIV, but in them the disease will take years longer to progress than usual. See J. C. Stephens et al. (1998) "Dating the Origin of the CCR5-Delta 32 AIDS-resistance Allele by the Coalescence of Haplotypes," *American Journal of Human Genetics* 62, no. 6 (June): 1507ff.

18. Benjamin R. Barber (1996) *Jihad Versus McWorld: How Globalism and Tribalism Are Reshaping the World* (New York: Ballantine).

19. Nathan Rosenberg and I. E. Birdzell Jr. (1986) *How the West Became Rich: The Economic Transformation of the Industrial World* (New York: Basic); and Paul Kennedy (1987) *The Rise and Fall of the Great Powers: Economic Change and Military Conflict from 1500 to 2000* (New York: Random House). The school of world systems theory, however, emphasizes that the core imperial nations have grown rich by plundering the less developed periphery. See Immanuel Wallerstein (1979) *Capitalist World-Economy* (Cambridge: Cambridge University Press) and (1991) *Geopolitics and Geoculture* (Cambridge: Cambridge University Press).

20. Clemens (1998) *Dynamics of International Relations*, chaps. 4 and 10.

21. Bruce Russett, John Oneal, and David R. Davis (1998) "The Third Leg of the Kantian Tripod for Peace: International Organizations and Militarized Disputes, 1950–1985," *International Organization* 52, no. 3 (Summer): 441–467; see also Clemens (1998) *Dynamics of International Relations*, chaps. 10 and 15.

22. See Hopf (1996) "The Promise of Constructivism," pp. 191–192, and David L. Rousseau, Christopher Gelpi, and Dan Reiter (1996) "Assessing the Dyadic Nature of the Democratic Peace, 1918–1988," *American Political Science Review* 90, no. 3 (September): 527.

23. Robert O. Keohane and Joseph S. Nye (1989) *Power and Interdependence*, 2nd ed. (New York: HarperCollins, an update of work begun in the 1970s).

24. These trends were evident in the 1970s if not before. See Walter C. Clemens Jr. (1979) *The U.S.S.R. and Global Interdependence: Alternative Futures* (Washington, D.C.: American Enterprise Institute).

25. Elsewhere, however, Nye argues the utility of promoting soft as well as hard power and leadership in the information revolution.

26. Hopf (1996) "The Promise of Constructivism," p. 176.

27. Clemens (1998) *Dynamics of International Relations*. The concept of creating and claiming values is developed in David A. Lax and James K. Sebenius (1986) *The Manager as Negotiator: Bargaining for Cooperation and Competitive Gain* (New York: Free Press); it parallels the distinction between mutual gain and exploitation in Walter C. Clemens Jr., "The Non-Zero Sum Hypothesis and the National Self-Interest," paper presented to the Peace Research Society (International), Central European Section, Vienna, August 29, 1971, inspired in part by Kropotkin's book *Mutual Aid*. For an update of Kropotkin, see Robert Wright (2000) *Nonzero: The Logic of Human Destiny* (New York: Pantheon).

28. Compare, for example, the Marshall Plan and the so-called Molotov Plan. From 1947 to 1951, the United States loaned or gave some $13 billion to Europe and helped generate a security community of prosperous partners. From 1945 until 1956, the Soviet Union extracted some $20 billion from its satellites, leaving them impoverished and ready to revolt. "Euratlantica" developed the ability to cope with complexity; the Soviet empire alternated between rigid order and anarchy.

29. Edward O. Wilson (1998) *Consilience: The Unity of Knowledge* (New York: A. A. Knopf).

4

Modern Technology and the Future of the Soldier

DAVID ROBERTSON

Soldiering—that pleasant, clubbable occupation compounded equally of regimental duties, minor imperial skirmishes, and field sports.
—Michael Howard, *Three People*

I am assuming that military force will continue to be used by those with political power well into the twenty-first century. But this is only uncontentious if we use *military force* in its widest sense. Even the most optimistic must surely expect that trade embargos and similar economic coercion will have to be used, perhaps often, in the decades ahead—and to make such embargos effective naval forces are essential. The arms-trade restrictions on states in the former Yugoslavia in the late 1990s were very demanding of naval resources. And there is little reason to believe that the United States will entirely give up its use of modern-day gunboat diplomacy via airpower—either manned or possibly entirely based on long-range precision-guided missiles.

But the thesis that military force in the narrower sense will continue to be useful and used is far less of a truism. Several important theoretical points can be highlighted by talking about the future of ground forces as opposed to soldiers per se (as the title of this chapter suggests). In its broadest sense this includes armies; in its narrowest, infantry.

Although I refer obliquely to those with political power, I need to specify that I am going to discuss the use of ground forces by advanced industrial states; but I am also going to assume that the targets of such use will not themselves be other advanced industrial states. Thus less advanced states and nonstate powers are the putative objects in the future of the soldier. Given these constraints, insisting that ground forces will have a major role in the policies of current NATO members well into the twenty-first century is far from obvious. Unlike naval and airpower, the use of ground forces involves a preparedness to do several things for which the political will in Western nation-states is in short supply.[1] Ground forces imply objectives that involve much more direct and complicated intervention in target nations and target societies; they constitute a more clear-cut breach of nonintervention assumptions; and they require an acceptance of much higher friendly casualty rates than any other form of military force. It must be said, however, that the experience of Kosovo may produce a different weakness of political will. When it finally comes home to the Western electorates that their governments effectively mounted a countervalue strategic air bombardment of largely civilian targets in an independent state in 1999, airpower may itself begin to attract serious political problems. U.S. advocates of airpower, finding the first ever apparent example of Douhet being right, might be wise to proclaim this less noisily than they are beginning to:

> To the surprise of many, airpower played the deciding role in a major theater war. In Operation Allied Force, airpower forced Slobodan Milosevic to the bargaining table and convinced him to withdraw thousands of troops, police, and paramilitaries while letting an international peacekeeping force enter Kosovo. Remarkably, this was accomplished without the loss of a single NATO airman in combat, despite 78 days in which NATO aircrews faced a dangerous, well-equipped enemy.[2]

As it happens, I believe ground forces will have an important role, a historically new rather traditional role, and possibly a role of greater rather than lesser importance vis-à-vis naval and airpower than has been true for a long time. But these are, as it were, fighting words, and my main aim here is to justify them. First we have to see why this proposition can (indeed, must) be seen as controversial.

There are two reasons to wonder whether the soldier has a future: politicosocial and technological. The politicosocial reason is not really my remit here, which is not to raise major theoretical issues about future conflict. However, I cannot accomplish my more mundane and technical task without some assumptions in this area. Thus, although I must state such assumptions, I cannot here defend or develop them.

My politicosocial assumptions are:

1. The thawing of the Cold War has unfrozen the world in such a way as to allow far more conflict far more easily to emerge, often with more dramatically vicious consequences, both within and between most societies outside the traditional Western powers of the old system.[3]

2. The old Western leaders, especially the United States, have entered into an interventionist mode even more intense than when the Cold War alliances made intervention geostrategically dangerous.

3. The electorates of those powers, though themselves largely responsible for the thrust toward intervention, are and will remain deeply
squeamish about the results, both in terms of friendly and hostile casualties and even in terms of wanting to minimize the political impact of
interventions. In other words, electorates and governments want to
stop civil wars and genocides and to respect national political autonomy; they want to intervene and to support the international law value
of nonintervention, and they want to do it without anyone being killed.
This point is reinforced by a growing concern for the impact of nonmilitary options like trade embargos on civilian populations. As
Western publics become concerned with, for example, children's
death rates caused allegedly by drug shortages in Iraq, some forms of
military action may come to be seen as actually preferable.

My technological assumptions are not really mine at all, but they must be
considered:

4. Modern military technology has reached a level at which military
force can be applied in the pursuit of the goals in assumptions 1–3
above. The restrictions built into them mean almost no use of face-to-
face combat on the territories of the target powers; through air and
naval power there is very little need for ground forces even to enter
the territories, let alone to combat troops of states or nonstate powers.

Such promises of the technology interact with the take-no-casualties-and-
cause-as-few-as-possible restrictions to make it seem that there really may be
no future for the soldier. This position, in its most extreme form, recently
received a tremendous boost from the Kosovo experience. (Still, it takes a
robust attitude to define an acceptably low number of opposition fatalities in
order to make air campaigns seem to satisfy that rule.) Commenting on the
Kosovo air war, a U.S. military officer writing in the U.S. Air Force's professional journal could, at best, come up only with the following formulation:
"Air superiority and aircrew confidence promoted morale among the NATO
coalition, and the collateral damage to civilians *was a miniscule fraction of
that witnessed in World War II.*"[4]
I think this is wrong, but I do believe that the future role of the soldier will
be unbelievably demanding, and we might not be able to find enough people
willing to take the job. But first I must examine the reasons behind the popularity of my fourth assumption, because the interaction of this supposed technological possibility with the politicosocial model suggests we might not need
soldiers anymore. By themselves neither set of assumptions does this. Without
the hope of technologically delivered safe intervention, there might be much
less of a demand to intervene. Without the expectation of intervention, tech-

nology would not lead to the reduction in importance of soldiers, because the
military machines would be geared up only for the extremely improbable traditional war between technological equals, where ground forces will naturally have a role. As such, they would be small contingency forces but would differ only incrementally from the opposing European armies of 1990. Why
technology is thought to raise questions about the future of the soldier can best
be studied through U.S. eyes.

THE REVOLUTION IN MILITARY AFFAIRS

The so-called revolution in military affairs (RMA) is the latest in the never-
ending battle over U.S. military doctrine, involving military professionals, the
defense intelligentsia, and politicians. What fuels U.S. confusion on military
planning at the moment is the unfortunate coincidence of the end of the Cold
War with the successes and failures of the Gulf War, further confounded by
U.S. experiences in Somalia, Serbia, and even Panama City and Haiti. Much
the same issues are debated in Western European defense establishments,
prompted more by the post–Cold War defense budget cuts. The future of the
Western European soldier will inevitably be deeply affected by what the
Americans decide to do. A semiofficial definition of a revolution in military
affairs is given by the U.S. Department of Defense (DoD; from the secretary's
Office of Net Assessment): "A Revolution in Military Affairs is a major
change in the nature of warfare brought about by the innovative application of
new technologies which, combined with dramatic changes in military doctrine
and operational and organizational concepts fundamentally alters the character and conduct of military operations."

This theory is merely the application of orthodox military history to current circumstances; historians have long analyzed military history in terms of
revolutionary changes brought about by new weapons or other scientific-technological breakthroughs. One of the best presentations of the current position
notes that previous RMAs have either been single-system revolutions—gun-
powder, atomic weapons—or of combined systems—the interwar development of weapons and ideas for armored warfare by the German army,
amphibious warfare by the U.S. Marine Corps, carrier warfare by the U.S.
Navy, and strategic bombing by the U.S. Army Air Forces. Collectively these
revolutionized warfare between 1918 and 1939. Now, the authors claim:

> Evidence suggests that the revolution unfolding today is neither a "combined
> system" or "single-system" RMA but rather an "integrated system" RMA.
> The outlook is for the rapid evolution of new technologies eventually lead-
> ing to the development of several advanced military systems. These systems,
> when joined with their accompanying operational and organizational con-
> cepts, will become "integrated systems." In contrast to developments during

the interwar period, this system of systems approach will aim to take advantage of the cumulative effect of employing each of the new capabilities at the same time. In World War II, each new form of warfare took place in its own operating medium—Armoured Warfare on land battlefields, Strategic Bombing in the air over homelands, Carrier Warfare at sea, and Amphibious Warfare at the intersection of land and sea—and only occasionally interacted with the others. In the current RMA, the integrated employment of all the new systems will be essential to take advantage of their true utility.[5]

There are, in fact, many different versions of the supposed revolution—and not a few dissenting voices—but the literature is too rich and complex to analyze properly here. One dissenting voice puts both the undoubted fact of the revolution and its possible irrelevance rather well:

> The drag-on debates as to whether or not there has been or is an RMA, what it portends, and how it differs from the "Military-Technical Revolution," are frivolous and irrelevant. The endless symposiums, studies, and articles are popular because they promise a new home to those intellectually dispossessed by the end of the Cold War. "Thinking" about the manageable secondary problem of the military application of technology in the future saves us from having to think meaningfully about the brutal, intractable issues immediately confronting our nation, our allies, and our interests.[6]

The revolution consists of three interweaving elements: very accurate, near-real-time information; near-complete accuracy and very long range in all weapons systems; and the ability to fight a parallel war in which an enemy's combat troops, command and control systems, logistics, state structures, and civilian economic targets can be hit simultaneously. It is a revolution in which airpower theorists feel they can finally make good the promises of strategic airpower but also in which ground forces can imagine total battlefield domination and the capacity to destroy the opponent's ground forces with near zero casualties. It is, in effect, a theoretical explanation of the Gulf War outcome combined with all the forces that used to advocate complex precision-guided weapons systems as force multipliers against Warsaw Pact tank armies. However realistic the expectations of the RMA advocates are hardly matters. In practice it is a theory about how to replicate an era when European armies fantastically outclassed their colonial opponents. It may be that high-technology will produce, for the most advanced economies, a soldier whose equipment is vastly more effective than his enemy's. The director of the U.S. Army Dismounted Battle Lab conjures up such an image:

> The 21st century land warrior will be a digitized soldier. Working with industry, we have a government contract for about $250 million to develop a system for the next-generation soldier. The system will include visual devices such as a daylight camera and thermal weapon imagery. The heart of

the system is a computer which has an 80 megabyte hard drive. Its menu includes a first aid quick reference, and it has the ability to capture still-frame imagery. The system is powered by a standard radio battery and transmissions go out over a small hand-held radio. It can send pictures and a digitized report up to eight miles in under sixty seconds. The entire system weighs 26 pounds and the cost should end up being $50,000 to $80,000 per soldier. . . . The costs must be weighed against the added lethality it provides for the soldier.[7]

Of course, allowing only a relatively modest cost creep, such battlefield equipment would cost $500 million to outfit 5,000 soldiers in a fighting division; those wearing it would not only have to be enormously more "lethal" to make it worthwhile but very nearly invulnerable.

In many ways the notion of the RMA is internally contradictory precisely because it is a bandwagon onto which classical airpower advocates and ground force theorists have jumped. The consequence is that we end up requiring both very high technology airpower and very high technology ground forces. From our point of interest, the ground forces are so highly and expensively equipped, with correspondingly high training and maintenance costs, that they would have to be used very sparingly indeed. The airpower advocates have to be able to show that only a gentle mopping-up operation would be required of the ground forces. Ground forces, therefore, could not be more than an ancillary force. And unless the rather odd and anachronistic nature of the Gulf War is repeated, it is unclear what their targets would be. Thus we need to look at the Gulf War to see why it is thought to provide a model for future military structures of would-be interventionist states.

The standard DoD analysis of the Gulf War states that airpower, using stealth technology and precision-guided ordnance, first suppressed Iraq's air defenses and then imposed massive materiel damage to its military assets so that a nearly outnumbered Coalition ground force aided by vastly superior weaponry was able to rout Iraqi land forces and drive them out of Kuwait in a nearly casualtyless offensive while inflicting massive Iraqi casualties. There have been several dissenting alternatives to this account, which I find considerably more plausible. Two in particular stand out. John Mueller mounts a convincing argument that the Iraqi troops, in addition to their poor morale, were in fact seriously outnumbered at all important times on the ground. He also notes that the estimates of Iraqi casualties, either during the bombing campaign or the land campaign, were massively exaggerated. In other words, there is very little evidence of a revolution.[8] In Mueller's words, "The Americans gave a war and no one showed up."[9]

This analysis is taken further in an important way by Stephen Biddle, who characterizes the approach of Mueller and others as amounting to saying "the Gulf War was less a revolution than merely the 'mother of all military anomalies.'"[10] Biddle suggests that there are two standard explanations for the

Gulf War's outcome: technical superiority on the part of the Coalition, or Iraqi shortcomings, including morale and numerical inferiority. Instead, he argues that the Coalition's better military technology would not have had such impact but for the tactical, training, and morale weaknesses of the Iraqis. Without the latter, the Coalition's victory would have been very much more costly. The most persuasive part of his article is based on simulation exercises run by the Institute for Defense Analyses, a major U.S. defense think-tank. His suggestion is so important that it is worth considering part of his technical analysis, covering the Battle of 73 Easting. In this engagement, what had been meant as a light reconnaissance probing force of three armored troops did not merely contact but utterly destroyed a major Iraqi brigade in forty minutes, with subsequent counterattacks leading to the complete destruction of the rest of the Iraqi division, supposedly part of the elite Republican Guard. The total loses to U.S. forces were two Bradley Armored Fighting Vehicles and one crew member.

Biddle states the Iraqis made two fundamental tactical errors: not setting up warning posts, and not digging in their tanks properly, which are not the consequence of low-technology or forced errors caused by U.S. military superiority. The highly sophisticated simulation allows the battle to be replayed assuming neither of these errors had been made. The real battle produced an exchange ratio of vehicle losses favoring the United States by a factor of around 43:1. The rerun produces an exchange rate of 1.5:1 in favor of the Iraqi army! Naturally, Biddle does not suggest that the ultimate outcome of the war could have been anything but a Coalition victory, perhaps a relatively cheap one. What is germane is that there can be no doubt that a ground campaign was necessary and that only a fool would regard any supposed revolution as being able to guarantee anything like so costless a war in the future. There is no doubt that the Coalition's air campaign, even counting its successes against purely military objectives, was not enough. Estimates vary, but something like 50–70 percent of all Iraqi armor was destroyed by tanks and army helicopter gunships—not airplanes. Its success against other targets in the parallel war was also not enough, demonstrated by the fact that after a six-week air campaign the land battle still had to be fought. What stands out is the inability of the air campaign to seriously weaken the Iraqi state, either by destroying the state apparatus or destroying civilian morale sufficiently.

In this context we need to consider the two other examples that airpower theorists state might reduce the role of the soldier. The first is NATO's air campaign against the Bosnian Serbs. Even from the beginning it was an unlikely campaign, and indeed many in the military opposed the campaign on the grounds that the relevant targets did not exist. It is impossible to say how much effect the campaign had in practical terms, but as one critic of the RMA-induced U.S. defense procurement plans put it: "In Bosnia . . . ground troops proved essential for a lasting truce. Moreover, to claim that NATO air strikes brought the Serbs to the negotiating table is to overlook the part played by the 100,000 Croatian troops advancing into Serb held territory."[11]

Again, presumably, one is looking at an interaction. There was nothing that NATO would have dared bomb that would have changed Serbian policy, and air strikes in and of themselves could not do more than attrite Bosnian Serb military capacity. Such attrition would not have prevented the Serbs from terrorizing Bosnian Muslims—but enough attrition would have made it even harder to fight against those 100,000 Croatians. Had the Croatian army not been around, only a NATO land campaign—and a huge one at that—could have replaced it. The problem of airpower is what it has always been: Is there a relevant target list available? Suppose it had been necessary, in the end, for European and U.S. military forces to be used in Rwanda to stop the genocide there, as it so nearly was. What, exactly, would even the most perfectly surgical strikes have been aimed at? What would deliberately unsurgical, deliberately dirty counterpopulation strikes intended to destroy civilian morale have been aimed at?

The second example may seem better evidence that soldiers are not really needed anymore: It is the Allied Force campaign to protect Albanian Kosovars against their Serbian neighbors. As Jeffrey Record has said, analyzing the impact of the Kosovo campaign on the U.S. Army's status vis-à-vis the Air Force, Allied Force "should trouble the Army not just because it advertised airpower as an apparently safe and relatively bloodless alternative to labor-intensive ground forces. Why Air*Land* Battle if pilots and missileers can do the job without ground pounders?"[12] Did Kosovo show that the soldier was simply unnecessary? This depends not only on why one thinks Milosevic withdrew his forces from Kosovo but also on whether the costs of achieving this result by airpower alone were less than the costs of doing it at least in part by using soldiers. It is actually very hard to analyze the costs and benefits of strategy in the Kosovo campaign given it was so recent. The real problems are twofold. First, the entire story worked out so very differently from NATO's intentions. It was hardly NATO's plan to force the Serbs to allow the Albanian Kosovars to return to Kosovo after complete ethnic cleansing. It is very hard to credit a strategy with success for achieving something necessary only because of an initial failure. Second, airpower was applied only after NATO had promised not only its own populations but also Serbia that it would not use ground forces. Because of this we cannot logically discuss the relative costs of airpower versus land power.

Some points can be made. The first is to acknowledge that the air campaign did produce a result that some anti-Douhetists had argued simply could not be achieved at all. One air force commentator put the actual results and their implication for theories of airpower rather neatly: "For the first time in history, the application of airpower alone forced the wholesale withdrawal of a military force from a piece of disputed real estate."[13] But even a military historian as wise and learned as John Keegan, who had denounced sole reliance on airpower throughout the major part of the campaign, reversed himself and, in a partial overturning of a lifetime of writing, stated outright "this was a victory for airpower" in an article evocatively, but misleadingly, entitled "So the Bomber Got Through After All."[14] The simplest point to make is that the bombers did indeed get through—*to Serbia*. No serious analyst arguing for the continued utility of ground forces would actually deny that a sufficiently savage attack on both the military and civilian infrastructure of a small and weak country could ultimately force its leaders to change a policy. We could, after all, have nuked Serbia, which might have made ethnic cleansing an unattractive policy option to its government. But are we really in the business of intervention war by strategic bombardment? A successful use of force in Serbia would have stopped ethnic cleansing as soon as NATO had made it clear it was prepared to go to war; it would have entailed a limited war against Serbian military forces inside Kosovo. President Bill Clinton specified several objectives in an early speech: to demonstrate the seriousness of NATO's opposition to aggression and its support for peace; to deter the Serbs from attacking helpless Kosovar Albanians; to make them pay a price for their actions if they continued to do so; and to damage Serbia's capacity to wage war against Kosovo by seriously diminishing its military capabilities.[15]

Obviously the first was satisfied, though the message may be ambiguous if it reinforces beliefs that rogue-state leaders may entertain about NATO, especially the unwillingness of the United States to accept the casualties and costs of ground commitment. The second was not achieved; Serbia's ethnic-cleansing campaign was accelerated to more or less complete success and had to be completely reversed. The third (related to the second) was satisfied; the Serbian population has paid heavily and will for some time to come. Whether moral retribution is an appropriate stance in international relations is somewhat doubtful. It is certainly beyond the scope of what we normally think of as military intervention strategy. Though the jury is still out, it looks almost certain that the fourth was not achieved; very little serious damage seems to have been done to the Serbian military. What was achieved was very costly and took enormous effort. As Earl H. Tilford Jr. says, NATO won

by applying a greater portion of the Air Force's total airframes during this operation than we did in the Korean War, during any period in the Vietnam War, or in Desert Storm. It took the air forces of 13 contributing NATO countries to batter Yugoslavia to the point that Milosevic agreed to withdraw his forces from Kosovo and permit the introduction of a UN peacekeeping force, including Russian troops, into the strife-torn province. And, while it is arguable whether air power was the deciding factor in changing Milosevic's mind, the wear and tear on aircraft, the huge expenditure of sophisticated weaponry, and the continued lowering of morale among service personnel in general and aircrews in particular are more evident.[16]

On top of all this are the straight financial costs. The U.S. Center for Strategic and Budgetary Assessments has estimated the total NATO costs of the campaign (up to the point that ground forces did enter Kosovo) as around $4 billion. The point here is that airpower is not, in fact, an easy option to go for in any respect but one: saving lives among the intervening force. Airpower is the option that can be followed by politicians anxious about their electoral standing. Airpower requires less political will. It might be argued however, that this is one of the many things wrong with it. Should intervening states go to war when the public is not willing to pay the price of the solution? It could be argued that the way in which ground intervention concentrates the mind of the would-be intervener is important.

In truth the debate about whether ground forces should have been used at an earlier stage is futile. The air campaign was precisely that—an early stage. There is now, and will be for an immeasurable time to come, a demonstrated need for soldiers in Kosovo: 50,000 of them, estimated by the same source quoted above as costing up to $3 billion per year just for the U.S. contingent (only 7,000). Allied Force was a campaign to minimize the casualties involved in getting intervention troops into Kosovo. The troops are there, and it cost no NATO lives. Now they have to get on with a job made arguably a good deal harder because the West chose that method of inserting them.

Enough has been said to suggest that any revolution in military affairs has, at best, limited consequences for the future of the soldier (excepting war between technological equals). Before we can make any further progress we need to revisit the question of what sorts of uses our governments might have for military forces in the future.

INTERVENTION SCENARIOS

One of the scenarios the future soldier must be capable of handling is a Gulf War equivalent. After all, the only other major external action of British forces in the last twenty years was also the expulsion of an invader by using the full panoply of military force (except armor) in the Falklands conflict. There are a great many third- and fourth-level national militaries with large conventional forces and political structures likely to reward external adventurism. Odd though the Gulf War seemed at the time, it must be highly likely that UN supporting forces will have to intervene to protect and liberate small countries from adventurism. It is equally likely that such aggressors will, like Iraq, prove difficult to deter or deal with by sophisticated parallel war air strikes; thus the equally traditional combat role of ground troops will endure. What leverage can be gained from advanced weaponry will be needed, if only because in raw manpower the interveners' logistical problems, as well as the fact that the invader is almost certain to use conscription, make it probable that the interveners will be outnumbered. Hence one conclusion about the future is at least in keeping with the RMA to a point: the future soldier, or some of them, will have to be well-trained and well-equipped conventional all-arms fighters.

But these are unlikely to be the most common form of operations for UN supporting troops in the future. Much theoretical effort is being put into attempts to categorize the various ways soldiers might be used in the future. These range on a continuum between the ill-defined notion of humanitarian intervention to the possibility of counterinsurgency warfare in support of a legitimate government threatened by rebellion. Somewhere in there fits the Somalia-type operation, where anarchy prevails without even the structure of organized civil war or a discernible ethnic conflict.[17] To the extent that these types of operations are different from orthodox warfare, they may require an entirely different conceptualization by the military. The fate of the U.S. Army's attempt to deal with this, via the concept of operations other than war, suggests this may not be a very useful activity. The U.S. Army's basic operations doctrine manual, FM100–5, is a sort of military soap opera with rather more plot variety. It has been revised nine times since 1945. Operations other than war were introduced in the 1993 rewrite to complement the standard principles of warfare. By the draft of the 1998 revision they had already been dropped, surely correctly, for something much more like the British army's "seamless web" approach.

However, this does not mean that there is no need to change doctrinal fundamentals or other expectations. It may rather be that the predominant likely mode of operation for the future soldier is new, or at least seems new against the assumptions of the last fifty years, and that traditional doctrine and expectations may not apply at all. John Keegan may have it right when he makes the point about traditional principles of warfare:

> One of the purposes behind the principles has been to make new and strange circumstances comprehensible, to draw a thread from one war to another, to force events into a mould, and to make conflicts obey the dramatic unities. . . A point is reached in the development of weapons systems beyond which one cannot compare the present and the past.[18]

He goes on to say that the principles, which always implied "maximization of means," could not be used for modern conventional war, which demands "subtle response, patience, self-control, firmness but not ruthlessness, and an ability to settle for something less than total victory." In our case it is not particularly the novel weapons systems that cause the gap with traditional war; the trend, when they do work, is a way from indiscriminate destructiveness. Rather it is a sociological change in war.[19]

What I mean by a *sociological change* is fairly complex. It refers predominantly to the expectations of intervening nations, as well as to the conditions under which soldiers will have to operate. It seems that Western nations have reached a stage where they are unprepared to sit back and allow massive suffering during civil wars, ethnic conflicts, and gang struggles in collapsing states. Typical of this sort of posture was the call in a *Foreign Affairs* article on Somalia that in the future "the United States, the United Nations and other intervenors" should be able to "declare a state 'bankrupt' and go in to restore civic order and foster reconciliation."[20] This was a U.S. perspective, of course, but the reactions of parts of the European electorates, and some of the major parties in the last few years, have been in the same direction. The current British government's defense review is openly aimed at making it easier for Britain to join intervention forces,[21] and this has been a large part of the official rhetoric behind President Jacques Chirac's defense reorganization plans, to name just two actors.

Realists can argue, if they wish, that such interventions are really carried out because of the national interests in world stability and the like. Yet they are sold to electorates on moral grounds, and the moral grounds then act as serious constraints. The trouble is that moral intervention carries with it the expectation that the interventions will be very gentle; this, combined with the increasing unwillingness of the same electorates to accept friendly casualties, requires a tremendously sophisticated use of force. As I suggested earlier, it is as though all operations are in the nature of aid to the civil power, even if the civil power in question is the UN or some multinational coalition of interveners. At the same time, the types of conflict—civil wars, mass ethnic violence, collapsed states turned into fields for tribal and gang conflicts, aid against large-scale armed subversion—are very much those that do not produce the target lists for airpower or any other form of indirect force application. (Similarly, these places are not usually open to trade embargos or other forms of economic sanctions, though arms embargos may well become more routine, requiring naval and naval aviation forces.)

The point can be seen more clearly if one considers the war aims of such interventions. A good way of describing the typical war aim is to alter the Clausewitzian norm slightly. In such situations war is not an extension of politics. Rather, war is used to give politics a chance, to stabilize and pacify long enough for some form of acceptable politics to be created in the area. In practice it means that the typical military problem is to get between conflicting groups and hold them apart, or to isolate and disarm groups, bands, and tribes. The truth is that the only useful form of force for these conflicts is ground force.

I have tried repeatedly above to hint that late-twentieth-century warfare is, in its own way, very traditional. The echoes are, of course, to the colonial experiences of European powers, the classic nineteenth- and early-twentieth-century occupation of British and French armies. The analogy to the "colonial gendarmerie" is very much in the minds of military professionals. The first time I heard that phrase to describe the traditional role of the British army was at the very beginning of the 1990s while interviewing a rising paratroop officer who was excited that the light infantry appeared to be coming back into prominence after an uncharacteristic period of dominance by the armored regiments during the Cold War.[22] There have even been lectures by senior RAF officers attempting to remind us that the RAF had a colonial policing role in Iraq and India between the wars. (Trenchard's arguments, when he was desperately seeking to justify an independent air force, were precisely the same: airpower was precise, cheap, and minimized casualties to both sides.)

These operations were often characterized as *subalterns' wars*—isolated and dispersed companies and platoons enforcing order of a sort over wide territories with tremendous local decisionmaking autonomy and corresponding needs for initiative and creativity. When the actual fighting intensifies, as with a more thorough counterinsurgency campaign, they may descend even farther. The British described their fighting against insurgents in Malaysia as a *corporals' war* because small patrols in the jungle became the dominant method of control; certainly an army that has to protect a dispersed ethnic minority in primitive conditions is unlikely to be able to place an entire platoon in every village that needs the intervener's presence.

WHAT SORT OF SOLDIERS WILL WE NEED?

The analogy to colonial policing needs to be understood very carefully, because what we do not need are lightly armed, cheaply equipped troops playing some version of friendly village policemen. Properly understood, the colonial gendarmerie never were like that. By comparison with those they fought, they were well armed and heavily equipped, and they certainly used deadly force whenever necessary; their rules of engagement, had they existed, would not have pleased modern humanitarians. The absolute necessity of minimizing at least friendly casualties cannot be overstated. Precisely because the motivation of modern intervening states is different than in the past, and because it is not in any very direct way the protection of vital national interests, it is impossible to demand of either the troops themselves or the electorates a tolerance for high casualty rates. In fact an intolerance for high casualties is itself a more common condition of the use of military force, dating at least from the widespread use of mercenaries—where the individual soldier was too expensive an investment to be lightly risked—and replicated through-out the history of colonial enforcement: there never were enough available troops to risk any of them easily.[23] When firefights happen, they must be won easily and rapidly, and troops must be maximally protected. They must also—in order to fight dispersed campaigns with too few troops—be highly mobile.

It is crucial to realize that there is an asymmetry to the sociology of future war. The need to minimize casualties, indeed to minimize casualties *to both sides*, is not shared by the likely opponents that are likely to have precisely the opposite profile. One U.S. military commentator lists the first of what he thinks are the myths behind U.S. military thinking: "Our most likely future adversaries will be like us"; "America will face [warriors] who have acquired a taste for killing, who do not behave rationally according to our definition of rationality, who are capable of atrocities that challenge the descriptive powers of language, and who will sacrifice their own kind in order to survive."[24]

Charles Dunlap cites John Keegan in defense of the notion that a form of warrior society is being reborn whereby the young are "brought up to fight, think fighting honourable, and think killing in warfare glorious." Even if this is both far-fetched and not exactly politically correct, the general idea that the opponents of future soldiers are more likely to behave like terrorists than like signatories of the Geneva Conventions is well put. In fact, what we are saying is that while most conflict for the professional soldier of the future will be much more like aid to the civil power, most conflict for the opponent will be normatively deeply unregulated. If soldiers have often been prone to complain that they have been obliged to fight with one arm tied behind their back, the complaint is likely to become nearly permanently true.

This point needs elaborating because quite the opposite theme is stressed often by U.S. advocates of the RMA, who continue to want to see war as somehow or other getting cleaner. One author will serve to typify this response. Steven Metz has argued that modern high-tech war will allow what he calls the *first-tier states* to avoid "the core dilemma for traditional civil-mil-itary relations," which he describes as

> finding a way to cultivate and sustain a body of people with the ability to do things considered abnormal by civilians—to transcend physical discomfort, master fear, and kill or coerce enemies—without undercutting the day-to-day comity that undergirds society. This has required simultaneously culti-vating a warfighter's ethos and instilling the belief that violence must be used only under very special circumstances and against specific targets.[25]

But he thinks this may become unnecessary because physical hardship and killing will be so much less common or demanding; in the same article he goes on to suggest: "This means that First Tier states will no longer have to erect a psychological and attitudinal wall between the military and the society. Soldiering will be much like any other white-collar job. The notion of a distinct military ethos will become quaintly archaic." This is frankly absurd: all the difficult demands from the first quotation will remain, but they will have to be suffered in increasingly frustrating and demanding circumstances. The military ethos will simply become every bit as necessary, though it may be less understood and even less valued or admired. The idea that the opponent will be willing to inflict high casualties, and probably to take them, is linked to another reason why a light force will usually be inappropriate. It is not so much that intervening forces will have to cope with opponents every bit as well armed as themselves, though this is at least occasionally possible; the disparity between state-of-the-art and slightly obsolete weaponry is not particularly great. Even the best main battle tank can, after all, be stopped by a relatively simple antitank weapon, and the most modern helicopter gunship is vulnerable to easily portable (and cheap to buy) missiles, especially when both such systems are wielded by those prepared to take casualties. And the sort of mortars the Bosnian Serbs used against Muslim towns are equally effective against Western soldiers in camp.

Consequently, within the very serious logistic constraints imposed by the fact that all interveners will always be projecting force from a distance, some form of mechanized and at least lightly armored forces would seem to be the norm, even if the main battle tank itself is rather hard to see as useful outside the Gulf War–type scenario. Their artillery and spotting systems certainly need to be as advanced as possible. In fact, there is no reason to expect that intervening ground forces need to be any less sophisticated or well armed than the ones that would be used under any more orthodox set of warfare expectations. Generally the logistics problem, second only to the training-recruitment problem I shall address shortly, is probably the biggest single factor in considering how feasible intervention will be. There is no room here even to begin to explore the complexities of the logistics problem, but one point must be made, because it runs contrary to much of the current political expectations of intervening powers. Recent history shows that governments that have been prepared to intervene have always seen intervention as a short-term process that must produce rapid results, because they are not prepared to keep their troops in position for very long. If I am right that the primary purpose of intervention is to impose a moratorium on conflict to give politics a chance, this is exactly the wrong approach. Troops must be sent in with the expectation that they may be in position—and not just in one or two convenient central bases—for lengthy periods. This means they must be supplied and maintained for lengthy periods. The implications are many. Although equipment must be as high-tech as possible, it must also be as robust and maintenance-free as possible; usage rates of ordnance may not be able to be very great; and the troops themselves may have to be trained and recruited with an eye to lengthy deployment. All our war thinking during and after the Cold War has tended to be short-term, or "burst," in nature, but that is no way to re-create colonial policing.

CAN WE RECRUIT SUCH ARMIES?

I have left to the end, and can only briefly raise, what may be the single biggest restriction on the ability of modern advanced states to intervene successfully in the rest of the world. The future soldier I have sketched may be very hard to find, train, and retain. Let us collect together some of the requirements of the role. The future soldier will have to:

1. Be fully competent with high-tech weaponry and capable of fighting a Gulf-style, all-arms war in cooperation with even more advanced air forces.
2. Be capable of extremely sophisticated intervention operations where an absolute minimum of violence will be permitted and enormous restraint will be required against an opponent who will not be so restricted.
3. Be capable at quite junior levels of commanding small units in isolation while exercising high degrees of initiative subject to the constraint in the second point above.
4. Be prepared for lengthy deployments not only away from home but from central, well-equipped bases.
5. Be prepared to do all this under intense and critical media attention for what may seem like small and undramatic successes.
6. Maintain throughout this a warrior orientation, allowing where necessary maximum and rapid use of violence.
7. In general accept a continual civil-political control at a detailed, even routine, level of activity.

We already know that the demands of modern weapons technology are very high in terms of troop ability; regular tests show that the real payoff of more advanced technology comes about only when the systems are operated by the most highly skilled. But if we add to these technical skills requirements of ability and psychology such as those listed above, then we are talking about a future soldiery that will be of much use only if it recruits the very best available in the interventionist societies. It must be stressed that those recruited must not only be willing but also eager to go into these combat and quasi-combat situations. It will be of no use at all to recruit, as the United States has at times done, able people who see the military as primarily a way to become skilled for later civilian life and who almost resent being sent on active service on the grounds that such duties were not really part of the package. The future soldier is far more likely to see action, perhaps regularly, than the garrison soldiers of the second half of the twentieth century. The future soldier will have to be extremely well trained but may have relatively little time for training; the force is going to be expensive, and the governments will inevitably never have as many troops as they need. There will be continual strain in the roles between the demands of the two sorts of action—the Gulf-style and the aid-to-the-civil-power style. Neither will it be helpful to recruit an officer corps that thinks of short-term commissions before a more sedentary life in commerce, because the most valuable quality of these troops will be experience. Yet the military establishments are never going to be so large that many people can hope for really high rank.

CONCLUSION

Can a modern military hope to compete against civilian employers for people of this ability level? Those with such abilities, little interest in affluence, and the requisite interest in international welfare can enter the civilian sides of the United Nations or their nation's foreign services. So why be a soldier? Those with purely traditional warrior interests will find much of their service life frustrating and indeed probably could not be entrusted with the roles. The problem with recruitment comes because the colonial gendarmerie analogy breaks down sociologically in terms of the structures of modern societies. The colonial officer corps were largely drawn from social classes for whom there were few alternative acceptable careers. The men they commanded were drawn from working classes and peasant strata where the chances of educational advancement were so low that by sheer chance many very able men filled the noncommissioned officer ranks that were the backbone of the services. Social orientations to family life meant long foreign deployments and were no barrier to recruitment, and for all classes and ranks an uncomplicated chauvinistic patriotism and sense of the legitimacy of colonial rule acted to legitimate and motivate. There are almost no analogues in modern society for the structures, beliefs, and institutions that provided the colonial gendarmerie, and yet we are proposing to deploy one quite dramatically more demanding. Where are they coming from?

I have followed a long and circuitous route to answer the question with an incredibly unexciting response: the future soldier will be very much like the current soldier in equipment, and half of him will be alike in training and role. The other half will be expected to bring that training and equipment into operation in ways that used to be, but for a long time have not been, what soldiering was all about. They will be like current soldiers, only better and very much scarcer and very much busier. But it is worth producing such a boring, if positive, response if only because so many seem to think soldiers really may become extinct—or indistinct from any other profession.

NOTES

1. I fully accept that the concept of political will is undertheorized and badly in need of serious investigation. I use it here to mean, very roughly, governments daring to do electorally unpopular things.

2. Lieutenant General William J. Begert (1999) *USAF Aerospace Power Journal* 13 (Winter): 4–10.

3. I am much in agreement with two articles that Edward N. Luttwak wrote on the theme of what he calls the "post-heroic" in defense matters in *Foreign Affairs* during the mid-1990s, though I do not accept most of his resulting prescriptions. In particular, see (1995) "Toward Post-Heroic Warfare," *Foreign Affairs* (May-June): 109–122; here he makes the case for expecting there to be much more to intervene in. See also (1996) "A Post-Heroic Military Policy," *Foreign Affairs* (July-August): 33–44, in which he makes force structure recommendations and outlines a theory of how to intervene.

4. Eric Ash (1999) "Terror Targeting: The Morale of the Story," *Aerospace Power Journal* 13 (Winter): 33–47 (emphasis added).

5. Jeffrey McKitrick et al. (1996) *The Revolution in Military Affairs*, chap. 3. It is worth noting that McKitrick, when he was still a serving U.S. Army officer in the mid-1980s, was a major proponent of the precursor debate to the RMA, the military reform debate. One of the arguments there, somewhat contrary to the current wisdom, was the importance of developing light infantry divisions.

6. Ralph Peters (1997) "After the Revolution" *Parameters* (Summer).

7. Quoted in Charles J. Dunlap Jr. (1997) "Twenty-first-Century Land Warfare: Four Dangerous Myths," *Parameters* (Autumn): 27–37.

8. John Mueller (1995) "The Perfect Enemy: Assessing the Gulf War," *Security Studies*, no. 1 (Autumn): 77–117.

9. Ibid., p. 106.

10. Stephen Biddle (1996) "Victory Misunderstood," *International Security* 21, no. 2 (Fall): 139–179.

11. William E. Odom (1997) "Transforming the Military," *Foreign Affairs* (July-August): 54.

12. Jeffrey Record (1999–2000) "Operation Allied Force: Yet Another Wake-Up Call for the Army?" *Parameters* (Winter): 15–23.

13. John A. Tirpak (1999) "Lessons Learned and Re-learned," *Air Force Magazine* (August): 23.

14. John Keegan (1999) "So the Bomber Got Through After All," *London Daily Telegraph*, June 4, p. 28.

15. Taken from Earl H. Tilford (1999–2000) "Operation Allied Force and the Role of Air Power," *Parameters* (Winter): 24–38.

16. Ibid., esp. 31.

17. I do not think the U.S. preoccupation with the military being used as an adjunct to police and coast guards in the drug wars has any relevance to us here. Neither is it in any way new, being surely not logically different from the age-old concern of regular navies with smugglers and pirates.

18. Quoted in Ralph J. Allen (1995) "Piercing the Veil of Operational Art," *Paremeters* (Summer): 111–119.

19. There is a point about frequent rewriting of doctrine that bears on our theme. The author recalls a conversation in 1984 with a major at West Point. He was worried about the effect on the operational coherence of a unit where almost every officer grade had done basic training under a different version of FM100-5. By my calculations, that man is now at least a colonel and has lived through three further versions. As an instructor at West Point, he was one of the U.S. Army's best and brightest. What chance is there for the less able officer to easily manage the increasing intellectual demands of future war?

20. Walter Clarke and Jeffrey Herbst (1996) "Somalia and the Future of Humanitarian Intervention," *Foreign Affairs* (March-April): 70–86.

21. Indeed, the plans of a Labor government to reverse a thirty-year-old policy set by a Labor government against large aircraft carriers speaks strongly to my point. The government is open about its ambitions to be active in the intervention area where "Britain can punch above its weight." *Daily Telegraph,* March 23, 1998.

22. It was ironic that the man in question, then-Brigadier Rupert Smith, was within months commander of the first British armored division actually to go to war.

23. Luttwak (1996) actually dates this casualty-avoidance policy on the part of colonial gendarmeries to the Romans.

24. Charles J. Dunlap Jr. (1997) "Twenty-first-Century Land Warfare: Four Dangerous Myths," *Parameters* (Autumn): 27–37.

25. Steven Metz (1997) "Which Army After Next? The Strategic Implications of Alternative Futures," *Parameters* (Autumn): 15–26.

5

New Conflicts:
Risks and Challenges

JAN WILLEM HONIG

A recent flurry of analyses has attempted to explain the supposedly new types of conflict that emerged after the end of the Cold War. Martin van Creveld, John Keegan, Samuel Huntington, Michael Ignatieff, and Barbara Ehrenreich have written some of the more popular books that seek to satisfy the demand to understand the nature of war and the ways in which it is changing.[1] Although they come to their subject from very different political and philosophical vantage points, they share a striking consensus: conflict is moving beyond the control of the state. Since the state represents the pinnacle in positive political development to many in the West, this is an unsettling finding. The modern democratic state so far has offered better security to its citizens than any other historical form of political organization. To be told that the state faces one of its greatest challenges yet is cause for serious worry.

Israeli military historian Martin van Creveld is the most pessimistic. He doubts that Western states can manage the challenge of low-intensity conflict fought by low-technology, irregular forces from the less developed parts of the world.[2] In his 1991 book *On Future War*, which was written under the shadow of the Intifada, he concludes bluntly that "either modern states cope with low-intensity conflict, or else they will disappear; the suspicion grows, however, that they are damned if they do and damned if they don't."[3]

Huntington, Ignatieff, Keegan, and Ehrenreich may not be quite as gloomy as van Creveld, but they also see grave dangers. Huntington singles out multiculturalism and Western universalism as the fundamental problems for the West in dealing with the most dangerous form of future conflict, that between inimical "civilizations." Multiculturalism threatens to undermine fatally the cohesion of Western civilization that is critical to its survival.

Universalism demands that the West forces its values on other civilizations—a tall order given the incompatibilities among civilizations and one that would entangle the West in endless war. Ignatieff, on the contrary, regards this universalism as a force for good and sees its weakness, rather than its strength, as a problem. Adolescent irregulars, fighting in "zones of testosterone" that are untouched by the authority of the state and the ethic of military professionalism, have little affinity with human rights. Keegan, in a variant of Huntington's worries on Western universalism, is concerned about the uncompromising form of war that the West has made its own. Nonetheless, he believes that "public tolerance of state violence in advanced societies has dwindled" and that nuclear weapons have made war "too big for mankind." As a result, it is only "mad and bad individuals" who continue to see force as a route to power.[4] Ehrenreich, finally, represents a familiar liberal idea, reinforced by a touch of fashionable sociobiology, which considers war to be a useless and parasitical social activity. She claims that mankind's control over war is tenuous because it has become "a self-replicating pattern of behavior" that is ingrained not in our genes but in our societies.[5]

The surprise in these treatments is the extent to which they emphasize sociocultural factors in their study of war. This represents a move away from the focus on the international system and international institutions as facilitators or inhibitors to war that prevailed in the academic study of conflict during the Cold War. Perhaps unsurprisingly, the dominant theories of realism and liberal institutionalism have not yet quite come to grips with the changed landscape. Apart from Huntington, none of the popular authors mentioned earlier are political scientists.[6] No treatment by a realist or liberal institutionalist can as yet claim the kind of popularity these books have achieved. Given that the state is so fundamental to realist and liberal-institutionalist theorizing, their adherents struggle to incorporate "stateless" forms of conflict.[7] Their failure to come to grips with the problem also means that they are of little help in finding ways of dealing with contemporary conflict.

The books discussed earlier are more helpful, but even they do not go as far as they perhaps should. Their authors, first of all, see their role as one of providing warning and expounding a major theory and not so much as one of offering solutions. Each author, in addition, often seems unduly influenced in their diagnoses and prescriptions by his or her personal circumstances and experiences. Huntington exposes himself as a good U.S. conservative, one who equates the woes of U.S. academia perhaps too readily with the ills of the world. He also displays a penchant to confuse U.S. culture with Western civilization in arguing for maintaining the West's internal strength through the defense of "the distinctive character of its values and institutions," which at its core is based on its "Christianity, pluralism, individualism and rule of law."[8] Ehrenreich fondly remembers her own days as an activist and sees "the antiwar movements of the late twentieth century" as a "crucial lesson" that "the passions we bring to war can be brought just as well to the struggle *against* war."[9] Keegan is clearly influenced by his exposure to the British army during his time teaching at Sandhurst. He sees the strong need for "skillful, disciplined warriors" in the service of the state who have learned the value of restraint in war and who can deal with "ethnic bigots, regional warlords, ideological intransigents, common pillagers and organized international criminals."[10] Ignatieff, via a different route, arrives at the same prescription. He suggests appealing to the paramilitaries "as warriors [rather] than as human beings, for warriors have codes of honour; human beings—qua human beings—have none."[11] In addition, as a good Western liberal, he argues for the need to reinforce this appeal through a process of rebuilding states, in the sense of creating "institutions that enable individuals to form civic identities strong enough to counteract their ethnic allegiances."[12]

These approaches to conflict suffer from two shortcomings. First, surveyed together they leave the reader confused as to what is the real nature of the conflicts we face and which poses the greatest danger. Second, each author proposes long-term solutions. As a result, how one goes about dealing with conflict on a more practical, political, and strategic level gets short shrift. In this chapter, I will not set out a grand theory of new conflicts. Instead I take a rather empirical approach and make two major points that are critical to any serious practical, immediate response to the conflicts we face.

First, I argue that it is important to recognize that force is a means to an end. If one rejects this principle—as many do who watched the horrors of Bosnia, Rwanda, and Somalia—not only does one become incapable of analyzing conflict; one also cannot devise a response to conflict. Clausewitz may not have been totally right, as van Creveld and Keegan argue, that war is the continuation of politics by other means, but—as they would agree—it never fails to serve some broader, more culturally defined purpose.[13] This recognition gives hope. If it were the case that terrorists, ethnic warriors, or rogue-state leaders were irrational and used force without any notion of aims, it would be impossible to influence them. The pursuit of aims, in contrast, gives them a certain rationality that enables us to understand their course of action and thus allows us, in principle, to influence them by denying them their objectives or offering them partial or alternative satisfaction.

Furthermore, the assumption that force is an instrument enables one to develop a unified approach to conflict that overcomes the terminological and analytical confusion by directing the analysis toward the question of who uses force to what end. I will therefore first discuss contemporary conflict by looking at the actors, including especially the most puzzling ones, that are commonly recognized as the main users of force in the modern world: states, rogue states, nonstate terrorists, and ethnic actors.[14] An instrumental approach clarifies several important issues about the extent to which the wars of these actors pose a real or imagined problem to the West.

The second major point in this chapter is that an effective Western response to all types of conflict requires acceptance of an idea of limited war, that is, that war should be fought for limited objectives that are subject to compromise. However, the acceptance by the West is constrained by two major factors, one related to the nature of our political system, the other to our understanding of the nature of war. In essence, politically and militarily, Western states find it difficult to conduct and terminate wars in a way that leaves room for compromise and that recognizes the possible validity of an adversary's objectives and his reasons for resorting to force.

INTERSTATE WARS

Interstate wars pose the least problem to the West because of the extensive and quite effective network of norms and institutions that has been built up to regulate international behavior. A normative framework exists that centers on the idea of just war. The key elements were already codified in the Middle Ages.[15] They posited that a war had to be fought for a just cause, with just intent, and under proper authority. Of course, implementation of this idea proved difficult, not least because of the room for dispute on the meaning of the terms. Nonetheless, their meaning was clarified to an important extent in the course of centuries of warfare, and it is now embodied in an extensive corpus of international law.

By this century, these norms had become more precise and more restrictive. Put simply, the criterion around which just cause revolves is only self-defense, which means that wars of aggression, for whatever just reason, are unlawful. Just intent has tended to coalesce with just cause because of, on the one hand, the difficulties of separating the just act of redressing a wrong from defending against the wrongful act of aggressive war and, on the other hand, the unattractiveness of just intent serving as a justification for aggressive war (although the principle of allowing force to redress a wrong is again beginning to play an important role in interventions in intrastate conflict; in interstate conflict it has not become acceptable). Proper authority has come to be seen to be vested in the sovereign state, the central building block in the modern international system. The commonly accepted notion is that the legitimate decision to go to war rests with the state alone.

There has been a further development, however, restricting the legitimate use of force even more. Particularly after 1945, the norm of self-defense by states was reinforced by international institutions, notably the United Nations. A legitimate war must have the benediction of the UN. Article 51 of the UN Charter explicitly recognizes only "the inherent right of individual or collective self-defense" by states, and then only "until the Security Council has taken the measures necessary to maintain international peace and security."

Preventive military action is still possible, but only by the Security Council and only if it determines, according to Article 42, "the existence of any threat to the peace, breach of the peace, or act of aggression." This right follows from the Security Council's fundamental responsibility under Article 39 "to maintain or restore international peace and security." However, preventive military action in interstate conflict sanctioned by the Security Council has not really caught on for understandable reasons. How can one avoid accusations of unnecessary and extreme meddling in a country's affairs by taking armed action against it? How can one ever know for certain that preventive action truly prevents and one does not waste valuable material and political capital for an uncertain cause? The Security Council prefers that armed conflict break out first and the issues crystallize themselves at least to some degree so that a political judgment can be made more readily that is defensible in the eyes of the world.

It is remarkable to what extent these norms of international behavior and the legitimacy of the United Nations have been accepted by the world's states. Although one could easily quarrel with the justifications given by states for why they go to war, it is nonetheless highly revealing of the success of international norms and international institutions that all states feel compelled to legitimize their case through them. Which state does not now claim to go to war but out of self-defense? Even Saddam Hussein, though he committed in the eyes of the world one of the most blatant acts of aggression of the century by invading Kuwait in August 1990, claimed to be acting out of self-defense. The dire economic situation in Iraq, coupled with the persistent Kuwaiti refusal to help the state to which it owed its protection during the Iran-Iraq War, gave Saddam, in his view, no choice but to defend Iraq against the economic war waged by Kuwait.[16] As he explained: "War is fought with soldiers and much harm is done by explosions, killing, and coup attempts— but it is also done by economic means. Therefore . . . this is in fact a kind of war against Iraq."[17] Ironically, whether he had wanted to or not, Saddam found that he had to play along with the UN system. Since the actions taken against him were undertaken in the name of the United Nations, his defense had to take place with reference to and largely within the parameters set by that body.

Similarly, the United States could not and, in contrast to Saddam Hussein, clearly did not want to escape the normative UN framework. Although realists would argue that the United States as a superpower can and must engage in the single-minded pursuit of its national interests irrespective of international law and international institutions, the example of the war over Kuwait illustrates that reality is more complex. Many believed that the war was first and foremost about the protection of a vital resource, namely, oil. Saddam arguably threatened a U.S. national interest by laying his hands on 20 percent of the world's oil reserves and threatening another 20 percent in Saudi Arabia.

When U.S. Secretary of State James Baker at one point explained that the conflict was about oil and U.S. jobs, he faced an avalanche of criticism. He never used the economic argument again. U.S. justifications for opposing Iraq centered on the undoing of an act of aggression and liberating Kuwait. As U.S. President George Bush explained in January 1991: "Our objectives are clear: Saddam Hussein's forces will leave Kuwait, the legitimate Government of Kuwait will be restored to its rightful place and Kuwait will once again be free."[18]

Realists would also expect major powers to act unilaterally. Despite the presence of some of the necessary ingredients that would have made unilateral action possible—like U.S. capabilities, an invitation to send troops from a Saudi Arabia that felt threatened, and an overwhelming perception that Iraq had committed naked aggression—again the Gulf conflict reveals more complexity. From the start, the U.S. administration tried to create as large a political and military coalition as was possible. Iraq faced repeated censure from all members of the Security Council, and very few states in the world came to its defense.[19] The Coalition arrayed against Iraq in the end comprised thirty-nine nations. The process of forging the Coalition was cumbersome and time-consuming. It involved some diplomatic U-turns (as in the case of Syria, which was heretofore considered a terrorist-sponsoring rogue state), significant compromise, and substantial sums of money (like canceling Egypt's outstanding $7 billion debt to the United States). In military terms, the coalition building did not make much sense. None of the allied contributions was critical to U.S. operations. Finally, the United States relied heavily on the UN Security Council instead of wholly on bilateral relations with important countries. The Security Council's resolutions provided the legal framework for action. Framing these resolutions involved hard work and, sometimes, significant compromise with countries that did not always matter much outside the Security Council. The United States resisted, however, turning the operation to liberate Kuwait into a UN undertaking and insisted that all allied forces operate under its command. It thus displayed some unilateral tendencies, but overall it showed a far greater sensitivity to international law and institutions and the requirements of coalition warfare than was actually necessary.[20]

The invasion of Kuwait thus provides an example of how the international community can cope in a straightforward and effective manner with interstate war. Interstate conflict has the great advantage over the other forms of conflict discussed below in that the parties to the conflict—sovereign states—are the element around which international law and institutions have been built. The mechanisms for dealing with international conflict are therefore there. Existing and widely shared norms allow a judgment on the lawfulness and justness of conflict, and the UN provides a process for addressing conflict. Interstate wars are, moreover, relatively rare. One survey of wars from 1945 to 1995 finds that they represented only 23 percent of a total of 164 con-

flicts.[21] Despite a huge increase in the number of states, the incidence of international war has decreased significantly, from 0.036 per state per year
between 1918 and 1941 to 0.005 in the postwar period to 1995.[22] An even
smaller number of these interstate wars directly affected or involved the West.
Remarkably, though the number of states in Europe after the end of the Cold
War increased from thirty-four to forty-seven, there seems little prospect of a
resurgence of international conflict. The causes for this are difficult to pin
down with precision and certainty, but surely one of them is the strength of
international norms and the faith in international institutions that can effectively mediate in conflicts.

ROGUE-STATE WARS

Some analysts distinguish rogue-state wars as a separate, new category of
conflict. This is a view that is particularly prevalent in the United States,
where states like Iran, Iraq, Libya, North Korea, Sudan, and Syria are habitually described as such. They are states that are believed not to be playing by
the accepted rules of international behavior. This is reflected, supposedly, in
the two forms of force they employ or threaten to employ. First, they sponsor
international terrorism. Second, they attempt to acquire weapons of mass
destruction. Both are means of prosecuting war that are especially odious to
the West. Yet do rogue states truly prosecute a distinct type of war?

Many people prefer to talk about rogue-state wars because of a desire to
distinguish a type of state that pursues supposedly irrational ends with unacceptable means. This is, however, a confused and confusing argument. First,
the literature often glosses over the first assumption, playing on the prejudi-
cial impressions of many readers in the West that these countries have strange
regimes that must be up to no good. But one must guard against assuming too
readily that some states pursue irrational ends. Saddam Hussein, for example,
may not have done a particularly good job in 1990 and 1991, and one may not
have had much sympathy with his policies and strategies, but he was clearly
trying to match means and ends. The same is true for the regimes in such
rogue countries as Iran, Libya, and North Korea. The literature tends instead
to engage in detailed discussions of means.[23] But can one usefully discuss
means without reference to ends? Because a state is able (or wants to develop
the capability) to do something truly nasty to another state, it does not necessarily follow that it will. One must consider the nature of the regimes in question and their political programs in detail before one should begin to worry
about their arsenals.

A second confusion is that the use of weapons of mass destruction (or, for
that matter, significant acts of state-sponsored terrorism—see the next section) would somehow not take place within the context of interstate war. It is

difficult to conceive of a significant attack, whether by missile or other means of delivery, that would not be regarded as a casus belli by the recipient.[24] There is, therefore, no reason to assume that the resulting conflict would not be dealt with in any other way than using the well-established mechanisms described above in the section on interstate conflict. Moreover, because it would most likely be considered a most heinous form of attack, it would meet an easily justifiable, strong response. In short, the category of rogue-state war suffers from a problem of logic. It cannot be readily distinguished from interstate war, as any state that uses force, except under the accepted norm of legitimate self-defense, must be considered a rogue state.[25] True, the more roguish a state's behavior, the easier the international response becomes. But the nature of the response is, in the first place, governed by the quality of the actor that used force rather than the quality of his behavior.

TERRORISM

I do not want to engage here in a difficult definitional debate,[26] but what we habitually call *terrorism* seems to exhibit the following traits: it is fought by nonstate entities who are relatively weak and therefore able to conduct only a low-intensity conflict and who target, usually deliberately and principally, though not exclusively, noncombatants. Terrorist actions aim to advertise a cause and, through sustained violence, impress and extend a support base while coercing an opponent by influencing public opinion into an accommodating position. Terrorists have a program, they are adapting means to ends, and hence they do not use violence indiscriminately. As they cannot assume that force speaks for itself, they have to communicate their program. As a result, terrorists habitually claim responsibility for their acts. They generally cannot hope to achieve their aims without making clear who their opponent is and what it is they are seeking to achieve.

The fundamental challenge for the terrorist, however, is avoiding the situation whereby the communication of responsibility and objectives gives the victim enough information so as to make possible reprisals or punishment. This leads to a complicated and usually ambiguous form of communication, often through proxies (think of the Irish Republican Army [IRA] and its so-called political wing, Sinn Fein). Nonetheless, there does not usually exist a lot of doubt as to who is doing what to what end. A problem, particularly for democracies, is to accumulate enough evidence that proves beyond reasonable doubt that specific people are guilty of specific crimes. A good case in point is the IRA.[27] By the early 1990s, if not long before, its key members were known to British security forces. It would have been feasible (as one former defense minister, the maverick member of parliament Alan Clark, suggested in 1998) to arrest these people in a dawn raid. The problem, however, was proving, in a way that would stand up in court, that these individuals had committed crimes. A failure to do so would have undermined the legitimacy of the British state, which rests on the idea of a due process of law and the protection of individual liberties. In effect, no democracy can pay this sort of price.

The same mechanisms that apply to terrorist organizations also apply to the rogue states that sponsor terrorism clandestinely or covertly. The reason for sponsoring terrorism is also a relative weakness that necessitates pursuing certain political aims without inviting easy punishment and reprisal. Having a nominally independent organization doing one's bidding reduces that risk for the sponsor state, but not to zero. Terrorist organizations would be foolish not to require a quid pro quo. Few would offer to commit risky acts without something in return.[28] There thus exists a link that may be tracked down and exposed. At the same time, the sponsor must also use terror to communicate a program for which he must claim some responsibility. He faces the same contradictory challenge as the active terrorist: while his relative weakness demands that he hides his tracks, his political program demands that he exposes them.

A second problem that terrorist organizations and their sponsors have to consider carefully is the amount and the nature of the damage they inflict.[29] If they inflict too much damage or kill the wrong people, they might not only undermine their own legitimacy but also make a strong response easier or even inevitable. When the so-called Real IRA—an IRA splinter movement that insisted on continuing the struggle after the IRA had decided to give up the use of force—exploded a bomb in Omagh that killed twenty-nine people in August 1998, it was counterproductive on both counts. It enabled the passing of draconian new antiterrorist legislation in the Irish Republic and Britain that would otherwise have been unacceptable to the public and its parliamentary representatives. At the same time, it undermined the legitimacy of the Real IRA among its sympathizers to such an extent that it was quickly forced to declare a cease-fire. Also, increasing the intensity of the conflict increases the amount of evidence that is scattered around and thus increases the chances of getting caught. Terrorism is of necessity a low-intensity form of warfare in which every act of terror is a coercive move in a drawn-out process that seeks to push an opponent toward accommodation. One peculiar characteristic of much terrorism that indirectly supports the contention that it must be low-intensity is the terrorists' restricted use of the available repertoire of violence. They appear very wary of resorting to the more destructive weapons and tactics that are readily available, especially with state sponsorship.[30]

Terrorism rarely poses a fundamental threat to the state. It is by its very nature a low-intensity, drawn-out game of cat-and-mouse. It cannot be easily defeated. Terrorists exploit the fact that Western states find it difficult to compromise their legal systems. Provided the terrorist takes care to keep his activities within bounds and avoids easy capture and condemnation, he can usually sustain his activities. Fighting terrorism involves an awareness that one is in for a long haul and that one ultimately, when the time is right, needs to bargain with the terrorists. The struggle is one for hearts and minds on both sides. The conflict is ultimately decided by an awareness that neither side can be completely victorious, and both have to compromise. The examples of Britain and the IRA and Israel and the PLO indicate that democratic states can contain and ultimately cope with terrorist organizations in their midst without fatally undermining the legitimacy of their state.

ETHNIC CONFLICT

Finally, let me turn to the most notorious and vexed new type of war: ethnic conflict. The term *ethnic conflict* is a misnomer, in part because the adjective is so difficult to define,[31] and in part because this type of conflict takes place within states, and we lack the normative and institutional mechanisms for guiding our judgment and actions. But most of all, the problem is one of stereotype: describing it as *ethnic* conflict appeals to prejudice, induces intellectual laziness, and often provides an excuse for inaction. Even more than with rogue states and terrorists, ethnic warriors are assumed to be irrational. They are driven by motivations that originate in the mists of history. They are not deemed to be open to the blandishments and threats that work with so-called normal people. Ethnic conflict is therefore deemed intractable, and interventions should best be avoided. Describing Bosnia, for example, as "an ethnic tangle with roots stretching back a thousand years" suggests that untangling the conflict is an almost hopeless task.[32] However, a careful consideration of the most notorious examples of this form of warfare—the former Yugoslavia and Rwanda—reveals this to be a short-sighted and fundamentally mistaken approach. Not only did these conflicts originate in recent history; they also exhibited a highly organized use of force. Force was a means to an end.

In the case of the former Yugoslavia, it was primarily what James Gow has called "the Serbian project for new borders," which included the use of paramilitaries and the Serb-dominated Yugoslav People's Army in the pursuit of a strategy of ethnic cleansing of weakly armed Bosnian, Croat, and Kosovar communities that accounted for most of the horrific violence of the war.[33] Without careful organization, the horrors could not have been so great and ethnic cleansing so successful. In one of the most notorious episodes of the Bosnian war, the fall of Srebrenica, an estimated 7,000 Muslim men were rounded up and massacred by Serbian soldiers in a matter of days. Such a "success" would have been impossible without good planning and organization.[34] The process, moreover, could not simply rely on ethnic hatreds "stretching back thousands of years." The crimes were not perpetrated in

Hobbesian fashion by all against all but usually only by a carefully selected minority of "special forces" and paramilitaries that executed their operations according to a carefully laid-out scenario.[35] Although the number of people who participated in the atrocities seems to have been higher than in the former Yugoslavia, the same principle of a highly organized use of force applied to Rwanda. The murder of as many as 800,000 people in the short span of about six weeks in April-May 1994 is inconceivable without good preparation and organization.[36]

Another problem with the term *ethnic:* it does not seem to apply well to all the conflicts that are clearly not interstate or terrorist in nature. The conflicts in Algeria, Somalia, Sierra Leone, and Liberia, for example, may be fueled to some degree by something one could call *ethnic* or *tribal* antagonism, but it is only a part of the picture. The response of some is to introduce still other categories of conflict. Algeria is said to be fueled by Islamic fundamentalism, Somalia by clan warfare, and so on. Such categories induce the same intellectual and political responses as ethnic conflict: there is nothing one can do.

This is patently not the case. Intervention can work. In 1995, a limited use of force by the international community in Bosnia brought the warring parties to the negotiating table in Dayton. In 1999, a more extensive, though still limited, use of force cost the Serbs control over Kosovo. As will be discussed in the next section, these uses of force have been marred by mishaps and confusions. Designing and implementing effective and efficient strategies of humanitarian intervention is no easy matter. Nonetheless, the Bosnia and Kosovo cases illustrate that the use of limited force can have positive results.

If *ethnic, fundamentalist,* or *tribal* are not the right adjectives to describe these conflicts, they do share a characteristic in that all are *intrastate.* Identifying them as such points to a problem, not so much of terminology (again, the key to a good understanding is to identify who is using force to what end rather than finding the right epithet) but of international law. Interventions in intrastate conflicts offend against the old principle of state sovereignty. The interventions in Iraq in favor of the Kurds, as well as in Bosnia and Kosovo, show though that this principle is no longer sacrosanct. As explained above, the UN Security Council has the power to override sovereignty if it deems that an internal conflict poses a "threat to international peace and security." The 1999 Kosovo intervention, in particular, showed that it is difficult to get the Security Council to agree on such a momentous judgment. Russian and Chinese opposition prevented it from passing the resolution sanctioning NATO action. NATO went ahead and intervened anyway. The legitimacy of the intervention was seriously dented. This could have posed major problems had the Serbs not started their massive ethnic-cleansing campaign when the first NATO bombs fell. What was legally suspect was thus legitimated on ethical grounds. Egregious human rights violations may make it possible to intervene without UN authorization, but one cannot count on that. The Kosovo example set a bad precedent. As the next section explains, building domestic and international support for effective humanitarian interventions is difficult enough. The process can do without the added complication of legal imperfections.

DEMOCRACIES AND INTERVENTION

One often hears that what makes interventions in intrastate conflicts so difficult is that there are usually no vital national interests at stake. This may be true if national interests are defined in a traditional sense. We do, however, worry about these conflicts, which is why "peacekeeping" troops are dispatched to many of them. This development, I would argue, is indicative of a growing shift in our understanding of *national interest*. We no longer go to war just for traditional reasons of security but primarily out of a moral imperative. It was the necessary precondition to make the interventions in Somalia, Haiti, Bosnia, and Kosovo possible. This is not to say that more traditional interests did not play a role. In the Haitian case, the refugees flooding the United States were an important consideration, as was the credibility of NATO in Bosnia and Kosovo. However, none of these four interventions would have begun without the deep concern over human rights violations.

One could argue that this humanitarian concern can now be classified as an important national interest. It appears that as we are provided with domestic security and protection of human rights by our governments, we expect that our governments will pursue policies that help provide the same kind of security and protection to other peoples and countries as well. Their provision is fundamental to the legitimacy of the modern, liberal state. Why can only we have it and not everyone else? Indications of the strength of this feeling are given by public opinion polls. They find great support for peacekeeping and peace-support missions and even a surprising willingness to accept casualties.[37]

Why does the West, nonetheless, find it so difficult to intervene effectively in conflicts such as in Bosnia, Rwanda, Somalia, Liberia, Sierra Leone, and even Kosovo? First, as mentioned above, an incorrect understanding, which claims that these conflicts are irresolvable, plays a part. Second, as also mentioned, the imperfections of an applicable legal framework, such as exists for interstate conflict, create problems. This can lead to serious disputes as to what responses are appropriate and lawful. The 1999 Kosovo intervention has been mentioned. An earlier example was the European Community's (EC) initial response to the breakup of Yugoslavia. The EC foreign ministers set up the Badinter Commission in 1991 and asked it to advise how the entities emerging from Yugoslavia should be approached under international law and thus, implicitly, what sort of responses were appropriate.[38]

A third factor is that some of the combatants make it deliberately difficult for outsiders to judge what is going on. The Serbs, for example, worked hard on creating opportunities for plausible deniability in Bosnia and pursued what can be described as a strategy of ambiguity. Key ingredients were the claim that the Bosnian Serbs acted independently from Belgrade and that the worst atrocities were committed by yet another, completely uncontrollable, criminal actor—the overly nationalistic paramilitaries. Because the nature of the links between Belgrade and Pale and between Belgrade and the paramilitaries was not immediately obvious (did not Belgrade itself admit that the paramilitaries engaged in criminal behavior?), and because the proof required the painstaking collection of masses of often circumstantial evidence, the Serbs succeeded in creating confusion as to what was going on and who was ultimately responsible. As a result, they made a targeted and effective response more difficult. In Kosovo they attempted the same strategy, though with less success. Belgrade could not easily deny responsibility, as the affair this time clearly took place within its own territory. The claim that NATO bombing caused the Kosovars to flee rang hollow given the scale and immediacy of the exodus. Nonetheless, the Serbian propaganda machine succeeded at least in sowing some doubts and muddying the waters. The surprisingly small number of NATO bombs that killed civilians was tirelessly exploited to feed into the deep Western concern about civilian casualties. Strategies of ambiguity are to be expected in cruel conflicts where those responsible for war crimes usually know they are engaged in morally repugnant, even criminal behavior. They will naturally try to cover their tracks and make punishment more difficult.

Western politicians are also innately cautious and hesitant about using force. War is a risky business, and many a politician has seen his career stumble as a result of a war gone wrong. Politicians also worry about the fickleness of public opinion. Sure, the people say they want to send in armed forces, but are they really willing to see the body bags come home? Humanitarian interventions also set a very demanding agenda. If high moral principle decides intervention, it is very difficult to compromise over these principles and accept a morally imperfect outcome to the conflict. Yet unless one is willing to expend vast resources and impose one's will completely, most conflicts will end in compromise. The question thus quickly arises as to what extent one can compromise with evil. Faced with such a situation, politicians will quickly display the common failing in being uncompromising in rhetoric— but more wobbly in practice. This virtually guarantees cautious behavior in interventions, usually an unhappy outcome, and, paradoxically, it can make them even more risky than they already are.[39]

Another problem for governments is that no nation intervenes by itself. They are undertaken by coalitions because a coalition makes intervention more legitimate and because, except for the United States, no country possesses sufficient military assets to intervene alone. As a result, a government has to go through the difficult domestic process of deciding on a potentially risky course of action, only to go through the same process with allies. Inevitably, the strength of the commitment to action will vary from ally to ally, as will the evaluation of the situation and opinions as to what is the best course of action. Coalitions, unless they find strong leadership, will tend to coalesce around the lowest common denominator.

If this were not enough to forestall any intervention, the militaries that have to perform the operation rarely advise their governments that intervention is a good idea. They are innately even more cautious than politicians and wary of not only interventions but of any use of force.[40] If they have to, they prefer to employ, as current U.S. doctrine calls it, "overwhelming force." The militaries are still heavily enamored by the nineteenth-century Clausewitzian idea that the aim in war is to make the enemy defenseless through the destruction of his means of resistance. In 1991, Operation Desert Storm to liberate Kuwait, for example, was designed to encircle and destroy the Iraqi armed forces. The key attractions of such an approach to military operations are that it provides a clear aim for planning and appears to maximize chances for success. The more force one uses from the start, it is believed, the more likelihood there is that the enemy is defeated. In addition, a defenseless enemy has no option but to agree to any political demand.

The problem with this approach to war is that the cost and effort required to fight are enormous, and that is politically difficult to accept in most cases. Despite the political and moral rhetoric, in practice the aim of interventions is generally a compromise outcome. Western governments are unwilling to expend the resources and incur the costs necessary to prosecute what is in effect a war of unconditional surrender. This political approach to conflict presents the military with a problem on a strategic level. Soldiers find it very difficult to plan for and execute a strategy that uses force not with the aim to make the enemy defenseless but that seeks to achieve something less. None of the conflicts we face, or are likely to face, easily warrant such a massive mobilization of military potential. As a result, our militaries adhere to a doctrine that is, in most cases, a recipe for paralysis. When force is used, the doctrine leads to serious civil-military tensions, an inefficient campaign, and an unhappy outcome.

The 1999 Kosovo campaign presents a good example of the political and strategic problems inherent in the doctrine of overwhelming force. For political reasons, force was restrained from the start. The use of ground forces was deemed unnecessary. In the mistaken belief that a limited demonstration of force would be sufficient to make Serbian President Slobodan Milosevic back down, the fight was to be undertaken exclusively by a relatively small number of aircraft. Nonetheless, the air forces set out to conduct a classic strategic bombing campaign that aimed at progressively and systematically destroying the Serbian capacity to prosecute war. The limited number of aircraft available just meant that targets were attacked at a slower pace and over a longer period of time. However, because of political sensitivities (especially regarding collateral damage and civilian casualties), the targeting was closely monitored by civilian authorities in NATO. This was deeply resented by the military, because it felt it undermined the campaign's effectiveness by excluding certain categories of targets. In the eye of the air force, the situation was made worse when demands grew to attack Serbian forces in the field in Kosovo to stop massive ethnic cleansing. The U.S. Air Force general commanding the operation, Lieutenant General Michael Short, vehemently opposed this and believed such attacks were a waste of his already scarce resources and that they went against the necessary nature of the campaign, further slowing down the attainment of the strategic objective of destroying Serbia's war potential.

General Short's attitude showed an overwhelming reluctance to accept the political realities of the intervention. Politically, then—assuming one wanted to impose a new constitutional arrangement for Kosovo and undo the effects of ethnic cleansing—destroying Serbia's entire war capacity was not necessarily the obvious or most direct way of forcing acceptance of these objectives. It is striking how little attention was paid to Serbian motives and strategies. There was little analysis of the weak points and sensitivities in the Serbian leadership, the targeting of which might have a major impact on their willingness to continue resisting NATO demands. One of the central puzzles of the conflict remains why Milosevic gave in. The U.S. Air Force has tried, but failed, to find a direct correlation between the progression of the air campaign and the end of the war.

What is needed—next to a less grudging political acceptance that compromise is the better part of valor in contemporary conflict—is a doctrine of limited war. Unfortunately, such a doctrine (or even a theory) does not exist. As I have argued elsewhere,[41] though the terms *limited war* and *limited war theory* have been around since the 1950s, this thinking applied to the particular dangers of nuclear war. It was a body of theorizing that (with little conceptual success, one must say) sought to limit the use of the all-destructive nuclear means. It did not generally see war as a pursuit of limited ends and as an exercise in bargaining with limited force.[42] Developing a doctrine of limited war requires, first of all, developing an understanding of one's enemy, as well as his motives, objectives, and strategies. The dominance of strategies that seek to make enemies defenseless has led to a damaging neglect of this old adage. A proper understanding can then lead to the development of a strategy that, at the very least, disrupts an enemy campaign or, better, denies him his critical objectives. This would force the opponent into a debate on the battlefield and at the negotiating table, which, if we are serious, he is bound to settle ultimately in our favor—as long as the West retains sufficient military capabilities for maintaining escalation dominance.

CONCLUSION

In conclusion, the conflicts of the post–Cold War world do not pose fundamental security risks to the West. Interstate conflict does not happen too often, and when it does we possess the political mechanisms to deal with it effectively. There exists a normative and institutional international framework that is remarkably strong. Terrorism is a low-intensity type of conflict that, by its nature, cannot really pose a fundamental threat to the state. Although the irritation factor may be high and it may last a long time, terrorism's very nature also makes it containable. If it develops into larger-scale violence, the victim state can more easily and legitimately bring to bear its overwhelming force potential—which is what the terrorist wants to avoid in the first place. If the larger-scale violence is fed or directed by foreign organizations or states (as some fear is possible with religiously inspired movements with weapons of mass destruction), it would take on the appearance of interstate conflict and can be dealt with as such. Because the West still possesses relatively massive arsenals and a potential for escalation dominance, it is again hard to see how any such threat could not be dealt with quite effectively.

Finally, ethnic conflict—or whatever one wants to call it—may not be a great risk, but it does pose the greatest challenge to the West. The domestic pressure to undertake humanitarian interventions can be expected to grow. If so, then we do need to be careful about not falling into the trap of moral absolutism. Effective intervention demands great political flexibility and will involve compromise with unsavory regimes and individuals. On the military side, we cannot rely on doctrines of overwhelming force. The militaries have to learn to achieve limited objectives with limited force. In striking contrast to the prevailing trend in the West to separate the military from the political, the militaries are an integral part of the political negotiating team. Effective intervention is possible, but it does require careful analysis. Success depends on understanding the aims of the protagonists, how they go about achieving them, and to what lengths they are prepared to go. A proper appreciation of the principle that force is a means to an end opens up the way to influencing them and forcing them to compromise. Fortunately, even in so-called ethnic conflict, the protagonists are sufficiently sane to continue to see force as a means to an end. Limited counterforce can therefore work.

NOTES

1. Martin van Creveld (1991) *On Future War* (London: Brassey's, published as *The Transformation of War in the United States* by Free Press); John Keegan (1993) *A History of Warfare* (London: Hutchinson); Samuel P. Huntington (1997) *The Clash of Civilizations and the Remaking of the World Order* (London: Simon and Schuster); Michael Ignatieff (1998) *The Warrior's Honour: Ethnic War and the Modern Conscience* (London: Chatto and Windus); Barbara Ehrenreich (1997) *Blood Rites: Origins and History of the Passions of War* (London: Virago).

2. Van Creveld (1991) *On Future War*, p. 20.

3. Ibid., p. 224.

4. Keegan (1993) *A History of Warfare*. The quotes are from an interview with Keegan: Harriet Swain (1998) "War, What Is It Good For? Absolutely Nothing...," *The Times Higher Education Supplement*, April 3.

5. Ehrenreich (1997) *Blood Rites*, p. 232.

6. Huntington is an interesting case. He is clearly sympathetic to the realist paradigm and its emphasis on national self-interest but feels that it underplays the role "values, culture, and institutions" play in defining interest and that these factors are often "civilizational" in nature: Huntington (1997) *The Clash of Civilizations*, pp. 33–35. In a sense, one could argue that Huntington's ideas represent a return to an earlier twentieth-century notion that saw the world as made up of nation-states, with the emphasis on *nation*, which not only meant that states often had pretensions beyond their borders but that they also claimed to defend broader civilizational interests. An example: the Nazis who presented their war against the "Jewish Bolshevik" Soviet Union as a "civilizational" struggle (*Kulturkampf*) that aimed to save "Europe." The so-called *Historikerstreit* that raged in West Germany in the mid-1980s was in part between historians who claimed that there was an element of truth to the Nazi claim and others who denied this; see, e.g., Historikerstreit (1987) *Die Dokumentation der Kontroverse um die Einzigartigkeit der nationalsozialistischen Judenvernichtung* (München: Piper).

7. They have attempted to branch out; see, e.g., contributions by Jack Snyder and Barry Posen (1993) in *Survival* (Special Issue, Ethnic Conflict and International Security) 35, no. 1 (Spring), and a collection of articles from *International Security* edited by Michael Brown (1993) *Ethnic Conflict and International Security* (Princeton: Princeton University Press). Others are looking for inspiration and reassurance in prestate history. See the rather funny and naive attempt to extend the realist paradigm to the Middle Ages in Markus Fischer (1992) "Feudal Europe, 800–1300: Communal Discourse and Conflictual Practices," *International Organization* 46 (Spring): 427–466. Some liberal institutionalists are now venturing into the new field of strategic culture; see, e.g., Judith Goldstein and Robert O. Keohane (eds.) (1993) *Ideas and Foreign Policy: Beliefs, Institutions and Political Change* (Ithaca: Cornell University Press); and Peter J. Katzenstein (ed.) (1996) *The Culture of National Security: Norms and Identity in World Politics* (New York: Columbia University Press). For an at times maladroit critique, see Michael C. Desch (1998) "Culture Clash: Assessing the Importance of Ideas in Security Studies," *International Security* 23, no. 1 (Summer): 141–170. The end of the Cold War was very soon seen as an event for some of the other academic disciplines to get their own back at the "golden children" of the bygone era; see, e.g., John Lewis Gaddis (1992–1993) "International Relations Theory and the End of the Cold War," *International Security* 17, no. 3 (Winter 1992): 5–58, and the resulting correspondence in *International Security* 18, no. 2 (Fall 1993): 202–210.

8. Huntington (1997) *The Clash of Civilizations*, p. 311.

9. Ehrenreich (1997) *Blood Rites,* p. 240; italics in original.

10. Keegan (1993) *A History of Warfare*, pp. 391–392.

11. Ignatieff (1998) *The Warrior's Honour*, p. 6.

12. Ibid., p. 7.

13. Martin van Creveld's 1991 book is admirably organized around the idea that war is a means to an end. It is unfortunate that at times he muddies the waters by suggesting, for example, on p. 226, that "it is simply not true that war is solely a means to an end" when he does not quite mean that. Van Creveld—and the same is true for Keegan—is so concerned with countering the Clausewitzian idea that war is a means only to a political end that the general proposition of war being a means to whatever end suffers as well. Ignatieff often appears to implicitly support the widespread idea that ethnic conflict is marked by mindless violence, although in places he points out that there is strategy; Ignatieff (1998), p. 132.

14. For a typical example, cf. François Heisbourg (1997) *The Future of Warfare* (London: Phoenix), pp. 17–18. Heisbourg distinguishes rogue-state wars, wars of secession, wars of disruption, and classical Clausewitzian wars.

15. Frederick H. Russell (1975) *The Just War in the Middle Ages* (Cambridge: Cambridge University Press).

16. Lawrence Freedman and Efraim Karsh (1993) *The Gulf Conflict, 1990–1991: Diplomacy and War in the New World Order* (Princeton: Princeton University Press), pp. 42–63.

17. Quoted in Freedman and Karsh (1993) *The Gulf Conflict*, p. 46.

18. Quoted in *New York Times*, January 17, 1991.

19. In the Security Council, only Yemen and Cuba opposed some of the resolutions (joined once by Zimbabwe, which also opposed Resolution 688, which established safe havens in Iraq). All condemned the Iraqi annexation of Kuwait, and Cuba also immediately condemned the invasion. The Yemeni ambassador failed to receive instructions in time and abstained; Freedman and Karsh (1993), p. 81.

20. See Andrew Bennett et al. (eds.) (1997) *Friends in Need: Burden Sharing in the Persian Gulf War* (New York: St. Martin's). Despite the valiant attempt to explain the burden-sharing in the Gulf War within the context of traditional international relations theory, the mostly Georgetown University–based contributors ignore the possibility of a normative, international law–based explanation. As a result, they find it very difficult to give a coherent explanation as to why the United States built such a broad coalition and why it was so successful.

21. K. J. Holsti (1996) *The State, War, and the State of War* (Cambridge: Cambridge University Press), table 2.1, p. 22.

22. Ibid., table 2.2, p. 24.

23. A favorite feature in this type of literature is the map with the ranges of missiles that suggests that as soon as the reader's country comes within range, there suddenly exists a threat that needs to be addressed.

24. It is possible, as some suggest, that rogue states will use their weapons of mass destruction in truly terrorist fashion, that is, without making clear who the author of the deed is. Not only do I regard this as unlikely for reasons that are set out in the section under terrorism, but were it to occur, the victim state can be expected to do all in its power to expose the perpetrator. If this happens to be a state, then what I have said about interstate war applies.

25. Initially, I did treat this as distinct, but as David Robertson pointed out to me at the original conference where this paper was presented, there is not really a distinction between rogue-state wars and interstate wars.

26. See, e.g., Bruce Hoffman (1998) *Inside Terrorism* (London: Victor Gollancz), chap. 1, "Defining Terrorism," pp. 13–44. Hoffman's ultimate definition of terrorism as "the deliberate creation and exploitation of fear through violence or the threat of violence in the pursuit of political change" (p. 43) is of little use since it could be said to apply equally to war or conflict in general. His preceding discussion, however, is useful in that it highlights some of the serious problems that complicate defining terrorism.

27. For the IRA, see M. L. R. Smith (1997) *Fighting for Ireland? The Military Strategy of the Irish Republican Movement* (London: Routledge).

28. Many terrorist organizations have become exceedingly wealthy as a result of state sponsorship. See Hoffman (1998) *Inside Terrorism*, pp. 187, 189. They also quite easily become involved in other criminal activity that pays well, like bank robbery (an IRA favorite), drug trafficking, and protection rackets.

29. "Terrorists want a lot of people watching and a lot of people listening and not a lot of people dead." This a view ascribed to Brian Jenkins in Hoffman (1998), pp. 198–200. Hoffman believes this may have applied to terrorists in the past but not to contemporary religiously inspired terrorists.

30. Hoffman (1998), p. 198. As said, Hoffman says this is changing with respect to religious terrorists. Note, however, that the bombings of the U.S. embassies in Dar-es-Salaam and Nairobi in August 1998 led to a speedy and quite massive U.S. response. One action, with seventy cruise missiles, was aimed at the man and organization held responsible in Afghanistan, the other at the Sudanese regime, which was not clearly connected with the bombings but seen as a sponsor of terrorism in general. The jury is still out as to whether such reprisals are effective. Hoffman, on the evidence of the U.S. air raid against Colonel Mohamar Qaddafi in 1986, is skeptical; Hoffman (1998), pp. 188, 192–193. Others are more sanguine: cf. Tim Zimmermann (1987) "The American Bombing of Libya: A Success for Coercive Diplomacy?" *Survival* 29 (May-June): 195–214.

31. See, for example, the literature cited in Note 7 above.

32. See remarks by the former chairman of the U.S. Joint Chiefs of Staff, in Colin Powell (1996) *My American Journey* (New York: Ballantine), p. 544. Such views were apparently widespread in the Clinton administration. Another notorious example was President Clinton's alleged reading of Robert Kaplan's best-selling *Balkan Ghosts,* which exemplified these ideas and made Clinton back away from intervention in 1993; see Elizabeth Drew (1994) *On the Edge: The Clinton Presidency* (New York: Simon and Schuster), p. 157. Powell apparently read the book as well.

33. James Gow (1997) *Triumph of the Lack of Will: International Diplomacy and the Yugoslav War* (New York: Columbia University Press).

34. For the details, see Jan Willem Honig and Norbert Both (1996) *Srebrenica: Record of a War Crime* (Harmondsworth, UK: Penguin).

35. For Srebrenica, see ibid. Many of the essential characteristics of the war were carefully laid out in the seminal "Final Report of the Commission of Experts Established Pursuant to Security Council Resolution 780 (1992)," UN Security Council S/1994/674, May 27, 1994.

36. See Gérard Prunier (1997) *The Rwanda Crisis: History of a Genocide* (London: Hurst), esp. pp. 237–268, and Alison Des Forges (1999) *Leave None to Tell the Story: Genocide in Rwanda* (New York: Human Rights Watch).

37. J. S. Van der Meulen (1997) "Post-Modern Societies and the Future Support of Military Missions," in G. C. De Nooy (ed.) (1997) *The Clausewitzian Dictum and the Future of Western Military Strategy* (The Hague: Kluwer Law International), pp. 70–71. See also Freedman and Karsh (1993), p. 285.

38. See Gow (1997) *Triumph of the Lack of Will*, pp. 67–77.

39. This is a key theme in Honig and Both (1996).

40. See the classic by Richard K. Betts (1991) [orig. ed. 1977] *Soldiers, Statesmen, and Cold War Crises* (New York: Columbia University Press).

41. Jan Willem Honig (1997) "Strategy in a Post-Clausewitzian Setting," in De Nooy (1997) *The Clausewitzian Dictum*, pp. 109–121. See also Jan Willem Honig (1994) "Interpreting Clausewitz," *Security Studies* 3, no. 3 (Spring): 571–580.

42. At stake in the Cold War—though this was often forgotten because it was so obvious—was the survival of either the capitalist West or the communist East. Although there is a lot of Cold War literature on bargaining, it is predicated on the central dilemma of the Cold War: how to avoid escalation into an all-out nuclear war. This makes its application to post–Cold War conflict rather less than straightforward and mostly highly problematic.

PART 2

European Security

6

Europe's Changing Security Role

ALPO M. RUSI

Creation of the euro will raise many policy issues that will require intensive cooperation, both across the Atlantic and in multilateral settings such as the Group of Seven and the IMF.

—C. Fred Bergsten

Security in Europe still comes with a price tag, but it remains affordable. And as we have learned again and again, the price of indifference is far higher than that of engagement.

—Javier Solana

A Greater Europe, I would say, will be the dominant power.

—Boris Yeltsin

In this chapter I discuss the evolving political-security role of the European Union. The aim is to elaborate this role within the changing international system and in the context of the Kosovo crisis. The primary question to be answered is whether it is possible for the European Union to strengthen its political-security influence commensurately with its economic power. The EU is already a global economic power, but it plays only a marginal political-security role at the global level. The EU aims at creating its political-security role primarily within a broad regional framework.

The international system is influenced by the process of globalization. A multipolar system is gradually replacing the existing post–Cold War system of fragile unipolarity. Regional trade areas are emerging, and the EU is paving the way to this new system of a multipolar world.

In the 1990s, the Balkan wars demonstrated the need to create independent crisis-management capabilities for the EU. As a result, the EU summits slowly promoted the agenda and capabilities, in the course of the 1990s, for a common foreign and security policy. In spring 1999, the Kosovo crisis revealed many problems in acting without Russia and the United States in solving any major crisis in Europe politically. It also showed shortages in the capabilities of the EU in acting alone militarily. Unfortunately the Kosovo crisis as well as the launching of the Stability Pact for Southeastern Europe revealed several flaws in the decisionmaking process of the EU. The Council of the EU and the Commission of the EU are not adjusted to constitute a coherent wholeness but easily compete with each other on mandates and competences. Basically the problem is related to the mandate of the Commission to decide upon the use of budgets. The Council does not have this power, which has caused many problems. The role of the European Parliament is also confusing because it may freeze the financing of a common foreign and security policy of the EU.

With the institutional decisions of the Amsterdam Summit, the European Union strengthened its role as a political-security actor. Former U.S. Secretary of State Henry Kissinger once asked, "Who do I call when I want to speak to Europe?" After two decades, he may finally have a formal answer. The mid-1997 Amsterdam Summit decided that when foreign leaders want to talk to the European Union about security matters they should dial the Secretary-General of the Council of Ministers. Javier Solana was appointed to be the first High Representative of the foreign and security policy of the EU, and he began to assume his responsibilities in October 1999. However, the High Representative of the common foreign and security policy of the EU has to deal with the EU presidencies: Commissioner Chris Patten deals with foreign relations of the Commission and the president of the Commission, and Romano Prodi, like Solana, wants to play an increasingly important role in foreign and security policy. Kissinger may yet ponder over the right phone number for a long time. One can also raise the question of whether the big powers of the EU have occupied all the key posts in the policy machinery (a bad omen in the longer term). The question is whether member states can adjust their policy cultures to promote a common foreign and security policy. Whereas southern states maintain a centralist tradition, northern states prefer more transparent decisionmaking processes. Although they may agree on goals, they may encounter problems agreeing on means and cultures.

The EU is also building a military arm for itself and strengthening its credibility as a political-security actor. The Helsinki Summit decided on the establishment of the European Rapid Deployment Force for crisis management with a size of 50,000–60,000 soldiers in December 1999. These forces could be deployed by 2003. The Interim Political and Security Committee, the Interim Military Body, and the military experts forming the nucleus of the future military staff were established, and the Committee for Civilian Crisis Management is yet to be established. But the military arm of the EU will remain in the hands of independent nation-states, not a unified command of one state.

AN EMERGING MULTIPOLAR SYSTEM

The global totality—the world system—can be seen in terms of the geography of economic development combined with the geography of politico-military development. The emerging international system will be very complex. Two factors are decisive. First, the bipolar stability has vanished, and no new stable system has yet replaced it. Second, the world will evolve into four to five politico-economic spaces, or blocs, that will gradually become the chief dramatis personae on the global stage. Consequently, this will make the blocs global geopolitical players in the longer term. The EU is developing its global role within this international transition.

It should be emphasized, however, that globalization (and regional integration, as its dynamic driving force) has flaws everywhere. In Europe, Russia and, in particular, the Balkan region remained outside the mainstream of European integration after the end of the Cold War. Furthermore, as new markets emerge and promote integration, smaller national and ethnic entities want autonomy and even independence throughout the globe.[1]

The center of gravity in economic development and growth is gradually shifting from Europe and the United States to Asia and the Pacific Rim. A global geopolitical transition is under way. As Joseph Nye reasons, the question is about the restoration of history to its former conditions. In 1820, in the early days of the industrial era, Asia's share of the world's gross domestic product (GDP) was 58 percent. By 1940 it had dwindled to 19 percent. It has now climbed back to 37 percent, and by 2020 at the latest Asia will have reattained the share it had two centuries earlier. Not even considerable setbacks will prevent this development trend from continuing in broad outline.[2] One has to be careful with forecasts. The economic growth rates may rapidly change, having an impact on these figures. In any case, the rise of new powers and the formation of a new international order is the key issue of the early twenty-first century. The ongoing transition, however, contains several unpredictable factors that create instabilities.

EUROPE: AN EVOLVING REGIONAL POWER

On the global role of Europe, Lester Thurow reasoned in the early 1990s as follows:

Just as the fall of the Berlin Wall in November 1989 marked the end of the old contest between capitalism and communism, so the integration of the European Common Market, on 1 January 1993, will mark the beginning of a new economic contest in a new century at the start of the new millennium. At that moment, for the first time in more than a century, the United States will become the second largest economy in the world. This reality will become the symbol for the start of the competition that determines who will own the twenty-first century.[3]

Although the EU's global role in general is so far patchy, the EU has developed into a "hard" regional power with considerable political and economic influence on the rest of the old continent. As Europe expands and integrates through EU and NATO enlargement, the boundaries for what is East and West are shifting eastward to Ukraine, Georgia, and Kazakhstan. Consequently, the future role of the EU as an international actor depends much on its internal evolution.

Undoubtedly the emergence of the single market, the enlargement of the EU, and in particular the introduction of the euro will have an important impact on perceptions about power relations in the world. However, in the strategic sense, the biggest challenge facing the international community in the twenty-first century will be the reemergence of Asia, and in particular China, as a major power center with global influence. From the point of view of Europe, another challenge is Russia, because it will desperately try to regain its status as a major power.

However, China, Japan, and several states in Southeast Asia have a growing dependence on world food markets and, for example, Middle East oil. It is forecasted that in the early half of the twenty-first century Asia will need considerably more Middle East oil than will Europe and the United States. The United States has stepped up purchases of oil from elsewhere, mainly from South America. Russia is forecast to become Europe's main source of oil and gas. This development has significant implications for the security configuration in Europe, in the Middle East, and consequently for the international situation more broadly as well.

Thus the world's food and energy resources will be shared by more and more inhabitants of the globe. Besides ethnic conflicts, possible nuclear accidents in Russia and mass migration pose security problems for Europe. Many environmental problems will continue to worsen for a long time to come. China will become the world's biggest acid-rain producer by the year 2010 and will have to import 5–7 million barrels of oil a day, the estimated amount produced in the entire Caspian Basin. This development will cause conflicts of interest, which could also engender military tension and armed conflicts.[4]

However, this fundamental geostrategic change—the core of which is the disappearance of division on a global scale and especially in Europe—has been widely challenged by scholars and decisionmakers alike. This has also misled many of them into drawing the wrong political conclusions. Professor John Mearsheimer has forecast the imminent decline of NATO and the European Community. He predicted that "the EC is likely due to the end of the Cold War to grow weaker, not stronger with time." He is of the opinion that "institutions have minimal influence on state behaviour and thus hold little prospect for promoting stability in a post–Cold War world."[5]

Mearsheimer was not right but not entirely wrong, either: a union of nation-states is likely to be a union of big states, giving an assertive Germany or an ambitious France too many liberties from the point of view of their smaller European partners. The decision by fourteen member states to punish Austria for its election results is a case in point. Was a democratic and stable member state punished only because it is a small state, as former Finnish President Mauno Koivisto indicated? Of course, the EU had an argument when taking a very strong position to isolate Austria (the EU is based on common values).

Regardless, enlargement is forcing the EU to face many of its unsolved internal questions. Most Europeans agree that the EU should absorb Eastern European countries as new members, but the EU will have to make hard choices on how to adapt and how to make itself strong enough to be able to tackle these challenges.

The biggest political question concerns leadership, not of the Union but rather of the continent. The unification of Germany, with the EU's biggest population and economy, undertook a gradual process of de facto control of the EU. Consequently, the geopolitical role of the EU is evolving. The EU has two basic concerns. It must be the vehicle for and the safeguard of the further unification of the whole of Europe, in particular the expansion of the EU institutions—and of the euro—toward Eastern Europe. Germany wants to avoid a situation whereby its eastern border is permanently the EU's eastern border as well. At the same time, however, it must ensure that the region does not turn itself into Fortress Europe; rather it must retain its extracontinental connections (acquis Atlantique).[6]

Closer cooperation on foreign and security policy is a prerequisite for the EU that the visionary founders of the European Community once sought. The EU faces traditional security risks, primarily in the Balkans, in the Mediterranean region, as well as in the Middle East and Algeria. The threats in the Balkans cannot be dismantled easily during the first decade of the twenty-first century. A strong commitment of the international community is needed in the region. The air campaign by NATO against the former Yugoslavia and the ensuing peace process in Kosovo paved the way for cooperation. This process, if successful, may become a turning point in efforts to create a more permanent security system for Europe as well as in strengthening the political-security arm of the European Union.

The EU's relationship with Russia will be central to the future European order in the long term. The border between Finland and Russia constitutes the border between the rich and poor in Europe. This fact is a security problem, if not necessarily a risk as such. One of the aims of the initiative of the government of Finland to launch the Northern Dimension of the EU is to eliminate these security problems by promoting cooperation between the EU and Russia. Finland has also been promoting trilateral cooperation among the EU, the United States, and Russia.[7] The steps taken in the Kosovo peace process in May-June 1999 may be seen as being the first tentative results of that process. The loss of the Russian nuclear submarine *Kursk* in the Barents Sea highlights the Finnish initiative.

The war in Chechnya became a critical factor in 1999 and may damage the relations of Russia with its Western neighbors. The EU states' Atlantic partnership keeps Russia balanced while preserving a distinction between a civilian EU and military transatlantic organs. A civilian EU can best stabilize Eastern Europe, as its civilian nature constitutes less of a problem to Russia. Much depends on Russia itself. However, the EU needs also to have credibility for its foreign and security policy role. This is not possible without arms. Lessons from Kosovo loom large. As George Robertson puts it, "In Kosovo we have all come face to face with the European future, and it is frightening."[8]

Kosovo prompted the EU member states to increase coordination, interoperability, and force projection capabilities. At the Cologne and Helsinki Summits (June and December 1999), European leaders pledged their support for improving Europe's collective military capabilities to address regional security challenges. These efforts focus on the capabilities needed to perform the kinds of tasks outlined in the Petersberg Declaration of 1992, ranging from humanitarian and rescue missions to peacekeeping, peacemaking, and combat crisis management. It is clear that this may prompt a change in strategic outlook among EU states, leading them to think more in terms of broader European interests that are affected on a global basis. Perhaps the hostage crisis on Jolo Island may prompt a debate on these broader interests. Thus the EU has to develop its military arm as well as its relationship with NATO. In the longer term, EU member states will likely be member states of a "new," larger NATO. This relationship, if created in due time, would constitute the so-called Grand Coalition, the core of the international community able to strengthen peace and security in Europe as well as other parts of the globe. But as James P. Thomas reasons, "The EU is unlikely to achieve a truly autonomous defence capability in the next 10–15 years which would allow it to carry out medium-sized combat operations such as Kosovo without the United States." I agree with Thomas that, paradoxically, "acknowledging this could lead EU states to accept a greater degree of dependence on the [United States] as a coalition partner in the short term, so as to achieve real military autonomy in the long term."[9]

PROSPECTS FOR THE GLOBAL ROLE OF THE EU

Through the gradual increase of its regional competence and influence, how-ever, the EU may be able to build a global political role in the early twenty-first century. Increasing global rivalry between the trading blocs may become the most crucial imperative for such a development. Despite its many short-comings, the EU could become the model actor of the emerging new international system based on a globalized economy and a structure of trading blocs.

One of the historical paradoxes is that even as European civilization expanded globally European political power diminished dramatically after World War II. At the end of the 1990s, the EU was in essence a trade bloc that "used money to buy international influence and power," as Loukas Tsoukalis correctly emphasized.[10] With the single market as one of the catalysts, the EU's external economic agenda has expanded. It has also expanded its agenda in the field of so-called soft security (environmental protection, development aid, and humanitarian aid). With respect to hard security, the EU has a troubled security role, and its emphasis is on regional security threats and stability. However, the EU is already a global player in several areas (discussed in the sections below).

Environmental Protection

In the 1960s and 1970s, when governments began taking serious action to protect the environment, Europe lagged behind the United States and Japan. This was particularly true in the case of vehicle pollution and efforts to combat acid rain. Now the EU is a global leader in environmental policies. It played a decisive role in framing the Montreal Protocol on the reduction of the use of ozone-depleting substances and the acceleration of the timetable for their elimination. The EU has its own internal legislation on waste disposal, including packaging waste. These rules are generally tougher than comparable legislation elsewhere. In Kyoto, Japan, the EU played the key role when the climate change conference was developed in December 1997.[11]

Development Policy

Besides environmental protection, development policy is one of the three pillars of the EU's external relations, alongside trade policy and the Common Foreign and Security Policy. Development policy is managed largely through the Lome Pact with seventy-one African, Caribbean, and Pacific (ACP) countries. Evolving out of the EU's postcolonial relationships with these regions, Lome's institutional framework for partnerships across a wide range of issues is the most ambitious development effort in the world. The focus of the EU-ACP partnership has shifted over the years, first from infrastructure to food security, then to structural adjustment and social welfare. But Lome's back-bone has remained development aid and trade preferences. However, the value of Lome trade preferences has been eroded by General Agreement on Tariffs and Trade (GATT) and World Trade Organization (WTO) multilateral liberal-izations, EU agreements with Central and Eastern European states, and the EU's proliferating regional trade arrangements. The Lome Convention was renegotiated and then signed in February 2000.[12]

Trade and Investment Liberalization

As trade and investment liberalization proceeds on a global scale, tensions will also increase between the EU and other (newly emerged) economic blocs. In these talks, the EU is well placed to lead the way in restoring the coherence of international economic and social policy. The EU could promote interde-pendence between the blocs. This would be in compliance with the goal of the EU that international cooperation must be based on strong social foundations. Unfortunately, economic globalization has its brutal face, too. The gap between per capita incomes in the richest and poorest countries tripled between 1960 and 1993. In the words of the UN's human development report, "We are witnessing jobless growth, ruthless growth, voiceless growth, rootless growth and futureless growth."[13] Globalization that breeds inequality on this scale is unsustainable and is a major challenge to all countries, not just to the advanced societies of Europe.

However, there is no good alternative to further liberalization of trade and investment. Protectionism is not a good alternative simply because of histori-cal experience. Opening new markets everywhere is a better solution. The role of the EU could be defined in two issue areas. First, the EU has to promote social development in a global market. That vision must be better tied to the globalization process and to trade and investment liberalization. The EU played a major role in drafting the relevant text on workers' rights at the WTO ministerial meeting in Singapore in 1996.

Second, the EU should serve as a mediator by promoting the admission to the WTO of China and some other countries. The EU has (in this respect) taken a more positive stance, and its position has been consistently based on stressing cooperation rather than confrontation. The U.S. trade legislation binds the hands of the executive branch. The U.S. legislation is intended to limit the room for maneuvering of other trade blocs (e.g., the Helms-Burton Act in the case of Cuba). In a similar way, the competition legislation of the EU may have the same result, as in the case of the mergers in the U.S. air-line industry. In the long term, however, the European Union and the United States have to work together through strategic partnership on a global scale.[14]

THE KOSOVO CRISIS: REFLECTING
A TROUBLED SECURITY ROLE

Throughout the 1990s, the Balkans remained outside the emerging post–Cold War European security system. Both the European Union and the United States failed to a certain extent to cope with the collapse of the former Yugoslavia. Four wars resulted: in Slovenia (1991), in Croatia (1992–1993), in Bosnia (1992–1995), and finally in Kosovo (1999). Now that Slobodan Milosevic has been voted out of power, the Federal Republic of Yugoslavia could become part of the emerging stability.

NATO has been instrumental in managing peace in the Balkans. The EU has been allocating economic assistance but has had a less influential, supportive role in the efforts to build peace in the region. Yet it was up to NATO to contain the establishment of greater Serbia in the 1990s. In Bosnia and Herzegovina, the NATO-led Peace Implementation Force united more than thirty nations, including Russia, in a unique coalition for peace and became a symbol of a new cooperative approach to security in 1995. Whereas the peace in Bosnia marked a turn for the better, the developments in Kosovo, which were not addressed by the Dayton process in 1995, took a turn for the worse in 1998 and 1999.[15]

Ever since Milosevic had extinguished the autonomy of this province in the late 1980s, the potential for unrest among its Albanian majority had been growing, with the predictable result of strengthening those who advocated violence to achieve independence. Over the course of 1998, fighting between Kosovar Albanian and Serbian forces grew, with the latter adopting a strategy that increasingly resembled the kind of ethnic cleansing seen before in Bosnia. The UN, NATO, EU, and the Organization for Security and Cooperation in Europe took preventive measures to stabilize the neighboring countries. Yet the situation deteriorated inside Kosovo.

In Security Council Resolution 1199 of September 1998, the UN demanded an immediate end to hostilities. But since the Security Council could not agree on a military response, the chances for inducing change from outside remained slim. As has been assessed, the international community faced the prospect of either witnessing a deliberately engineered mass expulsion of people in a region bordering NATO and the EU or addressing the Kosovo crisis in full.

The last opportunity to solve the crisis politically took place in Rambouillet in February 1999. Obviously, Milosevic never intended to accept a political solution. On 24 March, NATO began Operation Allied Force. For the first time in NATO's history, there would be sustained military action outside NATO territory against a sovereign state. The EU states basically accepted the political line of NATO, and several of them contributed to the air campaign. In April the Presidency of the EU (Germany) began consultations with Russia and the United States to elaborate the opening of a diplomatic track to end the air campaign. This was necessary because no immediate end to the air operations was in sight, and the internal factors became increasingly important, especially in Europe. Although NATO was the organization that actually used military force against Milosevic, the European Union took an initiative to establish a peace process on a trilateral basis, which led to the trip of President Martti Ahtisaari of Finland and Special Envoy Viktor Chernomyrdin to Belgrade on 2 June 1999. On 7 May, Chancellor Gerhard Schroeder of Germany invited President Ahtisaari to Hannover and "nominated" him to be a special envoy of the EU for the peace process. Of course, this decision was not approved by the EU summits or other meetings, but it marked a turning point in the implementation of the Common Security and Foreign Policy of the EU. Improvisation replaced rational bureaucracy. President Milosevic and the Yugoslavian government accepted the peace offer brought by Ahtisaari and Chernomyrdin to Belgrade, and the NATO-led military force was deployed to Kosovo after the military-technical agreement was approved by the Yugoslavian army and NATO on 9 June 1999. On 20 June 1999, Operation Allied Force was officially terminated.

The Kosovo crisis and its handling by the EU may become a turning point in the efforts to develop a political-security role for the European Union. The Kosovo peace process indicates that the EU should find an international role as a partner, in close cooperation with the United States; then, if possible, Russia should be included. The next step could be a trilateral meeting convened to deal with nuclear hazards related to the Russian fleet in the Barents Sea region.

CONCLUSION

The EU will be obliged to assume a more assertive global role in the future. However, its credibility is primarily based on its role in Europe. If the EU cannot create peace in the Balkans, what kind of role could it play elsewhere, even Africa, where it has close ties to some states? The problems related to the reconstruction of the Balkans and the interim administration of Kosovo indicate that the EU has not been able to play a leading role in the efforts to stabilize the Balkan region. Yet the EU has to develop an overall strategy for the region that should have its place within the European structures of unification and integration in the future.[16] First, its global role will evolve only through the expansion of European regionalism beyond Europe's historic geographic borders. This process has its geopolitical repercussions, although it is based on economic integration. Second, the EU as a trade bloc has to play a more decisive role within the framework of global trade and investment negotiations. Third, the EU will play a more important role in promoting a social dimension of the process of economic globalization. Fourth, the EU has to better define its security interests and to develop the Common Foreign and Security Policy, which contains the necessary defense capabilities for crisis management. Yet it must maintain its strategic partnership with the United States and the cooperative and integrative partnership with Russia, increasing its ties with other leading powers (based on EU dialogues). Outside Europe, the EU should cooperate with the United Nations and other international organizations and agencies to promote peace and common values on the basis of its own values. However, one of the obstacles to creating a global political-military role for the EU is the fact that France and Great Britain are occupying permanent seats in the UN Security Council. The EU should replace these seats in the longer term. Within the framework of Group of 8 (G-8) meetings, the EU should follow the same pattern. Sooner or later the EU itself should replace its member states as the legal representative within the G-8 framework.

NOTES

1. Alpo Rusi (1997) *Dangerous Peace: New Rivalry in World Politics* (New York: Westview); a paperback version with a new concluding chapter was published in June 1998), pp. 59–96 (on geopolitics and new geopolitical actors).

2. Joseph S. Nye (1997) "China and the Future of the Asia Pacific Region," paper presented to annual conference of the International Institute for Strategic Studies, Singapore, September 14, 1997.

3. Lester Thurow (1993) *Head to Head: The Coming Economic Battle Among Japan, Europe, and America* (New York: Warner Books), pp. 24–25.

4. Paul Hirst (1997) "The Global Economy: Myths and Realities," *International Affairs* 73, no. 3 (July): 409–425; Kent E. Calder (1996) *Asia's Deadly Triangle: How Arms, Energy, and Growth Threaten to Destabilise Asia* (London: Nicholas Publishing).

5. John Mearsheimer (1990) "Back to the Future: Instability in Europe After the Cold War," *International Security* 15, no. 1 (Summer).

6. Guy de Jonquires, "European Commission's Transatlantic Trade Initiative Clears First Political Hurdle," *Financial Times*, March 12, 1998.

7. Speech by Prime Minister Paavo Lipponen, in *Rovaniemi*, September 15, 1997, and speech by President of the Republic of Finland, Martti Ahtisaari, in *London*, October 18, 1995 (Royal Institute of International Affairs).

8. Chrystia Freeland, "Yeltsin Sees Role in 'Dominant World Power,'" *Financial Times*, March 27, 1998; see also Rusi (1997–1998), pp. 88–89.

9. James P. Thomas (2000) "The Military Challenges of Transatlantic Coalitions," Adelphi Paper 333 (IISS, Oxford University Press), pp. 66–70.

10. Loukas Tsoukalis (1997) "Why Europe's Global Record Is So Patch," the Philip Morris Institute for Public Policy Research, Brussels, September 1997, pp. 65–73.

11. Claude Cheysson (1997) "Defining Europe's Place in the World," in Philip Morris (1997) *What Global Role for the EU?*, pp. 33–40.

12. Ibid., pp. 38–40.

13. UNDP, Human Development Report 1995 (New York: Oxford University Press).

14. See Charlotte Bretherton and John Vogler (1999) *The European Union as a Global Actor* (London and New York: Routledge).

15. See Javier Solana (1999) "NATO's Success in Kosovo," *Foreign Affairs* (November-December): 114–120. The author of this chapter was a member of the delegation of President Ahtisaari in the Kosovo peace process in 1999.

16. See Andreas Wittkowsky (2000), "Der Stabilitatspakt fur Sudosteuropa und die 'fuhrende Rolle' der Eoropaischen Union," *Aus Politik und Zeitgesichte* B (29–30, 2000); see also Centre for European Policy Studies (March 2000) Report on the Western Balkans presented to the Lisbon European Council by the Secretary General/High Representative together with the Commission (SN/2032/200 REV 2), in *CEPS Europa South-East Monitor*, no. 9 (Brussels: Centre for European Policy Studies).

7

European Security, the Transatlantic Link, and Crisis Management

Heinz Gärtner

The Cold War system was based on the concept of balance of power. For Hans Morgenthau, alliances are the "most important manifestation of the balance of power."[1] In this observation, members of alliances have common interests based on the fear of other states. Stephen Walt has since modified this concept, viewing alliances as the result of a "balance of threat."[2] He shows that the overwhelming coalition led by the United States against the Soviet Union and its allies was a result not of the power of the Soviet Union but of its perceived threat. This traditional model, where the existence of alliances and a potential threat were inseparable, is consistent with the bipolarity of the Cold War.

Although the dramatic events of 1989–1990 indelibly transformed the global political landscape, the greatest changes remain visible in Europe. The main threat upon which defense planning was based during the Cold War has faded away, and global and European security requirements are undergoing profound change as a consequence. Today there is no major threat to deter, as in the past, and many of the new dangers tend to be smaller in scale, regional in nature, and located on the periphery or outside of Europe; the very nature of the security threat has changed. A single overriding threat originating from

For an earlier version of this chapter, with a different focus, see Heinz Gärtner, "European Security: A Small States Perspective," in Simon Duke (ed.) (2000) *Between Vision and Reality: CFSP's Progress on the Path to Maturity*. Maastrict: European Institute of Public Administration, pp. 91–116.

a monolithic source has been replaced by a multitude of different threats, including the resurgence of centuries-old ethnic conflicts frozen by the Cold War.

Security institutions are forced to adapt as the dissolution of the unique political and strategic milieu of the Cold War compels a reappraisal of national security policies from Portugal to Poland and beyond. European countries are seeking security for a continent that has undergone a major structural transformation. Crisis management is the paradigm that forms the cornerstone of a new system of international security, which in turn faces a far wider array of threats than during the Cold War. By far the greatest proportion of the operational efforts of NATO and the Western European Union (WEU) have already shifted away from collective defense toward this type of activity.

Members of an alliance, or in the framework of the Partnership for Peace (PfP) states, may have to participate in crisis management, peacekeeping, humanitarian action, and even peace-enforcement operations. All EU members, whether or not members of the WEU, could take part in crisis management, peacekeeping, and humanitarian action as well as peacemaking in the framework of the so-called Petersberg tasks. Concerning these operations, they also would have equal rights in decisionmaking. The tasks of allied and nonallied states would be blurred in the field of crisis management.

NATO

Based on the assumption that alliances can hardly survive without a sufficient threat, some analysts concluded after the end of the East-West conflict that "NATO's days are not numbered but its years are."[3] No alliance in history survived its enemy for very long. This is true for the coalition against Napoleon, the World War I entente against Germany, and the anti-Hitler coalition. Ten years after the end of the Cold War, however, NATO shows no signs of its demise. The prediction that alliances would weaken without threat appears to be wrong. NATO looks like it will be an exception to these rules and the fundamental logic of alliance theory. How can NATO endure in the absence of a serious opponent?

The reason lies in NATO's capacity for change. NATO is redeveloping its basic structure: preparing for a coalition war is no longer the only or even primary item on its agenda, and its focus now includes crisis-management and crisis-response operations, peacekeeping, humanitarian action, as well as peace enforcement. The new NATO looks and acts in part quite differently from the old NATO. Simultaneously, the definition of the NATO area (Article 6) is losing relevance—the NATO-led operations in Bosnia and Kosovo are cases in point. NATO will be focusing on new areas in the time to come. It can and will no longer focus on a single mission of collective defense as during the Cold War, for if NATO remains a traditional alliance of collective defense as enshrined in Article 5 of the Washington Treaty it is likely to die out or deteriorate. The new NATO's challenges lie beyond its territory in international terrorism, the proliferation of weapons of mass destruction, the disruption of Gulf oil supplies, and instability along NATO's southern and eastern flanks. Since these challenges do not represent a direct threat to NATO territory, the real issue for NATO's future is not territorial defense but rather its structural transformation into a crisis-management alliance. However, NATO's capabilities are still aimed at mobilizing large numbers of forces sent to defend against a major attack in Central Europe, not at the capability of quickly moving and supporting limited forces trained and equipped to perform specific crisis-management or peacekeeping operations.[4]

The PfP program has already been designed according to the new requirements. Cooperation of the PfP partners with NATO can be organized on an individual level through peacekeeping exercises, military-to-military contacts, and similar activities. The Implementation Force (IFOR) and the Stabilization Force (SFOR) in Bosnia were NATO's first joint operations with PfP partners and twenty non-NATO states. In Madrid in July 1997, NATO formally launched an enhanced form of PfP that widened the range of participation. Military exercises can now cover the spectrum of possible crisis interventions. PfP partners will be involved in planning and preparing for contingency operations. PfP partners will have a stronger presence at NATO headquarters. All in all, PfP will facilitate NATO's ability to integrate partner forces in future operations. In February 1998 PfP partners participated for the first time in a crisis-management exercise. The scenario focused mainly on actions that NATO might have to take to implement a UN-mandated peace-support operation.

The Euro-Atlantic Partnership Council (EAPC) provides a mechanism for productive consultation and more meaningful communication among PfP partners as well as a framework in which the enhanced PfP can develop. There will also be possibilities for closer political dialogue and consultations and greater scope for joint decisionmaking and coordination. With the creation of the EAPC, NATO carries forward its transformation on the basis of a broad, cooperative approach to security. PfP partners will have new opportunities to consult with the Alliance more regularly and more substantively. The EAPC is thus the logical political complement to a stronger, more operational Partnership for Peace. As the Basic Document of the Euro-Atlantic Partnership Council of 30 May 1997 states: "In addition, the Council will provide the framework to afford Partner countries, to the maximum extent possible, increased decision-making opportunities relating to activities in which they participate."[5]

The specific subject areas on which allies and PfP partners would consult within the framework of the EAPC might include, but are not limited to: political and security matters; crisis management; regional matters; arms control; nuclear, biological, and chemical weapons proliferation and defense issues; international terrorism; defense planning and budgets; defense policy and strategy; and security impacts of economic developments. EAPC's scope will include consultations and cooperation on issues such as: civil emergency and disaster preparedness; armaments cooperation under the aegis of the Conference of National Armaments Directors; nuclear safety; defense-related environmental issues; civil-military coordination of air-traffic management and control; scientific cooperation; and issues related to peace-support operations.

This array of options and cooperation provides for an innovative capacity in the face of new challenges not requiring an Article 5 (collective defense) response. This broad security approach encompasses not only military but also economic, political, societal, and environmental concerns. These occur simultaneously at global, regional, and local levels. As non–Article 5 contingencies, they will be addressed by "coalitions of the willing" that include, as in Bosnia and Kosovo, both NATO and non-NATO members. NATO will create flexible military assets suitable for use by varying coalitions, which it can employ when taking on crisis-management tasks itself and also lend to the Europeans according to the idea of "separable but not separate" capacities.

More than merely a new form of cooperation, NATO's new instruments and tasks will blur the differences between members and nonmembers (i.e., PfP partners). PfP/EAPC offers almost all the benefits of NATO except the collective-security guarantee articulated in Article 5. As former U.S. Secretary of Defense William Perry foresaw in December 1996 during a meeting of NATO defense ministers in Bergen: "The difference between membership and non-membership in NATO would be paper-thin." Indeed, in some cases non-members may play an even more important role in the new operations than NATO members as NATO's focus gradually shifts away from Article 5 missions (territorial defense) to non–Article 5 missions (crisis management).[6] Washington believes that PfP/EAPC will draw PfP partners much closer to NATO in the field of peace operations, humanitarian intervention, and crisis management. Non-NATO states could participate in those missions and cooperate with NATO while retaining their current defense profiles.[7]

NATO promised that it will provide PfP partners with all the standards required to allow them to interoperate with NATO with no loss to NATO's operational capability. Although PfP partners will not operate with the allies in Article 5 situations, it is vital for NATO that the high standards maintained by the allies also be used as the measures for PfP partners in non–Article 5 operations and exercises. Non–Article 5 standards for NATO must be the same for allies and PfP partners if true interoperability is to be achieved. Thus Article 5 training for allies has to be *in addition* to non–Article 5 training.[8]

At the Washington Summit, heads of state and government endorsed the report on enhanced and more operational PfP partnership and the development of an operational capabilities concept (OCC) as a new element of this partnership. The OCC seeks to improve the interoperability of PfP partner forces and the Alliance's capability to put together tailored force packages to mount and sustain NATO-led PfP operations such as SFOR and the Kosovo Force (KFOR) under NATO command. It also links regular PfP cooperation with the NATO force-generation process for specific NATO-led PfP operations, thereby reinforcing PfP's operational capability to support NATO-led PfP operations.[9]

The Combined Joint Task Forces (CJTFs) are specifically designed to include the participation of non-NATO countries for both non–Article 5 contingencies outside Alliance territory and Article 5 tasks. The concept builds on NATO's practice of multinational, multiservice operations and, therefore, could involve humanitarian relief, peacekeeping, or peace enforcement. The CJTF concept would also facilitate the use of NATO's collective assets by the WEU, as well as provide a mechanism for involving non-NATO PfP partners in NATO-led operations. Finally, as not all allies may be engaged in every non–Article 5 contingency, the CJTF concept is designed to deal flexibly with the ad hoc nature of participation without sacrificing cohesion, effectiveness, and reaction time.[10]

The Washington Summit communiqué of April 1999[11] and NATO's new Strategic Concept[12] stress that NATO will be larger, more capable, and more flexible. On the one hand, NATO still will be committed to collective defense; on the other hand, it will be able to undertake new missions, including contributing to effective conflict prevention and engaging actively in crisis-management and crisis-response operations. However, the latter are as yet undefined. In addition to territorial defense (covered by Articles 5 and 6 of the Washington Treaty), the Alliance security must also take into account the global context. Alliance security interests could be affected by risks of a wider nature, including terrorism, sabotage, organized crime, and disruption of the flow of vital resources (arrangements and consultations as responses to risks of this kind can be made under Article 4).

NATO will seek, in cooperation with other organizations, to prevent conflict or, should a crisis arise, to contribute to its effective management, consistent with international law, including the possibility of conducting non–Article 5 crisis-response operations. The Alliance's preparedness to carry out such operations supports the broader objective of reinforcing and extending stability and often involves the participation of NATO's PfP partners. NATO recalls its offer, made in Brussels in 1994, to support on a case-by-case basis, in accordance with its own procedures, peacekeeping and other operations under the authority of the UN Security Council or the Organization for Security and Cooperation in Europe (OSCE), including making available Alliance resources and expertise.[13]

The communiqué acknowledges the resolve of the European Union to have the capacity for autonomous action so that it can take decisions and approve military action where the Alliance as a whole is not engaged; Europeans (EU members and other allies) should strengthen their defense capabilities, especially for new missions, avoiding unnecessary duplication. Under the new Strategic Concept, issued at the NATO summit in April 1999, the European Security and Defense Identity (ESDI) is to be developed within NATO but in close cooperation with the WEU and, "if and when appropriate, the European Union." The objective of the Washington Summit–launched Defense Capabilities Initiative is to improve defense capabilities to ensure the effectiveness of future multinational operations of Alliance missions. This includes non–Article 5 crisis-response operations with a special focus on the interoperability among Alliance forces and, where applicable, between Alliance and PfP partner forces.

EAPC consultations[14] should contribute to conflict prevention and crisis management and develop practical cooperation activities, including civil emergency planning and scientific and environmental affairs. Although NATO pledges that it is committed to increasing the role the PfP partners play in PfP decisionmaking and planning and to making PfP more operational, this promise has not been put into practice. There was no involvement of the PfP partners in the planning and decisionmaking of a peacekeeping force in Kosovo.

In the plenary resolution entitled "NATO and Humanitarian Intervention" adopted by the NATO Parliamentary Assembly in Amsterdam on 15 November 1999, NATO emphasized that any intervention with the purpose of preventing or ending massive human rights violations can only be the last resort and that any intervention has to respect the principle of proportionality. NATO stressed its preparedness, according to the Alliance's 1999 Strategic Concept, to "contribute to conflict prevention and crisis management through non–Article 5 crisis response operations" in the Euro-Atlantic area.[15]

THE EUROPEAN UNION AND
THE WESTERN EUROPEAN UNION

The origins of Article 5 of the Brussels Treaty of 1948 can be found in the Cold War.[16] Since the so-called Petersberg declaration of 1992, the WEU will also focus on missions that include crisis management, peacekeeping, humanitarian action, and peacemaking. If the above observation of shifting challenges and tasks is correct, the Petersberg missions will become more important than Article 5. José Cutileiro, Secretary-General of the WEU, acknowledges: "Today the WEU is a politico-military tool for crisis management. It will run operations that Europeans decide to undertake and in which North Americans do not wish to participate directly."[17] At their meeting in Rome in November 1998, WEU ministers expressed the wish that a process of informal reflection be initiated by the WEU on the question of Europe's security and defense. As part of this process, it was decided to conduct an audit of assets and capabilities for European-led crisis-management operations.

The EU's Treaty of Amsterdam (June 1997) included the Petersberg tasks. It states in Article 17 that "the Union can avail itself of the WEU to elaborate and implement decisions of the EU on the tasks referred to." These are "humanitarian and rescue tasks, peace-keeping tasks and tasks of combat forces in crisis management, including peace-making." The treaty does not merge the WEU and EU. It simply states that "the WEU is an integral part of the development of the EU. . . . The EU shall . . . foster closer institutional relations with the WEU with a view to the possibility of the integration of the WEU into the Union." The precondition is a European Council decision and adoption of such a decision by the member states only "in accordance with their respective constitutional requirements." The Common Foreign and Security Policy (CFSP) of the EU shall, according to the treaty, "include all questions relating to the security of the Union, including the progressive framing of a common defense policy . . . which might in time lead to a common defense, should the European Council so decide." Such a decision has to be "in accordance with [the member states'] respective constitutional requirements."

Based originally on a Swedish-Finnish proposal, the Amsterdam Treaty allows "all [EU member states] contributing to the tasks in question to participate fully on an equal footing in planning and decision-taking in the WEU." Membership in the WEU, therefore, is not necessary to participate in the Petersberg tasks.[18] The European institutions—the WEU and EU—will limit their defense ambitions to crisis management and will try to build up separate force structures for this. The federal approach still aims to merge the EU and WEU, and Article 5 (collective defense and binding security guarantees of the WEU treaty) should be incorporated into the EU. This would lead to the creation of a new military alliance.[19] Such a radical development is very unlikely and not an option for a very long time.

The EU after Amsterdam focused on the Petersberg missions, including crisis management, peacekeeping, humanitarian action, and peace enforcement, rather than Article 5 operations (collective defense and security guarantees). The following options have been discussed after the conclusion of the Amsterdam Treaty:

- Britain proposed in October 1998 that mutual security commitments be included as a fourth pillar of the EU. The WEU would change dramatically and abandon Article 5 or dissolve entirely, and the main European defense role would remain with NATO. The fourth pillar would be based on NATO.

- The declaration issued by France and Britain at St. Malo in December 1998 stressed the necessity for Europe to develop the full range of capabilities needed for the sort of crisis-management tasks and humanitarian operations in which Europe might take the lead. The European Union "must have the capacity for autonomous action, backed up by credible military forces, the means to decide to use them and a readiness to do so, in order to respond to international crisis."[20]
- In March 1999 British Prime Minister Tony Blair criticized Europe's military capabilities as too modest for the security problems of the 1990s and twenty-first century. The Europeans need to restructure their defense capabilities to be capable to project force, to deploy troops, ships, and planes beyond their home bases, and to sustain them there. However, Blair underlined that the deployment of forces is a decision for governments and not for the European Parliament, the European Commission, or the Court of Justice.[21]
- According to the declaration of the European Council[22] in Cologne in June 1999, which is based on a proposal by the German EU Presidency,[23] a common European policy on security and defense requires "a capacity for action backed up by credible military capabilities and appropriate decision making bodies and procedures." The focus therefore should be to assure that the EU possesses the necessary capabilities (including military capabilities) to conduct crisis-management operations in the scope of the Petersberg tasks. The main characteristics include: deployability, sustainability, interoperability, flexibility, and mobility. Further arrangements to enhance the capacity of European multinational and national forces to respond to crisis situations will be needed.
- NATO remains the foundation for collective defense (Article 5). In the case of integration of the WEU into the EU, the commitment of Article 5 and of Article 5 of the Brussels Treaty will be preserved for the member states already party to these treaties. The document stressed that the policy of the EU shall not prejudice the specific character of the security and defense policy of certain member states. "States will retain in all circumstances the right to decide if and when their national forces are deployed."
- There should be the possibility of all EU member states (NATO members, neutrals, and nonaligned states) to participate fully and on equal footing in European operations drawing on NATO assets and capabilities; and there should be satisfactory arrangements for European NATO members who are not EU member states. EU-led operations using NATO assets and capabilities, as well as EU-led operations without recourse to NATO assets and capabilities, should be possible, and unnecessary duplication should be avoided.

- Planned are regular meetings of defense ministers, a permanent body of representatives with political and military expertise. This declaration included many changes proposed by European neutral and non-aligned states, explicitly excluding Article 5 commitments. The equal role of these states is underlined.

- On 20 July 1999, Prime Minister Blair and Italian Prime Minister Massimo D'Alema launched an initiative to improve European defense capabilities.[24] The declaration proposed to set criteria for improved and strengthened European defense capabilities and effective crisis management, including peacemaking. These efforts should be complementary to the Union's and the member states' capabilities concerning the nonmilitary aspects of crisis prevention and management, improving coordination between military and nonmilitary aspects.

- In November 1999, for the first time, the defense and foreign ministers of the European Union, including those from its quartet of neutral countries, launched the idea of developing a rapid-reaction corps that would act at the EU's behest in crises that were too big to ignore but not big enough to demand the involvement of the United States and, therefore, of NATO. Britain cited a number—40,000 men—to indicate the rough size of the force, which would come together only in times of crisis and therefore fall well short of becoming a standing European army. And Germany laid out a timetable: the EU, it suggested, should give itself a "defense identity" by 2003, if not sooner.

- The European Council in Helsinki in December 1999 adopted the two Presidency progress reports on developing the Union's military and nonmilitary crisis-management capability as part of a strengthened common European policy on security and defense. The Finnish Presidency of the EU[25] has given priority to the mandate given by the Cologne European Council to strengthen the common European policy on security and defense by taking the work forward in military and nonmilitary aspects of crisis management. The document stresses that NATO remains the foundation of the collective defense of its members. The common European goal has been adopted for deployable military capabilities based on a British and French proposal that called for a European rapid-reaction force of up to 60,000 troops capable of deployment within sixty days to tackle military crises without outside help. The European Council underlined its determination to develop an autonomous capacity to take decisions and, where NATO as a whole is not engaged, to launch and conduct EU-led military operations in response to international crises. (It is not clear whether the EU first has to ask NATO before it conducts an EU-led operation, however.) This process will avoid unnecessary duplication and does not imply the creation of a European army.

- The standing Political and Security Committee (PSC) has been established to address all aspects of the CFSP, including the Common European Security and Defense Policy. The Military Committee will provide for consultation and cooperation between the member states and give advice and make recommendations though the PSC. The report stresses that the European Union will contribute to international peace and security in accordance with the principles of the UN Charter. The Union recognizes the primary responsibility of the UN Security Council for the maintenance of international peace and security. Also, a nonmilitary crisis-management mechanism will be established to coordinate and make more effective the various civilian means and resources, in parallel with the military ones, at the disposal of the Union and the member states. The Portuguese Presidency of the EU established the Committee for Non-military Crisis Management.

TRANSATLANTIC LINK: PFP AND PETERSBERG

We have bifurcation within NATO and EU (i.e., the WEU). We have collective defense on the one hand and crisis management on the other. There also is a duplication of missions. We have the Amsterdam Treaty with the inclusion of the Petersberg tasks, and the new NATO with PfP and EAPC. We have crisis management here and crisis management there. We have non–Article 5 of the WEU here and non–Article 5 of NATO there. Clearly, there is a great deal of overlap. Why not combine some of the new elements? Rather than merge WEU and EU, it would be more logical to merge the non–Article 5 missions—to combine Petersberg and PfP.

Europeans and Americans face the same challenges: proliferation of weapons of mass destruction, disruption of world energy resources, international terrorism, transnational organized crime, ethnic conflicts, and so on. All affect U.S. as well as European interests.[26]

NATO's command structure is still focused on the defense of Europe and its territorial waters, however.[27] Designed for the now obsolete task of blocking Soviet military power, it is not appropriate for the new challenges. These crisis-management missions would require the members to rapidly deploy forces far from Europe's borders—in overwhelming strength if necessary. To date, only the United States has that capability. If Europe is given a major stake in power projection, it would have to share the burden as well. *The Economist*[28] concludes: "If America is to remain willingly engaged in Europe, increasingly Europeans must be willing to do their bit elsewhere." Table 7.1 compares the key areas of the EU and NATO.

Table 7.1 Key Areas of EU and NATO

Area	NATO Summit in Washington, April 1999 (Communiqué)	Cologne EU Summit, June 1999	Report of the Finnish EU Presidency in Helsinki, Dec. 1999
EU's capacity to act	• *We acknowledge the resolve of the European Union to have the capacity for autonomous action* so that it can take decisions and approve military action where the Alliance as a whole is not engaged. • We therefore stand ready to define and adopt the necessary arrangements for ready access by the European Union to the collective assets and capabilities of the Alliance, for operations in which the Alliance as a whole is not engaged militarily as an Alliance. . . . These arrangements . . . should address: a) Assured EU access to NATO planning capabilities able to contribute to military planning for EU-led operations; b) The presumption of availability to the EU of pre-identified NATO capabilities and common assets for use in EU-led operations.	• *The Union must have the capacity for autonomous action,* backed up by credible military forces, the means to decide to use them, and a readiness to do so, in order to respond to international crises without prejudice to actions by NATO.	• The European Council underlines its determination to *develop an autonomous capacity to take decisions and, where NATO as a whole is not engaged to launch and conduct EU-led military operations* in response to international crises. This process will avoid unnecessary duplication and does not imply the creation of a European army.
EU's contributions to crisis-response operations	• The European Union has taken important decisions and given a further impetus to its efforts to strengthen its security and defence dimension. • We applaud the determination of . . . EU-members . . . to take the necessary steps to strengthen their defence capabilities.	• For EU-led operations having recourse to NATO assets and capabilities, including European command arrangements, the main focus should be on the following aspects: Implementation of the arrangements based on the Berlin decisions of 1996 and the Washington NATO summit decisions of April 1999.	• *Further steps will be taken to ensure mutual consultation, cooperation and transparency between the EU and NATO on the development of the Union's capability* for military crisis management and on the appropriate military response to a crisis.
EU-NATO relations	• On the basis of decisions taken by the Alliance, in Berlin 1996 and subsequently, the European Security and Defence Identity will continue to be developed within NATO. *This process will require close cooperation between NATO, the WEU and, if and when appropriate, the European Union.* • *NATO and the EU should ensure the development of effective mutual consultation, cooperation and transparency.*	• *We shall ensure the development of effective mutual consultation, cooperation and transparency between the European Union and NATO.* • To ensure the development of effective mutual consultation, cooperation and transparency between NATO and the EU.	• The development of the common European policy on security and defence will take place . . . *with the maximum transparency between the EU and NATO.* • For the conduct of EU-led operations, the Union may use NATO assets and capabilities with NATO agreement.

Source: Compiled by Heinz Gärtner. The author received important suggestions from Johann Pucher.

A NEW COMMAND STRUCTURE

A new command structure[29] could be created dealing exclusively with non–Article 5 operations. Such a command structure would be based on both NATO and EU, which would provide the infrastructure and experience indispensable for the new mission. A political coordination group could discuss and plan the crisis-management tasks. The command should be headed alternately by an American and a European. Member states would assign special trained forces. It could be based on that part of the CJTF that focuses on non–Article 5 operations. The CJTF has become a tool for NATO crisis management while satisfying demands for a European identity. A first task could be a program for joint NATO-WEU crisis management. The first major crisis-management exercise—CMX 2000—took place in February 2000. This WEU-NATO joint exercise was based on a Petersberg mission scenario (peace support) leading to a WEU-led operation making use of NATO assets and capabilities. It demonstrated the culture of close cooperation developed between the two organizations. The aim was to test WEU and appropriate NATO crisis-management mechanisms and procedures as well as the consultation arrangements between WEU and NATO, including the interaction between each organization's headquarters and WEU-NATO nations. And more exercises are to follow.

The advantages of a new command structure are:

- The old part of NATO and WEU—the collective defense—would remain unscathed despite reduced capacity. The traditional function and obligations would not be diluted, and the cohesion would not be diminished as many fear. Still, it would permit PfP to demonstrate that it has its own role and rationale and is not just a waiting room for membership.
- Nonmembers of NATO and WEU (Austria, Sweden, Finland, Ireland) could participate in the new command structure, as only Article 5 commitments are inconsistent with their nonaligned or neutral status. The Gulf War, IFOR/SFOR in Bosnia, and KFOR in Kosovo show that international coalitions responding to crisis within or outside of Europe may include nonmembers. These states could and should participate in the decisionmaking process.
- It would also facilitate EU enlargement in the field of security to include nonmembers of the EU that are participants in PfP. NATO members who are not members of the EU (Hungary, Poland, the Czech Republic, Turkey, Norway, Iceland) can participate in these operations if they wish. The EU's PSC and the Military Committee could be enlarged by non-EU NATO members and other candidates to accession. They would then become mixed committees.

- This new structure would be nonthreatening to Russia. It could even include Russia at a later stage.
- Current NATO members can but need not take part in the new command structure. Those who do not want to take part in the new missions can limit themselves to traditional collective defense.

A common command structure could avoid the problem that would emerge if the WEU used NATO assets and capabilities for its own operations in which the United States does not want to take part and got into trouble; the United States eventually would have to come to its aid. The Americans would be part of the operation from the beginning. A UN or OSCE mandate for such operations would be preferable.

A new crisis management command structure would therefore meet the three fundamental objectives of NATO: to ensure its effectiveness, to preserve the transatlantic link, and to develop ESDI.[30] The overriding imperative is to develop a new structure that is mission-oriented.

It would also meet NATO Secretary-General Robertson's three *I*'s: the European Security and Defense Identity must bring an *improvement* in capabilities; it must be *inclusive* of all allies; and it must reaffirm the *indivisibility* of allied security. Thus it would also meet U.S. Secretary of State Madeleine Albright's three *D*'s: no *decoupling* of European from transatlantic security commitments; no *duplication* of defense assets; and no *discrimination* vis-à-vis non-EU NATO members. See Figure 7.1.

MODALITIES FOR CONSULTATION AND COOPERATION BETWEEN NATO AND EU

On a more operational level, modalities for consultation and cooperation between NATO and EU could be organized along the following lines.[31]

Routine *noncrisis phase modalities* of consultation that allow easy, regular, and frequent contacts may include: cross-representation by Secretaries-General for relevant agenda items; contacts between the respective councils, groups, committees, and staff, including periodic and ad hoc joint meetings and military staff liaison meetings; cross-representation between the EU and NATO Military Committees; cross-participation of EU and NATO military staff officers in EU meetings designed for the development of European defense capabilities and NATO meetings connected with the Defense Capabilities Initiative as well as in EU and NATO exercise conferences; regular briefings about the organizations' respective activities by the Presidency of the EU, EU and NATO secretariats, and, when required, by military staff of both organizations; and the establishment of EU and Supreme Headquarters Allied Powers Europe (SHAPE) offices in each other's headquarters.

Figure 7.1   Common Crisis Management

NATO	EU (WEU)

OLD

    Deterrence, collective defense   No military significance
    (security guarantees, Article 5)   (security guarantees, Article 5)

NEW

    Instruments
              PfP, EAPC   Petersberg Tasks
    Missions
    Crisis management (humanitarian actions,   Crisis management (humanitarian actions,
    rescue operations, peacekeeping, peace   rescue operations, peacekeeping, tasks of
    enforcement, non–Article 5)   combat forces including peacemaking,
                                     non–Article 5)

CRISIS MANAGEMENT

↓

Common exercises

↓

Common crisis management program

↓

Common coordination group?

↓

Common Command Structure for crisis management?
(non–Article 5)

Source: Heinz Gärtner.

Consultation and cooperation would cover key areas such as the elaboration of the headline goal, generic crisis management, and military advance planning for specific scenarios.

Once a crisis had been recognized and each organization had begun to monitor it, the two organizations would share intelligence and situation assessments and inform each other of their internal deliberations by means of an intensification of the mechanisms for consultation identified for the routine precrisis phase (see above). During this phase, close cooperation and transparency would be necessary between EU and NATO authorities, including SHAPE, to ensure a shared understanding of the possible requirements for NATO assets and capabilities to support the operation.

Coming at a point at which a common understanding would emerge (i.e., that the Alliance as a whole would not be engaged and that an operation under the political and strategic direction of the EU was envisaged *making use of NATO assets and capabilities*), intensified mechanisms of consultation would be supplemented by specific decisionmaking procedures: the EU Council would instruct the PSC (which is the body responsible for the political control and strategic direction of the operation) to select the headquarters for the operation, to appoint the operation and force commander, to approve the operation plan, and to decide on the mission and composition of the force.

Close cooperation would remain essential even if the EU mounted an operation *without recourse to NATO assets.* The operation commander, when provided by NATO, would receive political control and strategy direction from the EU's PSC, acting under the authority of the EU Council and bearing in mind the leading role of the Committee of Contributors in what regards the day-to-day conduct of the operation. Even if not the operation commander, the deputy Supreme Allied Commander Europe would be the principal point of contact with the EU at the military strategy command level. He would participate as an observer in meetings of the Military Committee and accompany the chairman of the Military Committee in briefings to the PSC, the General Affairs Council, and the European Council as necessary.

SELECTIVE ENGAGEMENT

There is a strong argument that European NATO members should spend far more money on modern arms and equipment to carry their share of responsibility in war. The Gulf War and the war in Kosovo demonstrated the huge disparities between U.S. and European forces, the growing gap between the two forces, and its effect on even the most sophisticated armies to react quickly in war.[32] According to the Brookings Institution, NATO countries spend roughly 60 percent of what the United States does and get about 10 percent of the capability. A lack of precision-guided munitions would have been chief among the European shortcomings during the Kosovo war. Transporting troops and equipment would be another large problem for the Europeans. Without changes, the Europeans would be unable to take the next step in creating their own defense and security arm within NATO. The London-based International Institute for Strategic Studies[33] reported that European military shortcomings highlighted in Kosovo included "command-and-control, in particular airspace management, secure . . . voice communications, targeting procedures and the proper integration of the collection and analysis of intelligence. . . . A major lesson of the campaign was that all participants, particularly the Europeans, held insufficient stocks of all types of precision-guided munitions." The WEU recommendations for strengthening European capabilities for crisis management of November 1999[34] concluded that the Europeans have available the force levels and resources needed to prepare and implement military operations over the whole range of Petersberg tasks. But it also identified several gaps and deficiencies with regard to collective capabilities: gathering and management of information and intelligence, including space-based imagery and the analysis of crisis situations; preparation, planning, political control, and strategic direction of crisis-management operations; and with regard to forces and operational capabilities: availability, deployability, strategic mobility, sustainability, survivability and interoperability, and operational effectiveness; multinational joint operation and force headquarters, with particular reference to airborne command, control, and communications and deployability of force headquarters. François Heisbourg[35] proposed a long list of remedies that the Europeans should acquire: professional armed forces, satellite surveillance, military electronics, heavy airlift, precision-guided weapons, and more versatile aircraft.

John Deutch, Arnold Kanter, and Brent Scowcroft have asked whether a European strategy of developing technologies internally ever could compete with the United States. Their answer is in the negative.[36] But the answer also cannot primarily be to "buy American." The Europeans should be spending more on defense, and for many Americans this implies that much of the spending would be with U.S. firms. With financial difficulties for many European governments and the absence of a direct threat, it is questionable whether Europeans should copy U.S. capabilities, however. Besides, the United States wishes to share with its European allies the burden stemming from its own commitments, new security problems, and regional crisis-management needs. Of course, the Europeans and Americans will have to share burdens, risks, and responsibilities in non–Article 5 areas, and European states will have to improve their ability to contribute militarily to the protection of common interests.

But there must be an appropriate division of labor. While the United States provided more than two-thirds of the aircraft in the campaign over Kosovo and Serbia, in the peacetime aftermath the EU provides five times as many peacekeeping forces as the United States.[37] Out of a force of some 45,000, the United States is providing roughly 6,000 troops, slightly fewer than the largest contributor, which is Italy. European nations, EU and non-EU together, are providing 80 percent of the KFOR forces. The same is true for the money. The European Union has provided some $16.5 billion to the Balkans since 1991 and has budgeted $12 billion through 2005.[38] During the past decade Europe has spent more than three times what the United States has spent on nonmilitary assistance. And nearly 90 percent of such costs in Kosovo are covered by Europeans. The overwhelming U.S. contribution is in war-fighting capability—what is by comparison a limited European contribution.

However, a capability to act does not only imply fighting a war; it also implies political capability in the sense of foresight, intelligence, planning, creativity, vision, and conflict prevention.[39] European forces and capabilities are designed more for peacekeeping, humanitarian action, and disaster relief than for the rapid deployment of larger forces over long distances. The United States will need to continue to project forces in high-intensity conflict. Smaller-scale operations can be conducted as an autonomous European operation without deployment of NATO assets and capabilities.

The increased importance of crisis-management operations has repercussions not only for the type of equipment procured for what is sometimes a wide diversity of operations but also for the operating costs, as severe demands are placed on the equipment during deployment. European states should not want more than they can control. They are not able to prepare for fighting, high-intensity combat, enforcing and making peace, peacekeeping, resolving conflicts, and participating in humanitarian and rescue operations. Although some militaries would like to get the equipment for this entire range of conflict contingencies, it is the involvement in low-intensity and soft-security operational missions that are most appropriate for European states, rather than high-intensity conflicts against opponents using traditional forces and strategies (see below). High-technology forces are not essential for soft-security and peacekeeping missions and not very helpful. Most highly developed military technology is poorly designed for use in crisis-response operations. Advanced technologies based on absolute information to increase the ability to strike with precision over great distances are not relevant to these missions.[40] Simulation centers like MITRE Corporation in Boston create virtual enemies and develop digital warfighting strategies based on the idea of absolute information. For them it is not important what capacities an enemy really has but rather what it might have. What counts is not what an enemy thinks but what it might think.

These technologies and correspondingly trained militaries are narrowly focused on high-end warfare, as was used in the operation against the former Yugoslavia. They are incapable of intervening in conflicts that require militaries trained for humanitarian action and peacekeeping. The technological requirements of advanced technology, combined with the emphasis on sensing equipment, simply do not translate well into low-intensity conflicts and may even be counterproductive in some cases. Peacekeepers have to be physically present, visible, and supportive to the population through mediation and advice (see below). A good soldier is not necessarily a good peacekeeper. A peacekeeper is a certain type of soldier. He should be qualified to perform police tasks, conduct civil-affairs operations, speak multiple languages, and be trained in some psychology.

Officers are expected to broker diplomatic deals, shelter the displaced, protect human rights, supervise the return of refugees, guard surrendered weapons, interact extensively with local people, ensure the safe delivery of food supplies, organize and monitor elections, rebuild government agencies or police forces, and support civil reconstruction.[41] People who are trained to be soldiers have to be retrained for the new role. The mandate defines in what way soldiers have to be trained and retrained. Each unit sent on a peace operation must be trained for several months.[42]

There is therefore a basic contradiction between this type of mission and the use of advanced technologies that are intended to reduce the need for forces on the ground. Such technologies are generally ill-suited to these missions.[43] Heavy airlift, precision targeting, absolute battlefield information, and advanced command-and-control systems do not have much relevance in environments where there is no war against an enemy with mass armies and heavy weapons.[44]

One important dividing line falls between the extended peacekeeping and peace-enforcement models. It does not presuppose the consent of the parties to the conflict or potential conflict (see line x in Figure 7.2). The relationship between consent and the use of force is a complex arrangement between a mandate and clear rules of engagement. The use of force remains the ultimate ratio (the area between x and y). As a rule of thumb, one may state that the stronger the international capability, the better the prospect for consent not being withdrawn.[45] In some cases, there could be a type of consensual Chapter 7, such as the Dayton Accord and the Kosovo peace agreement. In these cases the conflicting parties agreed to peace implementation by force. The other dividing line is the one between peace enforcement and war (line y). However, there is some room for interpretation about a clear distinction between peace-enforcement operations and war. Legally, one could argue that peace-enforcement operations that are authorized by the UN are not wars. Yet the differences are blurring, as the example of the second Gulf War between the U.S.-led Coalition and Iraq over the liberation of Kuwait in 1991 shows. The anti-Iraq Coalition was authorized by a mandate of the UN Security Council; the liberation of Kuwait could also, however, have taken place on the basis of self-defense (Article 51 of the UN Charter), which then would have counted as a war under the above definition.

A *war* describes a state when force is used by two or more conflicting parties on the basis of partiality and clearly designated enemies absent any mandate from an international organization. Conversely, UN peace operations are based on the three basic principles, namely, consent, impartiality, and the use of force only in self-defense.[46] These principles have occasionally been jeopardized by the use of humanitarian action as a pretense for political intervention with ambiguous and ill-defined objectives, as in Somalia.[47] A clear, appropriate, and realistic mandate has to be implemented in an impartial manner. Impartiality is not identical with consent, and it is not neutrality or passivity. Activities to implement mandates, including the use of force, do not mean taking sides, but they can be to one of the parties' detriment.[48]

Figure 7.2   Participation of European States

			Line y	
Crisis Response Operations—Petersberg Tasks *Participation of European States*				
Humanitarian action	Peace Operations (PSO)			War
Rescue operations	Peacekeeping	Peace enforcement		Kuwait
Refugee/ displaced persons assistance	Preventive deployment	Peace implementation		Kosovo (Operation Allied Force)
		Monitoring (Verification)		
CONSENT (Chapter 6)		Usually NO CONSENT but consensual Chapter 7 possible (Dayton, Kosovo UN resolution) AGAINST CONFLICTING PARTY BUT IMPARTIALITY (Chapter 7)		Designated Enemy
Use of force for self-defense		Use of force for the implementation of a mandate (agreement)		Use of force for defeat
e.g., early warning, pioneer, minesweeping, rescue, transport, disaster relief units		Troops prepared for combat		Troops in combat

Line x

Source: Heinz Gärtner. The author received important suggestions from Johann Pucher and Karl Schmidseder.

In principal, European states would be able to take part in all operations. This would demonstrate that international solidarity is not something to be left to military alliances. Operations between lines x and y (see Figure 7.2) must be based on international legitimation by the UN or the OSCE, whether it is in the framework of NATO-PfP or Petersberg. In such circumstances, the use of force requires strict impartiality. Limited force against any party that violates the mandate and impartiality will not be mutually exclusive.

In practice, European states should concentrate on the soft-security and nonmilitary crisis-response operations (left of line x in Figure 7.2). Their participation in combat is unlikely to be decisive. Their experiences range from infrastructure restoration to basic police, medical, and veterinary services.

Security goes beyond merely military aspects. The Cologne European Council recommended that the council examine all aspects of security with a view to enhancing and better coordinating the Union's and member states' nonmilitary crisis-response tools. The Finnish Presidency of the EU has developed this concept further, reflected in the report to the Helsinki European Council on nonmilitary crisis-management tools.

POLITICAL GUIDELINES

A mismatch between forces and missions, due to the lack of a clear mandate and the incomplete understanding of the missions, has been a common failing in many post–Cold War interventions.[49] For the involvement in operations mapped out on the right side of line x in Figure 7.2, European states should define conditions on whether and how to participate. Such a list of criteria could set guidelines for decisionmaking. This would demonstrate a European state's willingness to participate in international peace operations while preventing it from becoming entrapped in military actions that are doomed to fail, as in Somalia. The mandate for the 1993 operation in Somalia shifted back and forth between a humanitarian action, peacekeeping, peace enforcement, and peacebuilding.[50] This operation proved to be a failure because of the lack of knowledge about the differences among the different types of peace operations. A central point is to determine from the beginning the category to which an operation belongs. Rules of engagement will differ with the nature of the mandate. It is impossible to answer the question of *whether* to intervene without also considering *how* to intervene.[51]

Such guidelines for political and military feasibility could include the following:[52]

1. A participation in military operations is contingent on the Europeans' interests and/or on the promotion of international law and international principles.
2. It should be based on a mandate of an international organization—the United Nations or the OSCE. The mandate has to have clear political and military objectives that are both reasonable and attainable. The mandate of a humanitarian intervention must be strictly limited to ending the atrocities and building a new order of security for people in the country in question.
3. It has to be a multinational operation. It should be based on international solidarity and a fair distribution of responsibilities, burdens, and risks.

4. There can be no automatic process for the deployment of troops. Each mission requires a case-by-case political decision by the parliament.

5. The units of the European state will have to operate within a clear command structure of an international organization.

6. The financing of the participation has to be guaranteed. Overstretching the military capacities has to be avoided; the equipment and armaments must be adequate for the task. The risks for dispatched personnel must be kept at a minimum.

7. Rules of engagement have to be formulated unambiguously. The conditions governing when and how troops may use force must be clear. The use of force must be proportional to the humanitarian issue at hand. The level of risk must be reasonable.

8. The operation has to be limited in duration. There can be no open-ended commitments.

9. The operation must have a high likelihood of success.

10. Troops must have an exit strategy if the operation fails.

These criteria could also help in deciding on selective engagement. The participating state has to be associated with the conception, the planning, and the command of the operation. The precondition is that participation takes place on a voluntary basis and with UN or OSCE authorization. Participation could take place in the framework of NATO-PfP or as part of the Petersberg tasks. Under these circumstances, case-by-case action would be not only acceptable but likely.

CONCLUSION

Crisis management is the cornerstone of a new system of international security. Most operational efforts of NATO and the WEU have already shifted away from collective defense toward this type of activity. Whether members of an alliance or a PfP member, all of them will have to participate in non–Article 5 crisis-management operations such as humanitarian action, peacekeeping, and also peace enforcement. All EU members, whether or not members of the WEU, could take part in crisis management, peacekeeping, humanitarian action, and peacemaking within the framework of the Petersberg tasks. Concerning these operations, they also would have equal rights in decisionmaking. The tasks of allied and nonallied states would be blurred in the field of crisis management. A new command structure could be created dealing exclusively with non–Article 5 operations. It would be based on both NATO and EU. Modalities for consultation and cooperation between NATO and EU will have to be developed. European forces are more designed for peacekeeping, humanitarian action, and disaster relief rather than for the rapid deployment of larger forces over long distances. The United States will need to continue to project forces in high-intensity conflict. Selective participation in international peace operations is inevitable for Europeans. In principle, Europeans would be able to take part in all operations. In practice, European states should concentrate on the soft-security operations. The participation in peace enforcement should be decided on a case-by-case basis. For involvement in international operations, Europeans should define conditions. Participation in military operations is contingent on the Europeans' interests and/or on the promotion of international law and international principles. Peace-enforcement and peace-implementation operations must be based on international legitimation of the UN or the OSCE, whether it is in the framework of NATO-PfP or Petersberg. In such circumstances, the use of force requires strict impartiality. The mandate has to have clear political and military objectives that are reasonable and attainable. Rules of engagement have to be formulated unambiguously. The conditions governing when and how troops may use force must be clear. The level of risk must be reasonable. These criteria could also help in deciding on selective engagement. Such a list of criteria could set guidelines for decisionmaking.

NOTES

1. Hans Morgenthau (1985) *Politics Among Nations*, 6th. ed. (New York: Alfred Knopf), pp. 205–206.
2. Stephen M. Walt (1987) *The Origins of Alliances* (Ithaca: Cornell University Press).
3. Kenneth N. Waltz (1993) "The Emerging Structure of International Politics," *International Security* 18, no. 2 (Fall): 75–76; see also John J. Mearsheimer (1990) "Back to the Future," *International Security* 15, no. 1 (Summer): 52.
4. Dieter Mahncke (1999) "The Role of the USA in Europe: Successful Past but Uncertain Future?" *European Foreign Affairs* 4, no. 3 (Autumn): 353–370, 364–365.
5. Basic Document of the Euro-Atlantic Partnership Council, May 30, 1997.
6. F. Stephen Larrabee (1997) *NATO Enlargement and the Post-Madrid Agenda* (RAND, Santa Monica, Calif.: Cambridge University Press).
7. Stephen J. Blank (1999) "NATO Enlargement Between Rhetoric and Realism," *International Politics* 36, no. 1 (March): 67–88, esp. 69.
8. North Atlantic Military Committee, *NATO Military Authorities Advice on the Outline Operational Capabilities Concept—Assessment and Feedback*, October 28, 1999.
9. Euro-Atlantic Partnership Council ·(EAPC), *Political-Military Steering Committee on Partnership for Peace: The Operational Capabilities Concept for NATO-led PfP Operations* (OCC), November 10, 1999.
10. John Barrett (1996) "NATO Reform: Alliance Policy and Cooperative Security," in Ingo Peters (ed.) *New Security Challenges: The Adaptation of International Institutions—Reforming the UN, NATO, EU, and CSCE Since 1989* (New York: St. Martin's), pp. 123–152, esp. 136.

11. "An Alliance for the Twenty-first Century," Washington Summit Communiqué, issued by the heads of state and governments participating in the meeting of the North Atlantic Council in Washington, D.C., April 24, 1999.

12. The Alliance's Strategic Concept, approved by the heads of state and governments participating in the meeting of the North Atlantic Council in Washington, D.C., on April 23 and 24, 1999.

13. "An Alliance for the Twenty-first Century," p. 31.

14. See also "Chairman's Summary of the Meeting of the Euro-Atlantic Partnership Council at Summit Level," Washington, D.C., April 25, 1999.

15. NATO Parliamentary Assembly (1999), Annual Session Plenary Resolution, "NATO and Humanitarian Intervention," adopted by the NATO Parliamentary Assembly in Amsterdam, November 15, 1999.

16. Article 5 of the 1948 Brussels Treaty states: "If any of the High Contracting Parties should be object of an armed attack in Europe . . . the other High Contracting Parties will . . . afford the Party so attacked all the military and other aid and assistance in their power."

17. *International Herald Tribune*, December 17, 1998; *NATO Review*, no. 1 (Spring 1998): 18.

18. Austria currently occupies observer status in the WEU.

19. The WEU Treaty prohibits such a development, however. Article 4 states that "recognising the undesirability of duplicating the military staffs of NATO, the Council and its Agency will rely on the appropriate military authorities of NATO for information and advice on military matters."

20. The declaration also states that "the collective defense commitments to which member states subscribe [set out in Article 5 of the Washington Treaty, Article 5 of the Brussels Treaty] must be maintained." Text of French-British European Defence Statement, Saint-Malo, France, December 4, 1998.

21. Speech by Prime Minister Tony Blair at the United Services Institute, NATO 50th Anniversary Conference, March 8, 1999.

22. "Declaration of the European Council on Strengthening the Common European Policy on Security and Defence," June 3, 1999.

23. "Draft Presidency Reaction: Strengthening the Common European Policy on Security and Defence," July 5, 1999.

24. British-Italian Summit, "Joint Declaration Launching European Defence Capabilities Initiative," July 19–20, 1999.

25. The Finnish Presidency, *Presidency Report to the Helsinki European Council, Strengthening of the Common European Policy on Security and Defence: Crisis Management*, Helsinki, December 11–12, 1999.

26. David C. Gombert and F. Stephen Larrabee (eds.) (1997), *America and Europe: A Partnership for a New Era* (Cambridge: Cambridge University Press, p. 237).

27. James A. Thomson (1997) "A New Command for NATO's New Mission," in ibid., pp. 79–103.

28. *The Economist*, July 12, 1997.

29. This idea was first published in an earlier article by Heinz Gärtner (1998) "European Security, NATO, and the Transatlantic Link: Crisis Management," *European Security* 7, no. 2 (Autumn): 1–13.

30. General Klaus Naumann (1998) "NATO's New Military Command Structure," *NATO Review*, no. 1 (Spring): 11.

31. EU Presidency, "Draft Paper on "EU-NATO Relations," March 6, 2000.

32. See, e.g., George Robertson, "NATO Secretary General," Reuters, August 4, 1999.

33. International Institute for Strategic Studies, *The Military Balance, 1999/2000*. Oxford: Oxford University Press.

34. WEU recommendations, "Strengthening European Capabilities for Crisis Management," November 1999.

35. François Heisbourg (1999), "L'Europe de le defense dans l'Alliance atlantique," *Politique Etrangere* no. 2 (Summer).

36. John Deutch, Arnold Kanter, and Brent Scowcroft (1999) "Saving NATO's Foundation," *Foreign Affairs* (November-December): 55–67.

37. See Joseph S. Nye Jr. (2000) "The U.S. and Europe: Continental Drift?" *International Affairs* 76, no. 1: 51–59.

38. George Robertson, "NATO Secretary General, Unfinished Good Job in Kosovo," *Washington Post*, April 5, 2000.

39. Dieter Mahncke (1999) "The Role of the USA in Europe: Successful Past but Uncertain Future?" *European Foreign Affairs* 4, no. 3 (Autumn): 353–370.

40. Paul Van Riper and F. G. Hoffman (1998) "Pursuing the Real Revolution in Military Affairs: Exploiting Knowledge-based Warfare," *National Security Studies Quarterly* 4, no. 3 (Summer): 4.

41. Michael C. Williams (1998) "Civil-Military Relations and Peacekeeping," Adelphi Paper 321, International Institute for Strategic Studies, Oxford, p. 4; Congessional Budget Office, CBO Paper, December 1999, p. xii.

42. This was reaffirmed also by former U.S. Secretary of State Les Aspin (1995) "Challenges to Value-Based Military Intervention," Address to the Managing Chaos Conferences, United States Institute of Peace, *Peaceworks*, no. 3 (February).

43. Andrew Richter (1999) "The Revolution in Military Affairs and Its Impact on Canada: The Challenge and the Consequences," Institute of International Relations, University of British Columbia, Working Paper no. 28, March, pp. 36–50.

44. This does not mean that some advanced technologies are not helpful for soft-security operations, e.g., minesweeping, countermortar capabilities, technologies that can demobilize individuals without casualties, and peacekeeping simulation.

45. Winrich Kühne (1999) "Peace Support Operations: How to Make Them Succeed," *International Politics and Society* 4: 368–379, esp. 363.

46. Boutros Boutros-Ghali (1995) "Supplement to an Agenda for Peace: Position Paper of the Secretary-General on the Occasion of the Fiftieth Anniversary of the United Nations," January 3, paras. 33, 80, 85–87.

47. Michèle Griffin (1999) "Retrenchment, Reform, and Regionalization: Trends in UN Peace Support Operations," *International Peacekeeping* 6, no. 1 (Spring): 1–31, esp. 11.

48. Winrich Kühne (1999) "Peace Support Operations: How to Make Them Succeed," *International Politics and Society* 4, pp. 368–379, 363.

49. David Jablonsky and James S. McCallum (1999) "Peace Implementation and the Concept of Induced Consent in Peace Operations," *Parameters* (Spring): 64.

50. Restore Hope, UN Operation in Somalia (UNOSOM I and II) and the U.S.-led Unified Task Force (UNITAF). The U.S. troops started to hunt the leader of the rebels, Aidid.

51. Richard N. Haass (1999) "What to Do with American Primacy," *Foreign Affairs* 78, no. 5 (September-October): 46.

52. The Netherlands, as a small member state of NATO, defined criteria for participation in peace-support operations in 1995.

8

The Compatibility of Security Organizations and Policies in Europe

PETER SCHMIDT

One of the major questions facing security institutions in Europe today is how the cohesion and effectiveness of the current setting can be maintained and further developed in the context of its enlargement. Adding to the puzzle is how the relationship among the major organizations should evolve in light of the changed nature of Europe's security challenges. The October 1998 initiative by the U.K. government to strengthen the EU in security policy (leading to the EU's Helsinki Summit in December 1999) has given new impetus to the debate. In Helsinki, the EU decided on guidelines for the further evolution of its Common European Policy on Security and Defense, including the creation of a European force of up to fifteen brigades (50,000–60,000 persons) by 2003 capable of the full range of Petersberg tasks (including peacemaking), as well as substantial institutional changes aimed at taking over major Western European Union (WEU) tasks by the EU. The debate now includes the installation of the High Representative for the EU's Common Foreign and Security Policy (CFSP), a position taken over by former NATO Secretary-General Javier Solana.

All these changes have spurred a double debate: one on whether the two pillars of the EU's policy—the deepening and enlargement of the Union to a number close to thirty member states—are compatible;[1] another on how this development may fit into an ongoing, prosperous transatlantic relationship, especially in the framework of NATO.[2] Nevertheless, the doubts and questions are different in both cases. The European Union certainly suffers from several structural deficits that will become more prominent when the envisaged enlargement becomes reality. Nevertheless, its continued existence was and is not in question. There have been misgivings, however, concerning the future of the U.S.-European security relationship materialized in NATO. Why should it continue after the dissolution of the Soviet Union, whose military threat had constituted the major legitimizing factor for the Alliance? Should not an enlarged EU become the major security framework in Europe? In this chapter I focus on the institutional web of the two major security organizations in Europe: NATO and the EU. This will occur in light of current challenges, with a special emphasis on the transatlantic dimension.

The transatlantic security link embodied by NATO was of highest importance for the U.S.-European relationship during the Cold War. European efforts to develop a security system of their own failed even though they were supported by U.S. governments (the abortive European Defense Community of 1954 and the Fouchet plans of 1961–1962 being cases in point). It was always more a matter of feelings rather than rational analysis in deciding whether European integration and the advancement of the European Community (EC) into the field of foreign and security policy would endanger or support a strong Atlantic partnership. In a general manner, however, all U.S. presidents have regarded the strengthening of a European security and defense identity as beneficial to the transatlantic link. Still, many advocates of European integration for security and defense—especially in France—consider the development of an independent European security and defense policy as a counterpoise against perceived U.S. power and hegemony.[3] This is more evident today; for example, French Foreign Minister Hubert Védrine speaks of the United States as a so-called hyperpower (*hyperpuissance*) requiring an effective European counterweight, and Germany's chancellor echoed this critique during a visit to France.[4]

In addition, there are strategic differences with regard to rogue states, where European foreign policy—insofar as it can be said to exist—already differs from that of the United States (e.g., the treatment of Iraq and Israel, policy toward China and Southeast Asia).[5] It is difficult to assess whether this is the beginning of a drifting apart or whether this represents nothing more than a family quarrel.

Below I consider the vital factors influencing the transatlantic relationship. First, I will examine the basic policies of the major security institutions in the 1990s, namely, institutional enlargement, the reform of the functions and roles of major institutions, and the attempt to coordinate these two processes. Is it possible to discern the effect of these changes on the nature of the transatlantic link? Second, I peer into the near future by analyzing the currently identifiable trends in the development of European security institutions. This time I start from an institutional viewpoint. In this context I will focus on the evolution of NATO and the EU/CFSP/WEU—the major players in security affairs in Europe. How could the evolution of these institutions influence the transatlantic association during the next few years?

ADAPTATION TO A NEW WORLD: BASIC POLICIES AFTER THE DEMISE OF THE BIPOLAR ORDER IN EUROPE

The changed security environment in Europe after the demise of the Soviet Union forced security institutions to adjust more or less drastically. These processes took place in a very short period of time, threatening to overload the decisionmaking processes of the institutions involved. A basic reorientation of policy had to take place within less than ten years. Security institutions applied several principal policies, discussed below.

Policy 1: Enlargement

There have been applications for membership by Central and Eastern European states in all European security institutions. NATO has already taken in three new members (Poland, Hungary, and the Czech Republic) and—at least officially—NATO keeps open the door for additional members. The EU decided in Helsinki in December 1999 to accept thirteen states as candidate countries.[6] Concrete negotiations have already started with twelve of them. It was clear that this planned increase in member countries would cause problems of internal adaptation. Some political actors hope that the pressure to enlarge the EU's institutional structures will lead toward much more centralized decisionmaking in Europe. The greater question, however, is whether national political elites and societies are really able and willing to pass power fully to the EU.

NATO's problems of internal reform have certainly been hard to overcome, too. Even among established members, there have been differences about the scope and nature of the Alliance's reform and the outreach of its enlargement. Nevertheless, the Alliance was able to digest three new members and has substantially changed its strategy, institutional structure, and functions.[7] Currently, a serious problem is created by the special relationship of NATO with Russia. The creation of a partnership council and the involvement of Russia in the Partnership for Peace (PfP) program were meant to create a strategic partnership. This, however, has been damaged by NATO's enlargement and, even more, by NATO's bombing of Serbia without direct authorization by the UN Security Council and Russia.

These developments have had several effects on the Atlantic link. First, there are indications of an overburdening of institutional processes. NATO officials have to cope with too many negotiations and meetings in different circles and are under constant time pressure. From this fact arises the problem of managing institutional complexity. The overall effects on the U.S.-European relationship are not clear. It seems evident that this situation requires a guiding hand, which, during the reform process so far, has been provided by the United States. Although this might have a positive effect on U.S. decisionmakers and strengthen the case for further U.S. involvement, the current institutional complexity might ultimately lead to difficulties and disappointments arising from a lack of effective coordination mechanisms.

Second, NATO enlargement has been supported above all by Germany and the United States. Despite quarrels about the number of countries invited to join (e.g., the split between the United States and France over Romanian membership), enlargement is a fundamental policy consensus among all member governments. It represents a new task that supports the Alliance's cohesion.[8] Nevertheless, given Russia's current harsh critique of NATO and the European attitude to dampen Russian anger, quarrels regarding further enlargement are not unthinkable. There are, however, no major political actors on either side of the Atlantic pleading for immediate further enlargement.

Third, the enlargement of the European Union has brought about a quarrel between Europe and the United States. Whereas the United States pressed for the inclusion of Turkey for political and strategic reasons, the EU initially decided to put that country on the waiting list. In Helsinki, however, the EU reached out its hand to Turkey and declared it as a candidate country, excluding Ankara at the same time from immediate negotiations.

Finally, and closely related to the Turkish question, is the issue of Cyprus, whose application has been pending since 1990. The United States here complains about the EU's lack of strategic thinking and clout, whereas for the EU the offer of membership to Cyprus was nothing more than an internal bargain to obtain Greece's approval for enlargement toward Central Europe.

Regardless of whether it was a necessary action or not, it is evident that NATO's operation against Serbia has damaged the relationship with Russia. This had a double effect. On the one hand, Russia started to perceive the United States (and NATO) more as a serious opponent than a strategic partner, whereas the EU is regarded as a natural ally against Washington's strategic outreach; on the other hand, this event added to the EU's dynamic to become more independent in the security area. The French notion of the United States having the status of a hyperpower became an influential factor in Europe's endeavors to speed up cooperation in security and defense affairs.

Yet to draw an overall conclusion, the policy of enlargement pursued by the EU and NATO has helped to maintain and develop the relationship between the United States and Europe. Nevertheless, looking into the future, major risks for the relationship are visible.

Policy 2: Reform of Functions and Roles

All the institutions have extended their roles and functions since 1990. NATO has maintained its collective defense function but has become heavily involved in regional security issues (e.g., Bosnia, Kosovo). This was not done

on a conceptual basis: theory followed function; the revised functions have
not been based on an agreed concept. In addition, the Alliance has developed
a strong emphasis on cooperative security, as can be seen in the Euro-Atlantic
Cooperation Council, the PfP program, and the NATO-Russia and NATO-
Ukraine Councils.[9]

The EU, for its part, has moved toward the CFSP through the Maastricht
and Amsterdam Treaties, using the institutionally independent WEU as a military arm.[10] However, a broadening of scope always requires the deepening of
the institutional structure. With the provisions of the Amsterdam Treaty the
EU was not able to take a major leap forward: the possibility for qualified-
majority voting is very remote, and the hierarchical system of decisionmaking
indicates an immobile bureaucratic structure rather than a flexible institutional tool. This gave reason to install a new intergovernmental conference concentrating on streamlining the decisionmaking processes of the EU, as well as
the scope of qualified-majority voting[11] and a policy of the WEU's functions
being taken over by the EU.

In security and defense matters, the WEU has served as a link between
the EU/CFSP and NATO. At the same time, there exists a bilateral EU-U.S.
relationship (New Transatlantic Agenda/Joint U.S./EU Action Plan) including
regional security questions, at least on a general level.[12]

Yet NATO, being an alliance of sovereign states, has not had many opportunities to make decisionmaking structures more efficient. Concerning functions
and roles, there are growing overlaps between NATO and the EU/CFSP/WEU.
What have been the consequences for the U.S.-European link?

There have been transatlantic disputes over these changes, especially
where defense questions came into play. The United States has been keen to
avoid commitments through the backdoor to possible new WEU members that
are not part of NATO. In addition, the process toward a non–Article 5 role of
NATO was a troublesome one. Also, the vexing question of reforming
NATO's command structure has led to a U.S.-French split that has stopped
France's full integration into the Alliance's military structure. Nevertheless,
France remained rather isolated on these matters. It is therefore possible to
claim that all in all NATO's reform process was astonishingly successful,
especially if one considers the predictions of its demise in the beginning of the
1990s. At the same time, however, the Europeans themselves have been far
from united. In this situation, the CFSP cannot threaten the U.S.-European
link constituted by NATO.

Policy 3: The Coordination of Transformation
Among Security Institutions

Coordinating the transformation of Europe's security institutions was a difficult task for NATO as well as the EU/WEU. Linking NATO and the

EU/CFSP/WEU was a major issue of transatlantic disputes.[13] In the end, the Americans recognized the existence of the European Security and Defense Identity (ESDI) as personified by the WEU.[14] The Europeans agreed that NATO would remain the foremost security organization in Europe. Links between the WEU and NATO have been established.[15] In addition, the Europeans and Americans tried to put the transatlantic relationship on a broader foundation by institutionalizing a transatlantic EU-U.S. dialogue (the New Transatlantic Agenda). Astonishingly, the relationship between the WEU and NATO is better than the EU-WEU relationship.

Whereas the reform and enlargement of security institutions represent a traditional reform strategy, several new requirements and needs that will have an impact on U.S.-European relations have gained in importance in recent years.

First, the complex nature of modern regional security problems requires the cooperation of various institutions with different capacities and varying membership.[16] For example, to bring the Bosnian war to an end, a close coordination among NATO, the UN, EU, the Organization for Security and Cooperation in Europe (OSCE), and WEU was necessary. Regional security problems therefore cause difficult coordination problems among security institutions. This leads to a dilemma. On the one hand, the prerequisite for an effective policy is a close coordination among security institutions; on the other hand, this requirement increases the obstacles to reaching any agreement. The fundamental question remains how this coordination can be put into effect. Nevertheless, there are both positive and negative elements in this complex institutional structure. A major positive aspect has been institutional flexibility. Each crisis could be addressed by an institution suited for the situation.[17] However, there also have been discernible negative effects. The crisis in the former Yugoslavia was an example of how states have been able to shuffle discussions and decisions around the many institutions; in that crisis, each move toward a solution got stuck in complex interinstitutional bargaining processes, which took far too long. It was only the readiness of the United States to get involved in the crisis that finally convinced the Europeans to become seriously committed.

Second, in each crisis situation a precarious consensus has to be reached on the question of which organization should play which role in a given conflict. With regard to military operations, several frameworks exist that are capable of politically backing up military operations: the OSCE, UN, WEU, and NATO can form a coalition of the able and willing. In each individual case, the decision to form a coalition is taken against the background of difficult (and maybe varying) assessments of the crisis situation as well as a complex costs-and-benefits analysis.

Third, every institution as well as the nation-states have to redefine the relationship between the member states and security institutions. The EU included, for example, the possibility of qualified-majority voting, and within NATO there is a search for new flexibility. All this modifies the nature of the state-institution interrelationship. Ironically, the process of multi-institution-alization provides new freedom of action for the bigger states playing a major role in all organizations. There is therefore much evidence that the future power of each Western European country will depend on the capability to activate coalitions of countries and/or international organizations for the implementation of its political interests and goals.[18]

Finally, this situation has had contradictory effects on the U.S.-European relationship. On the one hand, the enduring institutional flexibility gave the United States a chance to form coalitions of the willing—like the countries of the Contact Group with regard to Bosnia, which took the function of a steering group for the many institutions involved; on the other hand, there is always the danger that the European Union will close ranks, thus risking a U.S.-European break.

To summarize: until now, the enlargement policies of the varying security institutions, the reform of their functions and roles in Europe, and the attempt to link these institutions in a synergetic way has led to a rather complex institutional setup. Interinstitutional coordination has become both a necessity and a problem. A complex type of coordination has evolved that creates the need for more flexible formations, including those countries having a strong interest in certain policies, as the United States certainly does (after some reluctance at the beginning of the 1990s, the United States has maintained a major role in European security matters). It has been able to mobilize coalitions of actors and institutions necessary to address the security challenges in Europe that are the driving force behind NATO's reform.

STRESSFUL CHANGE AHEAD: EUROPEAN SECURITY INSTITUTIONS IN THE YEARS TO COME

In this section, I look at the problems ahead for the major institutions, especially in the context of transatlantic relations.

EU/CFSP/WEU

In Helsinki, the EU states decided to create new EU bodies: a standing Political and Security Committee (PSC),[19] a nonpermanent Military Committee (MC), and a Military Staff (MS) within the European Council.[20] At the end, the United Kingdom offered the permanent joint headquarters at Northwood as a command structure; France suggested its own Centre Opérationel Interarmées.[21] Yet all these changes do not automatically bring about a stronger and more assertive EU. One has to look more closely at the

EU's current decisionmaking structure and the problems associated with taking over the WEU's functions. In addition, there is a need to look at one important and critical question with regard to the content of Europe's security policy—nuclear weapons and how they might fit into the development of a powerful CFSP.[22]

A substantially more assertive common foreign and security policy? The extent to which member states will use the CFSP's complex political structure—now enlarged to a Common European Security and Defense Policy (CESDP)—intensively and successfully is very difficult to predict. Nevertheless, several points indicate that the CFSP[23] will follow a rather bureaucratic structure, being much more capable in a stable environment in the long term but not performing well in the short term and under turbulent conditions (always the case in crisis situations where the military plays some role).

There are several reasons for this assessment. First, the hierarchy of decisionmaking from general guidelines to a common strategy and finally to common actions and positions is a rather bureaucratic and inflexible tool. The intention to establish a nonmilitary crisis-management mechanism apart from political bodies does not add to institutional cohesion but to complexity. Second, despite the possibility of applying the qualified-majority rule in common actions and positions, member states can still veto any move by stating reasons of national interest.[24] Qualified-majority voting will not be applied to military matters. At the same time, all member states are "entitled to participate fully and on an equal footing in all decisions and deliberations of the Council and Council bodies on EU-led operations."[25] Third, the reference to the formulated common guidelines and strategy as a precondition for the application of the qualified-majority rule allows a lot of room for member states to stop action by arguing that the envisaged action does not fit into the agreed strategy. Fourth, the planned enlargement process will bring in new states and increase the diversity of the Union substantially. Growing diversity might well urge the EU to concentrate much less on external than on internal affairs.[26]

Finally, the creation of the position of High Representative for the EU's CFSP[27] is often regarded as a "step in the right direction." It is argued that Europe now has a phone number. This is, however, a one-sided description. A more adequate analysis should take into account that the High Representative represents just one more actor in the EU's decisionmaking structure. Whether he will be able to play a strong role can be contested. There are several reasons for this. Certainly, if one of the bigger states holds the Presidency of the EU, Monsieur PESC will have only a limited role because of the Presidency's power. In addition, the Helsinki Summit has put the intergovernmental European Council in a central position; the High Representative is only "assisting" the Council.[28] Second, the Commissioner for External Relations of the EU will also have a strong say in the decisionmaking process. Third, it will be indispensable, for example, for any U.S. secretary of state (or any other actor in this field) to stay in close contact with European colleagues in major European capitals. French Foreign Minister Hubert Védrine clearly stated recently that the national foreign ministries will continue to be the major players.[29] Finally, the progress in decisionmaking structures has to be balanced against the great problems the Union faces and will face in the future.

Certainly, there are—with regard to the goal of integration—positive features in both treaties and/or political practice. Generally speaking, however, there is reason to assume that the CFSP is more likely to resemble a rather slow-moving supertanker when it comes to serious military questions than a fast and mobile speedboat; it will constitute a much more inward-looking than outward-looking actor.[30]

Merging the EU and WEU? The objective of creating new security- and defense-related bodies in the framework of the EU does not give a clear answer to the question of what happens with the existing WEU agencies. On the one hand, the Cologne declaration aimed at a merger of the WEU with the EU; on the other hand, the Helsinki material does not contain any clear indication that this goal is still valid. At the same time, the reference to possible treaty amendments still seems to keep the door open for some sort of a merger.[31]

If the EU aims in the longer term at a merger, there is no clear idea yet how this should happen, the reason being that there are several serious questions and problems related to such a step. First, in order to construct a tight system, all member states must agree on this step. This is still rather difficult in the case of the nonaligned members (Sweden, Finland, Austria)[32] opposing in different degrees a collective defense clause.[33] The use of the EU's flexibility clause might help but, at the same time, diminish the force of this solution. Second, the serious questions coming along with this solution include: What would be the big benefit between the former WEU and the new structure in case there will not be a single system?[34] What should happen with the WEU Assembly, to which the WEU governments must report under the WEU Treaty? Should it be dissolved? Or should the EU Parliament take over the duties and rights?

If the decision is to build up new bodies within the EU while merely thinning out the WEU, Europe will more or less accept the existence of a phantom structure. This may seem politically acceptable, but certainly not very reasonable.

The Atlantic Alliance

NATO faces major problems. First, with regard to enlargement, the most important question is whether there will be another enlargement round and, if so, who comes next. The reasons for this are twofold. NATO has not changed that much by welcoming three new members; yet any additional member may well paralyze the decisionmaking process within the institution. And a new round of enlargement will be opposed by Russia because former member states of the Soviet Union are involved.

Second, the changing role and functions of NATO represent a challenge, too. Although a fundamental agreement on a regional out-of-area role for NATO has now been reached in the NATO capitals, there remains a marked difference in emphasis on this role and the scope of this function in individual member countries. Although the United States is inclined to develop NATO as an institution acting all over the world,[35] many European states prefer to maintain its European focus. The new Strategic Concept of April 1999 has, however, only found bridging language in this regard.[36]

Third, NATO faces certain institutional overload. It is difficult to coordinate all the security institutions established after the Cold War while remaining a cohesive institution able to make substantial decisions. Organized relationships such as the NATO-Russia and NATO-Ukraine Councils, the Euro-Atlantic Partnership Council, and the vast PfP program are meant to integrate these countries into a broad area of cooperation. However, this leads to reduced cohesiveness and substance. This already constitutes a burning issue that will certainly continue.

If the EU realizes one day the idea to merge the WEU into the EU, this will lead to a discussion regarding the inclusion of a collective defense clause into the EU Treaty. This would greatly change the picture, because collective defense is still a major legitimization for NATO's existence.[37] In addition, the EU promised to enlarge to new countries, which will be accompanied by a debate on NATO's future size, quite likely leading to an even bigger difference between the NATO and EU memberships. This growing asymmetry in membership has been regarded by the United States—at least until today—with some suspicion because of possible backdoor commitments.

At the same time, the United States considers NATO as the main avenue for U.S. influence on European security matters and a prosperous U.S.-European relationship; the backbone of European collective defense; and an effective tool to manage security problems in Europe and probably beyond. Regardless of the fact that the United States and NATO have more or less accepted these changes on the European side, the EU's future evolution will raise some serious questions threatening NATO's area of traditional responsibility and decisionmaking.[38]

Several possible developments and problems will have a substantial impact on U.S.-European relations in the security arena (and possibly other areas as well). They might well change the nature of the relationship substantially. The United States and the Europeans should prepare themselves to understand these changes and challenges and search for adequate solutions to enable a prosperous relationship in security matters to continue.

Collective defense clause. If Europe were to decide to include a form of collective defense clause in the EU Treaty (as in the WEU Treaty), it must be accompanied by some defense and command arrangements, possibly separate from NATO. Such a modification might lead to several problems.

First, collective defense is still the major justification for NATO's integrated military command structure. The more the Europeans take over this task, the less this argument will represent a sound legitimization for NATO's unique command structure. Military integration has represented NATO's unique asset. Second, the more the Europeans claim to be responsible for their own defense, the less the United States will be prepared to undertake security investments in Europe. Third, the EU has already declared that it will develop a structure to implement the so-called Petersberg tasks (from peacekeeping to peace enforcement). At the same time, the Europeans accepted at NATO's Washington Summit a limited reach for NATO. If the Europeans take over—even only symbolically—the collective defense task, the question then becomes: What remains for NATO?

To a certain extent, this problem will arise as a result of existing EU plans. As the EU develops military capabilities for peace enforcement, NATO's crisis-management function will come under further scrutiny. In addition, there is no great difference any more between military formations established for collective defense and regional interventions, providing some reason to assume that Europe can take care of itself. A careful policy will be necessary to develop independent European structures while providing NATO with a real role in European security matters.[39]

The problem of a caucus in NATO. As Europeans develop a framework for their own foreign and security policy, questions will arise as to the role of North America. Until now, official rhetoric has proclaimed that NATO is the main body for this debate.

There are two major possibilities. First, following the traditional notion that Europe should speak in NATO with one voice, NATO would remain the main body of transatlantic consultation in security matters. This would, however, bring about two questions. How will they maintain the flexibility in European positions, which is a prerequisite for having a serious debate with the North American partners? And who should present European stances? The ambassadors represented at NATO? The Presidency of the EU?

Second, transferring the focal point for the transatlantic security dialogue from NATO to bilateral EU–North American channels would transform NATO into a kind of military toolbox without a strong political framework. It seems unlikely that NATO could survive this change in the long run. At the very least, it would not solve the problem of flexibility as long as the CFSP's High Representative had not become a powerful actor.

Finally, the NATO-EU relationship is a source of possible conflict. Although the Americans gave in on the issue of ESDI, and although the Europeans recognized NATO's leadership role in hard-security questions, further sources of conflict still exist. For example, the Middle East issue represents a disagreement between the United States and Europe. These differences are dealt with in two circles: the framework of the Transatlantic Agenda talks between the EU and the United States; and NATO's agenda. The Americans exert much pressure to give NATO a greater Mediterranean dimension; but the Mediterranean is an area in which the EU (since the Barcelona conference in November 1995) aims to establish a free-trade zone supported by regular political relations. Moreover, there are some conflicting trends in the development of military technology and tactics in the United States and Europe (and among Europeans themselves), complicating the issue of collective military operations within NATO (RMA, or the revolution of military affairs).

Certainly, there is always space for compromise, even for the crucial out-of-area question. One development would be dangerous for the relationship: if European countries present inflexible European positions within NATO, this would endanger the transatlantic link in the medium term. A full-fledged, tightly integrated European CFSP would require a different institutional setting based on a bilateral EU-U.S. link. Whether this would endanger the transatlantic partnership has not been analyzed here for the simple fact that this so far is only a long-term possibility.

CONCLUSION: THE NEED FOR FLEXIBILITY

In foreign policy and security matters, a European federation is a long way off. European foreign and security policy will—at least in the medium term—remain a mixture of national and European policies. This is to be welcomed at the moment for two mutually reinforcing reasons.

The complexity of security policy under current conditions raises the question of how the puzzling institutional setup can be managed. Some sort of an inner circle is necessary, at least while setting up the framework for a certain policy. This group has to be formed according to the principle of the capable and willing, trying to avoid leaving out major powers interested and engaged in the conflict. This may, as the Contact Group demonstrates, go well beyond an inclusion of only European countries.

In the current institutional framework, with NATO as the main link between the United States and Europe in security matters, flexibility is also a prerequisite for the smooth running of the system. One reason is that under current conditions a permanent and full-fledged European position within NATO could lead quite easily to stalemate because it would be difficult for the Europeans to negotiate seriously on this position. Due to the intricacy of European decisionmaking, such a policy will be difficult to change during negotiations. A true single European voice would ultimately require a substantial transformation of the existing security institutions. A purely bilateral relationship between the EU's CFSP and the United States would bypass NATO, which is still regarded by Washington as the major channel of U.S. influence.

In addition, there are many reasons for maintaining flexibility, especially where Europe's capacity to act is concerned, including: the differences of strategic cultures from Finland down to Portugal, the cleavages between the bigger and the smaller countries of the EU, the variances in the role and function of the armed forces in member countries, and the impossibility to find decisive mechanisms to overcome the divergences. Certainly, there are important attempts to establish a consensus on common interests and obligations (see the list of common goals in the EU Treaty) and to form some sort of a European strategic culture, for example, by the many multinational military formations in Europe. Nevertheless, the EU has not yet been able to come to grips with the two real options for overcoming decision blockage: the establishment of a permanent leading core group (*directoire*), and majority voting.

NOTES

1. The EU decided in Helsinki to accept thirteen countries as candidate countries, including Turkey. Concrete negotiations, however, are on their way with twelve countries only (excluding Turkey, so far).
2. See the discussions between Europeans and Americans during the Munich Conference on Security Policy.
3. President Chirac, e.g., is traveling throughout the world with the message that we have to fight U.S. hegemony. In a recent article, the head of the defense committee of the French Assemblée Nationale, Paul Quilès, criticizes the danger that NATO may become a meeting celebrating U.S. hegemony (see *Le Monde*, December 1, 1998, p. 16).
4. See the speech of Chancellor Schrœder in Paris on November 24, 1999.
5. For an account of the Greater Middle East, see Robert D. Blackwill and Michael Stürmer (eds.) (1997) *Allies Divided. Transatlantic Policies for the Greater Middle East* (Cambridge: MIT Press).
6. Bulgaria, Cyprus, Czech Republic, Estonia, Hungary, Latvia, Lithuania, Malta, Poland, Rumania, Slovakia, Slovenia, and Turkey.
7. For a most recent analysis, see Michael Rühle (2000) "Das neue strategische Konzept der NATO und die politische Realität," in Erich Reiter (ed.) *Jahrbuch für internationale Sicherheitspolitik, 2000* (Hamburg: Mittler Verlag), pp. 637–654.

8. For a more detailed argumentation in this regard, see Peter Schmidt (1997) *Stand und Perspektiven der NATO-Erweiterung: Österreichisches Jahrbuch für internationale Sicherheitspolitik* (Graz: Styria), pp. 245–259.

9. NATO has also tried to emphasize its nonmilitary functions (economic and environmental issues). This has, however, never really changed the military character of the institution.

10. For a full account of the WEU's history since the Maastricht Treaty, see Willem van Eekelen (1998) *Debating European Security* (The Hague: Sdu Publishers), pp. 105ff.

11. The instruction of the Amsterdam Treaty to install an intergovernmental conference to decide on the leftovers of Amsterdam originally did not address foreign policy and defense questions. Due to the most recent steps forward in security and defense matters, however, there is a discussion now to include this area into the discussion on majority voting.

12. This agreement, signed on December 3, 1995, aimed at a comprehensive partnership covering economic, political, and security questions; see John van Oudenaren (1996) "Die Transatlantische Agenda," *Internationale Politik* (May): 49–52.

13. See Rob de Wiyk (1997) *NATO on the Brink of the New Millennium: The Battle for Consensus* (London: Brassey's).

14. See the results of NATO's Berlin Summit on June 3, 1996.

15. Joint meetings between the councils and working groups on matters of common interests and agreements concerning the use by NATO of NATO's communications networks. Nevertheless, the envisaged framework agreement for the WEU's use of NATO assets has not yet been concluded.

16. Many private and semiofficial institutions experts estimate that there are about six hundred organizations active in Bosnia.

17. For an elaboration of this point, see Peter Schmidt (1996) "Security Challenges and Institutional Responses: A German Perspective," in Gunilla Herolf (ed.) *Europe: Creating Security Through International Organizations* (Stockholm: Swedish Institute of International Affairs), pp. 73–84.

18. See Peter Schmidt (1992) "Partners or Rivals: NATO, WEU, EC, and the Reorganization of European Security," in Peter Schmidt (ed.) *In the Midst of Change: On the Development of West European Security and Defense Cooperation* (Baden-Baden: Nomos), p. 236.

19. This body will be composed of national representatives and will deal with all aspects of the CFSP, including the Common European Security and Defense Policy.

20. See Presidency Reports to the Helsinki European Council (1999) "Strengthening the Common European Policy on Security and Defense," and on "Non-Military Crisis Management of the European Union," Annex 4, Helsinki, December 10 and 11, p. 24.

21. See "Britain Offers Europe Force HQ," *The Times*, November 26, 1999. It looks like these offers contain elements of competition and are not only based on a cooperative approach.

22. The inclusion of this part could be criticized by saying that this is no longer an issue of great importance. This argument, however, disregards the French (and to a certain extent British) approach that nuclear weapons can play a positive deterrent role in regional crises. The more the EU moves in the direction of regional crisis management (the so-called Petersberg tasks), the more the question comes up of how to link these weapons with the EU's CFSP. In this regard, the nuclear issue represents an important element in the question of how cohesive Europe's policy in the future may be.

23. In the following, no distinction is made between CFSP and CESDP.

24. Qualified-majority voting cannot be applied to military measures or operations.

25. Presidency Conclusions, Helsinki, December 10 and 11, 1999, p. 23. Nevertheless, a planned ad hoc committee of contributors may well provide more influence for the coalition of the capable.

26. Certainly, there is a countervailing trend: the pressure to stay together. Nevertheless, there are many ways to avoid strong engagement in foreign and security policy.

27. Mr. Solana, the former Secretary-General of NATO, started his work in November 1999. The decision was taken that he also take over the Secretary-General position at WEU.

28. Presidency Reports to the Helsinki European Council, p. 24.

29. See the interview with Joschka Fischer and Hubert Védrine, *Die Zeit*, October 28, 1999, p. 13. Hubert Védrine says clearly that Europe's CFSP will not prosper if it curbs the powerful national foreign policy of each country.

30. This incorporates the treatment of the neighborhood, including Russia.

31. Presidency Reports to the Helsinki European Council, p. 26.

32. For the difficulties of the Nordic countries, see "Sicherheitspolitische Sorgen der Skandinavier," *Neue Zürcher Zeitung*, June 4, 1999, p. S-3.

33. The Helsinki declaration clearly says that the measures to be undertaken do "not imply the creation of a European army" (paragraph 27 of the Presidency Conclusions).

34. On the one hand, after the merger the EU has a broader range of levers at its disposal than the WEU. This happens in one institutional framework, which would certainly represent an advantage. On the other hand, more actors are involved in the decisionmaking process.

35. Nevertheless, the United States will not press too hard in this direction. The likely outcome will be that NATO just transforms the Alliance's role toward a greater flexibility with regard to operations beyond the treaty area (see U.S. Secretary of State Madeleine Albright's remarks on this topic in "Süddeutsche Zeitung, Die NATO muß größer und flexibler werden," *Süddeutsche Zeitung*, December 7, 1998).

36. See *The Alliance's Strategic Concept.* Approved by the Heads of State and governments participating in the meeting of the North Atlantic Council in Washington, D.C., on 23–24 April 1999, sec. 6.

37. The argument that the change is marginal because this clause is already existing within the WEU Treaty is not valid. The WEU Treaty clearly states that WEU should rely in military matters on NATO. The EU now strives for some autonomy in military matters, too.

38. For a more recent account of the developments and problems, see the analysis of the former U.S. ambassador to NATO, Robert E. Hunter (2000) "The Future of NATO and Transatlantic Relations," in Erich Reiter (ed.) *Jahrbuch für internationale Sicherheitspolitik 2000* (Hamburg: Mittler Verlag), pp. 623–635.

39. In accordance to the Presidency Conclusions of the Helsinki Summit (p. 25), the EU looks for modalities for full consultation, cooperation, and transparency between the EU and NATO.

9

Strengthening Europe's Security Architecture: Where Do We Stand? Where Should We Go?

HEIKO BORCHERT

Recent experience permits us to form a more concrete picture of how Europe's security architecture will look in the next century. The most important steps have included the opening of the North Atlantic Treaty Organization through the Partnership for Peace (PfP) program, the signing of political charters with Russia and Ukraine, the entry of three new members, the Alliance-led military operations in Bosnia-Herzegovina and Kosovo, and the decision to enlarge the European Union. Most recently, we have seen the rapprochement between NATO and the EU, the latter's decision to integrate the Western European Union (WEU) and to be more actively involved in the so-called Petersberg tasks, and—finally—the agreement to create a Union of Freedom, Security, and Justice by integrating the Schengen and Dublin agreements into community law.

Against the background of these important developments, in this chapter I attempt to answer two basic questions: What are the central pillars of Europe's security architecture? and How do Europe's security organizations contribute to the strengthening of these pillars? I will concentrate on the second question and indicate what remains to be done in order to solidify Europe's current architecture.

I argue that the European security architecture, comprising the transatlantic community, the Central and Eastern European (CEE) states, and Russia and Ukraine, has to be multilateral in character, that is, it has to be built on a set of rules facilitating and strengthening cooperation. Multilateralism implies equal treatment of all actors (indivisibility) and the general applicability (nondiscrimination) of liberal norms.[1] Actors will therefore build up positive expectations favoring international cooperation and allowing them to overcome the security dilemma.[2] However, multilateralism has two potential

Figure 9.1   Main Components of Europe's Multilateral Security Architecture

---

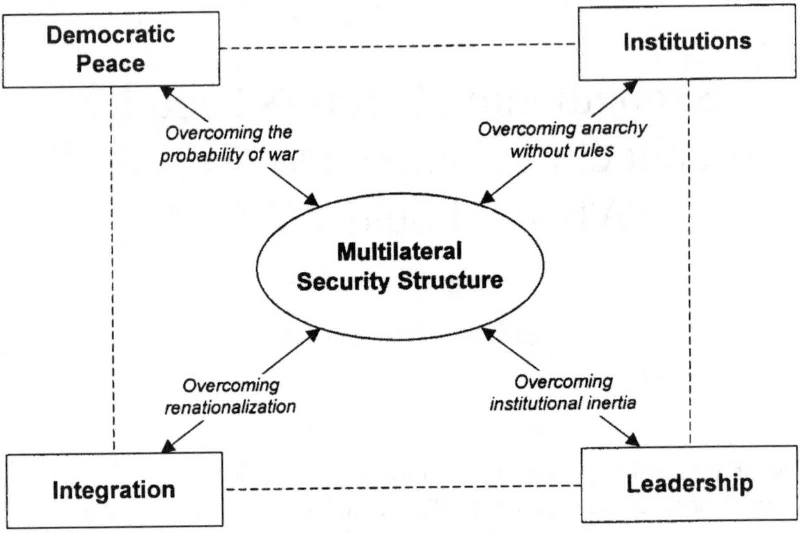

Achilles' heels. When cooperating, states form what Robert Keohane called "expectations of diffuse reciprocity."[3] States may expect, first, to benefit from international cooperation over time and are prepared to make concessions today, anticipating that the benefits of cooperation will outweigh concessions to other states. This approach may pose great risks if governments cannot expect others to play by the rules (security dilemma). There is thus, second, an implicit tendency to defect. Although favorable, cooperation is not certain. A multilateral security architecture therefore needs built-in safety devices that prevent backsliding or a "return to the future," as suggested by John Mearsheimer. I therefore propose an approach based on four pillars: democratic peace, institutions, leadership, and supranational integration (see Figure 9.1).[4]

Democratic Peace

Since the Cold War, the theory of democratic peace has become the guiding principle for the creation of a common European security architecture that includes the Atlantic, Western European, and the former communist countries. Building a security community does not only require "the realization of sufficient commonality of security interests" and "a substantial transformation of the security dilemma"; it also involves "the disappearance of the traditional security dilemma among a select group of states."[5] The disappearance of the traditional security dilemma has a lot to do with the foreign policy of the states involved. It is of paramount importance whether these states show a high or low propensity for war, and whether the likelihood of war in the international system is seen to be high or low. Democratic norms and structures reduce the probability of war between states.[6] Therefore, the theory of democratic peace can be interpreted as the first safety device to avoid relapse into war in Europe.

Institutions

In a multilateral order, actors develop common norms, follow them, and foresee enforcement procedures in the case of deviation. This implies the existence of institutions—understood as durable patterns of behavior based on norms, principles, rules, and decisionmaking procedures—ultimately based on a democratic and liberal worldview.[7] Since 1950, European countries, with the help of their transatlantic allies, have woven a tight web of international organizations, regimes, politically and legally binding international agreements, and common norms and principles, all serving as the backbone of Europe's security architecture. Because institutions "make certain things easier to do and other things harder to do,"[8] they help to overcome international anarchy. They can be regarded as the second safety device in order to avoid Mearsheimer's scenario.

Leadership

Despite its advantages, a multilateral system tends to show signs of institutional inertia, buck-passing, and inactivity—tendencies that undermine the credibility of the system. Therefore, a multilateral system cannot do without leadership—the third safety device—that helps to remedy such situations.[9] However, in contrast to hegemonic-stability theory, where material resources play a crucial role, recent studies have emphasized the importance of norms in persuading followers and the role of nonhegemonic states that can develop true leadership.[10] Following these lines, it can be argued that international organizations can provide leadership in two different ways. International organizations provide passive leadership either by facilitating decisionmaking (e.g., provisions for majority voting or mechanisms that improve flexibility) or by mandating international actions to be implemented outside international organizations (e.g., peace-enforcement missions authorized by the UN Security Council and conducted by a coalition of the willing). In contrast, international organizations acting independently can provide active leadership either by establishing international structures (e.g., the role of the European Court of Justice [ECJ] in developing the basic principles of European integration law), or by initiating cooperation (e.g., the role of the NATO Secretary-General in dealing with Russia on the first round of Alliance enlargement).

Supranational Integration

This distinctly European phenomenon can be understood as a process whereby governments act jointly and freely to create international bodies by transferring sovereignty, thus granting them executive power. Within such a framework, governments not only coordinate their policies but also initiate common policies that bind member states. The supranational body can act independently, and its norms are directly applicable, thereby enjoying precedence over national law. Hence, supranational integration, as the fourth safety device, helps to prevent the renationalization of European politics.[11]

*   *   *

In order to analyze the contribution of Europe's security organizations to the four-pillar concept, I distinguish between political, economic, and military security dimensions. On the one hand, this distinction reflects Europe's current security architecture. The Organization for Security and Cooperation in Europe (OSCE)[12] and the Common Foreign and Security Policy (CFSP) of the EU primarily deal with political questions; economic matters are dealt with by the EU; and military matters are referred to NATO and the WEU. On the other hand, this distinction makes clear that each pillar of my concept has three dimensions, although, as will be shown later, in varying proportions.

My analysis can be summed up as follows. First, and most important, Europe's security organizations tend to work on the basis of identical core values. At the national level, the democracy requirement (rule of law, separation of powers, free elections, and the guarantee of human rights) has become the rule. At the international level, openness, transparency, predictability, reciprocity, flexibility, abstention from the use of force, sufficiency, and cooperation form the constitutional norms of a multilateral European security architecture. Second, Europe's security organizations already make a twofold contribution toward bolstering stability and security. They strengthen the four pillars just outlined, and they influence member states' policies in economic, military, and political matters. In the realm of economics, the transfer of sovereignty has led to the creation of a robust supranational framework, especially in the European Community (EC).[13] In military matters, the aim of setting up multinational units and the required standardization of military doctrines and of equipment begin to encroach upon sovereignty. For multinational units to function, governments have to agree on decisions that limit their sovereignty. In politics, most prominently in security and foreign affairs, intergovernmentalism still reigns over supranationalism. However, most recent developments in the EU show that this distinction tends to get blurred. Third, improved coordination between political, economic, and military matters will be of foremost importance for Europe's future security. This requirement not only affects the enlargement process under way in NATO, EU, and the WEU. In the end it will also require a qualitative shift in the way that governments approach international politics. Transnational risks do not merely demand internationally agreed upon solutions and multilateral cooperation—they assume international instead of national interests.

This study has six sections. The first discusses the multiple activities of Europe's security organizations to promote democratic peace. The second turns to Europe's security organizations themselves. Among other things, it will show how they consult their member states, how decisions are made, and how they consult each other and cooperate. The third will deal with the question of institutional leadership by analyzing the degree of consent among the member states, defining the organizations' core competence, and giving four examples of executive leadership. Fourth, despite the strong resistance of states to transferring sovereignty in security issues, there are signs that international cooperation in this field is beginning to encroach upon sovereignty. Fifth, I address the question of what remains to be done in order to strengthen Europe's security architecture. Four concrete proposals are put forward, aimed at enhancing institutional contacts and augmenting institutional cooperation, improving rule orientation, managing peace building more effectively, and strengthening the European Security and Defense Identity (ESDI). Finally, I summarize the results.

DEMOCRATIC PEACE: BROAD INSTITUTIONAL SUPPORT

The contribution of international organizations to the promotion of democratic peace is often neglected.[14] Yet Europe's security organizations are active in many ways. They contribute to the development of norms, facilitate the monitoring of the application of jointly developed norms, and even provide enforcing mechanisms. Their assistance programs also support the building up of democratic structures.

Developing Norms

Joint liberal and democratic norms safeguard democratic peace,[15] and Europe's security organizations contribute to the establishment of such norms at the domestic and international levels.

At the domestic level, norms must accord with what is seen as appropriate international behavior.[16] Europe's security organizations strengthen national democratic norms in three different ways: they broaden the protection of human rights, set up rules for democratic structures, and enhance democratic control of armed forces. The OSCE has created the most far-reaching democracy and human rights regime worldwide, thereby placing special emphasis on the protection of human rights in times of public emergency and on the independence of the judiciary as well as the rule of law.[17] Additionally, the code of conduct on politico-military aspects of security adopted at the 1994 Budapest Summit contains detailed provisions on the democratic control of armed forces. The code's provisions refer, among other things, to a state's security and defense policy in peacetime, the domestic role of armed forces, and the human rights of military personnel.[18] The democratic control of armed forces is also on the PfP agenda. According to international experts, NATO officers thereby relate to the OSCE's code of conduct, which opens the door for interesting perspectives of cooperation.[19] Furthermore, the ECJ and the European Court of Human Rights (ECHR) in Strasbourg have contributed greatly to an effective protection of human rights. Because most states follow the Luxembourg and Strasbourg judgments, both courts have profoundly affected domestic law.[20]

At the international level, UN and OSCE norms as well as *ius cogens* can be seen as international constitutive norms. They include the principle of sovereign equality, the fulfillment of obligations in good faith, the peaceful settlement of disputes, abstention from the use of force, nonintervention in internal affairs, territorial integrity, and the inviolability of borders. These form the core of internationally binding norms. However, these norms are not uncontested, as the discussion on the legality of humanitarian interventions and various proposals to adapt the OSCE's decalogue have shown. On paper, at least, it is again the OSCE that has adopted the most far-reaching provisions by declaring that:

> The participating States emphasize that issues relating to human rights, fundamental freedoms, democracy and the rule of law are of international concern, as respect for these rights and freedoms constitutes one of the foundations of the international order. *They categorically and irrevocably declare that the commitments undertaken in the field of the human dimension of the CSCE are matters of direct and legitimate concern to all participating States and do not belong exclusively to the internal affairs of the State concerned.*[21]

This commitment implies that European states are, at least in principle, no longer willing to accept violations of human rights, and this constitutes a common identity based on the respect of the principles of the human dimension. It is therefore very difficult for a state, as tensions between the EU and Turkey have shown, "to consistently abuse human rights and still be deemed to belong to contemporary 'Europe.'"[22]

Let me now turn to international norms controlling the use of armed forces. Once more, the OSCE paved the way for what today is taken for granted: military cooperation between East and West. The detailed provisions for confidence and security building, developed between 1986 and 1989 in Stockholm and then enhanced by the Vienna Documents, established a regime built on the principles of openness, reciprocity, and predictability, allowing for a wide exchange of information. Recent conferences aimed at improving the Treaty of Conventional Forces in Europe (CFE), the cornerstone of military stability in Europe, also adopted the principle of sufficiency. *Sufficiency* means that every state should "maintain only such military capabilities, individually or in conjunction with others, as are commensurate with legitimate individual or collective security needs, taking into account their international obligations."[23] Interestingly, this quotation is taken from the NATO-Russia Founding Act, indicating that OSCE and NATO tend to work on the basis of the same norms.

Monitoring the Implementation of Norms

Obviously, the credibility of norms depends on their application by states. Playing by the rules is crucial, because perceptions play an important role in devising political strategies toward other states, and they determine whether a state is seen to behave democratically or not.

In the political and economic spheres, we can distinguish among three different approaches to the monitoring of norm application. Most international organizations require their executive bodies to monitor norm application (e.g., the UN Security Council, the European Commission, and the different Councils of the OSCE). In addition, most international organizations have developed special authorities to serve this purpose. The United Nations established the UN High Commissioner for Refugees (UNHCR); the OSCE developed the instrument of a High Commissioner on National Minorities (HCNM) and long-term missions as well as a Representative on Freedom of the Media. Second, political procedures, such as the monitoring and fact-finding missions of the UN and the OSCE, the OSCE's emergency mechanisms, or its review and implementation conferences, either help to clarify specific questions or to monitor the application of provisions in general. Finally, judicial proceedings often lead to legally binding judgments. Depending on who is allowed to appeal, a court's judgments are binding for different litigants: the International Court of Justice and the OSCE's Court of Arbitration and Conciliation accept only petitions received from member states or contracting parties. In contrast, after ratifying Protocol No. 11 that restructured the control machinery of the Council of Europe (CoE), the ECHR can receive petitions from natural persons, and the ECJ also accepts petitions from European Community institutions and legal persons.

The different approaches developed to monitor the application of military norms can be grouped as follows. Standard procedures normally entail the exchange of information and implementation meetings. Procedures for clarification are designed to facilitate decisionmaking and the search for specific temporary measures by providing structured forms of dialogue (e.g., the

Chemical Weapons Convention [CWC]). On-site procedures do not rely on information given by a state in question, but they do allow for routine inspections, challenge inspections, inspections for certification and reduction, visits, and observation flights.[24]

Enforcing Norms

Most norms and rules are not self-enforcing, therefore requiring implementation in the case of noncompliance. Enforcing norms raises two questions. First, is it legal to enforce them? Second, how can norms be enforced?

In order to answer the first question, we have to look at the basic treaties and charters of Europe's security organizations. The basic provision for the legality of enforcement actions can be found in the UN Charter, which empowers the UN Security Council to take all measures deemed necessary to safeguard peace and security worldwide.[25] The OSCE, which is based on a cooperative security approach, gives priority to mainly diplomatic instruments. However, the principles of the OSCE's human dimension are matters of direct and legitimate concern to all participating states. Thus the Prague Document (1992) says "that appropriate action may be taken . . . if necessary in the absence of the consent of the State concerned, in cases of clear, gross and uncorrected violations of relevant CSCE commitments."[26] The OSCE implicitly agreed to the possibility of imposing political and economic sanctions in accordance with the UN Charter.[27] In contrast, military sanctions or enforcement measures are categorically ruled out.[28] Hence, military enforcement measures—with the exception of the 1999 Kosovo intervention—can be undertaken only by the UN or by a coalition of the willing authorized by the UN Security Council. In 1992, both NATO and the WEU agreed to support such missions at the request of the UN Security Council and subject to agreement by their member states.[29] Finally, even the EU foresees enforcing measures. Although the Community institutions are entitled to enforce their decisions on the grounds of special treaty provisions (including economic sanctions), the Amsterdam Treaty introduced the possibility of imposing sanctions against a member state in the case of a "serious and persistent breach" of the principles of "liberty, democracy, respect for human rights and fundamental freedoms, and the rule of law." These sanctions may entail suspension of certain rights deriving from the Treaty on European Union, including the voting rights of the respective country.[30]

We can now turn to the different mechanisms to enforce norms. Again, it is useful to distinguish between political and economic mechanisms, on the one hand, and military procedures on the other. In the political and economic dimensions, five instruments are available. Normally, political and economic sanctions will be the first instrument the international community employs. If it is possible to appeal to a court in order to enforce commonly agreed norms, judicially binding judgments will be a second instrument. At least in European integration law, judgments by the ECJ may be combined with coercive payments or administrative fines imposed by the European Commission or the European Central Bank. To exert additional pressure, international organizations may decide to suspend treaty rights, as foreseen by the new Treaty on European Union or the CWC.[31] Finally, a member state can even be expelled or its membership suspended.[32]

Enforcing norms militarily remains the *ultima ratio*. Should the international community deem it necessary to rely on military force, four instruments are at hand. Collective self-defense will be the standard response to an attack directed at a member of NATO or the WEU.[33] Peace-enforcement measures authorized by the UN Security Council and directed by NATO/WEU, or a coalition of the willing, aim at enforcing either a cease-fire resolution or a peace agreement (e.g., Implementation Force [IFOR], Stabilization Force [SFOR]). Humanitarian interventions are feasible if a secure environment has to be created in order to help the civilian population. Finally, military enforcement measures (*bellum iustum*) are necessary to restore peace and security in cases where all other measures have proved inadequate.[34]

Building Up Democratic Structures

Let us turn to the contribution of Europe's security organizations toward the building of democratic structures within states. Most organizations provide consulting and general support. In politics, that means dealing with constitutional and legal issues, helping to solve minority problems and to repatriate refugees, reform the public sector, and establish a free press. Besides granting financial and technical assistance, international financial organizations, as well as the EU and the UN, help build up capital and venture capital markets. They also launch special programs for small and medium-sized firms and help integrate women in business, support the privatization of formerly state-owned enterprises, conduct seminars on all questions related to management, and advise on the setting up of social security systems and pension funds. In military matters, building up democratic structures means establishing and safeguarding democratic control of armed forces, a job NATO has undertaken in Albania.

Different monitoring activities contribute a second category. The UN, the OSCE, and the CoE monitor the implementation of human and minority rights, peace treaties, and international agreements. Occasionally, these activities can be supported by military forces, as in Bosnia-Herzegovina, where IFOR/SFOR provide for the monitoring of the cease-fire agreement and guarantee free movement of people. Finally, in countries where fighting has destroyed most of the infrastructure, international organizations may provide transitional authority. Transitional authority can also entail the organization and supervision of elections and the arrangement of negotiations between the parties to the conflict. International organizations may even negotiate international agreements on behalf of the parties of conflict as in the case of the OSCE, empowered to negotiate a regional arms control treaty under the Dayton Accords.

Summary

To sum up the results of this section, Europe's security organizations support democratic peace in four ways. First, they help to establish norms reorienting state behavior. Second, they provide various instruments to monitor the application of commonly agreed norms: monitoring by executive bodies, political and judicial procedures in politics and economics as well as standard procedures, procedures for clarification, and on-site procedures applied in the military dimension. Third, if necessary, Europe's security organizations help to enforce international norms. In this case, we can distinguish between sanctions, judgments, fines, the suspension of treaty rights, and suspension and expulsion of membership. Militarily we must differentiate among the right of collective self-defense, peace-enforcement measures, humanitarian interventions, and military enforcement measures. Finally, Europe's security organizations help build up democratic structures at a domestic level by consulting and supporting, granting economic aid, monitoring, and providing transitional authority.

COOPERATION AMONG EUROPE'S SECURITY ORGANIZATIONS: HIGH COMPLEXITY, LOW COORDINATION

This section presents an analysis of the structure of Europe's security organizations as well as their interaction. First, I will look at their decisionmaking procedures and the way they consult with their member states. Second, I turn to interinstitutional cooperation. Third, it will be shown whether Europe's security organizations facilitate deviation from commonly agreed rules or whether they render such behavior more difficult. Finally, relations between Europe's security organizations and nonstate actors are analyzed.

Consultation and Decisionmaking

What are the basic provisions for consultation and decisionmaking? How do Europe's security organizations consult with potential new entrants, and how did they prepare themselves institutionally for enlargement? This section provides some answers to these questions.

Basic structures: who, how, and for what? Intergovernmental bodies decide what Europe's security organizations should do and how they should approach their tasks. Within the OSCE as well as the CFSP, political guidelines are set by the heads of state, meeting either in the OSCE's summit meetings or at the European Council. All subsequent decisions to implement these guidelines will be adopted by the OSCE's various councils (Ministerial Council, Senior Council, Permanent Council) or by the EU's Ministerial Council. The WEU opted for a similar procedure. The guidelines will be adopted by the foreign ministers meeting as the WEU Ministerial Council, and day-to-day decisions are adopted by the Permanent Council meeting in different formats. In contrast, NATO's North Atlantic Council is the central body for decisionmaking, meeting as the summit of either the heads of state, the foreign ministers, or defense ministers.

Europe's security organizations basically decide by consent. However, this can mean different things. Within the OSCE, consent does not equal unanimity. Rather, consent means that no participating state vetoes a decision. In NATO, consensus is the basis for all decisions. In practice it requires consent. However, the "silence" procedure allows decisions to be taken as long as no ally feels so strongly that it believes it must block the decision. The same holds true for the WEU Ministerial Council, although a distinction is made between political and procedural matters. The former require unanimity (allowing for the possibility of opting out), whereas the latter do not require unanimous voting. Finally, the CFSP requires unanimity in the European Council, whereas the Ministerial Council may adopt decisions on the basis of qualified-majority voting; constructive abstention is possible.

The Secretaries-General play different roles. In NATO and in the UN, the Secretary-General plays an important administrative as well as political role, because both organizations grant him a right of initiative that gives him the possibility to influence internal decisionmaking. Additionally, NATO assumes that in case of disputes between member states, the Secretary-General can offer his good offices. In contrast, the Secretary-General of the OSCE acts rather as a civil servant by supporting the chairman in office and heading the administrative structures. So far, the CFSP has had no Secretary-General. However, the Treaty of Amsterdam established the position of a High Representative who is expected to give the CFSP a higher public profile. Javier Solana, who was appointed High Representative, also serves as the WEU's Secretary-General. Although the merger of the two functions is to be welcomed, the Union's external representation is still very confusing. Different persons can speak on behalf of the Union, among them the High Representative, the foreign minister of the country holding the Presidency of the EU, the commissioners for external relations and for enlargement, or a special representative appointed in the case of a crisis.

All of Europe's security organizations have parliamentary assemblies that serve four purposes. First, they serve as decisionmaking forums for various questions. Second, the parliamentary assemblies often criticize the information policies of intergovernmental bodies that are reluctant to pass on information. For this they have to build up their own expertise. Therefore, most parliamentary assemblies see themselves as critical counterparts—by questioning the governmental representatives addressing them and by developing independent positions on certain questions. Third, parliamentary assemblies support the democratization process within the former communist countries. The NATO Parliamentary Assembly has established the Rose-Roth Initiative, using the forum to facilitate interparliamentary cooperation. The Parliamentary Assembly of the OSCE adopted the Democratic Assistance Program and established the Parliamentary Assembly Network (PA-NET), an electronic system facilitating interparliamentary communications. Finally, all parliamentary assemblies are active in supervising elections.

Institutional framework for enlargement: who meets whom in what forum?
At present the OSCE is the only European security organization in which all participating states have the same rights and duties and take part in the same institutional bodies. The EU, NATO, and WEU, however, have adopted different procedures and established different institutions to manage enlargement.

EU. In order to cope with the demanding task of enlargement, the EU adopted four different institutional provisions. First, the European Conference serves as a general framework for consultations on a broad range of issues. The European Conference meets as twenty-eight (fifteen member states, ten CEE countries, Cyprus, Turkey, and Malta). Second, the Association Council was established as a framework for negotiations with those countries that will join the Union. Although the Union started admission talks in March 1998 in the format of twenty-six (fifteen member states, ten CEE countries, and Cyprus), it began its negotiations in the format of 5+1 (five CEE countries and Cyprus).[35] Most recently, the European Council decided to convene bilateral intergovernmental conferences to start negotiations with the other five CEE countries and Malta.[36] In general, the negotiations begin with the screening of secondary legislation by the Commission. While in transition, the preadhesion strategy will be reinforced, admission partnerships will mobilize all forms of assistance to the applicant countries, and financial support will be upgraded. Third, the Union has adopted a special framework for admission talks with Turkey. Although invited to the European Conference, the Union did not negotiate with Turkey in the Association Council.[37] In 1999, relations with Turkey gained new momentum when the European Council decided to draw up an accession partnership and to enhance its political dialogue and economic support.[38] Fourth, so-called

Agreements on Partnership and Cooperation have been signed with nine countries of the Commonwealth of Independent States, helping to institutionalize political dialogue with the EU.[39]

WEU. The WEU started accepting new members rather early.[40] Rights and duties of observers, associate members, and associate partners have been adopted by the Petersberg and Kirchberg declarations. Associate members take part in meetings of the Ministerial Council, have the right to address the Ministerial Council, and can contribute to military operations. Associate partners can join the Permanent Council (without the right to veto), and they can contribute to military operations. Observers participate in Ministerial Council meetings and can participate in Petersberg missions. Four different formats have been established for consultation. The Western European Armaments Group (WEAG), formed to improve armaments cooperation, meets as thirteen;[41] the Ministerial Council and the Permanent Council alternatively meet either at eighteen (member states, associate members, and observers) or at twenty-eight (eighteen and associate partners); in addition, the Parliamentary Assembly meets at twenty-eight, comprising parliamentary delegations of all WEU states, whereby only WEU members have the right to vote.

NATO. Before issuing the study on enlargement, NATO established the North Atlantic Cooperation Council (NACC) and adopted the PfP program in order to facilitate cooperation with CEE countries. In 1997, the NACC was replaced by the Euro-Atlantic Partnership Council (EAPC), NATO established special forums for communication with Russia and Ukraine, and it decided to receive three new members. Institutionally, the Alliance meets in different compositions. Meeting as forty-four (nineteen plus twenty-five) means that NATO members, EAPC, and PfP countries discuss matters of common interest. The format 19+n is the format for discussion between NATO members and a different number of partners, for example, to discuss the PfP's Planning and Review Process; 19+1 serves as the format for discussion of a country's Individual Partnership Program; 19+Russia is the format for meetings in the Permanent Joint Council established for discussion between NATO and Russia; 19+Ukraine is a similar format established under the NATO-Ukraine Charter; finally, 19+13 means that NATO members and thirteen former communist countries meet in the Parliamentary Assembly.

Interinstitutional Relations

In 1991, NATO ministers declared that the "challenges we will face in this new Europe cannot be comprehensively addressed by one institution alone, but only in a framework of interlocking institutions."[42] In order to be interlocking, institutions have to consult each other and must cooperate. Both issues will be addressed below.

Consultation. Because consultation schemes have become quite complicated, it seems useful to concentrate on specific interinstitutional relations.

OSCE, UN, AND COE. Under the Swedish chairmanship, the former Conference on Security and Cooperation in Europe (CSCE) and the UN signed a framework agreement on cooperation and coordination. Among other things, the agreement foresaw regular consultations between the UN Secretary-General and the chairman in office, and the exchange of documents, resolutions, and reports as well as coordinated activities. In addition, the UN General Assembly granted the CSCE observer status in 1993.[43] Most recently, the OSCE and the UNHCR extended their cooperation in the field and adopted various memoranda of understanding that aim at improving existing mechanisms for exchanging information. Relations between the OSCE and the CoE proved more difficult at the beginning. The main problems have included political differences, misunderstandings of each other's positions, and mutual fears of encroachment on authority.[44] Thanks to increasing cooperation in the field, these relations have improved greatly.[45] Besides organizing joint seminars and workshops, the CoE established a special working group in 1993. Since then, OSCE and CoE representatives come together in 2+2 high-level meetings involving the respective chairmanships and Secretaries-General. Finally, all three organizations form tripartite high-level meetings.

EU, OSCE, COE, AND UN. From the beginning, the EC and the former CSCE had good working relationships. The CSCE was one of the first organizations where EC member states began coordinating their foreign policy initiates. Today, the Presidency of the EU is to present the Union's positions regularly, and the Commission has established an OSCE bureau.[46] Due to its legal construction, the EU has not yet established its own charter of human rights but has accepted the European Convention on Human Rights to serve this function. This establishes a close link between the EU and the CoE. Following an exchange of letters in 1987, the president of the European Commission and the Secretary-General of the CoE paved the way for closer cooperation. Since then, quadripartite meetings with the presidents of the Commission and the Council, on the one hand, and the Secretary-General and the chairman of the Committee of Ministers of the CoE, on the other hand, take place. Furthermore, both organizations benefit from exchanging documents and participating at each other's meetings.[47] In 1974, the UN General Assembly granted the EC observer status. Since the EU is not a subject of international law, the EC remains the spokesman for the Union in areas of EC responsibility (e.g., trade, agriculture, fisheries). The exchange of information is facilitated by the fact that two EU members are permanent members of the UN Security Council.[48]

NATO/WEU AND OSCE/UN. There are no formal agreements between the two alliances and the OSCE or the UN. In 1992, NATO and the former CSCE agreed to exchange information regularly and participate at each other's meetings.[49] Exchange of information between NATO and the UN depends on case-by-case cooperation. The WEU Council will be informed by the chairman in office of the OSCE, and the WEU Secretary-General participates at OSCE summit meetings. He is also responsible for contacts with the UN.

NATO AND WEU. Joint meetings of the respective councils serve to exchange information. In 1996, NATO ministers agreed on the possibility of WEU having recourse to NATO infrastructure. In the same year, both organizations signed a security agreement allowing for the exchange of classified information. With regard to military planning, WEU is to be involved in NATO decisions, thereby allowing the newly established director of the WEU Military Committee to serve as a liaison officer between both organizations.[50]

NATO, WEU, AND EU. In 1999, relations among these three organizations were given a qualitative boost. During its spring meeting in Washington, D.C., NATO members agreed that the Alliance and the EU should "ensure the development of effective mutual consultation, cooperation and transparency." For this purpose the EU will have direct access to the collective assets and capabilities of the Alliance, especially for operations in which NATO is not involved.[51] Parallel to this, the EU decided to appoint the High Representative, who is Secretary-General of the Council, as Secretary-General of the WEU and to integrate the WEU into the EU. Coordination will be improved in the fields of decisionmaking, the holding of joint seminars, and, if possible, harmonization of their presidencies. Furthermore, the EU will establish new political and military bodies within the Council to tackle the setting up of the Common European Security and Defense Policy.[52] Despite recent progress, tricky questions remain to be solved. This is especially true for procedural questions, in the case of the EU availing itself of the WEU to conduct military operations, and for cooperation and exchange of assets between NATO and the WEU.

Cooperation. Consultation is one part of the idea of interlocking institutions; cooperation is another. In what follows I will look at interinstitutional cooperation with regard to preventive diplomacy, peacekeeping, and peace building.

PREVENTIVE DIPLOMACY. Preventive diplomacy rests on the assumption that conflicts can be avoided if all necessary steps are undertaken in advance. Preventive diplomacy is one of the main activities of the OSCE. In some cases the EU and the CoE support the OSCE. From a theoretical point of view, the EU's Pact on Stability is an extremely interesting example of interinstitutional cooperation. At the beginning of the 1990s, then French Prime Minister Eduard Balladur feared that contested borders and minority issues in the CEE countries could endanger European stability. His initiative aimed at reestablishing stability and improving early warning. The EU adopted the Pact on

Stability as a joint action and negotiated the final document with CEE countries. After signing, the Pact on Stability was transferred to the OSCE, now responsible for its development. This is an innovative way of combining the advantages of both organizations: monitoring and implementing common principles (OSCE) with financial support (EC), thereby creating incentives to agree on substantive solutions.

PEACEKEEPING. In 1992, the then CSCE declared it could conduct peace-keeping operations but excluded the possibility of military enforcement actions. The framework agreement already mentioned foresees that the UN in the case of such operations will support the OSCE. In addition, the OSCE and the UN can have recourse to NATO as well as WEU, which both decided in 1992 to support in such operations on the basis of a case-by-case evaluation of the alliances' own provisions. The conflict in former Yugoslavia became the first example of such interaction. NATO was responsible for monitoring and subsequently enforcing sanctions imposed on the former Republic of Yugoslavia (jointly with WEU in Operation Sharp Guard), supported the United Nations Protection Force in Bosnia, and subsequently enforced the UN's no-fly zones. In addition, the WEU, OSCE, and EU cooperated to implement sanctions on the Danube.

However, field operations between NATO and the UN were complicated by the dual-key procedure. In 1993, NATO and the UN agreed that the launch of NATO airstrikes must be authorized by both organizations. This provision was a continuous source of controversy and reduced the deterrent effect of NATO airstrikes. In order for such actions to be more effective, this aspect had to be changed. In the future, the UN will authorize peacekeeping or peace-enforcing operations. If NATO forces participate, the Supreme Allied Commander will keep the responsibility for the conduct of military operations, and the unity of the chain of command will not be challenged.[53] IFOR, established under the Dayton Accords, followed this approach.

PEACEBUILDING. The provisions of the Dayton Accords serve as an illuminating example. First, the Office of the High Representative has to oversee civilian implementation of the Bosnia peace agreement and has the right to make and impose decisions as long as the local parties cannot agree on measures.[54] Second, the Dayton Accords established specific fields of cooperation: the Commission on Human Rights, an OSCE-CoE joint venture, monitors and implements human rights. The OSCE provides the ombudsperson, and the CoE has established the Human Rights Chamber. In order to develop confidence- and security-building measures, IFOR/SFOR and the OSCE cooperate closely. The OSCE has been empowered to negotiate with the parties to the conflict an arms control regime for the whole Balkan region, its provisions monitored by armed forces. Although the OSCE is primarily responsible for organizing and supervising elections, it is supported by the CoE, the United Nations, and IFOR/SFOR (e.g., in technical assistance). Finally, economic recovery is a task managed by the EU and international financial organizations. Although the mere establishment of such fields of cooperation is not yet a guarantee for success, these examples are clear indicators of the potential inherent in interinstitutional cooperation in the field.

Defection or Playing by the Rules?

Whether institutional incentives to defect or play by the rules are high or low depends on at least two factors: the nature of the problems to be solved (collaboration or coordination), and the organization's institutional structure (regulative, normative, cognitive).[55]

Among Europe's security organizations, the EC and NATO primarily deal with coordination problems. Because member states mostly agree on the strategic tasks of these organizations and how to achieve them, collaboration is no longer a problem. In addition, within the EC supranational bodies, such as the Commission or the ECJ, have the possibility of adopting legal acts that are binding on the member states. However, both organizations are in a process of transition. While enlarging eastward the EU is also moving on to complete the final stage of the European Monetary Union, to which not all members belong. Hence, it may well be that collaboration will prove to be difficult on some questions. The same holds true for negotiations with new members. As has been demonstrated, enlarging the common market is a demanding task that is rendered more difficult by the fact that the necessary degree of commonality, reached between Western EU member states during some forty years, still remains to be framed with CEE countries. NATO faces a similar problem with respect to cooperation with Russia and Ukraine. In order to work as smoothly with these two countries as with its longtime members, NATO will have to overcome collaboration problems. In contrast, the CFSP, the OSCE, and the WEU all face collaboration problems from the start. In these three cases, disagreement over what should be done, and how, overshadows consent.

A similar picture is presented by the organizations' institutional structures. It will come as no surprise that the EC and NATO both follow regulative functions. The possibility of being sued for digression and the possibility of ECJ rulings against a member state set clear incentives to play by the rules. Similarly, a state will not take security commitments lightly. Since security is a precious good, most states will behave properly within NATO, although transgressions by single members cannot be ruled out. Where collaboration problems prevail, one should not expect an organization to provide for regulative functions; instead they mostly follow either normative or cognitive functions. This holds true for the OSCE and the CFSP. Although the OSCE foresees some obvious regulative functions, participating states tend to back away from the use of such instruments. The same holds true for the CFSP, where most decisions are adopted as voluntary declarations instead of taking

Table 9.1   Institutional Incentives for Defection

Criteria	OSCE	EU	CFSP	NATO	WEU
Institutional structure					
Regulative		X		X	(X)
Normative	X		(X)		
Cognitive	X		X		
Structure of the problem to be solved					
Collaboration	X	(X)	X	(X)	(X)
Coordination		X		X	X
Institutional directives binding for states					
Yes		X			
No	X		X	X	X
Enforcement mechanisms					
None					
Political sanctions	(X)	X	X		
Economic sanctions	(X)	X	X		
Military sanctions				X	X
Rulings by an international court					
Yes	(X)	X			(X)
No			X	X	X

Key:
X = Criteria comprehensively fulfilled by organization
(X) = Criteria partially fulfilled by organization

recourse to binding instruments, such as common positions or joint actions. The WEU, although a defense alliance, follows the same line. In contrast to NATO, the WEU has not really been tasked to prepare for the eventual case of an attack against one of its member states. This task has been delegated to NATO as part of a division of labor. Despite public statements, the WEU lacks a clear objective even today. The Petersberg Declaration can be interpreted as such a clear objective, but the organization still lacks robust backing by its members, hence they show the tendency to remain passive.

In sum, playing by the rules is to be expected in organizations that have the possibility of enforcing such behavior. In contrast, organizations that have to overcome collaboration problems can be expected to have greater problems convincing their members not to defect (see Table 9.1). This is so because for the most part these organizations provide normative or cognitive institutional structures. In these cases, playing by the rules is not the result of enforcement but of expectations or social learning. Hence, with regard to converging interests, the OSCE, the CFSP, and the WEU are more demanding. However, one should not interpret these findings as establishing a ranking. Rather, these results suggest different ways of influencing states' behavior, thereby suggesting that an organization that combines each of the three approaches shows particular promise in preventing members from defecting.

Access for Nonstate Actors

International organizations are said to suffer from a democracy deficit. This flaw can be overcome by stronger involvement of nonstate actors. Besides helping to improve democratic legitimacy, they serve additional purposes. They can help to facilitate fact-finding and monitoring, to inform about non-compliance with international rules, especially in the field of human rights, and to lobby international organizations and governments.[56] Therefore, this section examines how Europe's security organizations interact with nonstate actors.

Since 1990, the CSCE/OSCE has greatly improved its relations with non-state actors.[57] Nonstate actors are granted unrestricted access to conference buildings and infrastructure (except for rooms reserved for delegations); they can participate in all OSCE meetings and conferences; and participating states as well as OSCE institutions are asked to facilitate contacts with them by establishing liaison offices. At first, contacts concentrated on human rights and disarmament. In the meantime, nonstate actors dealing with conflict pre-vention have gained in importance. The OSCE consults with them regularly, and their representatives train members of OSCE long-term missions. In con-trast, nonstate actors have more difficulties influencing the CFSP. This is pri-marily due to the fact that the CFSP is an intergovernmental field where supranational institutions like the Commission play a subordinate role. Therefore, nonstate actors wishing to influence the Union's foreign and secu-rity policy have to address the member states. The situation is a little different with regard to the Community's development policy. The European Community Humanitarian Office has signed more than sixty partnership agreements with nongovernmental organizations (NGOs) that help to imple-ment Community decisions in the field.[58] Finally, neither NATO nor the WEU have official and formal contacts with nonstate actors. However, both can interact with them either in the field or within special programs. NATO enter-tains contacts with nonstate actors within the NATO Industrial Advisory Group, which deals with questions of logistics, and within the NATO Scientific Program. In addition, the parliamentary assembly of the WEU is in close contact with European armaments firms.

Summary

Europe's security organizations work and interact within a complex network of institutional relations. However, in most cases cooperation and coordina-tion rest not on formal but on ad hoc agreements. This holds especially true for peacekeeping and peacebuilding. From an institutional point of view, strategic guidelines are set by intergovernmental bodies deciding by consen-sus. Analyzing the way in which Europe's security organizations are able to influence the behavior of their member states leads to the conclusion that organizations faced with coordination problems, and thereby providing regulative institutions, diminish states' incentives to defect. In contrast, organizations faced with collaboration problems that provide either normative or cognitive institutional structures demand a higher degree of interest convergence among member states. Finally, the OSCE provides the broadest access to nonstate actors; they face bigger problems with the CFSP, NATO, and the WEU.

LEADERSHIP BY INTERNATIONAL ORGANIZATIONS?
UNDERESTIMATED POTENTIAL

Leadership is foremost an individual capacity. A liberal worldview may permit a leader to convince followers to act as he would like them to. Nonhegemonic leadership is possible within an established international system based on accepted liberal norms. Against this background, international organizations can be expected to act as leaders.[59] It is the purpose of this section to analyze this proposition. First, I will discuss how far the member states of Europe's security organizations agree on their roles and tasks. Second, their core competence will be analyzed. Finally, I will give four illustrations of executive leadership by international organizations.

Consensus Among the Participating States?

Basically, the OSCE covers activities in three fields: preventive diplomacy, consulting states in transition, and peacebuilding. Among other things, the discussion about a common and comprehensive security model for Europe for the twenty-first century, launched at the OSCE's 1994 Budapest Summit, aims at clarifying the OSCE's role. My impression of this discussion is that most states are, at least at the moment, neither willing to broaden the OSCE's agenda nor prepared to use the OSCE more intensively. The possibility of an OSCE peacekeeping mission for Nagorno-Karabakh has been discussed for several years without measurable results; proposals for institutional reforms have been opposed.[60] There is no chance to grant the OSCE legal status, and finally there is broad disagreement about the necessity to develop and adapt the OSCE's Helsinki decalogue. Therefore, Ingo Peters is correct in observing that the OSCE has been assigned a residual function by the participating states, since the organization is usually given tasks that no other organization wants to shoulder.[61]

So far the CFSP and the WEU have shared the same fate, because there seemed to be fundamental differences among member states about their development. However, at the end of 1998 the Franco-British St. Malo Declaration initiated a reform process.[62] Starting from the experience gained in Bosnia-Herzegovina, the heads of states declared that European military capacities needed to be backed up. During the most recent Kosovo crisis, this assertion was most obviously highlighted by the fact that NATO's air campaign was almost exclusively handled by the United States. It therefore comes as no surprise that EU states, at their Cologne and Helsinki meetings in 1999, decided to merge the WEU with the EU until the end of 2000 and to adopt measures that allow for EU-led crisis-management operations.[63] This is a welcome step that will help to establish a fairer sharing of the burden among the transatlantic partners. However, the political will to implement this decision will be most important. In a time of shrinking budgets and heavy competition among different governmental branches, it is not yet clear that the challenging aims can be realized. If this fails, the consequences will be far-reaching. Europe's strategic capabilities would depend even more strongly on NATO and on the degree to which Washington and its European allies agree on security issues.

The Kosovo intervention in spring 1999 made it clear that NATO seems to be the only European security organization that enjoys broad support by its members. However, even among NATO members there is disagreement on some important questions. Whereas Washington wants to keep the enlargement process open for everyone (thereby allowing for the possibility of Russian membership), European allies seem prepared to restrict membership in NATO. This question goes to the very core of NATO (i.e., the question of the future relationship between defense and non–Article 5 operations). Limiting NATO's membership implies that states want to uphold NATO as a defense organization, whereas extending the possibility of non–Article 5 operations implies using NATO as an organization to solve international conflicts, if necessary, by using force. Furthermore, the flexibility brought about by the decision on Combined Joint Task Forces (CJTFs) allows NATO members to not participate in NATO missions and also makes it possible for non-NATO members to participate. It remains to be seen if and how this trend will affect NATO's coherence.[64]

Core Competence

In the early 1980s, business managers asked how they could meet the challenges lying ahead. Puzzled by the success of Japanese companies, business economists like Gary Hamel and C. K. Prahalad began analyzing the secrets of Japanese success. Contrary to Western business strategies advocating decentralization and strategically independent units, Hamel and Prahalad saw that Japanese companies concentrate on what they do best. Sony was a champion of microtechnology, and Honda had an unmatched know-how in engines. They called the skills that allow a company to produce many different products *core competence*, which must meet three tests. First, core competence has to make a disproportionate contribution to customer-perceived value. Second, such a capability must be competitively unique, and thus almost impossible for other companies to imitate. Finally, core competence forms the basis for entry into new product markets.[65] Although international organizations are not privately run companies, it is evident that they, too, compete.

The OSCE works in many different areas: arms control, security and confidence building, questions of democracy, safeguarding human rights, preventive diplomacy, organizing and supervising elections, and peacebuilding; it competes with other international organizations in these areas. If we look closely at the way the OSCE is doing business, we can say that political dialogue is its core competence. This is reflected in the large number of different instruments of dialogue (e.g., seminars, meetings, implementation conferences, long-term missions, the HCNM and the Representative on Freedom of the Media, and general discussions within its councils). Dialogue is *the* precondition of every political process, thereby laying the groundwork for international cooperation. Although it is true that dialogue makes an important contribution to the "customer-perceived value" of the OSCE and opens the door to many "markets," it can be copied quite easily.[66] Furthermore, dialogue rests on the assumption that parties are willing to talk to each other. If this is not the case, the OSCE is in deep trouble—as many recent examples have made clear.

As long as foreign policy and security affairs among EU members are dominated by collaboration problems, the CFSP remains an invaluable instrument to harmonize different positions. Hence, its primary importance, although not a real core competence, is a domestic one. In this regard, the member states' approach to questions of foreign and security policy could benefit greatly from applying the EC's core competence: negotiating and adopting package deals. Let me illustrate this point with an example. In recent years, defense-related industries all over the world have undergone drastic changes shaped by the end of the Cold War. In the United States, the Pentagon has played an active role in helping to restructure this industry. Because Europe still lacks a common market for defense-related products and EU members act independently, Europe's defense industry has trouble competing with U.S. companies. In November 1997, the Commission submitted a proposal of implementing an EU strategy on defense-related industries to be adopted as a common position. The package deal the Commission proposed consists, among other things, of simplifying intracommunity transfers, creating a European Company Statute, allowing competitive bidding for public contracts, rationalizing standards, harmonizing common duties, and removing obstacles to European exporters.[67] The success of this proposal remains to be seen. However, it shows that the EU could greatly step up the quality of CFSP decisions by following the Community path, that is, by creating economic incentives to cooperate politically. It is no secret that harmonizing Europe's defense industry makes sense only if one is willing to act jointly on questions of foreign and security policy. According to the functional logic of integration, establishing a common market for defense-related products, or at least facilitating their trading, could build up economic pressure that might eventually lead to the necessary political steps to improve the CFSP.

So far the WEU has had no chance to develop core competence. However, the WEU has two favorable characteristics that have been underestimated. First, neither the United States nor Russia is a member of the WEU. At first sight, Washington's absence from the WEU could be interpreted as a flaw. In practice, however, it greatly facilitated dialogue between the WEU and CEE countries since there was no Russian opposition. The fact that Russia is not part of the WEU could be advantageous in regard to strengthening military cooperation with the former Warsaw Pact members. Many of them have been anxious that the Brussels-Moscow link could imply an indirect Russian veto over the question of enlarging NATO. Since neither the United States nor Russia is a member of the WEU, the organization does not face this problem. Second, the WEU has great institutional flexibility. Compared to the OSCE, in the WEU there is no overlapping competence between the different councils. Compared to NATO, the WEU has neither an integrated military structure nor a permanent command structure that could lead to problems over who should be given what command. However, both advantages have not been used effectively. WEU joint exercises started in December 1995, rather late if one takes into account the interest of CEE countries in cooperating militarily with the West. Despite numerous declarations on armament cooperation, most WEU members were hardly interested in initiating concrete talks with Russia or Ukraine over beefing up Europe's long-range airlift capacities. Furthermore, because the WEU has but a small-staffed military structure that has been strengthened only recently, there is no such thing as day-to-day working in integrated structures or provisions to standardize doctrines and military equipment.

NATO's survival at the end of the Cold War has been a puzzle to many commentators. It is no surprise when we consider the Alliance's core competence. Celeste Wallander and Robert Keohane have argued that NATO managed to survive because the Alliance has become a hybrid institution dealing both "with security problems created by external threats or problems and those problems posed by risks, mistrust, and misunderstandings among members." Such an organization can be termed a security management institution, denoting "an inclusive, risk-oriented arrangement with highly institutionalized practices."[68] Although, as Wallander and Keohane argue, changes in the external environment—from threats to risks as well as the hybrid character of an alliance—facilitate its transformation, NATO benefited greatly from its most distinctive core competence: commanding multinational contingents within integrated military structures. This is what NATO does best. It is precisely the ability to act together militarily that explains NATO's attractiveness at the end of the Cold War, where threats have diminished but risks remain to be solved. Adopting and modifying NATO's Strategic Concept in the 1990s would not have been possible without this core competence. If an organization such as NATO is able to command military contingents effectively, it does not matter whether these contingents have to defend a member state, help solve a crisis militarily, or serve as peacekeeping troops. For sure, all these tasks pose different demands. But without the organization being able to command troops effectively, none of these tasks can be achieved. Hence, the discussion about the future relationship between non–Article 5 operations and Article 5 operations is a futile one—at least with regard to the core competence of the Alliance.

Furthermore, it can be assumed that NATO will continue to play a central role within the Concert of Europe's security organizations, because its core competence not only adds disproportionately to customer-perceived value (military security) and is extendable to different markets (e.g., defense, crisis management, peacekeeping, or peace enforcement); it is almost impossible to copy because of the enormous amount of money that would be required to build a military organization comparable to NATO. Hence, NATO has an almost unfair competitive advantage over Europe's other security organizations.

Executive Leadership

To conclude this section, I would like to offer four examples that illustrate the possibility of active and passive leadership by international bodies. The Presidency of the EU and the chairman in office of the OSCE can be regarded as examples of passive institutional leadership, whereas the president of the European Commission and the HCNM should be interpreted as examples of active institutional leadership.

Taking over the Presidency of the EU is a very demanding task. The Presidency plays a vital part in organizing the work of the institution. It has to organize and chair all meetings and work out compromises capable of resolving difficulties. The Presidency also sets the agenda for its term of six months, thereby giving each country the possibility to lead on certain questions. Since every country acting as the Presidency attempts to do its job very well, it has become a driving force in the legislative and political decisionmaking processes. The chairman in office of the OSCE has a similar function. He is even more important, because the OSCE has no institution comparable to the Commission that guarantees continuity within the work of the organization. The OSCE chairman has become the central figure in decisionmaking; he mediates between different positions and tries to work out strategies that are acceptable to all participating states. Both positions can be seen as examples of passive institutional leadership because they facilitate governmental leadership by providing specific institutional procedures, especially the possibility to set the agenda.

In contrast, the president of the European Commission is a typical example of active institutional leadership. Of all presidents so far, Jacques Delors has had an enormous impact on the development of the Union. As Helen Drake has argued, Jacques Delors differed from his predecessors in many ways. When taking over the presidency he was willing to make contacts with national leaders in order to set the framework for his subsequent actions. He understood that *how* the Commission is doing its job is at least as important than *what* the Commission does. He therefore paid great attention to the Commission's public relations, maintained good relations with national leaders, and concentrated on some key issues (e.g., the European Monetary Union).[69] Within the OSCE, the HCNM performs a similar but almost unnoticed job. Max van der Stoel, acting as HCNM since 1993, usually points out that his job depends on three conditions. He is *impartial* because the HCNM is an instrument of conflict prevention; he does his work *confidentially* because matters of human rights are of great sensibility; and finally, his work rests on the *cooperation* of all parties involved.[70] Referring to the leadership categories developed by Oran Young,[71] we can assume that acting as the HCNM requires great intellectual as well as entrepreneurial leadership, because it will never be easy to convince a government that lacks interest in dealing with minority questions to undertake actions deemed necessary for their protection. However, the influence of the president of the Commission and the HCNM is limited. Discussions about Jacques Delors's successor made clear that his performance and his style might have been at the limit of what national leaders were willing to accept. Because national leaders appoint, with the consent of the European Parliament, the president of the Commission, they still decide whether the Commission is headed by a high- or low-profile personality. Despite the success of the HCNM, the HCNM's mandate is rather limited. Some participating states effectively blocked the extension of his mandate. Thus, he has no possibility to "communicate with and will not acknowledge communications from any person or organization that practices or publicly condones terrorism or violence."[72]

Summary

Analyzing the possibility of active or passive institutional leadership has revealed that such activities are subject to many preconditions. Consent among the member states and the institutions' core competence are two of the most important. One of the most promising examples of active institutional leadership is the president of the European Commission. Thus, it can be assumed that the creation of supranational bodies granted executive powers is an effective instrument to overcome inertia caused by differing national interests, thereby providing active institutional leadership. However, the

Commission plays only a subordinate role within the CFSP. This shows that the possibility of leadership by international organizations is, at least for the moment, subordinate to national interests. National resistance to international organizations acting independently can therefore be identified as one of the most fundamental obstacles to be overcome in the future.

SECURITY AND INTEGRATION:
CEDING SOVEREIGNTY SILENTLY

Integration means transferring sovereignty to supranational bodies. This process renders the renationalization of European politics more difficult. This section analyzes whether and to what degree European security organizations contribute to the process of transferring sovereignty in the area of foreign and security policy. Although the direct transfer of sovereignty remains an exclusivity of economic affairs, military cooperation begins to encroach upon sovereignty, and even political cooperation shows faint signs of moving away from intergovernmentalism. First, I will show how Europe's security organizations contribute to harmonizing the criteria that applicant countries are expected to fulfill. Next comes the question of coordinated or common policies in security affairs. Third, I will refer to majority voting as a clear indication of supranationality. Fourth, I will discuss whether documents and decisions of Europe's security organizations are legally or politically binding. Finally, I will look at the role of international courts in security and foreign policy affairs.

Converging Admission Criteria

Successful regional integration presupposes some degree of commonality. It can be argued that harmonized policies, comparable economic standards, and similar cultural values greatly facilitate regional integration. International organizations are able to support the process of regional integration by adjusting their admission criteria to the same values. This is what happens in Europe today.

With regard to political questions, the OSCE, the EU, NATO, and the WEU expect potential members to possess stable political institutions guaranteeing democracy, the rule of law, the protection of human rights, and effective and efficient administrative structures. Additionally, the extension of the Union's common market is leading to a growing convergence in most parts of a state's policies, including competition policy, environmental policy, social policy, transportation policy, agricultural policy, trade policy, and so on. This harmonization process facilitates the work of the EU and increases transparency as a political leitmotiv, thereby furthering predictability and stability.

A similar process is under way with regard to economic issues. At the regional level the EU plays an important role. At the global level, the World Trade Organization, as well as different financial organizations, support the harmonization of economic policies. In recent years, the World Bank, the International Monetary Fund, and the European Bank for Reconstruction and Development have come to place greater value on political considerations. The emphasis on good governance has greatly upgraded the value of programs aimed at fostering political stability, banning corruption, and creating stable conditions for foreign investments.[73] This shows that political and economic international organizations are beginning to reinforce one another.

The foregoing also holds true for military issues. NATO and the WEU expect future members to adhere to democratic principles. In addition, they want them to accept the decisions and documents that provide the basis for the work of both organizations. Through standardization, NATO has created a strong mechanism of harmonizing various aspects of military forces acting jointly. NATO introduced four different forms of standardization. Compatibility requires a smooth functioning of different components of a system. Interoperability requires different components of a system to work together. Interchangeability allows the exchange of different system components. Finally, commonality refers to common provisions that are required in order to command different multinational contingents.[74] NATO's current standardization priorities include commonality of doctrines and procedures, interoperability of command, control, and communications and major weapons systems, and interchangeability of ammunition and primary combat supplies. There are at present more than 1,200 agreements and publications that new members are expected to comply with.[75] Standardization thus has far-reaching consequences for national doctrines, the structure of national armed forces, and even for the production of weapons and related material.

In sum, we can say that belonging to Europe's security architecture requires a state to undertake adaptations with regard to its normative worldview, its political system, its economic policy, and its armed forces. In the words of James Robert Huntley, something new has appeared on the international scene: a union of states adhering to the same democratic principles and willing to exclude those states that do not apply them, thereby giving international organizations a prominent role.[76]

Coordinated or Common Policies?

The distinction between coordinated and common policies refers to the way the EC adopts political strategies. Common policies adopted by the Community are binding on the member states. Asking whether a security organization adopts coordinated or common policies therefore reveals whether and how it encroaches upon state sovereignty.

As will be shown later, the OSCE's decisions and documents are binding only politically. We can therefore not expect it to adopt common policies. Yet it is in a position to influence the normative basis of the participating states' policies due to its comprehensive norms and principles.[77] The same holds true for the CFSP. Although called *Common*, the CFSP cannot be compared to the Common Agricultural Policy or the Common Competition Policy. The search for an EU position on questions of foreign policy thus leads to some kind of coordination reflex requiring member states to adjust their interests to keep the Union's foreign policy workable.[78]

In contrast, NATO's impact on domestic military policy seems in some way comparable to the impact of the EC's common policies. Standardization as one way of influencing its member states' policies has already been mentioned. Another possibility stems from the fact of intensive daily cooperation within NATO's integrated military structure, which has been opened to EAPC countries within the enhanced PfP.[79] A third way of influencing national armed forces rests in NATO's force structure. Since 1990, NATO has distinguished among rapid-reaction forces, main defense forces, and augmentation forces—a distinction that has been applied by most NATO members. Fourth, multinationalization leads to a harmonization of defense doctrines as well as educational goals. Taken together, these processes have effectively blocked the renationalization of defense policies: "Very few European states would now be able, even if they were willing, to fight by themselves. They have the habit of co-operation. They regularly train and exercise together, buy the same equipment and occasionally set up joint units and headquarters."[80]

Majority Voting

Most textbooks dealing with integration list majority voting as one of the clearest signs of supranationality. Do Europe's security organizations decide by majority? Because neither NATO nor WEU have introduced majority voting, I will concentrate on the OSCE and the CFSP.

The OSCE deviates in many ways from the standard procedure of consensus. While the consensus-minus-one and the consensus-minus-two principles can be regarded as marginal deviations, the Parliamentary Assembly, the Court of Arbitration and Conciliation, and the Conciliation Commission decide by majority.[81] Additionally, the emergency mechanisms provide the most far-reaching digression from consensus. The political emergency mechanism can be activated by thirteen participating states (one state initiating the mechanism with the consent of twelve other states), and the humanitarian emergency mechanism requires the consent of ten participating states. Keeping in mind that the OSCE consists of fifty-four states, these provisions provide a significant departure from consensus voting.

Within the CFSP framework, decisions by the European Council and the Ministerial Council basically require unanimity while providing for constructive abstention. By derogating from this provision, the Ministerial Council may decide by qualified majority when adopting joint actions, common positions, or making any other decision on the basis of a common strategy or when adopting a decision implementing a joint action or a common position.[82] In the future, this provision could prove useful, because common positions and joint actions are binding on the Union's members. So far, declarations, introduced by the European Political Cooperation (EPC), remain the CFSP's main instrument. Although the Council adopted more then 160 declarations in 1998, it adopted only twenty-two common positions and twenty joint actions.[83] Declarations dominate because they are nonbinding. It is to be hoped that the clarifications brought about by the Amsterdam Treaty will lead to increasing adoption of common positions and joint actions.

Decisions and Documents: Politically and/or Judicially Binding

The doctrine of direct effect developed by the ECJ was praised as a cornerstone of successful European integration. It will be interesting to analyze the binding effects of the documents and decisions adopted by Europe's security organizations.

It has already been mentioned that all decisions and documents adopted by the OSCE are merely politically binding. Exceptions to this rule are the CFE Treaty and the Open Skies Treaty, both negotiated within the OSCE, as well as the OSCE's provisions on arbitration and conciliation. These documents are legally binding. The discussion on granting the OSCE legal status is as old as the organization. Different proposals have been put forward. Although most participating states oppose granting the OSCE legal status, the incoming Austrian chairman in office has declared its intention to shade new light on the pros and cons of such a step.[84]

Due to the complex structure of the EU, various differentiations are required in order to analyze the binding effects of CFSP instruments:[85]

1. Starting with the principles and guidelines, we can say that *principles* should not be considered as legally relevant acts but as a basis for guidelines. Concerning the tasks to be achieved, *guidelines* are legally binding for the Council, which will decide on their implementation by adopting common positions and joint actions. Therefore, we can assume that the Council must be given some leeway.

2. *Common strategies* are to be implemented by the Union in areas where the member states share important interests.[86] Because common strategies are required to set out their objectives, duration, and

means, they can be assumed to have the same legally binding effect as guidelines, but they restrict the authority of the Council even more.

3. *Common positions* are meant to define the approach of the Union to a particular matter of a geographical or thematic nature.[87] Their binding effects are contested. Some experts see them as only politically binding, whereas others consider them to be legally binding.

4. *Joint actions* address specific situations where operational action by the EU is deemed to be required.[88] Although adopted by the Council, joint actions are legally binding for the member states, thereby requiring them to adopt the necessary domestic measures.

5. *Economic sanctions* have a hybrid character. They are adopted within the framework of the EU but are implemented within the EC. Concerning the question of whether to impose sanctions, the EC will be bound by secondary Community law. However, the Union's decision to impose economic sanctions may not prejudice the way in which the Community implements the decision. If the Community adopts a regulation that is directly applicable, the Community institutions as well as the member states will be legally bound.

6. Finally, the EU has access to *military forces* by availing itself of the WEU. This raises the question of the legal relationship between the EU, which has no legal personality, and the WEU, which is a subject of international law. Whereas Christoph Thun-Hohenstein denies a legal subordination of the WEU to the EU, he contends that one might assume member states to be indirectly bound according to the *estoppel* principle.[89] By contrast, Matthias Pechstein and Christian Koenig and Jochen A. Frowein assume a tacit modification of the Brussels Treaty by its member states, which are at the same time members of the EU, thereby legitimating the EU's recourse to the WEU in advance.[90]

When analyzing the binding effects within NATO and the WEU, two points should be kept separate: documents and decisions on the one hand, and the relation between state sovereignty and the chain of command on the other.

NATO and WEU members join the alliances as sovereign states, thereby retaining the right to decide whether and how to contribute to alliance missions. It is argued that Article 5 of the modified Brussels Treaty implies a higher degree of automatism in case of an attack against a member than Article 5 of the Washington Treaty. However, it seems fair to assume that this formalistic interpretation will be more than compensated by the high degree of integration within NATO's military structures. Furthermore, we have to distinguish between politically and judicially binding documents. Within NATO the Washington Treaty, the Status of Forces Agreement, and the accession protocols for new member states are legally binding. The same holds true for

WEU's modified Brussels Treaty and the four protocols attached thereto. NATO's study on enlargement, the PfP program, the NATO-Russia Act, the NATO-Ukraine Charter, and WEU's Petersberg and Kirchberg Declarations, in contrast, are politically binding. Insofar as these documents are merely politically binding, NATO and WEU face the same problem as the OSCE: it is up to the member states to behave according to the rules established in these documents to safeguard the organizations' credibility.

With regard to assigning national armed forces to NATO and WEU, it is interesting to ask whether such an act constitutes a transfer of sovereignty. In 1994, the German Constitutional Court (Bundesverfassungsgericht) had to decide on complaints filed by the Social Democrats (SPD) and the Free Democrats (FDP) arguing that the German constitution (Grundgesetz) does not authorize out-of-area missions by the Bundeswehr and that, at least, parliament would have to give its consent.[91] In essence, the court freed Germany from military abstention by declaring that the Grundgesetz allows participation in a system of mutual and collective security, thereby using the Bundeswehr for actions within such a system. Assigning national armed forces to multinational armed forces requires the transfer of operational command or control. The Bundesverfassungsgericht argued that this act does not constitute a transfer of sovereignty, because parliament retains the right to withdraw German armed forces from such missions. However, the German government assents to a "limitation" of its sovereignty by accepting decisions of international organizations as binding.[92] The court's ruling makes clear that military cooperation within NATO, WEU, and within multinational contingents raises fundamental legal questions. Commanding such units is a very demanding task, because in many cases the legal provisions differ with respect to the authority of command, the disciplinary law, the basic rights of military personnel, the right of appeal, and provisions on the safety and stationing of the troops abroad.[93]

Discussing the relationship between sovereignty and military cooperation yields three conclusions. First, working day to day within highly integrated military structures raises fundamental legal questions that have to be solved in order to keep multinational contingents operable. Second, not every decision that is legally justifiable is politically feasible. Withdrawing national armed forces from multinational contingents risks paralyzing them. Third, military cooperation leads to a silent transfer of sovereignty resulting from the need to keep multinational contingents functioning.

What Role for the Courts?

When looking at the important role the ECJ played in developing the law of European integration, it follows naturally to ask what role the ECJ and other international courts play with regard to questions of foreign and security policy. The peaceful settlement of disputes was one of the basic provisions adopted in the 1975 Helsinki Charter of the then CSCE. In 1992, participating states adopted a decision on peaceful settlement of disputes, including the convention on conciliation and arbitration.[94] Among other things, the decision foresees provisions for the establishment of a Court of Arbitration and Conciliation (established in Geneva in 1995), the establishment of a Conciliation Commission, and the possibility of a directed conciliation. Although the document can be regarded as an important step toward the peaceful settlement of disputes within the OSCE area, it has a major flaw: neither of the institutions provided for by the document has so far been activated.

In the CFSP, the ECJ shares a similar fate. Although of major importance within the confines of the treaty establishing the European Community, the ECJ has only limited jurisdiction competence in the Treaty on European Union. There are a small number of cases where litigants could appeal to the ECJ. Basically, CFSP decisions must be interpreted as international, not supranational, law. Hence, they bind only member states but not legal or natural persons. However, if, for instance, the Ministerial Council implements a decision to impose economic sanctions by adopting a directly applicable legal act that binds natural and legal persons, they seem to have the possibility to appeal to the ECJ if the act violates individual rights. This suggests that appealing to the ECJ is theoretically possible if a CFSP decision violates the principle of Community loyalty or the principle of the inviolability of the Community treaties.[95] Such conflicts might occur in case of foreign-trade agreements, trade in arms, dual-use products and strategic goods, derogation from the common market on the grounds of protecting national security, and diplomatic protection.[96]

Finally, NATO and the WEU have not established their own courts. In 1956, NATO adopted a resolution on the peaceful settlement of disputes and differences, thereby referring to the Secretary-General's good offices.[97] In contrast, the WEU wants its member states to appeal to the International Court of Justice (ICJ) in order to settle disputes. However, this provision is subject to a declaration by the member states to recognize as compulsory the jurisdiction of the ICJ.[98]

Summary

The concept of integration should be used cautiously when talking about security and foreign policy. In coming years, there will be no direct transfer of sovereignty comparable to the process of integration taking place within the EC. Nevertheless, there are some clear but faint signs of possible change. First, the most promising finding is that Europe's security organizations tend to work on the basis of the same fundamental values, thereby leading to an increased harmonization of their members' policies while making admission contingent upon respecting these values. Second, in order to keep multinational military contingents operable, governments are prepared to cede sovereignty silently. Third, even highly political organizations, such as the OSCE and the CFSP, can encroach upon sovereignty, for example, by the possibility of directed conciliation within the OSCE or the possibility to adopt joint actions or common positions within the CFSP that bind member states.

Despite these positive facts, governments remain reluctant to have international organizations influence their sovereignty on matters of foreign and security policy. First, because joint actions and common positions are binding on EU members, they prefer adopting nonbinding declarations. Second, military personnel and infrastructure assigned to NATO, WEU, or multinational units remain subject to national jurisdiction. Third, majority decisions are still the exception. Fourth, international jurisdiction plays a negligible role in matters of foreign and security policy. Although disappointing, this is not surprising. Based on the political question doctrine established by the U.S. Supreme Court, most national courts exercise judicial self-restraint in matters of foreign policy.[99]

THE ROAD AHEAD

The above analysis shows that Europe's current security architecture is extremely complex. Although a lot has been accomplished in recent years, many problems remain unsolved. One of the most fundamental issues is the attitude of governments toward Europe's security organizations. Paraphrasing Clausewitz, we can say that these organizations are still regarded as politics by other means; hence, most governments see them as mere instruments toward achieving their own foreign policy goals. This must change. In the following I present four concrete measures to improve the situation. Contacts among Europe's security organizations should be enhanced, and cooperation should be augmented. Rule orientation should be improved. Peacebuilding should be managed more effectively. Lastly, ESDI should be strengthened.

Enhancing Contacts, Augmenting Cooperation

Europe's security organizations consult each other and cooperate, but in most cases they do so on the basis of ad hoc agreements. At least three steps are necessary to remedy this situation: improve the flow of information, start joint training and exchange of employees, and put problems before organizations.

First, information is one of tomorrow's decisive factors. Hence, it is vital to reorient the flow of information between Europe's security organizations in order to satisfy the organizations' true needs. Let me give a few examples. The stability of a political system is a precondition for successful economic transformation. Situation reports drafted by OSCE and UN missions should therefore be made available to the EU and international financial organizations and vice versa. The EU could, for instance, contact the HCNM when its own reports show that minorities are systematically discriminated against with respect to jobs, financial support, or unemployment benefits. The HCNM would then have to contact government officials in order to clarify these problems. Similarly, satellites do not serve only military ends. They also perform the tasks of monitoring crises, providing advance warning of aggression, monitoring the application of disarmament treaties, supervising humanitarian peace missions, and gathering strategic and tactical data.[100] Hence, satellite information should be made available not only to NATO and the WEU but also to the OSCE. The same holds true for the EU, which has substantially raised the demand for information by deciding to incorporate the Petersberg tasks into the new Treaty of Amsterdam. Conducting peacekeeping, peace enforcement, and crisis management, even if directed by the WEU, requires more information than the Union has received so far. Even NATO officials agree that the growing importance of non–Article 5 operations increases the Alliance's need for information to a degree formerly required only in times of warfare.[101]

Second, in addition to reorienting the flow of information, Europe's security organizations should start exchanging employees and training them jointly. The enhanced PfP foresees the possibility of assigning military personnel to NATO's integrated military structure in order to improve cooperation. The same could be done with the civilian employees of Europe's security organizations, thereby improving the understanding of these organizations, the restrictions they face, and the possibilities they offer. Training employees jointly serves the same purpose. Training programs for military personnel from all EAPC countries have become standard, but the same happens rarely with civilians. The OSCE summer school is a good example of how things can be done. However, such programs should no longer be restricted to one organization. By including all organizations, a comprehensive understanding of the problems ahead can be promoted. Seminars could advance the exchange of information by focusing on lessons learned. Simulation exercises, again standard procedure in the training of military personnel, would give civilian employees a real chance to practice cooperation among their organizations. Such exchange and joint training programs will promote the creation of truly committed elites at the international level.

Third, these proposals assume that form follows function or, put differently, that organizations must serve the problems they are meant to solve. Hence, Europe's security organizations should establish joint working groups to work out action plans in advance, thereby helping to use scarce resources more efficiently. Again, some examples illustrate this. Integrating minorities and guaranteeing their rights is not only a political issue but also a judicial, an economic, and even a psychological issue. Employees of the OSCE, the CoE, the UNHCR, and the EU could form a joint working group to deal with strategies of handling these issues. The same holds true for programs facilitating economic recovery. Granting financial and technical assistance is one problem. As experience in different countries teaches, building up robust small and medium-sized companies requires not only capital but also managerial skills. Although capital can be raised either via ordinary capital or venture capital markets, getting the necessary know-how is another problem that is much more difficult to solve. Therefore, the EU, international financial organizations, and consulting firms could set up plans to improve the diffusion of knowledge, to form business alliances (e.g., joint ventures in research and development), and to exchange employees.[102]

Improving Rule Orientation

I have argued that regulative institutions facilitate playing by the rules because they allow participants to calculate the costs of deviation. Normative and cognitive institutions, in contrast, force actors to behave properly either on the basis of common norms and values or social interaction, thereby decreasing the possibility of diversion. One way of improving rule orientation is to enhance cooperation in the legal dimension of security.

It has been said that the ECJ and the OSCE's Court of Conciliation and Arbitration are almost irrelevant when it comes to judicially monitoring the application of norms. States are reluctant to appeal to an international court in order to solve political problems. As long as there is no mandatory supranational jurisdiction, the idea of a community of law depends in large part on national courts.[103] It is understandable that the European Commission evaluates the judicial and administrative systems of the CEE countries, but I think it will not suffice. Following the concept of a community of law, these states should be included more strongly into the European legal cooperation scheme. I therefore propose that national judges be assigned to the ECJ and the ECHR in order to accustom them to European law and to the courts' legal culture. In addition, the EU should think about creating the position of ombudsperson for European law. Such a person would work together with the UN or OSCE missions active in those countries that are potential EU candidates. The ombudsperson would be asked to follow national legislation closely, to support and consult in cases of problems, and to report on the development of national legislation. Such an ombudsperson could hint at possible conflicts between national and European law, thereby helping to reduce such conflicts to an absolute minimum.

Managing Peacebuilding More Effectively

The idea of improving coordination between Europe's security organizations can be developed further. Our analysis has made clear that due to a lack of coordination there is a danger of interblocking instead of interlocking institutions. This holds especially true in the field of peacebuilding. Peacebuilding must be regarded as the first step in successful conflict prevention. It therefore has to be managed more professionally.[104] Again, two different approaches are possible. In the case of smaller international missions, Europe's security organizations should establish joint International Peacebuilding Bureaus, assigned to coordinate all activities in the field, similar to the mandate given to the Office of the High Representative under the Dayton Accords. Each organization would assign representatives to a bureau, thereby contributing to the establishment of a center of competence in the field. Resources could be shared, and cooperation with NGOs and local authorities could be greatly facilitated.

In the case of large and demanding missions such as the ones in Bosnia-Herzegovina and Kosovo, Europe's security organizations should no longer launch individual missions. Instead they should form an International Peacebuilding Mission.[105] Europe's security organizations would provide the necessary input, and the mission will no longer be organized along organizations but along the problems that have to be solved (see Figure 9.2).

At the top, such a mission would be run like the Office of the High Representative, with the head of mission responsible for communications with the international organizations as well as with the states. If necessary, he or she should be given the authority to impose decisions as long as the conflicting parties do not agree on measures. The steering committee would consist of the head of mission, the heads of the different units, and the military commander in the field.[106] The steering committee would be responsible for managing the mission and adopting the necessary strategies. Working groups organized according to different problem areas would have to implement the strategies adopted by the steering committee. There could be a working group dealing with military issues, such as the democratic control of armed forces. Other groups could deal with questions of infrastructure, rebuilding the economy, supporting the government, and handling humanitarian affairs. Of course, many problems do not fit into these categories. Working groups would therefore have to coordinate the repatriation of refugees, the establishment of minority laws, the rebuilding of the infrastructure, or the organization and supervision of elections.

Establishing an International Peacebuilding Mission has many advantages: by working together coordination will be greatly facilitated, personal communication will be easier, and the sharing of resources will improve efficiency. Situation analysis will be facilitated, because information flows will

Figure 9.2 International Peacebuilding Mission

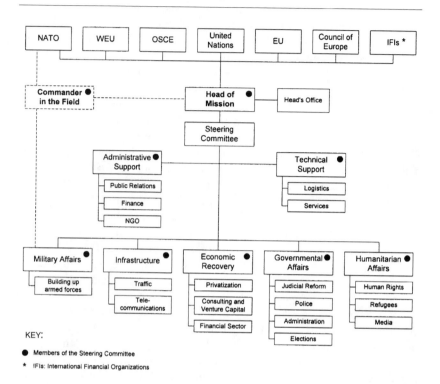

KEY:

● Members of the Steering Committee

* IFIs: International Financial Organizations

come together in the steering committee, which could also be given the right to rely on satellite information provided by NATO and the WEU. A mission of this kind would be organized jointly, thereby handling difficulties in logistics or the provision of additional resources more easily. Finally, there should be no doubt that the image of an international community acting coherently will influence the parties in a conflict.

Strengthening ESDI

It has become fashionable to demand the establishment of a European Security and Defense Identity. However, there is not a clear-cut definition of what ESDI stands for, and adequate strategies have not been presented to translate the concept into action. NATO's Berlin Council decision to implement the concept of CJTFs made clear that ESDI should be set up within NATO. Although this decision is to be welcomed, conceptual problems remain, because establishing the ESDI concept means many different things. First, it requires strengthening the European pillar of NATO. Second, it presupposes the readiness of European states to conduct non–Article 5 operations within the WEU or the EU. Third, conducting such operations requires a necessary agreement within the CFSP. Finally, establishing ESDI entails various transformation processes that are necessary in order to reorient national forces and improve their compatibility and interoperability.

In order to make the ESDI concept reality, several questions must be answered. European states have to first define their interests. Without defining the aims of the CFSP, there will be no ESDI. This also requires countries to clarify operational procedures between the EU, WEU, and NATO.[107] Second, military cooperation raises some fundamental legal questions that must be resolved in order to guarantee the operability of multinational contingents. This requires harmonization with regard to the authority of command, disciplinary law, basic rights of military personnel, the right of appeal, and provisions for the safety and stationing of troops abroad. The discussion of harmonizing European military law should not exclude the United States, the CEE countries, or neutral states. Therefore, a binding document on military cooperation should be put on the agenda of the EAPC or the OSCE.

Third, there is no doubt that the political goal of setting up multinational contingents and the requirements for standardization influence defense-related industries. But Europe still lacks the dramatic changes the U.S. defense industry has undergone in recent years. It is only too obvious that Europe's defense industry suffers from too many actors competing with each other, from governments still adhering to the idea of nationally independent defense companies, and from the absence of a common defense market. Several steps appear necessary. First, European governments will have to encourage international cooperation by establishing an adequate framework within the EU, by privatizing state-owned companies, and by encouraging transnational mergers and acquisitions. Second, experts warn that a growing technology gap between the U.S. and European defense industries could lead to problems in integrating their armies. Cooperation across the Atlantic and with CEE defense companies should therefore be strongly encouraged. Third, new methods have to be found to integrate the industry. The maintenance and modification of existing equipment is still a predominantly national concern that has a huge potential for increasing cooperation and cutting costs. Although outsourcing may ease the pressure on national defense budgets, there are fears of industrial dependency.[108] These fears might block the decisions needed to Europeanize defense-related industries. In order for Europe to envisage common solutions, enduring political support will be indispensable.

Finally, new risks—such as the proliferation of weapons of mass destruction, the technological vulnerability of the information society, and the problem of selling dual-use technologies to rogue states—have to be interpreted as questions that demand common European answers. The European Coal and

Steel Community rested on the assumption that war can be avoided by supranationalizing coal and steel and by inducing cooperation between former enemies. Following this principle, the establishment of a common European armaments market is a logical and long overdue step. However, it may not be enough. The new risks demand the establishment of cooperative frameworks to deal with the questions of biotechnology and genetics, microelectronics and microtechnology, and nuclear and information technology.[109] These industries have the potential to initiate cooperation between the committed elites not only in Western Europe but also in the United States and the CEE countries. This would extend the neofunctional logic into the twenty-first century and beyond the EU itself.

CONCLUSION

I have argued that multilateralism based on a liberal worldview, corresponding international rules, democratic principles, and the rule of law form the core of Europe's security architecture. Such a structure can be established by following four different paths. Democratic peace increases the probability that states will solve disputes peacefully; institutions create order by providing basic rules for the conduct of international relations; leadership initiates cooperation; and integration helps to overcome renationalization tendencies. Against this background, the contributions of Europe's security organizations can be summarized in three points. First, Europe's security organizations tend to work on the basis of identical core values, thereby paving the ground for Europe's security architecture in the twenty-first century. Second, Europe's security organizations strengthen the four pillars of my concept and influence member states' policies in economic, military, and political matters. Although the process of transferring sovereignty to supranational bodies is most advanced in economics, military and political issues are still solved by intergovernmentalism. However, military cooperation begins to encroach upon sovereignty. Third, coordination between these three issue areas must be substantially improved. In essence, this means shifting interests from the national to the international level. Let me elaborate on all three points.

Finding No. 1

By applying a set of common norms that potential member states have to respect, Europe's security organizations tend to frame the normative foundation of Europe's security architecture.

Being part of a democratic union requires governments to fulfill certain criteria, to which the OSCE, the EU, NATO, and the WEU subscribe:

1. Democratic principles, the rule of law, separation of powers, organizing free elections, and guaranteeing human rights;
2. Liberal economic constitutions that guarantee free trade, competition, and social justice;
3. Efficient political, judicial, and administrative structures that are indispensable for supranational rules to become effective;
4. Standardized military doctrines, equipment, and training of military personnel facilitating the establishment of multinational contingents; and
5. Democratic control of armed forces, ensuring that they are constitutionally governed and do not form a state within the state.

According to the theory of democratic peace, these principles guide a democracy's foreign policy. We can therefore define a set of norms that form the core of Europe's multilateral security architecture:

1. Existence of democratic domestic structures;
2. Openness with regard to all political processes, especially the enlargement of Europe's security organizations;
3. Transparency and predictability with regard to all political plans and as a condition of the way governments and organizations should behave;
4. Reciprocity as a condition applicable to all international agreements;
5. Flexibility as the basic principle that structures cooperation between states and organizations;
6. Abstention from the use of force to conduct foreign relations;
7. Sufficiency as a principle in the forming of defensive, not offensive, armed forces; and
8. Cooperation in order to resolve the challenges ahead.

Finding No. 2

Europe's security organizations strengthen the four pillars of my concept and influence member states' policies in economic, military, and political matters.

Apart from the economic integration taking place within the EC, there is no sovereignty transfer to supranational bodies such as the European Commission or the ECJ. Since they are endowed with certain powers, they can act as institutional leaders. By setting up specific standards of admission to the Union and its common market, these institutions contribute to the harmonization of the policies set by the member states. Whatever the positive effects of that process, we must not forget that the CEE countries find themselves in an economic, societal, and political transformation process. Because these countries are more prone to the negative effects of economic integration and worldwide competition, their political parties face heavy turbulence on the way to the common market. This requires the international community to coordinate its aid programs more effectively, thereby giving special emphasis to eliminating contradicting economic and political expectations. From a political point of view, higher inflation may seem a tolerable way to reduce unemployment and to boost the economy. From an economic point of view, however, rising prices increase interest rates, put pressure on the exchange rate, and worsen a country's economic performance in the long run.[110] Hence, it is time to form special working groups consisting of experts from all organizations involved in the rebuilding of the former communist countries.

Normally, one would not refer to military issues as an example of the transfer of sovereignty. I have shown that military cooperation is beginning to encroach upon sovereignty. In order to guarantee the operability of multinational units, governments cede sovereignty silently. Military cooperation therefore constitutes a large portion of Europe's stability and security. This is due to common procedures of standardization, the harmonization of defense planning, the adjustment of doctrines and the structure of armed forces, day-to-day workings in NATO's integrated military structure and in multinational military contingents, cooperation in PfP, and the military verification and security-building regimes that increase transparency and augment predictability.

With regard to politics, the last of our three security dimensions, there is no doubt that intergovernmentalism still reigns over supranationalism, particularly in defense and security policy. In contrast to the EC and NATO, the OSCE and the CFSP still face collaboration problems, which is an indication of a relatively high degree of disagreement among the member states. As long as collaboration is the dominant problem, political progress will be slow.

Despite the supremacy of intergovernmentalism, there are clear but faint signs of a departure from the status quo. These include the OSCE's decision to treat aspects of its human dimension not as exclusive issues in the participating states but rather as a matter of legitimate interest of all OSCE states; the possibility of conciliation directed by the Senior Council or the Ministerial Council; and the possibility of imposing political and economic sanctions in the case of enduring violations of the principles in the human dimension. There are also signs of a growing willingness to act jointly in the case of noncompliance with basic norms and principles. Furthermore, the OSCE has developed some highly innovative instruments of preventive diplomacy (HCNM, long-term missions, Representative on Freedom of the Media) that have a great potential for influencing local parties. Although successful, their leadership potential and their coordination with other international organizations can be improved. One promising example is the Pact on Stability initiated by former French Prime Minister Eduard Balladur, organized by the EU as a joint action, and now administered by the OSCE. Along these lines, I suggested establishing the position of an ombudsperson for European law, active in states that are to join the EU and where the OSCE has already deployed long-term missions.

Similarly, the CFSP would benefit greatly by increased application of community procedures. This means more than majority voting. When talking about the Union's core competence, I showed that one of its greatest assets is its possibility to adopt package deals. As an example, I referred to the Europeanization of defense-related industries and argued that future security challenges, such as the proliferation of weapons of mass destruction and dual-use technology, should be regarded as questions requiring joint action at a European level. In order to make substantial progress with the CFSP, European governments should change their attitudes. Instead of waiting for external crises to test the functioning of CFSP mechanisms, they should create more economic incentives that will increase pressure and require political action.

Aside from sovereignty transfer and leadership, I have also argued that institutions create rules and influence the behavior of governments. Rule orientation depends on the institutional structure underlying each of the three above-mentioned dimensions: economic integration in the EC and defense in NATO follow the logic of rational cost-benefit thinking. Because the costs of rule transgression can be calculated more or less clearly (e.g., lawsuits against a government for nonaction before the ECJ), governments tend to play by the rules. Where collaboration problems predominate, such as in the CFSP, the OSCE, and the WEU, governments act on the grounds of normative-cognitive institutions. In these cases, playing by the rules depends either on expectations of behavior or learning processes. When it comes to common goals, these organizations are much more demanding, because realizing common goals demands that collaboration problems be overcome. Hence, it is no surprise that political progress is slower and deviation is higher than in cases where regulative institutions reign. Furthermore, it should be added that both the OSCE and the CFSP are not supranational, that is, their norms are applicable solely to the participating states and the Community's bodies and not to legal or natural persons. Therefore, the ECJ and the Court of Arbitration and Conciliation in Geneva play a subordinate role in monitoring norm compliance. As long as this is the case, the promotion of a community of law requires that national courts interact closely with international or supranational courts.

Finding No. 3

The greatest challenge lies in increasing the coordination of activities taking place within the political, economic, and military dimension of security.

The ultimate strategy of transferring sovereignty to the Union in order to step up its efforts in the CFSP will be blocked for years to come. However, different instruments developed by the OSCE since 1990 and the multinationalization of armed forces have begun to encroach upon sovereignty. This is exactly the reason why adapting and enlarging NATO was the right strategy. Engaging the former communist armed forces in joint defense planning, training, and field operations, working with them in integrated command structures, and increasing common understanding will extend the habit of cooperation to these countries. This will lead to committed elites in the military sector who act according to democratic principles all across Europe.

Professionalizing peacebuilding and improving institutional relations serve various purposes. Strengthening Europe's security organizations is necessary, first of all, because only strong institutions can support governments effectively and efficiently. Second, organizations may act as leaders. So far their leadership has been subordinated to their members' interests. Since stability and security are collective goods that tend to be in short supply, strengthening Europe's institutional network is a necessary first step. Because institutions facilitate the shaping of common strategies and positions, they are indispensable to the defining of international interests. Thus, they should be strengthened and given more independence. But as long as governments do not change their attitudes toward international politics, every institutional effort will remain limited. In the coming years, there must be a fundamental shift in the way problems are addressed. Although we have already begun to see that transnational risks and problems can be addressed only multilaterally, national interests remain the common standard for evaluating international actions. This will no longer suffice. We need more than international instruments—we also need international interests.

NOTES

This chapter grew out of the author's dissertation, Heiko Borchert (1999b) *Europas Sicherheitsarchitektur: Erfolgsfaktoren—Bestandsaufnahme—Handlungsbedarf* (Baden-Baden: Nomos), which was conducted within National Research Program 42 sponsored by the Swiss National Science Foundation. I gratefully acknowledge the foundation's financial support (grant #4042–047350). Earlier versions of the chapter were presented in 1998 at the ECPR/ISA Joint Meeting in Vienna and at the Fourth Annual Graduate Student Conference, organized by the Center for German and European Studies, Georgetown University, Washington, D.C. I thank Jürg Martin Gabriel, Stanley Sloan, Celeste Wallander, and Ellen Russon for helpful comments.

1. Daniel H. Deudney and G. John Ikenberry (1996) *Structural Liberalism: The Nature and Sources of Postwar Western Political Order* (Philadelphia: University of Pennsylvania, Christopher H. Browne Center for International Politics), pp. 5–42.

2. John G. Ruggie (1996) *Winning the Peace* (New York: Columbia University Press), p. 20; (1993) "Multilateralism: The Anatomy of an Institution," in John Gerard Ruggie (ed.) *Multilateralism Matters: The Theory and Praxis of an Institutional Form* (New York: Columbia University Press), pp. 14–22.

EUROPEAN SECURITY

3. Quoted in Ruggie (1993) *Winning the Peace*, p. 11.
4. For a more detailed account of the theoretical arguments, see Borchert (1999b) *Europas Sicherheitsarchitektur*, pp. 71–152.
5. Brian L. Job (1997) "Matters of Multilateralism: Implications for Regional Conflict Management," in David A. Lake and Patrick M. Morgan (eds.) *Regional Orders: Building Security in a New World* (University Park: The Pennsylvania State University Press), p. 177.
6. Michael W. Doyle (1983) "Kant: Liberal Legacies and Foreign Affairs," in *Philosophy and Public Affairs* 12, no. 3 (Summer): 205–235; Colin H. Kahl (1998–1999) "Constructing a Separate Peace: Constructivism, Collective Liberal Identity, and Democratic Peace," *Security Studies* 8, nos. 2–3 (1998–1999): 94–144; Bruce M. Russett (1993) *Grasping the Democratic Peace: Principles for the Post–Cold War World* (Princeton: Princeton University Press).
7. For a general introduction into the different institutionalisms in political science, see B. Guy Peters (1999) *Institutional Theory in Political Science: The "New Institutionalism"* (London: Pinter).
8. Robert E. Goodin (1996) "Institutions and Their Design," in Robert E. Goodin (ed.) *The Theory of Institutional Design* (Cambridge: Cambridge University Press), pp. 1–53, esp. 16.
9. I define *leadership* as a person's ability to convince others to act as he would like them to. *Leadership* has to be distinguished from *dominance* or *power-wielding*, because it rests on a liberal worldview and common expectations, needs, and goals. Thus, a leader has the ability to initiate actions that will be followed by others and can even enforce such actions. Followers respect the leader's position as legitimated on the basis of a liberal worldview. Followers appreciate the leader deciding on their behalf and are occasionally prepared to change their own preferences if deemed necessary. For a similar understanding, see Burns MacGregor (1997) *Leadership* (New York: Harper and Row), p. 19. On the interplay between followers and leaders, see Jarrod Wiener (1995a) "'Hegemonic' Leadership, Naked Emperor, or Worship of False Gods?" *European Journal of International Relations* 1, no. 2 (June): 219–243; Andrew Fenton Cooper et al. (1991) "Bound to Follow? Leadership and Followership in the Gulf Conflict," *Political Science Quarterly* 106, no. 3 (Fall): 391–410, esp. 398ff.
10. Wiener (1995a) "'Hegemonic' Leadership'"; Jarrod Wiener (1995b) "Leadership, the United Nations, and the New World Order," in Dimitri Bourantonis and Jarrod Wiener (eds.) (1995) *The United Nations in the New World Order: The World Organization at Fifty* (New York: St. Martin's), pp. 4–163; Jarrod Wiener (1995c) *Making Rules in the Uruguay Round of the GATT: A Study of International Leadership* (Aldershot, UK: Dartmouth).
11. Most useful overviews of the vast literature on integration theory can be found in Claus Giering (1997) *Europa zwischen Zweckverband und Superstaat: Die Entwicklung der politikwissenschaftlichen Integrationstheorie im Prozess der europäischen Integration* (Bonn: Europa Union Verlag); Walter Mattli (1999) *The Logic of Regional Integration: Europe and Beyond* (Cambridge: Cambridge University Press), pp. 19–40; Andrew Moravcsik (1998) *The Choice for Europe: Social Purpose and State Power from Messina to Maastricht* (Ithaca: Cornell University Press), pp. 18–85; and Michael O'Neill (1996) *The Politics of European Integration: A Reader* (London: Routledge), pp. 21–53, 122–144.
12. For simplicity, I also use the acronym *OSCE* when talking about the former Conference on Security and Cooperation in Europe (CSCE), which was renamed in 1994.

13. We are used to referring to the *European Union* as denoting most of the institutions created within the European integration process. For clarification, it should be kept in mind that the European Union rests on three pillars: the European Communities (themselves consisting of the European Community, the European Coal and Steal Community, and the European Atomic Energy Community), the Common Foreign and Security Policy, and cooperation in the fields of justice and home affairs. Although the European Union is dominated by intergovernmentalism, the European Communities are dominated by supranationalism. I will therefore either refer to the *European Union* or the *European Communities* to highlight this distinction.

14. For a recent empirical study that describes the positive impact of membership in international organizations on peaceful external relations, see Bruce Russett, John Oneal, and David P. Davis (1998) "The Third Leg of the Kantian Tripod for Peace: International Organizations and Militarized Disputes, 1950–1985," *International Organization* 52, no. 3 (Summer): 441–467.

15. Russett (1993) *Grasping the Democratic Peace*, p. 42.

16. For a more general discussion of the role of international organizations in setting up and diffusing norms, see Martha Finnemore (1996) *National Interests in International Society* (Ithaca: Cornell University Press), pp. 34–127; and Michael Barnett and Martha Finnemore (1999) "The Politics, Power, and Pathologies of International Organizations," *International Organization* 53, no. 4 (Autumn): 699–732.

17. "Document of the Copenhagen Meeting of the Conference on the Human Dimension of the CSCE, Copenhagen," June 29, 1990; "Document of the Moscow Meeting of the Conference on the Human Dimension of the CSCE, Moscow," October 3, 1991. All OSCE documents are available online at <http://www.osce.org/docs/index.htm>.

18. "Code of Conduct on Politico-Military Aspects of Security," adopted as part 4 of the Budapest Summit Document, Budapest, December 6, 1994.

19. Jonathan Dean (1996) "Der OSZE-Verhaltenskodex—eine gute Idee, unvollkommen ausgeführt, ungenügend nachgearbeitet," in *Institut für Friedensforschung und Sicherheitspolitik an der Universität Hamburg* (Hrsg.) *OSZE-Jahrbuch 1996* (Baden-Baden: Nomos Verlagsgesellschaft), pp. 309–318, esp. p. 317.

20. For a comparison of the contributions of the ECJ and the ECHR, see Laurence Helfer and Anne-Marie Slaughter (1997) "Toward a Theory of Effective Supranational Adjudication," *Yale Law Journal* 107, no. 2 (November): 290–298.

21. "Document of the Moscow Meeting of the Conference on the Human Dimension of the CSCE," Moscow, October 3, 1991, preamble, italics added.

22. Emmanuel Adler (1997) "Seizing the Middle Ground: Constructivism" *World Politics: European Journal of International Relations* 3, no. 3 (September): 319–364, esp. p. 345.

23. "Founding Act on Mutual Relations, Cooperation, and Security Between NATO and the Russian Federation," Paris, May 27 1997, chap. 4, para. 8; <http://www.nato.int/docu/comm/m970527/uk-text.htm>.

24. These instruments are foreseen by the Treaty on Conventional Forces in Europe, the Vienna Documents, the Open Skies Treaty (all available online at the OSCE website) and the Chemical Weapons Convention <http://www.opcw.org/cwcdoc.htm>.

25. UN Charter, Article 1:1 and Article 24:1.

26. "Prague Document on Further Development of CSCE Institutions and Structures," Prague, January 30–31, 1992, chap. 4, para. 16.

27. Ingo Peters (1994) "Normenzund Institutionenbildung der KSZE im Widerstreit politischer Interessen: Die Durchsetzung des Gewaltverzichts als Prüfstein für die KSZE," in Bernard von Plate (ed.) *Europa auf dem Wege zur kollektiven Sicherheit? Konzeptionelle und organisatorische Entwicklungen der sicherheitspolitischen Institutionen Europas* (Baden-Baden: Nomos Verlagsgesellschaft), pp. 155–186, esp. p. 175.

28. Helsinki Document, June 10, 1992, chap. 3, para. 20.

29. NATO adopted its decision in Oslo and Brussels in June and December 1992. The WEU adopted its Petersberg Declaration in June 1992, thereby tasking the WEU to conduct operations of conflict prevention, crisis management, and peacekeeping.

30. Consolidated Version of the Treaty on European Union (CTEU), Articles 6–7, quoted according to the version reprinted in *European Union: Consolidated Versions* (Luxembourg: Office for Official Publications of the European Communities, 1997).

31. Chemical Weapons Convention, Article 12:2.

32. Suspension and expulsion are foreseen by the UN Charter. The OSCE can suspend a participating state. Even the European Bank for Reconstruction and Development (EBRD) has the possibility to suspend the membership of a member state (agreement establishing the EBRD, Article 8:3; <http://www.ebrd.com/english/Public/Basic documents/basic1.htm>.

33. UN Charter, Article 52; Washington Treaty, Article 5; Modified Brussels Treaty, Article 5.

34. UN Charter, Article 42.

35. The Czech Republic, Estonia, Hungary, Poland, and Slovenia participated in the first round of admission talks.

36. Presidency Conclusions, Helsinki European Summit, SN 300/99, December 10–11, 1999, paras. 6–10. Romania, Slovakia, Latvia, Lithuania, and Bulgaria will participate in the second round of admission talks.

37. *Agenda 2000* (Luxembourg: Office for Official Publications of the European Communities), pp. 69–79.

38. Presidency Conclusions, Helsinki European Summit, paras. 12–13.

39. Armenia, Azerbaijan, Belarus, Georgia, Kaszakhstan, Kyrghyz Republic, Moldova, Russia, and Ukraine.

40. In November 1992, Greece accessed as a new member, Denmark and Ireland as observers, Iceland, Norway, and Turkey as associated members. Since 1994, ten Central and Eastern European countries have accessed the WEU as associate partners.

41. The WEAG comprises Belgium, Denmark, France, Germany, Greece, Italy, Luxembourg, the Netherlands, Norway, Portugal, Spain, Turkey, and the United Kingdom.

42. "Declaration of the NATO Ministerial Council," November 7–8, 1991, S-1(91)86, para. 3.

43. CSCE Communication no. 166, Prague, June 1, 1993, and A/RES/47/5, October 13, 1993.

44. Thomas Buchsbaum (1993) "The CSCE and International Organizations: Expanding Cooperation with the Council of Europe," in Michael R. Lucas (ed.) *The CSCE in the 1990s: Constructing European Security and Cooperation* (Baden-Baden: Nomos Verlagsgesellschaft), pp. 125–142, esp. p. 131; Victor-Yves Ghebali (1996) *L'OSCE dans l'Europe post-communiste, 1990–1996: Vers une identité paneuropéenne de sécurité* (Bruxelles: Bruylant), pp. 547–565.

45. For more on this, see also the recommendations by the Assembly of the CoE in Recommendation 1381 (1998), General Policy: Council of Europe and OSCE; <http://www.stars.coe.fr/ta/ta98/erec1381.htm>.

46. Fraser Cameron (1993) "The European Community and the CSCE," in Michael R. Lucas (ed.) *The CSCE in the 1990s*, pp. 265–277; Heinrich Schneider (1997) "The Twelve/Fifteen's Conference Diplomacy: Has the CSCE/OSCE Remained a Successful Platform?" in Elfriede Regelsberger et al. (eds.) *Foreign Policy of the European Union: From EPC to CFSP and Beyond* (Boulder: Lynne Rienner), pp. 237–262.

47. Hans van den Broek (1996) "The Council of Europe and the European Union: Complementing Each Other," in *The Challenges of a Greater Europe. The Council of Europe and Democratic Security* (Strasbourg: Council of Europe), pp. 173–175.

48. *Partnership and Commitment: The European Union and the United Nations* (Luxembourg: Office for Official Publications of the European Communities, 1995), pp. 10-11.

49. Ingo Peters (1996) "Die Beziehungen der OSZE zu anderen internationalen Organisationen," in Institut für Friedensforschung und Sicherheitspolitik an der Universität Hamburg (ed.) *OSZE-Jahrbuch 1996* (Baden-Baden: Nomos Verlagsgesellschaft), pp. 417–434, esp. p. 425.

50. Assembly of WEU, WEU Military Committee, Document 1591, December 1, 1997, paras. 74–84.

51. Washington Summit Communiqué, Washington, D.C., NAC-S(99)64, April 24, 1999, paras. 9–10.

52. This has raised the question of whether the European Council is abolishing rather than integrating the WEU, because it now creates bodies that already exist within the WEU. See especially: Assembly of WEU, "WEU After the Washington and Cologne Summits—Reply to the Annual Report of the Council," Document 1652, June 10, 1999, paras. 59–64.

53. "Beyond IFOR, SFOR, DFOR: After the Combatant Comes the Legislator," North Atlantic Assembly, Sub-Committee on Defense and Security, AR 94 DSC/DC(93)3, April 16, 1998, paras. 36–43; Jean Klein (1998) "Interface Between NATO/WEU and UN/OSCE," in Michael Brenner (ed.) *NATO and Collective Security* (Basingstoke, UK: Macmillan), pp. 249–274.

54. His mandate derives from Annex 11 of the Dayton Accord <http://www.ohr.int>, from the London Peace Implementation Conference of December 8–9, 1995, and Security Council Resolution 1031 of December 15, 1995.

55. Collaboration problems occur when states want to cooperate but, due to different interests, do not agree on the way used to achieve cooperation. In contrast, coordination problems occur when states have the same interests. See Helga Haftendorn (1997) "Sicherheitsinstitutionen in den internationalen Beziehungen: Eine Einführung," in Helga Haftendorn and Otto Keck (eds.) *Kooperation jenseits von Hegemonie und Bedrohung. Sicherheitsinstitutionen in den internationalen Beziehungen* (Baden-Baden: Nomos), pp. 11–34, esp. pp. 16–18; Arthur A. Stein (1990) *Why Nations Cooperate: Circumstance and Choice in International Relations* (Ithaca: Cornell University Press), pp. 25–54; Celeste Wallander (1999) *Mortal Friends, Best Enemies: German-Russian Cooperation After the Cold War* (Ithaca: Cornell University Press), pp. 28–32. Regulative, normative, and cognitive institutions describe three different approaches to influencing an actor's behavior. Regulative institutions constrain and regularize behavior according to a rational cost-benefit analysis; normative institutions create expectations of behavior, thereby leading to compliance; cognitive institutions stress the importance of social interaction. They assume that the actor, his environment, and his expectations are socially constructed. In this case, compliance results from social interaction and learning. This distinction is developed by W. Richard Scott (1995) *Institutions and Organizations* (Thousand Oaks, Calif.: Sage), pp. 34–45.

56. Shaun R. Barcavage (1996–1997) "NGOs in the System of European Security," *ODIHR Bulletin* 5, no. 1 (Winter): 24–25; Rachel J. Brett (1992–1993) "NGOs and the Human Dimension of the CSCE," *ODIHR Bulletin* 1, no. 1 (Winter): 1–5; Margeret E. Keck and Kathryn Sikkink (1998), *Activists Beyond Borders: Advocacy Networks in International Politics* (Ithaca: Cornell University Press), pp. 1–38.

57. Brett (1992–1993), "NGOs and the Human Dimension"; Ritva Grönick (1993) "The CSCE and Non-Governmental Organizations," in Michael R. Lucas (ed.) *The CSCE in the 1990s: Constructing European Security and Cooperation* (Baden-Baden: Nomos Verlagsgesellschaft), pp. 227–248; Paul Gutlove and Gordon Thompson (1995) "The Potential for Cooperation by the OSCE and Non-Governmental Actors on Conflict Management," *Helsinki Monitor* 6, no. 3 (Fall): 52–64; OSCE, *OSCE Handbook* (Vienna: OSCE), pp. 88–90; Manne Wängeborg (1995) "The OSCE at 20: Breakthrough for 'Citizen Diplomacy'? Towards Closer OSCE-NGO Interaction?" *European Security* 4, no. 3 (Autumn): 393–399.

58. Fraser Cameron (1997) "Where the European Commission Comes In: From the Single European Act to Maastricht," in Elfriede Regelsberger et al. (eds.) *Foreign Policy of the European Union: From EPC to CFSP and Beyond* (Boulder: Lynne Rienner), pp. 99–108, esp. p. 105ff.

59. For a similar analysis, see Bob Reinalda and Bertjan Verbeek (1999) "Autonomous Policy Making by International Organizations: Purpose, Outline, and Results," in Bob Reinalda and Bertjan Verbeek (eds.) *Autonomous Policy Making by International Organizations* (London: Routledge), pp. 1–8.

60. However, during the 1999 Istanbul Summit the participating states decided to strengthen the OSCE's capacities by forming so-called Rapid Expert Assistance and Cooperation Teams (REACT), by establishing an Operation Center in Vienna to facilitate effective preparation and planning of field operations, and by establishing a Preparatory Committee designed to strengthen the consultation process.

61. Ingo Peters (1997) "Von der KSZE zur OSZE: Überleben in der Nische kooperativer Sicherheit," in Helga Haftendorn and Otto Keck (1997) *Kooperation jenseits von Hegemonie und Bedrohung*, pp. 57–100, esp. p. 99.

62. Reprinted in Assembly of WEU, "WEU and European Defense: Beyond Amsterdam," Document 1636, March 15, 1999, appendix. For an analysis of the document's importance with special emphasis on the British strategy, see Simon Duke (2000) *The Elusive Quest for European Security: From EDC to CFSP* (Basingstoke, UK: Macmillan), pp. 292–316, esp. p. 313ff.

63. Presidency Conclusions, Cologne European Summit, SN 150/99, June 3–4, 1999, annex 3: European Declaration on Strengthening Common European Policy on Security and Defence, pp. 33–42; Presidency Conclusions, Helsinki European Summit, paras. 25–28.

64. Paul Cornish (1997) *Partnership in Crisis: The U.S., Europe and the Fall and Rise of NATO* (London: Pinter, for the Royal Institute of International Affairs), pp. 81–111.

65. Gary Hamel and C. K. Prahalad (1994) *Competing for the Future* (Boston: Harvard Business School Press), pp. 223–233.

66. Emanuel Adler has argued that one of the most remarkable features "of the OSCE security model is how extensively it has 'traveled' throughout Europe. In other words, were the OSCE to cease to exist today, it still would continue to 'live' on, embedded in the practices of other European multilateral institutions." See Emanuel Adler (1998) "Seeds of Peaceful Change: The OSCE as a Pluralistic Security Community," in Emanuel Adler and Michael N. Barnett (eds.) *Security Communities* (Cambridge: Cambridge University Press), pp. 119–160, esp. p. 143.

67. "Implementing European Union Strategy on Defence-Related Industries," COM (97) 583 final, November 12, 1997, and "Action Plan for the Defence-Related Industries," COM (97) 583 final/Annex II, November 12, 1997.

68. Celeste A. Wallander and Robert O. Keohane (1999) "Risk, Threat, and Security Institutions," in Helga Haftendorn, Robert O. Keohane, and Celeste A. Wallander (eds.) *Imperfect Unions: Security Institutions over Time and Space* (Oxford: Oxford University Press), pp. 21–47, esp. pp. 22ff., 32–35, 40–46.

69. Helen Drake (1995) "Political Leadership and European Integration: The Case of Jacques Delors," *Western European Politics* 18, no. 1 (January): 140–160.

70. Max van der Stoel (1994) "The Role of the CSCE High Commissioner on National Minorities in CSCE Conflict Prevention," Address to the seminar entitled "The CSCE as a Security Tool in Europe: Which Role for the CSCE?" Brussels, June 4, 1994, p. 6.

71. Oran R. Young (1991) "Political Leadership and Regime Foundation: On the Development of Institutions in International Society," *International Organization* 45, no. 3 (Summer): 288–302.

72. Helsinki Decisions, Helsinki, July 10, 1992, chap. 2, para. 25.

73. OECD (1997) *Final Report of the Ad Hoc Working Group on Participatory Development and Good Governance* (Paris: OECD); World Bank (1994) *Governance: The World Bank's Experience* (Washington, D.C.: World Bank).

74. Gert Wessels and Günter Winzen (1996) "Interoperabilität und Ausrüstung," in Ernst Martin (Hrsg.) *Eurokorps und Europäische Einigung* (Bonn: Edition Zeitgeschichte), pp. 375–418.

75. NATO (1995) *Study on NATO Enlargement* (Brussels: NATO), paras. 75–78.

76. James Robert Huntley (1998) *Pax Democratica: A Strategy for the Twenty-first Century* (Basingstoke, UK: Macmillan), pp. 84ff.

77. Gregory Flynn and Henry Farrell (1999) "Piecing Together the Democratic Peace: The CSCE and the 'Construction' of Security in Post–Cold War Europe," *International Organizations* 53, no. 3 (Summer): 505–536.

78. Arnhild Spence and David Spence (1998) "The Common Foreign and Security Policy from Maastricht to Amsterdam," in Kjell A. Eliassen (ed.) *Foreign and Security Policy in the European Union* (London: Sage), pp. 48–58; Matthias Dembinski (1997) *Langer Anlaufkurzer Sprung: Die Aussenpolitik der Europäischen Union nach der Reform von Amsterdam* (Frankfurt: Hessische Stiftung für Friedenszund Konfliktforschung [HSFK-Report Nr. 7]), pp. 24–41.

79. Six staff officers from Austria, Bulgaria, Estonia, Finland, Romania, and Slovenia work closely with five staff officers from NATO members to form the Partnership for Peace Staff Element. Similar Partnership for Peace Staff Elements are also being established at seven other NATO military headquarters to support their staffs' work in all PfP efforts, including the development of PfP-related programs and the planning for NATO/PfP exercises and operations. See NATO, IMS Press Release 13.98, Brussels, September 4, 1998.

80. Lawrence Freedman and Anand Menon (1997) "Conclusion: Defence, States, and Integration," in Jolyon Howorth and Anand Menon (eds.) *The European Union and National Defence Policies* (London: Routledge), pp. 155–172, esp. p. 168.

81. The assembly's decisions are not binding for other OSCE bodies, and the court and the Conciliation Commission have so far not been appealed to.

82. CTEU, Article 23:2.

83. "Report on the Role of the Union in the World: Implementation of the Common Foreign and Security Policy for 1998," PE 299.885/fin, April 23, 1999, p. 21.

84. Statement by an Austrian representative at an OSCE workshop organized by the Center for OSCE Research in Hamburg, January 6, 2000.

85. Matthias Pechstein and Christian Koenig (1998) *Die Europäische Union: Die Verträge von Maastricht und Amsterdam,* 2nd ed. (Tübingen: Mohr Siebeck), pp. 106–122, 125–132, 145–152, 168–169, 174–176; Christoph Thun-Hohenstein (1998) *Der Vertrag von Amsterdam: Die neue Verfassung der EU* (Wien: Manz), pp. 62–77.

86. CTEU, Article 13:2.

87. CTEU, Article 15.

88. CTEU, Article 14:1.

89. Thun-Hohenstein (1998) *Der Vertrag von Amsterdam,* p. 68, and WEU, Declaration no. 3 ("Declaration of Western European Union on the Role of Western European Union and Its Relations with the European Union and with the Atlantic Alliance"), July 22, 1997, para. 6.

90. Pechstein and Koenig (1998) *Die Europäische Union,* p. 176; Jochen A. Frowein (1997) "Auf dem Weg zu einer gemeinsamen Sicherheitszund Verteidigungspolitik," in Christian Tomuschat (ed.) *Rechtsprobleme einer europäischen Sicherheitszund Verteidigungsidentität* (Heidelberg: C. F. Müller Verlag), pp. 11–18, esp. p. 13ff.

91. Markus Zöckeler (1995) "Germany in Collective Security Systems— Anything Goes?" *European Journal of International Law* 6, no. 2 (Spring): 274–286. The court's ruling (BVerfGE 90, 286) may be accessed at <http://www.uni-wuerzburg.de/dfr/bv090286.html>.

92. BVerfGE 90, 286 (346 f.).

93. Bernhard Gertz (1994) "Plädoyer für eine fortschrittliche Wehrverfassung in Europa," in Müller (1994) *Eurokorps und Europäische Einigung,* pp. 464–476; Paul Klein (1993) *Probleme in multinationalen militärischen Verbänden am Beispiel der deutsch-französischen Brigade* (München: Sozialwissenschaftliches Institut der Bundeswehr [SOWI-Arbeitspapier Nr. 83]), pp. 6–8; Torsten Stein (1997) "Rechtsfragen des Eurokorps und der deutsch-französischen Brigade," in Christian Tomuschat (ed.) *Rechtsprobleme einer europäischen Sicherheitszund Verteidigungspolitik* (Heidelberg: C. F. Müller Verlag), pp. 53–68, esp. pp. 60–64; Philipp Wassenberg (1999) *Das Eurokorps: Sicherheitsrechtliches Umfeld und völkerrechtliche Bedeutung eines multinationalen Grossverbands* (Baden-Baden: Nomos), pp. 203–214; Joachim Wieland (1999) "Ausländische Vorgesetzte deutscher Soldaten in multinationalen Verbänden," *Neue Zeitschrift für Wehrrecht* 41, no. 4 (July-August): 133–142.

94. Reprinted in *International Legal Materials* 32, no. 2 (March 1993): 551–571.

95. Consolidated Treaty establishing the European Community, Article 10; CTEU, Article 47.

96. Iris Canor (1998) *The Limits of Judicial Discretion in the European Court of Justice: Security and Foreign Affairs Issues* (Baden-Baden: Nomos), pp. 111–130.

97. See <http://www.nato.int/docu/comm/c/561214b.htm>.

98. Statute of the International Court of Justice, Article 36:2 <http://www.icjcij.org/icjwww/ibasicdocuments/ibasictext/ibasicstatute.htm>.

99. For an extensive overview, see Thomas Giegerich (1997) "Ver fassungsrechtliche Kontrolle der auswärtigen Gewalt im europäisch-atlantischen Verfassungsstaat: Vergleichende Bestandsaufnahme mit Blick auf die neuen Demokratien in Mittel–und Osteuropa," *Zeitschrift für ausländisches öffentliches Recht und Völkerrecht* 57, nos. 2–3: 409–564.

100. Assembly of WEU, "A European Intelligence Policy," Document 1517, May 13, 1996, para. 35.

101. Peter Van Rensen (1997) *Informationsbedarf der Gemeinsamen Aussen–und Sicherheitspolitik der Europäischen Union: Ansatzpunkte für eine Bewertung* (Ebenhausen: Stiftung Wissenschaft und Politik [IP 3046]), pp. 19–40.

102. By the way, such a strategy would greatly improve transnational relations, leading to grassroots movements in the business sector. See Charles Weiss (1997) "A Marshall Plan We Can Afford," *Foreign Policy* 106: 94–109.

103. Laurence Helfer and Anne-Marie Slaughter define a *community of law* as a "partially insulated sphere in which legal actors interact based on common interests and values, protected from direct political interference." Helfer and Slaughter (1997), pp. 277, 367–370.

104. This section draws on Heiko Borchert (1999c) "The Kosovo Conflict and the Swiss Contribution," *European Security* 8, no. 4 (Winter): 165–190; Heiko Borchert (1999a) "Den Friedensaufbau professionalisieren—Die institutionelle Zusammenarbeit verbessern," in Institut für Friedensforschung und Sicherheitspolitik an der Universität Hamburg/IFSH (ed.) *OSZE-Jahrbuch 1999* (Baden-Baden: Nomos Verlagsgesellschaft), pp. 459–472.

105. At least on paper, the United Nations Mission in Kosovo (UNMIK) established in June 1999 comes quite close to this proposal. UNMIK is headed by a Special Representative of the Secretary-General who has overall authority to manage the mission and to coordinate the activities of all UN agencies and other international organizations operating as part of UNMIK. Under the coordination of the UN, four international organizations should take the lead in their respective fields of activity. The UN is responsible for interim civil administration; the UNHCR deals with humanitarian affairs; the OSCE is responsible for institution building; and the EU manages reconstruction.

106. Experience in Bosnia-Herzegovina has shown that the military chain of command should not be split. However, in order to guarantee tight coordination between the military and civilian sides, the commander in the field should be part of the steering committee.

107. Assembly of WEU, "WEU: A European Instrument for Crisis-management—Reply to the Annual Report of the Council," Document 1647, May 18, 1999, Appendix.

108. Joachim Rohde (1997) *The Roles of Arms Industries in Supporting Military Operations* (Ebenhausen: Stiftung Wissenschaft und Politik [AP 3045]).

109. For a similar proposal, see David Long (1997) "The CFSP and Beyond: The EU's Territorial and Functional Conceptions of Security," in Michel Fortmann (ed.) *Multilateralism and Regional Security* (Clementsport: Canadian Peacekeeping Press), pp. 166–183, esp. p. 179.

110. For a similar argument, see Roland Paris (1997) "Peacebuilding and the Limits of Liberal Internationalism," *International Security* 22, no. 2 (Fall): 54–89, esp. 73–88.

PART 3

The OSCE

10

An Evaluation of the OSCE's Role in Conflict Management

P. Terrence Hopmann

Since the end of the Cold War, the security situation in Europe has been fundamentally transformed. The military confrontation between the two Cold War alliances of NATO and the Warsaw Pact has been replaced by a political-military fragmentation of the continent, especially on the territory of many of the former socialist states. This disintegration has created a particular dilemma as large multinational states such as the Soviet Union and Yugoslavia have broken up into their constituent republics. Thus, all fifteen of the former Soviet "union republics" emerged by early 1992 as fully sovereign and independent states, admitted into all major international organizations. Four of the six republics of the Federal Republic of Yugoslavia successively declared their independence, leaving a rump federation that consisted only of Serbia and Montenegro.

Yet within most of these newly independent states, persons belonging to national minorities also claimed a right to self-determination and frequently insisted that this should include the possibility of creating a territorial state by which the sovereignty of their nation would be acknowledged. This process became evident as the former Yugoslavia began to fall apart. Yugoslavia was a multiethnic federation created in the aftermath of World War I to unify under one authority those territories, inhabited mostly by southern Slavs, that had been fought over and divided for centuries among three rival empires: the Austro-Hungarian Empire to the northwest, the Russian Empire to the northeast, and the Ottoman Empire to the south. Its peoples also included other nationalities from the Balkan region such as Albanians, Bulgarians, Turks, Greeks, and Roma. After World War II, Yugoslavia consisted of six primary entities: Serbia, Montenegro, Bosnia-Herzegovina, Macedonia, Croatia, and Slovenia, as well as two autonomous regions within Serbia: Vojvodina and

Kosovo. After Marshal Tito's death in 1980, the country was governed by a rotating presidency coming from each of the separate entities. Economic crises and disputes between the federal center and the government of each republic weakened national unity over the next decade. In the chaos following the collapse of communism throughout Central and Eastern Europe, a variety of internal and external pressures came to a head on 15 May 1991, when the Serbian faction in the collective presidency refused to endorse the annual rotation of the chair to the Croatian representative, Stipe Mesic, signaling the effective delegitimization of federal authority and all that it represented.[1]

After Serbia began to crack down on the Albanian majority in Kosovo that was agitating for independence, Slovenia, the most ethnically homogeneous of the former Yugoslavian republics, declared its independence and eventually left the federation with relatively little blood being spilled. Shortly thereafter, however, Croatia also sought independence. In this instance, fighting broke out in several large Serbian enclaves within the country, supported by Serbian authorities in Belgrade and by Serbian paramilitary units; politicians on both sides fanned the flames of extreme nationalism, prompting an escalation of violence. Even more serious violence occurred after Bosnia-Herzegovina became independent from Yugoslavia, as conflict broke out among its three principal components: Serbs (predominantly Eastern Orthodox), Croats (mostly Roman Catholics), and Bosniaks (primarily Muslims). Nationalists from all three communities gained the upper hand and stimulated interethnic violence while preventing the formation of a multiethnic civil society in Bosnia. Next, the Former Yugoslav Republic of Macedonia declared independence; although this did not lead to large-scale violence immediately, the threat of such violence loomed large as a result of tensions between the Macedonian titular majority and the Albanian, Bulgarian, and Greek minority communities. Furthermore, ties between these groups and their neighbors threatened to cause these conflicts to be inflamed by conflicts in other regions or to spill over into those regions throughout the Balkans. Finally, within the Federal Republic of Yugoslavia, after 1992 composed only of Serbia and Montenegro, ethnic tensions appeared in three regions in particular: Kosovo (Albanians, mostly Muslims), Sandjak (Muslims), and Vojvodina (Hungarians). These tensions exploded into large-scale violence in 1998, which in turn provoked an eleven-week bombing campaign by NATO throughout the Federal Republic of Yugoslavia beginning in April 1999, followed by the establishment of a UN administration in Kosovo enforced by a NATO-led multinational force.

The breakup of the Soviet Union was also characterized by a significant number of violent and near-violent disintegrative processes. The Soviet Union was a multinational state that included over a hundred peoples, cultures, and languages. Although Russians mostly dominated the central institutions of the state, dozens of administrative units were created on the basis of ethnicity.

When the Soviet Union collapsed in 1991, the union republics, the most important of these national units, became independent and sovereign states. As soon as the possibility of independence became plausible during perestroika under Mikhail Gorbachev, the question of the external and internal borders of the union republics became problematic, triggering violence in some areas such as Nagorno-Karabakh. Due to the fact that most ethnic groups were dispersed and intermingled across much of the territory, when Stalin and other Soviet authorities created a series of national entities it was impossible to draw borders that would divide them into homogeneous entities. Therefore, all of the union republics contained multiple ethnic groups, even though the titular ethnic group was generally either a majority or the largest single group in each republic; many subregions where concentrations of minorities resided were given some form of autonomy, below the level of the union republic, but likewise these republics were seldom homogeneous in their ethnic composition.

Many of the ethnonational conflicts that broke out in the late Soviet period and immediately after its collapse reflected resentments and insecurities based on this division. Although it is often claimed that these borders were drawn arbitrarily and unjustly, and there are certainly reasons to give partial support to this argument, the resulting insecurity and conflict was largely a consequence of linking ethnicity to particular territorial regions in the first place. When the identity of a single ethnonational group becomes territorialized, conflicts over ethnic identity are turned into essentially zero-sum conflicts, since two groups cannot lay exclusive claim to the same territory simultaneously. This makes accommodation to one another's claims more difficult to achieve.

In the wake of suddenly becoming minorities, many national groups claimed the right to self-determination, namely, the ability to control their own destiny. This translated into declarations of independence (e.g., Abkhazia and Transdniestria) or into irredentist goals (i.e., the desire to be united with another state or territory as in Nagorno-Karabakh with Armenia, Crimea with the Russian Federation, Moldova with Romania, and South Ossetia with North Ossetia in the Russian Federation). Fighting appeared as a result of secessionist movements, including in Nagorno-Karabakh, a region populated mostly by Armenians within Azerbaijan; Abkhazia and South Ossetia within Georgia; Chechnya within the Russian Federation; and Transdniestria in Moldova. Violence also threatened to break out due to the disintegration of states in regions such as Crimea within Ukraine; Tatarstan within the Russian Federation; Ajaria and Javakheti within Georgia; eastern portions of Estonia and Latvia, where large numbers of ethnic Russians reside; in heavily Russian occupied regions of eastern and southern Ukraine (e.g., around the cities of Donetsk and Odessa); and in northern Kazakhstan. Ethnic tensions also arose in places such as the Prigordny raion of North Ossetia, heavily populated by Ingush peoples; and in the Ferghana Valley, which cuts across Uzbekistan,

Kyrgyzstan, and Tajikistan, where peoples mostly of Uzbek ethnicity inhabit regions outside of the boundaries of their titular state. Numerous conflicts have broken out on former Soviet territory as some of these regions have resorted to violence to secure their right to self-determination. This has undoubtedly been one of the most destabilizing aspects of the breakup of the Soviet Union.

In addition to ethnonational conflicts and movements for self-determination within regions of existing states, post–Cold War Eurasia has also witnessed the virtual collapse of several states. Collapsed, or failed, states are those in which the structures of a legitimate political order fall apart or become so weak that they are unable to govern at the national level. Sometimes the result is generalized anarchy, as appeared in Albania in early 1997, when the elected government collapsed following the failure of a pyramid scheme supported by the government. At other times, authority may devolve to local officials or to clan networks that undermine the legitimacy of the central state, as occurred in Tajikistan after the breakup of the Soviet Union. In Tajikistan, a low-intensity but continuing series of violent conflicts has occurred primarily among competing clientelistic networks and between Islamic groups and the remnants of the communist old guard. Collapsed states are typically accompanied by a breakdown in the social order. As Terrence Lyons and Ahmed Samatar note: "Without the state, society breaks down, and without social structures, the state cannot survive."[2]

These disintegrative processes also created serious dilemmas for international organizations operating in these regions, especially for the Conference on Security and Cooperation in Europe (CSCE). In its founding document, the Helsinki Final Act of 1975, the CSCE adopted ten principles as the foundation for European security. However, two of these appeared to collide dramatically in the aftermath of the collapse of communist regimes across Eurasia. The principle of the territorial integrity of states was directly challenged by the renewed call for self-determination, also one of the principles enshrined in the Helsinki decalogue. In all of the newly independent states, each of these two objectives appeared to be achieved simultaneously, at least for the titular majority. The dominant nationalities were able to realize self-determination for their own nationality through the creation of sovereign and integrated territorial states. However, the status of persons belonging to national minorities in these new states became increasingly problematic. For example, it was one thing to be a member of the Abkhaz nationality within the Soviet republic of Georgia when the members of the minority group could call upon the central government to recognize and protect its national identity. It was quite something else to be Abkhaz in a newly independent Georgian state, especially when Georgia's first post-Soviet president, Zviad Gamsakhurdia, declared Georgia to be a unitary state and abolished the former autonomy of regions including Abkhazia, Ajaria, and South Ossetia. Similarly, within the rump Yugoslavia, Serbia under the leadership of Slobodan Milosevic abolished the autonomous status of the regions of Kosovo and Vojvodina and imposed direct rule by Serbian authorities in Belgrade over all aspects of the daily lives of their people. Under these conditions, individuals belonging to minorities felt that their very existence as an identifiable nationality was at risk. It should hardly be surprising, therefore, that under these conditions violence became a widespread phenomenon as more and more nationalities sought to affirm their right to self-determination through violent means.

These violent conflicts have created numerous problems for security in the former Soviet Union, the former Yugoslavia, and elsewhere in the Balkans. First, they have retarded the consolidation of nation and state building in many of the newly independent states by diverting scarce resources and by depriving these states of their territorial integrity and sense of national unity. Second, they have impeded the growth of democratic institutions as political leaders adopted a nationalistic discourse to justify the restriction or abolition of democratic institutions and components of civil society in many states where they seized control. Third, they have provided numerous opportunities for outside parties to try to manipulate these conflicts to their own advantage contrary to the interests of the new governments in the region. And fourth, they have created massive refugee flows that often threaten the security of other states outside of the immediate region of chaos. In short, these ethnonational conflicts probably present the most serious security threat to emerge in Eurasia since 1990.[3]

International relations theorists have frequently debated the explanation for the onset of so many violent conflicts in the aftermath of the Cold War. Realists have generally interpreted these events as vindication of their predictions, which stressed the high probability of violent conflict in an anarchic international system at a time when the stability provided by the bipolar structure of the international system was undermined. John Mearsheimer has presented the neorealist argument most starkly in an essay written in 1990 in which he argues that the end of the Cold War would mean "that the prospects for major crises and war in Europe are likely to increase markedly." The absence of war in Europe during the Cold War, he asserts, was a consequence of three factors: "the bipolar distribution of military power on the Continent; the rough military equality between the two states comprising the two poles in Europe, the United States and the Soviet Union; and the fact that each superpower was armed with a large nuclear arsenal."[4] The frequent outbreaks of fighting throughout Eurasia since 1989 are thus believed by realists to confirm their prediction that the highly ambiguous system that has emerged, which combines simultaneously features of multipolarity and unipolarity, is far less peaceful than the bipolar system it supplanted.

By contrast, liberals, especially of the institutionalist school, saw in the end of the Cold War an opportunity to create a new international order based on principles of collective security. They viewed the spread of liberal democracies as potentially ushering in a new era of peace in Europe. They also believed that the new international system provided opportunities for the thick web of institutions that ties much of Europe together to function effectively for the first time in the domain of security, in addition to traditional domains such as the economy and the environment. Typical of this argument is the position taken by Robert Keohane and Joseph Nye, who argue that cooperation even on issues of security is possible in situations where mutual interests can be identified and reciprocal patterns of interaction can be established. With regard to the post–Cold War situation in Europe, they contend:

> Since west Europe was densely institutionalized when the Cold War came to an end, institutionalists anticipate more cooperation in Europe than would be expected if international institutions were insignificant, or merely reflected structural forces in world politics. Institutionalists agree with liberals that common or complementary interests can support cooperation, and that international institutions depend for their success on such patterns of complementary interests.[5]

Both of these theoretical arguments assume that international relations exists as an objective phenomenon to be observed and explained by the theorist; they both overlook the possibility that these theories interact with the phenomena that they seek to explain. Therefore, at least to some degree, international relations theorists, as well as policymakers who hold explicitly or implicitly to one or another theory, may behave on the global stage according to their own models about how the world works. Insofar as proponents of realism consider conflict to be inevitable, then they are not likely to be confident that institutions may in fact create cooperation where common interests exist; therefore, policymakers acting in accordance with the precepts of realism may not utilize institutional resources that are available, so that the result may match the expectations of realist theory. In other words, realism may create a self-fulfilling prophecy that manifests itself in a world that matches the predictions of realism. Conversely, if policymakers are confident in the ability of institutions to manage conflict, they may strive to strengthen institutions that are in fact able to play an important role in preventing and resolving conflicts, thereby reinforcing the claims of the liberal institutionalists. In this instance, actions based on the assumptions of a liberal paradigm may yield higher levels of institutional cooperation to restrain the outbreak of violent conflict.

This approach to international relations, sometimes referred to as *constructivist* or more generally as a *knowledge-based orientation*, stresses the impact that ideas about international relations have not only in describing, explaining, and predicting but also in actually creating the phenomena that scholars purport to analyze. Andreas Hasenclever, Peter Mayer, and Volker Rittberger summarize this argument as follows: "Cognitivists argue that these processes are shaped by the normative and causal beliefs that decisionmakers hold and that, consequently, changes in belief systems can trigger changes in policy."[6]

In this chapter, I proposes to evaluate these alternative theoretical arguments and apply them to an analysis of the ways in which the Organization for Security and Cooperation in Europe (OSCE)[7] has engaged in the tasks of conflict management, including conflict prevention through democratization, preventive diplomacy, third-party conflict resolution, and postconflict security building. I shall then evaluate the comparative advantages and limitations of the OSCE relative to other European security institutions and suggest some of the functions that it may perform better than or not as well as other multilateral institutions dealing with security in Eurasia. I shall also indicate how the OSCE may be strengthened in order to enhance its unique role in providing security for the Eurasian region, and I shall suggest ways in which multiple institutions may cooperate with one another, each drawing from its own particular comparative advantages, to enhance cooperative European security into the twenty-first century.

My central argument is that the Organization for Security and Cooperation in Europe has demonstrated the potential to fulfill many of the security functions that are directly relevant to the specific security challenges facing post–Cold War Europe at the beginning of the twenty-first century. At the same time, the prevalence of realist thinking on the part of many policymakers and scholars has inhibited this potential from being fully realized. Therefore, in practice the OSCE has not fully realized its potential for preventing violent conflict and building security in Europe. If policymakers affirm liberal principles and place greater confidence in the ability of multilateral security institutions like the OSCE to prevent and resolve conflicts like those that appeared throughout Eurasia during the last decade of the twentieth century, and if they translate those beliefs into concrete policies to strengthen multilateral security institutions, then there is every reason to believe that the OSCE, and the institutionalized structures of European security in which it is embedded, may be more effective in the early years of the twenty-first century.

THE OSCE ROLE IN DEMOCRACY BUILDING, PREVENTIVE DIPLOMACY, CONFLICT MANAGEMENT AND RESOLUTION, AND POSTCONFLICT SECURITY BUILDING

If the OSCE's conflict-management role is to be strengthened, it is first necessary to demonstrate to skeptical political elites in many member countries that the organization has established a sufficiently successful track record to date.[8] Only then can the proponents of a strengthened OSCE justify the claim that modest additional resources and support can enable the OSCE to play an even more active role in conflict prevention and resolution in the twenty-first century.

In this section, I shall argue that the OSCE has already established a more impressive record than most observers realize. The fact that its accomplishments are not more widely recognized is due to several factors. First, most of the OSCE success stories seem relatively minor in contrast to the dramatic stories of wars breaking our throughout post-Soviet and post-Yugoslavian regions of Eurasia. Only when one observes simultaneously the record of these many small successes does one begin to get a clearer idea of the cumulative impact that the OSCE had on Eurasian security in the last decade of the twentieth century. Second, when the OSCE is most successful, nothing happens; violence and war make headlines, but violence averted often goes unnoticed. Policymakers are preoccupied on a daily basis with the purported failures of preventive diplomacy that turn into wars, and this frequently causes them to downgrade or even to overlook the many small accomplishments that contribute to the prevention of violence in tense situations that might also turn violent.[9] My argument in this section is that the evaluation by policymakers and security specialists in many countries of the OSCE has been plagued by both of these shortcomings. I hope to demonstrate that the cumulative record of modest successes by the OSCE in many hotspots in post–Cold War Eurasia is far better than most observers have acknowledged.

Fundamentally, the OSCE has emerged as the only truly pan-European organization dealing with the full spectrum of security functions across all of Eurasia, Central and Western Europe, and North America since 1990. Its primary functions have included setting the normative framework for European security, developing military confidence- and security-building measures to reduce fear of war, and enhancing the human dimension of security, including human rights, democratization, and the rule of law. Here I will focus mostly on the role of the OSCE in the prevention and resolution of violent conflicts on the territory it covers. I will consider four different categories of conflict-management activities, although each new function typically incorporates some of the activities listed in the previous functions as well:

1. Democratization: this entails long-term conflict prevention through the promotion of democracy and human rights, including the creation of political conditions conducive to the peaceful resolution of disputes.
2. Preventive diplomacy: in addition to activities in the human dimension, this involves direct intervention in crisis situations that threaten to escalate to violence in the relatively near term if preventive action is not taken.

3. Conflict resolution: typically, these activities take place in the aftermath of violence and include specific efforts to promote a settlement of the underlying causes of the conflict while also engaging in preventive activities to avert the reoccurrence of violence.
4. Postconflict security building: in addition to the three activities already mentioned, this role involves efforts to rebuild war-torn societies through the reconstruction of the political system and the rehabilitation of the infrastructure required for normal human activity. In the aftermath of violence, this role entails efforts to build stable democratic societies capable of resolving differences peacefully but in the midst of the chaos and physical destruction that typically follows violent conflict.

Although most of the conflict-management activities of the OSCE involve all of these activities to some degree, I have selected certain missions to illustrate the performance of each function. The remainder of this section, therefore, will indicate the multiple roles that OSCE institutions played in responding to conflicts in Eurasia during the last decade of the twentieth century.

Democratization: Long-Term Conflict Prevention

OSCE member states have broadly accepted the democratic peace hypothesis, that is, the belief that democratic states seldom or never engage in violent conflict with other democratic states.[10] Therefore, they assume that the long-term foundations for peace may be constructed by encouraging the widespread development of democratic regimes throughout Eurasia. The basic argument is that liberal democracies promote nonviolent means to resolve conflicts, to build coalitions, and to achieve consensus about the basic goals of the state and relations among states. And since liberal democratic states can expect other democratic states to be similarly inclined, they can count on them to pursue nonviolent means to overcome differences of interest rather than resorting to wars and violence. Internally, democratic procedures also engender respect for the rule of law as well as recognition of the importance of the decision-making process through which citizens may seek redress for grievances and overcome differences. All of these factors are hypothesized to reduce the likelihood of domestic large-scale violence in liberal democratic states and to make war virtually unthinkable among democratic states.

Therefore, the OSCE has devoted considerable effort to the promotion of democratization. This has included the work of the Office of Democratic Institutions and Human Rights, which assists states seeking to democratize by establishing procedures for holding democratic elections, supervising the conduct of those elections, and then certifying the outcomes of elections as free and fair. Numerous OSCE missions and the High Commissioner on National

Minorities have worked to increase the capacity of minorities, often disen-
franchised or in other ways hindered from participating fully in the political
process, to achieve equal rights not only on paper but in practice as well. The
Office for Democratic Institutions and Human Rights (ODIHR) has a section
on the rule of law that also assisted states to develop legal principles to under-
gird democratic processes and to strengthen the norm that democracy requires
that the rule of law ought to prevail over the will of powerful individuals. The
Representative on Freedom of the Media, established at the Copenhagen
Ministerial Conference in 1997, also supports the principle of an independent
media as a foundation for civil society. Although most of these activities have
little direct influence on the occurrence or avoidance of violent conflict, they
are assumed to create the necessary long-term conditions for replacing
reliance upon coercion and force with a democratic process of give-and-take,
compromise, and bargaining as a way of overcoming differences.

Numerous OSCE missions such as those in Latvia, Estonia, Belarus, and
Central Asia[11] have had among the central elements of their mandates a charge
to assist the governments of transitional states in the process of complying with
democratic norms. In Latvia and Estonia, the primary OSCE focus has been to
assure that the new governments do not deprive the large Russian minorities
living in these two countries of their citizenship and other democratic rights out
of revenge for the perceived injustices suffered by Latvians and Estonians at
the hands of the Russian-dominated Soviet regime. Both countries had substantial populations of ethnic Russians, many of whom had moved to the Baltic
states following annexation by the Soviet Union in 1940. However, both governments at first refused to grant these individuals and their descendants citizenship, and they set high barriers, including fluency in the Latvian or Estonian
language, as a requirement for obtaining citizenship. The result was that substantial percentages of the population of both countries faced becoming stateless persons when their Soviet-era internal passports expired, and the Russian
Federation criticized these policies in very harsh terms.

In response to these dangers, the OSCE established missions of long
duration in Estonia on 13 December 1992, and in Latvia on 23 September
1993. Both mandates called upon the OSCE to assist the governments in their
efforts to deal with such issues as citizenship and language laws, migration
across borders, education, social services, and dialogue between the different
ethnic communities. In addition, the High Commissioner on National
Minorities, Ambassador Max van der Stoel, paid frequent visits to both countries, beginning in Estonia in January 1993. He issued a series of recommendations to both governments concerning those aspects of their national legislation that appeared to negatively impact ethnic Russian communities. The
most sensitive issue involved the citizenship laws, which effectively deprived
large portions of the Russophone community in both countries of civil rights.
Although both countries established tests through which these individuals

could become citizens, they were often difficult and required knowledge of the official state language.

The main efforts of the OSCE missions and of Ambassador van der Stoel were, therefore, directed to persuading these countries to modify the new citizenship laws in order to reduce their most discriminatory features. They also put great pressure on the governments to implement the existing laws more leniently, fairly, and expeditiously so that applicants for citizenship or for residence permits would not be harassed or subjected to intolerable delays. The OSCE representatives also encouraged national authorities to make it easier to pass citizenship tests and to expand significantly the opportunities for Russian speakers to learn the new state languages so that they had a reasonable chance of being successful in the examinations. Finally, Ambassador van der Stoel strongly encouraged both states to grant citizenship rapidly to stateless children born to parents who had lost their Soviet citizenship.

The OSCE tried to encourage both governments to achieve these goals in several different ways. First, it tried to persuade local authorities to modify procedures in implementing their own legislation. It also provided "good offices" to establish direct dialogue between leaders of the Russian communities and their counterpart Estonian and Latvian political elites. It established roundtables in which representatives of all ethnic communities were invited to participate, and it encouraged the governments to create an ombudsperson position to represent the interests of the minority communities before the government. In general, the OSCE pursued quiet diplomacy and operated outside the glare of publicity and the media. By early 2000, tensions had eased in these regions, but by no means had they disappeared altogether. Both governments strongly urged that the OSCE missions be terminated, but the Russian Federation in particular argued forcefully that OSCE participation was essential to prevent the situation from deteriorating again.

As tensions were being reduced in the Baltic states, fears of conflict emanating from a reversal of democratization arose in Belarus. Since Belarus is one of the few post-Soviet countries that is relatively ethnically homogeneous, consisting overwhelmingly of Slavs, including Belarusians, Russians, and Ukrainians, there was little danger of ethnic conflict. Yet conflict opened up between proponents of change and the supporters of a Soviet-style regime mostly made up of former communist elites. Under the government of President Alexander Lukashenko, who was elected in 1994, there was a substantial reversal of the trends toward democratic reform and economic liberalization; more than any other former Soviet state, Belarus seemed to be turning the clock back toward former Soviet times. Indeed, in a referendum on the constitution in November 1996, Lukashenko extended his term of office indefinitely into the future and effectively forced all political opposition out of the already weakened parliament. This was followed by an agreement in 1997 to establish a formal union between Belarus and the Russian Federation, enthusiastically embraced by President Lukashenko but reluctantly accepted by President Boris Yeltsin under pressure from his nationalist political opponents.

The OSCE Advisory and Monitoring Group in Belarus was established on 18 September 1997, to assist the government of Belarus in "promoting democratic institutions and in complying with other OSCE commitments" and to report on the results.[12] Although the Lukashenko government was ambivalent about allowing a resident international mission on its territory, it eventually bowed to Russian pressure to permit the advisory and monitoring group to set up shop in Minsk. It took up residence in February 1998 with a clear emphasis on providing a source of contact for the political opposition and for the many nongovernmental organizations (NGOs) that had been harassed and threatened by the Lukashenko government. Since that time, the mission has served primarily as a device to assist the remaining rudiments of civil society in Belarus to survive. It has sponsored seminars and workshops for NGOs, maintained close relations with key opposition political figures, and provided advice regarding election laws, laws regulating the media, and the rule of law. By late 1999, the OSCE group had successfully opened a dialogue between the government and opposition leaders concerning, among other issues, the possible scheduling of new elections.

In summary, the OSCE has acted since 1991 on the assumption that the construction of stable democratic political systems contributes in the long run to peace and security by reducing the risks of both intrastate and interstate violence. In the cases of Estonia and Latvia, it has encouraged two democratizing regimes with aspirations to join the Western European community of nations to pursue that process in a way that would not discriminate excessively against the large Russian minorities, widely perceived in these countries as former oppressors. Not only has the OSCE helped these countries move along the democratic path and closer toward a more significant relationship with the major Western European institutions; it has also reduced any pretext that Russian officials might have seized upon to intervene in the internal affairs of these two states in defense of the interests of brother and sister ethnic Russians who were victims of discrimination at the hands of the new majority. In Belarus, in contrast, the OSCE has recently taken up a role in trying to preserve the rudiments of civil society and institutions in a country that has turned its back on democratization and economic liberalization in favor of a more authoritarian route founded on nostalgia for former Soviet times and a pan-Slavic nationalism reflected in the Union Treaty signed between Belarus and the Russian Federation.

Preventive Diplomacy

The principle focus of OSCE's conflict-prevention activities is to identify and respond to brewing conflicts to prevent the outbreak of violence. It has become commonplace, but accurate, to assert that conflicts are easier to resolve before they become violent than afterward. This view has been expressed forcefully by Max van der Stoel, the OSCE High Commissioner on National Minorities:

> It is evident from the experience of Bosnia, of Chechnya, of Nagorno-Karabakh, of Georgia and elsewhere, that once a conflict has erupted, it is extremely difficult to bring it to an end. In the meantime, precious lives have been lost, new waves of hatred have been created and enormous damage has been inflicted. It is my firm belief that money spent on conflict prevention is money well spent, not only because it is cheaper, but especially because it saves so many lives.[13]

As van der Stoel suggests, once Humpty-Dumpty has fallen from his wall, it is extremely difficult to put him back together again. And so it is with states; once conflicts reach the stage of violence, peaceful accommodation may become extremely difficult to achieve. A significant challenge to preventive diplomacy, however, is that there is often only a very narrow window of opportunity during which outside parties may intervene to prevent the outbreak of violence. At early stages in a conflict, the gravity of the situation may not be recognized, so that no stimulus to intervene arises. Furthermore, premature intervention may actually create a self-fulfilling prophecy and even stimulate hostility and exacerbate conflict. Early interventions that are insensitive to local conditions—to the needs and interests of the parties and the nature of their conflict—may also widen rather than narrow differences between parties to a dispute. If outside parties and international institutions appear to buy into nationalist claims for self-determination at the outset of a conflict, they may legitimize extremist propaganda and undermine responsible political authorities. At the same time, if outside parties wait too long before intervening, the threshold of violence may be crossed before preventive diplomacy can be engaged. And once that threshold has been crossed, any opportunity to resolve the conflict may have been missed until a long time later.

Preventive diplomacy requires mechanisms for early warning about situations that may eventually turn violent. It also requires an ability to respond rapidly and effectively to escalating situations at the ripe moment for intervention. This is often a difficult task for multilateral security organizations, like the OSCE, that depend upon consensus among many members in order to react to developing situations. One of the advantages, however, of the OSCE's permanent missions and field activities is that the local head of mission has a great deal of discretionary authority to act in emergency situations without having to obtain consensus from the OSCE Permanent Council and its fifty-four participating states in Vienna. And the High Commissioner on National Minorities is permitted to act exclusively at his own discretion whenever he observes a serious threat to the peace involving persons belonging to national minorities. These two mechanisms have been especially helpful in enabling the OSCE to bypass some aspects of the consensus rule in order to respond quickly and flexibly to brewing conflicts.

The OSCE has engaged in a significant number of conflict-prevention efforts in regions where conflict appeared to be escalating and where the risk of large-scale violence was significant. Such activities have taken place in Ukraine (especially regarding separatist claims in Crimea and possible concerns about potential Russian intervention), in the Former Yugoslav Republic of Macedonia (especially in preventing conflicts in the Federal Republic of Yugoslavia—particularly the Kosovo region—and in Albania from spilling over into Macedonia), and in the Federal Republic of Yugoslavia (regarding separatist claims in Kosovo, Sandjak, and Vojvodina). Although some scattered violence and killing has occurred in all of these locations, only Kosovo has experienced large-scale violence, and even then not until 1998.

The first OSCE mission of long duration was created in the regions of Kosovo, Sandjak, and Vojvodina in the Federal Republic of Yugoslavia on 14 August 1992; it began its activities on 8 September. All three regions are inhabited by significant proportions of ethnic minorities—Albanian Muslims in Kosovo, Muslims in Sandjak, and Hungarians in Vojvodina—who fear for their safety at the hands of the majority Serbian population. The OSCE's mandate included monitoring the observance of the rights of individuals and persons belonging to national minorities in each region, with the purpose of promoting peaceful dialogue between representatives of the minority populations and the central government in Belgrade. It was to collect information on human rights violations, to encourage negotiated settlement of issues that arose regarding the treatment of the minority populations, and to provide local authorities with information about OSCE and other international standards regarding the protection of the rights of individuals and persons belonging to minorities.

The government in Belgrade was suspended from active participation in the OSCE in May 1992, however, due to charges about its behavior in the fighting in Croatia and Bosnia. Partially in retaliation for this action, the regime refused to renew the memorandum of understanding concerning the mission's operation after it expired following an initial six-month period. In a special protocol it was briefly extended, but this agreement expired on 28 June 1993, and the OSCE missions were withdrawn. In 1997, the Danish chair in office appointed the High Commissioner on National Minorities, Max van der Stoel, as his special representative in Kosovo. However, he was not permitted to travel there as an OSCE official, since the government in Belgrade responded to its suspension from the OSCE by refusing to recognize it as having any legitimate role to play in what it asserted to be its internal affairs. The expulsion of the Belgrade government from active participation in the OSCE undoubtedly limited the organization's influence in the country after 1993, especially in the regions most likely to experience violence. Due to the OSCE's inability to intervene more effectively in Kosovo as the crisis escalated, the prospects for a diplomatic solution became more remote. If the OSCE—or the so-called Contact Group consisting of the United States, Russia, France, the United Kingdom, and Germany—had successfully initiated meaningful negotiations between the Kosovar Albanian leadership and the government in Belgrade in late 1997 or early 1998, before positions hardened even further, violence possibly could have been averted.

In the absence of international intervention at an early stage, however, tensions escalated between an increasingly radicalized Kosovar population and the government of the Federal Republic of Yugoslavia throughout 1998. Hostilities broke out in the summer and fall of 1998 between Serbian police and paramilitary units, on the one hand, and the Kosovo Liberation Army. As a result, U.S. Special Envoy Richard Holbrooke stepped in and brokered an agreement in October 1998 calling for a cease-fire to be monitored by the OSCE. Under that agreement, the OSCE agreed to send in approximately 2,000 unarmed civilian monitors, the Kosovo Verification Mission (KVM), to verify compliance with the cease-fire on both sides and to assist in the return of refugees to their homes. This was by far the largest operation undertaken by the OSCE in terms of personnel, and it was also one of the most risky. The volatile nature of the political situation in Kosovo, and the vulnerability of a large number of unarmed monitors to attacks from militants on either side who might wish to disrupt the cease-fire, placed the OSCE in the most sensitive position in its history. The OSCE's dependence on volunteers, seconded by member governments, became especially problematic in this case. By the time the mission was withdrawn in March 1999, the KVM had reached fewer than 1,400 personnel, and many of them were poorly trained and equipped for the complex duties they were required to perform.

The establishment of the KVM recognized dramatically the expanded role that the OSCE might be able to play in conflict prevention in volatile regions, especially if military force could not be deployed. However, under the conditions in which the KVM entered Kosovo in late 1998, it was too little, too late to contain the rapidly escalating conflict. Although the force of unarmed observers was often successful in resolving many disputes at the local level, including securing the release of hostages and investigating charges of police brutality, it was unable to resist the pressures created by political extremists both within the Kosovo Liberation Army and within the Serbian government in Belgrade. Their nationalistic policies and personal gambits to enhance their own power base contributed to a serious deterioration of the security situation by the spring of 1999. After an abortive attempt by the Contact Group to impose a settlement on the factions at Rambouillet in February 1999, NATO began an eleven-week aerial bombardment in March to try to dislodge Serbian control over Kosovo and, at least indirectly, to force Milosevic from power in Belgrade.

The outbreak of overt war in Kosovo in 1999 represented a dramatic failure of preventive diplomacy. Indeed, at the OSCE Istanbul Summit in November 1999, the organization sought to remedy some of the deficiencies of the KVM and to enhance its conflict-prevention capability by creating Rapid Expert Assistance and Cooperation Teams (REACT). The OSCE will establish and maintain a registry of individuals from member countries who will be trained in advance and available for rapid deployment when civilian peace monitoring and police functions are required in potential conflict situations. The REACT units will thus enable the OSCE to respond quickly to emergency situations with personnel trained to respond to complex situations where monitoring and diplomatic skills are more important than the use of force to maintain the peace.

The second OSCE mission focusing on preventive diplomacy, officially known as the OSCE Spillover Monitor Mission to Skopje,[14] was established on 18 September 1992, and began its work very shortly thereafter. Its primary mandate was to monitor developments on the border with Serbia and other neighboring states that might spill over into Macedonia and create conflict there. Of special concern was a significant Albanian minority that would inevitably be very much influenced by events in contiguous Kosovo, as well as smaller Greek and Bulgarian minorities that might also be sources of tension. The OSCE mission of eight persons also worked closely with a European Community Monitor Mission at the outset. The small OSCE and EC missions were eventually complemented by the stationing of UN peacekeeping forces in Macedonia, initially a division of the UN Protection Force deployed elsewhere in the former Yugoslavia. This force was eventually renamed the UN Preventive Deployment Force and included some 800 soldiers, later supplemented by about 360 U.S. soldiers under UN command, all eventually withdrawn in 1999.[15] Its major function was to deter Serbian intervention in the affairs of Macedonia, although much attention subsequently shifted to the internal scene as well, where tensions have frequently arisen between the Albanian minority and the titular majority of Macedonians. Although scattered incidents of violence have broken out from time to time, large-scale fighting has largely been averted, due in part to the frequent intervention of both the High Commissioner on National Minorities and the OSCE Monitor Mission.

The third major mission engaged primarily in conflict prevention was the mission in Ukraine. This mission was established on 15 June 1994, largely on the recommendation of the High Commissioner on National Minorities, who was concerned about the seriously deteriorating relations between officials in the Crimean region and the central government in Ukraine following two visits in February and May 1994. The region of Crimea (67 percent of the population being ethnic Russian) had been part of the Russian Federation until it was given as a gift by Nikita Khrushchev to Ukraine in 1954. This change in status made little practical difference until the Soviet Union collapsed; Crimean Russians suddenly found themselves to be a minority in the new Ukrainian state. Tensions between Crimean authorities and Kiev worsened dramatically in January 1994 when Yuri Meshkov, a nationalistic Russian, was elected as the first president of Crimea. He immediately proposed changing the Crimean constitution to declare that Crimea was not an integral part of the Ukrainian state but an independent and sovereign state in its own right. This set off a strong response by the central government in Kiev, which wanted to preserve the territorial integrity of the Ukrainian state.

The principal mandate of the OSCE mission was to assist in settling the status of Crimea as an autonomous region within the state of Ukraine. Both the mission, with offices in Kiev and Simferopol, and High Commissioner van der Stoel began providing advice to the governments and parliaments of both Crimea and Ukraine concerning the drafting of their constitutions in an effort to harmonize the provisions of the two constitutions in such a way as to ensure the outcome of an autonomous Crimea within Ukraine. Van der Stoel organized several conferences and seminars, inviting political leaders from the region and experts from outside, in order to examine these constitutional issues, first in Locarno, Switzerland; subsequently in Yalta; and then in Noordwijk, Holland. On the basis of these seminars, he drafted a series of recommendations for both governments, including detailed language designed to bridge the gaps between the two constitutions. By December 1998, these recommendations made it possible for Crimea to adopt a constitution that was effectively consistent with the Ukrainian constitution. Both documents acknowledged that Crimea was within the territorial state of Ukraine while granting the region substantial autonomy. As a result of this success, the OSCE Mission to Ukraine was downgraded to Project Coordinator in Ukraine in early 1999. Operating with a reduced professional staff, it was mandated to monitor the implementation of the agreements achieved between Crimea and the central government and to provide assistance for large numbers of Crimean Tatars returning to their ancestral homeland, from which they had been deported during Soviet times.

The Crimean case has become a model illustrating how regions with significant ethnic minorities can successfully negotiate self-determination through substantial autonomy as an alternative to insisting upon complete independence, thereby also preserving the de jure territorial integrity of the state. The Crimean case thus serves as an excellent example of how a regional security organization like the OSCE can assist newly independent states to recognize the rights for self-determination of nationalities within their borders without undermining the formal territorial integrity of the larger state in which they are situated.

Conflict Management and Resolution

In regions where violent conflict occurred recently but has largely ceased, OSCE activities focus on managing conflicts to avert the reappearance of violence and on resolving underlying issues to remove conditions that led to conflict in the first place. In a few instances, the OSCE has played an active role in negotiating cease-fires; however, in the vast majority of cases, fighting has simply ceased either because one party achieved its immediate objective and the other was unable to resist by force, because the parties became exhausted and turned to other means to pursue their conflicts, or because an outside party, such as Russia, intervened to help bring an end to the fighting.

Once a cease-fire is in place, typically some kind of peacekeeping arrangement has been set up, usually under the auspices of the Commonwealth of Independent States (CIS) or NATO. In those cases where individual countries such as the Russian Federation have provided peacekeeping forces, the OSCE has been mandated to observe their performance, to assure their neutrality, and to verify that they do not themselves instigate incidents that might lead to a renewal of violence. These activities have been most prominent in the South Ossetia region of Georgia, the Transdniestria region of Moldova, and in Tajikistan, especially near the frontier with Afghanistan, where Russian border patrols play a major role in trying to prevent the infiltration of illegal traffic.

But most important, the OSCE has frequently entered into regions of violent conflict after a cease-fire has been reached in order to assure that violence does not reignite and to help resolve some of the underlying issues that led to violence in the first place. Quite frequently, this has entailed mediating between central governments and authorities in secessionist regions to find an acceptable formula that will assure rights to self-determination while maintaining the formal territorial integrity of the state, consistent with the 1975 Helsinki principles.

Several techniques have been utilized by OSCE representatives performing third-party roles in conflict management and resolution. The High Commissioner on National Minorities has often played a significant role in trying to move parties to a dispute along the path of resolution. One technique employed by Ambassador van der Stoel is to organize seminars, typically in conjunction with the Foundation on Inter-Ethnic Relations, an NGO that works closely with the office of the High Commissioner in The Hague. The High Commissioner has also undertaken shuttle diplomacy, traveling between disputing parties and listening to their grievances and suggestions, following up with a set of recommendations to the parties involved.

A second approach often utilized by the OSCE, especially by missions of long duration, has been to provide good offices and other fairly passive forms of mediation to assist parties to a dispute to reach agreement. The OSCE mission head can serve as a go-between or mediate meetings between parties. For example, OSCE missions have served as mediators between the government of Moldova and the breakaway region of Transdniestria and between the government of Georgia and the separatist regime in South Ossetia. The mission in Dushanbe has also mediated between the government of Tajikistan and rival clans and political opponents of the ruling regime who have sometimes resorted to violent means in an effort to bring down the central government. Finally, the OSCE Assistant Group to Chechnya, under the leadership of Ambassador Tim Guldimann of Switzerland, played a critical role in mediating the agreement reached at Khasavyurt in August 1996 between the Chechen leaders and the Russian government that temporarily ended that bloody conflict.

A third approach at mediation has been to establish formal groups of states operating under the auspices of the OSCE to assist disputing parties to resolve their differences peacefully. These may take the form of "contact groups," "friends" of a particular country, or a formal group such as the Minsk Group, which was established in 1992 to mediate the conflict over Nagorno-Karabakh. The Minsk Group is currently cochaired by the United States, France, and the Russian Federation, and it frequently operates at senior diplomatic levels (including foreign ministers from member countries) to hammer out a political solution to what has been one of the most deadly conflicts in post–Cold War Eurasia.

Finally, where agreements have been reached, the OSCE may play a role in overseeing their implementation. For example, the OSCE set up special missions to assist in the implementation of bilateral agreements between Russia and Latvia concerning a Russian radar station at Skrunda and a joint commission on military pensioners, as well as an agreement between Russia and Estonia to set up a similar joint commission. Its field missions may also be mandated to supervise specific agreements. For example, the mission in Moldova is charged with monitoring the 1994 treaty between Russia and Moldova (not ratified by the Russian Duma) on the withdrawal of the Russian 14th Army and associated equipment and supplies stored on the left bank of the Dniester River in the separatist region of Transdniestria. In principle, but thus far not in fact, the OSCE may undertake a peacekeeping operation under its auspices, perhaps with assistance from NATO, other military alliances, or individual participating states, to oversee political agreements between disputing parties. Such a possibility has been anticipated as part of a political settlement between Azerbaijan and the Armenian community in Nagorno-Karabakh since the 1992 Helsinki Summit, and at the 1994 Budapest Summit the OSCE created the High Level Planning Group to prepare for such an operation. However, to date a political settlement has remained elusive so that there is no agreed mandate under which an OSCE peacekeeping force might function.

Altogether, there have been five OSCE missions whose primary tasks have involved the management of conflicts after a cease-fire has been achieved and the promotion of a longer-term resolution of the underlying issues to those conflicts: these include Georgia, Moldova, Tajikistan, Chechnya, and Nagorno-Karabakh.[16]

The first such mission was established in Georgia on 6 November 1992, with a mandate to "promote negotiations between the conflicting parties in Georgia which are aimed at reaching a peaceful political settlement." The OSCE mission entered into Georgia in the aftermath of a cease-fire reached on 24 June 1992 at Sochi, on Russia's Black Sea Coast. It was specifically charged with mediating the conflict in order to make recommendations for holding an international conference, in cooperation with the UN, aimed at resolving the conflict and settling the status of South Ossetia within the Georgian state. Although the conflict had not been completely resolved by late 2000, substantial progress toward its resolution had been made, and both parties to the conflict generally credit the OSCE with having, at a minimum, prevented a resumption of the fighting. More significant, most believe that it has contributed to a slow improvement in confidence between the parties that appeared to be enhancing prospects for a political settlement of the status of the South Ossetian territory.

The second OSCE mission of this type is the mission to Moldova, created on 4 February 1993. Its mandate called for the mission "to facilitate the achievement of a lasting, comprehensive political settlement of the conflict in all its aspects" including "the reinforcement of the territorial integrity of the Republic of Moldova along with an understanding about a special status for the Trans-Dniester region." About two-thirds of the population is made up of Russian- and Ukrainian-speaking peoples; the Russian 14th Army was (and still is) stationed in this region. During the Gorbachev period, Moldovan nationalists began calling for the independence of Moldova from the Soviet Union, and some even called for unification with Romania. Residents east of the Dniester resisted moves toward the Romanization of Moldova and responded by declaring themselves to be the Transdniester Moldovian Soviet Socialist Republic within the Soviet Union; their leadership continued to proclaim its loyalty to the Soviet Union even after its collapse. In the spring of 1992 the authorities in Chisinau, Moldova's capital, insisted on enforcing the primacy of Moldovan law throughout the country, and this led to fighting between the Moldovan army and the Transdniestrian Republican Guard supported by elements of the Russian 14th Army. A cease-fire was reached in Moscow on 6–7 July 1992, after approximately 800 people had lost their lives in the fighting, and a peacekeeping force of Russian, Moldovan, and Transdniestrian units was established to police the cease-fire.

The CSCE mission in Moldova was created in the aftermath of the Moscow agreement. As in Georgia, it was to oversee the performance of the peacekeeping forces, report on the human rights and security situations, and assist the parties to achieve a permanent political settlement that would recognize some form of autonomy for the Transdniester region within the Moldovan state. By 1999 several confidence-building measures had been negotiated along the security zone separating the two parties, but by early 2000 no agreement had been reached on the political status of Transdniestria in relationship to the Republic of Macedonia. A treaty, signed between the governments of Moldova and the Russian Federation in 1994, called for the complete withdrawal of Russian troops not involved in peacekeeping as well as the large stocks of equipment and ammunition stationed in Transdniestria. The OSCE mission was mandated to assist the parties to verify this withdrawal. By early 2000, only token withdrawals had taken place, and the OSCE mission was powerless to enforce the treaty (which had set a November 1997 deadline for withdrawal). The OSCE formally called on Russia to speed up withdrawal and to complete it by 2002; a fund was created to receive voluntary contributions to assist with the high costs associated with the withdrawal of armaments and equipment.

The third mission is that in Tajikistan created on 1 December 1993. Here, the issue involves internal competition for power among competing clientelistic groups. Several issues arose due to the situation along the southern border with Afghanistan, where the Tajikistan government, with the support of Russia and other Central Asian leaders, feared that Islamicist political forces could easily enter the region. The border was also a frequent route for trafficking in drugs and other contraband, so Russian border guards were stationed along the frontier even after the Soviet Union collapsed, and the CIS also took on a peacekeeping role. In this instance, Russian forces generally played a one-sided role in helping to defend the central government against its opponents and to limit the rights of the opposition.[17]

With the encouragement of the CSCE mission, talks took place between the government and opposition leaders in Moscow in April 1994. Subsequently, the CSCE put considerable pressure on the government to allow for free and fair elections to take place in the fall, and some resulting changes in the electoral law apparently encouraged the opposition to agree to a cease-fire during negotiations in Tehran in September 1994. After many sporadic violations and repeated extensions of the cease-fire, a major breakthrough came on 27 June 1997, when the terms of an agreement on peace and national accord were accepted by all parties in inter-Tajik negotiations in Moscow. The Commission of National Reconciliation was created, and the OSCE assumed substantial responsibility for aiding and advising this commission as it set about creating conditions in which the civil conflict could be brought to a halt.

The fourth OSCE activity of this type was the Assistance Group to Chechnya, established on 11 April 1995, the first such mission to operate inside the Russian Federation. Chechnya is a predominantly Sunni Muslim region in the northern Caucasus, with a population consisting largely of mountain-dwellers who resisted Russian occupation for centuries. Its population in 1989 consisted of about 65 percent ethnic Chechens and 25 percent Russians, the latter mostly living in the capital of Grozny and the plains north of the Terek River. Following the Moscow coup attempt in August 1991, General Dzokhar Dudayev seized power in Chechnya and shortly thereafter declared independence from Russia. Dudayev subsequently refused to sign Yeltsin's proposed federation treaty, and on 11 December 1994, some 40,000 Russian troops entered Chechnya, resulting in full-scale war, by far the bloodiest of the post–Cold War conflicts in Eurasia. The war lasted off and on for some two years.

It was in this context that the OSCE Assistance Group was created with a mandate to "promote the peaceful resolution of the crisis and the stabilization of the situation in the Chechen Republic in conformity with the principle of the territorial integrity of the Russian Federation and in accordance with OSCE principles." In addition, the OSCE group was assigned to monitor compliance with the usual set of human-dimension norms. The head of the OSCE Assistance Group, Ambassador Tim Guldimann of Switzerland, interpreted his mandate broadly in order to assume an activist role in promoting talks between Russian and Chechen leaders. He arranged a secret meeting in the Kremlin on 30 July 1995, at which a military accord calling for a cease-fire was negotiated. Even though this was frequently violated, following the death of Dudayev during a Russian rocket attack, Guldimann was able to arrange another meeting between the new Chechen leader, Aslan Maskhadov, and Yeltsin's newly appointed security adviser, General Alexander Lebed, at Khasavyurt in neighboring Dagestan in August 1996. The two men agreed to a cease-fire to take effect on 13 August 1996, and to hold parliamentary and presidential elections in Chechnya on 28 January 1997. The Khasavyurt agreement, signed on 31 August 1996, postponed final resolution of Chechnya's status for five years, leaving an element of ambiguity surrounding the most important political issue dividing the parties.[18]

Tragically, however, the peace agreement did not bring lasting security to Chechnya. By early 1998, the situation in Chechnya had deteriorated into almost complete anarchy, as economic conditions became hopeless, human rights abuses became abundant, and guns became available for all. In early 1999, the mission moved from Grozny to the Norwegian Embassy in Moscow. Shortly thereafter fighting resumed. Although a major effort was made at the 1999 Istanbul Summit to position the OSCE as a mediator between the Russian government and the Chechens under President Aslan Maskhadov, those efforts eventually failed. Consequently, the destruction and killing continued in what has been one of the most violent episodes of the post–Cold War period.

The fifth OSCE activity whose primary function was to promote conflict resolution is the Personal Representative of the Chairman-in-Office [CiO] on the Conflict Dealt with by the OSCE Minsk Group, appointed initially on 10 August 1995. The goals of this mission, based in Tbilisi, Georgia, are among the most ambitious to be mandated by the OSCE Permanent Council: the personal representative will "represent the OSCE Chairman-in-Office in issues related to the Nagorno-Karabakh conflict, assist the CiO in achieving an agreement on the cessation of the armed conflict and in creating conditions for the deployment of an OSCE peace-keeping operation, in order to facilitate a lasting comprehensive political settlement of the conflict in all its aspects." The conflict was in Nagorno-Karabakh, a formerly autonomous region within the union republic of Azerbaijan populated mostly by ethnic Armenians. The conflict in Nagorno-Karabakh began even before the breakup of the Soviet Union. On 1 February 1988, the regional council petitioned the Supreme Soviets of Azerbaijan and Armenia to transfer sovereignty over the region from the former to the latter. This action was followed by the killing of Armenians in Azeri regions and of Azeris by Armenians. When the Soviet Union collapsed and both republics became independent, the fighting became more intense as the Armenians in Nagorno-Karabakh drove virtually all ethnic Azeris out of the territory and began to fight in earnest to separate from Azerbaijan and join with the newly independent Armenian state.

Both Armenia and Azerbaijan had joined the CSCE in January 1992.[19] During the Helsinki Summit in July 1992 there was some optimism about the possibility that the CSCE might broker a peace agreement in Nagorno-Karabakh, and the CSCE leadership began to discuss the possibility of undertaking the organization's first peacekeeping operation to monitor whatever agreement might emerge. The communiqué issued at the Helsinki Summit envisioned the possibility of such an operation; it also noted that the CSCE might call on regional military arrangements such as NATO, the WEU, and the CIS to support such an operation.

Unfortunately, the situation on the battlefield largely prevented serious negotiations from getting under way. By May 1994, when a cease-fire was agreed upon, the Armenians had forced a one-sided military outcome that encouraged the Karabakh and Armenian parties to dig in their heels; and the Azeris have also been reluctant to negotiate from a position of military weakness. Outstanding issues included the formal, legal status of the Nagorno-Karabakh region; security guarantees; safe return of refugees; and the extent and role of peacekeeping forces to monitor the agreement.

Diplomatic misfires and changes in political leadership occurred over the next several years, and many OSCE officials were optimistic that a settlement to the conflict might be attainable in time for the Istanbul Summit in November 1999. Dialogue was opened between the presidents of Azerbaijan and Armenia during this period, and, with the assistance of the Minsk Group cochairs, tangible progress seemed to be achieved. However, the assassination of the Armenian prime minister and other senior parliamentarians only a few weeks before the Istanbul Summit seemed to derail the negotiation process when it appeared to be making progress. In summary, this conflict has probably been the most frustrating thus far. Perhaps because the OSCE began this operation with such high expectations in early 1992, the lack of progress remains a source of disappointment. However, the process undertaken by the Minsk Group has been subject to manipulation by the powerful member states who have sometimes pursued their own divergent interests rather than seeking a resolution that truly serves the needs of the parties to the conflict.

Postconflict Security Building

The OSCE has also frequently been engaged in promoting long-term peace and security in regions where conflicts have occurred and where a political settlement has been formally achieved, but where the bitterness and destruction of war have left a legacy of hatred and animosity that must be overcome. This often involves efforts to promote reconciliation between the parties to the conflict that goes beyond a formal settlement and moves toward a deeper resolution of differences. It may also involve building democracy to resolve differences nonviolently rather than through coercion and violence. The construction of civil society, holding of elections, assistance in the creation of new constitutions and the promotion of the rule of law, and all other aspects of the OSCE human-dimension activities may be stressed in these situations.

In addition, the OSCE may assist in the verification of disarmament agreements. It may arrange and provide training for civilian police and other institutions required to maintain law and order. Since economic distress is frequently a major obstacle to postconflict rehabilitation, the OSCE may assist the parties in identifying donors to obtain external economic relief or in helping humanitarian organizations become established in zones where violence has created severe social needs. In short, it provides assistance to help relieve the conditions that breed conflict and make reconciliation difficult to realize. Finally, in several cases the OSCE has assisted with the return of refugees and internally displaced persons to their prewar homes. In some cases, such as the Eastern Slavonia region of Croatia, the OSCE has worked directly with returning refugees to facilitate their return.

The most dramatic illustration is the implementation of the Dayton Accords on Bosnia-Herzegovina. When fighting broke out in the former Yugoslavia in 1991, the CSCE Conflict Prevention Center was just being created, and no adequate mechanism existed to engage the organization in conflict-prevention or -resolution activities. Therefore, international responsibility was passed to the European Union, which sought to demonstrate its bona fides under the Common Foreign and Security Policy that was formalized in the Maastricht Treaty in December 1991. For the next several years, the European Union, sometimes in tandem with the United Nations, sought to broker an end to the fighting in Croatia and Bosnia-Herzegovina. The CSCE played only a minor role at this stage, providing ombudspersons to assist individuals under the human dimension role of the CSCE. On 2 June 1994, the OSCE created a mission in Sarajevo to assist and advise the ombudspersons.

The OSCE role was substantially upgraded following the signing of the Dayton Accords on 21 November 1995. The mission to Sarajevo was replaced by a much larger mission to Bosnia-Herzegovina on 8 December 1995, to carry out all tasks assigned to the OSCE by the Dayton Accords. The OSCE was charged specifically with preparing and supervising all national, republic-level, and municipal elections and with implementing the results of those elections, including the return of elected officials to those communities from which they had been forcibly evicted during the fighting. It was assigned with oversight of the implementation of the regional stabilization and arms-control measures under Articles 2 and 4 of the Dayton Accords, including supervising the disarmament of combatant forces, the surrender of weapons by individuals, and aerial surveillance to verify compliance with the arms-control provisions and to enhance confidence among the parties to the conflict. Finally, the OSCE played a leading role in promoting the development of pluralistic and independent media and the use of fair techniques in connection with elections and other political activities. In short, with the exception of the direct military enforcement role under the leadership of the NATO-led Implementation Force (IFOR) and Stabilization Force (SFOR), the OSCE has played the leading role in implementing the Dayton Accords, especially the political dimensions of the security-building process. The mission became larger than any previous activity launched by the OSCE and was headed by Ambassador Robert Frowick of the United States through December 1997; he was replaced at the beginning of 1998 by Ambassador Robert Barry, also a senior U.S. diplomat. Its 2000 budget was some 41 million euros, about 22 percent of the entire OSCE operating budget for the year.

The OSCE role in implementing the Dayton Accords has gone almost unnoticed in the media, especially in the United States. Yet the political and arms-stabilization and arms-control provisions of the Dayton Accords were at least as important as the military components, and the fulfillment of these tasks by the OSCE has perhaps demonstrated most clearly the value of its unique role, namely, linking military security issues to the human dimension, especially democratic processes and human rights. Just as the OSCE could not have implemented these provisions without the physical security provided by IFOR and SFOR troops, so the conditions that may make the reduction and eventual withdrawal of these troops possible could not have been created without the role that ODIHR and other OSCE personnel have played. Their involvement was essential in conducting elections and implementing their results as well as in carrying out the stabilization and arms-control measures called for in Articles 2 and 4 of the Dayton Accords.

Similarly, the OSCE mission in Croatia has played a key role in the post-conflict process in that country. This mission was created on 18 April 1996, largely to assist the government of Croatia with the settlement of the many issues left over after an end to the violence in the Eastern Slavonia (Danube) and Krajina regions of Croatia, areas that had been heavily populated by Serbs prior to the outbreak of fighting. The mission's mandate focused on implementation of democratic processes and the rule of law. Primary responsibility for peacekeeping and other security functions at that time was lodged with the United Nations, especially with the UN Transitional Administration in Eastern Slavonia, Baranja, and Western Sirmium (UNTAES). The mandate for this force was scheduled to expire on 15 January 1998, and full responsibility for administration in this region was to revert to the government in Zagreb. However, most Serbian residents and refugees had little confidence in the Croatian authorities' commitment to implement these agreements fairly, so the OSCE mission agreed to step into the breach.

In January 1998, some 250 OSCE officials took over tasks formerly undertaken by the UNTAES. A principal responsibility for mission officials has been to assist and oversee the Croatian government's implementation of agreements concerning the two-way return of refugees in an effort to undo at least partly the ethnic cleansing that took place in this region of Croatia. A UN police training unit stayed on to assist Croatian civilian police in protecting all parties involved in the return of refugees, but all other responsibilities for advising the government on how to implement its commitments reside with the OSCE.

Third, the OSCE played a major role not only in resolving the conflict that broke out in Albania in early 1997 but also in the process of trying to rebuild political and social order in Albania after the fighting was brought to an end. This mission was established on 27 March 1997, in the aftermath of the collapse of civil order in Albania. The major precipitating event was the failure of a pyramid scheme supported by the government of President Sali Berisha, which led to widespread chaos and violence throughout the country. The Italian government responded by leading a coalition of the willing to create a small Multilateral Protection Force to enter Albania and restore order; known as Operation Alba, it was sanctioned by both the United Nations and the OSCE.

Following the restoration of some semblance of order, a tentative agreement was reached on 9 March among the Albanian political parties to hold new elections. Shortly thereafter, the OSCE decided to establish its presence in Albania, and one of its major tasks was to assist in the preparation of elections, to monitor them, and to aid in their implementation. The mandate adopted by the Permanent Council on 27 March was even broader, however, including the provision of "the co-ordinating framework within which other international organizations can play their part in their respective areas of competence, in support of a coherent international strategy, and in facilitating improvements in the protection of human rights and basic elements of civil society." Specific areas of OSCE specialization would include, as in many other missions, responsibility for preparing and monitoring elections; oversight of democratization, media, and human rights; and monitoring the collection of weapons.

The Danish Chairman-in-Office appointed former Austrian Chancellor Franz Vranitzky to head the OSCE presence. Vranitzky's personal role was essential in the effective operation of the OSCE mission, as his prominence in European political circles gave him access to high-level officials of major European governments to assure that the OSCE presence had the support it needed from those governments. The OSCE presence also worked closely with the Italian-led Multilateral Protection Force, relying on it to provide the security necessary to undertake its major tasks. The entire operation was conducted with little warning or advance preparation. It demonstrated clearly the flexibility of the OSCE to react rapidly and creatively to a fast-developing crisis to which other organizations, more tightly bound by bureaucracy, were unable to respond so quickly.

The ODIHR was able to prepare and mount presidential elections by the scheduled date of 29 June; the elections proceeded peacefully, with the selection of the opposition leader, Fatos Nano of the Social Democratic Party, as prime minister. Following the election, the OSCE mission was reduced in size, and the Multinational Protection Force was withdrawn as political stability returned for the most part to Albania. The OSCE continued to make some progress in overseeing the return of some 1–1.5 million light weapons looted from storehouses during the violence and restoring the foundations of civil society in Albania. Although many aspects of the situation in Albania remain precarious, there can be little doubt that the OSCE played a major role in coordinating the international response to a severe crisis. The OSCE assistance was critical in preventing that state's collapse, and Albanian authorities credit the OSCE with being the key to preventing a major tragedy in their country.[20]

Once again, in 1999 the OSCE presence played a critical role in helping Albania survive the consequences of the war in Kosovo, especially assisting with the problems created by the massive flows of refugees, mostly ethnic Albanians, who fled Kosovo during the NATO military campaign. In addition, it has focused on advising the Albanian government in a thoroughgoing reform of its public administration, bringing it closer in line with Western European standards. A new law on the status of the civil service, prepared with advice from OSCE experts, was passed in November 1999, and it promised to reduce significantly the politicization that had previously infected the governmental structures.[21]

The primary reason for the OSCE success in Albania was perhaps ironically the same factor that has hindered its success in other cases, namely, its small staff and resource base. Yet this ability of a small organization to react flexibly, under the firm leadership of prominent individuals and concerned and willing states, also gave the OSCE a capability to respond quickly when no other international organization was able to. The personal representative of the Chairman-in-Office, Franz Vranitzky, and his deputy, former Austrian Ambassador Herbert Grubmayr, were given virtual carte blanche by the OSCE to take charge of the mission, and they acted promptly and decisively. Their personal leadership of the OSCE presence, and the fact that their hands were not tied by the Permanent Council in Vienna, were undoubtedly major factors in enabling the OSCE to play a significant role in putting Humpty-Dumpty back together again in Albania. This case thus seems to offer optimism that a regional security organization can play a role in managing crises in collapsing states that may endanger international security.

Finally, an OSCE mission in Kosovo was established in June 1999 as a consequence of the accords, brokered by former Russian Prime Minister Viktor Chernomyrdin and Finnish President Martti Ahtisaari, bringing an end to NATO's aerial campaign. In this instance, duties for postconflict restructuring in Kosovo were parceled out among several different international institutions and agencies, with the United Nations taking the lead role. Nonetheless, the OSCE was charged with organizing and monitoring elections and training and putting into the field a civilian police force that would treat all nationalities fairly. In addition, this provided the OSCE an opportunity to show that it could work effectively alongside many other international organizations, including the UN, the Council of Europe, the UN High Commissioner for Refugees, NATO, and the European Union, to name only the most salient. The result was the creation of the largest OSCE field mission to date (with a 2000 budget of some 85 million euros, constituting about 44 percent of the overall operating budget).

At the time of this writing, it is too soon to evaluate the effectiveness of this mission, which must operate in the wake of the failed Kosovo Verification Mission and the massive military campaign launched by NATO. As the small number of remaining ethnic Serbs clustered into enclaves and as the vast majority of Serbs formerly residing in Kosovo fled to Serbia proper, the prospect for the re-creation of any kind of multinational Kosovo appears to be beyond the reach of the OSCE or any other outside party. This case unquestionably illustrates the great importance of conflict prevention, since reconstruction of a multinational civil society in the aftermath of large-scale violence and attempts at ethnic cleansing are extremely challenging tasks. The failure of the international community, including the OSCE, to take timely action to prevent this tragedy left much of Southeastern Europe in shambles.

This sad outcome highlights how much harder it is to put Humpty-Dumpty back together than it is to prevent him from falling in the first place.

EVALUATING AND STRENGTHENING THE OSCE'S ROLE IN CONFLICT MANAGEMENT

Strengths and Limitations of the OSCE

As the preceding review of OSCE activities suggests, the OSCE has successfully fulfilled several of the major security functions with which it has been charged, whereas tangible results are less evident in some other areas of its responsibility.

1. The OSCE has contributed significantly to strengthening democratic processes and institutions in countries undergoing transformation, and this activity has helped prevent conflicts from escalating to violence, as in Latvia and Estonia, for example.
2. The OSCE is the one European security institution that explicitly links the human dimension of security with the political-military dimension. It has recognized and reacted to the principle that threats to the rights and self-identity of individuals and persons belonging to minority groups also endanger peace and security.
3. The OSCE has become the principal coordinator of European-wide nonnuclear arms–control measures, including confidence- and security-building measures and limitations and reductions of military personnel and armaments throughout Eurasia.
4. The OSCE has proven to be remarkably flexible in reacting to potential crises, which has made it possible for the OSCE to respond more rapidly than most other institutions and to adapt its responses more appropriately to specific issues. The rapid and creative way in which the High Commissioner on National Minorities, Ambassador Max van der Stoel, brokered a constitutional agreement between Ukraine and Crimea, as well as the rapid response of the OSCE presence in Albania under Franz Vranitzky as the Albanian state effectively collapsed, provide clear examples of how rapid yet low-level responses by the OSCE have prevented or brought a rapid conclusion to episodes of violence.
5. The reconstruction of civil society and democratic institutions after violent conflict is another area in which the OSCE has registered some mixed successes. Throughout the entire region, the OSCE has become the major institution assisting newly independent states to

conduct elections, and its supervision and monitoring of the process has made it the most authoritative single source on the openness of elections in this region. In addition, it has played a role in training civilian police and assisting in the return of refugees to their homes in the aftermath of violence in places such as Bosnia-Herzegovina, Croatia, and Kosovo.

Perhaps because its hands have often been tied politically by the need to maintain a certain basic consensus among OSCE's diverse membership, the OSCE and its field missions have often been reluctant to be proactive in promoting resolution of existing conflicts, especially between secessionist regions and central governments. Patient OSCE mediation has achieved some modest progress in the cases of Georgia and South Ossetia, Moldova and Transdniestria, and Nagorno-Karabakh (supported by Armenia) and Azerbaijan. At a minimum, the OSCE has kept the parties at the negotiation table. The OSCE successfully brokered a cease-fire between Russia and Chechnya in 1996, only to watch helplessly while the region plunged into anarchy and another war in 1999. The OSCE entered Kosovo in 1998 in order to monitor a cease-fire, only to withdraw on the eve of a full-scale air campaign launched by NATO in March 1999 in response to further hostilities. Thus, it seems that OSCE missions come up short in their efforts to preserve cease-fires and to promote a resolution of the issues underlying conflict in regions that experienced violence during the final decade of the twentieth century.

There are two sorts of problems that the OSCE confronts that have limited its effectiveness in conflict management. First, there are numerous structural problems. The budgets of OSCE missions are very limited and normally have a duration of one year or less. The missions also depend heavily on seconded personnel, which makes them dependent on the quality of the individuals provided by member governments. Recruitment also tends to depend on the ability of governments to find appropriate personnel, which may take far too long, especially in the case of large missions like those in Bosnia-Herzegovina, Croatia, and Kosovo. Many individuals are sent into the field with little or no prior training about the region where they are assigned, or about the processes of conflict management. Furthermore, the missions are supported only by a very small staff in Vienna, which lacks the necessary personnel and resources to provide adequate assistance for the missions. As a consequence, the level of professionalism of the missions falls short of expectations. Thus, it is hardly surprising that most OSCE missions have met with only limited success, especially when it comes to the resolution of conflicts in the regions where they work. Structural factors mean the OSCE operates better in a reactive rather than a proactive mode; it responds fairly rapidly and flexibly compared to other multilateral institutions, but it is seldom able to seize the initiative in promoting solutions to the underlying causes of conflict.

Second, the OSCE confronts several political problems in taking a more proactive role in conflict management, transformation, and resolution. Some degree of consensus is necessary within the OSCE to take major decisions, at least among the largest and most powerful states and regional organizations, which increasingly operate in bloc structures. The fact that missions can operate somewhat independently of the Permanent Council and its collective decisionmaking enables them to act flexibly within the constraints of their mandates. Still, most heads of mission are reluctant to push beyond their formal mandates or go beyond the role of passive facilitator. Within the clear guidelines provided by their mandate, most feel no need to get guidance from the Permanent Council in Vienna regarding day-to-day decisions. Yet most fear exceeding their mandates in ways that may cause any party—perhaps the host state, perhaps an ally of the host state, or possibly another major state within the OSCE—to call for the withdrawal of the mission. If they take a political decision that incurs the wrath of any major OSCE participating state, they risk such an outcome. Therefore, most OSCE heads of mission have been fairly cautious in interpreting their mandate, and they have tended to avoid excessive involvement in the political disputes in the country where they are stationed.

Although the OSCE has developed and promoted several important universal norms as a multilateral organization, in the final analysis it is also a political organization composed of states with their own interests. Thus, it has not totally escaped from the realists' worldview, in which the interests of powerful states may prevail over the interests of parties locked in conflict or over the larger interests of the international community. These political constraints have severely limited the ability of the OSCE to play a more active role in engaging the parties to disputes in meaningful dialogue and in searching for long-term solutions. It has also made it possible for stronger multilateral institutions such as the United Nations, NATO, and the European Union to push the OSCE aside once they determine to take the lead.

Strengthening the OSCE's Role in Eurasian Security

This analysis of institutional and political obstacles to a more effective OSCE role in conflict management suggests several policies that OSCE participating states and the OSCE Secretariat could promote to strengthen the organization's potential to be a more active player in European security policy.

First, the OSCE must clarify its relationship to other multilateral institutions dealing with European security, and those relationships should become increasingly complementary rather than competing. Particularly destructive has been the perceived competition between the OSCE and NATO. In the United States and some Western European countries, there has often been a fear that anything that strengthens the OSCE will weaken NATO; this attitude is also held in many Central European countries that, after the end of the Cold War, were among the strongest proponents of the OSCE, but whose interest waned after they became candidates for NATO membership. In reality, this perceived competition is largely a myth. In fact, NATO and the OSCE have different comparative advantages that could be mutually reinforcing. The OSCE is a broad-based security organization with universal membership, explicit links between military and nonmilitary dimensions of security, and a political role to play in conflict prevention and resolution that cannot possibly be played by a military alliance like NATO, no matter how it is transformed. At the same time, in the few instances where the OSCE's policies require military force for their implementation, including making and keeping peace, close links can be forged between the two, building especially on NATO's Partnership for Peace program. Such links were envisioned in the final communiqués of NATO's ministerial meeting in Copenhagen in June 1992 and the OSCE Helsinki Summit in July 1992.

Similarly, the OSCE is extremely dependent on the European Union and on powerful and relatively wealthy countries such as the United States. Those states and multilateral organizations provide the economic resources for the OSCE to carry out its missions as well as the economic foundations for security in regions of Eurasia where scarcity, poverty, and unemployment breed instability and insecurity. Even though economic and technical cooperation constituted one of the three so-called baskets of the Helsinki Final Act, it is now apparent that the comparative advantage of the OSCE does not lie in the field of economics, given the extremely limited resources that it commands. Therefore, although it can facilitate cooperation with other institutions more generously endowed with economic resources, the OSCE should not compete with organizations like the European Union. Instead, it should rely on the EU's support wherever economic resources need to be brought to bear to assist in the resolution of problems that lead to conflict and violence.

The OSCE must also enhance its cooperation with other institutions that have overlapping functions, such as the Council of Europe. In the recent past, there have sometimes been conflicts over the similar roles of the OSCE and the Council of Europe in human-dimensions activities, especially with regard to setting and implementing norms in areas such as human rights, the rule of law, and democratization through free elections. Similarly, work on the environment does not represent a particular strength of the OSCE, and it ought to yield leadership to the Council of Europe and other institutions with a stronger capability in this area. Cooperation between the OSCE and the Council of Europe increased considerably in the second half of the 1990s, a positive development that needs to be replicated elsewhere. Finally, the United Nations and the OSCE have at times become embroiled in disputes over the division of tasks in postwar Kosovo, due in large part to the ambiguous nature of authority granted in the June 1999 agreement that led to their deployment and the apparent overlap of tasks assigned to these two large security institutions.

Second, the OSCE needs to take a series of modest but comprehensive steps to improve and professionalize its conflict-prevention mechanisms. Missions should have longer mandates, with specific, goal-oriented tasks and budgets that are adequate to meet the requirements of the mandate. With a 2000 budget of some 191 million euros, the overall OSCE budget is still extremely small, especially compared to the costs of military operations—both peacemaking and peace enforcement—that may be necessary when the OSCE's conflict-prevention efforts fail.

The recent steps to create the REACT force of standby volunteers and a support center in the Conflict Prevention Center should add to the ability of the OSCE to respond rapidly and competently to future conflicts that break out in Eurasia. But better training of mission members and volunteers for programs like REACT are necessary if they are going to be able to play a proactive role in conflict settlement; sadly, efforts by untrained mediators too often exacerbate rather than resolve conflicts. Finally, the OSCE ought to be able to evaluate when missions have realized their goals and thus close down successful missions so that limited attention and resources can be redirected to the areas of greatest potential danger.

Finally, the OSCE and its member governments need to stop selling the organization short. Too often they have viewed the OSCE as having a role to play only on the margins of European security. As a result, they have often failed to seize opportunities to inject the OSCE into potential zones of conflict where prevention might be far more valuable than a subsequent cure, especially if that cure involves military action of the kind taken in Kosovo. If national governments were confident in the potential of the OSCE and gave it the support it needs—not only materially but politically—then it could become demonstrably more successful in producing clear and recognizable joint benefits in terms of improved security for all of its members. This would positively reinforce the confidence that member governments and their populations have in the OSCE, so that they would be more likely to assign it a central role in conflict management whenever violence threatens to break out. In the absence of such confidence, the OSCE will inevitably fall short of expectations. This will cause its critics to dismiss it as another weak and ineffective multilateral organization upon which states cannot depend to preserve national security. States may consequently withdraw their support from the OSCE and put greater confidence in military alliances and unilateral self-help.

CONCLUSION

The future of the OSCE depends not only upon its objective accomplishments but upon the premises with which today's leaders approach European security. Like Jean Monnet and others who inspired a vision of a united and peaceful Western Europe after World War II, in the aftermath of the end of the Cold War leaders in Europe, Eurasia, and North America could adopt a new vision of a collective approach to European security for the twenty-first century. Belief in that vision might create the political environment in which strengthened multi-lateral security institutions could flourish. As Robert Keohane and Stanley Hoffmann note, "international institutions change realities and expectations."[22] Alternatively, they could fatalistically resign themselves to accept the inevitable future of conflict and insecurity prophesied by the realists. Instead of building and strengthening multilateral institutions, they could fall back on self-help strategies in which states act unilaterally to protect their own security, thereby reinforcing security dilemmas that in the end make everyone more insecure.

The OSCE alone, of course, is not a panacea for a new, stable, and secure European order, and excessively optimistic expectations could lead to almost certain disappointment and disillusionment. At the same time, the denial of the potential of multilateral security institutions like the OSCE by realists, and political leaders in many countries who subscribe to their views, generates a self-fulfilling prophecy. It undermines their ability to reach their potential and may even condemn them in advance to almost certain failure. What is needed is a recognition of the concrete accomplishments already made by the OSCE and support for the optimistic, but not unrealistic, belief that some modest efforts to strengthen the OSCE could make a significant positive contribution to a more secure common future for all Europeans "from Vancouver to Vladivostok."

NOTES

This chapter was originally prepared for the Third Pan-European International Relations Conference and joint meeting with the International Studies Association in Vienna, September 16–19, 1998. The first draft was written while the author was a Jennings Randolph Senior Fellow at the United States Institute of Peace (USIP) in Washington, D.C., from February through August 1998 and updated in 2000. This chapter is based largely on field research conducted by the author while he was a Fulbright Senior Fellow to the OSCE in Vienna from September 1997 through January 1998, based at the Austrian Institute of International Affairs in Laxenburg. At USIP, I am especially grateful for the assistance of Dr. Joseph Klaits, director of the Jennings Randolph Program; Dr. Sally Blair, program officer; and Simon Limage, my research assistant. For their generous assistance during my period as a Fulbright Fellow, I wish to thank Dr. Richard Pettit of the Council for the International Exchange of Scholars in Washington and coordinator of the Fulbright Program in Western Europe; Mr. Stanley

Schrager and Ms. Ileen Jennison of the Public Affairs Office, U.S. Mission to the OSCE in Vienna; Mr. Finn Chemnitz, Diplomatic Officer, and Ms. Kitty Weinberger of the OSCE Conflict Prevention Center in Vienna; and Professor Dr. Otmar Höll, director, Professor Dr. Heinz Gärtner, and Ms. Monika Stepanovsky, of the Austrian Institute for International Affairs in Laxenburg, who provided a most hospitable home for my research. I am also grateful to Heinz Gärtner, Victor-Yves Ghébali, and Peter Liotta for comments on the draft of this chapter presented in Vienna in September 1998.

1. For a comprehensive analysis of the factors accounting for the dissolution of Yugoslavia, see Susan L. Woodward (1995) *Balkan Tragedy: Chaos and Dissolution After the Cold War* (Washington, D.C.: Brookings Institution).

2. Terrence Lyons and Ahmed I. Samatar (1995) *Somalia: State Collapse, Multilateral Intervention, and Strategies for Political Reconstruction* (Washington, D.C.: Brookings Institution), p. 1. See also I. William Zartman (ed.) (1995) *Collapsed States: The Disintegration and Restoration of Legitimate Authority* (Boulder: Lynne Rienner Publishers).

3. See P. Terrence Hopmann, Stephen D. Shenfield, and Dominique Arel (1997) *Integration and Disintegration in the Former Soviet Union: Implications for Regional and Global Security* (Providence, R.I.: Thomas J. Watson Institute for International Studies, Occasional Paper no. 30). The only serious competition as a major new regional threat might be the potential for runaway proliferation of armaments of all kinds and loosening control in Russia over weapons of mass destruction. At the time of this writing, however, this threat remains largely hypothetical, whereas ethnic violence has already appeared frequently and thus constitutes a major and immediate threat to security in many parts of Eurasia.

4. John J. Mersheimer (1991) *Back to the Future: Instability in Europe After the Cold War,* reprinted in Sean M. Lynn-Jones and Steven E. Miller (eds.) *The Cold War and After: Prospects for Peace* (Cambridge: MIT Press), pp. 142–143.

5. Robert O. Keohane and Joseph S. Nye (1993) "Introduction: The End of the Cold War in Europe," in Robert O. Keohane, Joseph S. Nye, and Stanley Hoffmann (eds.) (1993) *After the Cold War: International Institutions and State Strategies in Europe, 1989–1991* (Cambridge: Harvard University Press), pp. 5–6.

6. Andreas Hasenclever, Peter Mayer, and Volker Rittberger (1997) *Theories of International Regimes* (Cambridge, UK: Cambridge University Press), p. 136.

7. The organization was known as the Conference on Security and Cooperation in Europe (CSCE) from its founding in 1973 through 1994; beginning in 1995, following the Budapest Summit, its name was changed to reflect its transformation from a series of conferences into an organization with a permanent secretariat.

8. The analysis in this section is based largely on on-site research by the author at the OSCE headquarters in Vienna for two extended periods in 1992 and in 1997–1998, including interviews with numerous OSCE staff members, heads of mission, and national delegations.

9. In the social-science jargon, this is often referred to as the problem of *sampling on the dependent variable*. In other words, if one focuses only on conflicts that end in violence, one may identify conditions that are presumed to cause violent outcomes (dependent variables); one may overlook, however, the fact that many of these factors may have also been present in situations that ended nonviolently. As a result, the observer may fail to identify those factors that make the critical difference between conflicts that end with violence and those that do not.

10. See Michael Doyle (1993) "Kant, Liberal Legacies, and Foreign Affairs," in *Philosophy and Public Affairs* 12, no. 3 (Summer): 205–235; Bruce M. Russett (1993) *Grasping the Democratic Peace: Principles for the Post–Cold War World* (Princeton:

Princeton University Press); and Michael W. Doyle (1997) *Ways of War and Peace* (New York: W. W. Norton), chap. 8.

11. The status of the missions in Central Asia is somewhat ambiguous. There is an OSCE liaison office for Central Asia based in Tashkent and reporting directly to the OSCE Secretary-General. There are also OSCE centers in Almaty, Bishkek, and Ashkabat under the Conflict Prevention Center. The OSCE Advisory and Monitoring Group in Belarus functions more or less like a mission of long-term duration, although the government of Belarus refused to accept an OSCE presence, established in early 1998, if it were called a "mission," leading the OSCE member states to find another appropriate euphemism to describe its resident activity based in Minsk. Similar reasoning led the OSCE to call its activity in Chechnya an "assistance group" and to refer to its role in Albania as the OSCE "presence."

12. OSCE, "Memorandum of Understanding Between the Government of Belarus and the Organization for Security and Co-operation in Europe on the OSCE Advisory and Monitoring Group in Belarus," SEC.GAL/37/97, December 18, 1997.

13. Max van der Stoel (1997) "Minorities in Transition," *War Report*, no. 48 (January-February): 16.

14. The convoluted title for this mission is a consequence of Greek objections to the name of Macedonia, by which this region was known when it was one of the six republics in the Yugoslav federation but which, according to the claims of the Greek government, refers to a much larger region including significant segments of modern Greece. Although there has subsequently been a compromise decision to call this state the Former Yugoslav Republic of Macedonia, this name has not been accepted by the government of the country. Therefore, the OSCE mission has been referred to under the name of the republic's capital city, Skopje.

15. Allan Rosas and Timo Lahelma (1997) "OSCE Long-Term Missions," in Michael Bothe, Natalino Ronzitti, and Allan Rosas (eds.) *The OSCE in the Maintenance of Peace and Security: Conflict Prevention, Crisis Management, and Peaceful Settlement of Disputes* (The Hague: Kluwer Law International), p. 184.

16. Although Kosovo might also be considered to constitute such a case after the NATO air war was brought to an end in June 1999, the OSCE role was mostly restricted to promoting measures of democratization rather than seeking a solution to the conflict. Responsibility for administering Kosovo fell instead to the United Nations, which is also charged with seeking an eventual settlement of the political status of Kosovo in relationship to the Republic of Serbia and the Federal Republic of Yugoslavia.

17. Ettore Greco (1997) "Third Party Peace-keeping and the Interaction Between Russia and the OSCE in the CIS Area," in Bothe et al., *The OSCE in the Management of Peace and Security*, p. 281.

18. Tim Guldimann (1997) "The OSCE Assistance Group to Chechnya," paper presented at the Carnegie Endowment for International Peace, Washington, D.C., March 11, 1997, p. 3.

19. Although technically the dispute is between Azerbaijan and the secessionist forces in Nagorno-Karabakh, their extensive support from Armenia has in effect made the government in Yerevan a party to the conflict, whose participation is required for its resolution.

20. Interview with Ambassador Roland Bimo, Albanian representative to the OSCE, Vienna, January 21, 1998.

21. Giovanni Porto (1999) "Albania's Path to Democracy—New Law on Civil Service," *OSCE Newsletter* 6, nos. 11–12 (November-December): 8–10.

22. Robert O. Keohane and Stanley Hoffmann (1993) "Conclusion: Structure, Strategy, and Institutional Roles," in Keohane et al., *After the Cold War*, p. 392.

11

Targeting Its Constituency: Political Will, Public Relations, and the OSCE

Walter Kemp

This chapter is an insider's view on how to improve the outsider's knowledge of the Organization for Security and Cooperation in Europe (OSCE). It looks at the relationship between political will and public awareness, asks what the OSCE's constituency is, and examines whether or not that audience is being reached.

THE POLITICAL WILL/PUBLIC AWARENESS RELATIONSHIP

Almost every organization, private or public, needs to generate publicity about its work in order to raise public awareness. The underlying assumption is that raising public awareness can generate support (political, financial, sympathetic) for one's activities. Where democratic governments are concerned, public support is crucial, hence the obsession with image—even to the detriment of substance.

Increasingly, the linchpin between political will and public opinion is the media. Twenty-four-hour news, on-the-spot reporting, investigative journalism, spin doctors, and the Internet have revolutionized the dynamics of domestic politics and international relations. In many respects, the media has become, to quote former U.S. Secretary of State Warren Christopher, the North Star of foreign policy.

There is a symbiotic feedback relationship between political will and public opinion. Sometimes political will is mobilized to raise or manipulate public awareness. At other times, public opinion can create a groundswell of support that can generate the political will necessary to effect change.

The pivotal role of the media in society has long been recognized by the OSCE. The need for freer dissemination of information and improved working conditions for journalists was laid out in the so-called third basket of the 1975 Helsinki Final Act. This recognition of the importance of the freedom of expression was an inspiration to many journalists and human rights activists during the Cold War; as a result, they brought their leaders to account when free speech was muzzled. Although governments could still suppress outspoken critics, such actions came at a heavy price, for they showed the incongruence between public opinion and the state. Over time that incongruence helped to erode the legitimacy of the communist governments of Eastern Europe and the Soviet Union and contributed to their collapse.

Further evidence of the OSCE's concern for the role of the media in society can be seen in the Moscow Document of 1991, which states that "independent media are essential to a free and open society and accountable systems of government and are of particular importance in safeguarding human rights and fundamental freedoms." This point is frequently reinforced in the day-to-day work of the OSCE. Media activities are routinely observed as part of OSCE long-term election monitoring, and some OSCE missions, most notably Bosnia-Herzegovina and Croatia, support media development as part of their democratization activities. Furthermore, since January 1998 the OSCE has had a Representative on Freedom of the Media whose mandate is "to strengthen the implementation of relevant OSCE principles and commitments as well as to improve the effectiveness of concerted action by the participating States based on their common values."

Clearly, there is a recognition by OSCE participating states that the media is a powerful tool and that it can influence the relationship between governments and their electorate as well as relations among states. There is also a clear correlation between public accountability, transparency and openness, and cooperative security and good governance. However, the OSCE has been slow to apply these lessons to itself. How does one account for this?

SHEDDING THE CONFERENCE CULTURE

The OSCE began life as the Conference on Security and Cooperation in Europe (CSCE) in 1973. During the Cold War, the CSCE was an open-ended series of conferences. Only recently has it evolved out of this conference culture—one of smoky meeting rooms, closed to the press and public, where all-night negotiations resulted in rather cryptic decisions. Furthermore, the CSCE was not institutionalized. It was, quite simply, a self-perpetuating and self-contained diplomatic process that moved from meeting to meeting with an accumulating catalog of decisions and principles but without permanent bodies and support staff. Its principles and decisions generated its publicity, as did the application (or lack of implementation) of those principles by the people who took them to heart—groups like Charter 77, Amnesty International, and Soviet dissidents who held their governments accountable to their CSCE commitments.

The CSCE process, despite the closed doors and lack of public-relations staff, struck a chord with the public. People associated the CSCE with the principles of the Helsinki Final Act, the linkage between human rights and security, and negotiations between representatives of the Eastern bloc, the West, and the neutral and nonaligned countries over the most pertinent issues of the era. The CSCE mattered to diplomats and the man in the street because it was seen as a potential vehicle for fostering security through cooperation in a divided Europe. Because the CSCE was a child of the Cold War, it had to retool itself in the postcommunist period. The point was still to build security through cooperation. But as ideological bipolarity was replaced by greater cooperation, relative stability gave way to new insecurities. Due in large part to a lack of bureaucratic inertia, the CSCE was able to quickly adapt to these new challenges.

Arguably, the changes that the CSCE undertook in the early 1990s made it more difficult to understand for the outside world. Since the challenges to security were less cut and dried than those faced between 1975 and 1990, the response had to be more subtle and multidimensional. This widened the already comprehensive view of security. It also meant becoming involved to an unprecedented extent in intrastate conflicts that defied conventional paradigms of international relations. New mechanisms and institutions like missions and other field activities, the High Commissioner on National Minorities, and the Office for Democratic Institutions and Human Rights (ODIHR) were relatively successful, but they were little known partly because they usually operated discretely, partly because they were so new and novel, but mainly because there was no organizational apparatus to explain what they were doing.

Not only was there practically no public information; the activities of the CSCE/OSCE were all but out of bounds to those few journalists and academics who were interested in what was going on. Almost all meetings and documents were restricted. The few people in the know were those like Radio Free Europe journalist Rollie Eggelston and Swiss professor of international studies Victor Yves Ghebali, who had inside contacts and access to information. As a result, on many occasions they became filters and sources of information to the outside world for what was going on behind closed doors.

Another reason why the CSCE/OSCE was (and arguably still is) hard to crack for an outside observer is because its approach to security is unique. Cooperative security, because of its nonconfrontational nature, is both low-key and long-term. So, too, is democracy building and the so-called human dimension of the OSCE's work—itself a cryptic expression to the uninitiated. Most of what the OSCE does is undramatic. Developing civil society is like pouring concrete: it is essential for building strong foundations, but it takes time, and watching it solidify is rather uneventful. Successful preventive diplomacy is hard to quantify (in other words, nothing happens when it works) and post-conflict rehabilitation can take years just to achieve normalization. For these reasons, much of what the OSCE does is considered unnewsworthy for the media and public and their relatively short attention spans.

In the early 1990s, the OSCE evolved from a process to an institution with specific expertise in all phases of the conflict cycle—preventive diplomacy, crisis management, and postconflict rehabilitation—particularly through its field activities and specialized institutions. As a result, its character and profile changed. The public impression of an organization of gray men in gray suits sitting around the conference table changed to a much more action-oriented organization involved in election monitoring, troubleshooting, and conflict management. In the mid-1990s, the OSCE's public profile was raised by its activities in Kosovo, Bosnia, Albania, and Chechnya. There were a growing number of references to the OSCE on the Internet, over the wire services, and in library catalogs. Reuters began to refer to the OSCE as either "Europe's watchdog" or "Europe's leading security organization."

Part of the process of institutionalization was to introduce a press and public-information officer in 1994. By 2000, this one post had evolved into a press and public-information section with seven people in the OSCE Secretariat, as well as press and public-information officers or contact points in most OSCE institutions and missions. Related activities now include a comprehensive website, a monthly newsletter, regular information for the press (including briefings, press releases, and press trips), and a series of publications, including a handbook. Most of this information is available in all six working languages of the OSCE (English, French, German, Italian, Russian, and Spanish). In short, the OSCE now has a well-functioning, professional press and public-information section. There is also broad acceptance among participating states that press and public information is important. This commitment can be noted by the fact that the 2000 budget for press and public information is approximately 775,000 euros, an increase of 110 percent over the 1999 budget.

Nevertheless, the OSCE remains a relatively unknown and opaque organization. Except for the occasional news story, the organization's constituency remains limited to political elites, specialist nongovernmental organizations, and security experts. Because of the relatively restricted nature of OSCE information, even this constituency finds it hard to find out what is going on. What are the reasons for this?

WHY SO MODEST?

After the end of the Cold War, low public awareness of the CSCE/OSCE was the result of a lack of openness and the absence of a public-relations strategy. Until the mid-1990s, the fact that few people knew about the OSCE stemmed in part from the fact that it was almost impossible to find out anything about the organization. A low profile became a self-fulfilling prophecy: few resources were devoted to raising public awareness, which meant a lack of public interest in the OSCE, which suggested that there was no point in spreading the word about its activities. Fortunately, as the developments above would suggest, this shortsighted perspective is changing.

Still, the organization is a hard sell. One reason is the fact that most of the areas where it is engaged are of little interest to the average person—until things go horribly wrong. Who had ever heard of Chechnya or Kosovo until a few years ago? How many people understand the complexities of national reconciliation in Tajikistan or the intricacies of the political settlement processes in places like South Ossetia, Abkhazia, Transdniestria, or Nagorno-Karabakh? Sadly, crises in some OSCE countries are sometimes regarded by the popular press in the same disinterested way that Neville Chamberlain referred to Germany's annexation of the Sudetenland in 1938: "a quarrel in a faraway country between people of whom we know nothing."

The OSCE does not easily lend itself to "branding," to use the marketing vernacular. Its logo is fairly nondescript, it has no recognizable headquarters, and it has few high-level personalities with the exception of the Chairman-in-Office and the High Commissioner on National Minorities. It has the additional handicap that its name is a mouthful in any language; the acronym *OSCE* doesn't roll off the tongue like *NATO* or *UN*.

At the same time, the OSCE's low profile can be attributed to a conscious strategy to avoid the limelight. Many of the OSCE's activities are designed to avoid creating conflicts or crises—in other words, news. If prevention works, it stops dramatic or newsworthy things from happening. If someone told Humpty-Dumpty to get down off the wall at an early stage, nothing would have happened—no nursery rhyme, no work for all the king's horses and all the king's men. If a forest ranger goes through the forest and prevents fires, this is rather uninteresting. But if half of Florida or large tracts of Greek forest burn to the ground, this is news. Preventing crises may not make dramatic headlines—but that's the point.

The work of OSCE missions is also usually quite low-key. Because OSCE missions and other field activities pursue a cooperative approach to security, they seek to work with and maintain the confidence of the host government. In most cases the OSCE, through its missions and other field activities, does not want to overly politicize or sensationalize situations. Negative press coverage of the missions' activities or criticism by the mission of the host country's behavior could cause friction.

Of course, there are exceptions where pressure needs to be brought to bear on the host government in order to prod it into living up to its commitments or to follow a course of action favorable to the majority of OSCE states. This is particularly the case in violations of commitments in the human dimension (e.g., elections, freedom of the media, human rights abuses, and resettlement of refugees and displaced persons), when public pressure can focus attention and mobilize support against an errant state. Through this approach, states can be brought back into line before the situation gets worse. The fact that criticisms are seldom made in public means that the use of a public pronouncement (a critical election report, a statement by the Chairman-in-Office or another high-ranking OSCE official, or a publicized remark by a head of mission) is in itself a demonstration of the organization's resolve. Because it is a departure from the usual way that the organization does business, when it does happen, the state in question usually takes notice.

For the most part, however, the cooperative approach to security usually results in a soft and constructive line. This tactic has proved successful in many instances. In terms of European security, this is a good thing. In terms of publicizing the work of the OSCE, it creates a paradox: the same reasons that make the organization successful keep it out of the public eye.

One result is that the OSCE is often overlooked when credit is given for success. This would not be so bad if critics did not apply a double standard when apportioning blame. When there is a success story in which the OSCE has played a significant role, the same observers who are quick to criticize the OSCE for being ineffective vaguely refer to the success of the international community (if they acknowledge the success at all). When there is a failure, it is the OSCE rather than the international community that is to blame.

MORE OPENNESS AND PUBLICITY?

Therefore, wouldn't the OSCE benefit by more openness and publicity? Let's look at both sides of the argument, starting with "yes." The assumption here is that there is a correlation between media attention and political will. Like it or not, politicians and diplomats are conscious of, and in some cases driven by, the media. Following this argument, wider recognition of the OSCE will generate greater interest among decisionmakers and therefore make it easier for officials dealing with the OSCE to forward their policy and budgetary aims. Furthermore, an organization that prides itself on the human dimension should reach out to the people who are impacted by its decisions. Besides, very little that the OSCE does is secret. For example, is it really necessary for the Permanent Council to be closed to the press and public? In the past few years, the Permanent Council has become less of a negotiating body and more of a rubber stamp for negotiations that have taken place in the Informal Permanent Council, the corridors, and the capitals.

This was indirectly acknowledged by the creation of the Preparatory Committee at the 1999 Istanbul Summit. If the Permanent Council is now more symbolic than substantive, why not open it to the public? Ministerial and summit meetings are already heading in that direction. Following this logic, more documents could be made publicly available. In a similar vein, although too much publicity might compromise the work of the organization in specific situations, it would not hurt for its overall profile to be enhanced. As noted earlier, more resources are being devoted to this task. The twenty-fifth anniversary of the OSCE in 2000 is a good impetus to go even farther in this regard.

But let us look at the other side of the argument, that is, the case against opening up the OSCE. The OSCE is an international organization. One could even argue that the OSCE is merely a collection of states or that it simply represents the framework and parameters for a collection of states that share a common interest, principles, and commitments. There is no need for raising the profile of this process for its own sake. It serves no purpose. The OSCE is not a private enterprise—it doesn't have to sell itself. Its stockholders are its participating states, and it is their organization. Besides, because of the characteristics already described, even if the OSCE was more widely understood, its profile in many activities would still not be very high—and this is one of the secrets of its success. The real work in implementing OSCE principles and commitments rests with the states themselves. The OSCE is only a midwife and/or watchdog in this process. For those reasons, it is the commitments and principles that need to have a higher profile in participating states, not the organization itself.

The truth lies somewhere between. But even following the "no" logic, there is a case for increased public information, albeit of a different kind. The closed circle of OSCE participating states, as well as its related circles of parliamentarians and other international organizations, need more than internal OSCE information. National delegations and OSCE institutions need information about OSCE-related topics in order to make informed policy decisions. Of course, delegations can draw on their own foreign ministries and experts, but there is also a case for receiving specialized information and analytical studies from nongovernmental organizations (NGOs) and academics. This is especially the case for OSCE institutions that do not have their own information-gathering services. If members of NGOs and the academic community—which I will refer to as the *second constituency*, as opposed to the primary target audience (i.e., the press and general public)—are familiar with the OSCE, their work on OSCE-related subjects can have a knock-on effect, first by spreading the word about the organization, and second by infusing new ideas and insights into the OSCE process. After all, the OSCE is no longer strictly a diplomatic process. It is engaged in a wide range of activities that are supported by very limited institutional structures and resources. Staff turnover is high, and there is limited institutional memory or in-house analytical expertise and resources (for example, there is no library in the OSCE Secretariat). Furthermore, the organization is often dealing with issues in which nonstate actors have more expertise and flexibility.

Another argument in favor of opening OSCE, especially to this second constituency, is that NGOs and academics, more than the general public, have a bearing on policy formation and the opinions of decisionmakers and decisiontakers. Following the logic of the relationship between public awareness and political will, if NGOs and academics are more engaged in the activities of the OSCE, they could have an important impact on the political will needed to make most effective use of the organization's capabilities.

This second constituency is seldom targeted. Rectifying this shortfall is in the enlightened best interests of the OSCE.

ENGAGING THE SECOND CONSTITUENCY

How can the OSCE reach this important audience? One basic idea would be to create an OSCE Academics Network. This network, which could be attached to the OSCE website or hosted by a think-tank, would be an Internet clearinghouse of sorts that could include a chatroom on OSCE and OSCE-related issues, a bulletin board to post information on publications and upcoming meetings, as well as a bibliography of information on the OSCE. It could also link people and institutions interested in and/or working on the OSCE. In this way, people doing research on the OSCE and subjects of interest to the OSCE community could be in contact with each other, the OSCE would have a better sense of what expertise it could tap, and in the process a mechanism would be created to galvanize ideas on how to more closely integrate interested outsiders into the work of the organization. This idea has already been raised in the context of the Swiss government's OSCE Cluster of Competence (part of its Partnership for Peace commitment), but it has yet to be developed.

In addition to this virtual clearinghouse, an annual symposium bringing together practitioners and analysts could be arranged to take stock of a range of pertinent issues facing the OSCE. A precedent has already been set with the input of NGOs and academics into discussions on the OSCE Security Model.

Another consideration would be to have a contact point within the OSCE Secretariat to coordinate contacts with the second constituency. For the moment, most contact on subjects of interest to this constituency is made through the ODIHR (on human-dimension issues), or on a case-by-case basis with OSCE institutions, usually in the context of seminars. With a permanent database and regular contacts, the OSCE could tap into the expertise of NGOs and academics on a more regular basis—for either broad-ranging discussions on issues like regional security, or for more specific issues like small arms or mission member training; the second constituency would have an open window on the OSCE process.

This information could also regularly feed into an analytical unit within the organization, perhaps in the Conflict Prevention Center. This unit could act as a filter for information from the second constituency that could enrich the organization's activities across a wide range of subjects.

However, there are those who feel that this type of activity should not be carried out by the Secretariat. But that is not to say that it should not be carried out at all. This is one of the reasons why it has been suggested that the OSCE should, at least indirectly, support the establishment of a think-tank. Some have called it an OSCE Academy; I prefer Institute for Cooperative Security (ICS).

Currently there are a few institutions doing work on the OSCE. Among the most notable are the Institut für Friedenforschung und Sicherheitspolitik an der Universität in Hamburg (which has recently opened the Center for OSCE Research), the Graduate Institute of International Studies in Geneva, the Stockholm International Peace Research Institute, and the Working Group of the German Political Science Association, as well as several individual scholars scattered throughout the OSCE area. But there is no OSCE brain trust as such along the lines of the Western European Union's Institute for Security Studies. The ICS should be at arm's length from the OSCE to maintain a certain amount of independence but, at the same time, should be plugged into the OSCE so that both can benefit from a synergistic relationship. It could also be a center for preserving the organization's institutional memory.

CONCLUSION

This is all just food for thought. But the main point should be reemphasized: now that the OSCE has the means to better project its image and to explain its principles and operations, it must concentrate on targeting and reaching its primary constituency or, as has been argued, other constituencies. Developing press and public-information strategies is a major step forward. But as has been argued above, more efforts are needed to reach and involve NGOs and academics (what I have called the second constituency). If they are better informed about the OSCE and are given more opportunities to be involved in its activities, the organization will profit by gaining valuable allies that can help raise awareness, lend support, and contribute expertise to its work. These assets can help to make the OSCE as effective and dynamic as it looks to its golden anniversary.

12

The High Commissioner
on National Minorities:
His Work, Effectiveness, and
Recommendations to Strengthen
the HCNM as an Institution

WOLFGANG ZELLNER

This chapter addresses the activities and the effectiveness of the OSCE's High Commissioner on National Minorities (HCNM). First, it analyzes the High Commissioner's basic views on carrying out his responsibilities in the area of prevention, including questions about understanding fundamental ethnopolitical categories, basic views on conflict prevention, and the principles by which the HCNM works and employs the instruments at his disposal. Second, the content and tendency of the HCNM's recommendations are investigated on the basis of the recommendations given by the HCNM with regard to Hungarian minorities in Romania and Slovakia; Russian minorities in Estonia, Latvia, and Ukraine; and the Albanian minority in Macedonia. The third section deals with the effectiveness of the High Commissioner's activity. This is, politically speaking, the most important question but also the most difficult to answer in a scholarly sense. Fourth, an attempt will be made to formulate several recommendations for strengthening the institution of the High Commissioner on National Minorities of the OSCE.

One of the most tragic ironies since the end of the Cold War lies in the fact that the disappearance of a global and continental risk of war has made possible a series of small and medium-sized wars and civil wars. Nagorno-Karabakh, the former Yugoslavia, and Chechnya are names that stand for hundreds of thousands of deaths and millions of refugees, for enormous economic losses and profound traumas that will go on for decades. The indirect effects of these violent disputes undermine the foundation of common values

265

and the stability of the entire OSCE area. If one had to identify a single cause common to these very different cases, it would be in the area of ethnopolitical conflicts.

This development has taken most countries and international organizations by surprise; after all, "a new era of democracy, peace and unity in Europe"[1] had been predicted, so described in the Charter of Paris for a New Europe. The original Conference on Security and Cooperation in Europe (CSCE), the forerunner to the OSCE, was one of the first international organizations to create instruments for dealing with new ethnopolitical conflict situations. The decisions of the Helsinki Summit in 1992 contain not only a detailed section on early warning, conflict prevention, and crisis management but also the mandate of the HCNM. Its core sentence says:

> The High Commissioner will provide "early warning" and, as appropriate, "early action," at the earliest possible stage in regard to tensions involving national minority issues which have not yet developed beyond an early warning stage, but in the judgement of the High Commissioner, have the potential to develop into a conflict within the CSCE area, affecting peace, stability or relations between participating States, requiring the attention of and action by the Council or the CSO [Committee of Senior Officials].[2]

Because the HCNM's mandate has been dealt with extensively and authoritatively in the scholarly literature,[3] and an investigation of the way in which the office of the High Commissioner has actually been used would appear to be more productive than an analysis of the mandate's text, I shall concentrate on the way in which the incumbent High Commissioner, Max van der Stoel,[4] has carried out and interpreted his mandate and thus put his stamp on the new OSCE institution, as outlined in the opening passages of this chapter.[5] The following four areas to be investigated are: the High Commissioner's basic views on carrying out his responsibilities in the area of prevention; the content and tendency of the HCNM's recommendations; the effectiveness of the High Commissioner's activity; and possible recommendations for strengthening the institution.

This chapter is based on preparatory work for a more comprehensive research project, "On the effectiveness of the OSCE minority regime. Comparative case studies on the implementation of recommendations of the High Commissioner on National Minorities (HCNM) of the OSCE,"[6] in the course of which the degree of implementation of recommendations of the HCNM on Estonia, Latvia, Ukraine, Romania, Slovakia, and Macedonia is to be subjected to a comparative analysis. As the empirical results of this project have not been available in time for this chapter, considerable parts will be devoted to asking questions rather than providing answers; even then, the statements will have only a provisional character.

BASIC VIEWS OF THE HIGH COMMISSIONER

Fundamental Ethnopolitical Categories

Definition of minorities. It is a known fact that because of the varying interests of members, not one of the large international organizations has been able to agree on a definition of *minority* as a concept, let alone that of *national minority.* The High Commissioner brushed this dilemma aside with a statement, which has become famous, to the effect that "I would dare to say that I know a minority when I see one."[7] Even so, he proposed a working definition: "First of all, a minority is a group with linguistic, ethnic or cultural characteristics which distinguish it from the majority. Secondly, a minority is a group which usually not only seeks to maintain its identity but also tries to give stronger expression to that identity."[8] In addition, van der Stoel frequently refers to paragraph 32 of the Copenhagen Document of 1990, which states: "To belong to a national minority is a matter of a person's individual choice."[9] Here, van der Stoel has captured two of the essential characteristics of a minority. First, every minority has at least one characteristic related to its own identity that distinguishes it from the majority; and second, it wants to preserve such characteristics and the dissimilarity constituted by them.

Relationship between majority–minority–kin state; the nature of ethnopolitical conflicts. Like more recent approaches in the theory of nationalism[10] the incumbent HCNM assumes a triangular relationship between state (majority), minority, and kin state, in the process assigning priority to the internal state relationship between majority and minority, both in analytical and practical terms: "Solutions should be sought as much as possible within the framework of the state itself."[11] In van der Stoel's view, the relationship between state and minority is characterized by a balance of reciprocal rights and obligations that in the optimal case can be described in terms of three categories: communication, participation, and integration.[12] The more substantial communication between majority and minority is the greater the level of social and political participation by the minority, the more the minority is integrated into a joint society with the majority, and the more likely it is that the differing identity of the minority can find expression without creating interethnic tensions and conflicts. It follows from this that interethnic tensions can be the result of exclusionary or assimilationist strategies on the part of the majority, or of isolationist strategies of the minority, or of reciprocal effects emerging from both. The High Commissioner clearly addressed both of these aspects in his report to the Human Dimension Implementation Meeting in November 1997. Speaking to both the majorities and the states, he wrote: "integration cannot occur if whole groups of persons remain excluded from being a legitimate and recognized part of the polity in which they live and on which they most depend for the enjoyment of their human rights." Turning to minorities, he said:

> If persons belonging to minorities refuse to recognize that they share a common destiny with the majority in the State within which they live, if they constantly seek to isolate themselves from the rest of society and insist on institutional arrangements which would promote such isolation, the reaction on the other side might be increasingly suspicious and negative.[13]

Van der Stoel emphasizes in this connection the political and politically caused character of interethnic conflicts: "I have been repeatedly struck by the relative harmony between ethnic groups at the inter-personal and community levels. At the political level, however, this harmony can be quite fragile, particularly during periods of transition."[14] On interethnic conflicts, the High Commissioner spoke of "so-called ethnic conflicts"[15] that emerged from the political level and resulted from the strategies of "small groups of radicals"[16] "of very small cliques,"[17] which, to serve their own power interests, exploit and aggravate tensions, particularly those that have arisen during the current transformation processes in Central and Eastern Europe. Thus interethnic conflicts are not, as it were, automatic and hence unavoidable; interethnic tensions turn into conflicts only as a result of extremist strategies that deliberately exploit them. This is the basis for the High Commissioner's assessment that "ethnic conflicts . . . can and should be avoided."[18]

As to the relationship between the minority and the kin state, van der Stoel sees a balance similar to the one between the rights and obligations of majority and minority. On the one hand, he grants that the interest of a kin state in "its" minority is logical and understandable, but "on the other hand the kin state has also the duty to see to it that such expression of concern will not develop into a sort of system of interference into the affairs of the other state. Here there is a fine line which is not always easy to draw."[19] Bilateral treaties between a state containing a minority and the relevant kin state could, in his view, be helpful, but they are no panacea. At a minimum, the following two aspects would have to be taken into consideration in drawing up such treaties:

> First, where relations between neighboring states are already difficult, efforts to conclude a bilateral treaty may only serve to underline their differences. Second, even in cases where bilateral treaties might be within reach, any attempt to force the tempo of negotiations may actually disrupt the process of rapprochement.[20]

This makes clear that van der Stoel regards approaches to conflict regulation within the state concerned as more important than bilateral/international attempts at regulation. With regard to such internal efforts, the two elements of "state" and "minority" are by no means of equal importance. The way in which the High Commissioner's strategy is oriented toward the state becomes clear, for example, from the fact that, even though during the course of his visits he consults with representatives of both the state and of minority associations or parties, his written recommendations are directed only to the state. At the same time, the High Commissioner never tires of stressing that protection of minorities lies in the strategic interest of the countries involved: "The protection of persons belonging to minorities has to be seen as essentially in the interest of the state. If the state shows loyalty to persons belonging to minorities, it can expect loyalty in return from those persons."[21]

Minority rights and self-determination. Van der Stoel bases his view of minority rights on an expanded interpretation of individual rights: "The concept of minority rights rests on the concept of individual human rights but it is only the joint exercise of certain rights in the fields of language, culture and religion that enables the persons belonging to a minority to preserve their identity."[22] However, he makes a distinction between this position and the minimalist view that the observance of human rights in general is sufficient to guarantee the rights of minorities.[23] Yet one can find in van der Stoel's thinking a clear dislike of autonomy arrangements, especially territorial autonomy:

> Secondly, I wonder whether there are not good reasons for minorities to consider a pragmatic approach. Even though the Copenhagen Document mentions territorial autonomy as an option, minorities should take into account the fact that such a demand will probably meet maximum resistance, whereas they might be able to achieve more if they concentrated on legislation that enabled them to have a greater say in fields of special interest for them.[24]

The "mere mention of the term 'autonomy' leads to a large number of concepts that may underlie it, but unfortunately, it does not lead directly to a solution."[25] Thus, the High Commissioner is of the opinion that realizing a minority's right of self-determination—van der Stoel also speaks of "self-realization"—need not be expressed in any territorial way.[26]

Even though this position of the High Commissioner is shared by the majority of OSCE participating states and, as van der Stoel rightly points out, "no international instrument commits or obliges a State to the acceptance of territorial autonomy,"[27] this remains an unsolved normative problem of fundamental importance for the OSCE (which will not be discussed in this chapter but must at least be mentioned). Autonomy arrangements, apart from their nonbinding mention in the Copenhagen Document of 1990 as one possible kind of solution, are not included in the OSCE's set of norms. Even so, the OSCE has in several conflicts—including those in former Yugoslavia, Koso-

vo, Moldova/Transniestria, Georgia, and Nagorno-Karabakh—either worked
out territorial autonomy arrangements itself or at least provided political support for them.[28] The fact that these were all conflicts in which the force
threshold had clearly been crossed gives rise to the provocative question
whether the OSCE and its participating states were not, in these cases, operating with a double standard or with a split set of norms: territorial autonomy
for the settlement of conflicts that take on violent form, no territorial autonomy in cases of tension that remain clearly below the threshold of violence.
This raises several fundamental questions. Does the OSCE need to have a
consistent position on autonomy arrangements? Or are conflicts so varied in
nature that such a position can be dispensed with? What will be the consequences of the current way of dealing with autonomy issues, which is largely opportunistic in character? Is it possible that some minority associations
might draw the wrong conclusions, that is, in view of such an attitude on the
part of the international community, will escalation better serve their purposes than de-escalation?

The main point is that the High Commissioner, in light of the discussion
among political scientists, takes a modern view of ethnopolitical conflicts that
stresses their politically created character. With regard to minority rights, van
der Stoel can be regarded as representative of the mainstream that supports an
expanded concept of the protection of minorities based on the collective exercise of individual rights and takes a skeptical view of ideas of autonomy and
collective rights.

Early Warning, Conflict Prevention, and the Responsibilities of the High Commissioner

Although the mandate of the HCNM, in van der Stoel's estimate, "is the most
elaborate CSCE text on early warning and preventive diplomacy,"[29] it contains
no definitions of *early warning* or *conflict prevention*. For that reason, the
incumbent HCNM has presented several working definitions: "As a working
definition I would say that early warning should provide the relevant CSCE
bodies with information about escalatory developments . . . far enough in
advance in order for them to react timely and effectively. . . . This also
includes what I would call the 'tripwire function.'" And: "As far as preventive
diplomacy is concerned I would say that it should contain particular disputes
and threats and prevent them from escalating into armed conflict. If possible
it should try to dissolve those disputes but that may be too much of a task for
preventive diplomacy alone."[30] Van der Stoel distinguishes between "early
and late preventive diplomacy" and sees a close relationship between early
warning, preventive diplomacy, and short-term conflict prevention, whereas
long-term conflict prevention calls for a comprehensive approach.[31] This
comprehensive approach refers to the broad security concept of the OSCE,

which includes all of its dimensions. However, the High Commissioner rightly criticizes the fact "that, alone among the various dimensions of the CSCE, the economic dimension is virtually lacking from the range of CSCE conflict prevention tools."[32] Considering the importance of economic and social factors for the transformation processes in Central and Eastern Europe, there is no doubt that this lack substantially diminishes the effectiveness of the OSCE's instruments for conflict prevention.

The mandate of the High Commissioner, according to van der Stoel, "puts me first and foremost in the category of short-term conflict prevention. At the same time, however, to be effective I cannot pass by the important longer-term aspects of the situations with which I have to deal."[33] And yet the High Commissioner has a dual job to carry out: "first, to try to contain and de-escalate such tensions, and second, to act as a 'tripwire.'"[34] All in all, the HCNM has to fulfill "a self-standing conflict prevention function."[35] If one compares the text of the mandate with van der Stoel's interpretative statements and the practical work of the High Commissioner, it becomes clear that the incumbent HCNM takes a proactive approach: "Early action is required."[36] In comparison with early warning, which is strongly emphasized in the mandate, active conflict prevention has clearly taken center stage. The formal early-warning notice, to which a whole section of the mandate was devoted, has become almost meaningless; the High Commissioner has so far undertaken only a single use of this instrument.[37] Indeed, van der Stoel equates the issuance of an early-warning notice with his failure in a case: "If I would have to issue an early warning notice, it means that I would not have been able to fulfil the most essential of my tasks which is to prevent the matter from getting out of hand."[38]

The High Commissioner sees the limits of his effectiveness as being reached if tensions have already led to a violent conflict. However, the HCNM could once again play a useful role in the phase of postconflict rehabilitation: "One could imagine, however, that the Commissioner could make a contribution once a conflict situation involving violence has come to an end, but the underlying causes which led to the conflict have not yet been removed."[39] This means that the instrument of the HCNM can in principle be used in all phases of a conflict where violence has not yet broken out or does not continue, that is, when there remains among the parties to the conflict minimum willingness to cooperate, something that is indispensable for the successful use of the instruments of preventive diplomacy.

Methods and Instruments of Work

The High Commissioner's basic methods and instruments of work are partly provided for in his mandate and have partly been developed by the incumbent himself.

Principles and methods emerging from the mandate. Along with the independence of the HCNM, which is a necessary condition for carrying out his activities, impartiality, confidentiality, and cooperation[40] can be mentioned. At first glance, impartiality would appear to be perfectly obvious, but when one looks more closely, some farther-reaching conceptual dimensions of this principle begin to appear. It follows logically from the principle of impartiality that the HCNM "has not been defined as an instrument of the human dimension";[41] neither is he "an instrument for the protection of minorities or a sort of international ombudsman who acts on their behalf. This is reflected in the title: OSCE High Commissioner *on* National Minorities and not *for* National Minorities."[42] The High Commissioner's involvement in cases of tension related to minorities represents an indirectly effective "security-oriented approach to minority rights,"[43] because his direct mandate is concerned with "*tensions* [emphasis added] involving national minority issues which . . . have the potential to develop into a conflict within the OSCE area, affecting peace, stability or relations between participating States."

This indirect strategy is possible only because the comprehensive security concept of the OSCE ties together all causes and dimensions of conflict in such a way that violations of minority and human rights, traditionally the internal affairs of states, come to represent an endangerment of stability and security, a classic problem in international relations. The comprehensive OSCE security concept—and this is the real innovation—thus allows for the involvement of international institutions, in this case the HCNM, in traditional *domains reservés* of national sovereignty. Still, to be sure, this is only on the basis of an indirect strategy that ties the two areas together and thus legitimates what is a new effect under international law. For this reason, the High Commissioner *must* be an instrument of the security dimension; assigning him to the human dimension would put at risk the entire basis of his legitimation.

The principle of confidentiality, also contained in the mandate, makes it possible to control any escalation risks that might be associated with the involvement of the HCNM: "It is, however, possible that early involvement might actually escalate the disputes if parties are encouraged to exploit outside attention. This risk can be considerably reduced if a low profile is adopted."[44] In practice, this means that the High Commissioner gives press conferences only in coordination with, and with the agreement of, the parties involved. Van der Stoel's numerous speeches and articles deal almost exclusively with general aspects of his activity and rarely go into the detailed conflict situations in the countries where he is active.

A principle that can be at least derived from the spirit of the mandate (and from the entire construction of the OSCE) is that of a cooperative, or noncoercive,[45] way of proceeding. The incumbent has on many occasions put particular stress on this principle: "Coercion would certainly never have a lasting positive effect. In other words: if solutions are found, it is essentially because parties themselves want a solution, but require some advice or assistance in getting there."[46] Moreover, van der Stoel has called attention to the relationship between a cooperative manner of proceeding and international involvement in fields of national action: "It is in the light of this crucial aspect of cooperation that we should look upon the process of increasing CSCE intrusiveness in the affairs of participating states."[47] Along with the strategy of indirect legitimation, the principle of cooperation is a further condition for enabling international organizations to act at the national level—especially in fields such as interethnic relations, among the most sensitive that exist.

This makes clear in a general way that the principles of impartiality, confidentiality, and cooperation provided for in the HCNM's mandate are not just working principles for the HCNM as an instrument of conflict prevention; politically and under international law, they are also a necessary condition for the sort of international involvement in areas of national interest that may be regarded as a *conditio sine qua non* of effective conflict prevention.

Instruments of work created by the High Commissioner himself. The incumbent HCNM has developed further approaches contained in the mandate while creating new working instruments within the framework of the mandate. In the first place, mention should be made of the recommendations that the High Commissioner sends in the form of letters to the foreign ministers of various states. The category of recommendations has scarcely been elaborated in the mandate; the idea appears only in the section on the High Commissioner and involvement of experts (in the appendix on sources of information about national minority issues). Here, van der Stoel, making use of the most rudimentary approaches in the mandate, has created a new instrument that has come to be one of the most important ones in the hands of the HCNM (as well as one of the most fruitful for interested scholars).

Another instrument developed by van der Stoel himself includes recommendations for the practical interpretation of OSCE norms: The Hague Recommendations Regarding the Education Rights of National Minorities and Explanatory Note,[48] the Oslo Recommendations Regarding the Linguistic Rights of National Minorities and Explanatory Note,[49] and the Lund Recommendations on the Effective Participation of National Minorities in Public Life and Explanatory Note.[50] These three sets of recommendations were worked out by expert groups set up by the Foundation on Inter-Ethnic Relations, which supports the work of the HCNM. The need for such recommendations arises from the gap that exists between relatively abstract OSCE norms and the disputes over educational, linguistic, and participatory issues, which are often of a highly concrete nature and confront the High Commissioner in individual countries. Thus, the recommendations of The Hague, Oslo, and Lund cover precisely that middle level of abstraction that is most relevant for the purposes of taking action. According to the report of the High Commissioner to the 1997 Human Dimension Implementation Meeting, "*The Hague Recommendations* were very well received by relevant parties as a practical and balanced guide for resolution of many specific issues."[51] Neither the High Commissioner nor the expert groups he puts together have a mandate to develop new OSCE norms; even so, it cannot be overlooked that with his recommendations on the concrete interpretation of existing OSCE norms van der Stoel has created a new instrument that is highly relevant for action and has de facto advanced the development of norms by making them more concrete.

A third instrument is constituted by the project-oriented approach[52] that the High Commissioner has used in several cases in which it was clear that the classic methods of preventive diplomacy would not be adequate. Examples are "projects in the educational field . . . for the improvement of minority education, including the training of teachers and the publication of school books . . . inter alia, in Albania, . . . Macedonia, Kyrgyzstan and Ukraine."[53] Other projects have to do with roundtables—for example, in Croatia, Estonia, Macedonia, and Kazakhstan—and information projects such as the ones in Estonia and Latvia on citizenship issues. The project approach shows that classic preventive diplomacy (mediation, good offices, recommendations, etc.) quickly reach the limits of their effectiveness and must be embedded in a more comprehensive approach involving an expanded range of instruments.

All in all, it is fair enough for van der Stoel to claim that "the HCNM has developed his own approach to his tasks through his understanding of the notion of comprehensive security."[54] This applies to the whole spectrum of application, exercise, interpretation, and concretization of his mandate, with regard both to the principles and instruments of his work and to the OSCE norms that underlie them. In this way, van der Stoel has established a substantial number of precedents that his successor will have to take into account.

CONTENT AND TENDENCY OF THE HCNM'S RECOMMENDATIONS

Theoretical and Methodological Considerations

This section deals with the question of whether a specific tendency can be discerned in the recommendations of the High Commissioner and, if so, what its nature is. On the one hand, it is correct to say: "What might be a useful solution for the position of minorities in the context of one State, can be totally inappropriate in the context of another."[55] This could mean that the recommendations of the HCNM are so specific that they can hardly be subjected to comparison. On the other hand, the High Commissioner is again and again confronted with certain issues in several countries, especially those dealing with education and language policy. The elaboration of the recommendations of The Hague, Oslo, and Lund makes clear that it is quite possible to formulate recommendations for differing countries and minority situations. In what follows, I will investigate the question of whether there is a specific tendency to be seen in those recommendations as well as in the recommendations of the HCNM to the governments of Estonia, Latvia, Ukraine, Romania, Slovakia, and Macedonia. Because the recommendations of the High Commissioner have not yet been fully evaluated here, the results must be regarded as provisional.

In order to compare the High Commissioner's recommendations to the various governments, a common standard is needed to apply to their content, one that can be formulated only in abstract terms owing to the differences between the various situations. Since ethnopolitical conflicts have to do with the relations between nations as well as those between nations and the state, the quality of nation-building and state-building strategies appears to be suitable as the central analytical category. Juan J. Linz and Alfred Stepan distinguish between unifying and differentiating nation-building strategies and between inclusionary and exclusionary state-building strategies on the part of the majority and, through the superimposition of these two strategy levels, arrive at a four-field table concerning four types of ethnopolitical strategies: an exit strategy involving an exclusionary state-building and a unifying nation-building strategy in which the minority is either driven out or at least encouraged to leave the country on its own initiative; an isolation strategy made up of an exclusionary state-building and a differentiating nation-building strategy that grants the minority civil and social rights but not political rights; an assimilation strategy made up of an inclusionary state-building strategy and a unifying nation-building strategy that does give political rights to the minority but at the price of their ethnocultural identity; and, finally, a strategy of balance based on an inclusionary state-building strategy and a differentiating nation-building strategy that draws the minority into the construction of the state but does not seek in the process to take away their cultural particularity.[56]

This concept has the significant advantage of describing both the relationship between nations and their relationship to the state in terms of general schemes of values and preferences. However, Linz and Stepan limit themselves to the state- and nation-building strategies of the majority and thus fail to take account of the interactive nature of the relationship between majority, minority, and kin state. Moreover, they leave out the factor of territoriality, to which both Rogers Brubaker[57] and Claus Offe[58] ascribe central importance as a criterion of ethnopolitical institutionalization. Since the factor of territorial

Figure 12.1   State- and Nation-Building Strategies

		State-Building Strategy			
		No Territorial Differentiation		*Territorial Differentiation*	
		Inclusionary	Exclusionary	Inclusionary	Exclusionary
Nation-Building Strategy	Unifying	Assimilation	Expulsion Emigration	—	Secession Expulsion Division
	Differentiating	Balance	Isolation	Territorial Autonomy	Confederation

differentiation play a big role in the relationship between majorities and minorities—the latter frequently demand territorial autonomy, whereas the former generally fear that there is a desire for secession—we have combined the approaches of Brubaker and Linz and Stepan. We distinguish, in connection with state building, between ethnoterritorial and nonethnoterritorial strategies and between inclusionary and exclusionary strategies; and, in connection with nation building, between unifying and differentiating strategies. When these three characteristics are superimposed, the result is an eight-field scheme that we view as an ethnopolitical value, or preference table, for one group of actors, namely, the majority (or, as the case may be, the state dominated by the majority), the minority, the kin state, and the High Commissioner as external mediator. This analytical instrument makes it possible to apply general value categories to individual lines of action as well as to the institution-building strategies of the three groups of actors and external actors, thereby permitting comparisons (see Figure 12.1).

The High Commissioner's Ethnopolitical Value Table

The following section looks at the ethnopolitical value table of the High Commissioner by examining his recommendations on problems of state and nation building in Estonia, Latvia, Ukraine, Macedonia, Romania, and Slovakia.[59] It also makes use of The Hague Recommendations, the Oslo Recommendations, and the Lund Recommendations, as the High Commissioner himself initiated the development of these documents and refers to them in a favorable way. For reasons of space, the investigation can only be illustrative and make use of examples.

Problems of State Building

Citizenship. Citizenship can be considered to be the most fundamental issue in state building. It has at least three important dimensions. First, members of national minorities may not exercise political rights until they have acquired the status of citizens; second, many states will not recognize ethnically differing groups as a national minority until they have acquired citizenship; and third, there are certain service functions of the state that are open only to citizens.

The High Commissioner has become involved in citizenship questions especially in Estonia and Latvia. In contrast to Lithuania, these two countries have not granted citizenship automatically to those persons living in their territory who do not belong to the majority nation but have made the acquisition of citizenship dependent on a more or less complicated and difficult naturalization process. In dealing with the Estonian and Latvian governments, the High Commissioner advocated in principle a "policy . . . to aim at the integration of the non-Estonian population by a deliberate policy of facilitating the chances of acquiring Estonian citizenship for those who express such a wish, and of assuring them full equality with Estonian citizens."[60] The HCNM filled out this basic recommendation with a wealth of detailed proposals, among them the automatic granting of citizenship to children born in Estonia or Latvia who would otherwise be stateless, simpler language tests, lower administrative fees, and the inclusion of the unemployed in the group of people entitled to acquire citizenship.[61] With respect to Latvia, he pressed again and again for the elimination or liberalization of the quota system in use there.[62] Overall, these recommendations are aimed at achieving integration of national minorities through the granting of citizenship.

Participation of national minorities in public life. As the Lund Recommendations[63] represent the most comprehensive document on this issue drawn up under the aegis of the HCNM, I start from this basis. Under the "General Principles" section, the Lund Recommendations define their starting point as follows: "These Recommendations aim to facilitate the inclusion of minorities within the State and enable minorities to maintain their own identity and characteristics, thereby promoting the good governance and integrity of the State."[64] Van der Stoel himself related this basic objective more openly to the dominant pattern of conflict in the 1990s: "The basic idea behind [the Lund Recommendations] is that there are many other methods than secession to ensure the interests of national minorities. Secession has played quite a role in Europe in the nineties." And further: "The basic question I asked the experts to study was whether sufficient attention had been given to the question of what could be done to safeguard the interests of various ethnic groups living in a multiethnic state while maintaining the territorial integrity of the state."[65]

This basic objective shall be accomplished by a set of recommendations under the sections entitled "Participation in Decisionmaking" and "Self-Governance."[66] The first recommends a series of "Arrangements at the Level of the Central Government," from special representation of minorities in parliament (the case in Romania), "formal or informal understandings for allocating to members of national minorities cabinet positions,"[67] up to "special measures for minority participation in the civil service."[68] Thus, the HCNM pressed in November 1994 for the inclusion of more representatives of the Albanian minority in the armed forces, police, and public offices of Macedonia.[69] Concerning elections, the Lund Recommendations point out that the "electoral system should facilitate minority representation and influence."[70] In June 1994, the High Commissioner had urged the Slovakian government to take account of ethnic considerations in its planned administrative reform; he went on to emphasize "that the electoral system should guarantee adequate representation of minorities on deliberative and executive bodies."[71] Finally, various "Advisory and Consultative Bodies" are proposed "to serve as channels for dialogue between governmental authorities and national minorities."[72] In September 1993, the High Commissioner had recommended that the Romanian government give additional responsibilities to the Council for National Minorities it had established, including certain rights: making "recommendations on legislation," "making proposals on Government decisions," and "monitoring problems at the local level of administration."[73] In November 1993, he recommended to the Slovakian government that it establish a minority council along the lines of the Romanian model.[74] The High Commissioner also suggested to Estonia and Latvia that they set up similar organs or make full use of ones available.[75]

The politically most sensitive part of the Lund Recommendations ("Self-Governance") is divided into two paragraphs on "Non-Territorial Arrangements" and "Territorial Arrangements."[76] The first type of arrangement is seen as most amenable to regulating such issues as "education, culture, use of minority language, religion, and other matters crucial to the identity and way of life of national minorities."[77] *Territorial arrangements* are basically defined as transfer of central governmental competences to lower territorial levels:

> Experience in Europe and elsewhere shows the value of shifting certain legislative and executive functions from the central to the regional level beyond the mere decentralization of central government administration from the capital to regional or local offices. Drawing on the principle of subsidiarity, States should favourably consider such territorial devolution of powers.[78]

The explanatory note to this recommendation, however, makes it very clear that this territorial devolution does not mean arrangements of autonomy on an ethnic basis: "With regard to territorial governance, in no case [among the

OSCE states] does this apply on an ethnic criterion."[79] The incumbent HCNM admits that territorial autonomy has been

> a success in a number of cases. . . . However, we also have to face the fact that quite a number of states are reluctant to grant territorial autonomy. They suspect, rightly or wrongly, that this will prove to be a step in the direction of eventual secession. But there are also ways other than territorial autonomy to ensure that the vital interests and needs of national minorities will be adequately safeguarded. I am thinking for instance of decentralisation, devolution and various forms of participation of representatives of minorities in decisions which are of special interest for them. The twenty eminent persons that drafted the Lund recommendations have concentrated especially on these fields.[80]

Asked directly in which cases he would support solutions of territorial autonomy and in which cases he would not, van der Stoel answered: "I tend to favour a pragmatic approach, taking into account the specific situation in a given country, and then to opt for formulas which would provide the best chance of relative stability. One could also formulate it in a negative way. I would oppose the choice for territorial autonomy if such a formula would lead to potentially dangerous tensions."[81] Following this line, the High Commissioner was in favor of a balanced model of territorial autonomy for Crimea. In contrast, he never supported arrangements for territorial autonomy in Romania and Slovakia, even though the Hungarian minority associations in these two countries have strongly pushed in that direction.[82] On the contrary, in August 1996 the HCNM expressly told the Slovakian government "that no international instrument commits or obliges a State to the acceptance of territorial autonomy."[83] At the same time, however (and in view of threatening tendencies in Slovakia's governing coalition), the HCNM vigorously opposed the criminalization of peaceful efforts aimed at achieving territorial autonomy.

All in all, it is fair to say that the incumbent HCNM is strongly in favor of a regional decentralization on the basis of the subsidiarity principle but very cautious of arrangements of territorial autonomy. The reason lies in the fear that ethnically motivated solutions might quickly develop into (at least the perception of) secession scenarios and thus endanger fundamental stability goals. Thus, the HCNM tries to reach the sometimes nearly impossible and at the same time absolutely necessary objective: to satisfy ethnopolitically motivated needs by basically nonethnic means.

Problems of Nation Building

In his recommendations, the High Commissioner has raised several specific problems of nation building and of the balancing of claims put forward by the majority nation with those of the minority nations. Because of their special

importance, I would like to confine my discussion here to two groups of problems that come up again and again: education rights and language rights of
national minorities.

Education rights of national minorities. The most systematic of the documents drawn up under the aegis of the High Commissioner on the education
rights of national minorities are The Hague Recommendations (1997). In its
first paragraph, this document identifies two main goals. On the one hand,
members of national minorities have the right to maintain their identity, which
can only be assured "if they acquire a proper knowledge of their mother
tongue during the educational process." On the other hand, "persons belonging to national minorities have a responsibility to integrate into the wider
national society through the acquisition of a proper knowledge of the State
language."[84] Realizing these two goals, which are to some extent contradictory, leads to the search for the right balance between instruction in the minority language and the majority language. Satisfactory solutions call for "the
attainment of the highest possible level of bilingualism."[85] For practical purposes, this needs to be done by having all instruction at the preschool and
kindergarten levels in the native language, whereas at primary and secondary
schools the majority language would figure as a subject of instruction and
would be used, in increasing measure, as the language of instruction in other
subjects. Instruction at vocational schools and at universities should be provided in the minority language if the numerical strength of that minority justifies it and if there is a need. Existing structures could be used for this purpose, but independent institutions for minority education at the tertiary level
could also be created.[86] However, Guillaume Siemienski and John Packer
point out in their commentary on The Hague Recommendations that "it is not
absolutely necessary to establish entirely separate institutions of higher learning for national minorities."[87]

In a public statement in September 1995, the High Commissioner recommended to the Romanian government the creation or maintenance of
groups, classes, sections, or schools in which instruction would be given in the
minority language. In addition, he supported more minority-language instruction at vocational schools and argued that the founding of private schools
should not be made more difficult than it already was under the prevailing criteria. As for university education, the HCNM simply pointed out that under
Romanian law "possibilities exist for additional private university education."[88] He did not go into the demand by the Democratic Alliance of Hungarians in Romania that the Hungarian Bolyai University in Cluj-Napoca,
which had been forced to unite with the Romanian Babes-University in 1959,
should be allowed to reopen.[89] In 1998, the High Commissioner welcomed
"efforts of the Government of Romania to find a compromise solution for a
difficult problem in the field of tertiary education by initiating the procedure

regarding the establishment of the 'Petofi-Schiller' multicultural State university with [instruction] in Hungarian and German."[90]

With regard to university education, it was natural that the High Commissioner attached special importance to faculties for teacher training in minority languages; thus, he recommended to the governments of Macedonia and Slovakia that they establish or expand such faculties.[91] Even in Macedonia, where an Albanian minority that constitutes about a quarter of the population has been exerting particularly strong political pressure for an Albanian-language university of its own, the HCNM did not give in to such pressure. Instead, he recommended a privately operated Higher Education Center for Public Administration and Business in which instruction would be offered in Macedonian, Albanian, and English.[92]

Language rights of national minorities. The Oslo Recommendations,[93] which were also worked out by a group of experts on the initiative of the High Commissioner, are based on the same principle as The Hague Recommendations:

> The [Oslo] Recommendations do not propose an isolationist approach, but rather one which encourages a balance between the rights of persons belonging to national minorities to maintain and develop their own identity, culture and language and the necessity of ensuring that they are able to integrate into the wider society as full and equal members. From this perspective, integration is unlikely to take place without a sound knowledge of the official language(s) of the State.[94]

In particular, this is to be achieved by ensuring that there are no limitations on the use of the minority languages in the giving of names, in the exercise of religion, and in the carrying out of business. Members of minorities are to have the right to set up their own media organizations and to receive broadcasts or other media products from abroad; in addition, they are to be given "access to broadcast time in their own language on public funded media."[95] There is to be free choice of language in economic life; the state is allowed to prescribe the additional use of the official language only to the extent that the interests of third parties are involved (e.g., in consumer protection, security matters in the workplace, etc.). Public agencies are to use the minority language, both spoken and written, when the minority is present "in significant numbers" and "where the desire for it has been expressed."[96] In court proceedings (in both criminal and civil cases), use of the minority languages is to be allowed; when necessary, interpreters or translators are to be made available without charge.

In his recommendations to the Slovakian government, the High Commissioner offered more detail about the abstract phrase *in significant numbers* and suggested adding to the state language law an article specifying that the minority language, in communities where the minority has a share of at least 20 percent of the population, be permitted for official communications.[97] This had, in fact, been the applicable rule in Slovakia until the state language law went into effect. In a recommendation to Ukraine, where law provided that the minority language could be used in official intercourse along with Ukrainian wherever the minority constituted a majority, the HCNM proposed that the percentage be set below 50 percent but did not offer a specific number.[98]

Summary

All in all, it is clear that the High Commissioner provided varying recommendations in different countries. Nevertheless, they exhibit a large measure of consistency and differ less from one another than one would expect in view of the diversity of conditions in the six countries under review.

According to the categories of our ethnopolitical values table, the HCNM's state-building strategy is clearly inclusionary and tends to introduce territorial elements in cases only where, for historical or other reasons, it seems unavoidable. His nation-building strategy should be classified as differentiating, the overall strategy as one much more of balance than of territorial autonomy. At the same time, it became clear in applying our analytical categories that the category of differentiating nation-building strategy is too crude to do justice to the character of the High Commissioner's recommendations. For that reason, we further subdivide this category according to the level of institutionalization: a differentiating nation-building strategy can, ideally, fill a spectrum ranging from without institutionalization, to institutionalization within the framework of joint or majority institutions, to autonomous institutionalization under the administration of a minority. If we apply this extended category (i.e., the degree of institutionalization of a differentiating nation-building strategy) to the recommendations of the HCNM, it can be seen that most of them lie in the middle range of the institutionalization spectrum; the extremes of (without institutionalization and autonomous institutionalization) are scarcely to be found.

The reason for this probably lies in the incumbent High Commissioner's fundamental view on the balance that must be created or maintained between the reciprocal and interlocking rights and obligations of the majority *and* the minority. This idea of a necessary balance between interrelated actors is also the basis for the three guiding principles of the High Commissioner for the organization of interethnic relations: communication, participation, and integration. Thus, there is reason to suppose that the High Commissioner regards too high a level of autonomy and the related tendency toward isolation as a risk for the integration of the society as a whole, and for that reason rejects it.

At the same time, the concept of balance gives the HCNM's actions the flexibility they need. Since balance can be the result of varied combinations of factors on both sides of an equation, the notion of a balance between the rights and obligations of a majority and a minority provides a good basis for finding a variety of solutions under differing conditions—without departing from the principles themselves.

THE EFFECTIVENESS OF THE HIGH COMMISSIONER'S ACTIVITY

The question that is most important politically but most difficult to answer in a scholarly sense concerns the actual effectiveness of the High Commissioner. The OSCE participating states, in review meetings and implementation meetings on human-dimension issues, have always given the work of the High Commissioner a positive evaluation;[99] the Permanent Council thanked Max van der Stoel on 2 July 1998, on the occasion of extending his term, "for his outstanding service."[100] The tenor of the scholarly literature, insofar as it deals with the effectiveness of the HCNM, is also entirely positive: the High Commissioner must "in the final analysis . . . be regarded as an effective instrument."[101] Brigitte Reschke adds another dimension to this: "The results of the High Commissioner's work are, in the final analysis, hard to measure; even so, his efforts are generally regarded as *the* success story of the C/OSCE from 1990 on."[102]

The difficulty of measuring the effectiveness of the HCNM leads to several questions: What precisely are we to understand by *effectiveness of the HCNM*, and what criteria should be applied to measure, or at least evaluate, effectiveness? Is effectiveness assured when the recommendations of the HCNM have been put into practice? Or can we speak of effectiveness only once the stability objectives that the HCNM's recommendations are intended to serve have been attained? If there is a discernible effectiveness of the High Commissioner, what factors explain this effect?

Answers to these questions would go beyond the limits of this chapter. Moreover, as far as is known, there has as yet been no thorough, empirical study of the effectiveness of the High Commissioner. For this reason, I will sketch the research plan that we used, within the framework of the above-mentioned project, to come to terms with the question of the HCNM's effectiveness.

In the first place, an investigation of the effectiveness of the HCNM calls for identifying areas of agreement or similarities between his recommendations and the actual behavior of the government in the country concerned. Second, if correspondences are found, we must ask whether the actions of the state have actually been influenced by the recommendations of the HCNM or by other factors or, as the case may be, what the relationship is between these two groups of factors. Third, not only the implementation of the recommendations of the HCNM must be examined but also the more important question of the extent to which the goals of prevention and stability that those recommendations were meant to serve have been in fact realized. The investigation of the first stage means that in each of the countries under investigation the recommendations of the HCNM and the behavior of the state in question must be compared in detail, over the entire period of investigation, in accordance with the unified classification of our preference structure. The second and third questions call for a process analysis that would include the domestic political process in the relevant countries, *all* related activities of the HCNM and other OSCE bodies, as well as the political process between the state in which the relevant minority lives and its kin state, along with other international influences at the bilateral and multilateral levels. Taken together, this constitutes the first part of the empirical section of the project.

The theoretical goal of the project lies in the attempt to explain whatever efficiency or inefficiency has been found in the work of the HCNM by identifying the factors that explain the implementation or nonimplementation of his recommendations by the states. In the course of this analysis, we take several steps, which build upon one another.

As a first step, we assume that the strategies of both majority and minority, as well as the recommendations of the HCNM, represent a specific ethnopolitical value structure. The contradictions between the preference structures of the majority and the minority constitute the ethnopolitical conflict potential; the preference structure of the HCNM represents a possible, flexible, and usable offer of a solution. Our basic preference structural hypothesis asserts that indicators as to the effectiveness of the OSCE's minority regime can be found in the points of agreement and the differences between the three preference structures.

As a second step, we want to examine whether and to what extent ethnopolitical preference structures and their political/tactical instrumentalization by particular groups of actors are influenced by progress in the transformation process, especially by the various phases of democratic consolidation. Our starting hypothesis here is that as consolidation moves forward the latitude for the tactical instrumentalization of preference structures at first becomes less, whereas in the later phases the latitude for changes in the preference structure itself increases.

As a third step, we investigate internationally the influence of asymmetrical interdependence relationships on the development of majority-minority conflicts, distinguishing between noncomplex interdependence (in the sense of the kin state's classic superiority based on power) and complex interdependence[103] based on intensified cooperation with or integration in the EU and NATO. Here, our starting hypothesis is that complex interdependence relationships influence majority-minority conflicts more powerfully than do noncomplex ones, bearing in mind that the arrangement of the various interdependence relationships must be taken into consideration in each case.

As a fourth step, we shall examine the relative influence of transnational communications processes between the minority and the kin state on the relationship between majority and minority within the host state. Our starting hypothesis for this purpose is that the relative density of the transnational communications process in comparison with the internal one, the level of democratic consolidation in the kin state, and the relative distance between the preference patterns communicated by the kin state and the minority and those of the majority in the host state can provide indicators as to whether the transnational communications processes are likely to aggravate or alleviate the internal relationship between minority and majority.

The theoretical question, broadly stated, has to do with the relationship between the various explanatory dimensions and the reciprocal influences they have on each other. To attempt an answer, one must formulate a series of hypotheses, operationalize them, and test them for plausibility,[104] at first in one dimension and then tied together by way of multilevel games.[105] That would be the second part of the empirical section of the project.

We think that this elaborate research design is worthwhile not only because it promises general findings on the effectiveness of the High Commissioner but also answers two questions: Under what conditions can the HCNM be an effective instrument? and How successful can he be? This would make it possible to discuss on the basis of an empirical analysis the options for strengthening this OSCE institution.

CONCLUSION: RECOMMENDATIONS FOR STRENGTHENING THE INSTITUTION OF THE HIGH COMMISSIONER

The OSCE's efforts in the areas of early warning and conflict prevention appear to be confronted by four major problems.

First, the OSCE is faced with ensuring better implementation, not only in connection with conflict prevention but in all areas of its activity. This is a problem of fundamental political importance, because continuing and serious failures of implementation by a large number of participating states threaten, over the long term, to undermine the durability of the OSCE's normative (and thus its political) foundation.

Second, we have witnessed the development of a wealth of early-warning instruments—including the missions, the HCNM, the OSCE Representative on Freedom of the Media, and the Coordinator of OSCE Economic and Environmental Activities—whose activities, both theoretically and practically speaking, appear to be inadequately coordinated.

Third, neither theoretically nor in a practical, political sense is the OSCE's broad concept of security being fully applied by coordinating all its dimensions. Although the human dimension is effectively tied to the OSCE's conflict-prevention activities, a relationship to the economic dimension hardly exists.

Fourth, the main problem, as can be seen in the case of Kosovo, is not to be found in early warning but in the lack of capacity for effective and timely early action.

On this basis, I present the following four recommendations. Their central point is to strengthen the High Commissioner's office as an institution; they necessarily touch upon other areas of the OSCE's range of instruments for early warning and conflict prevention.

First: The recommendations of the High Commissioner should not be made binding, but their implementation should be subjected to intensified review. The proposal to make the High Commissioner's recommendations binding, which has repeatedly been brought forward, would not under current circumstances result in a strengthening of his effectiveness; on the contrary, it would undermine the foundations and the conditions for functioning of the HCNM as an institution. The participating states tolerate intrusion into an extraordinarily sensitive area only because the High Commissioner works on the basis of an indirect, security-oriented strategy and proceeds exclusively with cooperative, noncoercive methods. Any change in this balance between internal affairs and international intrusion would inevitably put at risk the foundation of the High Commissioner's activity. This, however, does not mean that it is unnecessary to subject the implementation of his recommendations to regular and detailed review. One problem is that between the Human Dimension Implementation Meetings and the Annual Implementation Meetings of the Forum for Security Cooperation there is a substantial institutional gap with regard to conflict-prevention activities, especially those of the High Commissioner, which touch on both dimensions. From a pragmatic standpoint, the review of the HCNM's recommendations could take place at the biannual Human Dimension Implementation Meetings, which already— despite a certain incongruence—have the review of the High Commissioner's activities on their agenda. The current format allows for a general discussion of the activities of the HCNM, but not for a detailed review of his recommendations to specific countries. Whether Decision 241 (Modalities for OSCE Meetings on Human Dimension Issues)[106] has changed this situation in any way depends on how it is interpreted and applied. At a minimum, it would be necessary to give the activities of the HCNM and the issue of implementation of his recommendations a working group of their own.

Second: Efforts should be made toward better coordination of the various early-warning functions within the OSCE and toward intensified discussion of these activities in the Permanent Council. A whole series of OSCE institutions have by now come into being that, among other things, fulfill early-warning functions. Coordination of these different institutions faces a twofold problem. The various early-warning agencies receive differing indicators, so only when they have been fitted together can a realistic picture of the situation emerge; and there is no adequate institutionalization of steady cooperation among the various institutions so as to provide a realistic picture of the situation. The Conflict Prevention Centre, which (at least by virtue of its name) might serve this purpose, has as of today become almost exclusively a division for mission support. The only conclusion to draw from this is to give the Conflict Prevention Centre the means to create a basis for institutionally guaranteed cooperation among the various early-warning agencies and to present the consolidated results from the various early-warning agencies to the Permanent Council for discussion and decision. Whether the new Operation Centre within the Conflict Prevention Centre (established by decision at the Istanbul Summit)[107] can fulfill this remains to be seen.

Third: Include the economic dimension in the conflict-prevention activities of the OSCE. Although there is a close connection between the economic and social transformation crises in Central and Eastern Europe and ethnopolitical tensions and conflicts, the economic dimension is given almost no attention in the conflict-prevention activities of the OSCE. In order to mitigate this deficiency, the following measures might be considered. Include in the catalog of responsibilities of the Coordinator of OSCE Economic and Environmental Activities a reference to the relationship between economic/social crises and ethnopolitical tensions; on this basis, have him report to the Secretary-General and the Permanent Council and cooperate with the HCNM. All of this, including any reference to the relationship between ethnopolitical tensions and the economic dimension, is missing from the Coordinator's mandate.[108] Then, based on these modifications to the reporting requirements for the Coordinator and the HCNM, discussions could be held in the Permanent Council regarding cases of ethnopolitical tension viewed against the background of the economic dimension. This would be only a modest beginning in the process of drawing the economic dimension into the field of conflict prevention.

Fourth: Strengthen the High Commissioner's project-oriented approach by creating a conflict-prevention fund. Since the political and economic costs of conflict settlement grow with the level of escalation (nonlinearly), such a fund would be both politically and economically cost-effective. This measure, however, would require rethinking the categories of preventive diplomacy in favor of an integrated conflict-prevention strategy, already under way in the practical activities of the incumbent HCNM and the ODIHR. It is true that "conflict prevention is cheaper than peacekeeping measures and these, in turn, are cheaper than a war";[109] even so, this kind of rethinking would force us to admit that effective conflict prevention calls for different budgets than those needed for the dispatch of a few diplomats. One idea that the HCNM has frequently raised—that of a contribution equivalent to 1 percent of the defense expenditures of the OSCE participating states—could be a useful basis for discussion. The first step could be the establishment of an OSCE conflict-prevention fund financed by obligatory and voluntary contributions. Upon approval by the Permanent Council, this fund could be used to finance concrete projects (of small and medium size) of the HCNM, the missions, and other OSCE institutions, the need for which might arise from the ongoing process of conflict prevention.

APPENDIX: DOCUMENTS

Recommendations of the High Commissioner

Estonia. Letter by the OSCE High Commissioner on National Minorities to His Excellency, Mr. Trivimi Velliste, Minister for Foreign Affairs of the Republic of Estonia, The Hague, 6 April 1993, in Bloed (ed.) (1993), pp. 1065–1070.

Letter of the CSCE High Commissioner to the President of Estonia, 1 July 1993, in Bloed (ed.) (1993), pp. 1087–1091.

Latvia. Letter by the CSCE High Commissioner on National Minorities to His Excellency, Mr. Georgs Andrejevs, Minister for Foreign Affairs of the Republic of Latvia, The Hague, 6 April 1993, in Bloed (ed.) (1993), pp. 1071–1077.

Letter by the OSCE High Commissioner on National Minorities to His Excellency, Mr. V. Birkavs, Minister for Foreign Affairs of the Republic of Latvia, The Hague, 14 March 1996, <http://www.osce.org/inst/hcnm>.

Letter by the OSCE High Commissioner on National Minorities to His Excellency, Mr. V. Birkavs, Minister for Foreign Affairs of the Republic of Latvia, The Hague, 28 October 1996.

Macedonia. Letter by the CSCE High Commissioner on National Minorities to His Excellency, Mr. Stevo Crvenkovski, Minister for Foreign Affairs of the FYROM, The Hague, 1 November 1993, in Bloed (ed.) (1997), pp. 724–726.

Letter by the CSCE High Commissioner on National Minorities to His Excellency, Mr. Stevo Crvenkovski, Minister for Foreign Affairs of the FYROM, The Hague, 16 November 1994, in Bloed (ed.) (1997), pp. 729–732.

Letter by the OSCE High Commissioner on National Minorities to His Excellency, Mr. Stevo Crvenkovski, Minister for Foreign Affairs of the Former Yugoslav Republic of Macedonia, The Hague, 28 April 1995, in Bloed (ed.) (1997), pp. 735–738.

Romania. Letter by the CSCE High Commissioner on National Minorities to His Excellency, Mr. Teodor Melescanu, Minister of State, Minister for Foreign Affairs of Romania, The Hague, 9 September 1993, in Bloed (ed.) (1997), pp. 741–746.

Statement by the OSCE High Commissioner on National Minorities on the occasion of his mission to Romania on 28–31 August 1995, in Bloed (ed.) (1997), pp. 751–753.

Slovakia. Letter by the CSCE High Commissioner on National Minorities to His Excellency, Mr. Jozef Moravcik, Minister for Foreign Affairs of the Republic of Slovakia, The Hague, 8 November 1993, in Bloed (ed.) (1997), pp. 754–756.

Letter by the CSCE High Commissioner on National Minorities to His Excellency, Mr. Eduard Kukan, Minister for Foreign Affairs of the Slovak Republic, The Hague, 20 June 1994, in Bloed (ed.) (1997), pp. 760–763.

Letter by the OSCE High Commissioner on National Minorities to His Excellency, Mr. Juraj Schenk, Minister for Foreign Affairs of the Slovak Republic, The Hague, 24 August 1995, in Bloed (ed.) (1997), pp. 769–775.

Letter by the OSCE High Commissioner on National Minorities to His Excellency, Mr. Juraj Schenk, Minister for Foreign Affairs of the Slovak Republic, The Hague, 13 August 1996.

Ukraine. Letter by the OSCE High Commissioner on National Minorities to His Excellency, Mr. Anatoly Zlenko, Minister for Foreign Affairs, The Hague, 15 May 1994, in Bloed (ed.) (1997), pp. 785–787.

Speeches of the High Commissioner

Acceptance speech to the Stockholm Meeting of the Council of Ministers of Foreign Affairs of the CSCE, 15 December 1992, Stockholm, Sweden.

Intervention of Mr. Max van der Stoel, CSCE High Commissioner on National Minorities, Warsaw, 24 May 1993.

"International Response to Ethnic Conflicts: Focusing on Prevention," Keynote Address by Max van der Stoel, CSCE High Commissioner on National Minorities, to the Fourth International PIOOM Symposium: "Ethnic Conflicts and Human Rights Violations in Europe," 25 June 1993, Leiden, The Netherlands.

"Early Response to Ethnic Conflicts: Focusing on Prevention," Address by Max van der Stoel, CSCE High Commissioner on National Minorities, to the Parliamentary Assembly of the Conference on Security and Cooperation in Europe, 8 July 1993, Helsinki, Finland.

Intervention by Max van der Stoel, High Commissioner on National Minorities, at the Human Dimension Implementation Meeting, 28–29 September 1993, Warsaw, Poland.

Remarks of M. van der Stoel, High Commissioner on National Minorities of the Conference on Security and Cooperation in Europe (CSCE), Global Panel, 6th International Conference: "Patterns of a Changing World," Maastricht, 26 November 1993.

Address by Mr. Max van der Stoel, CSCE High Commissioner on National Minorities, to the Rome Meeting of the Council of Ministers for Foreign Affairs of the CSCE, Rome, 30 November–1 December 1993 (long version).

Keynote speech by Max van der Stoel, CSCE High Commissioner on National Minorities, to the CSCE Seminar on Early Warning and Preventive Diplomacy, Warsaw, 19 January 1994.

"Preventive Diplomacy in Situations of Ethnic Tensions: The Role of the CSCE High Commissioner on National Minorities," Remarks of M. van der Stoel, High Commissioner on National Minorities of the Conference on Security and Cooperation in Europe (CSCE), Bonn, 27–28 January 1994.

"Political Order, Human Rights, and Development," Introduction by Max van der Stoel, CSCE High Commissioner on National Minorities, The Hague, 24 March 1994, to the Seminar "Conflict and Development: Causes, Effects, and Remedies, Instituut Clingendael."

Speech by Max van der Stoel, 13 May 1994.

"The Role of the CSCE High Commissioner on National Minorities in CSCE Conflict Prevention," Address by Max van der Stoel, CSCE High Commissioner on National Minorities, to the Seminar "The CSCE as a Security Tool in Europe: Which Role for the CSCE?" Brussels, 4 June 1994.

"Preventing Conflict and Building Peace: The CSCE and Conflict Prevention in Europe," Address by Max van der Stoel, CSCE Commissioner on National Minorities, to the Meeting of the Third Committee of the CSCE Parliamentary Assembly, Vienna, 6 July 1994.

"Controlling Ethnic Tensions in Europe: The Experience of the CSCE High Commissioner on National Minorities," Address by Mr. Max van der Stoel, CSCE High Commissioner on National Minorities, to the Oxford University Civil Liberties Society, Oxford, 28 October 1994.

"Human Dimension Issues," Warsaw, 2–19 October 1995, Report of Mr. Max van der Stoel, OSCE High Commissioner On National Minorities, Warsaw, 2 October 1995.

"OSCE Review Meeting," Vienna, 4–21 November 1996, Report by Mr. Max van der Stoel, OSCE High Commissioner on National Minorities, Vienna, 4 November 1996.

High Commissioner on National Minorities of the Organization for Security and Co-operation in Europe (OSCE), Max van der Stoel, Rede vor dem Institut für Friedensforschung und Sicherheitspolitik (Speech at the Institute for Peace Research and Security Policy), Hamburg, 17 March 1997.

High Commissioner on National Minorities, OSCE Human Dimension Implementation Meeting, November 1997.

NOTES

1. Charter of Paris for a New Europe, Paris, November 21, 1990, in Arie Bloed (ed.) (1993) *The Conference on Security and Co-operation in Europe: Analysis and Basic Documents, 1972–1993*, p. 537.

2. CSCE Helsinki Document 1992: "The Challenges of Change," Helsinki, 10 July 1992; Helsinki Decisions, Section 2, CSCE High Commissioner on National Minorities, para 3, in ibid., p. 716.

3. Rob Zaagman (1994) "The CSCE High Commissioner on National Minorities: An Analysis of the Mandate and the Institutional Context," in Arie Bloed (ed.) *The Challenges of Change: The Helsinki Summit of the CSCE and Its Aftermath* (Dordrecht: Martinus Nijhoff), pp. 113–175; The Foundation on Inter-Ethnic Relations (FIER) (1997) *The Role of the High Commissioner on National Minorities in OSCE Conflict Prevention: An Introduction.*

4. At the third meeting of the CSCE Council in December 1992, the former Dutch Foreign Minister, Max van der Stoel, was chosen as High Commissioner on National Minorities for a term of three years; the fifth meeting of the Ministerial Council in December 1995 in Budapest extended van der Stoel's term for three more years, until the end of 1998. The maximum term of office provided for in the mandate was thus reached. Nevertheless, the Permanent Council recommended on 2 July 1998, to the Ministerial Council that Max van der Stoel's term be further extended "as an exceptional measure" until 31 December 1999 (cf. PC.DEC/240 of 2 July 1998). Finally, at the OSCE Istanbul Summit in November 1999, the heads of state and government expressed their gratitude to van der Stoel "for his willingness to continue in his position until a new High Commissioner on National Minorities has been appointed at the latest at the OSCE Ministerial Meeting in Vienna in November/December 2000." <http://osce.instanbul-summit.org/summit_declaration.htm>, para. 46.

5. I agree with Estebanez that the fact that "the concept of the High Commissioner was conceived of as one person, and all CSCE institutions have Directors who are explicitly instructed to do something" (Zaagman, "The CSCE High Commissioner on National Minorities," p. 124) is not sufficient to call the institutional character of the High Commissioner into question. Maria Amor Martin Estebanez (1997) "The High Commissioner on National Minorities: Development of the Mandate," in Michael Bothe, Natalino Ronzitti, and Allan Rosas (ed.) *The OSCE in the Maintenance of Peace and Security: Conflict Prevention, Crisis Management and Peaceful Settlement of Disputes* (The Hague: Kluwer Law International), p. 157. In accordance with the

normative variant of "new institutionalism," the core characteristic of an institution lies in the presence of a set of norms and rules that govern the decisions and behavior of the actors. B. Guy Peters (1996) "Political Institutions, Old and New," in Robert E. Goodin and Hans-Dieter Klingemann (eds.) *A New Handbook of Political Science* (Oxford: Oxford University Press), p. 208.

6. Cf. Wolfgang Zellner (1999) "On the Effectiveness of the OSCE Minority Regime: Comparative Case Studies on Implementation of the Recommendations of the High Commissioner on National Minorities of the OSCE," a Research Project of IFSH, Hamburg (Hamburger Beiträge zur Friedensforschung und Sicherheitspolitik, Heft 111). First results will be published in the Working Papers series of the Centre for OSCE Research (CORE) at the Institute for Peace Research and Security Policy at the University of Hamburg in summer 2000.

7. Van der Stoel, 24 May 1993, p. 45 (abbreviated citation for the speeches of the High Commissioner, most of which are reprinted in Max van der Stoel (1999) *Peace and Stability Through Human and Minority Rights, Speeches by the OSCE High Commissioner on National Minorities*, ed. Wolfgang Zellner and Falk Lange; the rest can be found on the OSCE website at <http://www.osce.org/inst/hcnm>. Pages refer to van der Stoel 1999, if the text is contained, and to the website printout, if this is not the case.

8. Van der Stoel, 24 May 1993: 45.

9. "Document of the Copenhagen Meeting of the Conference on the Human Dimension of the CSCE," Copenhagen, 29 June 1990, in Bloed (ed.) (1993) *The Conference on Security and Co-operation in Europe: Analysis and Basic Documents, 1972–1973* (Dordrecht: Kluwer Law International), p. 456.

10. Rogers Brubaker (1996) *Nationalism Reframed. Nationhood and the National Question in the New Europe*, pp. 55ff.

11. Van der Stoel (1998), p. 74.

12. Van der Stoel, 1 December 1993, p. 4.

13. Van der Stoel (1998), pp. 74 and 75.

14. Van der Stoel, 8 July 1993, p. 2.

15. Van der Stoel, 25 June 1993, p. 1.

16. Van der Stoel, 28–29 September 1993, p. 54.

17. Van der Stoel, 26 November 1993, p. 55.

18. Van der Stoel, 8 July 1993, p. 1.

19. Van der Stoel, 13 May 1994, p. 79.

20. Van der Stoel, 27–28 January 1994, p. 7.

21. Van der Stoel, 24 May 1993, p. 47.

22. Van der Stoel, 17 March 1997, p. 135.

23. Van der Stoel, 24 May 1993, p. 46.

24. Van der Stoel, 2 October 1995, pp. 111–112.

25. Van der Stoel, 17 March 1997, p. 137.

26. Van der Stoel, 1 December 1993, p. 6.

27. Rec. HCNM to Slovakia 13/8/1996, abbreviated citation, which will be used henceforth, for: Letter by the OSCE High Commissioner on National Minorities, Mr. Max van der Stoel, to His Excellency, Mr. Juraj Schenk, Minister for Foreign Affairs of the Slovak Republic, The Hague, 13 August 1996. The recommendations of the High Commissioner are reproduced in part in the literature; see esp. in Bloed (ed.) 1993, Arie Bloed (ed.) (1997) *The Conference on Security and Co-operation in Europe: Basic Documents, 1993–1995*, and *Helsinki Monitor*) most of them are available on the OSCE website <http://www.osce.org/inst/hcnm>.

HIGH COMMISSIONER ON NATIONAL MINORITIES

28. Hansjörg Eiff (1999) "Autonomy as a Method of Conflict Management and Protection of Minorities Within the OSCE Framework," in Institute for Peace Research and Security Policy at the University of Hamburg/IFSH (ed.) *OSCE Yearbook 1998*, pp. 255–264.

29. Van der Stoel, 19 January 1994, p. 63.

30. Ibid.

31. Van der Stoel, 24 March 1994, p. 76; van der Stoel, 4 June 1994, p. 3.

32. Van der Stoel, 4 June 1994, p. 9.

33. Van der Stoel, 28–29 September 1993, p. 52.

34. Van der Stoel, 4 June 1994, p. 4.

35. Van der Stoel, 27–28 January 1994, p. 4.

36. Van der Stoel, 13 May 1994, p. 80.

37. On 12 May 1999 the High Commissioner, addressing the OSCE Permanent Council, issued a formal early-warning notice regarding the tense situation in Macedonia. On 3 June 1999 he repeated this early warning (cf. *OSCE Newsletter* 6, no. 5 [May 1999], p. 8; 6, no. 6 [June 1999], p. 12).

38. Van der Stoel, 24 May 1993, p. 4.

39. Van der Stoel, 15 December 1992, p. 31.

40. Van der Stoel, 19 January 1994, p. 65.

41. Van der Stoel, 28 October 1994, p. 51.

42. FIER (1997), p. 22.

43. Gudmundur Alfredsson and Danilo Türk (1993) "International Mechanisms for the Monitoring and Protection of Minority Rights: Their Advantages, Disadvantages and Interrelationships," in Arie Bloed, Liselotte Leicht, Manfred Nowak, and Allan Rosas (eds.) *Monitoring Human Rights in Europe. Comparing International Procedures and Mechanisms* (Dordrecht: Martinus Nijhoff), p. 175.

44. Van der Stoel, 24 May 1993, p. 4.

45. Ibid., p. 5 (author's emphasis).

46. Van der Stoel (1998), p. 2.

47. Van der Stoel, 6 July 1994, p. 90.

48. FIER (1996) *The Hague Recommendations Regarding the Education Rights of National Minorities and Explanatory Note.*

49. FIER (1998) *The Oslo Recommendations Regarding the Linguistic Rights of National Minorities and Explanatory Note.*

50. FIER (1999) *The Lund Recommendations on the Effective Participation of National Minorities in Public Life and Explanatory Note.*

51. Van der Stoel (1998), p. 72.

52. Van der Stoel (1998), p. 4 (emphasis added).

53. Van der Stoel, 4 November 1996, p. 130.

54. Van der Stoel (1998), p. 76.

55. Van der Stoel (1998), p. 73.

56. Juan J. Linz and Alfred Stepan (1996), *Problems of Democratic Transition and Consolidation: Southern Europe, South America, and Post-Communist Europe* (Baltimore: Johns Hopkins University Press), p. 429.

57. Brubaker (1996), p. 30.

58. Claus Offe (1994), *Der Tunnel am Ende des Lichts. Erkundigungen der politischen Transformationen im Nahen Osten* [The Tunnel at the End of the Light. Inquiries into the Political Transformations in the Near East], pp. 145–146.

59. The two groups of cases involving Russian (Estonia, Latvia, Ukraine) and Albanian (Macedonia) minorities were chosen because they illustrate the High Commissioner's current lines of emphasis; the one involving Hungarian minorities (Roma-

nia, Slovakia) because they represented an important focal point for the CSCE at the time when the HCNM first became engaged with this issue; Zaagman (1994), p. 172.

60. Rec. HCNM to Estonia 6/4/1993.

61. Rec. HCNM to Estonia 6/4/1993; Rec. HCNM to Latvia 6/4/1993; Rec. HCNM to Latvia 14/3/1996.

62. Rec. HCNM to Latvia 28/10/1996.

63. FIER (1999).

64. FIER (1999), p. 4.

65. Interview with the OSCE High Commissioner on National Minorities, Max van der Stoel, on 28 May 1999, at The Hague, in van der Stoel (1999), p. 24.

66. FIER (1999), pp. 4–8.

67. FIER (1999), p. 5.

68. FIER (1999).

69. Rec. HCNM to Macedonia 16/11/1994.

70. FIER (1999), p. 5.

71. Rec. HCNM to Slovakia 20/6/1994.

72. FIER (1999), p. 6.

73. Rec. HCNM to Romania 9/9/1993.

74. Rec. HCNM to Slovakia 8/11/1993.

75. Rec. HCNM to Latvia 6/4/1993; Rec. HCNM to Estonia 1/7/1993.

76. FIER (1999), pp. 6–7.

77. FIER (1999), p. 7.

78. FIER (1999), p. 7.

79. FIER (1999), p. 16.

80. Interview van der Stoel, in van der Stoel (1999), pp. 24–25.

81. Interview van der Stoel, in van der Stoel (1999), p. 26.

82. Wolfgang Zellner and Pál Dunay (1998), *Ungarns Außenpolitik 1990—1997: Zwischen Westintegration, Nachbarschaftszund Minderheitenpolitik* [Hungary's Foreign Policy 1990—1997. Between Western Integration, Neighborhood, and Minority Policy], pp. 258–262, 310–312.

83. Rec. HCNM to Slovakia 13/8/1996.

84. FIER (1996), p. 5.

85. Guillaume Siemienski and John Packer (1997) "Integration Through Education: The Origin and Development of The Hague Recommendations," in *International Journal on Minority and Group Rights*, no. 4 (1997): 195.

86. FIER (1996), pp. 6–8.

87. FIER (1997), p. 194.

88. Statement by the High Commissioner on National Minorities on Romania (1 September 1995), in Bloed (ed.) (1997), pp. 751–753, esp. p. 753. This was one of the few occasions when the High Commissioner (in prior agreement with the parties) issued a public declaration that included recommendations on various issues.

89. Zellner and Dunay (1998), pp. 249–250.

90. Statement by Max van der Stoel, OSCE High Commissioner on National Minorities, HCNM 4–98 <http://www.osce.org/inst/hcnm/news/08oct98.htm>.

91. Rec. HCNM to Macedonia 1/11/1993; Rec. HCNM to Slovakia 13/8/1996.

92. Rec. HCNM to Macedonia 28/4/1995.

93. FIER (1998).

94. FIER (1998), p. 14.

95. FIER (1998), p. 6.

96. FIER (1998), p. 7.

97. Rec. HCNM 24/8/1995.

98. Rec. HCNM to Ukraine 15/5/1994.

99. Thomas Buchsbaum, Stefan Hammer, Walter Suntinger, and Hannes Tretter (1994) "The First Human Dimension Implementation Meeting: Analysis of the Informal Recommendations," in *Helsinki Monitor* 5, no. 2 (1994): 76; Merja Pentikäinen (1997) "The Human Dimension of the OSCE in the 1996 Vienna Review Meeting," in *Helsinki Monitor* 8, no. 1 (1997): 10; Merja Pentikäinen (1998) "The 1997 Implementation Meeting on Human Dimension Issues of the OSCE," in *Helsinki Monitor* 9, no. 2 (1998): 31.

100. PC/DEC/240, 2 July 1998.

101. Brigitte Reschke (1997) "Der OSZE-Hochkommissar für nationale Minderheiten" [The OSCE's High Commissioner on National Minorities], in *Humanitäres Völkerrecht—Informationsschriften*, no. 2 (1997): 103 (own translation).

102. Reschke (1997), p. 116 (emphasis in the original, own translation).

103. Robert O. Keohane and Joseph S. Nye (1989) *Power and Interdependence: World Politics in Transition*, pp. 24–25.

104. Harry Eckstein (1975) "Case Study and Theory in Political Science," in F. I. Greenstein and N. W. Polsby (eds.) *Handbook of Political Science* pp. 97–108.

105. Robert D. Putnam (1988) "Diplomacy and Domestic Politics: The Logic of Two-Level Games," in *International Organization* 42, no. 3 (Summer 1988): 427–460.

106. PC.DEC/241 of 9 July 1998.

107. Cf. <http://osce.istanbul-summit.org/summit_declaration.htm>, para. 36.

108. cf. PC.DEC/194 of 5 November 1997.

109. Van der Stoel, 17 March 1997, p. 139.

PART 4

Regional Security

13

The Challenge of Collective Action: Security Management in European and Regional Contexts

Kari Möttölä

Early warning, conflict prevention and dispute settlement, crisis management, peacekeeping and peace enforcement, as well as conflict resolution and post-conflict rehabilitation provide a complex and growing area of security management, one in which states test and demonstrate their capacity for collective action as an international community. In fact, the post–Cold War security order in Europe is being shaped, in an evolutionary and ad hoc manner, by the means chosen by states to protect joint values and tackle common threats, rather than by the implementation of a grand design or contract.

Alongside states as the principal actors, the scene of security management is increasingly dominated by intergovernmental or supranational and transnational institutions. Within the space of the Organization for Security and Cooperation in Europe (OSCE), the challenge of collective action is being met increasingly through a network of security-related arrangements and regimes of various degrees of institutionalization. Consequently, a central part of the security model process that led to the adoption of the Charter for European Security by the OSCE Istanbul Summit in 1999 was devoted to elaboration of rules, principles, and mechanisms for cooperation and coordination among institutions and organizations.[1]

The understanding of the concept of security has undergone a change that fundamentally affects security management. The willingness of the OSCE community to undertake concerted actions reflects the recognition and adoption of the comprehensive concept of security and, consequently, of the need to respond to a broad spectrum of risks, threats, and challenges to common, state, and civic security. Moreover, since the common acceptance in the 1990 Charter of Paris for a New Europe of the OSCE acquis of values, norms, and principles on democracy, human rights, and economic liberty, the new activity in security management has been norm-driven, aiming at implementing the joint values and principles through the accountability of all the actors and their commitment to mutual support and cooperation. Through such a conceptual transformation in the international environment, security management has taken on a societal and economic dimension in addition to the traditional political and military aspects. The needs for organizing and taking action vary in the different sectors of comprehensive security.[2]

As a consequence of the lifting of the Cold War overlay, cooperative institutions have been proliferating at all levels while new tasks for security management such as bridging political and economic gaps, strengthening human rights regimes, and resolving ethnic and nationality disputes have emerged. Both trends have emphasized a need for bilateral and regional-subregional efforts to complement the functioning of European, transatlantic, or OSCE-wide arrangements. Regionality has replaced bipolarity as a dominant structural feature of the security order. States feel a more intensive security interdependence with their neighbors and partners than with more distant actors or with the global system as a whole. Accordingly, regional security relationships are formed and institutionalized to deepen partnership and integration and to tackle problems related to mutual suspicion, historical legacies, and military instability.[3]

The efficiency of international security management is dependent, first, on the credibility of the common norms adopted as the guidance for the historical unification of Europe after the Cold War division. Second, the success or failure of joint efforts will depend on the political, economic, and military capabilities available for states and institutions, determining the power structures that underlie efforts at security management. Third, the outcome is intertwined with the institutionalization of the overall security order, where the unification of the OSCE space is driven and dominated by the exclusive processes of political, economic, and military integration and alignment within the European Union/Western European Union (EU/WEU) and NATO—Western-originated institutions that have survived the transition from the old era through adaptation and enlargement.

Fourth, states need to have a sufficient degree of unity in their political objectives. The incentives and motivations for security cooperation are based on the need of the traditional political West—the EU and NATO countries—to support political, social, economic, and military transition in order to enlarge and consolidate the stable zone of peace based on democracy and integration, as well as to prevent the escalation of local conflicts in partnership with the new and broad coalition of likeminded countries that make up the New Europe. Still, countries aspiring to join the Western-based core institutions strive to meet the standard of such a cooperative and responsible behavior, which is viewed as part of their membership requirements. In parallel with the orientation toward consensus-based action, there is a competition for status and influence in the construction and management of the security order, where Russia, in particular, is looking for a legitimate place within the increasingly Westcentric security architecture and challenging each case of decisionmaking on collective actions, most notably in regard to Kosovo and Chechnya. The common overall objectives for joint actions are most conveniently found in the OSCE norms, but they rarely provide a guideline for concrete measures in any particular situation.

Immediately after the end of the Cold War, it became clear that the new European security order was not to be based on the ideal model of collective security but on a more ambiguous and ad hoc but pragmatic model of cooperative security.[4] Whereas the UN system of collective security provides the uncontested global and legal framework for joint action by states or groupings of states, security management in the OSCE space is based on a wide spectrum of political and institutional solutions. The political will of states and institutions, as well as their political, economic or military capabilities, determine outcomes, which are varied and uncertain, providing a pattern of ad hoc coalitions in security management. Furthermore, broad security calls for responses across the conflict cycle; special attention is devoted to enhancing the possibility for early warning and preventive action.

The interinstitutional order is evolving through several key means: the central position of NATO in military crisis management; the uncontested position of the EU in political and economic stability promotion as well as its more recent interest, incorporating the functions of the WEU, in a role of its own in military crisis management;[5] and the consolidation of the OSCE's position, together with the Council of Europe, as an inclusive political forum and a specialized actor on the ground. In this setting, made up of European and transatlantic structures, regional and subregional efforts, with a limited group of states interacting in a territorially limited space, can reach across former lines of division and produce innovative solutions to practical needs while drawing upon the legitimizing and stabilizing effect of the wider security order with its common norms, institutions, and capabilities.

To summarize: the outcome of collective, cooperative, concerted action in international security management depends on four types of factors—the normative and conceptual basis for action; the institutional framework in which cooperation takes place; the military, economic, and other capabilities available for common use; and the political will and decisionmaking capacity of states, individually and jointly, to respond to security risks and challenges.

Comments are made below on the impact of these factors on security management in the wider European and regional contexts. The normative, institutional, structural, and political dimensions of security management will be a determining factor in the overall evolution of the security order in the OSCE space. Whether the architecture will evolve toward a more unified and centralized structure, continue to develop on the basis of selectivity and ad hoc practice, or possibly turn into a capability-based hierarchy provides an agenda for alternative futures worthy of analysis.

THE EUROPEAN CONTEXT OF
SECURITY MANAGEMENT

The increased readiness of states to take part in joint security management is one of the formative features of the international order in the post–Cold War era. Shaping and controlling security in a continually changing Europe imposes two kinds of tasks, which are interconnected; support for political and economic transition in Central and Eastern European countries and societies; and preventing, managing, and resolving conflicts and crises by collective action as they appear in Europe's more unstable regions.[6]

Transition support is conflict prevention in the deepest sense, as it aims at consolidating democracy and the respect of joint international norms and standards, as well as promoting the competence of reforming countries to participate in full European integration. On the one hand, support for reform and restructuring provides fundamental and deep social change with a stability that affects both the domestic and foreign policies of the transition countries. On the other hand, stability promotion—applying the theory of democratic peace—aims in the longer run at a sustainable change in the international order based on the inherent effects of democracy and interdependence on security. The first post–Cold War decade has demonstrated that such a transition will be an uneven and long process.

Conflict management draws more political and public attention than transition support, as its success or failure not only affects real and concrete security interests of states in the conflict region (in its vicinity and more broadly in Europe); it also has become a credibility test of the new security order and its constituent parts. In particular, it is unhelpful to compare security-related institutions and put them in a ranking order according to their competence, capability, and authority in tackling more or less violent disputes and conflicts. Although the EU and the Council of Europe are natural leaders in transition support, and the OSCE has a special niche in early warning and conflict prevention, NATO is the uncontested central institution for crisis management requiring the use of deterrent or forcible means.

Conflict management calls for responses across the full conflict cycle: conflict prevention/early warning, fact-finding, preventive diplomacy, and peaceful settlement of disputes; crisis management/political mediation and support, humanitarian intervention and peacekeeping, and peace enforcement; military compulsion, military sanctions, and warmaking; and political resolution/reconstruction, rehabilitation, and peacebuilding.

Emphasis is placed on the importance and possibility of early warning and preventive action, which has become even more evident and understandable as Europe embarks on the post–post–Cold War era. On the one hand, political and economic transition has made progress, and the zone of stable or democratic peace is enlarging, consolidated by political and economic integration in the core and making apparent new lines of division further eastward. On the other hand, experience in the former Yugoslavia has shown the difficulty of limiting and controlling ethnic and national conflicts connected with power struggles once they break out in full. Within the concept of, and as a follow-up to, the Stability Pact for South Eastern Europe, postconflict political and economic rehabilitation is combined with reinforcing and opening long-term prospects for regional and European integration for the transition states of the conflict-ridden region.[7]

Norms and Concepts

The new activeness in security management is driven by norms and principles, since the post–Cold War acceptance of the OSCE documents on democracy, human rights, and economic liberty has made these true criteria for action. Security management aims at implementing joint values and principles through support and cooperation. A few norms and guiding principles stand out as particularly relevant for the more mature stage reached in the evolution of the New Europe that has entered the second post–Cold War decade in the 2000s.

As the pace of integration quickens through the deepening and enlargement of the EU and the adaptation and expansion of NATO, and as several transition countries have achieved considerable results in their political, economic, and even military reform and adjustment, the principle of the freedom of choice in security policy has been brought into focus. A struggle over respect for the freedom of states to make independent decisions is evident in the context of the eastward enlargement of NATO and Russia's opposition to its extension into the space of the former Soviet Union. In a more subtle and complex manner, this principle is being tested and applied in numerous other situations involving political and economic decisions.[8]

The criteria governing the collective and individual rights of minorities and the relationship between national self-determination and the inviolability of borders are highlighted not only because they touch upon the core causes of current disputes and conflicts in Europe; they also involve key preconditions for EU membership and are among the requirements for accession to NATO. In broader terms, then, human rights have become not only a yardstick but also a central incentive and motivation for states' efforts in security management, in particular through humanitarian intervention.[9]

The willingness of the OSCE community of states to undertake concerted actions reflects recognition and adoption of the broad concept of security and, by extension, of the need to respond to new risks and challenges to common international security as well as to accept values and structures essential for the survival and welfare of states and civic societies.

The comprehensive security concept calls for a wide array of instruments for establishing the international presence and influencing the outcomes of dynamic and unpredictable situations. Innovative solutions have been found, such as OSCE missions or the work of the High Commissioner on National Minorities in the field of early warning and conflict prevention, as well as the pattern of comprehensive or enlarged peacekeeping in the military field undertaken within the Partnership for Peace (PfP) program. A recent addition to this set of tools is the introduction of capabilities for rapid response in civilian crisis management within the framework of the OSCE (through its so-called REACT teams) and the European Union.[10]

Although the adoption of common norms calls for the accountability of states to one another for their behavior, the goal of common security calls for actions based on the concepts of assistance and solidarity in cases of noncompliance with joint norms and threats against partner states from external actions or internal breakdowns of stability. Although such mechanisms are outlined in the OSCE Security Charter, they will not replace the mechanisms for self-defense that states possess under Article 51 of the UN Charter. This fact highlights the contradiction within the OSCE regime between broad normative commitments and the insufficiency of the capabilities for resolving serious and violent conflict and crises as states look for security guarantees and support. It is also the reason why ripostes to more violent breaches of the common norms require a response by an orchestra of institutions rather than a single player.

Institutional Framework

The rules and practices for interinstitutional cooperation and coordination, key items in the new OSCE Security Charter, provide a framework for and contribute to the shape of the evolving security order in Europe. There is consensus on the nonhierarchical nature of interinstitutional cooperation, as well as on the principles of mutual reinforcement and comparative advantage as guidelines. As various solutions to post–Cold War situations in Europe have shown, the division of labor between institutions and the coordination of actions in concrete situations on the ground remain open or unpredictable.

In political and economic conflict prevention, crisis management, and postconflict rehabilitation, the outcome of burden sharing in resource allocation and the attainment and recognition of political status in decisionmaking are becoming for states critical issues regarding the relationship between security-related institutions and their own contributions to collective action. This dilemma, whereby the EU members feel that their organization pays the bill while the United States through NATO takes the credit, is one of the most important factors determining the EU effort to create a capability for autonomous action in military crisis management.

The interinstitutional order is evolving through the central position of NATO in military crisis management, where the PfP serves as a vehicle for interoperability and as a channel for contributions for joint operations. NATO is not, however, the only potential institution for military crisis management, as the OSCE has a competence for traditional peacekeeping and the EU has adopted crisis management as one of the tasks in the common foreign and security policy. The EU has an uncontested leading position in political and economic stability promotion, given its resources for support and assistance and its influence in international financial institutions. The OSCE has consolidated its contribution as an inclusive political forum and an actor on the ground specializing in early warning and conflict prevention and, moreover, in postconflict presence. The Council of Europe has a similar role in the promotion of democratic security.[11]

Yet a contest for the position of leading institution is possible if individual states that are members of several security-related institutions have differing or conflicting preferences for the choice of institution in a particular case. Whereas NATO is constructing a broadly based readiness capability for crisis management based on the partnership model, the EU and the WEU are yet to launch a full-scale operation between themselves. The Treaty of Amsterdam provides the EU with a competence and a mechanism for a crisis-management role in Europe. Whether it will be used depends not only on military-related capabilities but also on political considerations. The triangle connection linking the EU, the WEU, and NATO is yet to be fully clarified for possible European-led operations using NATO assets. However, mechanisms are being created and streamlined for such an eventuality, initially for the WEU-NATO interface, to be replaced by an EU-NATO interface as the relevant functions of the WEU are incorporated within the EU.

The situations in Bosnia, Albania, and Kosovo as well as Chechnya have demonstrated the difficulty of choosing between institutions and the effect of political, including domestic, considerations. Although NATO had the necessary capability for intervention in Bosnia (used after a longer period of hesitation), the Albanian mission was undertaken by a group of WEU states but not under the competence of the organization itself. In the case of Kosovo, NATO, the WEU, and the EU as well as the OSCE were all in action politically, trying to apply pressure for a peaceful resolution, including through a monitoring presence on the ground; the demonstration and use of military force were left to NATO. In the aftermath of the war in Kosovo, the international community is present in Kosovo on the broadest possible basis, with the UN, the EU, and the OSCE dividing the main tasks of humanitarian, economic, and political reconstruction among themselves under the security umbrella provided by the NATO-led peacekeeping force (KFOR). As for an international contribution to the Chechnya conflict, the OSCE was the only forum for any meaningful political dialogue on the crisis,[12] while the UN and the EU made efforts to assist in the humanitarian situation in the region.

Military Capabilities

An enlarged role for military organizations within the broad range of security-management tasks is an outcome of the adaptation of defense policies and military doctrines to the changing political and integration environments. The military objectives involved reflect the dual role of national defense, where traditional territorial defense is accompanied by new kinds of international assignments and responsibilities. Transformation in national contexts is under way, which in some cases turns a peacetime defense establishment into a crisis-management resource, instigating at times a discussion on the merits of volunteer and conscription armies. The military scene in Europe, which was fundamentally changed by the dissolution of the threat of a central war, is finding its focal point in cooperation for crisis management and other defense-related activities, such as procurement and technology.[13]

A refocused determination to meet the challenge in military crisis-management capability is witnessed by such projects and programs as the Defense Capabilities Initiative of NATO, the Planning and Review Process within the Partnership for Peace, the WEU audit of available European capabilities, and the overall headline goal and the capability goals targeted to command and control, intelligence, and strategic transport that were adopted by the EU in the Helsinki Summit for its joint readiness force.[14]

In military crisis management, meeting the challenge of interoperability differentiates countries (alliance members, partners) in terms of their rights and responsibilities in planning and decisionmaking. Interoperability as a joint commitment plays a dual role, supporting the growth of partnership capabilities and membership competences in the applicant countries' relationship with NATO while creating a closer working relationship between the nonallied and formerly neutral partners and NATO. The fundamental fact remains, however, that NATO retains the decisionmaking competence for NATO-led operations and the use of NATO resources, and a developing PfP provides a network as well as a resource base for auxiliary contributions to joint operations. In a similar manner, the EU will retain its decisionmaking autonomy while creating partnerships of its own with non-EU European NATO members and other associated countries, as well as other interested states in military crisis management.

A cooperative practice that transcends military alignments and traditions is emerging both within the PfP framework and in the EU-WEU context. It is significant that participation in crisis management remains open-ended and flexible within the frameworks offered by the mandating institutions of the UN and the OSCE and the implementing arrangements such as the NATO/Euro-Atlantic Partnership Council/PfP and the forthcoming EU consultation and cooperation structures with contributing non-EU states. Such a flexible system calls for the development of interoperability of defense forces that offer their services for international tasks on the basis of their national competences. Participation would be based on the will and capability, case by case, and not so much on formal alignments or commitments.

Political Objectives

The political incentives and motivations for security cooperation are based on the need, in particular for EU and NATO countries, to support political, social, economic, and military transition as well as to prevent the escalation of local conflicts. Both contributions are inherent elements in an enlarging zone of democracy and stability in Europe.

At the same time, there is a competition for power and influence in the construction and management of the security order. Russia is looking for a legitimate position as a recognized great power within what is an increasingly Westcentric security architecture. Although Russia is using the opportunities offered by the bilateral relationship with NATO—despite its being politically hindered by the Kosovo crisis—it has been unwilling to contribute fully to multilateral NATO outreach activities such as the PfP. Russia does not want to legitimize a NATO-centered security order and devotes its diplomatic activities to bilateral Russian-NATO relations, the promotion of an OSCE-centered order, and regional initiatives such as those related to the Baltic Sea region.

At times, the idea of a great-power concert has gained prominence in discussions on the future European security order. NATO enlargement, which has been connected with the institutionalization of a Russian-NATO partnership and an enhanced PfP, has made that model less likely, but an inconclusive enlargement leaves several options open.

Although the UN system of collective security provides the global framework, security management in the OSCE region is based on the concept of cooperative security. The political will of states and institutions and their political-economic-military capability determine outcomes, which are varied and uncertain, providing a pattern of ad hoc coalitions in security management. A critical aspect of the future order in the overall OSCE space is the degree of equality and indivisibility—called for by the concept of a common security space—in a situation where all states are competent producers of security.[15]

Through risk evaluation and parliamentary control, domestic determinants in foreign and security policy have an emphasized effect on states' participation in crisis management. Although the U.S. Congress plays a well-known role, the situation is in different ways similar in other great powers and smaller states as well. The domestic component leaves the future of crisis management open, as joint action will ultimately depend, in each case, on the political will of governments and, in many cases, on the consent of parliaments and the opinion of publics. For smaller states, the demands for resource, the risks involved, and the degree of enforcement or compellence envisaged or mandated are factors that affect their willingness to participate in military crisis-management operations.

REGIONALITY IN SECURITY MANAGEMENT

A growing regionality is one of the key formative outcomes of the post–Cold War change in Europe. In security management, the regional context brings added value to transition support, whereas conflict management would in most cases call for the presence of European or transatlantic institutions. A dominant trend in regional and subregional cooperation is concentration on stability policy in such areas as energy, transport, and the environment and the networking of civic societies.

Accordingly, the reemergence of regions and subregions has a special relevance for institutional and political aspects of security management, whereas the normative base is common to regional and wider activities, and military capabilities are not regularly deployed in regional institutions or processes.

A particular consequence of the end of the Cold War has been the creation or reconstitution of regions and subregions that draw states to closer interaction across the former line of division and increase their interdependence in promoting transition and overcoming political and economic gaps. Regions may also facilitate a common identity or promote mutual responsiveness in joint institutions and arrangements.

The increasingly prominent place for regionalism and subregionalism is also an outcome of the changing concept of security. With the new and broad agenda of risks and challenges to state and civic security, joint problem solving and collective action may be more opportune among neighbors facing the common security environment than in a wider context.

Regionality can both draw upon and consolidate the OSCE model of common security, but it does not compensate for the benefits to be achieved by EU integration or NATO membership, which remain as strategic goals for transition states in Central Europe. The Baltic Sea region is a case in point of regionality in security management.

A Case Study: The Baltic Sea Region

The Baltic Sea region is both a test case and a proof of the significance of security management combining regionally based and region-targeted efforts for tasks in transition support, early warning, conflict prevention, and conflict resolution.[16]

The Baltic Sea region bridges a former line of political, ideological, economic, and military division, brings together transition countries as well as EU and NATO members, involves Russia as a leading indigenous participant, constitutes an arena for the enlargement and outreach activities of the EU and NATO, and borders on territories of military-strategic centrality as a legacy of the era of confrontation.

In the normative sphere, a challenge is created by the application of the freedom-of-choice principle in the changing constellation in wider Europe and the region itself. For the Baltic States—Estonia, Latvia, and Lithuania—membership in the EU and NATO is vital for concluding their political, economic, and social transition and returning to the core of Europe as equal and sovereign partners. For Finland and Sweden, the security benefits of the principle of equal sovereignty are preserved by the maintenance of the option of changing their current policy of military nonalliance, although they are not seeking NATO membership.

Russia is faced with accommodating respect for the OSCE rules and norms, including freedom of choice, with the requirements of meeting the geopolitical challenge of NATO enlargement. Although accepting the right of the Baltic States to choose their security arrangements, Russia stresses the obligation of NATO to take account of its legitimate security interests, which go against NATO enlargement farther eastward. At the same time, Russia is ready to support EU membership for the Baltic States, which it regards as economically beneficial and not strategically challenging. Moreover, Russia is drawn into regional cooperation by the EU's Northern Dimension initiative.[17]

Although the discussion on security arrangements in the Baltic Sea region has touched upon future choices, the naturalization of Russian-speaking noncitizens in Estonia and Latvia and the conclusion of border agreements between Russia and Estonia and Russia and Latvia have remained on the agenda as open issues of concern to a wide international audience. Although few direct efforts in the area of mediation or good offices have been made in the case of the border negotiations, the issue of Russian minorities has been targeted by the OSCE and other institutions as a prominent and visible case in their security-management activities.

In the institutional field, the OSCE missions in Estonia and Latvia, assistance in the implementation of bilateral agreements related to the withdrawal of Russian troops and the abolition of the Russian military infrastructure, and the sustained activity and referee's role of the OSCE High Commissioner on National Minorities provide for a strong OSCE presence in the region. In addition, the expertise and technical assistance of the Council of Europe and the UN have contributed to the international attention given to Baltic issues. Moreover, regional and subregional institutions, such as the Council of the

Baltic Sea States and the Nordic Council, regularized cooperation among the Nordic countries and the Baltic States in the 5+3 format, and bilateral assistance programs between Nordic and Baltic countries have made contributions to stability promotion.

In the military sphere, the Baltic Sea region is one arena for a high level of PfP activities among partners in the region. Although no crisis-management operations are foreseen for the region itself, countries of the region have cooperated in the NATO-led IFOR/SFOR peacekeeping operation in Bosnia within a Nordic-Polish brigade that has given the Baltic States their first experience in peacekeeping. At the same time, partners assist the Baltic States in the creation of national defense establishments capable of both territorial defense and international peace missions. Initiatives have been taken to promote military confidence- and security-building measures among neighboring countries in the region, and the Conventional Armed Forces in Europe Treaty in its adapted form continues to incorporate a flank regime aimed at strengthening stability in the potentially sensitive region bordering Russia.[18]

Politically, the situation in the Baltic Sea region is affected by both indigenous and external developments. The United States takes a strong interest in the region because of the domestic political significance of supporting the Baltic States and the strategic significance of the region for NATO enlargement. Russia, while seeking a sustainable new identity and policy recognizing the Baltic States as equal neighbors, is activating its cooperation with other countries of the region and trying to manage its relations with the United States and NATO in a bilateral context. The Nordic countries, which have a strong interest in regional stability and security, seek to combine their bilateral and regional policies with contributions to an effective role for the EU and NATO and ad hoc groups assisting the Baltic States in the region. The Northern Dimension of the common policies of the EU will place the Baltic Sea region in the focus of a broad range of long-term efforts in transition and stability support.[19]

Results have been achieved in security management for the Baltic Sea region through a wide selection of policies and institutions without an all-embracing structure or a hegemonic power. Both small and large actors have made their contributions based not only on their capability but also on the intensity of their interests and the effectiveness of their political and diplomatic skills. In many ways, the region is a reflection of what the OSCE space as a whole is experiencing.

CONCLUSION: FUTURE PROSPECTS

Security management is shaping the OSCE space and its regions as a continuous process. Normative, institutional, structural, and political factors will determine whether security management will be based on a more unified and centralized model, continue to develop on the basis of selectivity and ad hoc practice based on partnership, or turn into a capability-based hierarchy. It seems that the middle variant will prevail, whereas the two other models may act as background factors and political thresholds, when states make decisions on contributing to dispute settlement or conflict management.

Participation will depend on political will, and equality is offered by an open-ended partnership. The overall order will remain uneven and complex, consisting of the position of the EU as an anchor of stability and a promoter of change; the status of NATO as a guarantor of hard security for its members and an organizer and resource base for joint crisis management; the evolving (albeit unaccomplished) security and defense identity of the European Union; and the inconclusive definition of the role in security tasks of the inclusive OSCE.

Supported by systematic work to create a credible joint capability, the international community was politically capable of undertaking another massive operation in Kosovo after and in parallel with IFOR/SFOR, but the future of humanitarian intervention as a pattern of collective action remains uncertain. The requirements for transition support will be long-lasting, and they may be increasingly difficult to satisfy in some cases, whereas others will reach their objectives in integration in the foreseeable future. However, EU enlargement has become a more credible strategy, after the initial decision in Luxembourg in 1997, as a result of the decisions taken in Helsinki in 1999 on furthering its pace and extent. Likewise, the differences between regions in Europe may grow as they face different challenges in security management. It is likely that a wide range of instruments will be needed and used in the future for security management in Europe.

NOTES

1. The mandates for the work on the Security Model and a document charter on European Security were laid down in the documents of the Budapest 1994 (A Common and Comprehensive Security Model for Europe for the Twenty-first Century) and Lisbon 1996 (Lisbon Declaration on a Common and Comprehensive Security Model for Europe for the Twenty-first Century) CSCE/OSCE summits and in the Copenhagen 1997 Ministerial Council (Guidelines on an OSCE Document-Charter on European Security). Principles and modalities for interinstitutional cooperation and coordination are defined in the Platform for Cooperative Security, attached as an operational document to the Charter for European Security signed by the Participating States in the Istanbul Summit on November 19, 1999.

2. On a broad approach to the concept of security, see Barry Buzan, Ole Wæver, and Jaap de Wilde (eds.) *Security: A New Framework for Analysis* (Boulder: Lynne Rienner Publishers).

3. David A. Lake and Patrick M. Morgan (1997) "The New Regionalism in Security Affairs," in David A. Lake and Patrick M. Morgan (eds.) *Regional Orders:*

Building Security in a New World (University Park: Pennsylvania State University Press), pp. 3–19; on the concept of security complex, see "Introduction," in Buzan et al. (eds.) (1998) *Security*, pp. 1–20.

4. Kari Möttölä, "Collective and Co-Operative Security Arrangements in Europe," in Martti Koskenniemi (ed.) *International Law Aspects of the European Union* (The Hague: Kluwer Law International), pp. 87–98.

5. The determination of the European Union for resurgence in military crisis management, complementing steps in bettering coordination in civilian response as well, is documented in the decisions of the Cologne and Helsinki European Councils, respectively, of 1999. See, in particular, the Presidency Report on Strengthening the Common European Policy on Security and Defence, included in annex 4 of the Presidency Conclusions in Helsinki, and the corresponding Presidency Report on the same topic adopted by the Cologne European Council.

6. Kari Möttölä (1997) "The OSCE: Institutional and Functional Developments in an Evolving European Security Process," in Michael Bothe, Natalino Ronzitti, and Allan Rosas (eds.) *The OSCE in the Management of Peace and Security: Conflict Prevention, Crisis Management, and Peaceful Settlement of Disputes* (The Hague: Kluwer Law International), pp. 1–33.

7. The Stability Pact, modeled after the Balladur Plan of the early 1990s, was initiated in the aftermath of the Kosovo crisis by the EU, and joined by the United States, Russia, and other key actors, as a long-term strategy for the engagement and integration of the Balkans, including ultimately the Federal Republic of Yugoslavia, into the unifying Europe. Complementing and supporting the immediate objectives of the UN-led presence of the international community on the ground in Kosovo, the Stability Pact process aims at bringing to bear sufficient resources for reconstruction and transition support, predicated upon efforts by the recipient states for national reform and regional cooperation. See Stability Pact for South Eastern Europe (Cologne, June 10, 1999).

8. The principle is stated in the most elaborate form in section 4 of the Code of Conduct on Politico-Military Aspects of Security adopted in the CSCE Budapest Document 1994.

9. For an analytical discussion of the the political and legals aspects of the issue, see *Humanitarian Intervention: Legal and Political Aspects* (Copenhagen: Danish Institute of International Affairs, 1999).

10. For instruments and tools of security management, see various articles in Bothe et al. (eds.). The model of REACT (Rapid Expert Assistance and Co-operation Teams) is outlined in paragraph 42 of the Charter for European Security; see also, Presidency Report.

11. Coordination and cooperation among security-related institutions were dealt with in the proposals of the European Union on a common concept and a platform for cooperative security that was discussed in the context of the OSCE process that led to the adoption of the new Charter for European Security.

12. Russia agreed to a joint commentary on "the events in North Caucasus," emphasizing humanitarian aspects, in the Istanbul Summit Declaration (November 19, 1999) and gave a commitment to receive a visit by the OSCE Chairman-in-Office to the region as a contribution to a political solution of the conflict. The OSCE had established a presence, the OSCE Assistance Group, in Chechnya in connection with the first Chechen conflict, although the group had to withdraw to Moscow as a result of the new hostilities. The political arm-twisting over the recognition of the Chechen conflict as an international concern delayed the signing of the Charter for European Security by a day in the Istanbul Summit.

13. For the discussion on new dimensions of defense policies, see materials from the OSCE Seminar "Defence Policies and Military Doctrines," Vienna, January 26–28, 1998.

14. The DCI adopted by the Washington Summit is presented as a response to the deficiencies observed in the Kosovo air campaign and the deployment of the ground troops in KFOR; the EU headline goal constitutes both quantitative and qualitative criteria for a credible joint EU force to be fulfilled by national decisions and contributions assessed and supported by peer review in the Council of Ministers; the work toward the specific capability goals is spearheaded by larger EU members bilaterally and those members involved in the multinational Eurocorps.

15. On multiple factors affecting the formation of security policy, see Ronald L. Jepperson, Alexander Wendt, and Peter J. Katzenstein (1996) "Norms, Identity, and Culture in National Security," in Peter J. Katzenstein (ed.) *The Culture of National Security: Norms and Identity in World Politics* (New York: Columbia University Press), pp. 33–75.

16. Kari Möttölä (1998) "Security Around the Baltic Rim: Concepts, Actors, and Processes," in Lars Hedegaard and Bjarne Lindström (eds.) *The NEBI Yearbook, 1998: North European and Baltic Sea Integration* (Berlin: Springer), pp. 363–404.

17. The Northern Dimension for common external crossborder policies of the EU was adopted by the Vienna Summit in 1998 at the Finnish initiative. In a ministerial meeting of the members and partners in Helsinki in 1999, a decision was made to initiate a concrete program of action. The European Council in Helsinki invited the Commission to prepare an action plan, which was endorsed by the European Council in June 2000 under the Portuguese Presidency.

18. In the offer made by Finland and Sweden in 1998, additional CSBMs (evaluation visits and inspections) could be agreed among neighboring states in the region to complement the OSCE-wide regime.

19. The Northern Dimension will contribute to the future shaping of a region of strategic importance together with the interests and objectives pursued by the Union within its common strategy on Russia and its transatlantic dialogue with the United States and Canada, involving key actors for the future of the region and Europe as a whole.

14

Arms Control as a Spatial Practice: Challenges in the Baltic Region

PERTTI JOENNIEMI

Security has turned into a unifying theme in current-day Europe. Charac-terizations such as *collective* or *common* are increasingly outdated and *coop-erative* is in vogue. The efforts are not those of all against one or all against the common threat of annihilation but all with all in the endeavors to avert unpredictability and contain local, site-specific conflicts. Security, in such a context, calls for a joint front and has functions of inclusion rather than exclu-sion. Instead of being undivided, security becomes, if not divisible, at least separable and thereby also conducive to regionalization. It descends from interbloc relations to regional, subregional, and bilateral levels and even far-ther down to local relations.

The alterations that have taken place bring about far-reaching changes in many security-relevant spheres, including arms control. The new arms control does not pertain—as the old one used to do—to a balance-of-power system and management of confrontation but rests on a rather different logic. The task is no longer one of operating within the framework of a balance system by facilitating the operation of such a system with a minimum amount of costs and risks. To aspire to that would be quite futile; there is no need for such an endeavor within a setting that has moved beyond balance of power. In a Europe with no given enemies, with no ideological conflicts of the Cold War type, and void of competing blocs and traditional power-political conflicts, arms control obviously has to be rethought and provided, to a large extent, with new meaning.

However, some relationship to balancing remains, although it has turned into one of contrariety. In other words, instead of operating within the context of a balance-of-power system—as arms control used to do—the aim has become one of preventing such a system from reentering that stage. Endeavors of control are thus not about regulating enmity—with enmity seen as an integral part of interstate relations. Rather, they aim at preserving and fortifying—with the help of intrusive surveillance and other similar measures—a situation with no given enmity. Arms control is there to assure, in an auxiliary manner, that Europe does not slide—due to mistrust or a mismanagement of local conflicts that allow them to spread and poison the atmosphere—back into a historical pattern, with balance of power as one of its constitutive elements.

Another way of putting it would be to argue that the otherness that gave rise to a bipolar Europe with a distinct division into opposite blocs has evaporated, although there is some otherness present also in post–Cold War Europe. There is still something to resist and struggle against. However, the Other no more consists of some particular major power, the nuclear arms race, opposing bloc, or threatening actor; it is now made up of Europe's chaotic and unstable past and the threat that it also forms the future. The power-politics logic itself—once a progressive thought that allowed for religious and thus spiritual liberty—has become the new enemy and the target of security policies.[1]

Arms control is hence provided with the task of contributing to political management in aiming at the downgrading of uncontrolled developments that might, in the worst of cases, refurnish power politics with some breeding space. The need for arms control is still there, but its very purpose has changed profoundly in the context of partnership, conflict management, and containment of islands of conflict. It has become part of a setting—imbued by cooperative arrangements such as the Partnership for Peace (PfP) program or Euro-Atlantic Partnership Council—where the goal consists, according to one interpretation, "of integrating all of Europe militarily—particularly Russia."[2]

It appears that arms control has to take into account the existence of quite different security neighborhoods and focus particularly on areas or pockets within broad zones of peace where stable development is threatened. Obviously, with the emergence of a variety of nonstate actors, arms control may not exclusively focus on states or alliances. Neither can it be premised on fixed boundaries and established divisions; it must function across boundaries.

IN SEARCH OF CLARITY

With these extensive transformations in the sphere of security, the concept of new arms control recently achieved some standing in the debate.[3] However, as security has become increasingly difficult to define and pin down in precise terms, many of the new conceptualizations remain obscure. This goes for arms control. The content of the new conceptualizations lack in clarity, and the dividing line between the old and new has remained diffuse.

In order to pinpoint the difference and provide the new concept with a more distinct profile, one might speak, as does Robert Cooper,[4] of *postmodern arms control*. The term signals that arms control has profoundly altered in content and assumed new functions in the context of a postbalance system. It has become part of a setting, Cooper argues, that does not rely on balance; neither does it emphasize sovereignty, tight territorial control, strict borders, or the separation of domestic and foreign affairs. The conceptualization of security underlying such arms control does not solely refer to relations between states but locates the problems within some particular states. It recognizes that there exist other referent objects than the state actors in the sphere of security; it is less technical and pregiven in its orientation and thus increasingly brings politics into the picture. Postmodern arms control pertains, in other words, to the formation of political space no longer premised on the key principles of the modern era.

Endeavors to control armaments turn, within such a context, into an integral part of a highly developed pattern of mutual intrusion. Normative standards of domestic behavior—democratic procedures, treatment of minorities, freedom of the press—have been set up and are internationally monitored. Various arms-control agreements, such as the Conventional Forces in Europe (CFE) Treaty in its more recent form or the Chemical Weapons Convention, infringe upon areas normally within state sovereignty. "Intrusive verification breaks with the absolutist tradition of state sovereignty," Cooper argues. For example, parties to the CFE Treaty have to notify the location of their heavy weapons (which are in any case limited by the treaty) and allow various forms of inspection and monitoring. "The legitimate monopoly of force, which is the essence of statehood, is thus subject to international—but self-imposed—constraints," Cooper remarks. "The normal, logical behavior of armed forces is to conceal their strength and hide their forces and equipment from potential enemies and hence treaties to regulate such matters are an absurdity in strategic logic." In the first place, one does not reach agreements with enemies, and if they are enemies, they cannot be trusted. In the second place, one does not let the enemy come snooping around your bases counting weapons, he argues.

And what has brought about this weird behavior? The roots are contained in the paradox of the nuclear era, Cooper claims. In order to defend oneself, one had to accept the idea of self-destruction. To avoid a nuclear catastrophe in such a setting, the European countries had to go beyond the normal strategic logic of hostility and suspicion. The solution to the prisoner's dilemma lay in ending previous secrecy. The mutual vulnerability that provided stability in the nuclear age has now been extended to the conventional end of the spectrum where it becomes mutual transparency: "The result is that transparency remains but enmity and balance have effectively gone."

As one step led to another, the parties discovered—due to the transparency introduced—that the assumed enmity was no longer there. It could not be upheld under conditions of far-reaching transparency. The previous modern order collapsed, but "unlike the pre-modern it is collapsing into greater order rather than into disorder," Cooper claims. The use of force in resolving disputes could be rejected and rules of behavior codified. Rigid borders have turned into more flexible boundaries, and territoriality is no longer the absolute principle it used to be. And in a system that does not depend on balance, it has become possible to incorporate large and potentially powerful states. The peaceful unification of Germany offers, according to Cooper,[5] proof of the system having changed.

AN AREA IN-BETWEEN?

In a sense, these ideas are quite convincing; the essence of arms control has to alter in a postmodern Europe. It has to be tuned in with a security system that is built on openness, mutual surveillance, and extensive insight into everybody's internal affairs in matters such as democracy, freedom of the press, and minority rights. Arms control is not to stay as a remnant of the previous system. It has to be viewed, in order to preserve its relevancy, as part of a profound break and be linked to open cooperative security.

But does the new system cover all of Europe and involve all the relevant actors? Is it not conceivable that there is also something left of the old and that such a disjuncture labels areas located at the fringes of Europe, including the Baltic region? Is the Baltic Sea area an integral part of the new, or does it rather belong to a sphere where one has to revert to double standards and primarily stay with concepts and the more rough methods of the modern era: force, secrecy, security guarantees, and arms control as an aspect of a balance-of-power system?

Obviously, the Baltic Sea area is an area in-between. Much has changed with the demise of the Cold War, the unification of Germany, the disappearance of the Soviet Union, and the reemergence of the Baltic States. Political space is no longer defined by a binary division into two major camps with some neutrals softening, to a degree, a bifurcated setting. The Baltic Sea region is far less divided, bordered, and determined by the traditional security concerns, but some aspects of the old nonetheless remain. The traditional logic feeds in particular on the Baltic-Russian tangle; in this regard, the relevant actors have a very diverse security status. One may conclude that the security landscape does not hinge on the substitution of one logic by another, at least not in the short run. It rather reflects a mixture between the old and the new, and is labeled by a contest between these two understandings.

The outside world more often than not has chosen a new perspective, although there are clear differences between the U.S. approach[6] and that of the European Union. It seems that outside actors increasingly try to handle the frictions that are still there as local issues, apply ad hoc approaches, downplay linkages to larger confrontatory constellations, and endeavor to downgrade and contain rather than approach the issues at stake as being part of a more general power-politics problem. Actors that are part of the CFE adaptation talks—and this goes for Denmark, Germany, Poland, and Russia around the Baltic region—are clearly more accustomed to ideas of stability zones or region-specific ceilings. They are prepared to discuss deeper verification, greater transparency of military structures, and expanded confidence-building measures, whereas the countries outside (Finland, Sweden, and the Baltic States) are far more hesitant about such measures.

This is to say that the postmodern approach has considerable support, but there are voices present that still feel at odds with such an understanding. These voices are found all over the region, but they are clearly more distinct in the Baltic States. In their assessment, the issues at stake are not region-specific and separable. The relevant security space is not to be narrowed down and delinked from broader constellations. They argue—very much in contrast to a postmodern view—that issues of security have a much more general background and should therefore not be approached as something local. The Baltic States still tend to articulate security space in a familiar us-versus-them manner.

These divergent perceptions provide ample ground for misreadings, competition, and clashes. There is a mixture of departures and a contest between different understandings. Ideas that look good on one agenda appear quite problematic on another; many have the feeling that the Baltic case is not properly understood, that too little importance is attached to the hard military issues, and that they are in danger of being sold out by providing Russia—due to Western disregard, selfishness, naïveté, or appeasement—with the option of establishing a regional hegemony. The Baltic States would like to be part of the more general norms originating with the traditional agenda, as well as arrangements that furnish them with the backing deemed to be needed in order to bolster their endangered security. The threat of interstate war is felt to be acutely alive, and they look upon violence as something calculated and instrumental in pondering issues like preventing occupation and countering aggression against sovereignty and territorial integrity.

Although it seems evident that the holders of the more traditional views are no longer able to define and settle the agenda in the way they once did, this grouping is still present in the debate and has a certain influence on policymaking around the Baltic region. They take issue with those who focus more on crisis prevention, preserving stability, or joint effort to avert unpredictability. However, there are no strict dichotomies, and it would be erroneous to assume the Western side of the Baltics is altogether postmodern in its approach while categorizing the Eastern side as engaged in a reconstruction of nation-states with the consequent understandings of sovereignty, territoriality, and security.

Some of the contrast is there—with a postmodern West and a remodern-izing (or even traditionalizing) East—but there is also much that deviates from this pattern. There are reflections of postmodernity in the East as well; it has just taken different turns from most Western debates given the challenges of postcommunism,[7] and the West is indeed filled with modernist attempts to contain and discipline postmodern challenges.[8] There is a temporal disjunc-ture, but it is not crystal-clear, although postmodern approaches are in gener-al better anchored on the western than the eastern shores of the Baltic Sea. The dividing lines are hence not very sharp, but they are sharp enough to allow broad categorizations of the postures of the different actors relevant for the development of the region.

THE POLICIES OF THE MAJOR ACTORS

With a new European order based on openness and mutual interference, there are good reasons to assume that EU countries are part of the postmodern sphere. Security—comprehended in the traditional statist sense—has been downgraded, and it now has less importance. It has lost preeminence as an organizing principle, whereas other concerns have grown in significance.

However, the postmodern logic does not necessarily apply to the conduct of relations with states and regions that do not fall into the same pattern; if the more postmodern cases are challenged by actors that operate according to the rules of Clausewitz rather than those of Kant, then they may have to respond on the same level and revert to more traditional views. This has not been much of a problem around the Baltic region, where the approach has primarily been postmodern, as indicated by initiatives such as the Stability Pact, the estab-lishing of a Baltic table within the context of the OSCE, the U.S. Northern European Initiative, and the U.S.-Baltic Charter of Partnership of January 1998. The EU countries may well be assumed to continue with such integra-tive policies, downplaying traditional security concerns and treating security as something separable.

Robert Cooper[9] views the United States—in listing actors with a truly postmodern mind—as a more doubtful case. It is not clear that the U.S. gov-ernment and Congress accept either the necessity or desirability of interde-pendence or its corollaries of openness, mutual surveillance, and mutual inter-ference to the same extent as most European governments now do. Its relative reluctance to accept, for example, challenge inspection in the Chemical Weapons Convention, and its hesitations about certain OSCE ideas, are exam-ples of U.S. caution about postmodern concepts, he adds.

It should be taken into account, however, that the United States is a driv-ing force in the context of the CFE talks; it has experience in transparency in the nuclear field, although the policies pursued in the naval sphere are clearly directed against any mutual intrusion and transparency. The U.S. policies seem to reflect a certain duality around the Baltic region. On the one hand, the United States is interested in tuning down local tensions so that they do not have a negative impact on questions of high value, such as U.S.-Russian relations and Russia's ability to adapt to the post–Cold War situation. On the other hand, the United States may capitalize on the concerns of the smaller countries in the region, being seen as the only credible "protector," and thereby having a legitimate presence and a say in the affairs of the region. Downgrading security and turning it into something separable would reduce the position of the United States as a central actor on the regional scene.

Yet developments seem to point toward a postmodern route in the U.S. case. Considerable attention has been devoted to the Baltic area, and since 1996 it has been turned into a testing ground for cooperative security and efforts to overcome old-fashioned geopolitical thinking. Several key decisions will continue to be made, primarily on a bilateral U.S.-Russian basis (for example, in the context of the SALT II process), but there is also much emphasis on local and region-specific initiatives. For example, Deputy Secretary of State Strobe Talbott stated, in providing the background to U.S. policies in the Baltic region, that a strengthening and thickening of a web of subregional cooperation will become a "guarantee that Northern Europe avoids the kind of trouble that has proved so devastating and dangerous in southeastern Europe."[10] The more particular aim has been to optimize the security of the Baltic countries without further antagonizing Russia. This has been done by deliberately blurring various binary categories (either-or and inside-outside), including those that pertain to NATO membership. The Baltic States, as well as Finland and Sweden, are in as well as out, and even Russia has been offered several opportunities to link in, above all in the context of PfP. Peter van Ham concludes, on the basis of an analysis of the U.S. politics around the Baltic region, that the area functions as a testing ground for more soft, regionalized policies that go beyond the usual power-politics approach.[11]

Russia, for its part, comes out as having accepted some elements of the postmodern setting while resisting others. The security doctrine launched during the late 1990s seems to indicate that many new ideas on security have been embraced, including the idea that the probability of some general interstate war—relevant for Russia's security—is quite marginal.[12] Robert Cooper argues that there are postmodern elements in Russia trying to get out: "Russian acceptance of the CFE Treaty and the OSCE observers in Chechnya suggest that it is not wholly lost to the doctrine of openness."[13]

Russia also seems to be able to deal with several proposals that rest on specific rules and norms. It has, in some cases, put forward similar ideas, advocating the establishment of a representative post to deal with issues of democracy, human rights, and national minorities in the context of the Council of the Baltic Sea States. Russia has insisted, in its recent contest of wills with Latvia, on an extensive application of minority rights. Obviously, the understanding of security has become decentered, various societal elements have been upgraded, and Russia shows increasing signs of being willing to lean on the concept of cooperative security in combating uncontrolled developments—and to do so jointly with several other state actors.

However, various schemes to extend NATO membership to Northern Europe have been met with resistance, and the reading of such ideas has primarily been rather traditional. NATO's announcements concerning moves to transform the alliance "to bring confrontation between East and West to an end,"[14] its downgrading of military capabilities in the context of the Strategic Concept,[15] and general moves toward cooperative security and reducing the impact of divisive borders have not convinced Russia.

Yet NATO's policy of dealing with Russia as a partner has provided some space for a dialogue and a meeting of minds. The aspiration for "no more Yaltas or new dividing lines in Europe"[16] has brought results. It has been openly admitted that Russia has a say, although not a veto power, as to the security structures to be established. These inclusive policies have been clearly evidenced by the NATO-Russia Charter, whereby Russia is involved in certain NATO decisions. Moreover, Russia has agreed to operate under NATO command in Bosnia and has also become a member of the PfP, although not a very active one. The features of partnership have increased in strength, and there is little left of any previous confrontation, although some memories of mistrust are still there.

In the duality that NATO represents, Russia has paid more attention to the deterrence elements of Article 5, whereas NATO more generally works along a postbalance and postmodern logic promoting military openness, application of accepted norms, and building of confidence.[17] Over time, Russia's attitude may change, and there are some signs pointing to this, but the process of discovering the new NATO will in all probability be slow.

Needless to say, Russia's attitude is quite decisive for either keeping the old agenda alive or for ensuring that Europe moves over to the new one. Russia's recent initiatives on arms control in the Baltic Sea region seem to indicate that the understanding of security is moving into a cooperative direction.[18] There also seems to be a move toward increasing openness in a regional context, a preparedness to reduce the centrality of security in relation to neighboring states, and to pave the way for increased participation in European integration. However, the signals pointing in this direction are still weak, and the security sensitivities of Russia's Baltic Sea partners are not always taken sufficiently into account. The signals have not been clear and strong enough for all the neighbors to be convinced that this is the way things are now moving.

THE BALTIC STATES AND THE
NORDIC COUNTRIES

The Baltic States are more easy to categorize, as they constitute rather clear-cut cases. They tend to perceive security as working strictly in terms of inclusion or exclusion and aspire for a firm position within the Western security structures. Their ultimate goal is to be embraced by collective defense and firm security guarantees, and there is the fear that accepting region-specific arrangements would reduce the chances of being included in the broader ones. Their arguments have almost exclusively been grounded in the logic of the traditional agenda, and the influence of such a reading has been strengthened by different Russian moves and concepts such as that of the near-abroad. The discourse has very much been about security guarantees, balances, buffer areas, military vacuums, and spheres of interest. Conceptualizations pointing to separable security have usually been rejected out of hand, although some rethinking seems to have occurred over time. Now that the major NATO and EU enlargement decisions have been taken, the Baltic countries are less reticent of regional fora.[19]

As membership in NATO has not been available, the Baltic countries have maintained a close relationship with the West through Partnership for Peace and agreements with the EU, and by becoming associate partners of the WEU. The Western hesitation to extend NATO membership to the Baltic countries has been seen as a concession to Russia. The Baltic countries fear that they are left in a kind of strategic ghetto, although the disappointment has to some extent been softened by the U.S.-Baltic Charter.

Clive Archer concludes, in talking about a bifurcation in the sphere of security, that the Baltic countries have been in danger of placing themselves outside the security dialogue within NATO and between NATO and the Central and Eastern European states and the Russian Federation. "They were therefore less likely to obtain the answer for which they hoped than had they been asking a different question, one less reliant on collective defense and a plea for military help."[20] The Baltic States risk, in positioning themselves firmly on the old agenda, finding themselves on the periphery, where the realist perspective of security dominates.

Archer further argues that the Nordic countries have functioned as friendly interlocutors for the Baltic States once choices have to be made between the old and the new. After the Cold War, the Nordic countries themselves rather quickly embraced new understandings of security,[21] although some differences surfaced as Denmark and Norway saw NATO as a major framework for the military aspect of action and Finland and Sweden shied away from involvement in any military alliance. These differences have to some extent leveled out, as Finland and Sweden have contributed actively to various forms of cooperation in the context of the new NATO.

However, in a regional context the differences tend to prevail. Both Finland and Sweden are quite reserved about security turning spatially separable. For example, the Swedish Parliamentary Defense Commission talked about an "increased risk of security policy regionalization of the Baltic," confirming that it was "a Swedish interest to counteract such security policy regionalisation."[22] Various official statements seem to confirm that the policy pursued is one that approves regionalization in soft-security matters but not the harder, distinctly military, matters.[23] Finland followed a similar line, although the aversion against regionalization of hard security has been spelled out more softly.

It seems obvious that there is a certain duality present in the policies of the two nonaligned Nordic countries. They tend to subscribe to the new agenda in European questions at large but remain—to a degree—within the old one around the Baltic region. The regional setting is, in their view, still unchanged. Deterrence and the balance of power continue to function as crucial organizing concepts. The nearby environment is seen as lacking in balance with only one major power, Russia, present around the Baltic region, and thus balancing has to be encouraged by assuring a strong U.S.-NATO presence in the region.

As Russia is interpreted as being old-thinking, or in danger of some day slipping back to power politics, it is felt that there are limits for the renewal of Finnish and Swedish policies as well. Consequently, these two countries have refused to shoulder any responsibility within a more narrow, regional context. They fear that acceptance would reduce the need of the United States and NATO to develop a distinct profile in the region. It also follows that agreeing to inspection, monitoring, and openness in sensitive military questions—including their systems of mobilization—is perceived as unwarranted. The consequences are seen as negative, as too much intrusion would add to vulnerability in case of an attack.

In general, Finland and Sweden refrain from contributing to anything that could cut off the Baltic region from a wider (and, in their view, more balanced) context. They are worried about moves that could constrain their room for maneuver and remain firmly of the opinion that arms control proper is a pan-European issue, that is, it should not take differentiated and regionalized forms. They do not object to cooperation with Russia as such or the inclusion of Russia in the structures to be established, provided that the setting is broad enough to deny Russia the advantage of being the only participating major power.

It thus appears that the two nonaligned Nordic countries are not that far from the Baltic States in issues pertaining to hard security in the nearby environment. They function as interlocutors between the old and the new, and they also help the Baltic States to cross the threshold. In some questions, they are actually holding back. They strengthen the view that it is quite advisable, in the sphere of hard security, to stay with the old. They caution against region-specific arms control and are among the actors that are partly responsible for the little progress made over recent years. Their nonaligned position has allowed them to stay with somewhat traditional views and concepts of hard security as the sphere where sovereignty, tight territorial control, strict borders, and the separation between domestic and foreign affairs still count.

CONCLUSION

Obviously, the issue of arms control around the Baltic region remains complicated. There is scant support—and in some cases outright resistance— among the littoral actors for such measures. Some of them feel that there is no need for arms control in the first place. The Baltic States in particular tend to think that such control would not promote but hamper their security. They have dropped out of the CFE talks[24] and do not seem inclined to use the recent option of rejoining.

Finland and Sweden appear almost equally hesitant about the new features of arms control. On the one hand, they feel that they should grasp direct access to the CFE talks, as they are bound to have an impact on their security environment. On the other hand, they oppose the idea of having to expose themselves extensively to openness and intrusion. Their reading of arms control remains basically modern, and the more recent postmodern features create confusion. As Finland and Sweden feel that the regional constellation is unbalanced, they tend to resist solutions pointing to zoning. The two nonaligned Nordic countries find it difficult to stay out, but it is equally difficult for them to participate, let alone agree with the results that the CFE adaptation talks will yield.

In responding to this dilemma, Finland and Sweden have offered to unilaterally raise passive quotas for evaluation visits and inspection as provided under the 1994 Vienna Document and suggested that their neighbors could take similar steps on the basis of reciprocity. The effort is one of breaking the stalemate by signaling that they are not just passive bystanders; they also have views and initiatives of their own. Some minimal steps are proposed, but at the same time the endeavor is one of preempting more far-reaching proposals. Sweden in particular seems to resist ideas harbored by Germany and France for establishing a Baltic-specific regional table in the context of the OSCE.

Finland and Sweden are certainly correct that passiveness does not suffice. Results may be expected from the CFE adaptation talks in due time, and it is also obvious that the various Russian proposals call for some kind of response. The Western countries are keen to build upon the proposals made (although not accepting them as such). The Western powers will in all probability raise some ideas of their own in trying to engage Russia in a dialogue concerning the future of the Baltic region.

Finland and Sweden have no doubt been involved in the search for some common ground, yet they have found it difficult to join a broad Western front. Instead, they have put forward their own proposal, trying to direct the process toward regional security cooperation rather than regional arms control. In other words, the spatial underpinnings of arms control are seen to be in conflict with efforts at regionalization. Embarking down a road of their own seems to confirm that Finland and Sweden have difficulties in joining the ranks of the Western powers and instead have to adopt a position closer to that of the Baltic countries.

The crux of the issue is that many influential European actors—and increasingly also the United States—look for local remedies in the context of postmodern arms control. They are prepared to pursue inclusive policies within regional constellations, and the Baltic Sea region is no exception to this (although in the U.S. case such policies seem acceptable only in this context). The danger of a major interstate war is felt to be quite limited, and therefore local and specific issues are seen as needing the most attention. Moreover, NATO's enlargement brings about some diversification in the sphere of security. As enlargement tends to meet with approval in general but encounters resistance in some particulars, these residual issues may be handled by measures of specific cooperation, including arms control. The question of Kaliningrad—and its treatment in the CFE adaptation talks—is a case in point.[25]

Moreover, the major actors feel that the need or prospects for arms control on a pan-European level are limited; thus attention is directed toward local concerns and region-specific measures. They think that—with security having increasingly turned separable—the prospects for the implementation of such ideas are bright. With a conceptual preparedness growing in strength, the matter turns into one of implementation.

The Baltic region appears to have many features that may turn it into a testing ground for postmodern arms control. The legacy of the Cold War security structures has remained heavy, but the region is nevertheless an integral part of Europe and may not remain an outpost of the old forever. Region-specific systems of mutual intrusion have already been established in monitoring democratic procedures, treatment of minorities, as well as freedom of the press. The postmodern logic underpinning these systems will over time spill over into the sphere of hard security. The major European actors seem to be inclined to move forward in the context of the OSCE, the CFE adaptation talks, the Euro-Atlantic Partnership Council, and the Partnership for Peace. The United States works in the context of its North European Initiative and U.S.-Baltic Charter. Besides, the enlargement of the EU also calls for a certain normalization and tuning-down of the traditional security agenda.

It thus seems clear that the two nonaligned Nordic countries and the Baltic countries continue to remain at the sidelines, even though they are profoundly affected by region-specific arms control; otherwise, they would reverse their policies and accept participation. They are confronted with a choice as regionalization progresses. One may expect, on good grounds, that regional cooperation that is indirectly security-relevant will continue to move forward, that the span of soft security will be extended, but that regionalization increasingly will reach the hard sphere of security. The Russian Proposals for a Pact of Regional Stability and Security, as well as the more recent proposals on Kaliningrad,[26] point to this. The Western responses—to be tabled once there is more clarity about the future of the CFE talks and NATO enlargement—will further strengthen the tendency.

The Baltic Sea region has already become quite transparent due to openness, intrusion, and inspection. However, growing transparency has not been traded for enmity and balance to the same extent as in Europe at large. The two latter qualities are still there to some extent. The transparency has not yet been sufficient for all the parties to discover that the enmity has, in fact, gone away, although the regional grouping is still too weak to draw conclusions. It may remain so, as it is quite diverse, yet one may assume that the broader European trends will sooner or later be valid as well for the Baltic region, and in some cases the region may even turn into a testing ground for a spatially new type of arms control.

NOTES

1. Pim Den Boer (1995) "Europe of 1914: The Making of an Idea," in Pim den Boer et al., *The History of the Idea of Europe* (London: Routledge); Ole Wæver (1996) "European Security Identities," *Journal of Common Market Studies* 1, no. 34 (March): 103–132, esp. 122.

2. Bertil Heurlin (1998) "NATO, Security, and the Baltic States: A New World, a New Security, and a New NATO," in Birthe Hansen and Bertil Heurlin (eds.) *Baltic States in World Politics* (Copenhagen: Curzon), pp. 65–85, esp. p. 72.

3. Neil Cooper (1998) "An Agenda for Demilitarisation After Post-Modern Conflicts," paper for the Third Pan-European International Relations Conference, ECPR-ISA, September 1998; Zdzislaw Lachowski (1999) "Prospects for Regional Arms Control in the Baltic Sea Area," in Pertti Joenniemi (ed.) *Confidence-Building and Arms Control: Challenges Around the Baltic Rim* (Mariehamn: The Åland Islands Peace Institute), pp. 9–32.

4. Cooper (1998) "An Agenda for Demilitarisation," pp. 22–25.

5. Ibid., p. 26.

6. Peter van Ham (2000) "Testing Cooperative Security in Europe's North: American Perspectives and Policies," in Dmitri Trenin and Peter van Ham (eds.) *Russia and the United States in Northern European Security* (Helsinki: Finnish Institute of International Affairs), pp. 57–88.

7. Krzysztof Zydowics (1997) "Nationality Versus Regionality: A Central–East European Perspective Pertaining to the Southern Baltic," in Pertti Joenniemi (ed.) *Neo-Nationalism or Regionality? The Restructuring of Political Space Around the Baltic Rim* (Stockholm: NordREFO), pp. 54–84.

8. Ole Wæver (1997) *The Baltic Sea: A Region After Post-Modernity?* in Pertti Joenniemi (1997) *Neo-Nationalism or Regionality?* pp. 293–342, esp. p. 315.

9. Cooper (1998), p. 33.

10. Strobe Talbott (1998) "Address to the Paasikivi-Society," January 21, 1998 (Helsinki).

11. Van Ham (2000) "Testing Cooperative Security."

12. Alexander Sergounin (1998) *Russia: A Long Way to the National Security Doctrine.* Copenhagen Peace Research Institute, Working Papers, no. 10.

13. Cooper (1998), p. 33.

14. NATO (1995) *Study on NATO Enlargement* (Brussels: NATO), pp. 34–35.

15. Ibid., pp. 40.

16. Heurlin (1998) *Baltic States in World Politics*, pp. 76.

17. Cooper (1998), pp. 28–29.

18. Lachowski (1999) "Prospects for Regional Arms Control."

19. Zaneta Ozolina (1998) "The Impact of EU and NATO Enlargement on Baltic-Nordic Cooperation," in Aivars Stranga (ed.) *The First Round Enlargements: Implications for Baltic Security* (Riga: The Latvian Institute of International Affairs, University of Latvia), pp. 41–101, esp. p. 94.

20. Clive Archer (1999) "Nordic Swans and Baltic Signets," *Cooperation and Conflict*, no. 7 (March): 47–73.

21. Clive Archer and Christopher Jones (1997) "The Security Policies and Concepts of the Baltic States," in *Danish Foreign Policy Yearbook, 1997* (Copenhagen: Danish Institute of International Affairs), pp. 81–100.

22. Försvarsdepartementet (1995) *Sverige i Europa och världen* (Stockholm: Försvarsdepatermentet), p. 121.

23. Archer (1998), p. 13.

24. Jane M. O. Sharp (1998) "CFE and the Baltic Rim," in Lars Hedegaard and Bjarne Lindström (eds.) (1998) *The NEBI Yearbook, 1998: North European and Baltic Sea Integration* (Berlin: Springer), pp. 423–437.

25. Lachowski (1999).

26. P. Joenniemi, S. Dewar, and L. Fairlie (2000) *The Kaliningrad Puzzle—A Russian Region Within the European Union* (Karlskrona: The Baltic Institute and the Åland Islands Peace Institute).

15

New Global Politics: Reflections on the Return of Geopolitics to Central Asia and Its Effect on European Security

ERICH REITER

If one asks what is really new after the end of the Cold War, one must accept the notion that there is much inertia that extends the life of old-order concepts, causing many to think in terms of East-West and North-South confrontation. New, modern order concepts in security policy theories are not prevalent. Today, this bipolar thinking happens in categories that are free of ideology but still according to geopolitical perceptions of balances and counterbalances. And one must not forget that the main opponents in the Cold War—the United States and Russia—still maintain their strategic nuclear arsenals; an antagonistic base component thus continues in their relations.

Beyond that it is necessary to develop new scenarios for new thinking, perhaps something like mind games based, of course, on perceptions from the past and the present. Extrapolations are permitted and useful when dealing with future scenarios and help us move beyond historic reflections and current analyses. The future is open; occasionally, we may encircle it with unbrushed thinking.

Is the East-West conflict really over? Or has it only declined in importance because of a much weaker Russia? Because there still exists a confrontational situation between the West and Russia—and that is undeniable—then the basis for it must be geopolitical thinking, particularly on the part of Russia. This distilled East-West conflict applies only to Eastern Europe and

A previous version of this chapter was published by the Bureau for Military Scientific Studies, Ministry of Defense (2000) *Studien und Berichte zur Sicherheitspolitik* 1 (January), Vienna.

Central Asia, including the Caspian Sea region. The old East-West confrontation has experienced a rejuvenation thanks to the competition between China and the United States in East and Southeast Asia.

Security policy relations are influenced by geographical factors. All the warnings in respect to NATO enlargement—that it would deepen the confrontation—attest to the fact that such a confrontation exists despite the end of the Cold War. Any attempt by a particular state to establish hegemony will be met with power politics. As Russians attempt to assert hegemony over the countries of the Commonwealth of Independent States, they will challenge Americans for world leadership. The question is *how* the great powers will react to this (antagonism or cooperation?) in order to maintain a multipolar world, which has existed since China shook off Russia's supremacy in the 1960s, since Japan became a great economic power, and since the common market made the European Union an economic world power. A bipolar system after the 1960s existed only in a military-political sense and in respect to the situation in Europe. And a unipolar world with clear U.S. leadership existed probably only for a very short time, that is, after the breakdown of the Soviet Union and the U.S. prosecution of the Gulf War against Iraq.

DECOLONIZATION AS THE BASIS
OF THE FUTURE WORLD ORDER

With respect to fundamental prerequisites for the development of new geopolitics, the principal change is the progress of decolonization during the Cold War. Since the end of World War II, the number of sovereign states has increased from sixty-eight (including a few tiny states in Europe) to 183 or more. But the new states could not become real players in international relations because of the global domination of the two military superpowers who—along with China—influenced their policies, politics, and ideological, social, and economic orientations in different ways. Partially, these new sovereign states were integrated into coalitions or spheres of interest led by the great powers; partially, they tried to make their own way. However, they lacked a common strategic goal within the organization of unaligned states. Therefore, they were not very successful in wielding global influence or in shaping a world order conforming to their respective interests.

Although its importance was not so obvious, decolonization brought about the major change in the world in the twentieth century and will be of even greater importance in the future. The developing countries, with less than 20 percent of the world's total gross national product, represent four-fifths of the world's population; different as they may be, they all are up against a world dominated by the United States. After the disintegration of bipolar hegemony, the importance of regional powers increased. Regional powers have become self-reliant players whose relations to the United States, or their strategic triangle relations to each other, shape the regional political structures that define the global situation. Thus the sheer number of countries and their newfound ability for action make a unipolar world practically impossible. Regional conflicts become difficult to predict. Added to this equation is the independence of the former Soviet republics and satellite states, a continuing and open-ended process.

WESTERN INTERESTS IN CENTRAL ASIA
AND THE CASPIAN SEA REGION

The fact that the emergence of new independent countries leads to completely new conditions for geopolitics is demonstrated in Central Asia and the Caspian Sea region. These places illustrate the return of geopolitics.

These regions possess important economic and strategic considerations in which U.S. and European enterprises are interested. At the moment part of this area is a power vacuum and undergoing political and cultural reorientation. This area borders—apart from Russia and China—Turkey, Iraq, Iran, and Afghanistan. These countries are of strategic importance to the United States and to Europe and are, in fact, potential or actual sources of crisis.

Although oil and gas resources will be expensive to extract, the region (consisting of the former Soviet republics in Central Asia and south of the Caucasus) offers a strategic reserve for these raw materials. Therefore, measures were taken for later exploitation, including the planning and construction of new pipelines. Thus, in November 1999, an agreement on the construction of an oil pipeline was actually signed, according to the wishes of the United States and Turkey, by the presidents of Azerbaijan, Georgia, Turkey, and the United States (with further agreements on trans-Caucasus energy routes, including Kazakhstan and Turkmenistan). Under the consortium leadership of British BP-Amoco, oil is to be transported on the Baku-Ceyhan route from Azerbaijan via Georgia to the Turkish Mediterranean port of Ceyhan starting in 2004. After construction of a pipeline through the Caspian Sea, Kazakhstan and Turkmenistan could also be connected later on. The establishment of a Eurasian transportation corridor from Kazakhstan to Turkey would decisively reduce the dependency of the producing countries on Russia. This assistance in escaping Russian influence parallels the expansion of Western influence east of Europe. Russia's defense against growing Western influence in Central Asia is relatively weak, because the big Russian companies are above all concerned with selling Russian oil; stronger engagement in the Central Asia/Caspian Sea region in order to increase production would compete with their own production. So the Russian companies are in a wait-and-see mode, even as Russia tries to expand its own pipelines.

Strategic and economic interests are not always in line: some Western companies thought that one should include Russia to a higher degree in the exploitation of oil and gas resources, because long-term stabilization and peacemaking in this conflict-prone region is not possible without Russia. The strategic interest of the United States, however, aims at pushing back Russian influence. And due to their financial strength and technical expertise, U.S. companies have advantages (e.g., U.S. politics sets the political framework for private investment). Turkey has a certain presence in the region but does not dominate it; as a threshold country, it is not able by itself to shape economic development in the region persistently. It therefore is the natural U.S. partner and offers itself as the country for the pipeline routes.

Up to now one of the priorities of U.S. policy has been to exclude Iran as much as possible from the oil and gas business in this region. Numerous Western, especially European, companies would like to include Iran for reasons of economic advantages (especially shorter transportation routes) and are ready to invest. The policies of several important EU member states are strongly influenced by that, and they pursue a policy vis-à-vis Iran that is different from U.S. policy.

TRADITIONAL GEOPOLITICAL
IDEAS AND CONCEPTS

Looking at geopolitics from a historic point of view, this geographic area is also of strategic importance, as it is the center of Eurasia.

Sir Harold Mackinder argued that the Western maritime coalition should underline the importance of the Eurasian heartland (including Central Asia and the Caspian Sea region) and predicted that Moscow's victory in World War II would make the Soviet Union the greatest land power on the globe, which could dominate Eurasia and the world. After World War II, U.S. security planners (based on Mackinder's theories) saw the Soviet Union—as the heartland power—as the fundamental threat to U.S. security interests; this led to the containment policy directed against Soviet geographic and ideological expansion during the Cold War. The Central Asia/Caspian Sea region belongs to Mackinder's heartland, but according to him the basic element for global domination was the control over Eastern Europe. Whoever controls Eastern Europe rules the heartland; whoever rules the heartland rules the world island; and whoever rules the world island rules the world. Central Asia is an important, but not the essential, part of the heartland, according to Mackinder.

However, this was surely valid only with respect to the former Soviet Union; to a sea power, the heartland was invulnerable, according to Mackinder. These are theories, and Nicholas Spykman, for instance, who carried Mackinder's analysis further, formulated that whoever controls the Eurasian rimland rules Eurasia, and whoever rules Eurasia controls the destiny of the world. For that reason, U.S. foreign policy made it impossible for the Eurasian landmass to host an overwhelmingly dominant power, especially a hostile, totalitarian nation. Control over Central Asia is still of geopolitical importance, although the need for continued Western emphasis on the Eurasian heartland has decreased because of the regained independence of many countries in the heartland. In the longer run, the geopolitical importance of this area could increase because the Eurasian rimland still abounds in potential threats to world order.

Thus, Central Asia cannot be disregarded with respect to current geopolitical situations. The strategic triangles that are probably decisive to the global balance of power today are those between the United States, China, and Japan in the Far East and between the United States, the EU, and Russia in the Euroatlantic. The critical connection between both is the long Russia-China land border and Central Asia. Therefore, in Central Asia Russia will try to build counterweights to the United States, which may concern China and India and thus influence relations within the triangles. The power structures in this area will have effects that reach beyond its borders.

CHANGING POLICIES

The new situation may change some policies, because national interests today are economic and strategic in nature. National policy often supports economic interests. U.S. policies and politics especially support economic goals in the Central Asia/Caspian Sea region. This has already brought and will continue to bring the United States and Western Europe into conflict with the interests of Russia and other bordering countries.

Relations with Iran

The dual containment policy of the United States toward Iraq and Iran may change with respect to Iran for the sake of economic interests; at least some groups in the United States will seek cooperation with Iran, and important parts of Iran's society are ready. Thus, Iran may be able to challenge Russia's control of oil and gas resources and the means of transportation. Eliminating Russia as a power factor in this area is what the United States really wants. Therefore, there is no guarantee that Russia and Iran will become stable partners in the future. If political pressure on Iran diminishes and it becomes more integrated into the international political structures, which some European countries are already trying to do, it will be a potential rival of Russia. The

Western economic interests are thus combined with strategic interest, not only to weaken Russia and gain influence in the region but also to control the shipping lanes in the Persian Gulf.

In addition, Russia is trying to contain Islamic influence in this region, and Iran is the promoter of this influence. Even after the conclusion of its fundamentalist phase, Iran will remain an important factor of cultural influence on the Islamic world. It is also in China's interest to contain Islamic influence, and China has a common interest with Russia to balance U.S. influence in Central Asia and the Caucasus.

Russia-China Relations

All of this constitutes a basis for strategic cooperation between Russia and China. One could argue that there are too many political, economic, and strategic obstacles for their long-term strategic cooperation. But there is enough ground for interim strategic cooperation against specific U.S. interests. Therefore, one could say that U.S. engagement in the Central Asia/Caspian Sea region is creating a new basis for Chinese-Russian common political goals.

Not to be overlooked is the Chinese interest in cooperating with the country occupying the largest geographic area in Central Asia, Kazakhstan, for supply of oil and gas. But this need not cause a confrontation with Russia in the short or medium term, because China is not directly interested in a zone of influence in this area; it will be much more interested in Russia fulfilling the function of an order power in Central Asia.

The normalization of Chinese-Russian relations works well; they are deepening, and Russia is supporting the Chinese armed forces in modernizing their equipment. Due to NATO enlargement, extension of the security agreements with Japan, and the activities in Central Asia, it makes sense to find this sort of common ground. This does not necessitate a long-term strategic partnership, but it can lead to medium-term tactical concepts against Western interests.

Turkey and Iran

It is hard to predict the internal development in Iran and Turkey, but one can imagine that the differences in their social and cultural self-understanding will diminish due to increasing Islamic influence in Turkey and Iran's gradual liberalization. Iran is, of course, leveraging the dwindling credibility of the U.S. Gulf policy to normalize its relations with some Arabic countries, especially Saudi Arabia but also the smaller Gulf neighbors.

Turkey is not really a decisive player in the region, although Azerbaijan and all Central Asian countries except Tajikistan are ethnically and linguistically predominantly Turkish (Turkic-speaking). However, because of its economic situation, Turkey does not qualify for generous and large-scale investments in this region. The Turkic-speaking countries tend toward differentiated politics; they are open-minded to all potential investors, believing any investment would support their independence. Turkish attempts at gaining influence in this area are in competition especially with Russia and Iran.

The continuation of Turkish cooperation with the United States and Israel will depend on internal developments in Turkey, which may not always be Western-oriented. Turkey has become skeptical toward the European Union, and general anti-Western trends can be noticed. The perspective of Turkey's possible admission into the EU since the end of 1999 has changed this, but membership remains undetermined, and there will be no negotiations for some time to come. If Turkish skepticism resurges in this regard, it will promote better relations with Iran, with the potential for strategic cooperation. Both countries, especially Turkey, are in a phase of reorientation. Thus, it makes sense for two relatively important regional powers to cooperate to enhance their role in the Middle East and reduce U.S. and Russian influence. This would affect transatlantic as well as U.S.-Russian relations.

India's Role in Central Asia

The influence of India in this area is limited by Pakistan, which could offer new routes for oil transportation via Afghanistan, and by China, especially because of its strategic cooperation with Pakistan. Cooperation with Russia is more difficult and will depend to a degree on Russian strategic cooperation with China. Therefore, India—in spite of the new situation in Central Asia—is not a potentially important player outside the South Asia subcontinent.

Yet the fact that two new nuclear powers (India and Pakistan) exist in South Asia may lead to a reorientation of these powers toward one another as well as toward the great powers. Poor relations between India and Pakistan, their possession of nuclear weapons, and their unresolved problems (especially Kashmir) raise the danger of nuclear war, yet the official nuclear powers can be more easily integrated in a control mechanism for nuclear weapons and tests. This would put U.S. problems with regard to India in perspective; at the same time, Islamic and anti-American tendencies in Pakistan would make its relations with the United States more difficult. It would be too early to predict a course change in this case; but it is a given that India will experience a political-military increase in power.

As to the stabilization of the Indian subcontinent, there will be no way around India. And since stabilization has reached high priority for China (i.e., with regard to the independence aspirations in the Chinese province of Xinjiang), a stronger willingness to move closer to India on the part of China can be noticed. In any case, India will in the future influence the relations of the great powers. One will have to take into account the strategic triangles: China-India-Russia, United States–India–China, and possibly United States–India–Russia. India may well project its power into the region, but one cannot be certain at this time.

Blocs of Interest

Based on current international relations, two big blocs of interest can be detected vis-à-vis interests in Central Asia: the United States, Western Europe, Turkey, and Pakistan; and Russia, Iran, and India. China cannot belong to the second bloc of interest because up to now its relations with India were hostile and characterized by rivalry. Will the situation bring about a change in this case? Many things seem possible, including enhanced U.S. interest and better China-India relations. Of course, this has to be seen in the context of developments in Europe, as a decisive new order of security policy arose there through NATO enlargement.

NATO ENLARGEMENT AND CENTRAL ASIA

With NATO enlargement to Poland, the Czech Republic, and Hungary, there is for the first time a component of Western order in the so-called crisis belt from the Baltic Sea to the Black Sea. It means an extended engagement of the United States in European security policy and a further extension of its scope of influence.

According to Russian geopolitical and imperial thinking, NATO enlargement is a reason for taking measures to safeguard Russia's influence at least in the former Soviet republics in the south, Russia's so-called soft belly. A second step toward NATO enlargement must also be evaluated, and limiting or forestalling any further NATO enlargement (e.g., as a consequence of a U.S. requirement for strategic cooperation with Russia) will depend on the situation in the Central Asia/Caspian Sea region. Of course, Russia's future zone of influence will be determined as well by geostrategic possibilities, that is, by the space for power projection left to it by the West; this will depend on NATO enlargement (as well as on the process of integrating former Warsaw Pact countries) and on internal development in Russia (i.e., whether it becomes a democracy). If not, then it will be a hegemonistic and imperialistic country at least vis-à-vis the commonwealth countries and the Baltic States.

Does development in Russia depend on, or is it determined by, Western policies and politics, particularly the extent and speed of NATO enlargement? Not necessarily, because NATO enlargement is not a real threat for Russia; still, such a perception does exist in Russia, and it is suitable for political manipulation by Russian nationalists. The conjured danger does not lie in aggressive actions by NATO against Russia but in statements that NATO might expand up to the Russian border, which would in itself demonstrate Russia's current weakness.

Thus, the West can put these anxieties to rest only by "good behavior," which would in the end mean complying with Russian ideas in Eastern, Southeastern, and Northern Europe. A positive Western influence on internal Russian development is extremely difficult; only marginal influence is possible, and even that may prove to be counterproductive, as financial aid supports the anarchic economic system instead of transitioning it to a market economy. Thus one must consider Russia's self-perception of its role as a great power. In the end, Russian development is decided within Russia; Western policies and politics are not decisive. If Russia becomes a normal state—a Western-type democracy—then it will also behave normally, that is, peacefully. If, however, it becomes authoritarian and imperialistic again, then it is good if it does not find a large sphere of influence and is limited in its imperialistic ambitions.

NATO is without doubt the first factor of order for Europe. A second enlargement, possibly including Romania, would reposition the southern flank of NATO and result in a stronger scope of influence in the Black Sea area, which up to now—with the exception of the Turkish coast areas—has practically been controlled by Russia. This would be a serious challenge to Russian geopolitics.

The political arrangements resulting from the first round of NATO enlargement mean that Russia has practically been integrated into NATO's stability and security net, albeit in a limited way. In any case, the first step of NATO enlargement did not strain U.S.-Russian relations as much as some critics had expected. Looking at it from this point of view, it becomes more difficult to envisage what countermeasures Russia could take against its gradual encirclement. There are few possibilities, even after a resurgence of strength for Russia. And Russia has noted that its quasi-integration into NATO structures has given it no possibility of shaping the decisionmaking process. Thus, Russia may form new alliances, even with more obscure countries like Iraq, or establish a strategic triangle with India and China. The obstruction of Western policies is and will continue to be one core element of Russian politics in portraying the importance and great-power role of Russia.

The NATO air war in the Kosovo conflict merely damaged Russia's relations with the West. Russia took on a mediator position to influence Western measures; however, Russian influence on Serbian leadership proved weak, and it is disputed whether Russia was able to exert decisive influence with regard to the acceptance of NATO's peace conditions. Relations with the West have in any case deteriorated due to the Kosovo war, because it exposed Russia's relative lack of influence.

In any case, for the United States, Central Asia is a new power vacuum, an attractive target for U.S. politics and business. The questions are how U.S. interests in this area can be balanced with Western security interests in Eastern Europe, and whether U.S. engagement in Central Asia will be counterproductive to NATO enlargement. A more severe confrontation with Russia runs counter to U.S. long-term global interests. Intense pursuit of U.S. interests with the parallel elimination of Russia from business in this region, plus a second enlargement of NATO, especially to sensitive countries like Romania, could prepare the ground for more internal radicalism inside Russia and increase its tendency toward imperialistic and aggressive politics. The result could be long-term strategic cooperation with China, additional pressures on commonwealth and Baltic countries, refusal to cooperate on strategic arms control and reduction, and the formation of anti-Western coalitions in Asia and Africa.

THE EUROPEAN SECURITY SITUATION

Perspectives toward European security and the European security architecture are also influenced by constellations outside of Europe; they depend heavily on the evolution of Russian-Chinese and U.S.-Chinese relations but especially on U.S.-Russian relations. Russia sees itself in a struggle for influence with the United States. Japan will possibly in the future become a global player, including militarily. A Japan armed with nuclear forces would transform the situation in East Asia, with global effects.

U.S. Policy Toward Russia

What would be more helpful for the development of European security: U.S. containment of Russian influence in Central Asia or in Eastern Europe?

If the United States really aims at a unipolar strategy of global hegemony by strengthening its leading role in NATO, tightening its control over Europe, and dominating the Western Pacific region, it also aims at a policy of enclosing, containing, and weakening Russia. NATO enlargement, Ukrainian independence, and economic and political support of countries of the former Soviet Union will shrink Russia's space for strategic survival. For the time being, Russia has neither the intention nor the capability to confront the United States. Even after economic recovery, Russia will not have sufficient means to seriously challenge the United States.

U.S. Interests and Europe

Are there general and definite U.S. objectives in the long term toward Europe, or are they dependent on changing factors: revolving political administrations, domestic politics, and trends and moods? How about Europe? Does Europe long for its Cold War role as junior partner of the United States? Russia remains a potential adversary, and so Europe cannot separate from the United States in security affairs. Still, there are signs of disagreement. The United States is demanding more international engagement by the Europeans to maintain the transatlantic link, in particular the readiness and willingness for military engagement in the Middle East, as well as at least symbolic contributions in the Far East. At the same time, Europeans seek U.S. support and leadership in European conflicts. Based on Europe's apparent unwillingness to shoulder global responsibility, it does not seem to be a reliable U.S. partner. Still, the United States has no real alternative allies for global engagement.

A Common Foreign and Security Policy of the EU deserving of the title may well emerge, but it will still take some time. A European Security and Defense Identity is another story entirely, as illustrated by the difficulties the EU encounters in reforming its institutions. Nevertheless, a Common Foreign and Security Policy will be easier to achieve than fitting the United States into a coordinated transatlantic foreign and security policy, as that country is accustomed to doing things its own way. For the United States, a common policy means U.S. leadership, with the others following only in the execution of policy, not in decisionmaking.

CONCLUSION

European integration is—in principle—the opposite of hegemony and balance of power. On the one hand, it is directed against hegemony of a European power; on the other hand, it serves the purpose of avoiding U.S. hegemony over Europe. European integration is a contrary development to decolonization, a process of reducing players, and it will completely change geopolitics throughout the world.

16

Peace Operations:
An Assessment

ERWIN A. SCHMIDL

At a first glance, one might be tempted to believe that by the end of the twentieth century we had already achieved a high level of international and collective security management. Mandated by the United Nations or some other body, international peace operations are undertaken. Observer, monitor, and verification missions are dispatched to crisis regions. Collective measures are applied against so-called rogue states such as Libya, Iraq, and Serbia. International courts punish some of the perpetrators of horrible crimes in the former Yugoslavia and Rwanda. Are we finally on the way toward a better world, one in which national interests of the major powers are limited in favor of the welfare of all nations?

If we examine these apparently positive developments more closely, however, it becomes clear that the increased international character of these measures is cosmetic rather than substantial. True, nowadays the powers find it often more appealing to act through (or disguised by) international institutions or arrangements rather than on an outspoken national or unilateral basis. But national interests still play the dominant—and decisive—role in executing security policies, for the United States as well as for other powers.

PEACE OPERATIONS AT THE END
OF THEIR FIRST CENTURY

The evolution of peace operations in recent years demonstrates these developments. Contrary to popular opinion, peace operations were not invented by the UN in 1948 (when the first observer missions were created) or 1956 (with the establishment of the Emergency Force in Egypt, and the advent of the blue helmets). Rather, peace operations gradually developed in the nineteenth century as one element of the increasing international cooperation between the European powers after the Napoleonic Wars.[1] The emergence of international organizations in the place of the earlier Concert of Europe and its congress diplomacy made it easier to streamline the execution of these missions, and the powers' political and/or economic interests played an important role, as they do today.

To distinguish peace operations from other forms of interventions or war, I use the following five criteria:

- an international mandate or authorization;
- a multinational composition of the force;
- the aim of either preserving a status quo or effecting a peaceful transition to a new, agreed-upon status (i.e., postcolonial transition to independence);
- acting in the interest of the population concerned; and
- adhering to the principle of "minimum damage" (i.e., the application of measured force, not minimum force).[2]

The first operations fulfilling all five criteria were the international operations in Crete (1897–1908) and in Albania (1913–1914), followed by several missions staged under the umbrella of the League of Nations in the interwar years, notably the Saarland operation of 1934–1935.[3]

IN WHOSE INTEREST?

One crucial element in the criteria outlined above is the notion of acting in the interest of the population. In traditional literature, one usually finds the term of *host-country consent* instead.[4] I believe that this criterion is important to distinguish peace operations from old-fashioned conquest. However, host-country consent appears to be too narrowly defined and legalistic. What do we do when the host country's authorities do not represent the interests of the population, or when they lack the proper authority, or when there is no government left at all (as was the case in Somalia)? Admittedly, *in the interest of* is rather vague and leaves room for interpretation. Also, in realistic terms, one has to admit that this principle is flawed in most missions and that the real long-term interest of the host country's population rarely enjoys top priority in the minds of those planning or authorizing peace missions. At best, the aim of a peace operation might reflect (in a very paternalistic fashion) what the participating countries consider to be in the best interest of the country in question. What really has precedence, however, is undoubtedly the national interest[5] of each of the organizing powers or of various participating countries—which hopefully does not conflict too openly with the needs of the target country (or, to use the euphemism, the *host country*) for a peace mission. Actually, it is here that international organizations channel the national interests of countries, hopefully for the benefit of the host country.

To illustrate this point by example, when Austria sent a hospital unit to the Congo operation in 1960, Foreign Minister Bruno Kreisky was not really interested in the Congo at all—at that time he wanted to bring the issue of South Tyrol before the UN General Assembly. Participation in the Congo operation was seen as a means to advance Austria's national interests—while helping the people in the Congo at the same time.[6] To use a more recent example, German participation in the Somalia operation took place primarily because of German national interests not linked to Somalia. UN peace operations enable the tapping of resources less easily available otherwise.

THE ROLE OF THE UNITED NATIONS

If one took the UN Charter seriously, only the UN Security Council would be in a position to authorize missions involving force (the so-called Chapter 7 missions). However, often force is used—or implied in a threat—even without such a mandate, and the Security Council's consent is not always sought, even for enforcement operations. Sometimes, ad hoc coalitions might act without a proper mandate from the Security Council. Practice also shows that even when such a mandate is issued, it does not imply that the Security Council really is an *actor* in international politics. Rather, it remains a *tool* at the hands of the powers, notably the five Permanent Members (P-5). A look at the French-led intervention in Rwanda in 1994 (Operation Turquoise) is useful to illustrate this point: the Security Council finally approved the mission when the planes were less than an hour's flight time from the Kigali airport—and few observers believe that France would have aborted the mission if the mandate had not been given in time. Yet this is one of several cases sometimes cited as proof that the UN Security Council plays a larger role today than during the Cold War.

Immediately after the end of the Cold War and following the role played by the UN in the Gulf War, people like UN Secretary-General Boutros Boutros-Ghali, in his 1992 Agenda for Peace, envisaged a more active role for the organization, including the establishment of standing UN forces. However, these ambitions were short-lived: the operations in Somalia and the former Yugoslavia most clearly demonstrated that although the UN has the necessary apparatus and infrastructure for limited peacekeeping missions, such as interposition forces after an armistice and to organize and coordinate military as well as nonmilitary (police, election) observer missions, it is less suited for larger military operations. Such capabilities could easily be established, of course, but at this time (and for the foreseeable future) none of the powers appears willing to limit its own options by delegating such abilities to the UN.

This assessment was recently confirmed when the allied powers intervening in Kosovo in spring 1999 demonstrated their lack of respect for the UN Charter by mounting an air war without a proper Security Council mandate. However, even in this case some form of international legitimation was sought (and granted) by NATO's North Atlantic Council.[7]

Nonetheless, some improvements have been made in the UN system, such as the establishment of a proper department of peacekeeping operations within the UN Secretariat in New York, as well as the revival of the standby arrangements originally introduced in the 1960s. Still, there is a long way to go—and in come cases action might be more difficult now than in the 1950s and 1960s. As Sir Brian Urquhart recently stated, it had taken Dag Hammarskjöld only seven days to send the first blue helmets into the Sinai, but "they're lucky now if they can do it in seven months!"[8] The necessary unification of the operational and administrative chain of command (always a sore point in UN operations) was briefly effected but then quickly abandoned. The improvements within the department of peacekeeping operations were jeopardized when the Third World countries forced the General Assembly to terminate the practice of "gratis personnel" being seconded from European and North American countries (which allowed this department to function at all). The performance of the Lessons Learned Unit established by Kofi Annan in April 1995 has been disappointing so far[9] (which might indicate, incidentally, that there are elements within the organization that are not really dedicated to improvements, besides the big powers' reluctance to grant more power to the UN).

AIMS AND PURPOSES

Operations like those in Rwanda and the former Yugoslavia also indicate that the host countries for peace operations are not really taken seriously as partners (or even opponents) in international policy. Rather, it shows a difference in status that is not too different from a colonial or protectorate setting. This is not bad per se—colonial administrations had their positive aspects, too—but it appears to be one more reason to doubt the image of a better, more internationalized world.

When lecturing on peace operations, one is sometimes confronted with the question of whether the involvement of organizations like the UN and the Organization for Security and Cooperation in Europe (OSCE) in conflicts such as those in Kosovo and Albania would eventually lead to similar international missions in Northern Ireland or in Spain's Basque region. The answer clearly is no: Great Britain and Spain are both "real" and respected countries, which no organization could dare to target for a peace mission (both countries would certainly prevent any such intervention in their internal affairs). It is only among second league and Third World countries that target (sorry, *host*) countries for peace operations can be found, if such missions are deemed useful by the countries undertaking such operations.

But there is more to this issue: in the popular image, international organizations are often and wrongly considered as actors rather than as tools at the hands of the great powers. This leads to false and exaggerated expectations, and when these organizations fail to act accordingly, they are duly accused of being ineffective, which further harms their public image. In reality, the leading powers, especially the United States, play the dominant role in most international organizations. This is true not only for the United Nations and NATO but also for other, more democratically structured ones like the OSCE, which has since 1995 developed into a tool of U.S. foreign policy in Eastern and Southeastern Europe, complementary to NATO for nonmilitary tasks.

Another case of false expectations has to be mentioned here: public opinion often demands international organizations to end or solve a conflict. Conflicts can only be solved by those involved in the conflict. Outsiders can provide assistance (and exert pressure), but they cannot solve somebody else's conflict.

Public opinion in the contributing countries is increasingly important, yet this does not mean that the publicly stated aims always match the real motives. A good example was the Multinational Protection Force in Albania that Italy organized in 1997 to protect itself against Albanian refugees. This was achieved (as was the secondary purpose of entrenching the position of the Italian joint chiefs of staff vis-à-vis the different services), but the short military intervention had little effect on the situation in Albania itself.[10] Even at the time, few contemporaries believed that this force, with its very limited mandate, could stabilize the chaotic situation in Albania.

PUBLIC INTEREST AND THE MEDIA

However, slight changes have become apparent in recent years. Traditionally, in most countries foreign affairs remained the domain of unfettered policy-making for those in power, with comparatively few restraints either by democratic institutions (such as a parliament) or by the public. Recently, this has changed: more than before, foreign policy decisions are under the scrutiny of the public and the media, at least when they refer to European issues. This, in due course, makes it more appealing to governments to use international institutions to play a part (and provide a useful cover or, eventually, take the blame). Although there are no guarantees, there is at least a chance that this might at some point strengthen the role of international organizations.

In some cases, public opinion pressured governments to mount a peace mission—as was the case with the UN-mandated, U.S.-led Unified Task Force (UNITAF) in Somalia in 1992–1993; politicians supported the international operation to prevent accusations of inaction when pictures of starving children appeared on TV screens at Christmastime.[11] But even in this example, where the so-called CNN factor generated an operation, public interest dwindled rapidly. Experience shows that the public attention spans in Europe or North America are limited (a German Red Cross spokeswoman confirmed in the mid-1990s that public interest could be raised only for one crisis area at a time and only for about six months).[12] In contrast, peace operations are by their very nature lengthy undertakings, especially if they are to assist in rebuilding a country after an internal conflict. Dwindling public support can tempt politicians to press for fixed exit dates instead of a properly defined end state, as was the case in the first year of the NATO presence in Bosnia-Herzegovina in 1996. Fears of mission creep can limit the execution of a mandate and might actually jeopardize the success of an operation altogether.

If staged only for the benefit of audiences at home, international operations can sometimes cause more harm than good to the countries in which they take place. Examples of recent actions undertaken with little regard for the host country include U.S. muscle-flexing vis-à-vis Yugoslavia and Iraq.

By and large, the public in Europe and North America is more interested in European affairs than in developments elsewhere, which allows the powers more leeway to follow their interests in the Third World, leading to several examples of postimperial policing in Africa as well as in the former Soviet Union. In Africa, the two recent UN operations in the Central African Republic (after the earlier intervention by a French-led force) and in Sierra Leone (following the intervention by the Economic Community of West African States [ECOWAS] Observer Group) clearly show a pattern of UN operations taking over from or observing interventions by hegemonic and/or regional powers—not unlike the UN observers dispatched to the Dominican Republic following the U.S.-led intervention in 1965.

CONTRACTING OUT AND COALITIONS OF THE WILLING

Following the debacles in Somalia and the former Yugoslavia, new models of international action were tried. Where military enforcement actions were necessary, these were carried out outside the UN system, with a lead nation gathering a coalition of the willing or acting through existing organizations or regional arrangements (such as NATO). Professional UN staff, also known as *onusiens* from the French acronym ONU, usually deplore this contracting out as undermining the authority of the UN. However, this model has proven quite

effective in Haiti and Bosnia-Herzegovina. Experience has shown that contracting out is not at all incongruent with UN peacekeeping—actually, a forceful military intervention might be succeeded by a more traditional UN mission
once the situation had been stabilized.

The Haiti operation in 1994 showed how this could work with well-
planned, gradual, and overlapping transitions, from the U.S.-led Multinational Force to the UN operation, then to the new local government supported by
the UN, as well as bilateral programs. In contrast, the operations staged in
Bosnia-Herzegovina after the 1995 Dayton-Paris Accords and in Kosovo after
the 1999 war, demonstrated the problems caused by a parallel (rather than a
consecutive) approach: the political direction comes from the United States
through the OSCE, the money is provided by the Europeans, the police
aspects are provided by the UN, and a strong NATO presence caters for the
military security. Cooperation between all these players (and the hundreds of
nongovernmental organizations present in both theaters) still is not what it
should be, with many organizations not really aware of what their counterparts do.[13]

In general, there now exist three different models for international interventions:

- The first is the UN approach. Although the highly ambitious and complex operations in Somalia,[14] Angola, and Rwanda are considered failures, the UN is still the institution of choice for small to medium-sized
  traditional peacekeeping operations as well as specialized tasks like
  police assistance and election monitoring. In recent years, limited missions, like the operation in Mozambique and the observer mission in
  South Africa, worked successfully.
- For more forceful interventions (more or less staged along the lines of
  classic counterinsurgency operations), a lead nation–type multinational intervention has proven to be better suited. With limited aims and a
  more military organization, these operations were comparatively successful in Somalia (UNITAF) and Rwanda (Operation Turquoise, as
  well as the U.S. humanitarian support mission). However, the pressing
  urgency not to miss an exit date might jeopardize long-term achievements.
- Not unlike the lead-nation model, recent operations also show that
  occasionally regional organizations play an increased role in security
  issues. The role of the European Community in ending the war in
  Slovenia in 1991 has to be mentioned here, as well as the military
  operations under ECOWAS auspices in Liberia and Sierra Leone.
  Although particular nations still play a dominant role, this model
  might also indicate a tendency by regional organizations to become
  players themselves.

CONCLUSION

At the end of the twentieth century, more than one hundred years after the staging of the first international peace operation on Crete, there were fundamental questions that remain unresolved—some cannot be resolved, in fact, because they address the political motives behind such operations—and thus were bound to lead to problems again and again. Thus, it should be elementary that an operation should be customized according to the situation on the ground and the political aim envisaged. Also, the duration of such a mission should be determined by an end state rather than an end date. Despite all anniversaries (including fifty years of UN peacekeeping), peacekeepers are still sent into missions lacking proper preparation for their tasks, including crucial areas like cultural-awareness training. Experiences are still not properly collected, let alone disseminated.

Was this the disappointing state of peace operations at the end of the twentieth century? Not necessarily: from an optimistic point of view, it shows that there is still wide room for improvement.

NOTES

1. I have included a brief summary of this evolution in my recent (1998) booklet "Police in Peace Operations," *Informationen zur Sicherheitspolitik* 10 (Vienna: BMLV/MWB, September). See also Erwin A. Schmidl (1997) "Im Land der Skipetaren: Die internationale Friedensoperation in Albanien 1913 –1914," *Österreichische Militärische Zeitschrift* 35, no. 4 (July-August): 431–440.

2. In traditional UN operations, the basic notion was to use force only in self-defense or in defending the mandate (whatever that could mean)—again, with different interpretations in different missions. In accordance with police practice, *measured force* (or *minimum collateral damage*) appears a more correct term than *minimum force*.

3. The evolution of peace operations is covered in more detail in the introductory chapter to my book, Erwin A. Schmidl (2000) *Peace Operations Between Peace and War* (London: Frank Cass).

4. See also Antonietta Di Blase (1978) "The Role of the Host State's Consent with Regard to Non-coercive Actions by the United Nations," in Antonio Cassese (ed.) *United Nations Peace-keeping: Legal Essays* (Alphen/Rijn: Sijthoff and Noordhoff), pp. 55–94.

5. In the course of the discussions at the conference at the Landesverteidigungsakademie in April 1998, the question was put forward whether there are ways to measure national interest. Basically, the only question is whether or not the national interest is sufficient to support an operation. When examined in detail, this vague entity of national interest shows itself to be a conglomerate of various opinions and interests—in practice, medium-level bureaucrats might be able to torpedo an endeavor even if higher-ranking politicians favor it, and vice versa.

6. This is covered in more detail in my study on the Austrian medical unit in the Congo: Erwin A. Schmidl (1995) *Blaue Helme, Rotes Kreuz: Das österreichische UN-*

Sanitätskontingent im Kongo, 1960 bis 1963, Innsbrucker Forschungen zur Zeit-geschichte 13 (Innsbruck–Wien: StudienVerlag). See also, in English, Erwin A. Schmidl (1995) "The Austrian Medical Unit in the Congo, 1960–1963: Austria's First Participation in a UN Operation," *Maintien de la Paix de 1815 à aujourd'hui, Actes 21* (Ottawa: Commission Canadienne d'Histoire Militaire), pp. 629–635.

7. For an excellent summary of the war of 1999, see Erich Reiter (ed.) (2000) *Der Krieg um das Kosovo 1998–1999* (Mainz: v. Hase and Koehler).

8. I am grateful to Sir Brian for granting me an interview in October 1997.

9. When a symposium was held to discuss the failure of the Somalia operation, some participants complained that the sessions were arranged in a fashion that opin-ions critical of the performance of UN Headquarters and some key personnel could easily be left out. The resulting recommendations are published in neat little booklets and are phrased in rather watered-down fashion (e.g., "The deployment was slow. . .") so as to cause no harm.

10. Albanians I have since talked to about this intervention have different opin-ions about its effects. Those who didn't expect anything from it (perhaps the more real-istic approach) said that it was useless but at least did not cause much harm. In con-trast, more optimistic Albanians (who apparently really hoped that this mission would help to stabilize the situation in the country) showed disappointment, often claiming that the short international presence only made matters worse.

11. This was recently exposed in a brilliant article by Gérard Prunier.

12. I owe this information to Dr. Maren Köster-Hetzendorf, who worked for the German Red Cross at the time.

13. I shall address this aspect in more detail in my forthcoming study on the Euro-pean Community Monitor Mission.

14. Literature on Somalia abounds. Here, I would like to mention only Mohamed Sahnoun (1994) *Somalia: The Missed Opportunities* (Washington, D.C.: United States Institute of Peace), which well illustrates (from the point of view of the special repre-sentative who resigned in protest to the Secretary-General's actions) the difficulties encountered in communications between UNHQ in New York and the mission in the field.

PART 5

The Role of
Major Powers

17

Great Powers and
Global Insecurity

DANIEL N. NELSON

What will be the role of states—particularly large and powerful ones—in global affairs in the twenty-first century? States possess a principal role in human affairs not because of their vitality but because there is yet no clear successor. States are now far more permeable and less autonomous, yet they confront demands for empowerment, self-determination, and devolution.

Postinternational dynamics evoke turbulence, rendering state institutions, processes, and laws archaic.[1] Matters of state—most notably national security—increasingly are not seen in terms of the nation-state alone; if there are national interests, they are more and more the concern of subnational or transnational businesses and institutions that can address critical issues such as employment.[2]

States aren't what they used to be. The authoritative allocation of values and resources is less and less vested in the state and its institutions. These critical functions have shifted to multinational business, worldwide crime syndicates, global media, international financial institutions, and a stratum of advocacy-focused nongovernmental organizations (NGOs).[3] A "gross criminal product" from global organized crime, for example, may have reached $1 trillion by the late 1990s, more than any sovereign state except the United States and Japan.[4]

In many cases, these extrastate institutions perform functions more efficiently than the state itself. The state's institutions continue to operate, but they do so with less efficiency, fewer resources, and reduced legitimacy.[5] In

An earlier version of this chapter appeared in Michael Klare and Chandrani Yogesh (eds.) (1998) *World Security: Challenges for a New Century* (New York: St. Martin's).

Africa, states have been destructive, preventing development and democracy, and in Latin America land owners, business elites, drug traffickers, armies, and the church have meant that political systems and regimes may come and go with little effect.[6] A number of Islamic states have had a somewhat different fate, being co-opted or subsumed by a fundamentalist clergy or dominated by militarized one-party regimes. Where strong central government does not prevail, quasi-states[7] proliferate; micro–self-determination—beyond regionalism, where small minorities insist on separate, sovereign political authority—leads to state fragmentation. And as the imperatives of the world capitalist order weigh in on every country, the fracturing of states leads to more peripheral economies with substantial dependence on or absorption into dominant economies.[8]

At the very least, political, economic, and social functions of human organization are no longer vested in the territorial control exerted by states.[9] And when political leaders woodenheadedly insist that greater sovereignty is their aim, reduced economic performance usually follows.[10]

Yet states remain the principal organizing unit of human society and a key plane upon which global peace and prosperity depend. Overtaken and underthrown, states hold fewer cards than ever before, but they are still important players. Between the most powerful states and groups of states will rest the potential to build or destroy security for the foreseeable future. In large part, this is because states still dispose of most armies and weapons and still maintain large bureaucracies for obtaining and distributing resources.

The United States, China, Russia, Japan, and the European Union (EU) are, for now, the only states or associations of states that might be labeled as *great powers*. Although other analysts have preferred terms such as *potential challengers* or *major contenders* for states with ample military or economic capacities, the same five were identified in 1990 as principal actors on the global stage.[11] Adjustments down or up in the capacities of each to "control their political environment and to get other nations to do what [they] want"[12] have clearly occurred; Russia as the principal successor to the former Soviet Union certainly is far weaker, China has accumulated economic and military resources, and the EU is likely to become more of a unified economic (and perhaps politico-military) actor.

But the real issue here is broader. How will these major states and relations among them affect global security in the twenty-first century? Although such a far-reaching question has no definitive answer, below I consider the potential role of these principal actors in maintaining a regional and global balance between threats and capacities—the ratio that lies at the core of what we mean by *security*.[13] Such an imprecise ratio implies the degree to which military, economic, or political resources possessed by an actor address or ameliorate dangerous conditions. Although this ratio cannot be reduced to a science, neither is it mere speculation. States have resources and capacities; if those are substantial, threats from domestic or foreign origins can be balanced and neutralized.

Disorder and conflict implicit to human nature require the creation of an authority—the state—to ensure physical security and socioeconomic well-being. Only derivatively are states providers of justice, equality, and other political goods.[14] States ally with one another not because of principles but because there are tangible benefits that outweigh the costs. Alliances are formed essentially because of a common threat and not because of shared values; they operate as self-help systems in which states cooperate to enhance their capacities to deter or defeat an actor that poses a common threat.[15]

Are the world's great powers, their associations, and their alliances willing and able to fulfill such a role? Do principal states and their bilateral and multilateral relations provide humankind with greater order, more peace, and enhanced prosperity? States are unquestionably involved in matters of security, but achieving a balance between threats and capacities depends less and less on actions by, or decisions within, the state. States are capacity-driven, concentrating on accumulating wealth, expanding markets, strengthening defense, and protecting interests. They have yet to fashion mechanisms for conflict avoidance or resolution. Instead, states are a milieu in which resources are amassed for conflict and thereby encourage such events.

THREATS AND CAPACITIES

For everyone—individuals, groups, regimes, people, and nations—danger can be physical or psychological, real or perceived, imminent or latent, internal or external.[16] The degree to which individuals, groups, and societies confront economic distress, social malaise, political violence, dangers to environment and health, and the specter of armed attack—and the immediacy with which these and other perilous conditions are perceived—all contribute to insecurity unless they can be abated, or capacities enlarged, to achieve a balance.

Physical or psychological threats can rise or fall, but that never determines net security. Rather, the ratio of threats to capacities defines security. When threats exceed capacities, and the ratio is larger than 1:0, one can expect—at any level of analysis—suspicion, vulnerability, turmoil, indecision, dissolution, and evasion. When capacities exceed threats, and the ratio is less than 1:0, the inverse can be expected—violent assertiveness, authoritarianism, elitism, autarky, confrontation, and abuse. Many intervening variables affect such behavioral consequences, and there is a typology of such responses to threat (see Table 17.1).

Table 17.1   Behavioral Consequences of Threat

	Nation	State	System	Regime	Group	Individual
More threats than capacities	xenophobia	invasion, annexation, absorption	revolution, anarchy	political turmoil, indecision, policy fluctuation	dissolution	fear, evasion
Balance between threats and capacities	integration	cooperation	democracy, egalitarian	alliances, collective endeavors	negotiation/ accommodation	cooperation/ joining
More capacities than threats	ethnic cleansing, genocide	militarism, aggression	dictatorship/ authoritarianism	elitist and unitary, eschews alliances	demands and confrontation	abuse, violence

Note: The ratio between threats and capacities represents an aggregate estimate for one country's cumulative risk or danger from internal and external sources vis-à-vis the same country's aggregate resources with which such threats can be addressed, countered, or mitigated. Threats may be perceived more than tangible, and capacities can be more potential than current. As such, these estimates by the author are offered as a heuristic device, illustrative rather than precise, to suggest the dynamic nature of the relationship between threats and capacities inherent to the concept of security.

Security lies at the intersection of threats and capacities. From nations and their organization into states down to individuals, an equilibrium between threats and capacities offers the potential of peace and prosperity. When threats exceed capacities, states become inviting victims; when capacities exceed threats, a classic security dilemma ensues.[17]

Ambient threat for a state may be generated by other states. In the twenty-first century, however, cumulative threat is far more likely to derive from forces above, below, or within the state. Indeed, for the United States, the European Union, Russia, China, and Japan, other states are not the problem—even if old thinking continues to insist that danger looks like it always did. Even these principal states and groups of states confront forces bigger and more pervasive than their own budgets can address, yet the threats are more elusive than their armies and police can target. Criminal syndicates burrowed deeply within society and bureaucracy and transnational links among extremist and anarchist groups both add to social violence, the prevalence of drugs, and the danger of terrorist attacks.[18] Ethnic hatreds, massive refugee flows, ecological devastation, and other phenomena lie well beyond what one state could stop with traditional tools of diplomacy, economic sanctions, and military action.[19] Speculation about information warfare and cyberattacks suggests, as well, that states no longer have borders denoted by territorial control defended with divisions, flotillas, laws, and courts.[20] Most broadly, the world economy and the effects of technological diffusion can no longer be redirected through the policies of a major state or alliance.[21]

Capacities are resources with which an actor can pursue desired outcomes. Security is a universally desired outcome, and capacities are used to deter threats or defeat those who try to implement their threats.

Among the five cases sketched below, capacities are proportionately greater than other states in the contemporary international system. But by no means are the resources of these cases either complete or uniform. As Joseph Nye discussed in 1990,[22] and as was apparent in earlier attempts to quantify states' power, the capacities of great powers are highly varied and, in different degrees, partial.[23] We can, however, recognize that resources in economic, social, political, and military realms can gain credibility and utility if they are more autonomous, unique, large, flexible, durable, and qualitatively superior. Self-sufficiency in microchips and satellite imagery can be a highly useful and applicable resource. A unique missile defense system, a very large army, a small but flexible police strike force, long-term economic and political stability, advanced and precise technology, and social cohesion—any or all can add to capacities that may be deployed as a balance against threats.

Among great powers today, however, capacities are increasingly missing the mark. The sheer weight of accumulated power indicators can no longer pin down security. In other words, states that pursue a national security strategy through capacity-driven behavior create armies, defense industries, and an intelligence infrastructure all dressed up but with no place to go. Much of the surge in peacekeeping, peacemaking, and humanitarian interventions, NATO's metamorphosis and enlargement, and other multilateral trends, in retrospect, may be understood as new activities for old capacities.

THE UNITED STATES AND GLOBAL INSECURITY

Hubris hung thickly in the air over Washington, D.C., during 1989–1991. European communist regimes had come apart at the seams as popular movements led ruling parties to hand over the reins of power. To many in the U.S. national security establishment and business elite, this was a victory over evil denied on the battlefields of Korea, the Bay of Pigs, and Vietnam—a vindication of military expenditures, global competition, and, ultimately, U.S. values, will, and strength.

The November 1990 summit of the Council for Security and Cooperation in Europe (CSCE), a multilateral process involving all countries from the Atlantic to the Urals begun amid the Cold War in the early 1970s, concluded with the Charter for a New Europe. The fifty-plus leaders who convened, however, were in no position to implement much, if any, of the New Europe Charter. The U.S. sentiment was already clear that its national interest required not the destatized collective security framework encouraged by the charter but rather a new and pumped-up NATO.[24]

Then, in the fall of 1990, an unequivocally bad Middle East dictator decided to invade a small, neighboring, undemocratic state that happened to supply much of the industrialized West with critical oil supplies; with its interests joined, consciences clear, and ample Cold War weapons at the ready, the U.S.-led Coalition provided a convincing victory in the brief Gulf War in early 1991. And when the Soviet Union itself fractured at the end of 1991 and the United States' archnemisis of the Cold War appeared defeated, no tangible threats seemed to loom on the horizon.

Soon after the last victory parades exited U.S. Main Streets, however, the horizon began to quickly darken. Yugoslavia's end was anything but velvet, erupting into Europe's most deadly conflict since World War II. Fighting began in 1991, pitting Serbs briefly against Slovenes; then came months of vicious warfare against Croatia. In 1992, warfare spread further into Bosnia-Herzegovina, which continued to suffer from combat until the U.S.-led NATO intervention in late 1995.

Further, military intervention to overthrow elected politicians in Haiti, renewed warfare in Afghanistan, and terrorist incidents in many locales gave U.S. leaders and the U.S. public little respite. These threats were perceived as distant by most U.S. voters, as evidenced by the 1992 presidential campaign, which focused almost exclusively on domestic issues such as crime, health care, and related matters. But the persistence of peril affecting the United States, and the increasingly diffused nature of such threats—that is, no longer presumed to be primarily political and military or emanating from one source as in the Cold War—were worrisome nonetheless.

Between late 1992 and late 1996, the litany of international crises in which U.S. lives were at stake was lengthy, and tragic outcomes were many. The deaths of eighteen U.S. troops in one day in Mogadishu effectively ended U.S. participation in the UN's Somalia intervention and led to the eventual withdrawal of all foreign forces in the next year. Meanwhile, the 1994 U.S. intervention in Haiti obtained uncertain success, with democracy hardly ensured and neither social peace nor economic recovery thus far evident; both supporters and opponents of U.S. action agree that little economic improvement was evident in Haiti several years later and that the threat of violence permeated the country's politics through the end of the 1990s.[25]

U.S., French, and other forces entered Central Africa about the same time to ensure relief for hundreds of thousands of refugees from war and genocide in Rwanda; two years later, a regional war ensued that spread into Zaire. U.S.-brokered negotiations between Israel, Palestinians, and Syrians have ended neither violence nor fear of renewed war. Twenty thousand U.S. troops in a

NATO-led Implementation Force (IFOR, later renamed SFOR with a reduced U.S. component) to keep the post-Dayton peace in Bosnia-Herzegovina have separated combatants without achieving any of the conditions for lasting peace in civilian society. In Bosnia, a threat-rich environment remained after the large and prolonged deployment of U.S. and NATO forces; refugees did not return, weapons were still plentiful, war criminals carried on with impunity, poverty was endemic, and the economy lay in shambles.

Likewise, the warfare in and over Kosovo during 1999 involved a U.S.-led NATO force bombing Serbia and Serbian forces to insist on their withdrawal from Kosovo, after which the province was occupied by more than 40,000 NATO troops and thousands of NGO personnel. But even this huge presence in a tiny geographical confine was unable to stem murderous retribution by Kosovar Albanians against Serbs and others or to restore a semblance of police and administrative functions.[26]

In these instances, U.S. power was deployed through the injection of military force. Success was always incomplete and transient. U.S. armed forces have the equipment and training to constitute a formidable instrument of international policy. Yet U.S. military force offers no silver bullet; Marines do not wade ashore as midwives to democracy, and cruise missiles make bad diplomats. A show of force might have some temporary utility to delay or redirect action; but it will not change minds, spawn a new political culture, or make friends out of enemies.

Most conditions that may set U.S. nerves on edge cannot be ameliorated with the strengths amassed by the United States during generations of confrontation with the communist menace. Post–Cold War wars, fought with the cast-off weapons of erstwhile superpowers and their erstwhile allies, have turned out to be vicious affairs in which there are few opportunities to identify sympathetic victims led by noble heroes. But most threats have little to do with overt aggression and much more to do with incremental processes that enfeeble, undermine, and erode the social fabric and political institutions within a state.

In the United States, neither the public nor elites see it as threatened in the same manner that it was for two generations after World War II.[27] But unease can be heard from Main Street to Pennsylvania Avenue—a palpable concern that arsenals and command centers do little good when endangered by organized criminals from Asia, Russia, and South America who export violence with a plutonium or cocaine bonus. At the top of all U.S. foreign policy goals in the mid- to late 1990s was "stopping the flow of drugs."[28] More broadly, Americans are confronted by images of a tidal wave of boatpeople, by whispers of terrorists' intentions, and by probabilities of a nuclear catastrophe. To such frightening notions, Americans see their own capacities as limited and their vulnerability to be quite high. A typical news day of the late 1990s suggested the very limited U.S. capacity to deter or deflect drug imports from Latin America.[29]

360 THE ROLE OF MAJOR POWERS

In the 1990s under Republican and Democratic presidents, the United States stayed the course in national and international security policy. Whereas U.S. armed forces were bottomed-up and quadrennially reviewed, downsized, and redeployed since 1989–1990, most of the commands, types of weapons, and missions retain greater similarities to, than differences from, a decade ago.[30] The United States continues to plan to fight two major regional wars almost simultaneously and to order new ships and aircraft for global force projection; the Department of Defense (DoD) investment plan for the late 1990s and early 2000s "include[d] enough C-17s so that DoD could conduct a variety of other military missions [beyond fighting two major regional conflicts]."[31] U.S. allies have remained the same since the end of World War II, and U.S. links to NATO have gained added weight, given promises to enlarge the Alliance's functions and membership. Not surprisingly, U.S. defense expenditures remained at levels about 92 percent of the Cold War average, expressed in 1997 dollars.[32] That figure went down to only 85 percent or so before additional spending began to increase defense allotments in the late 1990s.

From the quiet cataclysm of the mid- to late 1980s, when European communism was eroded and then pushed aside peacefully, through a period of post–Cold War turmoil evident in the Balkans, Caucasus, Central Africa, and elsewhere, the United States has sought to maintain its preeminent role.[33] To do so, the United States has relied on the same capacities, among which are the same friends in the same organizations backed by a military force structure that looks like a smaller version of its Cold War antecedent. U.S. security policy remains dominated by a capacity-driven strategy.

This is a risky game made riskier because the United States does not seem to know it is playing it. When the Cold War ended, the United States was the only player left holding cards. Such is no longer the case; having intervened militarily to restart democracy, to enforce peace, to feed refugees, and to assert order, the United States has fewer options. The American public is wary, and money is scarce. But it is the waning credibility and reduced efficacy of such intervention that make it harder to revisit the military option with each new crisis.

In the 1992 presidential campaign and in the heady days of the early Clinton administration, talk of assertive multilateralism was heard from new policymakers.[34] A first draft of a 1993 presidential decision directive (PDD-25) would have sanctioned U.S. military participation in UN or other peacekeeping efforts not under U.S. command. But Somalia, the intractable crises in the former Yugoslavia and Haiti, dangers in Korea and the Middle East, and innumerable other post–Cold War tensions generated harsh criticism of U.S. commitments to supranational authorities. President Bill Clinton's foreign policy team spent most of the next three years trying to find firm strategic and political footing—offering a variety of sound bites such as "engagement and enlargement" in 1994–1996, and then "integration" in lieu of the Cold War theme of "containment" while backing away from many principles (e.g., human rights vis-à-vis China or other states) for which they could not produce political support.[35]

In the first post–Cold War decade, U.S. relations with the world were like the efforts of a physician who, believing that he has just cured the world of a devastating disease, tries to apply the same analysis and techniques against other illnesses. Clinton's foreign policy and defense teams spoke, instinctively, about the changes the world had seen in the 1980s and early 1990s, but they had no new strategy and no new tools. In part because they were unable to create adequate political support, they fell back to adapting old capacities and instruments, applying them as Band-Aids to address gaping wounds made by new, transnational threats.

For Bosnia, the United States urged a lift-and-strike option—lifting the arms embargo with respect to the Bosnian Muslim–led government, then using air strikes to halt Serbian aggression. Secretly, the United States tacitly aided the arming of Croatian and Muslim armies through a pipeline of money and weapons from other sources. The key to the U.S. response was military, not participation in the United Nations Protection Force (UNPROFOR), much less any farsighted effort in 1990–1991 to deploy peacekeepers when there was a peace to keep. For the nascent democracies of East-Central and Southeastern Europe, the enlargement of an alliance for common defense has been the core of U.S. policy in the mid- to late 1990s. To Latin America, the message has been sent through the prosecution of the U.S. war on drugs and the coercive Helms-Burton Act, which threatens retribution in U.S. courts against any foreign company that does business with Cuba involving expropriated U.S. assets.

At the same time, the United States assumed and maintained post–Cold War leadership in global arms exports. The United States in the 1990s "overwhelmingly domina[ted] the commercially driven arms market"; total U.S. arms shipments from 1991 through 1995 exceeded $70 billion (in 1997 dollars); Great Britain's shipments, at $24.1 billion, ranked second. Russia's shipments (in third place) were valued at $16.4 billion during the same period. U.S. dominance of the licit arms market remained total through 1999, as U.S. sales and transfers continued to exceed the nearest competitors by several times.[36]

Meanwhile, as to the other great powers over which the United States could not exert direct military pressure, the rule was accommodation at any cost. Business must be conducted as usual with China no matter what human rights violations occurred, regardless of missile sales and technology transfers, and despite an extraordinary trade imbalance assisted by deplorable labor conditions in China.[37] Russia can, with impunity, bomb civilians in Chechnya, sell arms to China, Iran, and elsewhere, and allow deep and pervasive Mafia control—anything as long as they ultimately play ball on NATO enlargement and controlling their own nuclear arsenal. Japan can ignore or comply mini-mally with trade agreements provided Tokyo accepts minimal changes with the status-of-forces agreement and supports U.S. policy vis-à-vis China and Russia.

Abandoning any alternatives that might have addressed the world's changing panoply of threats, the United States speaks the rhetoric of U.S. leadership, enlargement, and engagement. All the while, the United States accommodates presumed interests of presumed great powers while dealing with the rest of the world on a crisis-by-crisis basis using familiar resources: cruise missiles to send diplomatic messages, airborne divisions to deliver democracy, mechanized brigades to ensure peace, and arms transfers to bal-ance power.[38] The fact that the United States has ample capacities of different kinds—dominance in technology and information science, for example[39]—seems lost on policymakers, just as the option of a security strategy focused on threat abatement, not capacities, appears to be beyond the ken of these same political elites.

GREAT POWERS' POWERS AND GLOBAL SECURITY

Do any of the world's principal states or associations of states use their pow-ers to enhance global security? Is the balance between threats and capacities more or less likely as a consequence of policies pursued by the European Union's largest members, Russia, China, and Japan?

Among these large powers with a reach beyond their immediate area—by virtue of some combination of economic strength or rapid growth, population and geographic size, military prowess, nuclear arms, or cultural influence—the new millennium finds varying degrees of democracy, market principles, and other measures of adherence to higher standards. In each, however, lead-ers continue to apply political, economic, and military capacities in ways that are oblivious to the limits of state efficacy. The dysfunctional role of great powers in global security is, indeed, the story of the post–Cold War. Each struggles to preserve prerogatives its elites expect and its masses viscerally believe, relying on makeshift policies, recycled capacities, and techniques that no longer fit specifications. By doing so, they help no one, including their own populations.

In the European Union, principal members such as Germany and France pursue foreign policy trajectories that, at the very least, offer little chance for the much-vaunted Common Foreign and Security Policy (transformed as the European Security and Defense Identity, or ESDI, and then the European Security and Defense Policy [ESDP], after the EU summit in Cologne in June 1999) and a rocky road for European Monetary Union (EMU), to which EU members agreed at the 1992 Maastricht Summit. Publics evince little sympathy for the notion of multilateralism or for EMU. Some observers even think that "the impending crisis in Europe is the eventual failure of EMU."[40] Although the EMU has certain identifiable standards and a timetable, the ESDI has none and is unlikely to ever materialize. Europe's potential to unravel, rather than to progress further toward integration, was being given serious thought by the mid- and late 1990s, in part because of the EMU difficulties and due to the obvious inability of European countries to act in concert in a crisis such as Bosnia or without U.S. leadership in Kosovo.[41] Even in the case of Helmut Kohl's Germany, where the government spoke as if it were a staunch advocate of foreign and defense policy coordination, public support dwindled for such multilateralism.[42]

Despite its rhetoric as the most European of Europeans, Kohl's Christian Democratic Union (CDU) government fashioned a distinctly traditional foreign and defense policy after reunification, using its new constitutional latitude to deploy military assets in Bosnia while employing arms transfers to further German contacts in countries such as Turkey, providing minimal support to international peacekeeping, and vigorously pressing ahead with the expulsion of refugees in order to placate extremist public opinion. The German government under Kohl did not utilize anything other than the standard resources of a powerful state for which the Weltanschauung is viewed through realists' lens.[43] And notwithstanding Maastricht rhetoric, Kohl was unable or unwilling to roll back a strong public desire to delay or scrap the EMU.[44] Gerhard Schroeder's Social Democrat/Green coalition government and Foreign Minister Joschka Fischer, rather than reversing such realpolitik, continued Germany's so-called maturation—committing the country to a combat role in the NATO air attacks against Serbian targets, ordering a major deployment within Kosovo after Serbian withdrawal, and taking the lead role in advocating a Balkan stability pact. Nothing in the Schroeder government suggests reverting to an inactive, reactive foreign and defense policy.

For France, too, security issues have been framed in unilateral terms. President Jacques Chirac, then Foreign Minister Herve de Charette, and former Defense Minister Charles Millon often spoke in the late 1990s of their concerns for Mediterranean security and conflicts in the south, that is, terrorists of Islamic origin or uncontrolled migration from Northern Africa.[45] The latter concern, one should add, flew in the face of data that clearly refuted any notion of an immigration surge into France; the proportion of foreigners within France's population remained stable at about 6.5 percent for the two decades between 1975 and 1995.[46] In the public mind, immigration destroys national culture and, with globalization, takes away jobs.[47] The latter is also a codeword for inroads of U.S. influence. French leaders during this period also emphasized in the mid- to late 1990s the need to restructure and modernize the French military and the chance to rejoin NATO's military councils. The latter step, however, could occur only on terms recognizing the importance of

France, for example, by transferring the Southern Command at Naples from the United States to a European state.[48] Despite words of conciliation in early 1997, this issue continued to fester into 1999, when several East-Central European states joined NATO. As a consequence, the Alliance confronts its biggest challenges without unity among its oldest members.

The doubt and fears that underlie such issues have not, however, generated fundamental change. Instead, the French have tended to retreat into a culturally defensive posture and to political conservatism sans vision, à la President Chirac, or reactionary politics à la Jean-Marie Le Pen's Front Nationale. In the face of clear and present evidence that domestic socioeconomic conditions—13 percent unemployment in 1998, social unrest, and a growing appeal of extremist politics—are moving in perilous directions, the weak French state has little to offer.[49]

In such behavior, Germany and France during the 1990s evinced many of the dysfunctional roles played by states within associations of states. Although governments seek to protect sovereignty and territoriality by, for example, expelling refugees or expanding their role in or exerting control through alliance structures, they pander to the same fears that stoke neofascist flames in France or an insidious rightward drift in Germany while dismissing issues that generate fear and political volatility.[50]

From the standpoint of public opinion, fears are rooted in socioeconomic conditions. "Profound changes in trade, finance and technology" have given us an "age of widespread economic insecurity" and worker disaffection.[51] In Europe, joblessness had soared from very low levels in the first decades after World War II to 12 percent by 1994 and more than 13 percent in the last years of the 1990s; "to make matters worse, a large part of Europe's jobless have been unemployed for a year or longer."[52] In Germany, the 1996–1998 unemployment rates in the 12–12.5 percent range were the highest recorded since the 1930s. Socioeconomic crises will soon assume an added dimension in Europe as the percentage of pensioners in the population exceeds 20 percent in much of the EU by 2020, and worker-to-retiree ratios will be only about 1.4–1.6:1 (versus 2.1:1 in the United States) by the same year.[53] Such ratios mean that more retired people will be supported by fewer wage earners, putting greater strain on taxes, budgets, and the allocation of scarce resources (e.g., health care). To these concerns, European states singly or conjoined in the EU have thus far offered no solution or strategy. The nation-state's inability "to keep unemployment at a tolerable level while maintaining the social safety net," writes John Newhouse, "has accelerated Europe's growing devolution of authority."[54]

Such current or impending threats, when intermingled with anti-immigrant sentiment, provide the nutrients for demagogues of the right and left and weaken interest in or commitment to further integration. The Austrian vote in late

1999 that propelled Jörg Haider's FreihelLiche Partei Österreichs into a coalition government in early 2000 raises serious questions about the direction of Central European democracy.[55] Germany's intellectual debate now resonates with voices from a resurgent new right that speak the language of national "self-confidence," which provides a theoretical defense of neo-Nazi actions. Rejection of the postwar Bonn government and its participants and glorifications of renewed Germanness are recurrent themes. And while the views of controversial figures like Botho Strauss are not those of the CDU as a whole, new right messages are easily seen in the nationalism of the CDU's youth movement, in major newspapers, which now print characterizations such as "the Jew Rifkind" (referring to British Foreign Minister Malcolm Rifkind),[56] and in the writings of Wolfgang Schauble, who talks about German identity being derived from the "emotional, connective power of the nation."[57] The rumblings of unrest in Germany, although still distant, are no longer impossible to imagine.[58]

These narrow interests and rhetoric of national identity do not sound much like the promised New Europe. Fueled by economic insecurity and immigration, such views slow momentum toward integration and make the ascent toward a united Europe longer and steeper. The European Union, far from being a strong partner, has a gossamer-like visage in global security.

Principal Asian states, out of the great-power business for more than two generations, are now members of the club once again. China's economic surge in the 1980s and 1990s sets a trend that could make it the world's largest economy, surpassing the United States, before 2020.[59] Although per capita measures would still place China among the developing countries, its gross output (gross domestic product at purchasing power parity) might reach more than $20 trillion, versus $13.5 trillion for the United States and a projected $5 trillion for Japan. These projections assume a continuation of China's extraordinary growth rate (over 9 percent in the mid- to late 1990s)[60] and that the incorporation of Hong Kong in 1997 enhanced the overall trend. Regardless of the exact pace of China's economic expansion, the Deng Xiaoping–inspired growth has been accompanied by a significant enlargement of China's military capacity, supported by a bigger defense budget.[61] Purchases of advanced Russian aircraft,[62] the transfer of U.S. missile and avionics secrets via Israel,[63] an expansion of China's own ballistic missile arsenal in size and sophistication, the addition of blue water–capable surface and submarine combatants,[64] and more professional ground forces all add up to a regional if not global presence in the twenty-first century.

Chinese nationalism is a predictable, if not a comfortable, counterpoint to domestic uncertainty and flux. "No one dares to be anything but a strong nationalist in such circumstances," Michel Oksenberg said of China in the mid-1990s.[65] Having lunged into state capitalism while trying to retain political control, the Chinese Communist Party cannot be sanguine about its own

future. The death of Deng Xiaoping in February 1997 did not precipitate turmoil, collapse, or any other cataclysm, in part because he had been on the
precipice of death for years and because Chinese reform has generated its own
"conservative but energetic" foundation.[66]

Yet the Communist Party leaders such as Chairman Jiang Zemin no
longer dictate; they must manage, in a very political fashion, all of the social,
economic, and cultural tensions that accompany rapid change. Crushing student democrats in spring 1989 with military force killed hundreds or thousands, but it did not eradicate ideas of a more plural and tolerant China. Jiang
Zemin may be a politician who sings in many keys, but the music is far different today.[67]

Regardless, China's outlook is one of unreconstructed realism—a state,
its interests, and its power against all threats. As "the high church of realpolitik in the post–Cold War world [whose] analysts think more like traditional
balance-of-power theorists than do most contemporary Western leaders,"
China eschews normative ends or multilateral means.[68] Instead, Beijing acts
unilaterally to accumulate comprehensive national power through military
and economic capacities with which to intimidate, to aggrandize, and to support the enemies of its enemies. Beijing's principal approach to Taiwan, which
it regards as a renegade province, is the path of military intimidation. The
most egregious example was during the 1996 Taiwanese presidential elections, but similar techniques were used earlier.[69] When the South China Sea
and Spratly Islands became matters of competition in the early 1990s, China
resorted quickly to the deployment of warships in the region. And to counterbalance India—still seen in Beijing as a challenge to Chinese regional security—China has sold M-11 ballistic missiles to Pakistan in clear violation of its
pledges to the United States.[70] Although Deng's counsel of "acting calmly"
and "not seeking confrontation" can be traced in cases where China reacted
rhetorically, not militarily, to perceived external provocation,[71] Communist
Party conservatives and the People's Liberation Army have criticized moderation and pulled China inexorably toward a more hard-line position. China's
military capabilities still pose no imminent threat to the United States, but
Beijing's regional role is not reassuring.[72]

China's leaders talk and act with militaristic bravado. But just beneath and
behind this image of strength lies a weak state and uncertain political legitimacy of the ruling elite.[73] Turmoil such as the June 1989 Tiananmen Square
incident led quickly to a reemergence of China's old antihegemonist theme,
reflecting fear of international policemen and foreign intervention.[74] The
Chinese worry about Japanese militarism,[75] U.S. commitments to Japan and
Taiwan, Taiwanese moves toward independence, and an alleged China-threat
conspiracy to isolate and contain Beijing.[76] But they also worry about labor
unrest if the economy ceases to grow rapidly, as well as political and cultural

dissent among urban intellectuals. By the late 1990s, Chinese authorities also had to confront minority uprisings (as erupted in early 1997 among Uighurs in Xinjiang Province and in sporadic terrorist bombings in Beijing).[77] Any of these could begin to tear away the shroud that conceals a China that is far less unified and far more questioning than Western observers typically assume.

Japan, a U.S. ally by treaty and historical exigency, is often in conflict with the United States. The conflicts are nonviolent but vehement, and they stir public antipathy in both countries. Disputes about trade have been the most frequent, but increasing friction was created in the mid-1990s because of the violent attacks by U.S. armed forces personnel on Japanese women on the island of Okinawa and elsewhere and the harm (and sometimes death) suffered by Japanese visitors in the United States. Yet the United States and Japan saw the Soviet Union and communist China as threatening, which helped to ensure their defense cooperation for several decades after the end of postwar U.S. military occupation. Today, signs that the two countries view their security differently, and that differences are rather substantial, are evident.

By 1997–1998, the luster of Japan's economy had diminished considerably; growth had slowed, small and medium-sized banks had begun to fail, unemployment had appeared and grown (although still far below any European country), and the Tokyo stock market had lost almost half its value as compared with the late 1980s. The beginning of the end of Japan, Inc., was being foreseen by some observers.[78] An attack in March 1995 on the Tokyo subway using sarin nerve gas killed twelve people and injured several thousand. Although the Aum Shinrikyo cult leader, Shoko Aasahara, was taken into custody in May, the shaken Japanese public found that it had been targeted for mass terrorism.[79] Fears accompanying these indicators had led to a rollback of voter interest in alternative political leadership and much of anything that resembles reform; Prime Minister Ryutaro Hashimoto's Liberal Democratic Party government constituted a return to power of the old guard, albeit a new generation of old cliques and factions. The mid-1998 selection of Keizo Obuchi as Hashimoto's successor further cemented this turn to the past. As in other states, elites and masses reach for the familiar and comfortable when uncertain conditions loom.

Japan expressed doubt about working with the United States in developing a theater missile defense (TMD) system, not only because burden sharing with the United States has little political benefit but also because other threats are perceived. Whereas U.S. difficulties with the unsophisticated Iraqi Scud missiles in the 1991 Gulf War led U.S. officials to see North Korea's tests of a Rodong medium-range ballistic missile in the early and mid-1990s as cause to accelerate a TMD system for Northeast Asia, Japan considered such a system as too costly given the negative signals this would send to China.[80] Although U.S. pressure produced by 1999 some form of Japanese engagement

in TMD, differing perceptions between Washington and Tokyo were painful-
ly evident.[81] Yet Japan has begun to reconsider unilateral measures that might
someday be required to protect its security with military means, including
nuclear weapons.[82]

As states are wont to do, Japan and its leaders have been drawn inexorably toward what appear to be Japan's problems: economic malaise
(unheard of for two generations), domestic terrorism, and a visceral reaction
against a U.S. presence. Husbanding resources while responding to voters'
resentments and fears, Japan fulfills far less of an international or multilateral role than its extraordinarily important and powerful economic role would
otherwise lead one to expect.

Russian capacities have eroded so much that only within certain locali-
ties, such as Moscow and its Mafia-ridden government, do things work at all.
As a state Russia functions poorly, although economic activity in Russia
began its recovery by 1995 and seemed, by 1996–1997, to hold some promise.[83] But new prosperity affected only a narrow stratum of the population, and
various economic woes dominated the top worries for the Russian population
in 1997.[84] When the ruble collapsed in 1998, such fears appeared fully justi-
fied. For ordinary Russians, where there was once a fear of the centralized
state and its secret policy, one now finds a new brand: the "decentralization of
fears."[85] In an atmosphere characterized by Mafia influence, intimidation, and
assassinations, anyone with talent or ambition in any field is vulnerable and a
target to be frightened into submission. In the threat-rich, capacity-poor environment of Russia today, questions are being raised (harkening to 1917) as to
how long Russians can take it, as well as the direction they will turn.

For many Russians the answer was provided in Chechnya in late 1999
and early 2000, when state forces destroyed through unsophisticated means
(massive artillery and air attacks) the remnants of Grozny. Pursuit of Chechen
rebels at any cost was the simple rule of engagement. Emerging from the
shadows at this moment in Russian history was President Boris Yeltsin's
declared successor, Vladimir Putin. His KGB history and careful avoidance of
specifics during the campaign prepared Russia for possible administrative
authoritarianism. But his own personal credibility for ordinary Russians had
been enormously enhanced by events in Chechnya.

An enfeebled Russia still deploys thousands of nuclear warheads, exports
vast quantities of sophisticated weaponry to governments with uncertain
intentions, and has a capacity to hurt neighboring peoples through outright
violence or holding back energy supplies. Several Kilo-class diesel sub-
marines and nuclear technology have been provided to Iran. Russia has provided scores of Su-27s and other advanced combat aircraft plus tanks, missiles, and other weapons to China.[86] The vicious air and artillery attacks
against Chechen cities and towns in 1996 and again in 1999 did not lead to

victory, but both campaigns killed tens of thousands of civilians and Chechen rebels. Less directly, Russian pressure through the control of energy supplies can be a potent weapon against Ukraine, the Baltic States, and others.

Propelled by fear, Russia may not engage in direct military provocations but could well obstruct multilateral efforts (using its veto in the UN Security Council), support unfriendly rogue governments (by selling weapons, oil, and gas), or use pressure and intimidation on vulnerable targets such as the Baltic States. Domestically, Russian fears turn easily toward the authoritarian tendencies embodied in Putin.

The United States and, to an even greater extent, Germany have sought to deal with Russia in this delicate and dangerous period by first supporting and then relying on the presidency of Boris Yeltsin. Such a one-man policy, followed almost unflinchingly through 1995 and by default through 1999, may have been derived from the romantic vision of Yeltsin atop the tank in August 1991 and then reinforced by the absence of strategic thinking in the West. This dependency on one leader in Moscow was criticized, and broader and far-reaching engagement was advocated.[87]

As the United States as well as NATO's other principal members pressed ahead with plans to extend membership to some former Warsaw Pact members, Russian objections became increasingly strident in 1996, 1997, and 1998. Whereas in Washington and Western Europe the enlargement of NATO seemed unthreatening, benign, and an appropriate reward for the anticommunist struggles and transitions of Poles, Czechs, and their Central European neighbors, the view from the Volga was entirely different.

From inside the Kremlin walls, it appeared that a victorious military alliance, already in a dominant position, was to edge closer and perhaps forward-deploy its weapons and troops. Even among savvy Russians who rejected such a simplistic interpretation of NATO's motives, there was no way to depoliticize the Alliance's enlargement. Quickly and deeply embedded in Russian politics, opposing NATO's growth became de rigueur—a ticket that every national figure had to punch. Consequently, Moscow's demands for compensatory security gestures—revision of the Conventional Forces in Europe (CFE) Treaty, more military collaboration with the United States and other structural ties codified in a binding charter, and other steps—escalated as Russian politicians and generals outmaneuvered one another.

In months leading up to NATO's Madrid Summit in July 1997, the United States and NATO sought to mollify Russian concerns. The 27 May 1997 Paris Charter solidifies Russian presence in a consultative council with NATO members but explicitly excludes Russia from voting on Alliance matters and offers no promises regarding the disposition of forces or weapons. The CFE renegotiation was sought by Moscow for several years because of Russia's perception that the original CFE Treaty, negotiated in the 1980s between a

Soviet-dominated Warsaw Pact and NATO, disadvantaged Russia after its erstwhile allies sought to join Western security institutions. In the CFE revision, negotiated in earnest during 1998 and 1999, Russians obtained national weapons ceilings and expanded rights to deploy forces from central to flank areas (as they have done in the Caucasus).

Still, in the NATO enlargement debate the core insecurities of Russia and Russians remain unattended; CFE changes, joint brigades, and a host of consultancy fora in Brussels neither control Russians' decentralized fears nor abate the sense of impotence that generates the rhetoric of extremism. Even after NATO allies gathered with Yeltsin in Paris to sign the founding charter for NATO-Russia consultation, Russian commentary focused on the continued exclusion of Russia from Europe, as well as Russia's loss of face.[88]

CONCLUSION: STATES, POWER, AND INSECURITY

This cursory glance at great-power behavior tests no hypothesis. Yet such observations evoke the dilemma of large and ostensibly influential states today. Even though they may intervene in far-flung corners of the world, rattle their sabers, and throw around their economic weight, such states are neither very strong nor very secure. Some have far greater capacities than others. But their insecurity derives less from having too few capacities than from a failure to abate threats. Transfixed by the flamboyance of their militaries on parade, or compelled to advocate economic growth and territorial control, rulers still push the same old buttons of power no matter whether they work or not.

And they do not work well at all. In large, muscle-bound states, the state itself may be weak, that is, it may lack sociopolitical cohesion.[89] In that condition, trying to push the buttons of power may precipitate a performance crisis from which a regime, government, and system will not recover. But even a strong state that is also well endowed with the accouterments of industry and armies has no guarantee of security.

A few years ago, it might have been possible to tell a weak state from a strong state based largely on the degree of sociopolitical cohesion.[90] But just as the capacities of such modern, complex states to control society and to extract labor and material from it had risen to unprecedented levels, the security agenda expanded once again, ratcheting up the threshold of threats. The Soviet Union had the world's largest nuclear arsenal but rotted from within— a weak state with huge military and industrial capacities that were irrelevant and counterproductive to its political survival. In other words, the security of such a system rested on the amount of threat within itself, not its accumulation of military-industrial capacities.

By comparison, the United States is still in the business of global leadership, enlargement, and engagement; it looks and acts like the sole remaining superpower. But the victor of the Cold War and guardian of the world's freedom for almost sixty years cannot pay for its foreign policy establishment, is unable to slow, much less halt, the drug trade, confronts mounting incidents of domestic terrorism, remains at the pinnacle of murders per capita among advanced industrial countries,[91] and mutely accepts social stratification that excludes tens of millions from health care and education. Perhaps the United States is a strong state relative to others, but the direction of its internal evolution might be questioned, even by the most ardent patriot.

Externally, the stronger the state, the more it is likely to be engaged elsewhere and thus become enmeshed in tensions, disputes, and conflicts. And because strong states are not necessarily democratic, the potential for bellicosity is high. In other words, strong states may not be good news for security—their own or that of their neighbors.

When the strength of today's great powers wanes, there is still no good news. Hemorrhaging political legitimacy, ebbing social cohesion, faltering economic momentum, or a combination of these deadly ills for states can be harbingers of conflicts, cold or hot. The potential for violent conflict between the largest, most resource-rich states may increase not when great powers cease to be great but when leaders of principal states fear that their domain may soon become less great. When a loss of capacity can be foreseen or inferred, for example, due to the diminished availability of resources such as energy supplies, water, lines of commerce, and the like, confrontations and military clashes are more, not less, likely. Oil and gas resources are available or anticipated in the Caspian Sea and South China Sea, and Russia, China, the United States, and clients in those regions may well confront each other.

The genesis of rivalries among the largest powers stems, in part, from ebbing power or from the increasing irrelevancy of some kinds of capacities. When perceived, such a trend can prompt desperate last stands to protect control over essential resources. From such a cornered-animal psychology, we have little protection.

Insecurity follows from an inability to use resources that states typically accumulate—wealth, military assets, cultural influence, diplomatic skills—to address threats in the twenty-first century. Capacities that states garner are fungible when threats are unequivocal and univariate (i.e., primarily and consistently of one type, as was the Soviet and Warsaw Pact military danger). When capacities can be mobilized and targeted at one kind or source of threat, its effects can be deterred and defeated. But the convenient image of a communist menace emanating from one command post in the Kremlin is no longer present.

States and associations of states have done well in amassing capacities; they can create large armies, extract resources to foster extensive (bigger if not more efficient) economic growth, and mobilize society through hierarchy and coercion. They do much less well, or ignore completely, the mitigation of internal and external peril through negotiation, arbitration, the redistribution of material and political resources, confidence-building measures, and peacekeeping.

Because states are capacity-driven, relations between and among great powers will have less and less to do with twenty-first century security. Indeed, states may get in the way. Were the United States and other principal states to plan military forces and economic development into the twenty-first century assuming only worst-case scenarios, then we are likely to get the international environment for which we plan. When states persist in building capacities (whether military, economic, or political) for power projection, the global environment responds as other actors restructure their capacities in similar fashion. By shunning the international system's interactive character, we may be blinding ourselves to promising insights regarding how capacity-driven policies construct threats, which, if not thought to be balanced by further capacities, generate dangerous behavioral consequences.[92]

Balancing threats and capacities will not soon be done without states. But it is becoming increasingly difficult to do it with them. More and more, states are the harbingers of global insecurity, whether rogue actors or great powers. For supranational and subnational agents to pursue peace and prosperity, overcoming the obstacle of states that traffic in arms, harbor criminals, enlarge inequalities, and suppress expression has become a raison d'être.

Left to their own devices, states conduct bilateral relations and form associations and alliances based on balance-of-power machinations among territorially defined sovereign actors—a calculus offering counterthreat to deter and defeat, not a path to avoid conflict. States using power, guided in a vague fashion by presumed national interests, lurch toward an illusive security, trying to accumulate the capacities they know best. And as they do so, the biggest and most capacity-endowed states inexorably generate security dilemmas for the next generation; as the ratio of threats to capacities falls under 1:0 (as described in Table 17.1), what had seemed a chimera of security for one great power becomes a harbinger of threat for others. The more one actor stockpiles capacities, the more neighbors will begin to exhibit security envy.

Opportunities and solutions lie elsewhere—with shared resources and inclusive institutions to confront global problems. Balancing threats and capacities—not ensuring that one's own strengths exceed all adversaries—is a twenty-first-century route to the next century's security challenges. No longer utopian but urgent and pragmatic, this wider security perspective for the twenty-first century may allow states to retain a place in the quest for a balance between threats and capacities by becoming agents of threat abatement instead of capacity enhancement. But to do so, there is much to be learned, and we see few signs that the great powers are ready to begin.

NOTES

1. James N. Rosenau (1990) *Turbulence in World Politics: A Theory of Change and Continuity* (Princeton: Princeton University Press), pp. 12–13. Rosenau discusses five forces that characterize the world's transition from international to postinternational. These are: (1) the dynamics of technology; (2) transnational issues; (3) reduced capacity of governments to provide satisfactory solutions to major issues; (4) international and national tendencies toward decentralization and subgrouping; and (5) populations with enhanced analytical skills that can less easily be manipulated by governments. The threat to states from within, not from the anarchical nature of the international system, is an important related theme developed superbly by Heinz Gärtner (1997b) "States Without Nations: State, Nation, and Security in Central Europe," *International Politics* 34, no. 1 (April): 7–32.

2. John Newhouse makes this point in (1997) "Europe's Rising Regionalism," *Foreign Affairs* 76, no. 1 (January-February): 67–84.

3. A similar theme is echoed in Jessica T. Matthews (1997) "Power Shift," *Foreign Affairs* 76, no. 1 (January-February): 50–66. Matthews cites an estimate by McKinsey and Company that global financial markets will expand to reach $84 trillion by 2000, "triple the aggregate GDP of the affluent nations of the [OECD]" (p. 57).

4. Vincent Boland (1997) "Earnings from Organized Crime Reach $1,000 bn," *Financial Times*, February 15, p. 1.

5. One examination of the state's dwindling functionality is John W. Meyer (1980) "The World Polity and the Authority of the Nation-State," in Albert Bergesen (ed.) *Studies in the Modern World System* (New York: Academic), pp. 109–137.

6. I am indebted to David Kanin for these comparative insights. See his provocative essay, David Kanin (1997) "The State, Its Dysfunction, and Ours," *International Politics* 34, no. 4 (December): 335–370.

7. Robert H. Jackson (1990) *Quasi-States: Sovereignty, International Relations, and the Third World* (Cambridge: Cambridge University Press).

8. Edward A. Kolodziej (1997) "Order, Welfare, and Legitimacy," *International Politics* 34, no. 1 (March).

9. David J. Elkins (1995) *Beyond Territoriality: Territory and Political Economy in the Twenty-First Century* (Toronto: University of Toronto Press), pp. 121–146.

10. Branko Milanovic (1996) "Nations, Conglomerates, and Empires: The Tradeoff Between Income and Sovereignty," World Bank Policy Research Working Paper, no. 1675 (October).

11. See, for example, Joseph S. Nye's listing of "major contenders" according to his estimate of their power resources in 1990 in Joseph S. Nye (1990) *Bound to Lead: The Changing Nature of American Power* (New York: Knopf), p. 173.

12. Ibid., p. 174.

13. Concerning the notion of security as a balance between threats and capacities, see Daniel N. Nelson (1996) "Civil Society Endangered," *Social Research* 63, no. 2 (Summer): 345–368, and the same author's "Great Powers and World Peace," in Michael Klare and Thomas Daniel (eds.) (1994) *World Security: Challenges for a New Century*, 2nd ed. (New York: St. Martin's), pp. 27–42. An alternative, and somewhat ironic, view of security is that of author Germaine Greer, for whom "security is when everything is settled—when nothing can happen to you. Security is the denial of life." But for most people, risk is not life-enriching; Greer's notion of security qua death won't wash.

14. J. Roland Pennock (1996) "Political Development, Political Systems, and Political Goods," *World Politics* 18, no. 2 (April).

15. This realist perspective on alliances is, for example, clear in George Liska (1962) *Nations in Alliance* (Baltimore: Johns Hopkins University Press).

16. Bobrow Davis (1996) "Complex Insecurity: Implications of a Sobering Metaphor," *International Studies Quarterly* 40, no. 4 (December).

17. See, for example, Robert Jervis (1978) "Cooperation Under the Security Dilemma," *World Politics* 30, no. 1 (January): 167–214. Generally, Jervis and a long lineage of other authors see such a dilemma as arising when one state's efforts to achieve unassailable protection from threats pushes other actors to seek added capacities (e.g., by arming more heavily) to counter the first state's actions.

18. Despite years during which the United States pursued a "war on drugs," the State Department concluded, in early 1997, "that [the war on drugs] has had 'little discernible effect' on the price or availability of narcotics on North American streets." *The Economist*, March 8, 1997, p. 44.

19. Refugees, for example, expanded by over seven times between the mid-1970s and the mid-1990s—from about 2.4 million in 1975 to over 18.2 million in 1993. States, unable to respond, have thrown the problem to a once-tiny UN agency, the High Commissioner for Refugees (UNHCR), the budget of which rose from a mere $69 million in 1975 to $1.3 billion in 1993. See *World Refugee Report* (New York: UNHCR, 1995).

20. Regarding cyberconflict see Richard E. Haynes and Gary Wheatley (1996) "Information Warfare and Deterrence," *Strategic Forum 87*, Washington, D.C., Institute for National Strategic Studies (October).

21. Good, if cursory, discussions of these many new threats and their effects at the end of the twentieth century are in Karl Kaiser and Hans-Peter Schwarz (eds.) (1995) *Die neue Weltpolitik* (Baden-Baden: Nomos Verlagsgesellschaft); see esp. section 2, "Determinanten der neuen Weltpolitik," pp. 73–300.

22. Nye (1990).

23. One novel effort to quantify measures of relative power was attempted by Ray S. Cline (1980) *World Power Trends and U.S. Foreign Policy* (Boulder: Westview).

24. For a detailed discussion of this emerging U.S. policy, which rejected any alternative to NATO in post–Cold War security, see Daniel N. Nelson (1994) "American and Collective Security in Europe," *Journal of Strategic Studies* 17, no. 4 (December): 105–124.

25. John Sweeney (1996) "Stuck in Haiti," and Robert I. Rotberg (1996) "Clinton Was Right," *Foreign Policy* 102 (Spring).

26. See, for example, Daniel N. Nelson (1999) "NATO Emerges with Blood on Its Hands," *Boston Globe*, June 14, 1999; (1999) "Balkans Need More than Stability," *Los Angeles Times*, July 30, 1999; and (2000) "Kosovo One Year Later," *Boston Globe*, March 24, 2000.

27. Gallup polls regularly ask "What do you think is the most important problem facing this country today?" The proportion of Americans who said that superpower confrontation, nuclear weapons, or related issues was "most important" dropped from 20–27 percent in the mid-1980s to 2 percent at the beginning of 1996. See Jeremy D. Rosner (1995–1996) "The Know-Nothings Know Something," *Foreign Policy* no. 101 (Winter): 124. Data is from the Chicago Council on World Affairs annual survey in 1995.

28. Data is from the Chicago Council on World Affairs annual survey in 1995.

29. See, for example, Douglas Farah (1997) "Colombia Suspends Anti-Drug Crop Effort," and Molly Moore and John Ward Anderson (1997) "U.S. Officials Visit Mexico for Parlay on Drug Policy," both in the *Washington Post*, March 6, 1997. The same month, other reports carried similar ominous messages, e.g., Doug Farah and

Molly Moore (1997) "Mexican Drug Traffickers Eclipse Colombian Cartels," *Washington Post,* March 20, 1997.

30. A May 1997 Quadrennial Defense Review (QDR), for example, reconfirmed assumptions under which the Pentagon was operating since the end of the Cold War and, while suggesting a small cut in active-duty personnel, advocated the maintenance of all the same commitments for all the same scenarios with a broadly identical array of commands, weapons, and strategy. See Department of Defense (May 1997) *Quadrennial Defense Review* (Washington, D.C.: Department of Defense). A nine-member independent panel created by Congress to examine the QDR offered a sharp critique of the Pentagon's effort, indicting the Defense Department for "fail[ing] to go far enough in revamping military structures and investment plans to meet projected new threats and international conditions" and for "avoid[ing] a bolder commitment to transforming the U.S. military into a smaller, more flexible 21st century force." See Bradley Graham (1997) "Pentagon Faulted for Short-Sighted Plans," *Washington Post,* May 23, 1997.

31. Congressional Budget Office (February 1997) "Moving U.S. Forces: Options for Strategic Mobility" (Washington, D.C.: Congressional Budget Office).

32. As calculated by the Center for Defense Information, Washington, D.C., and cited in its *Defense Monitor* periodical (April 1997).

33. See John Mueller (1995) *Quiet Cataclysm: Reflections on the Recent Transformation of World Politics* (New York: HarperCollins).

34. In Madeleine Albright's confirmation hearings in the U.S. Senate for the post of ambassador to the United Nations in January 1993, she used this phrase that was later repeated in private conversations before various think-tank audiences.

35. See The White House (February 1995) *A National Strategy of Engagement and Enlargement* (Washington, D.C.: The White House). Regarding the newer theme of integration, see Jonathan S. Landay (1997) "Clinton Team Forges Foreign Policy Vision," *Christian Science Monitor,* April 2, 1997.

36. Federation of American Scientists, *Arms Sales Monitor* no. 33 (February 24, 1997), citing Congressional Research Service data. See also *SIPRI Yearbook, 1998* (and prior years) for such data.

37. David M. Lampton (1994) "America's China Policy in the Age of the Finance Minister: Clinton Ends Linkage," *The China Quarterly* 139 (September): 597–621.

38. On the latter point, see "USA: Arms Sales Superpower," *Boston Globe,* February 11, 1996, p. B-2.

39. Joseph S. Nye Jr. and William A. Owens (1996) "America's Information Edge," *Foreign Affairs* 75, no. 2 (March-April): 20–36.

40. These comments were made by Lucio Caracciolo, editor of *Li Mes,* in a seminar at the Eurowatch Group, Center for Strategic and International Studies, Washington, D.C., on December 2, 1996. See also "Sweating for that Euro," *The Economist,* February 15, 1997, wherein it is opined that "some of the single currency's keenest proponents are starting to doubt that it will take shape on time" (p. 45).

41. George Soros (1996) "Can Europe Work?" *Foreign Affairs* 75, no. 5 (September-October): 8–14.

42. German public opposition to a common European security identity rose to 28 percent in 1995 and 31 percent in 1996. Although still a minority, this trend was clearly different than elsewhere on the continent. See USIA (September 1995) *The New European Security Architecture* (Washington, D.C.: USIA Office of Research and Media Reaction), p. 31, and Eurobarometer reports in 1996.

43. For a more detailed discussion, see Daniel N. Nelson (1997) "Germany and the Balance Between Threats and Capacities in Europe," *International Politics* 34, no. 1 (March): 63–78.

44. See the Lou Harris Poll reported in *The Independent* (June 19, 1996) that reported 67 percent of the German public was opposed to EMU. Some other polls found even greater opposition.

45. This French view was noted by Jim Hoagland (1997) "South of Europe," *Washington Post*, March 6, 1997.

46. Barry James (1997) "Immigration to France Unchanged in 20 Years," *International Herald Tribune*, February 28, 1997.

47. See Jim Hoagland (1997) "Debating Immigration the French Way," *Washington Post*, March 2, 1997.

48. On French foreign and defense policy priorities particularly vis-à-vis NATO, see R. P. Grant (1996) "France's New Relationship with NATO," *Survival* 38, no. 1 (Spring): 58–80.

49. A couple of reports that convey this mood are Roger Cohen (1997) "A Somber France, Racked by Doubt: Under Pressure to Modernize, Nation Clings to the Old Ways," *International Herald Tribune*, February 12, 1997, and Barry James (1997) "New Victory of Far Right Stirs Doubts in France," *International Herald Tribune*, February 11, 1997.

50. In the French case, Prime Minister Alain Juppe has advocated that intellectuals not protest a government bill against illegal immigration because their protests would "undermine democracy" by giving arguments to the extreme right. Essentially, then, the government must do much of what the extremists want to prevent them from becoming stronger. Such pandering to extremism understandably drew the wrath of French intellectuals. See Barry James (1997) "French Face Off over Immigration," *International Herald Tribune*, February 18, 1997.

51. Ethan B. Kapstein (1996) "Workers and the World Economy," *Foreign Affairs* 75, no. 3 (May-June): 37.

52. Ray Marshall (1995) "The Global Job Crisis," *Foreign Policy* no. 100 (Fall): 50.

53. These data are from the World Bank and U.S. Department of Commerce as reported by Marshall N. Carter and William G. Shipman (1996) "The Coming Global Pension Crisis" (Special Supplement) *Foreign Affairs* 75, no. 6 (November-December).

54. Newhouse (1997) "Europe's Rising Regionalism," p. 67.

55. See Daniel N. Nelson (2000) "Dangerous Assumptions," *Bulletin of the Atomic Scientists* (July-August): 24–28.

56. The *Frankfurter Allgemeine Zeitung*, perhaps Germany's most respected conservative newspaper, used such a phrase in late February 1997, as reported in the *Washington Post* on February 23, 1997.

57. Wolfgang Schauble (1994) *Und der Zukunft zugewandt* (Berlin: Siedler Verlag).

58. For a journalist's reflections on such troublesome indicators, see E. J. Dionne Jr. (1997) "Germany's Problems Should Trouble Us, Too," *International Herald Tribune*, February 11, 1997.

59. Central Intelligence Agency (1995) *World Factbook* (Washington, D.C.: Central Intelligence Agency).

60. Steven Mufson (1997) "Major Speech Puts Li Peng in Spotlight," *Washington Post*, March 2, 1997, p. A-22.

61. See, for example, "Soldiering Pays," *The Economist*, July 4, 1994, and Nicolas Kristof (1993) "China Raises Military Budget," *New York Times*, March 17, 1993.

62. The Sukoi Su-27, one of the best Soviet-Russian combat aircraft to be developed in the 1980s, was sold to China in large numbers during the mid-1990s—perhaps as many as forty-eight units in two batches. Russia, eager for exports and to repair relations with China, apparently agreed to transfer Su-27 technologies to China and to license Beijing's production of this potent supersonic aircraft. See "Russia: Largest Aircraft Deal to Be Signed with PRC," *Kommersant Daily*, February 7, 1996, as translated in FBIS-SOV-96–028, February 9, 1996, p. 21.

63. The Israeli-China connection has long been rumored. CIA briefings in 1991 to congressional leaders and, later, newspaper reports based on those CIA findings suggested that Israel had supplied missile and avionics technology to China in the late 1980s and early 1990s. See, for example, "China Has U.S. Missile Secrets," *Washington Times*, January 5, 1993, regarding the Patriot system used in the Gulf War. Israel has also helped China develop its J-10 fighter, a system based on the Israeli Lavi, which in turn had benefited greatly from avionics in the best U.S. fighter-bombers of the late 1980s. See "Israel Co-Operates with China on Secret Fighter," *Flight International*, November 2–8, 1994.

64. Many reports have addressed these naval additions, including Ben Barber (1995) "Beijing Eyes China South Sea with Sub Purchase," *Washington Times*, March 7, 1995.

65. Oksenberg, quoted in the *New York Times*, December 19, 1994.

66. An upbeat assessment of China's evolution is William H. Overholt (1996) "China After Deng," *Foreign Affairs* 75, no. 3 (May-June): 63–78.

67. Steven Mufson's report about the Chinese leader's vocal and piano efforts, and Jiang's larger political savvy, was carried in the *Washington Post*, February 23, 1997, with the title "China's Musical Leader Sings in Many Keys."

68. See Thomas J. Christensen (1996) "Chinese Realpolitik," *Foreign Affairs* 75, no. 5 (September-October): 37.

69. "Chinese Weapons Tests Seen Targeting Taiwanese Politics," *New York Times*, August 16, 1995. Before and during the 1996 Taiwanese elections, the Chinese held huge military exercises just across the strait between the island and mainland and repeatedly fired ballistic missiles into target areas less than thirty miles from the Taiwanese coast.

70. Many sources have reported these sales. See, for example, Martin Sieff (1995) "U.S. Probes China on Missiles," *Washington Times*, July 9, 1995, and Douglas Jehl (1993) "China Breaking Missile Pledge," *Washington Times*, May 6, 1993.

71. This more charitable view of Chinese foreign policy intentions is exemplified by Joseph Yu-shek Cheng (1996) "China's America Policy," *Journal of Chinese Political Science* 2, no. 2 (Summer): esp. 58–61.

72. A well-written example of concern and scenarios of impending conflict between the United States and the Beijing regime is Richard Bernstein and Ross Munro (1997) *The Coming Conflict with China* (New York: Alfred Knopf).

73. An insightful discussion of this thesis is Samuel S. Kim (July 29, 1996) *China's Quest for Security in the Post-Cold War World* (Carlisle, Pa.: Strategic Studies Institute Monograph, U.S. Army War College).

74. See, for example, the *South China Morning Post* (Hong Kong), September 25, 1989, which quotes the official Beijing daily *Remin Ribao* (September 24, 1989) in this regard. By mid- and late 1995, there was substantial talk of a new U.S. containment strategy and hegemonist policy toward China. See Cheng (1996) "China's America Policy," p. 66.

75. Japanese militarism is a theme in, for example, *Jiefangjun Bao*, April 2, 1996, p. 1.

76. See Cheng (1996), pp. 69–70, and his citations of *Renmin Ribao* (December 22, 1995, and January 26, 1996).

77. See Steven Mufson (1997) "Ethnic Turmoil Roils Western China," *Washington Post*, February 23, 1997.

78. Sandra Sugawara (1997) "Japanese Face Up to Need for Change," *International Herald Tribune*, March 10, 1997.

79. A good account of this episode was in *Jane's Intelligence Review*. See E. Croody (1995) "Urban Terrorism: Chemical Warfare in Japan," *Jane's Intelligence Review* 7, no. 11 (November): 521.

80. Clifford Krauss (1997) "U.S. Doubtful Japanese Will Join Plan for Missile Defense," *New York Times*, February 14, 1997.

81. See Gwen Robinson (1997) "Targeted by Washington," *Financial Times*, April 29, 1997.

82. Charles J. Hanley (1995) "Japan Keeps Open Unthinkable Option," *Washington Times*, May 12, 1995, and "Japan Shifts Its Stand on Ruling Out A-Bomb," *Los Angeles Times*, July 9, 1993.

83. A more upbeat economic assessment of Russia was conveyed in Avraham Shama (1996) "Inside Russia's True Economy," *Foreign Policy* 103 (Summer): 111–127.

84. *The Economist*, March 8, 1997, p. 55, cites data from a "Visions" survey in which the top ten "worries" were, with the exception of crime, dominated by strictly economic matters.

85. This is Vladimir Shlapentokh's term from his "Decentralization of Fears: Life in Post-Communist Society," unpublished manuscript, Department of Sociology, University of Michigan, January 1997.

86. *Jane's Intelligence Review* (1996) "Sino-Russian Arms Bazaar," *Jane's Intelligence Review* 8, no. 7 (July): 30.

87. See, for example, Senator Bill Bradley (1995–1996) "A Misguided Russia Policy," *Foreign Policy* no. 101 (Winter): 81–101.

88. For example, see commentaries by Alexei Malashenko in *Nezavisimaya Gazeta*, May 7, 1997, and George Boyt in *Sogodnya*, May 16, 1997.

89. Barry Buzan discusses this notion in detail in Barry Buzan (1991) *People, States, and Fear* (Hemel Hempstead, UK: Harvester Wheatsheaf/Lynne Rienner), chap. 2.

90. Barry Buzan (1995) "Security, the State, the 'New World Order,' and Beyond," in Ronni D. Lipschutz (ed.) *On Security* (New York: Columbia University Press), pp. 187–211.

91. World Bank data on murder rates per 100,000 population for the late 1980s and early 1990s ranked the United States ninth in the world, "behind" eight Latin American states but far higher than any other advanced industrial democracy (at 10.1 murders per 100,000).

92. This is the argument of constructivists; see, e.g., Alexander Wendt (1994) "Collective Identity Formation and the International State," *American Political Science Review* 88, no. 2 (June): 384–396.

18

Farewell to Russia:
The Decay of a Superpower

GERHARD MANGOTT

The loss of the outer empire and then the inner empire, the massive rollback of frontiers, the emergence of new independent states on the post-Soviet stage, and the massive penetration of the region by external actors—Western powers, Turkey, Iran, Pakistan, India, China, and Japan—have left Russian leaders in geopolitical confusion and have altered Russian foreign, security, and defense policies. Russian foreign policy planning does not expect a serious strategic threat—let alone a threat of a strategic military nature—to the Russian Federation to emerge in the next decades.[1] In the very center of its concern, however, is the further downgrading of Russia's international status and remarkable losses of influence in the European, Caucasian, Central Asian, and Asian-Pacific theaters.

Due to multidimensional structural weaknesses and deficiencies, Russia's scope and means of action will be quite limited in the decades to come. Russia has been and will continue to suffer many weaknesses stemming from internal upheavals—the economic, political, cultural, and social reshuffling of affairs—and a fundamentally altered external setting. According to Paul Marantz, "During the Cold War, the outside world was so preoccupied with Soviet capabilities, strengths and potentially aggressive intentions that it is not always easy now to comprehend fully the magnitude of Russia's weakness and the very different challenge this poses." He continues: "Instead of having to hedge against the threat of a soon-to-be-powerful-again Russia, the West

A previous version of this chapter appeared in *International Politics* 37, no. 4 (December 2000) and is reprinted here with the kind permission of Kluwer Law International.

must deal with a weak Russia and address the challenge of continuing Russian instability."[2]

Russia, therefore, will be a restrained though highly ambitious power longing for an influential role in international relations. The following variables and factors can be listed as the most important constraints, limitations, and vulnerabilities regarding Russia's international performance:

A first set of variables is related to problems of identity after the collapse of the Soviet Union. Russia is still searching for an inclusive, integrative postimperial identity and a sustainable definition of the very essence of the post-Soviet Russian state. "Russia is a state without a state concept."[3] The issue of Russia's self-definition has serious implications for Russia's external behavior. Is Russia finally accommodating to a nonnational definition of the Russian Federation? Or will it eventually resort to an ethnically defined statehood, which could ultimately lead to the violent revision of post-Soviet borders given that more than 20 million ethnic Russians—roughly one-sixth of the Russians living in Russia—still settle outside the borders of the Russian Federation? Or is there a third option? Is Russia heading to a nonnational restoration of an empire designed to fulfill a spiritual mission in Eurasia?

Furthermore, a large segment of Russia's political elite has still not adjusted to the slump in Russia's international prestige and influence. The psychological trauma of the collapse of the Soviet Union—which by a vast majority is perceived as having been a serious error by Russian and Ukrainian leaders—will remain a major factor in both their perceptions of and their behavior in the international arena. Verbal radicalism quite often is a vaccination against the acceptance of bleak realities.

Radical-nationalist outbursts of rhetoric are often linked to domestic political power struggles but hardly and rarely correspond to actual policies. "Ambitious politicians, such as Alexander Lebed and Yurii Luzhkov, continue to use strident nationalism to advance their strive for power."[4] However, this sort of behavior, a successful tactic, causes frequent irritation and concerns for external observers and partners. Russian verbal radicalism thus turns out to be counterproductive, as it nurtures Western public and elite perceptions of Russia still being a potentially aggressive, expansionist power.

A second set of factors constraining Russia's external activities is related to the process of regime change and (democratic) institution building or rebuilding. Russia is still in a political transition period, hardly having taken the first steps on the path of democratization. No societal and/or elite consensus on the overall direction of Russian reforms and politics has been established as of yet. The political regime in Russia can best be described as authoritarian-presidentialist, further aggravated by a widespread disregard for legal norms, constitutional rules, institutional power sharing, and accountability of political decisionmakers. Russia still suffers from political strife and divisions. The political capacity of most state institutions is very low.

Furthermore, the Russian leadership is still struggling to preserve the economic, legal, and political coherence and integrity of the Russian Federation. Economically and/or ethnically motivated separatism is still on the agenda. The current method of selectively delineating federal and regional competencies by a confusing set of treaties and agreements between the center and its subjects has not yet produced a stable framework for efficient, coherent, and consistent policies on the whole Russian territory. Russian domestic developments are hardly predictable, and major shifts in domestic as well as in external behavior cannot be ruled out, which makes Russia an unpredictable and partly reliable actor in the international arena.

The Russian political elite has become increasingly pluralistic, with new actors and interests—business groups (the fuel and energy sector especially), regional actors, and the like—emerging. They are influencing both the decisionmaking and implementation processes in foreign and security policies. Coordination of differing views and initiatives at least on the level of central government has been quite weak. In particular, interaction between the Foreign Ministry and the Defense Ministry and the Russian Security Council has all but worked well. The Foreign Ministry has been unable to take over this role from the central committee departments of the Communist Party of the Soviet Union; this was true particularly under the tenure of Foreign Minister Andrei Kozyrev. This improved only when Yevgeni Primakov took over the office of foreign minister in 1996. In the foreign policy concept approved by the Security Council on 23 March 2000, this problem has reportedly been addressed, and the Foreign Ministry has been given the central coordinating role in foreign policy.[5]

Due to the lack of coordination and the emergence of a myriad of federal, regional, and sectoral players in foreign policy, the formulation of Russian foreign and security policy has lost much of its Soviet coherence, consistency, and predictability.

Much like the political process in general, foreign and security policy has become the subject of intensive media coverage and public debate. This situation is challenging for most of the Russian foreign policy cadres and diplomats, as they had been accustomed to formulating and implementing policies outside public scrutiny. In addition, the new context of decisionmaking limits the range of available options for the Russian authorities, as the positions and actions taken must—at least to a certain extent—be sold on the domestic front. Moreover, external policies are more than once utilized for domestic battles, straining both coherence and consistency of Russian foreign policy.

A third set of constraining variables that needs to be addressed includes the socioeconomic structure and development of the Russian Federation. Russia currently—and for the foreseeable future—lacks the economic and financial potential for a leading role in international relations; it is too weak in financial and economic terms to pursue a noncooperative approach to the

Table 18.1   Gross Domestic Product of Russia, 1990–2000 (real change in percent against preceding year)

1990	1991	1992	1993	1994	1995	1996	1997	1998	1999[a]	2000[a]
–3.0	–5.0	–14.5	–8.7	–12.7	–4.1	–3.4	0.9	–4.6	1.7	2.0

Sources: Data are taken from Peter Havlik et al. (1999) *The Transition Countries in 1999: A Further Weakening of Growth and Some Hopes for Later Recovery,* Research Report 257 of the Vienna Institute for International Economic Studies, June, p. 3; Josef Pöschl et al. (2000) *Transition Countries Clamber Aboard the Business Boom in Western Europe: Upswing Masks Persistent Transition-Related Problems,* Research Report 264 of the Vienna Institute for International Economic Studies, February, p. 18.
Note: a. Prognosis.

Western countries and to be an attractive partner for potential anti-Western powers. Russia's gross domestic product (GDP) has been shrinking since 1989, falling to a level of 62.1 percent of the 1991 value in 1999.[6] The Russian government's hope that the decline had bottomed out in 1997 when the country experienced modest GDP growth soon collapsed. With the financial crash in August 1998—when the government defaulted on the domestic debt (short-term T-bills and bonds), posed a moratorium on debt payments by Russian banks to Western creditors for ninety days, and effectively devalued the ruble, first by broadening the corridor for the exchange rate to float, then by deciding to let the ruble float freely—the Russian (and many Commonwealth of Independent States [CIS]) economies melted down, and GDP decreased again by 4.6 percent (see Table 18.1).

However, the crisis of 1998 had a positive short-term effect on the Russian economy. The collapse of the ruble (which currently is undervalued) and the sharp decline in real wages (by about 15 percent in 1999) have made many imported commodities overly expensive and noncompetitive on the Russian market. This led to an increased utilization of domestic production capacities, and domestic industrial production increased sharply in 1999 (by 8 percent), especially in areas substituting for imports, resulting in an overall growth of GDP of 1.7 percent.[7] Devaluation has also led to a slight increase of foreign direct investment in the real sector by about 1.5 percent and lower unemployment rates. An additional factor for the rather positive economic development in 1999 has been the rising price of oil on the international markets, which almost doubled state budget revenues from the fuel and energy sector.[8]

The massive decline of Russia's GDP since 1989 can be explained by two factors: the low rate of capacity utilization in Russia caused by cheaper imports within the framework of liberalized foreign trade and by the decline in domestic consumption due to shrinking real wages; and the decay of domestic production facilities due to lacking or low rates of state and/or private investment. The low investment rate is the result of a lack of capital and the unwillingness of private actors to invest money in the Russian economy. Current growth, however, has a limited potential as the devaluation takes effect; import substitution by domestic producers will soon be exhausted, and fuel prices are expected to fall again. In addition, the Russian government has not taken advantage of the current positive climate to initiate structural reforms in the economy. In any event, even if Russian GDP growth were to continue, the growth rates will most likely be quite modest in the medium term. The level of Russian GDP in 1990 will be achieved only late in the first decade of the 2000s.

Making full use of domestic production capacities can generate overall growth in Russian GDP of 8–12 percent at maximum over the next few years.[9] This potential is limited by growing infrastructural deficiencies of the Russian economy, particularly in the energy and transportation sectors. Without large-scale state investment in these sectors, further GDP growth could be hampered by a lack of energy resources and transport capacities for higher industrial production turnout.[10]

Capital assets of the Russian economy are remarkable, however, they are often not usable for high-quality production at reasonable cost. Russian natural resources—oil, gas, coal, metal ores—are considerable, but exploration, extraction, transport, and processing of these resources is economically viable only if prices for these goods are or remain high on the world markets. The slump in world market prices for crude oil revealed the weakness of the Russian oil sector regarding the cost of extraction. In addition, Russia needs technical aid to make exploration and extraction possible. Furthermore, Russian economic growth cannot be sustained in the long run by its natural-resources potential only. Such a strategy could foster a negative trend of deindustrialization.[11] Labor as a production factor will remain more than abundant in Russia. The current Russian workforce is estimated at roughly 73 million people, whose standard of training is fairly high; wages remain very low. This considerably large workforce is further increased by immigration of Russians and Russian-speaking people from the other CIS members.[12]

Large-scale state investment, however, would require both an overhaul of current state expenditure and a significant increase of revenues. In 1998, federal tax and tariff revenues made up only 8.8 percent of Russian GDP; better tax compliance and increased efforts on the part of authorities to collect taxes increased this to approximately 10 percent in 1999 (with more taxes being paid in cash rather than in commodities than ever); a rate of 12 percent is expected for 2000. This rate would still be far below Western standards; it is highly optimistic in any event.[13]

That being said, one can predict that a long-term strategy of industrial growth is unlikely without large-scale foreign direct investment and technology transfers in the real sectors of the Russian economy. These factors are also, though not exclusively, dependent on the external behavior of Russia. In addition, measures to encourage and enforce domestic investment are also indispensable. At the moment, capital flight makes up U.S.$1–1.5 billion per month, money that is urgently needed for investment in the Russian economy.

Russia's socioeconomic weakness also becomes clear from per capita income. Russia's GDP per capita currently amounts only to roughly one-third (32 percent) of the average European Union (EU) rate; in 1990 Russia achieved almost double that amount.[14] Russia currently does not qualify for the top forty countries listed by GDP at purchasing power parities per capita.

An additional barrier to the anti-Western course is Russia's huge debt problem. Russian sovereign debt (not accounting for private foreign debt, including banks, and the foreign debt of regional and local governments) amounted to approximately U.S.$156.2 billion by early 2000. In terms of Russian GDP, foreign debt skyrocketed after the collapse of the Russian ruble in August 1998. In 1990 Russian sovereign foreign debt amounted to 10.4 percent of GDP; in July 1998 this figure had risen to 31 percent, exploding to 113 percent in December 1998.[15] In the meantime, this share has fallen to 87.3 percent due to the modest economic recovery. Russia was unable to service all its foreign debt in 1999 (some U.S.$17.5 billion)[16] and will not be able to deliver all the debt-service payments due in 2000 (approximately U.S.$15.2 billion). The Russian budget for 2000 envisages debt servicing accounting for 27.3 percent of total state expenditures. This allows Russia to live up to about 40 percent of its total debt-service obligations in 2000. This dire situation was aggravated when the International Monetary Fund (IMF) suspended disbursements from the U.S.$4.5 billion standby loan in December 1999, allegedly due to Russia's failure to implement structural reforms in the economy.[17]

Russia has been partially successful in its debt-rescheduling negotiations with Paris and London creditors. In August 1999, Russia reached an agreement with Paris creditors on restructuring the Soviet debt inherited by Russia until the fall of 2000, which significantly lowered debt payments.[18] In February 2000, Russia reached a preliminary agreement with the London creditors, transforming U.S.$31.8 billion in Soviet debt into Russian eurobonds, writing off an average of about 36 percent (approximately U.S.$10.6 billion), prolonging debt servicing up to thirty (from twenty-five) years and applying very modest interest rates.[19]

Russia still needs the disbursement of further tranches of IMF and World Bank loans to service its debt to these organizations and to fulfill the obligations from the eurobonds.[20] Not mentioning the enormous financial and economic implications of Russia's debt, from a political point of view one has to state that Russia's high vulnerability prevents it from following an anti-Western agenda. It is in Russia's vital interest to ask for Western assistance in dealing with the debt crisis. An overall default on its sovereign debt would for years make Russia a pariah in the international financial markets and might cut it off from desperately needed foreign direct investment.

Put simply, Russia lacks the economic and financial means to pursue confrontational foreign policies. Quite the contrary: cooperation with external actors is an indispensable prerequisite for economic stabilization. "Russia's need for foreign economic assistance, investment and trade limits Moscow's freedom of action and provides a powerful incentive for restraint and moderation."[21] Russia thus lacks the economic and financial status to be attractive as a coalition partner with other countries in the international system. This feature, more than anything else, spoils the prospects of Russia entering political, military, and economic alliances that are anti-Western in character.

Another socioeconomic constraint is demographics. The radical decrease in Russia's population may endanger economic recovery and control of the entire territory. Despite sharp productivity increases, a modernizing Russian economy could lack an adequate skilled labor force in about 2020 and fail to populate the vast territory. The population of Russia has decreased sharply in the past decade. Negative population growth began in 1985, preceded by a marked decrease in birthrates; in 1996 the birthrate reached an all-time low (1.28 children per fertile woman).

In 1993, the entire population of Russia was 148.3 million; as of December 1999 this number had fallen to 145.6 million, despite the influx of Russians and Russian-speaking people from post-Soviet countries.[22] In 1999 alone, the population decline was 0.5 percent, the highest since 1992. Current trends will lead to a population of 138.4 million in 2015; in 2050, only 80–100 million Russians will remain.[23]

The reasons for the population decline are manyfold. The birthrate is low; the death rate has increased sharply; and socioeconomic problems are legion: a dramatic increase in cardiovascular diseases, alcohol and tobacco abuse, malnutrition, a massive deterioration in health care, a dramatic increase in tuberculosis, HIV, and syphilis, increasing rates of infertility, ecological threats due to contaminated water and air, and so on.

The last fundamental constraint is the military. The military pillar of Russian foreign, security, and defense policy has been weakened since and due to the dissolution of the Soviet Union; the current state of affairs is both depressing and alarming. "Not since June 1941," Alexei G. Arbatov puts it, "has the Russian military stood as perilously close to ruin as it does now."[24] The Russian military suffers from organizational, financial, technological, and social problems, which are unlikely to be overcome in coming years. Meanwhile, the cohesion and combat capability of the Russian armed forces have eroded to the extent that its ability to carry out a comprehensive conventional operation is in question.[25]

Military reform—designed to adapt to the altered international and domestic environments—has been delayed far too long. The military was left untouched in order to maintain its loyalty to the political leadership in domestic political crises. Serious military reform started only after Igor Sergeev was appointed defense minister in May 1997. The main elements of reform are laid down in a classified document signed by then President Boris Yeltsin on 30 July 1998 ("On the Principles of State Policy on Military Development till 2005").[26] Its key elements are the reorganization of relations between the armed forces subordinated to the Ministry of Defense and the paramilitary forces of other ministries and agencies, the restructuring of the military districts and the command structure of the armed forces, the reduction of service branches from five to three (as of March 2000, four branches existed: air, navy, ground forces, strategic forces), reductions in manpower, measures to improve operational readiness, and modernization of equipment.

A sober and thorough comparison of ambitions and capabilities in defense planning has long been indispensable. Defense resources are not as abundant or easy to mobilize as they were during the communist period. The cost factor can no longer be ignored in a political setting that is linked (at least in theory) to public acceptance.

However, it is still difficult to assess actual defense expenditures due to the various definitions of *expenditures* to be calculated, continuous revision of budget allocations, and significantly lower actual spending. It can be said, however, that actual state spending on defense has been decreasing since 1992 both as a share of total state expenditures and as a share of Russian GDP. Russia spends 5–7 percent of GDP on defense.[27] Despite several verbal commitments by President-elect (now President) Vladimir Putin to increase spending on arms procurement and research and development, the Russian budget for 2000 still marks "only" 17.1 percent of the total budget for defense, which is even less than in 1999. Using the projected figures of GDP development in the state budget for 2000, this would bring defense spending down to 3.8 percent of GDP in 2000; this is the lowest rate since 1992 (see Table 18.2).

It is important to notice, however, that actual state spending on defense is primarily used for salaries and maintaining day-to-day operations. Important sectors for the middle- and long-term status and development of Russian armed forces (i.e., procurement, research and development), however, are lacking the appropriate investments (see Table 18.3).

The implosion of Russian spending on arms procurement was considerably strong until 1996, with the air force and the navy most strongly affected. This drop in procurement has resulted in increasing aging of Russian weapons systems. Obsolete or worn-out equipment can hardly be replaced. In addition to dwindling procurement, the Russian military has serious problems in operating and maintaining its weaponry. The Ministry of Defense is notorious for long delays in paying off domestic producers for delivered weaponry.

These reductions in spending on military research and development threaten Russia's status as a military superpower in the medium and long

Table 18.2   Russian Defense Expenditures, 1993–2000 (in redenominated millions of rubles)

	1993[a]	1994	1995[a]	1996	1997[a]	1998	1999	1999[a]	2000[b]
Defense budget	8,327	40,626	59,379	80,185	83,000	81,765	93,702	109,000	146,500
Federal budget (in percent)	n.a.	20.9	21.3	18.4	19.7	16.4	16.3	19.0	17.1
Defense outlay (DO)	7,210	28,028	47,800	63,900	79,700	56,700	n.a.	n.a.	n.a.
DO in % of initial budget	86.6	69.0	80.5	79.7	96.0	69.4	n.a.	n.a.	n.a.
DO in percent of GDP (IISS estimates)	8.9	8.3	7.4	6.5	5.8	5.2	n.a.	n.a.	n.a.

Source: Data from International Institute for Strategic Studies (1999) *The Military Balance, 1999/2000* (Oxford: UK: Oxford University Press), pp. 109–110.
Notes: a. Revised budget.
b. Budget 2000 has been passed by the Duma in second reading only.

terms. With the partial exception of the nuclear sector, Russia could lose the capability of producing competitive products across the whole range of weapons, which would impede its share of the international armaments market. Revenues from arms sales abroad, however, are significant for the state. In 1997, Russia sold arms totaling U.S.$2.5 billion on the international weapons market; after a slump in 1998 (U.S.$1.7 billion), arms sales were

Table 18.3   Estimated Russian Defense Budget by Function, 1999 (redenominated millions of rubles)

Function	Rubles (m)	In Percent of Total Spending
Personnel	33,900	31.1
Operations and maintenance	29,600	27.2
Procurement	23,800	21.8
Research and development	14,000	12.8
Infrastructure	3,500	3.2
Nuclear	1,900	1.7
MOD	500	0.5
Other	1,800	1.7
Total defense budget	109,000	100.0

Source: International Institute for Strategic Studies (1999) *The Military Balance, 1999/2000* (Oxford: Oxford University Press), p. 109.

boosted to U.S.$3.5 billion in 1999. Deputy Prime Minister Ilya Klebanov expects a further increase in 2000, with a sales value of U.S.$4.3 billion.[28]

Prospects for modernizing weaponry are bleak. Most Russian defense elites probably agree in concentrating defense planning on preventing local conflicts (particularly on the southern periphery), which requires the creation of highly mobile rapid-reaction forces and the strengthening of the nuclear component, with particular emphasis on promoting strategic and maritime nuclear forces.[29] The Ministry of Defense has therefore focused on moderniz- ing nuclear forces as the core element of Russia's military power. The mod- ernization of the arsenal of intercontinental ballistic missiles with the new Topol-M and the maintenance of strategic nuclear parity with the United States have been at the center of recent military planning. The Russian defense establishment has also taken decisions on modernizing tactical nuclear weapons. Responding to NATO action against the former Yugoslavia, the Security Council reportedly agreed at its closed meeting on 29 April 1999 to implement a long-prepared program[30] on developing a new generation of tactical nuclear weapons with limited destruction capacities. These nuclear arms are designed for regional conflicts and should make nuclear warfare pos- sible on a nonstrategic level.

Highly contested within the Russian military is Defense Minister Sergeev's plan to create a combined supreme command for Russia's strategic deterrence forces. Furthermore, opposition is building against a further decline in spending for conventional forces. This became particularly apparent in the course of the second Chechen conflict that started in September 1999.

These financial and weapons-related problems are exacerbated by social problems within the military: unpaid or delayed salaries (forcing soldiers to look for legal or illegal jobs); lack of food, housing, and medical care; corrup- tion; crime; drug problems; shrinking discipline and morale; poor recruitment of new cadres (draft-dodging, draft exemptions, corruption); poor retention of junior officers. As a result, the intellectual quality of Russia's officer corps is decreasing, many units are understaffed, and combat-readiness is lacking.

A reasonable military reform—downsizing and restructuring the armed forces—requires considerable financial resources. This is even more true for the transition to an all-professional army. The currently allocated resources, however, are insufficient. The reduction in the military's manpower until 1 January 1999, to 1.1–1.2 million, is not radical enough to solve the current financial crisis. A further downsizing of the Russian armed forces to 600,000 personnel is inevitable if state spending is to remain somewhat level and if spending on procurement and research and development (announced by the government on 27 January 2000) is to be implemented.

But even if reasonable military reform is carried out successfully and even if the economy regains strength, Russia will be unable to respond to mil- itary challenges on more than one flank. Russia will hardly be able to withstand an adversary armed with modern, highly sophisticated weaponry. "However, Russian armed forces should prove adequate in regional conflicts with states possessing poorly developed technology, as long as they are able to raise the morale of their soldiers and provide sufficient funding and materials for exercises and training."[31]

GEOPOLITICAL OPTIONS:
FOREIGN AND SECURITY POLICY

Having addressed several constraints upon Russian action in the international arena, we now turn to three geopolitical options that have been intensively discussed and pursued in the foreign policy debate to promote Russian interests. The advantages and disadvantages, the gains and losses, of these options will be analyzed. These options are not mutually exclusive; some elements of each may well be combined and pursued simultaneously. However, the overall direction of Russian foreign and security policy will follow the lines of one of these alternatives.

Reintegration of the Post-Soviet Space

The territory of the former Soviet Union is important to Russia's status as a global player. The post-Soviet region is still considered to be a sphere of Russian influence, with Russia having special rights and responsibilities to protect its vital interests. Yet many political elites have not accepted the collapse of the Soviet Union, not to mention the sovereignty and independence of the post-Soviet countries. They share the belief that if Russia fails to reestablish hegemonic control over the post-Soviet region, it will not be able to regain sustainable and credible great-power status. In the early months of Russian independence, Russia lacked a comprehensive concept for the post-Soviet region, be it within or outside the CIS, because foreign policy cadres (inspired by Foreign Minister Kozyrev) were notoriously fixed on the Atlanticist agenda, which has changed since the fall of 1992. Russia's "basic aim" since 1992 "has been to reconstitute strategic order in a huge region that became anarchical when the Soviet Union collapsed." Thus, its "minimalist objectives have been to prevent a wave of chaos and violence from sweeping over the region" with potentially serious spillover effects on Russian territory and to "prevent the newly independent states from aligning with Russia's adversaries."[32] Russia's maximalist objective has been to draw states into closer bilateral and multilateral relations with Russia, leading finally to the reintegration of the entire post-Soviet region.

Assessing the overall development, it can be argued that Russia failed to achieve both objectives. Russia has failed to reassert hegemonic control over the post-Soviet region, whether within the CIS or through various bilateral and multilateral initiatives. Russia seriously miscalculated the ability of the other post-Soviet countries to consolidate statehood and independence, however fragile and weak they seemed at the end of 1991. "Particularly since 1996 most of the CIS states have consolidated their independent status . . . and shown a burgeoning tendency toward emancipation from Russia. The only exceptions are Belarus and Tajikistan, the latter being militarily and financially completely dependent on Russia."[33] Armenia should now be added to that list. Furthermore, Russia overestimated its economic potential as the vehicle for speedy reintegration.

The integration dynamic of the CIS has been limited due to the economic impotence of Russia to promote economic reintegration. In addition, the interests and objectives of the newly independent states are often divergent, sometimes even diametrically opposed. There is currently "no external or internal threat that is perceived by all the states as a common danger or even, for that matter, a common threat perception shared equally by all states. On the contrary, the threat perceptions of the CIS states are frequently incongruent if not indeed diametrically opposed."[34] In addition, leaders of the other post-Soviet states share a genuine distrust of Russian intentions, which caused several CIS countries to oppose reasonable integration initiatives despite apparent advantages.

The multilateral reintegration within the framework of the CIS must be judged an overall failure. As of today, the CIS is nothing more than an institutional-organizational structure without impact on real politics; it is a form without function, there to disguise the failure of meaningful reintegration. In December 1998, the chairman of the Russian Federation Council—the upper chamber of the Russian parliament—stated that "the CIS as such does not exist. It is only an outward form."[35] Still, Russia will embrace the CIS as a forum to reach common decisions related to the international and external security of member states; financial and economic issues, however, can be expected to be dealt with increasingly on bilateral and selectively multilateral bases.

Intra-CIS trade has been characterized by a downward trend reflecting administrative-structural constraints and the efforts of many CIS members to reorient trade away from the Russian market. Russian exports to the CIS made up 19.2 percent of total Russian exports in 1998 (valued at U.S.$13.7 billion). Russian imports from the CIS accounted for 26 percent of total imports (U.S.$11.3 billion).[36] Russian trade with the CIS has been particularly affected by the Russian financial crisis in August 1998; both exports to and imports from the CIS decreased radically in the second half of 1998 and in 1999.

Russia failed to promote exclusively vertical cooperative structures within the CIS, thus preventing horizontal patterns of cooperation—potentially excluding Russia—among CIS members, let alone with external actors. The post-Soviet states have meanwhile established intensive cooperative relations—politically, economically, as well as in the defense and security field—on selectively multilateral and bilateral bases, with other post-Soviet countries and external actors (which have massively penetrated the southern flank of the post-Soviet region).[37] The most apparent examples of this differentiation process are the cooperation efforts within the institutionalized Central Asian Union or the informal cooperation of Georgia, Ukraine, Uzbekistan, Armenia, and Moldova (the so-called GUUAM group).[38]

The collective security agreement signed in May 1992 by all CIS members (with the exception of Turkmenistan, Moldova, and Ukraine) has never achieved practical importance for conflict resolution in the CIS. Meanwhile, Uzbekistan, Georgia, and Azerbaijan withdrew from the body in April 1999.

Russia has also come to realize the limited means available to pursue the ambitious CIS agenda and overcome the divergent interests of members. "There are increasing signs that the Russian leadership is beginning to distance itself from its original idea of reintegrating the post-Soviet area. Russia's above mentioned maximalist objectives apparently have been dropped meanwhile."[39] Recently, it can be discerned that Russia has reoriented its integrationist efforts from the multilateral CIS level; this includes the Commonwealth of Integrating States (SIG) (Sodruzhestvo Integrirovannykh Gosudarstv) with Kazakhstan, Kyrgyzstan, and Belarus (1996, with Tajikistan joining this group in February 1999) and the Russian-Belarusian Union (SBR, based on various agreements and treaties since 1996). However, these initiatives also fell well short of expectations.

The efforts to create a free trade area and customs union within the framework of the SIG have failed so far due to Russian economic and financial problems. This holds true even for the highly ambitious SBR (Soyuz Belarusi i Rossii). The current legal framework for the SBR is the Treaty on the Union of Belarus and Russia and an operative action program, signed on 8 December 1999; both documents entered into force on 26 January 2000.

Despite the considerable interests of various Russian lobbies—armed forces, defense industries, energy producers, and transportation agencies—in promoting the integration process between Russia and Belarus, the Russian leadership has been unwilling to risk the financial, economic, and political costs of any sort of unification or integration with Belarus. Despite the rhetoric on both sides, the actual depth of Belarusian-Russian reintegration is still weak. This can be explained by the different motives for and interests in eventual merger, the very concept underlying the nature of the emerging new entity, and the fact that domestic political consensus (at least in Russia) over the issue is still missing.

The very nature of the new entity to be created is subject to debate. The Belarusian regime of Alyaksandr Lukashenka seeks a union of sovereign states with equal rights for both parties and equalized decisionmaking structures. Most Russian supporters promote the concept of unification with Belarus becoming an autonomous republic within the framework of the Russian Federation, at best endowed with some additional rights than current federation members.

The primary motive for Belarus is to strengthen the economic basis of the Lukashenka regime. Russia is still by far the most important market for Belarusian products (in 1997, 56 percent of Belarusian exports were directed to the Russian market; in 1999 this figure is estimated at roughly 60 percent),[40] and the Belarusian economy depends on Russian energy carriers delivering goods below world market prices (paid for primarily through barters). The Russian motives are far more diverse; various groups have different objectives for promoting unification. The Russian military-industrial complex (*voenno-promyshlennyj komplex*, or VPK) stresses the strengthening of Russia's strategic position and defense capabilities by absorbing the territory of Belarus; in this respect, radar, defense, and intelligence installations on Belarusian territory are among the Russian gains. Furthermore, access to the Russian exclave of Kaliningrad would be much easier. The energy lobby (*toplivo-energeticheskij komplex*, or TEK) promotes unification, as Belarus could serve as a reliable conduit for Russian gas and oil exports to Western European markets (which would undermine Ukrainian bargaining power vis-à-vis Russia, with Ukraine losing much of its current status as the major conduit for Russian energy exports). The Russian export business could use Belarus, with decent roads and rail, as a major infrastructure bridge to Western and Central Europe.

The reformist camp in Russia opposes unification. Russian liberals in particular have been afraid of the huge financial burden the unreformed Belarusian economy would impose if the economies were united and a common currency adopted.[41] Another sticking point is the role Lukashenka could play in domestic Russian politics. Finally, reformers and centrists are afraid of potential centrifugal effects on the federal structure of Russia if the strongest constituents demanded constitutional status equal to that of a unified Belarus; Tatarstan has more than once raised the issue were Belarus to be included as a special subunit.[42]

The steps toward real union taken thus far—the foundation of the Russian-Belarusian Community on 2 April 1996[43] and the creation of the Russian-Belarusian Union on 2 April 1997[44] (with the Charter of the Union signed by the presidents of both countries on 23 May 1997),[45] the Declaration of Intent of 25 December 1998, and the Treaty on the Union of Belarus and Russia of 8 December 1999—have turned out be rather modest.[46] The current Union Treaty envisages the introduction of a common currency no later than 2005. In the meantime, key financial and economic legislation should be harmonized, in particular tax laws, banking regulations, trade laws, and customs tariffs. The Union Treaty creates a Supreme State Council consisting of the presents, prime ministers, and heads of parliaments of both countries; voting rights are given only to the presidents. Lukashenka was elected head of this council on 26 January 2000. The head of the executive Council of Ministers is Russian First Deputy Prime Minister Mikhail Kasyanov. The union will also have a bicameral parliament, with the lower house being elected directly (presumably in 2001). The union also possesses a small common budget. In 1999, the budget was a mere U.S.$35 million; in 2000, it was raised to U.S.$76 million.[47]

However, with the crash of liberal-reformist policies in Russia in August 1998 and the subsequent changes on Russia's domestic political scene, together with the rising economic difficulties and social unrest in Belarus, the likelihood for real progress on unification is much higher than in previous instances. Yet it seems that Russia is pushing defense and security while slowing down on the costlier aspects of economic integration.

In any event, it is important to note that any integration effort that is not shared and supported by Ukraine is of limited value for the Russian Federation. The loss of Ukraine as a result of the Soviet Union's dismemberment has undermined Russian statehood and identity and weakened its ability to project economic and military power southward. Without Ukraine, any attempt to reestablish some sort of unified entity in the post-Soviet region is considerably less likely and less conducive to Russian interests, as it would further enhance the non-European character of the Russian state. Without Ukraine, Russia moves steadily eastward, transforming into a predominantly Asian power.[48]

Antihegemonial Coalitions and Counteralliances

The main objectives of the antihegemonial coalition-building approach—discussed intensively among Russian foreign political elites—are: to counterbalance U.S. dominance in international relations after the demise of the Soviet Union; to advance Russian economic interests (arms trade, the fuel and energy sector, etc.); and to increase Russia's bargaining potential in its relations vis-à-vis Western powers, particularly the United States.

Among the most prominent partners for such coalitions are countries like Serbia, Iran, Iraq, India, and China. Below I analyze Russian relations with China.

RUSSIA'S RELATIONS WITH CHINA

In April 1996—with the third presidential summit since the dissolution of the Soviet Union—relations between Russia and China started to moved beyond bilateralism, entering a stage of closer cooperation on the international level.

At this summit, the presidents of Russia and China signed the Common Declaration on Strategic Partnership, based on equality and trust. In April 1997, the Declaration on a Multipolar International System was signed by both countries, directed against alleged unipolarism, that is, U.S. hegemonism, in international relations. In December 1998, then Russian Prime Minister Yevgeni Primakov even hinted at the possible emergence of a strategic triangle consisting of Russia, India, and China. Declarations like these and several other joint initiatives and agreements have fostered the impression of an emerging anti-Western bloc similar to the Sino-Soviet alliance of the 1950s. A closer look at the relations between Russia and China, however, reveals the limits of that alliance. Both countries do share short-term interests and objectives, as cooperation is mutually beneficial. But in the long term, disagreements, diverging interests, and strategic courses may well erode the alliance.

There are several short-term interests and objectives that we can discern. Both countries share—on the elite and mass levels—strong anti-Western resentments, particularly vis-à-vis the United States, that can be—and increasingly often are—utilized in the domestic political discourse. Among the many factors underlying and causing this indignation are the ultimate failure of Russia's strategic partnership with the United States, ongoing Western pressure on China to liberalize its trade regime and improve its human rights record, and the shared unease about the 1996 U.S.-Japanese security agreement.

Both China and Russia are opposed to the idea of a world led by the United States and favor a multipolar international order. The common appeal for multipolarism is the recurring theme in Russian-Chinese declarations and policy statements. When economic instruments of power projection are widely lacking and military strength eroding, the resort to blocs and alliances seems quite reasonable. This is where the interests of a fading power and an emerging one seem to coincide, as least for a time.

Russia and China are interested in fostering the perception of a far-reaching alliance, as both can use that perception as a powerful bargaining chip in relations with other countries, especially the United States. Russian and Chinese leaders seek to receive concessions from the United States for refraining from entering an ever closer alliance with each other. This is not to say, however, that the idea of a Russian-Chinese partnership boils down to a tactical maneuver, although tactical considerations remain a crucial element.[49]

China and Russia are keen to develop mutual trade relations, with arms trade being the crucial element. "Russia is selling technology that would take China a very long time and huge financial resources to develop by itself and which it absolutely could not get anywhere else."[50] Chinese leaders are particularly interested in strengthening the air and maritime components of its armed forces. Soviet/Russian arms deals with China were reentered in 1990.

Table 18.4 Chinese Imports from Russia, Exports to Russia, and Total Chinese Imports/Exports, 1997–1999

		Russia (in thousand U.S.$)	Total (in thousand U.S.$)	Russia as Percentage of Total
1999[a]	Imports	3,886,623	148,298,492	2.62
	Exports	1,290,927	174,696,541	0.74
1998	Imports	3,640,860	140,166,300	2.60
	Exports	1,840,370	183,757,110	1.00
1997	Imports	4,085,700	142,370,360	2.87
	Exports	2,038,060	182,791,660	1.12

Source: Data provided to the author by Waltraud Urban, an expert on China at the Vienna Institute for International Economic Studies, in March 2000.
Notes: a. 1999 data are from January to November only.

In the subsequent years, China developed into the leading market for Russian arms producers, which are keen to remain beneficiaries of Western arms embargos imposed after the Tiananmen Square massacre in 1989.[51] Russia is selling air-to-air and surface-to-air missiles, tanks (T-72s), fighters (Su-27s), armored fighting vehicles, and modern electronic devices. Between 1992 and 1997, China spent at least U.S.$5 billion on Russian arms.[52] Russia has become the largest source of arms purchases, providing almost 70 percent of China's arms imports in 1996.[53] The value of Russian arms sales per year since then is estimated at approximately U.S.$1.2–1.5 billion.[54]

Besides weaponry, China is importing Russian resources, metals, and machinery. Chinese exports to Russia are primarily consumer goods of low quality. Total Russian-Chinese trade, however, is still quite small. Chinese exports to Russia made up only 1.1 percent of total Chinese exports in 1996 and remained fairly stable in 1997 and 1998. This rate decreased to 0.74 percent in 1999 (see Table 18.4). Chinese imports from Russia made up only 3.7 percent in 1996 and decreased to 2.6 percent in 1999.

Russian exports to China have been decreasing over the past years as a share of total Russian exports; in 1998, China's share in Russian total exports was 5.34 percent. Russian imports from China as a share of Russian total imports have been increasing from 2.6 percent in 1995 to 3.5 percent in 1998 (see Table 18.5).

It has to be taken into account, however, that economic cooperation and trade relations are significantly stronger when looking at the border regions of China and Russia; this trade is for the most part not reflected in the official statistics of both countries.

Table 18.4   Russian Imports from China, Exports to China, and Total Russian Imports/Exports, 1996–1998

		China (in thousand U.S.$)	Total (in thousand U.S.$)	China as Percentage of Total
1998	Imports	1,154,000	32,791,000	3.52
	Exports	3,146,000	58,937,000	5.34
1997	Imports	1,266,000	39,365,000	3.21
	Exports	4,015,000	69,959,000	5.74
1996	Imports	1,016,000	32,798,000	3.10
	Exports	4,750,000	70,975,000	6.69

Source: Handbook: Russia in Figures, 1999 <http://www.gks.ru/scripts/eng/lc.exe?XXXX12F.26.3.4.1/021500R>.

Despite the ambitious plans to substantially increase bilateral trade—agreements concluded in 1997 called for a trade volume worth U.S.$20 billion by the year 2000—bilateral trade is still weak in value, size, and structure. Total trade in 1997 amounted to a modest U.S.$6.12 billion. Moreover, trade turnover in 1998 shrunk by about 10 percent to a new low of U.S.$5.48 billion due to Russia's financial crisis and the fall of the ruble. In 1999, total trade turnover recovered insignificantly, to U.S.$5.65 billion.[55] The decline or stagnation in recent years has been largely due to sharply decreasing Chinese exports to the Russian market.

The sorting out of bilateral tensions first and foremost involves controversial territorial claims of considerable bilateral and regional importance to both countries. The delimitation and demarcation of the Russian-Chinese border and the confidence-building measures of demilitarization have helped to stabilize the border areas of China and Russia considerably, particularly by including the Central Asian countries (Kyrgyzstan, Kazakhstan, and Tajikistan) in the agreements (the so-called Shanghai Group); a Russian-Chinese conflict is a very remote scenario for the foreseeable future.

It is highly doubtful, however, that the Russian-Chinese partnership will be maintained in the long term. Most of the above-mentioned factors pushing for Russian-Chinese cooperation are most likely to wane or be outweighed by other factors. The modernization of the Russian economy—itself a precondition for Russia's status as a global player—is highly dependent on Western technological, financial, and trade assistance. These supportive elements will not be provided for profit interests only but will result from political decisions by Western governments. Russia simply cannot afford to pursue a coherent and strict anti-Western course. The same holds true for China, though perhaps to a lesser extent. The United States is the single largest market for Chinese exports. U.S. investment is crucial for the modernization of the Chinese economy.[56] Moreover, it can be said, neither side of this alliance can fulfill this support role for the other partner. Therefore, both Russia and China cannot regard each other as credible partners for an anti-Western strategic alliance in the long term, let alone as an alternative partner for economic modernization.

It goes without saying that the economic modernization of Russia is not only a precondition for its international status vis-à-vis the West but a sine qua non for all alternative scenarios for Russia's foreign and security policy orientation. An economically weak, technologically backward, and politically unstable Russia is hardly a reliable partner for any other country.

Assuming continuous economic growth, China will be able to establish highly efficient domestic arms industries, especially if China manages to transfer Russian technology instead of just Russian hardware. In the medium term, Chinese demand for Russian weaponry will decrease further due to the technological decline of Russian weapons. Moreover, should China gain access to Western arms dealers, Russia could be pushed from the Chinese market even before that. Moreover, the economic benefits of Russian arms sales will increasingly be outweighed by the potential security risks of delivering sophisticated arms technologies to China. This causes increasing concern, particularly within the Russian armed forces. Highly indicative of these sentiments was the identification of China as a potential military challenge to Russian security by then Russian Defense Minister Igor Rodionov in December 1996.[57] This statement reflects a growing unease among Russia's military leadership about the sale of weaponry to China, which is barely even available for the Russian military itself.

Among the security threats to Russia emanating from China is the slow Chinese penetration of the Russian Far East and eastern Siberia. Due to severe social and economic crises, the outmigration of ethnic Russians from these areas is considerable and started long before the dissolution of the Soviet Union. Meanwhile, these regions are thinly populated and highly unstable in political terms, and the Russian center's grip on these provinces is loose. Roughly 5 million Russians are facing about 130 million Chinese along the border rivers—the Amur and Ussuri.[58]

The adjacent Chinese areas, however, suffer from high population density and a lack of land and resources. Given this setting, many Russian observers expect increasing Chinese pressure on Russia's eastern territories in order to meet the domestic challenges of its resource-lacking economy and massive overpopulation.

China's lack of resources, food, and settlement areas could also challenge Russian interests on its southern flank in Central Asia and the Caspian Sea region. China may well seek to expand its current political and economic rela-

THE ROLE OF MAJOR POWERS

tions to a sort of special relations with Central Asian countries, which could be detrimental to Russian interests in the region. The cooperation between Kazakhstan and China in the oil and gas sector—foremost, Chinese investments in the exploration, production, and transportation of Kazakh gas and the construction of new transport routes from the Caspian Sea to the Chinese Pacific Coast agreed upon in September 1997—is of particular concern to Russia, as it undermines Russian efforts to preserve the Central Asian countries' dependence on Russian pipeline nets for their energy carrier exports.

Particularly in the Asian theater Russia more and more assumes the role of a junior player, whose very acceptance as an actor depends on Chinese support and assistance. "Security relationships between China, Japan, the two Koreas, and the United States are conceptualised and negotiated with little regard for Russia's interests or wishes. Increasingly Asian states are taking scant notice of Russia when formulating their security policies."[59] The power-projection capabilities of Russia's military in the Far East since 1990 have become more and more limited. This refers to the general shift in the international status of Russia in China's eyes: Russia is a declining world power, whereas China is a slowly ascending one. Never before in bilateral relations has Russia been closer to the role of junior partner; and it is most likely that Russia will remain the weaker and less prospective pole of the axis for a long time.

Certainly, the arguments raised here underline the limited scope of any long-term Russian partnership with China, but they are not fully valid for other potential antihegemonic coalitions.[60] It can be said that Russian special relations and alliances with China, Iran, and India are not serious, permanent alternatives for Russia's external orientation. These relations are based on short- and medium-term common economic interests (arms trading) and political interests (variable and bargaining chip in relations with other states, particularly with the United States) and resemble tactical coalitions. Russia's Western orientation will and can be balanced, but not substituted, by these special affiliations.

In addition, potential Russian alliances are far from being mutually reconcilable. If Russia were to form an alliance with China, Russian relations with India would seriously be strained; the same holds true the other way around. When Russian Prime Minister Primakov, on the occasion of his visit to India, launched the idea of a strategic triangle made up by Russia, India, and China,[61] it may have reflected wishful thinking, but this can hardly be assessed as a probable development in the near future.

Moreover, substance, depth, and development of any of these alliances—particularly the alliances Russia is seeking with China and Iran—can be influenced and shaped by policy decisions and actions on behalf of the Western countries, particularly the United States. If the United States is not going to push China into the arms of Russia—which is unlikely—the prospects for any anti-Western alliance of Russia and third parties is extremely unlikely, very definitely so without any serious political, economic, and military threat potential.

Western Orientation

Atlanticism and the illusionary concepts of strategic partnership and or alliance. In the initial months after the dissolution of the Soviet Union, the outright Atlantic orientation of Russian foreign and security policy was seen as the crucial variable in promoting marketization, democratization (as a means to overcome Russia's traditional backwardness), and the preservation of Russia's great-power status. The major protagonists of this approach have been Kozyrev, Yuri Gaidar, and Yeltsin. In a sort of strategic trade-off of interests and values, the following premises were accepted: Russia promotes the development of liberal-democratic institutions in the economic and political spheres; Russia delivers support for U.S. policies in the defense and security fields; Russia receives massive Western financial and technical aid in the marketization process, underpinned by quick integration of the Russian economy into the world market; and Russia is allowed by the United States and the West to play a leading role in the post-Soviet space with the ultimate goal of reintegrating the area. The basic—and illusory—understanding of the concept of alliance and partnership by Russian leaders was that of a value-based, genuine equality, with Russia being involved in all relevant decisions and actions by Western institutions.[62] The United States, however, was never inclined, willing, and capable to meet such expectations; moreover, Russia was far too weak to qualify as a credible partner for the United States.

The limited Western economic and financial support, and the U.S. policy of consolidating the political independence of the post-Soviet states, made Russian leaders realize, in the second half of 1992, that the results of the Atlantic orientation not only did not meet initial expectations but had seriously undermined the position of the reformers on the domestic front. It had become obvious that the benefits of Atlanticism had been far lower than expected due to illusory premises and that Russian interests are by no means identical, even compatible, with Western interests. In an address to the Russian Foreign Ministry, President Yeltsin harshly criticized the attitudes of Western countries toward Russia: the West "sees Russia as a state that says only yes," ignoring that "Russia is a great power." Yeltsin noted a "certain disappointment with the attitude of some Western countries, including the United States." Russia had shied away from defending its national interests "because of the apprehension that such actions would be criticised as imperialist. But the only ideology the Foreign Ministry should follow is the defense of Russia's interests and Russia's security."[63] Having overcome the outright confusion after the honeymoon went sour and after alternative policy options

turned out to be no more conducive to Russians interests, a more realistic rein-
terpretation of Russia's Western orientation is discernible.

*Moderated Western orientation: Realism, civilized partnership, and
cooperation.* The realist cooperative approach is based on several sober
assessments and perceptions of Western positions vis-à-vis Russia.[64]

The United States is interested in preserving the power constellation that
emerged after the collapse of the Soviet Union. Despite verbal commitments
to partner with Russia, the United States is pressing ahead with its own interests and agenda. In particular, NATO enlargement to Central Europe in 1998,
as well as the Alliance's military action in the former Yugoslavia in Kosovo
without any mandate by the United Nations and despite strong Russian opposition, are perceived as blatant violations of the very essence of partnership
relations. Furthermore, Russia is anxious about U.S. initiatives in arms control and disarmament, which, as the Russians see it, could undermine global
nuclear stability and Russia's ability for nuclear deterrence; in this respect,
U.S. proposals to amend the 1972 Anti-Ballistic Missile Treaty, U.S. nonrati-
fication of the Comprehensive Nuclear Test-Ban Treaty, and the differences
between Russia and the United States on the timing and scope of START III
are at the center of Russian complaints.[65]

Due to its current multidimensional weaknesses—economic, political,
military, and ideological[66]—Russia is unable to claim rightfully the same status as the United States in international relations. Western policies are perceived as both reflecting Russia's current weakness and preventing it from
regaining its previous status, particularly by undermining the reintegration of
the post-Soviet space under Russia's hegemonic control. U.S. policies on the
southern Caucasus and the Caspian Sea region nurture Russian perceptions of
isolation and encirclement.

The West is reluctant to open Western markets to Russian products and
sticks to a policy of limited economic and financial assistance for and engagement in Russia. In Russia's view, the United States is actively driving Russia
from international markets, particularly from the arms markets. In particular,
U.S. objections against Russian contracts with India (the nuclear reactor in
Tamil Nadu) and Iran (the nuclear plant in Bushehr) on nuclear reactors and
missile technology have raised anger in Moscow. Russia will most likely not
give in to external pressure in this field. On 31 March 2000, Putin stated that
Russia will even expand nuclear exports abroad.[67]

Based on these assessments, illusory Atlanticism has been replaced by the
concept of civilized partnership. This approach implies mutual respect for
vital national interests; mutually advantageous cooperation in various policy
fields, with particular emphasis on defense, security, and the economy; and
civilized competition in the international system. Cooperation is deemed to be
in Russia's interest by preventing or settling regional conflicts (excluding the

post-Soviet space), continuing disarmament while preserving Russia's capability of nuclear deterrence, nonproliferation of weapons of mass destruction, military-technological cooperation, economic aid, investment and technical assistance, as well as cooperation in space research and activities.

Within the Russian elite, there is consensus that, despite conflicting interests and basic reserves vis-à-vis the motives of Western policy toward Russia, cooperative relations with the countries of the Organization for Economic and Cooperative Development are indispensable. The modernization of Russia's economy—which is the indispensable precondition for the preservation of Russia's global role—cannot be achieved with alternative partners. Russian external policies should therefore reflect genuine capabilities and resources and be linked to the requirements of domestic modernization and reform. The dominant aim of Russian foreign policy, therefore, is to achieve beneficial cooperation at the lowest political and military costs, for example: to limit Western conditions and criteria for the full integration of Russia into the European and transatlantic institutions; to limit the influence, interference, and engagement of Western countries in the post-Soviet area; and to implement to the maximum extent possible Russian vital interests in the post-Soviet area without threatening relations with the West. These positions are reflected in the new Russian National Security Concept, signed by Putin as interim president on 12 January 2000, and—reportedly—in the new Foreign Policy Concept adopted by the Russian Security Council on 24 March 2000.

Disappointment regarding the Atlanticist orientation and the wrangling over NATO expansion caused deep anti-Western suspicion, primarily toward the United States. Such anti-American resentment partly explains Russia's partial shift away from the United States and toward Europe, a predictable long-term trend. This shift became clear in the fall of 1997 when President Yeltsin—at the Strasbourg Summit of the Council of Europe in October—launched the troika initiative, bringing together Germany, France, and Russia in a regular series of summits to be held in the respective countries. Although this big-powers approach is somewhat reminiscent of nineteenth-century alliances, it nevertheless reflects the growing interest of Russia in a political dialogue with Western Europe.

At the very center is the European Union. The importance of EU relations, based on the Partnership and Cooperation Agreement signed in 1994 and the EU's Joint Strategy for Russia of 1999, has been growing over the past three years. Initially, Russia had been primarily interested in economic and financial cooperation, whereas the EU had been stressing the importance of institutionalized political dialogue. Since late 1997, Russia has shifted away from its initial reluctance to engage in political dialogue with the EU. It seems that the political relevance of the EU in Russian external relations is growing along with the EU's increasing economic engagement in Russia.

The European Union is of crucial importance to Russia's economy. The EU is leading in foreign direct investment in Russia; furthermore, it is Russia's single largest trading partner, although the share of Russian exports to the EU as a percentage of total exports has been decreasing since 1992. Russia primarily delivers energy,[68] raw materials, and metals, having achieved substantial trade surpluses over the past years. Just over 33 percent of Russia's total exports in 1997 were directed to the EU market, with Germany as the single largest trading partner; this is by far the highest proportion of exports to the EU by any country of the CIS. In 1998, the value of Russian exports to the EU was U.S.$23.2 billion, 32.5 percent of overall exports.[69] Russian exports to the ten EU associated countries in Central and Eastern Europe (EU-10) plus Croatia and Albania made up another 14.7 percent of total Russian exports in 1997; in 1998 this rate was roughly the same (14.6 percent). Imports from the EU accounted for 36.1 percent of all Russian imports in 1998, with a nominal value of U.S.$15.7 billion. Nine percent of Russian imports in 1998 came from the EU-10 plus Albania and Croatia. Both Russian imports from and exports to the EU declined substantially in the second half of 1998 and in 1999 as a result of the financial crash of August 1998. Exports decreased by 17.1 and 13.2 percent in 1998 and 1999, respectively, imports by 19.6 and 42.7 percent. Germany is the leading Russian trading partner in the EU. In 1998, Germany accounted for 17.5 percent of all Russian imports, and 10.9 percent of Russia's exports were directed to Germany.

CONCLUSION

Based on a rational-choice assumption, Russia has no alternative to undertaking cooperative relations with Western countries. Russia lacks the means and resources to pursue a strategy of confrontation. If it were to choose such an option, it would be irrational and most likely come at the detriment of Russia. Russia would also be without any powerful allies in an aggressive anti-Western campaign; rogue states such as Iraq and Libya can hardly be considered reliable and helpful comrades-in-arms. But the most important factor for Russia's Western initiative is its dependency on Western assistance in modernizing its moribund economic, financial, and social structures. This modernization effort, in contrast, is a sine qua non for Russia's reemergence as a great power.

The pragmatic, cooperative Western approach Russia has opted for since 1997 is most likely to prevail for years to come. However, this holds true only if the benefits outweigh the political costs. As long as Western partners of a transforming Russia are willing and able to provide reasonable opportunities, the structural imperative of Russia's Western orientation will prevail for any Russian leadership. Nevertheless, Russia will—for a long time to come—

remain a tumbling actor in the international arena, struggling hard to retain a position considered dignified for a power seeking to recapture a glorious past.

NOTES

1. Both the Russian National Security Concept of December 1997 and the revised version of the Security Concept signed by interim President Putin on January 12, 2000, state that the main threats to Russian security are primarily of domestic origin, many of them having a nonmilitary nature. The report addresses prominently the socioeconomic crisis as a threat to the national security of Russia, the erosion of Russia's scientific-technological basis and the growing dependence on external technologies and know-how, the expanding position of foreign firms in various sectors of the Russian market, and ecological threats. Moreover, the threat to the society by organized crime and the penetration of state structures by criminal elements are highlighted in the report. To avert these threats, political, economic, demographic, and ecological means are required. For the current Security Concept, see *Nezavisimoye Voennoye Obozreniye*, January 14, 2000.

2. Paul Marantz (1997) "Russian Foreign Policy During Yeltsin's Second Term," *Communist and Post-Communist Studies* 4, no. 199: 345–352, esp. 348.

3. Gerhard Simon (1997) *Rußland auf der Suche nach seiner politischen Identität: Visionen und Wirklichkeiten* (Köln: Berichte des BIOst 33).

4. Marantz (1997) "Russian Foreign Policy," p. 349.

5. The Security Concept had not been published at the time this article was finished.

6. Interfax, January 25, 2000.

7. The Russian State Committee for Statistics even speaks about 3.7 percent GDP growth in 1997. This number, however, is heavily contested by most economists. See *Moscow Times*, January 27, 2000.

8. Data from Josef Pöschl et al. (2000) "Transition Countries Clamber," p. 38.

9. *Voprosy ekonomiki* 12, 1999, p. 12.

10. *Nezavisimaya gazeta politekonomija*, November 23, 1999.

11. See especially Roland Götz (1994) *"Deindustrialisierung" Rußlands: Unabwendbares Schicksal oder Problem der Struktur–und Währungspolitik?* (Köln: Aktuelle Analysen des BIOst 50 [13.9.]); and Roland Götz (1994) *Regionale Aspekte der "Deindustrialisierung" in Rußland. Problemregionen kristallisieren sich heraus* (Köln: Aktuelle Analysen des BIOst 56 [30.9.]).

12. For a comprehensive overview on these issues, see Roland Götz (1997) *Wirtschaftswachstum in Rußland: Faktoren und Perspektiven* [Economic Growth in Russia: Factors and Prospects] (Köln: Berichte des BIOst 32).

13. Ognian Hishow (1999) *Der russische Haushalt 2000: Ein Beitrag zur finanziellen Konsolidierung?* (Köln: Aktuelle Analysen des BIOst 56 [30.11.]), p. 3.

14. According to the forecast, Russia's rating will roughly be the same as that of Bulgaria and Romania in the decade ahead, lagging dramatically behind Central European countries.

15. See Ognian Hishow (1999) *Rußland in der Schuldenfalle: Bedingungsloser Schuldenerlaß unzulässig* (Köln: Aktuelle Analysen des BIOst 4 [19.2.]).

16. Russia has paid only U.S.$5–6 billion in 1999. See Roland Götz (2000) *Die russische Wirtschaft im Jahr der Präsidentenwahl* (Köln: Aktuelle Analysen des BIOst 13 [10.2.]).

17. The real reasons for the suspension are more likely the effect of the money-laundering scandal with the Bank of New York made public in August 1999 and the Russian war against Chechnya.

18. By the end of March 2000, Russia had reached agreement with Austria and Spain on a further restructuring of its debt.

19. Interest rates will start with 2.5 percent and only after six years will rise to 7.5 percent. Previously, the interest rates had been 8.5 percent.

20. According to cautious calculations, Russia will need at least U.S.$5 billion to service its debt vis-à-vis the IMF and the World Bank and approximately U.S.$1.7 billion for its eurobond obligations.

21. Marantz (1997), p. 348.

22. *Segodnya*, January 26, 2000.

23. See Murray Feshbach (1999) "A Sick and Shrinking Nation," *Washington Post*, October 24, 1999. See also *Kommersant—Vlast'* 5, 2000; Trud, 22.2.2000.

24. Alexei G. Arbatov (1998) "Military Reform in Russia: Dilemmas, Obstacles, and Prospects," *International Security* 4 (Spring): 83–134, esp. 83.

25. Dale R. Herspring (1997) "The Future of the Russian Military," *Problems of Post-Communism* 2 (March-April): 47–56, esp. 51. The "rapid decay" of Russia's combat readiness has more recently been confirmed in a report by the U.S. State Department handed over to Congress on February 19, 1999. See *Moscow Times*, February 23, 1999.

26. Joachim Schmidt-Skipiol (1997) *Die Militärreform in Rußland, Teil I: Sachstandsbericht* (Köln: Aktuelle Analysen des BIOst 48 [25.9.]) and *Teil II: Ausblick* (Köln: Aktuelle Analysen des BIOst 49 [25.9.]).

27. The International Institute for Strategic Studies (IISS) estimated Russian defense expenditure as 7 percent of GDP in both 1996 and 1997, down from 12 percent in 1992. See IISS (1997) *The Military Balance, 1997/1998* (London: Oxford University Press), p. 107.

28. RFE/RL Newsline, February 29, 2000; Reuters, March 7, 2000.

29. See Alexei G. Arbatov (1998) "Military Reform in Russia: Dilemmas, Obstacles, and Prospects," *International Security* 4 (Spring): 83–134, esp. 87–88. In an interview with the Russian daily *Segodnya* on December 29, 1998, Russian Defense Minister Sergeev once referred to the nuclear potential as the cornerstone of Russian defense.

30. This program is usually referred to as the "Mikhaylov Plan," after a previous Russian minister for nuclear energy and nuclear industries.

31. Hans-Henning Schröder (1997) *Die russischen Militärausgaben, 1995–1997: Eine Auswertung der Haushaltsdaten* (Köln: Berichte des BIOst 23), p. 38.

32. Richard L. Kugler (1996) *Enlarging NATO: The Russia Factor* (Santa Monica, Calif.: Rand), p. 41.

33. Olga Alexandrova and Heinz Timmermann (1997) *Rußland—Belarus—GUS: Integrationsbestrebungen und Desintegrationstendenzen* (Köln: Berichte des BIOst 30), p. 26.

34. For a recent assessment of the CIS since its creation, see Richard Sakwa and Mark Webber (1999) "The Commonwealth of Independent States, 1991–1998: Stagnation and Survival," *Europe-Asia Studies* 51, no. 3 (May): 379–415.

35. Quoted in *Jamestown Foundation Monitor*, December 8, 1998.

36. United Nations Economic Commission for Europe (1999) *Economic Survey of Europe, no. 3* <http://www.unece.org/ead/ead_h.htm>.

37. Andrei Zagorski (1997) "Die Politik Rußlands gegenüber der GUS—zwischen Anspruch und Wirklichkeit," *Österreichische Zeitschrift für Politikwissenschaft* 3 ("Rußländische Transformationen: Räume, Akteure, Felder"): 319–329.

38. The cohesion of GUUAM was fading in the early months of 2000. Both Moldova and Uzbekistan have signaled reservations about security cooperation within that group; several prescheduled meetings have been cancelled, notably one of defense ministers. On the occasion of Ukrainian President Leonid Kuchma's visits to Georgia and Azerbaijan in March 2000, however, plans for forming a peacekeeping battalion involving Ukraine, Georgia, and Azerbaijan have reportedly been discussed.

39. Olga Alexandrova and Heinz Timmermann (1997) *Rußland—Belarus—GUS*.

40. Interfax, March 26, 1998.

41. In an interview with the radio station Echo Moskvy on January 10, 1999, however, former First Deputy Prime Minister Boris Nemtsov suggested that the Russian government had calculated in 1998 that monthly costs for the integration of Belarus would be roughly U.S.\$100 million per month. In this interview Nemtsov—in a remarkable U-turn—suggested that the price would be worth it for geopolitical and military reasons. Nemtsov has repeated and elaborated on this new position by Russian liberals at the meeting of the organizing committee of the right-of-center political coalition Pravoye Delo (Just Cause); see ITAR-TASS and Interfax, January 20–21, 1999.

42. Interfax, December 28, 1998.

43. For the full text of the agreement, see *Diplomaticheskij Vestnik* 5 (May): 39–42.

44. See *Rossiskaya gazeta*, April 3, 1997.

45. For the text of the charter, see *Rossiskaya gazeta*, May 24, 1997.

46. The common budget of the Union is in fact very small—only a few million dollars are dedicated for common projects. In 1998, Russia has paid only 27 percent of its share of the budget, whereas Belarus has lived up to 90 percent of its financial commitments. See *Jamestown Foundation Monitor*, January 22, 1999.

47. Figures provided by ITAR-TASS, February 12, 1999.

48. This "decapitation" of Russia's status as a great power by the perseverance of an independent Ukraine is particularly strongly emphasized in Zbigniew Brzezinski (1997) *The Grand Chessboard: American Primacy and Its Geostrategic Imperatives* (New York: Basic Books).

49. The same holds true to a certain extent for Russian relations with Iran.

50. *The Economist*, April 26, 1997, p. 19.

51. The crucial role in Russian arms deliveries holds true also for India. Approximately 80 percent of the Indian army's equipment is Russian. The latest deal was signed on December 18, 1998, ordering ten Russian Su-30K fighters for the Indian air forces.

52. *The Economist*, April 26, 1997, p. 20.

53. Jennifer Anderson (1997) *The Limits of Sino-Russian Strategic Partnership*, Adelphi Paper 315 (Oxford: Oxford University Press), p. 36. Robert J. Art (1998) "Creating a Disaster: NATO's Open Door Policy," *Political Science Quarterly* 113, no. 3 (Fall): 383–404, esp. 391.

54. Interfax, November 14, 1999.

55. ITAR-TASS, February 6, 1999. Similar figures are given by the Chinese Customs Office. See Xinhua (in English), February 22, 1999. These figures were confirmed by the Vienna Institute for International Economic Studies. Total trade volume in U.S. dollars for 1999 has been calculated by the author on the basis of data given for January–November 1999.

56. Art (1998) "Creating a Disaster," pp. 383–404, esp. p. 393.

57. See Interfax, December 25, 1996. Rodionov made this assessment while addressing a Moscow conference of CIS members on military cooperation. He also mentioned Iran as a potential threat to Russian security.

58. Dmitri Trenin (2000) "Russian-Chinese Relations: A Study in Contemporary Geopolitics," in Erich Reiter (ed.) (2000) *Jahrbuch für Internationale Sicherheitspolitik 2000* (Hamburg: E. S. Mittler), pp. 913–930.

59. Stephen Blank and Alvin Z. Rubinstein (1997) "Is Russia Still a Power in Asia?" *Problems of Post-Communism* 2 (March-April): 37–46, esp. 41.

60. On Russian relations with Iran, see Vitaly Naumkin (1998) "The Russian-Iranian Relations: Present Status and Propsects for the Future," *Perceptions* 3, no. 1 (March-April): 67–85.

61. See Reuters, December 21, 1998.

62. These expectations were clearly expressed in the address of President Yeltsin to the Security Council of the United Nations on January 31, 1992; see Reuters, January 31, 1992.

63. Interfax, October 28, 1992.

64. Interview by Foreign Minister Primakov in *Izvestya*, March 6, 1996.

65. The ratification of START II—signed back in January 1993 by Presidents Bush and Yeltsin and ratified by the U.S. Senate in January 1996—has still (as of April 2000) not been ratified by the Russian Duma. However, it seems likely that the Duma that was elected in December 1999 will allow ratification of the treaty in the forthcoming months. President Putin as well as the Ministries of Defense and Foreign Affairs are pushing for a speedy ratification in order to start negotiations on START III. A framework agreement between the United States and Russia on the scope of ICBM reductions under START III and a common understanding of the future of the ABM Treaty would definitely make ratification easier.

66. Ideological competition, which had been a crucial element in the U.S.-Soviet conflict in the past decades, however, has gone, since Russia is unable to provide a credible and viable alternative concept for sociopolitical development.

67. See *Jamestown Foundation Monitor*, April 3, 2000.

68. In 1997, total Russian exports were worth U.S.$88.7 billion, 48 percent of which came from the export of crude oil, oil products, natural gas, and petrochemical products. In 1998, the revenue from the export goods was expected to be down to U.S.$28.4 billion (41.8 percent of total export revenues); see Reuters, November 23, 1998.

69. United Nations Economic Commission for Europe (1999) *Economic Survey of Europe, no. 3* <http://www.unece.org/ead/ead_h.htm>.

19

China: Global or Regional Player? Great Power, Partner, or Chaotic Power?

KAY MÖLLER

Since the mid-1990s,[1] much of the outside view of the People's Republic of China (PRC) has been based on the assumption of its more or less peaceful evolution into a more or less authoritarian, but certainly strong and unitary, actor.[2] Although the details of this process are uncertain,[3] China's economic success and its leadership's supposed ability to cope with domestic and external challenges have been taken as proof for the inevitable emergence of a new international player whose historical aversion to cooperation and interdependence might be diluted through cognitive learning.[4] As soon as the United States had understood that the PRC could not, and possibly never would, be able to challenge U.S. dominance of Pacific markets and sea-lanes by military means,[5] constructive engagement was the logical outcome. Through this approach, Washington proposed "to act with China where we agree, to foster greater consensus where the picture is mixed, and to prevent or minimize conflict where we disagree."[6] This allowed China to decide for itself whether, and in which field, bilateral progress would be made. When Presidents Bill Clinton and Jiang Zemin met for their first official summit in Washington in October 1997, and when the United States went as far as offering Beijing consultations on its alliance with Japan,[7] the PRC found itself recognized as the most important strategic partner of the United States in the Western Pacific. Earlier, the Clinton administration had actually abandoned enlargement as an operative strategy to be applied to China, had accepted Beijing's terms for the settlement of the Korea problem, and had tacitly consented to a more visible Chinese security role in much of mainland Southeast Asia as well as on the western shores of the South and East China Seas. Taiwan was the last immediate obstacle to a long-term U.S.-Chinese understanding, with both Clinton and Jiang trying to prolong the status quo through symbolic concessions made by the island republic. At the global level, the PRC's great-power status had been much less evident, but Beijing appeared increasingly ready to accept international norms in areas that had little or no immediate relevance for East Asia.[8]

The U.S. (and general outside) approach remains problematic in the sense that it may be questioned whether the Chinese side has actually started accepting interdependence as a fact or life or, conversely, whether it still conceives of interdependence as a threat and whether there will be sufficient time available for the economic imperative to prevail over Beijing's traditional obsession with power politics. In attempting an answer, I examine China's foreign policy perceptions and actual policies since the early 1990s, the premises for continued economic growth, and, by implication, domestic political stability, as well as possible alternative power configurations involving the PRC.

THE DISSATISFIED POWER

Its permanent seat on the UN Security Council and nuclear-power status notwithstanding, the PRC fulfills certain quantitative qualifications for great-power status (territory, human and natural resources, historical continuity). Its military modernization remains slow and selective, but there are pockets of excellence that have already impressed smaller neighbors and will be further developed.[9] By focusing its external strategy on politics, the region, and sovereignty, however, the PRC appears to have undermined this theoretical status by a lack of flexibility and global reach.

The Political Imperative

China's economic success is to a significant extent driven by exports. Including Hong Kong, the export share of gross domestic product (GDP) was around 40 percent during the first half of the decade. Of this, 40 percent was consumed by the U.S. market. This explains why Beijing, following the Tiananmen Square incident in June 1989 and preceding President Clinton's delinkage of most-favored-nation status (MFN) and human rights in May 1994, made occasional and short-lived concessions to the United States on the protection of intellectual property, arms exports, and human rights. Since then, both sides have been occasionally balancing on the brink of a trade war, and Beijing confined most dissidents to prison and labor camps before exporting a few prominent ones to the United States in 1997 and 1998. For the time being, China has no alternative export markets. One may therefore assume that constructive engagement has been partly responsible for the failure of interdependence, prompting China to assume a more responsible global role.

In 1986, the PRC had applied for membership in the General Agreement on Tariffs and Trade (GATT). Negotiations with the United States were successfully concluded in late 1999, but it remains to be seen whether China can build on this success to accelerate the opening of its markets. At the time of this writing, fears of an uncontrolled collapse of the state sector and subsequent social unrest have not abated, and the political imperative remains dominant in Beijing. During the early days of the Deng Xiaoping era in 1979, the PRC, provoked by Hanoi's intervention in Cambodia, invaded its Vietnamese neighbor. Ten years later, China's nascent democracy movement was smashed on Tiananmen Square. In that case, the context of power politics was evident. As to the Vietnamese conflict, it has emerged that the campaign was meant as a test for the People's Liberation Army (PLA), which withdrew under humiliating circumstances.

If one were to adopt the Chinese line of reasoning, many elements of this policy could also be explained in economic terms.[10] Whereas this may explain Beijing's latent disposition to resort to force, it does not make it any more acceptable.

The Regional Imperative

China has been a member of the UN and a permanent member of its Security Council since 1971, and it has twice vetoed Security Council decisions that were unrelated to the nomination of the UN Secretary-General. In the first veto, in 1972, it opposed Bangladesh's UN membership; in the second, in January 1997, it vetoed a peacekeeping mission in Guatemala that would have supervised observation of the cease-fire between the Guatemalan government and guerrillas. The second veto was imposed because Guatemala had diplomatic relations with Taiwan and had supported Taipei's campaign for readmission to the UN. It was dropped as soon as the Central American state promised to discontinue that support.[11]

Samuel Kim has characterized China's contributions to the development of internationally binding norms and global political order as "symbolic rather than substantial."[12] The picture is somewhat different if one looks at international power politics and power balances, a field in which China has been feeling at home since at least the third century B.C. When the Beijing politburo in September 1993 decided to challenge Pax Americana and thus risk MFN, it was stated that there were "serious internal contradictions in the West [that] prevent the [United States] from making . . . relations with China entirely acute."[13] Western Europe was seen as one possible counterweight, as it had demonstrated more pragmatism during the months following Tiananmen. That is why the PRC was initially skeptical about German unification,[14] and it took post-Maastricht irritations and Europe's failure in the former

Yugoslavia to convince China of the continued importance of strong national states such as Germany.[15]

Russia and Japan were potential new poles, but Beijing felt even more suspicious about them than it felt about a German Europe. It is true that since 1991 the PRC has imported Russian arms worth about U.S.$10 billion and that Russia has been the only partner with whom substantial CSBMs were agreed. Since 1996, China has even spoken up against NATO's eastward extension.[16] Yet Beijing always suspected Yeltsin of being tempted to sell out his independence to the West. Furthermore, the PRC has been more than reluctant to help Moscow make a diplomatic impact on the same Northeast Asia that it had been unable to conquer by military means.[17]

Japan had to be kept on a leash, as it presented a theoretical obstacle to China's power projection in Northeast and Southeast Asia. Until the late 1980s, the leash was a combination of U.S. hegemony and the PRC's own economic attraction. Based on a small anti-Soviet triangle, Beijing had occasionally been able to play U.S. military power against Japan and Japanese economic power against Washington. Following the demise of the Soviet Union, China's regional ambitions and Tokyo's preventive defense have increasingly become contradictory. The United States has tried to defuse the situation through a trilateral exercise in confidence building, yet Tokyo remains faced with dilemmas in Korea and Taiwan, and Beijing harbors no illusions about the U.S.-Japanese alliance being anything but a bulwark against itself. In the sense that military China has been obstructing economic China, any decrease in PRC economic attraction would make the security problem much more acute.

One hastens to add that Beijing's global strategic thinking is not founded in theoretical ambition, let alone hopes for a peace dividend. It is rather based on a hierarchy of objectives, in which national interest and the PRC's periphery continue to play the most important part. This can cause miscalculations as to third-party responses. Concessions on world order and regional order have been made vis-à-vis Washington, for example, so as to make the United States reaffirm its adherence to the principle of Chinese unity. Nuclear proliferation has been a concern insofar as Beijing would like to avoid it on its own periphery. Nuclear weapons–free zones have been addressed only in areas of little interest to the PLA and the Chinese navy. If, in 1990, the PRC abstained from vetoing the allied military intervention against Iraq, it was because of a desire to break out of its post-Tiananmen isolation and to convince the U.S. administration under George Bush to revoke several sanctions.

The major conclusion to be drawn from this regional imperative: one should not expect China to act more responsibly in the region and worldwide because it is being offered global prestige or is being threatened with international sanctions. Beijing's participation in the 1991 Cambodian peace process was motivated by the correct understanding that this would help minimize third-party involvement in Cambodia and thus automatically increase the PRC's own influence (since 1996, Beijing has even been cultivating former adversary Hun Sen). As to the nuclear problem in Korea and an armistice regime, however, China has prevented the UN from playing a major role, because geography and history suggested that only bilateral secret diplomacy would maximize PRC influence. Whenever Beijing has signaled its readiness to respect international arms-control agreements such as the Missile Technology Control Regime, it was only because Beijing correctly expected a quid pro quo from its negotiating partner (the United States, in most cases). One may ask, however, whether regional pressure or the offer of regional prestige would make a difference.

The Sovereign Principle

One need not read books such as *A China That Can Say No* and *Will the Chinese Army Win the Next War?* to find an explosive mixture of nationalism, anti-Americanism, and anti-Japanism. Deng Xiaoping himself, when defending the June 1989 suppression of China's democracy movement, talked about a "CIA-led conspiracy" designed to subvert a PRC that had become vulnerable to "peaceful evolution" through economic opening-up.[18] At the very moment when the disappearance of the Soviet Union and the liberation of its productive potential had removed the most important obstacles to China's regional dominance, the "civilization pretending to be a state"[19] whose worldview matched "the late 16th rather than the late 20th century"[20] found itself besieged and contained by a U.S.-led coalition.[21]

In September 1993, the Beijing politburo, pushed by the PLA leadership, agreed on the following guidelines for relations with Washington: China will not seek confrontation, but neither will it try to avoid it, and China will not shy away from confrontation if Washington provokes it.[22] Prior to this, the United States had stopped and inspected a Chinese cargo ship suspected of transporting chemical weapons components to Iran (the suspicions could not be confirmed). Shortly afterward, the PRC blamed "Western interference" for the failure of Beijing's bid for the 2000 Olympics. Since March 1993, China had accused Washington of obstructing its accession to GATT. In October 1994, both sides narrowly avoided a military clash in international waters in the Yellow Sea.

Had the PLA's foreign policy role become visible on these occasions, it could no longer be overlooked during the escalation following the Taiwanese president's "private" visit to the United States in June 1995. Confronted with a domestic power struggle and military pressure, Jiang Zemin was practically forced to try out certain strategies for raising the ante in the Taiwan Strait. When Jiang tried again during Taiwan's March 1996 presidential election campaign, Clinton dispatched two carrier groups, and the PLA's maneuvers were less than successful. However, no blame was attributed in public.

It is over Taiwan that the contradiction between the Westphalian world-view and the world of enlargement becomes most visible. Since 1972, Beijing has repeatedly told Washington that it views Taiwan as being at the center of its own national agenda and of the U.S.-Chinese relationship. It was not before the 1990s, however, that the PRC showed some urgency in trying to solve this problem. Washington had accepted the principle of Chinese unity in 1972 on the condition that realization, let alone realization by force, was not a medium-term perspective. This caused misunderstandings between policies based on future expectations, on the one hand, and those of the U.S. national security adviser on the other. By 1996, Clinton had understood the risk and tried to offer China compensation. By 1999, it had become clear that compensation was not enough, with the PRC raising the ante over the bombing of its Belgrade embassy by a U.S. cruise missile. On Taiwan proper, Washington has so far had little leeway for mediation. As long as this remains the case, there is considerable potential for conflict. And because of Beijing's attempt to replace Marxism with nationalism, such conflict has considerable potential for escalation.

There is no historical precedence for the successful binding of an irredentist power that has only started to develop into a modern national state. If many analysts have been cautiously optimistic, however, then it is because of their belief that European experiences cannot be transplanted onto East Asia and that it would be possible to stabilize the region even in the absence of a high degree of verifiable and sanctionable CSBMs. This, in turn, must be explained by economic and cultural factors.[23] East Asia's economic crisis undermined many of these premises in the late 1990s, but even in the absence of economic crisis it would have been easy to understand that a country of China's size, were it to solve its multiple conflicts without resorting to force, required constitutional change. Minimal conditions to be fulfilled would include replacing the political imperative with an economic imperative, providing transparency at home and abroad, and viewing the world in functional rather than moral categories. In the following section, I examine whether China's current domestic context could be conducive to such a change.

THE FRAGMENTING STATE

Leninist China has survived Tiananmen, but Tiananmen will continue to haunt it if economic reform comes to a halt. Recently, there have been indications that this may be the case.[24]

In 1997, East Asia's hitherto booming economies fell victim to a dramatic economic crisis. Backed by governments and encouraged by foreign investors, local businessmen had borrowed money at home and abroad, which was frequently invested into overcapacity or prestige projects. International financial speculators were alerted to the resulting weakness and launched attacks against regional currencies, which subsequently fell 50 percent and more against the U.S. dollar. To avoid a gigantic wave of insolvencies, some governments had to call in the International Monetary Fund, whose initial austerity prescriptions contributed to social and political instability in cases like Indonesia.

Basically, Jiangist China is confronted with similar, albeit much larger, problems. Some 50–70 percent of the liquid assets of state enterprises are covered by short-term commercial credit. Property speculation escalated during the early 1990s. Three of four state-owned commercial banks are technically insolvent. Almost two-thirds of all liquid bank assets consist of savings, but people would start withdrawing their money if they lost confidence in the regime's economic management. Irretrievable credit adds up to about 20 percent of GDP (Japan 15 percent, South Korea 8 percent), or about U.S.$200 billion (currency reserves were U.S.$140 billion in 1997). A bailout package announced in February 1998 could yet backfire if it does not inspire more lending discipline. That is much less likely, however, as the central bank has so far been unable to cut through the net of relationships among state-owned banks and local politicians.

Prior to 1998, a nonconvertible currency, strong domestic demand, and the steady inflow of foreign direct investment (FDI) more or less cured China of the East Asian flu. However, all three barriers have become porous. If the PRC does indeed join the World Trade Organization (WTO), the renminbi has to be gradually made convertible. Domestic demand for consumer goods, which has so far accounted for 50 percent of GDP, has been stagnating, with sellers trying to undercut one another. The real estate market has also stagnated, and enterprises are having problems repaying loans. With markets for consumer goods and investment goods saturated, a decrease in domestic demand can hardly be fought by lowering interest rates. There is less foreign capital than in neighboring countries that might be withdrawn at short notice,[25] but with FDI drying up the entire system risks collapse. Investments into Southeast Asia have become cheaper and offer considerably higher returns. Devaluation of the renminbi, which would confront the entire region, especially Hong Kong, with dramatic consequences, cannot be ruled out in the short term.

Since the late 1980s, foreign investors have not made substantial profits on the Chinese market.[26] Whereas joint-venture costs most of the time exceeded expectations, returns on the Chinese market were disappointing. Chinese partners often turned out to be unable or insolvent. Corruption escalated, and the domestic market remains overregulated. Agreed FDI has decreased since 1997. With more than three-quarters of all FDI originating in East Asia, the overall volume is likely to stagnate in years to come, and so could PRC exports.

In October 1997, the Fifteenth Congress of the Chinese Communist Party (CCP) addressed, but did not solve, a few of the fundamental problems. Reelected to the position of CPC chairman, Jiang Zemin called on China's 118,000 state enterprises[27] to start issuing shares. As transpired later, 512 large enterprises, representing about 50 percent of the state sector's overall value, were to be exempted, with others to be taken over by the CCP. The rest would survive through the issuing of shares to individuals and other state enterprises, the founding of joint ventures, or the dismissal of workers. In these cases, too, the state would maintain at least a significant share.[28]

Most of the enterprises in question have been taking losses, and had the program been consequently applied, one-third of 100 million industrial workers would have lost their jobs (surplus labor in the countryside has been estimated at 150 million people).[29] Some 70 million inhabitants in the countryside have already migrated to the cities. Of these, about 20 percent have found employment; the remaining workers would have incurred dramatic losses in their social welfare. A social net would have to be put in place by the privatizing enterprises themselves, but most of them do not have sufficient capital for this task. Privatization was slowed down in mid-1998, but social pressures had already risen. Since 1997, there has been a dramatic increase in demonstrations by unemployed workers, in addition to endemic rural unrest.

China requires a GDP growth of at least 8 percent to create sufficient employment to contain large-scale social conflict. In 1996, official GDP growth decreased from 9.7 percent to 8.8 percent over the previous year (in 1993, growth was still more than 13 percent). Estimates for 1999 are about 7 percent, the lowest growth rate since 1990.[30] Furthermore, official statistics are unreliable, and actual growth may have been 2–3 percent lower than declared. New employment has been created only by rural collectives and private enterprises, but even in these cases growth has started to flatten. Between 1996 and 1997, state-sector productivity decreased from 17.7 to 11 percent. Up to 1997, China's exports continued to grow by about 20 percent per year, but this sector has come under the pressure of devaluations in neighboring countries. In early 1998, a three-year infrastructure program worth U.S.\$750 billion was announced. Even in the unlikely case that such a goal can be realized, the program came too late to stimulate growth in 1998 and 1999. All this makes a new round of privatization less than likely.[31]

Jiang Zemin found himself confronted with these problems at a time when his position at home had consolidated and the PRC's international standing had improved. On 1 July 1997, he brought Hong Kong home. In October 1997, he succeeded in purging most potential challengers, not least the military ones, from the politburo's standing committee.[32] Also in October, he agreed with President Clinton on a far-reaching improvement in bilateral relations and had implicitly been offered U.S. recognition of a Chinese zone of influence in East Asia. As early as 1994, Clinton had delinked MFN and human rights because of business lobbying and mounting tensions on the Korean peninsula.

By 2000, this consolidation had been called into doubt once again. Jiang had clamped down on the democratic and religious opposition and had once again raised the ante in the Taiwan Strait. Relations with Washington looked increasingly shaky over these developments, as well as allegations of large-scale Chinese spying by the United States. The 2000 U.S. presidential campaign threatened to bring all these issues into the spotlight.

Jiang's personal dilemma reflects China's fundamental problems. He views market forces as subversive, and he is part of a coalition that has profited from continued restrictions. Still, he knows that any attempt to obstruct market dynamics will endanger further growth and thus undermine social cohesion. He used to believe that an adjustment of Beijing's and Washington's national interests was possible even with regard to Taiwan, but such an adjustment has repeatedly been sabotaged by domestic factions on all three sides. If Jiang were a strong leader in the mold of Mao or Deng, he could solve some of these contradictions through courageous policies. But instead of being a strong leader, he remains the compromise candidate of 1989 who owes his office to political murder and the final decoupling of the ruling elite from Chinese society. Therefore, and because China is still unprepared for "normal" authoritarian politics (as in Singapore), peaceful evolution, at least for the time being, remains the most unlikely scenario. Under a best-case scenario, Jiang would steer his rolling ship through the shallow waters of more, perhaps smaller, Tiananmens. In the worst case, civil war could break out, accompanied by tensions along the periphery. The Pacific century would have to be postponed indefinitely, but it has already been postponed anyway, and from the viewpoint of global and regional order, it would have been more problematic in the guise of a Chinese century than anything else.

PAX SINICA

Pax Sinica, from the Han Dynasty down to Deng Xiaoping, has rarely meant occupying territories. It has instead implied assuring China's dominance by establishing a balance of powers among smaller neighbors and by denying third parties a major role along China's borders.[33] On the one hand, this classic realist policy, exercised by an autocratic state, confronts the contemporary region and world with several risks. On the other hand, Pax Americana has so far imposed limits on Beijing's influence, and Pax Americana could in the medium term be replaced only by a new multipolar balance or common/cooperative security. There is no new hegemony on the horizon.

Cooperative Security

Profiting from the end of the Cold War and general prosperity, regional players, including a reluctant United States and a reluctant China, have experimented with cooperative models since the early 1990s, both viewing them as a supplement to rather than a replacement of power politics. Beijing's participation in CSBMs has been ad hoc and conditional. As China's lingering trade conflict with Washington shows, the PRC until recently has been reluctant to let itself be tied in economically. Beijing has accepted multilateral exchanges at a low level of obligations whenever it expected to win privileges and prestige in the absence of major concessions. In the framework of the Asia-Pacific Economic Cooperation (APEC) forum, for example, none of the problems that continued to obstruct China's accession to the WTO could be brought closer to resolution.

Since the end of the Cold War, the PRC has introduced certain elements from the catalog of European CSBMs into its relations with several continental neighbors (Russia, Kazakhstan, Kyrgyzstan, Tajikistan, and India). In contrast to the situation in Europe, the solution of unsettled border problems was more a principal motive of than a precondition for discussing or implementing CSBMs. In practice, this has involved only minor changes. The stabilization of the territorial status quo was used only in a few exceptional cases as a means to arrive at further security arrangements. Whenever China was unsatisfied with the status quo (e.g., Vietnam, because of related maritime claims), CSBMs were only discussed (if Tajikistan has been an exception to this rule, it is only because of the larger Russian context; see below). Wherever the status quo was to China's advantage (as in India), CSBMs could be implemented even in the absence of a border agreement. As Russia represents the only case in which confidence and security building has significantly progressed beyond the stage of discussions, it would appear that the combination of a serious potential adversary and good or satisfactory overall relations has been a stronger incentive for Beijing than, for example, the Vietnamese case at the other end of the spectrum. To the extent that good relations presuppose similar approaches to Western interference, Beijing's assertions regarding the insignificance of ideology as a determining factor should be read with reservations. Therefore, if the PRC understands its April 1996 agreement with Russia, Kazakhstan, Kyrgyzstan, and Tajikistan as a model for the future organization of Asia-Pacific security, this does not constitute a quantum leap in Chinese strategic thinking. China's interest in a multipolar world is an interest in balances, not in regimes. And even in cases where the above-mentioned condition is fulfilled, several years may pass before an agreement in principle is technically implemented.

The Vietnamese case also attests to a Chinese reluctance to solve territorial conflicts with a maritime dimension. This aversion is due to an increased importance of territorial seas and exclusive economic zones for the PRC's economic and military strategies, as well as to the expectation to be in a better position to realize maritime claims following successful overall modernization. Therefore, apart from agreement on certain principles, maritime

CSBMs have been implemented neither with Japan nor with Southeast Asian neighbors. Whereas Japan and the United States fulfill the qualifications for serious potential adversaries, they do not live up to the criteria of good or satisfactory overall relations. Chinese concessions made to Washington and Tokyo, therefore, do not enter the context of confidence and security building but are rather offered on a quid pro quo basis, with Japan being additionally confronted with its historical guilt.

Beijing's bilateral diplomacy has been dictated by a hierarchy of interests (priority for strategic goals in maritime areas to the east and southeast, lower priority for similar goals to the north and southwest) and expectations as to related responses by the parties concerned. Those expectations could prove deceptive to the extent that China, in applying its own realist parameters, has tended to ignore the role played by society and world order in the foreign policies of others. Under this approach, Washington and Tokyo automatically became competitors trying to subvert the PRC from the inside (through peaceful evolution) and from the outside (through engagement). Actually, both tried to avoid a Chinese collapse as much as they tried to prevent Chinese expansionism and held on to their respective security dialogues with China even after Beijing had seriously damaged them. Taking into account public opinion, Delhi could not have become a strategic partner, even if the PRC had stopped supporting Pakistan and if India had not tested the atom bomb. And with regard to Moscow, structural incompatibilities among two neighboring continental powers would eventually have outweighed the relative advantages of a common anti-Western policy.

Beijing's participation in multilateral fora of confidence building (especially in the context of the South China Sea problem) has not been prompted by an expectation to solve territorial problems along the lines of bilateral dialogues with continental neighbors. As a matter of principle, the softening of state sovereignty inherent in multilateral processes is viewed with suspicion. To the PRC, participating in the Association of Southeast Asian Nations (ASEAN) and the ASEAN Regional Forum (ARF) has been a matter of prestige. At the same time, ARF's terms of reference inspired hopes for improving relations with ASEAN at the expense of the United States while sparing China binding agreements on hard issues. It was helpful that Washington, too, has not been ready to modify its dominating role and its preference for strategic ambiguity for the sake of far-reaching transparency in areas such as weapons technology and military doctrine. The same reluctance has applied to many regional middle powers. Yet the United States and most Western Pacific nations share a common interest in maintaining the status quo, an interest that is underdeveloped in China, to put it mildly. Adherents of Eastern ways and constructivism may claim that readiness to talk is a confidence-building measure in itself. In the case of China, one would like to emphasize that military modernization, threatening gestures, and expansionist tendencies have continued independently of Beijing's participation in respective fora and that latent conflict could turn violent before this kind of confidence building will have produced operative conclusions.

Multipolar Balancing

Shortly before, for the first time in decades, economic crisis made it possible to meddle in East Asian domestic affairs and to extend the camp of democracies and market economies, the Clinton administration had factually abandoned enlargement in this part of the world. It had been replaced with more or less constructive dialogues with China, Indonesia, and North Korea, and Beijing had at least implicitly been offered a new strategic partnership during the October 1997 Washington Summit. The motive was foremost economic, only secondly related to regional strategies: since 1994, the United States has formulated its Pacific interests in a national rather than in a world context, has believed in China's inevitable rise to regional great-power status, has at the same time stopped believing in a serious military challenge emanating from Beijing, and has tried to defuse regional flashpoints such as Korea and Taiwan with Chinese help. As a consequence of these assumptions and objectives, an increase of PRC influence has been accepted on the periphery of Washington's own maritime sphere of interests. Thereby helping a relatively weak Jiang Zemin acquire prestige, the administration also tried to avoid the kind of 1995–1996 scenario under which military hardliners had prevailed over the politburo in provoking tensions in the Taiwan Strait.

Modernized in September 1997, the U.S.-Japanese alliance has prevented this constellation from turning into a new strategic triangle. However, Washington, by encouraging China and Japan, Japan and Korea (maybe both Koreas?), as well as Russia and Japan (significantly not Russia and China) to entertain their own security dialogues,[34] has implicitly accepted a higher degree of intraregional diversity. It was hoped that, for nonmembers, too, U.S. alliances could be turned into clearinghouses for the identification of joint objectives, thus making hegemony more cooperative.[35] In this case, too, the underlying assumption was that Washington's maritime dominance would not be threatened in the foreseeable future by any single player or coalition of players. Residual risks would be reduced by encouraging confidence building among regional players, and economic multipolarity might even turn out to be beneficial to the United States in its bilateral trade conflicts. Have these expectations been vindicated?

Russia–China–United States. Meeting with Bill Clinton in October 1997, PRC President Jiang Zemin promised stricter controls on the export of Chinese nuclear technology and renounced nuclear cooperation with Iran. In response, Clinton lifted an embargo on the export of nuclear technology to

China. Beijing also said it would reconsider delivery of cruise missiles to Iran. The two sides agreed on a regular strategic dialogue at all levels, on the creation of a government communications link for emergencies, and on negotiations for an agreement to avoid clashes at sea (the latter was signed by U.S. Secretary of Defense William Cohen in Beijing in January 1998). China announced it would buy fifty U.S. passenger aircraft. "Fundamental differences" prevented an agreement on human rights issues.[36]

At first glance, this result was the culmination of four years of comprehensive engagement. The compartmentalization of U.S. China policies into segments that could be alternatively activated had, among other things, led to the most extensive exchange on security ever, albeit one in which results often did not match efforts (it remains to be seen, for example, to what extent and for how long China's nuclear cooperation with Iran will indeed be frozen).

Lingering suspicions notwithstanding, Beijing has accepted engagement for as long as it promises relative gains, both ideally and materially. If the Washington Summit otherwise did not evolve beyond commonplaces, then it was because it was not the culmination of a successful security dialogue but an attempt to overcome the lowest point in U.S.-Chinese relations since the 1989 Tiananmen massacre, namely, the 1995–1996 crisis over Taiwan. In the Taiwan Strait, Beijing had formulated its challenge to Washington's leading role in the Pacific, and Beijing's propaganda had gone as far as questioning worldwide Pax Americana. The Chinese leadership was much too realist to believe in its own ability to terminate U.S. dominance through the Washington deal. Yet it had experienced how engaging the United States over Korea and Taiwan had temporarily led to an almost neutral U.S. stance between the opposing camps, and how the gradual expansion of China's own sphere of influence on the Southeast Asian mainland and in the South China Sea had been tacitly accepted. In 2000, China's leadership once again discussed the merits of forcing Taiwan to the negotiating table by military means.

As has been shown above, Russia is the only neighbor of the PRC with whom almost all territorial problems have been solved and with whom substantial CSBMs have been agreed. Russia remains China's most important source of arms technology. The United States, in its bilateral contacts, urged Moscow not to sell equipment at the technological level of the MiG-31, which could change the East Asian balance of power. However, not even these kinds of sales can be ruled out anymore, and licensed production of Russian arms inside China has been a cause of apprehension.

The strategic partnership proclaimed in April 1996 for the twenty-first century by Boris Yeltsin and Jiang Zemin in a sense only follows these developments. Even before this agreement, however, Moscow had threatened to intensify its relations with Beijing in case of an eastward extension of NATO,[37] and China had followed up with similar warnings. As a matter of principle, there is indeed a common Chinese-Russian interest in balancing the United States as the only remaining superpower. In this sense, NATO's extension is to Moscow what a modernized U.S.-Japanese alliance is to Beijing, and parallels were easily drawn between developments in Kosovo on the one hand and Taiwan, Tibet, and Chechnya on the other. Furthermore, both sides share an interest in maintaining stability and in containing religious and nationalist influences in Central Asia.[38]

Nevertheless, several political, economic, and strategic obstacles stand in the way of a further improvement of relations. Russia's Far East is home to 150 million citizens of the Russian Federation. On its Manchurian borders, Russia finds itself exposed to the demographic pressure of a few hundred million Chinese, and the number of Chinese immigrants to Siberia has been estimated at 1–8 million. Even if officially dropped, the PRC's territorial claims remain a source of friction at the local level. The region in question is six thousand kilometers and six time zones away from Moscow and is basically connected by two vulnerable links—the Transsiberian and Baikal-Amur railways. Russia's diplomats have tried to respond to U.S. and East Asian concerns over uncontrolled weapons sales. Even within Russia's Ministry of Defense, Chinese hegemony remains a future possibility.[39] China, for its part, expects a revival of Russian hegemonic ambitions and has been less than enthusiastic about Moscow's diplomatic initiatives in Northeast Asia. Arms exports notwithstanding, bilateral trade mainly consists of Russian imports of Chinese consumer goods, which has prevented respective industries from developing in Siberia. Moscow and Beijing are competitors for Western capital and Western economic aid.

Washington has been talking to each of the two about each of the two. That is no coordination of foreign policies, and a coordination of China's and Russia's U.S. strategies seems even more unlikely. In the words of Winston Lord, the U.S. State Department's assistant secretary for Asia and the Pacific at the time, "They [Russia and China] will stay between these extremes of hostility and a dangerous alliance, and we're very comfortable and therefore we welcome this improvement in their relationship."[40] The creation of an alliance as a counterweight to the Washington-Tokyo axis would serve as a self-fulfilling prophecy. There is still no strategic triangle among Russia, China, and the United States.

Russia-Japan-China. In the coming years, Russia and Japan could bring about the long-delayed rapprochement that would be a precondition for the creation of a regional triangle among Moscow, Beijing, and Tokyo. On paper, at least, then President Boris Yeltsin and Japanese Prime Minister Ryutaro Hashimoto, during their meeting in Siberia in October 1997, agreed to conclude a peace treaty by 2000, an agreement that would presuppose some kind of arrangement over the Kuriles question.[41] Subsequent normalization of relations is also hoped to stimulate Japanese participation in the economic development of the Russian Far East. A security dialogue has already been launched, and Moscow has promised to reprogram its nuclear missiles away from Japanese targets.[42]

It remains to be seen how and to what extent these intentions will be put into practice. With the standing at home of Japan's LDP government damaged by economic crisis and related scandals, political leaders may not be strong enough anymore to push through a Kuriles compromise. Given Russia's domestic situation, its economic attraction remains largely theoretical, and economic crisis is likely to even further diminish Japan's importance as a source of aid and FDI. Trade with Russia represents less than 1 percent of Japan's (and just about 7 percent of China's) total foreign trade.

So far, Tokyo, not unlike China, has tried to avoid giving Moscow a say in the future of Northeast Asia. Russia's initiatives on Korea, for example, have been met with reservations. The same has been true for Beijing's policies vis-à-vis Japan. Tokyo is even more concerned than Washington with Russian contributions to the PLA's modernization, but when raising this issue in Moscow, Japanese emissaries have received even more noncommittal replies than have the Americans. Beijing would not necessary welcome a far-reaching Russian-Japanese entente, but neither need it fear such a development as long as Tokyo is not a security player in its own right. Trilateral economic cooperation could be imagined under the UN's Tumen River Development Project, but Japan has so far been reluctant to look into this possibility.

If a strategic triangle among Moscow, Beijing, and Tokyo has not progressed beyond some rudimentary beginnings, then it is because of one long-standing feature of the Pacific security equation that would be difficult to change: the U.S.-Japanese alliance.

Japan–China–United States. As shown above, China had become concerned with Japanese unilateralism during the early 1990s. Beijing subsequently tried to win over Tokyo for joint regional initiatives.[43] Japan succeeded in convincing China to accede to the Nuclear Nonproliferation Treaty and to participate in several arms-control regimes. Within APEC, China and Japan together opposed U.S. demands for rapid and far-reaching trade liberalization. In May 1993, they agreed on a bilateral security dialogue to improve transparency in defense policies and to discuss regional issues.

Also in 1993, due to China's armed forces modernization, Japan's defense establishment came to view the PRC as a long-term threat. In May 1994, Japanese Prime Minister Morihiro Hosokawa failed to convince his Chinese counterparts of the merits of a higher degree of transparency on defense spending, military doctrine, and arms acquisitions, as well as common strategies vis-à-vis North Korea.[44] Provoked by continuing Chinese nuclear tests, Japan in 1995 suspended a small portion of its economic aid.

In November 1995, Jiang Zemin, on a visit to Seoul and in the presence of South Korean President Kim Young Sam, said that the future of Chinese-Japanese relations would depend on whether Tokyo would adopt a "correct view of its former militarism" or whether a "militaristic minority" would once again prevail in Japan.[45] The following year, tensions mounted over the Senkaku Islands in the East China Sea, a small group of rocks controlled by Japan and claimed by China.

Washington and Tokyo had recognized in 1995 that their permanent trade conflict was undermining their alliance at the very moment when new risks had surfaced in Korea and Taiwan. In April 1996, Clinton and Hashimoto agreed on maintaining a U.S. military presence in Japan at existing levels and signed an agreement on Japan's logistical support of these units in times of peace. In September 1997, this agreement was supplemented with new guidelines on cooperation during times of conflict. The necessity to review the 1978 guidelines transpired after U.S.–North Korean negotiations over Pyongyang's nuclear weapons program deadlocked in the summer of 1994 and the Pentagon began preparing for a preventive strike against North Korean facilities. The new guidelines provide for U.S. forces using Japanese airfields and ports in the event of conflict "in areas surrounding Japan"; for the support of U.S. operations by Japanese intelligence, minesweepers, and logistics (provision of weapons and ammunition excluded); as well as more extensive Japanese participation in UN peacekeeping measures.[46]

Beijing interpreted the expression *areas surrounding Japan* to mean Taiwan and launched a public-relations campaign against the revised guidelines. Tokyo and Washington refused to elaborate on the geographic scope,[47] but they tried to use the controversy to win China for the kind of trilateral dialogue that the United States was going to offer as a new strategy in January 1998. In March 1997, Hashimoto lifted the above-mentioned sanctions against the PRC, and China had started viewing him as a more predictable partner than his domestic rivals. In September 1997, China and Japan agreed on annual summits and the participation by uniformed personnel in their security dialogue.[48] The following year, Japan and the United States, as a consequence of a North Korean missile test, agreed to develop a theater missile defense system. Beijing viewed the initiative as a further setback for its effort to bring Taiwan home and responded with an accelerated modernization of the PLA and its missile force.

WHAT PLAYER? WHAT STRATEGY?

As has been shown, China in 2000 is not a great power with global reach or even a power with major global interests. The PRC remains a traditional regional player that has increased its foreign policy leeway since the reforms of Deng Xiaoping and the end of the Cold War.

With economic reform reaching its limits, double-digit economic growth no longer guaranteed, and an opaque power constellation, China's evolution into a dominant regional player, let alone global actor, becomes increasingly doubtful. Fragmentation, accompanied by power struggles at all levels and their crossborder projection, is at least as likely. However, the latter scenario is only slightly more encouraging than the authoritarian great-power perspective. One might believe, however, that constructive engagement, by implicitly according China regional—and some global—great-power status, could serve as a self-fulfilling prophecy. That would be true if the PRC had a few more decades to develop along these lines. Again, the sheer number of latent domestic and crossborder conflicts would appear to rule this out.

So what kind of player is China? It is a frustrated pluralist player, if you like, where foreign policy interests are being formulated at many levels and in many strata while the central leadership tries to preserve its monopoly. Nationalism has already entered this equation, but nationalism is even more difficult to control and may in turn inspire regionalism. The country is simply too large to be governed by a self-serving group of sexagenarians legitimized by their grip on power rather than anything else. Federalism would be the obvious way out, but again, a constitutional transition is less than certain.

In sum, the material and intellectual potential is great, but due to a lack of central vision it cannot be put to optimal use. Frustration is greater and risks are growing much faster than is the center's resolve to address constitutional reform. Hopes to engage China bilaterally or multilaterally will not come to much, because the partners to be engaged understand this as a tactical gamble, and those in the provinces or among the intellectuals who might have a strategic vision cannot yet be engaged. Fortunately, the tactical factor also applies to Beijing's own involvement in balancing exercises, and the state of the country and its body politic simply does not allow any major third party to treat the PRC as a reliable, long-term strategic partner.

This has been tried out, nevertheless, with the result that certain conflicts (Taiwan, Burma, possibly Korea) may be perpetuated rather than solved peacefully and that power politics has made a dangerous comeback in the East. It is possible that the challenges posed to national politics by economic globalization will bring about yet another turnaround. Economic crisis in East Asia could be the first sign of a new global and regional order. The West may at last be confident about the victory of its system. Enlargement will witness an Eastern renaissance. In such a context, China will literally shrink to its commensurate size. It will, however, probably not shrink gracefully. Conflict cannot be ruled out on the Chinese periphery. The rest of the region must thus be prepared and united. One may, of course, ask, whether such a contingency can realistically be prepared for and whether attempts at preparation might not themselves become a self-fulfilling prophecy. This is indeed a diplomatic balancing act that to succeed would require a high degree of transparency. Such an approach should not be confused with constructive engagement, however, where problems can at least be temporarily swept under the carpet. It is a carrot-and-stick strategy centered on the very region where Beijing locates its vital interests. But carrots and sticks are a feature of any diplomacy, including the Chinese variety.

NOTES

1. Paper presented at the conference "Security Concepts for the Beginning of the Twenty-first Century," Vienna, April 2–4, 1998.

2. E.g., Harry Harding (1994) "On the Four Great Relationships: The Prospects for China," *Survival* 36, no. 2 (Summer): 22–42; Joseph S. Nye (1997–1998) "China's Re-emergence and the Future of the Asia-Pacific," *Survival* 39, no. 4 (Winter 1997–1998): 65–79.

3. Harding (1994) "On the Four Great Relationships"; David Shambaugh (1996) "China in 1995: A Balance Sheet," *The Official Journal* (London: American Chamber of Commerce, January), pp. 34–38.

4. John J. Schulz (1998) "China as a Strategic Threat: Myths and Verities," *Strategic Review* 26, no. 1 (Winter): 5–16.

5. David Shambaugh (1996) "China's Military in Transition: Politics, Professionalism, Procurement, and Power Projection," *The China Quarterly*, no. 146: 265–298.

6. Winston Lord (1995) "For China, Not Containment but True Integration," *International Herald Tribune*, October 13, 1995, p. 8.

7. As early as 1997, Washington had offered Beijing a formal trilateral dialogue of U.S., Chinese, and Japanese defense ministers. Nye (1997–1998) "China's Re-emergence," p. 76.

8. In 1992, 1993, and 1996, respectively, the PRC signed the Nuclear Nonproliferation Treaty, the UN Convention on Chemical Weapons, and the Nuclear Test Ban Agreement. In 1990, Beijing had voted for economic sanctions against Iraq and had acquiesced in Operation Desert Storm.

9. Chong-Pin Lin (1994) "Chinese Military Modernization: Perceptions, Progress, and Prospects," *Security Studies* 3, no. 4 (Summer): 718–780; Stephen P. Aubin (1998) "China: Yes, Worry About the Future," *Strategic Review* 26, no. 1 (Winter): 17–20.

10. Deng Xiaoping, for instance, on the eve of the attack against Vietnam, said that the latter's "expansion in Southeast Asia and disturbances in Chinese-Vietnamese border areas . . . have actually already destroyed the calm that China requires for its modernization." Shi Hua (1997) "Deng Xiaoping's Internal Speech on the Eve of the Sino-Vietnamese War," *Qishi Niandai* (Hong Kong), no. 4 (April): 25–26.

11. Notimex News Agency (Mexico City, in Spanish), January 20, 1997, as quoted in *Summary of World Broadcasts* (SWB), FE/2824/G/2, January 23, 1997.

12. Samuel S. Kim (1994) "China's International Organizational Behaviour," in Thomas W. Robinson and David Shambaugh (eds.) (1994), *Chinese Foreign Policy: Theory and Practice* (New York: Clarendon), pp. 401–434.

13. *Tangtai* (Hong Kong), September 15, 1993, p. 9.

14. In October 1990, China's official news agency Xinhua (XNA) identified a new German "superpower" able to compete with Washington and Moscow for preeminence in Europe. XNA (in English), October 1, 1990, as quoted in SWB, FE/0884/A1/1, October 2, 1990.

15. Wan Lingying (1993) "Mayue fengbo jiqi yingxiang" (Disputes About the Maastricht Treaties and Their Implications), *Guoji wenti yanjiu*, no. 3: 13–19; Su Huimin (1993) "'Ouzhoude Deguo' haishi 'Deguode Ouzhou'?" ("European Germany" or "German Europe?"), *Guoji wenti yanjiu*, no. 1: 20–22.

16. E.g., XNA (in German), April 26, 1996, as quoted in *Deutsche Welle Monitordienst Asien* (DW), April 29, 1996.

17. Tao Bingwei (1996) "Dongbeiya jushide fazhan bianhua" (Changes in the Development of the Northeast Asian Situation), *Guoji wenti yanjiu*, no. 2 (April): 13–16.

18. Jacob Kovalio (1991) "The 1989 Tiananmen Square Incident: Retrospective and Prospective Considerations," *Asian Perspective* 15, no. 1 (Spring-Summer): 5–36.

19. Lucian W. Pye (1990) "China: Erratic State, Frustrated Society," *Foreign Affairs* 69, no. 4 (Fall): 56–74.

20. David Shambaugh (1992) "China's Security Policy in the Post–Cold War Era," *Survival* 34, no. 2 (Summer): 88–106.

21. In 1996, the director of the Institute of American Affairs at the Chinese Academy of Social Sciences wrote: "Engagement [is] an attempt to infiltrate U.S. economic, political, cultural, and ideological influences into China and to force international norms approved by the [United States] on it." Jisi Wang (1996) "China-Politik der USA: Eindämmung oder Engagement?" *Beijing Rundschau*, October 22, 1996, pp. 6–9 (author's translation). Another analyst characterized *engagement* and *containment* as "opposites on the surface but identical in reality." Yang Wie (1995) "How China Views the World and How It Should Face It," *Liaowang* (the official journal of the Communist Party of China), December 11, 1995, p. 1, as quoted in SWB, FE/2491/G5–6, December 20, 1995.

22. *Far Eastern Economic Review* (FEER), October 7, 1993, pp. 12–13.

23. E.g., Sukhumband Paribatra (1994) "From ASEAN Six to ASEAN Ten: Issues and Prospects," *Contemporary Southeast Asia* 16, no. 3 (December): 243–258.

24. William A. Kerr and Ed MacKay (1994) "Is Mainland China Evolving into a Market Economy?" *Issues and Studies* (Taipei) 33, no. 9 (September): 31–45.

25. However, according to a January 1998 report by Hong Kong's *Ching Chi Tao Pao*, there is a considerable amount of "hidden foreign debt." FEER, January 15, 1998, p. 28.

26. According to figures released by the Chinese Ministry of Finance, in 1996, 61 percent of a total of almost 56,000 enterprises in which foreigners held a stake were in the red. Overall losses reached R55.2 billion, a 50 percent increase over the preceding year. FEER, December 18, 1997, pp. 52–54.

27. In 1996, state enterprises produced 41 percent of GDP, communal enterprises 35 percent, and private enterprises/joint ventures 24 percent. The former employed 25 percent of the industrial workforce. The state was holding 59.8 percent of the shares of the then 4,300 partly privatized state enterprises. Remaining shareholders were "collective owners" with 17.8 percent, "ordinary citizens" with 8.3 percent, employees with 6.5 percent, foreigners with 6 percent, and others with 1.6 percent. State Commission for the Restructuring of the Economic, as quoted in FEER, September 25, 1997, pp. 14–15. By late 1997, the preceding year's rather modest partial privatization had resulted in 12 million workers losing their employment, with only half of them having found new jobs. FEER, January 15, 1998, pp. 46–47.

28. Ibid.

29. In January 1998, the state-run railway announced the planned dismissal of 1.1 million workers, one-third of the total, by 2000. Another 1.2 million workers are to be released by the textile industry. *International Herald Tribune*, January 21, 1998, p. 2.

30. Ibid.

31. On the one hand, the commission recommended further liberalizing the currency and accelerating the privatization of state enterprises. On the other hand, development of the domestic market was accorded priority over export-led growth, with capital imports being channeled into "productive use." *Wen Wei Po* (Hong Kong), January 4, 1998, p. 1, quoted in SWB, FE/3117/S1/3–4, January 6, 1998.

32. This did not mean that Jiang was able to replace them with his own followers in every case.

33. Kay Möller (1993) "China in Ostasien: Die Renaissance der Pax sinica," in Albrecht Zunker (ed.) *Weltordnung oder Chaos?* (Baden-Baden: Nomos), pp. 317–327.

34. Speech by U.S. Secretary of Defense William Cohen in Singapore on January 15, 1998, as quoted in *U.S. Information and Texts* (Washington, United States Information Service), January 22, 1998, pp. 6–9.

35. "Today they [the alliances] are not reactive, they are pro-active. Standing not against anyone, but standing for shared objectives." Ibid.

36. The White House (October 29, 1997) "Fact Sheet: Accomplishments of U.S.-China Summit," Washington, D.C., available at <www.whitehouse.gov>.

37. Minister of Defense Paval Grachev, quoted in *Financial Times*, April 24, 1996, p. 1.

38. Both sides are also interested in exploiting Central Asian resources, which may become a future source of conflict. In June 1997, China's state oil corporation bought a major share in Kazakhstan's oil industry. Beijing has started constructing a 3,000-kilometer pipeline from Kazakhstan to Sinkiang and farther eastward.

39. In late 1996, Minister of Defense Igor Rokhionev speculated about the possibility of a Chinese threat. See *Washington Post*, December 28, 1996, p. 1.

40. FEER, March 13, 1997, pp. 20–21.

41. FEER, October 30, 1997, p. 30.

42. Interfax, May 26, 1997, as quoted in SWB, FE/2955/E/1, June 26, 1997.

43. Gaye Christoffersen (1996) "China and the Asia-Pacific: Need for a Grand Strategy," *Asian Survey* 36, no. 11 (November): 1067–1085.

44. Radio Japan International (in German), March 22, 1994, quoted in DW, March 23, 1994.

45. Yonhap, November 14, 1995, as quoted in SWB, FE/2461/D/4–5, November 15, 1995.

46. Joint Statement of U.S.-Japan Security Consultative Committee (Washington. D.C., Office of Assistant Secretary of Defense), September 23, 1997.

47. FEER, October 9, 1997, pp. 24–28.

48. Kyodo News Service (in English), September 4, 1997, quoted in SWB, FE/3018/G/5–6, September 8, 1997.

Acronyms

ACP	African, Caribbean, and Pacific
APEC	Asia-Pacific Economic Cooperation forum
ARF	ASEAN Regional Forum
ASEAN	Association of Southeast Asian Nations
CCP	Chinese Communist Party
CDU	Christian Democratic Union
CEE	Central and Eastern European
CESDP	Common European Security and Defense Policy
CFE	Treaty of Conventional Forces in Europe
CFSP	Common Foreign and Security Policy
CiO	Chairman-in-Office
CIS	Commonwealth of Independent States
CJTFs	Combined Joint Task Forces
CoE	Council of Europe
CWC	Chemical Weapons Convention
DoD	Department of Defense
EAPC	Euro-Atlantic Partnership Council
EC	European Community
ECHR	European Court of Human Rights
ECJ	European Court of Justice
ECOWAS	Economic Community of West African States
EMU	European Monetary Union
EPC	European Political Cooperation
ESDI	European Security and Defense Identity
ESDP	European Security and Defense Policy
EU	European Union
EU/WEU	European Union/Western European Union
FDI	foreign direct investment
FDP	Free Democrats

GATT	General Agreement on Tariffs and Trade
GUUAM	Georgia, Ukraine, Uzbekistan, Armenia, and Moldova
HCNM	High Commissioner on National Minorities
ICJ	International Court of Justice
IFOR	Implementation Force (NATO-led, Bosnia)
IGOs	international governmental organizations
IMF	International Monetary Fund
KFOR	Kosovo Force (NATO-led)
KVM	Kosovo Verification Mission
MFN	most-favored-nation status
NAA	North Atlantic Assembly
NACC	North Atlantic Cooperation Council
NATO	North Atlantic Treaty Organization
OCC	operational capabilities concept
ODIHR	Office for Democratic Institutions and Human Rights
OSCE	Organization for Security and Cooperation in Europe
P-5	five Permanent Members (of UN Security Council)
PA-NET	Parliamentary Assembly Network
PARP	Planning and Review Process
PfP	Partnership for Peace program
PJC	Permanent Joint Council
PLA	People's Liberation Army
PRC	People's Republic of China
PSC	Political and Security Committee
REACT	Rapid Expert Assistance and Cooperation Teams
RMA	revolution in military affairs
SBR	Russian–Belarusian Union
SFOR	Stabilization Force (NATO-led, Bosnia)
SHAPE	Supreme Headquarters Allied Powers Europe (NATO)
SIG	Commonwealth of Integrating States
SPD	Social Democrats
TMD	theater missile defense
UNHCR	UN High Commissioner for Refugees
UNITAF	Unified Task Force
UNTAES	UN Transitional Administration in Eastern Slavonia, Baranja, and Western Sirmium
WEAG	Western European Armaments Group
WEU	Western European Union
WTO	World Trade Organization

Bibliography

Acharya, A. (1997) "The Periphery as the Core: The Third World and Security Studies." In K. Krause and M. Williams (eds.) *Critical Security Studies: Concepts and Cases*. London: UCL, pp. 299–328.

Adler, Emanuel (1998) "Seeds of Peaceful Change: The OSCE as a Pluralistic Security Community." In Emanuel Adler and Michael N. Barnett (eds.) *Security Communities*. Cambridge: Cambridge University Press, pp. 119–160.

———. (1997) "Seizing the Middle Ground: Constructivism." *World Politics: European Journal of International Relations* 3, no. 3 (September): 319–364.

Adler, E., and M. Barnett (eds.) (1998) *Security Communities*. Cambridge: Cambridge University Press.

Agenda 2000 (1997) Luxemburg: Office of Publication of the European Communities.

Albright, M. (January 9, 1997) "Madeleine Albright Reviews Foreign Policy Agenda." USIS Official Text, U.S. Embassy, London.

Alexandrova, Olga, and Heinz Timmermann (1997) *Rußland—Belarus—GUS. Integrationsbestrebungen und Desintegrationstendenzen*. Berichte des BIOst 30, Köln.

Alfredsson, Gudmundur, and Danilo Türk (1993) "International Mechanisms for the Monitoring and Protection of Minority Rights: Their Advantages, Disadvantages, and Interrelationships." In Arie Bloed, Liselotte Leicht, Manfred Nowak, and Allan Rosas (eds.) *Monitoring Human Rights in Europe: Comparing International Procedures and Mechanisms*. Dordrecht: Martinus Nijhoff, pp. 169–186.

Alker, Hayward R. (1996) *Rediscoveries and Reformulations: Humanistic Methodologies for International Studies*. Cambridge: Cambridge University Press.

Alker, Hayward R., and Fraser Simon (1996) "On Historical Complexity: 'Naturalistic' Modeling Approaches from the Santa Fe Institute." Paper delivered at the American Political Science Association annual meeting, San Francisco, August 31, 1996.

Anderson, Jennifer (1997) *The Limits of Sino-Russian Strategic Partnership*. Adelphi Paper 315. London: IISS.

Arbatov, Alexei G. (1998) "Military Reform in Russia: Dilemmas, Obstacles, and Prospects." *International Security* 4 (Spring): 83–134.

Archer, Clive (1997) *Nordic Involvement in the Baltic States Security: Needs, Motives, and Success.* Working Papers, no. 19. Copenhagen Peace Research Institute.

Archer, Clive, and Christopher Jones (1997) "The Security Policies and Concepts of the Baltic States." In *Danish Foreign Policy Yearbook, 1997.* Copenhagen: Danish Institute of International Affairs, pp. 81–100.

Art, Robert J. (1998) "Creating a Disaster: NATO's Open Door Policy." *Political Science Quarterly* 113, no. 3 (Fall): 383–404.

Ash, Eric (1999) "Terror Targeting: The Morale of the Story." *Aerospace Power Journal* 13 (Winter): 33–47.

Aubin, Stephen P. (1998) *China: Yes, Worry About the Future. Strategic Review* 26, no. 1 (Winter): 17–20.

Axelrod, Robert M. (1997a) "Advancing the Art of Simulation in the Social Sciences." International Conference on Computer Simulation and the Social Sciences, Cortona, Italy, September 22–25, 1997.

———. (1997b) *The Complexity of Cooperation: Agent-Based Models of Competition and Cooperation.* Princeton: Princeton University Press.

Ayoob, Mohammed (1997) "Defining Security: A Subaltern Realist Perspective." In K. Krause and M. Williams (eds.) *Critical Security Studies: Concepts and Cases.* London: UCL Press, pp. 121–148.

Baldwin, D. (ed.) (1993) *Neorealism and Neoliberalism: The Contemporary Debate.* New York: Columbia University Press.

Barber, Benjamin (1995) "Beijing Eyes China South Sea with Sub Purchase." *Washington Times,* March 7, 1995.

———. (1996) *Jihad Versus McWorld: How Globalism and Tribalism Are Reshaping the World.* New York: Ballantine.

Barcavage, Shaun R. (1996–1997) "NGOs in the System of European Security." *ODIHR Bulletin* 5, no. 1: 24–25.

Barnett, Michael, and Martha Finnemore (1999) "The Politics, Power, and Pathologies of International Organizations." *International Organization* 53, no. 4 (Autumn): 699–732.

Barrett, John (1996) "NATO Reform: Alliance Policy and Cooperative Security." In Ingo Peters (ed.) *New Security Challenges: The Adaptation of International Institutions, Reforming the UN, NATO, EU, and CSCE Since 1989.* New York: St. Martin's, pp. 123–152.

Bauböck, Rainer (1994) *Changing Boundaries of Citizenship: The Inclusion of Immigrants in Democratic Polities.* Paper prepared for the annual convention of the American Political Science Association. New York, September 1–3, 1994.

Baumann, R., V. Rittberger, and W. Wagner (1999) "Neorealistische Aussen politiktheorie und Prognosen über die deutsche Aussenpolitik nach der Vereinigung." *Zeitschrift für Internationale Beziehungen* 6, no. 2 (December): 245–286.

Baylis, J., and N. Rengger (eds.) (1992) *Dilemmas of World Politics: International Issues in a Changing World.* Oxford: Clarendon.

Begert, William J. (1999) USAF *Aerospace Power Journal* 13 (Winter): 4–10.

Bennett, Andrew, Joseph Lepgold, and Danny Unger (eds.) (1997) *Friends in Need: Burden Sharing in the Persian Gulf War.* New York: St. Martin's.

Bergesen, Albert (ed.) (1980) *Studies in the Modern World System.* New York: Academic.

Bernstein, Richard, and Munro Ross (1997) *The Coming Conflict with China.* New York: Alfred Knopf.

Bertalanffy, Ludwig van, Ervin Laszlo, and Jay W. Forrester (1971) *World Dynamics.* Cambridge: Wright-Allen.

Betts, Richard K. (1991, orig. ed. 1977) *Soldiers, Statesmen, and Cold War Crises.* New York: Columbia University Press.

Bhaskar, R. (1979) *The Possibility of Naturalism.* Brighton: Harvester.

Biddle, Stephan (1996) "Victory Misunderstood." *International Security* 21, no. 2 (Fall): 139–179.

Blackwill, Robert D., and Michael Stürmer (eds.) (1997) *Allies Divided: Transatlantic Policies for the Greater Middle East.* Cambridge: MIT Press.

Blank, Stephen J. (1999) "NATO Enlargement Between Rhetoric and Realism." *International Politics* 36, no. 1 (March): 67–88.

Blank, Stephen, and Alvin Z. Rubinstein (1997) "Is Russia Still a Power in Asia?" *Problems of Post-Communism* 2: 37–46.

Di Blase, Antonietta (1978) "The Role of the Host State's Consent with Regard to Non-coercive Actions by the United Nations." In Antonio Cassese (ed.) (1978) *United Nations Peace-keeping: Legal Essays.* Alphen/Rijn: Sijthoff and Noordhoff, pp. 55–94.

Bloed, Arie (ed.) (1993) *The Conference on Security and Co-operation in Europe: Analysis and Basic Documents, 1972–1993.* Dordrecht: Kluwer Law International.

———. (1997) *The Conference on Security and Co-operation in Europe: Basic Documents, 1993–1995,* The Hague: Martinus Nijhoff.

Boland, Vincent (1997) "Earnings from Organized Crime Reach $1,000 bn." *Financial Times,* February 15, 1997.

Booth, K. (1991) "Security and Emancipation." *Review of International Studies* 17, no. 4: 313–326.

Booth, K., and S. Smith (eds.) (1995) *International Relations Theory Today.* Oxford: Polity.

Borchert, Heiko (1999a) "Den Friedensaufbau professionalisieren—Die institutionelle Zusammenarbeit verbessern." In Institut für Friedensforschung und Sicherheitspolitik an der Universität Hamburg/IFSH (ed.) *OSZE-Jahrbuch, 1999.* Baden-Baden: Nomos Verlagsgesellschaft, pp. 459–472.

———. (1999b) *Europas Sicherheitsarchitektur: Erfolgsfaktoren—Bestands-aufnahme—Handlungsbedarf.* Baden-Baden: Nomos Verlagsgesellschaft.

———. (1999c) "The Kosovo Conflict and the Swiss Contribution." *European Security* 8, no. 4 (Winter): 165–190.

Bothe, Michael, Natalino Ronzitti, and Allan Rosas (eds.) (1997) *The OSCE in the Management of Peace and Security: Conflict Prevention, Crisis Management, and Peaceful Settlement of Disputes.* The Hague: Kluwer Law International.

Boulding, K. (1978) *Stable Peace.* Austin: University of Texas Press.

Bradley, Bill (1995–1996) "A Misguided Russia Policy." *Foreign Policy* 101 (Winter): 81–101.

Brett, Rachel J. (1992–1993) "NGOs and the Human Dimension of the CSCE." *ODIHR Bulletin* 1, no. 1 (Winter): 1–5.

Brown, Michael (ed.) (1993) *Ethnic Conflict and International Security.* Princeton: Princeton University Press.

Brubaker, Rogers (1996) *Nationalism Reframed: Nationhood and the National Question in the New Europe.* Cambridge: Cambridge University Press.

Brzezinski, Zbigniew (1997) *The Grand Chessboard: American Primacy and Its Geostrategic Imperatives.* New York: Basic Books.

Buchsbaum, Thomas (1993) "The CSCE and International Organizations: Expanding Cooperation with the Council of Europe." In Michael R. Lucas (ed.) *The CSCE in the 1990s: Constructing European Security and Cooperation*. Baden-Baden: Nomos Verlagsgesellschaft, pp. 125–142.

Buchsbaum, Thomas, et al. (1994) "The First Human Dimension Implementation Meeting: Analysis of the Informal Recommendations." *Helsinki Monitor* 5, no. 2: 68–80.

Bull, H. (1977) *The Anarchical Society: A Study of Order in World Politics*. London: Macmillan.

Bulloch, Gavin (1996) "Military Doctrine and Counterinsurgency: A British Perspective." *Parameters* (Summer): 4–16.

Buzan, Barry (1993a) "From International System to International Society: Structural Realism and Regime Theory Meet the English School." *International Organisation* 47, no. 3 (Summer): 327–352.

———. (1991) *People, States, and Fear*. 2nd ed. London: Harvester Wheatsheaf.

———. (1995) "Security, the State, the 'New World Order,' and Beyond." In Ronni D. Lipschutz (ed.) *On Security*. New York: Columbia University Press, pp. 187–211.

———. (1993b) "Societal Security, the State, and Internationalization." In O. Wæver et al., *Identity, Migration, and the New Security Agenda in Europe*. London: Pinter.

Buzan, Barry, and David Held (1998) "Realism Versus Cosmopolitanism." *Review of International Studies* 24, no. 3 (July): 387–398.

Buzan, Barry, and Ole Wæver (1997) "Slippery? Contradictory? Sociologically Untenable? The Copenhagen School Replies." *Review of International Studies* 23, no. 2 (April): 241–250.

Buzan, Barry, Ole Wæver, and Jaap de Wilde (eds.) (1998) *Security: A New Framework for Analysis*. Boulder: Lynne Rienner Publishers.

Calder, Kent E. (1996) *Asia's Deadly Triangle: How Arms, Energy, and Growth Threaten to Destabilise Asia*. London: Nicholas Publishing.

Cameron, Fraser (1993) "The European Community and the CSCE." In Michael R. Lucas (ed.) *The CSCE in the 1990s: Constructing European Security and Cooperation*. Baden-Baden: Nomos Verlagsgesellschaft, pp. 265–277.

———. (1997) "Where the European Commission Comes In: From the Single European Act to Maastricht." In Elfriede Regelsberger et al. (eds.) *Foreign Policy of the European Union: From EPC to CFSP and Beyond*. Boulder: Lynne Rienner Publishers, pp. 99–108.

Canor, Iris (1998) *The Limits of Judicial Discretion in the European Court of Justice: Security and Foreign Affairs Issues*. Baden-Baden: Nomos.

Carter, Marshall N., and William G. Shipman (1996) "The Coming Global Pension Crisis." Special supplement to *Foreign Affairs* 75, no. 6 (November-December).

Cassese, Antonio (ed.) (1978) *United Nations Peace-keeping: Legal Essays*. Alphen/Rijn: Sijthoff and Noordhoff.

Cederman, Lars-Erik (1997) *Emergent Actors in World Politics: How States and Nations Develop and Dissolve*. Princeton: Princeton University Press.

Central Intelligence Agency (1995) *World Factbook*. Washington, D.C.: Central Intelligence Agency.

Cheng, Joseph Yu-shek (1996) "China's America Policy." *Journal of Chinese Political Science* 2, no. 2 (Summer).

Cheysson, Claude (1997) "Defining Europe's Place in the World." In Philip Morris Institute for Public Policy Research, *What Global Role for the EU?* Brussels, September, pp. 33–40.

Choucri, Nazli, and Robert C. North (1975) *Nations in Conflict.* San Francisco: Freeman.

Christensen, Thomas J. (1996) "Chinese Realpolitik." *Foreign Affairs* 75, no. 5 (September-October).

Christoffersen, Gaye (1996) "China and the Asia-Pacific: Need for a Grand Strategy." *Asian Survey* 36, no. 11 (November): 1067–1085.

Clark, I. (1997) *Globalization and Fragmentation: International Relations in the Twentieth Century.* Oxford: Oxford University Press.

Clarke, M. (ed.) (1993) *New Perspectives in Security.* London: Brassey's, for the Centre for Defence Studies.

Clarke, Walter, and Jeffrey Herbst (1996) "Somalia and the Future of Humanitarian Intervention." *Foreign Affairs* 75, no. 2 (March-April): 70–86.

Clemens, Walter C. Jr. (2000) *America and the World, 1898–2025: Achievements, Failures, Alternative Futures.* New York: St. Martin's.

———. (2000) *The Baltic Miracle: Complexity Theory and European Security,* Lanham, Md.: Rowman and Littlfield.

———. (1990) *Can Russia Change? The USSR Confronts Global Interdependence.* Boston: Unwin Hyman.

———. (1998) *Dynamics of International Relations: Conflict and Mutual Gain in an Era of Global Interdependence.* Lanham, Md.: Rowman and Littlefield.

———. (1972–1973) "Ecology and International Relations." *International Journal* (Special Issue: "Earth Politics") 28, no. 1 (Winter): 1–27.

———. (1971) "The Non-Zero Sum Hypothesis and the National Self-Interest." Paper presented to the Peace Research Society (International), Central European Section, Vienna, August 29, 1971.

———. (1978) *The U.S.S.R. and Global Interdependence: Alternative Futures.* Washington, D.C.: American Enterprise Institute.

Cohen, Roger (1997) "A Somber France, Racked by Doubt: Under Pressure to Modernize, Nation Clings to the Old Ways." *International Herald Tribune,* February 12, 1997.

Cooper, Neil (1998) *An Agenda for Demilitarisation After Post-Modern Conflicts.* Paper for the Third Pan-European International Relations Conference, ECPR-ISA, September.

Cooper, Robert (1996) *The Post-Modern State and the World Order.* London: Demos.

———. (1998) "The Post-Modern State and the World Order." *Demos,* no. 144.

Cornish, Paul (1997) *Partnership in Crisis: The U.S., Europe, and the Fall and Rise of NATO.* London: Pinter, for the Royal Institute of International Affairs.

Cox, Robert W. (1992) "Towards a Post-Hegemonic Conceptualisation of World Order: Reflections on the Relevance of Ibn Khaldun." In James N. Rosenau and Ernst-Ottto Czempiel (eds.) *Governance Without Government: Order and Change in World Politics.* Cambridge: Cambridge University Press.

Croody, E. (1995) "Urban Terrorism: Chemical Warfare in Japan." *Jane's Intelligence Review* 7, no. 11 (November).

Danish Institute of International Affairs (1999) *Humanitarian Intervention: Legal and Political Aspects.* Copenhagen: Danish Institute of International Affairs.

Davis, Bobrow (1996) "Complex Insecurity: Implications of a Sobering Metaphor." *International Studies Quarterly* 40, no. 4 (December): 435–450.

De Jonquires, Guy (1998) "European Commission's Transatlantic Trade Initiative Clears First Political Hurdle." *Financial Times*, March 12, 1998.

De Nooy, G. C. (ed.) (1997) *The Clausewitzian Dictum and the Future of Western Military Strategy.* The Hague: Kluwer Law International.

Dean, Jonathan (1996) "Der OSZE-Verhaltenskodex—eine gute Idee, unvollkommen ausgeführt, ungenügend nachgearbeitet." In Institut für Friedensforschung und Sicherheitspolitik an der Universität Hamburg (Hrsg.) *OSZE-Jahrbuch, 1996.* Baden-Baden: Nomos Verlagsgesellschaft, pp. 309–318.

Dembinski, Matthias (1997) *Langer Anlauf—kurzer Sprung: Die Aussenpolitik der Europäischen Union nach der Reform von Amsterdam.* Frankfurt: Hessische Stiftung für Friedens und Konfliktforschung (HSFK-Report nr. 7).

Den Boer, Pim (1995) "Europe of 1914: The Making of an Idea." In Pim den Boer, et al., *The History of the Idea of Europe.* London: Routledge.

Des Forges, Alison (1999) *Leave None to Tell the Story: Genocide in Rwanda.* New York: Human Rights Watch.

Desch, Michael C. (1998) "Cultural Clash: Assessing the Importance of Ideas in Security Studies." *International Security* 23, no. 1 (Summer): 141–170.

Deudney, Daniel (1990) "The Case Against Linking Environmental Degradation and National Security." *Millennium: Journal of International Studies* 19, no. 3 (Winter): 461–476.

———. (1991) "Environment and Security: Muddled Thinking." *Bulletin of the Atomic Scientists* (April).

Deudney, Daniel H., and G. John Ikenberry (1996) *Structural Liberalism: The Nature and Sources of Postwar Western Political Order.* Philadelphia: University of Pennsylvania, Christopher H. Browne Center for International Politics.

Deutch, John, Arnold Kanter, and Brent Scowcroft (1999) "Saving NATO's Foundation." *Foreign Affairs* 78, no. 6 (November-December): 55–67.

Deutsch, Karl (1968) *Die Analyse Internationaler Beziehungen.* Frankfurt am Main: Fischer.

———. (1957) *Political Community and the North Atlantic Area.* Princeton: Princeton University Press.

De Wiyk, Rob (1997) *NATO on the Brink of the New Millennium: The Battle for Consensus.* London: Brassey's.

DiMaggio, P., and W. Powell (eds.) (1991) *The New Institutionalism in Organizational Analysis.* Chicago: Univesity of Chicago Press.

Dionne, E. J. Jr. (1997) "Germany's Problems Should Trouble Us, Too." *International Herald Tribune*, February 11, 1997.

Donnelly, C. (1996) "Defence Transformation in the New Democracies." *NATO Review*, no. 6 (November): 20–23.

Doyle, Michael W. (1993) "Kant: Liberal Legacies and Foreign Affairs." In *Philosophy and Public Affairs* 12, no. 3 (Summer): 205–235.

———. (1997) *Ways of War and Peace.* New York: W. W. Norton.

Drake, Helen (1994) *The Commission Presidency of Jacques Delors: The Theory and Practice of Political Leadership.* Manchester, UK: University of Manchester, European Policy Research Unit (EPRU Paper no. 3).

———. (1995) "Political Leadership and European Integration: The Case of Jacques Delors." *Western European Politics* 18, no. 1: 140–160.

Drew, Elizabeth (1994) *On the Edge: The Clinton Presidency.* New York: Simon and Schuster.

Duke, Simon (2000) *The Elusive Quest for European Security: From EDC to CFSP.* Basingstoke, UK: Macmillan.

Dunlap, Charles J. (1997) "Twenty-first-Century Land Warfare: Four Dangerous Myths." *Parameters* (Autumn): 27–37.

Dunne, T. (1995) "The Social Construction of International Society." *European Journal of International Relations* 1, no. 3 (September): 367–389.

Eckstein, Harry (1975) "Case Study and Theory in Political Science." In F. I. Greenstein and N. W. Polsby (eds.) *Handbook of Political Science.* Reading, Mass. VII: 79–138.

Ehrenreich, Barbara (1997) *Blood Rites: Origins and History of the Passions of War.* London: Virago.

Eiff, Hansjörg (1998) *Autonomie als Mittel der Konfliktbewältigung und des Minderheitenschutzes im Rahmen der OSZE* [Autonomy as a Means of Conflict Settlement and Minority Protection Within the OSCE Framework]. In Institut für Friedensforschung und Sicherheitspolitik an der Universität Hamburg [Institute for Peace Research and Security Policy at the University of Hamburg]/IFSH (ed.) *OSZE-Jahrbuch* [OSCE Yearbook], *1998.* Baden-Baden: Nomos Verlagsgesellschaft, pp. 255–264.

Elkins, David J. (1995) *Beyond Territoriality: Territory and Political Economy in the Twenty-First Century.* Toronto: University of Toronto Press.

Enloe, C. (1987) "Feminist Thinking About War, Militarism, and Peace." In B. Hess and M. Ferree (eds.) *Analysing Gender: A Handbook of Social Science Research.* London: Sage.

Epstein, Joshua M., and Robert Axtell (1996) *Growing Artificial Societies: Social Science from the Bottom Up.* Cambridge: MIT Press.

Estebanez, Maria Amor Martin (1997) "The High Commissioner on National Minorities: Development of the Mandate." In Michael Bothe, Natalino Ronzitti, and Allan Rosas (eds.) *The OSCE in the Maintenance of Peace and Security: Conflict Prevention, Crisis Management, and Peaceful Settlement of Disputes.* The Hague: Kluwer Law International, pp. 123–165.

Euro-Atlantic Partnership Council (1999) *Political-Military Steering Committee on Partnership for Peace: The Operational Capabilities Concept for NATO-led PfP Operations.* November 10, 1999.

Farah, Douglas (1997) "Colombia Suspends Anti–Drug Crop Effort." *Washington Post,* March 6, 1997.

Farah, Doug, and Molly Moore (1997) "Mexican Drug Traffickers Eclipse Colombian Cartels." *Washington Post,* March 20, 1997.

Fenton, Cooper, et al. (1991) "Bound to Follow? Leadership and Followership in the Gulf Conflict." *Political Science Review* 106, no. 3 (Fall): 391–410.

Feshbach, Murray (2000) "A Sick and Shrinking Nation." *Washington Post,* October 24, 1999.

Finnemore, Martha (1996) *National Interests in International Society.* Ithaca: Cornell University Press.

Fischer, Markus (1992) "Feudal Europe, 800–1300: Communal Discourse and Conflictual Practices." *International Organizations* 46 (Spring): 427–466.

Flynn, Gregory, and Henry Farrell (1999) "Piecing Together the Democratic Peace: The CSCE and the 'Construction' of Security in Post–Cold War Europe." *International Organizations* 53, no. 3 (Summer): 505–536.

Försvarsdepartementet (1995) *Sverige i Europa och världen.* Stockholm: Försvarsdepatermentet.

Foundation on Inter-Ethnic Relations (FIER) (1997a) *Bibliography on the OSCE High Commissioner on National Minorities: Documents, Speeches, and Related Publications.* The Hague: FIER.

————. (1996) *The Hague Recommendations Regarding the Education Rights of National Minorities and Explanatory Note*. The Hague: FIER.

————. (1999) *The Lund Recommendations on the Effective Participation of National Minorities in Public Life and Explanatory Note*. The Hague: FIER.

————. (1998) *The Oslo Recommendations Regarding the Linguistic Rights of National Minorities and Explanatory Note*. The Hague: FIER.

————. (1997b) *The Role of the High Commissioner on National Minorities in OSCE Conflict Prevention. An Introduction*. The Hague: FIER.

Frankel, Benjamin (ed.) (1996) *Roots of Realism*. Ilford, UK: Frank Cass.

Freedman, Lawrence (1998) "International Security: Changing Targets." *Foreign Policy* (Special Edition "Frontiers of Knowledge") no. 110 (Spring).

Freedman, Lawrence, and Efraim Karsh (1993) *The Gulf Conflict, 1990–1991: Diplomacy and War in the New World Order*. Princeton: Princeton University Press.

Freedman, Lawrence, and Anand Menon (1997) "Conclusion: Defence, States, and Integration." In Jolyon Howorth and Anand Menon (eds.) *The European Union and National Defence Policies*. London: Routledge, pp. 155–172.

Freeland, Chrystia (1998) "Yeltsin Sees Role in 'Dominant World Power.'" *Financial Times*, March 27, 1998.

Frowein, Jochen A. (1997) "Auf dem Weg zu einer gemeinsamen Sicherheits—und Verteidigungspolitik." In Christian Tomuschat (ed.) *Rechtsprobleme einer europäischen Sicherheits—und Verteidigungsidentität*. Heidelberg: C. F. Müller Verlag, pp. 11–18.

Gaddis, John Lewis (1992–1993) "International Relations Theory and the End of the Cold War." *International Security* 17, no. 3 (Winter): 5–58.

Gärtner, Heinz (1999) "Crisis Management and Small States." In Olof Palme International Center (ed.) *Northern Europe and Central Europe: Hard, Soft and Civic Security*. Stockholm: Olof Palme International Center, pp. 41–63.

————. (1998) "European Security, NATO, and Transatlantic Link: Crisis Management." *European Security* 7, no. 3 (Autumn): 1–15.

————. (1997a) *Modelle Europäischer Sicherheit. Wie entscheidet Österreich?* Vienna: Braunmüller.

————. (1997b) "States Without Nations: State, Nation, and Security in Central Europe." *International Politics* 34, no. 1 (March).

Gallie, W. (1962) "Essentially Contested Concepts." In Max Black (ed.) *The Importance of Language*. Englewood Cliffs, N.J.: Prentice Hall, pp. 121–146.

Gertz, Bernhard (1994) "Plädoyer für eine fortschrittliche Wehrverfassung in Europa." In *Eurokorps und Europäische Einigung*. Bonn: Edition Zeitgeschichte, pp. 464–476.

Ghebali, Victor-Yves (1996) *L'OSCE dans l'Europe post-communiste, 1990–1996: Vers une identité paneuropéenne de sécurité*. Bruxelles: Bruylant.

Giegerich, Thomas (1997) "Verfassungsrechtliche Kontrolle der auswärtigen Gewalt im europäisch-atlantischen Verfassungsstaat. Vergleichende Bestandsaufnahme mit Blick auf die neuen Demokratien in Mittel—und Osteuropa." *Zeitschrift für ausländisches öffentliches Recht und Völkerrecht* 57, nos. 2–3: 409–564.

Giering, Claus (1997) *Europa zwischen Zweckverband und Superstaat: Die Entwicklung der politikwissenschaftlichen Integrationstheorie im Prozess der europäischen Integration*. Bonn: Europa Union Verlag.

Goldstein, Judith, and Robert O. Keohane (eds.) (1993) *Ideas and Foreign Policy: Beliefs, Institutions and Political Change*. Ithaca: Cornell University Press.

Gombert, David C., and Stephen F. Larrabee (eds.) (1997) *America and Europe: A Partnership for a New Era.* Cambridge: Cambridge University Press.

Goodin, Robert E. (1996) "Institutions and Their Design." In Robert E. Goodin (ed.) *The Theory of Institutional Design.* Cambridge: Cambridge University Press, pp. 1–53.

Gottlieb, Gidon (1993) *Nation Against State: A New Approach to Ethnic Conflicts and the Decline of Sovereignty.* New York: Council on Foreign Relations.

Götz, Roland (1994) *"Deindustrialisierung" Rußlands: Unabwendbares Schicksal oder Problem der Struktur- und Währungspolitik?* Köln: Aktuelle Analysen des BIOst 50 (13.9.).

———. (2000) *Die russische Wirtschaft im Jahr der Präsidentenwahl.* Köln: Aktuelle Analysen des BIOst 13 (10.2.).

———. (1994) *Regionale Aspekte der "Deindustrialisierung" in Rußland: Problemregionen kristallisieren sich heraus.* Köln: Aktuelle Analysen des BIOst 56 (30.9.).

———. (1997) *Wirtschaftswachstum in Rußland: Faktoren und Perspektiven.* Köln: Berichte des BIOst 32.

Gould, Stephen Jay (1989) *Wonderful Life: The Burgess Shale and Nature of History.* New York: W. W. Norton.

Gow, James (1997) *Triumph of the Lack of Will: International Diplomacy and the Yugoslav War.* New York: Columbia University Press.

Graham, Bradley (1997) "Pentagon Faulted for Short-Sighted Plans." *Washington Post,* May 23, 1997.

Grant, R. P. (1996) "France's New Relationship with NATO." *Survival* 38, no. 1 (Spring): 58–80.

Griffin, Michèle (1999) "Retrenchment, Reform, and Regionalization: Trends in UN Peace Support Operations." *International Peacekeeping* 6, no. 1 (Spring): 1–31.

Grönick, Ritva (1993) "The CSCE and Non-Governmental Organizations." In Michael R. Lucas (ed.) *The CSCE in the 1990s: Constructing European Security and Cooperation.* Baden-Baden: Nomos Verlagsgesellschaft, pp. 227–248.

Guldimann, Tim (1997) "The OSCE Assistance Group to Chechnya." Paper presented at the Carnegie Endowment for International Peace, Washington, D.C., March 11.

Gutlove, Paul, and Gordon Thompson (1995) "The Potential for Cooperation by the OSCE and Non-Governmental Actors on Conflict Management." *Helsinki Monitor* 6, no. 3 (Special Issue, "Twenty Years Helsinki Final Act"): 52–64.

Haass, Richard N. (1999) "What to Do with American Primacy." *Foreign Affairs* 78, no. 5 (September-October): 37–49.

Haftendorn, Helga (1997) "Sicherheitsinstitutionen in den internationalen Beziehungen: Eine Einführung." In Helga Haftendorn and Otto Keck (eds.) *Kooperation jenseits von Hegemonie und Bedrohung: Sicherheitsinstitutionen in den internationalen Beziehungen.* Baden-Baden: Nomos, pp. 11–34.

Hakala, Terhi (1998) "The OSCE Minsk Process: A Balance After Five Years." *Helsinki Monitor* 9, no. 1: 10–11.

Halliday, F. (1996) "The Future of International Relations: Fears and Hopes." In S. Smith, K. Booth, and M. Zalewski (eds.) *International Theory: Positivism and Beyond.* Cambridge: Cambridge University Press, pp. 318–327.

Hamel, Gary, and C. K. Prahalad (1994) *Competing for the Future.* Boston: Harvard Business School Press.

Hanley, Charles J. (1995) "Japan Keeps Open Unthinkable Option." *Washington Times,* May 12, 1995.

Harding, Harry (1994) "On the Four Great Relationships: The Prospects for China." *Survival* 36, no. 2 (Summer): 22–42.

Hasenclever, Andreas, Peter Mayer, and Volker Rittberger (1997) *Theories of International Regimes.* Cambridge, UK: Cambridge University Press.

Havlik, Peter, et al. (1999) "The Transition Countries in 1999: A Further Weakening of Growth and Some Hopes for Later Recovery." Research Report 257 of the Vienna Institute for International Economic Studies (WIIW), June.

Haynes, Richard E., and Gary Wheatley (1996) "Information Warfare and Deterrence." Strategic Forum 87. Washington, D.C., Institute for National Strategic Studies, October.

Hedegaard, Lars, and Bjarne Lindström (eds.) (1998) *The NEBI Yearbook, 1998: North European and Baltic Sea Integration.* Berlin: Springer.

Heisbourg, François (1997) *The Future of Warfare.* London: Phoenix.

———. (1999) "L'Europe de le defense dans l'Alliance atlantique." *Politique Etrangere,* no. 2 (Summer).

Helfer, Laurence, and Anne-Marie Slaughter (1997) "Toward a Theory of Effective Supranational Adjudication." *Yale Law Journal* 107, no. 2 (November): 290–298.

Herspring, Dale R. (1997) "The Future of the Russian Military." *Problems of Post-Communism* 2 (March-April): 47–56.

Heurlin, Bertil (1998) "NATO, Security, and the Baltic States: A New World, a New Security, and a New NATO." In Birthe Hansen and Bertil Heurlin (eds.) *Baltic States in World Politics.* Copenhagen: Curzon, pp. 65–85.

Hirst, Paul (1997) "The Global Economy—Myths and Realities." *International Affairs* 73, no. 3 (July): 409–425.

Hishow, Ognian (1999) *Der russische Haushalt, 2000: Ein Beitrag zur finanziellen Konsolidierung?* Köln: Aktuelle Analysen des BIOst 56 (30.11.).

———. (1999) *Rußland in der Schuldenfalle: Bedingungsloser Schuldenerlaß unzulässig.* Köln: Aktuelle Analysen des BIOst 4 (19.2.).

Historikerstreit (1987) *Die Dokumentation der Kontroverse um die Einzigartigkeit der nationalsozialistischen Judenvernichtung.* München: Piper.

Hoagland, Jim (1997a) "Debating Immigration the French Way." *Washington Post,* March 2, 1997.

———. (1997b) "South of Europe." *Washington Post,* March 6, 1997.

Hobsbawn, E. (1994) *Age of Extremes: The Short Twentieth Century, 1914–1991.* London: Michael Joseph.

Hoffman, Bruce (1998) *Inside Terrorism.* London: Victor Gollancz.

Hoffman, M. (1987) "Critical Theory and the Inter-Paradigm Debate." *Millennium: Journal of International Studies* 16: 231–249.

Holm, Hans-Henrik, and Georg Sørensen (eds.) (1995) *Whose World Order? Uneven Globalisation and the End of the Cold War.* Boulder: Westview.

Holsti, K. J. (1993) "Armed Conflicts in the Third World: Assessing Analytical Approaches and Anomalies." Paper presented at the annual meeting of the International Studies Association, Acapulco, Mexico, March 23–27.

———. (1996) *The State, War, and the State of War.* Cambridge: Cambridge University Press.

Homer-Dixon, T. (1994) "Environmental Scarcities and Violent Conflict: Evidence from Cases." *International Security* 19, no. 1 (Summer): 5–40.

———. (1991) "On the Threshold: Environmental Changes as Causes of Acute Conflict." *International Security* 16, no. 2 (Fall): 76–116.

Honig, Jan Willem (1994) "Interpreting Clausewitz." *Security Studies* 3, no. 3 (Spring): 571–580.

———. (1997) "Strategy in a Post-Clausewitzian Setting." In G. C. De Nooy (ed.) (1997) *The Clausewitzian Dictum and the Future of Western Military Strategy.* The Hague: Kluwer Law International, pp. 109–121.

Honig, Jan Willem, and Both Norbert (1996) *Srebrenica: Record of a War Crime.* Harmondsworth, UK: Penguin.

Hopmann, Terrence P., Stephen D. Shenfield, and Dominique Arel (1997) "Integration and Disintegration in the Former Soviet Union: Implications for Regional and Global Security." Providence, R.I.: Thomas J. Watson Institute for International Studies (Occasional Paper 30).

Horgan, John (1996) *The End of Science: Facing the Limits of Knowledge in the Twilight of the Scientific Age.* Reading, Mass.: Addison-Wesley.

Hua, Shi (1979) "Deng Xiaoping's Internal Speech on the Eve of the Sino-Vietnamese War." *Qishi Niandai* (Hong Kong), no. 4 (April): 25–26.

Huimin, Su (1993) "'Ouzhoude Deguo' haishi 'Deguode Ouzhou'?" ("European Germany" or "German Europe"?). *Guoji wenti yanjiu*, no. 1: 20–22.

Hunter, Robert E. (2000) "The Future of NATO and Transatlantic Relations." In Erich Reiter (ed.) *Jahrbuch für internationale Sicherheitspolitik, 2000.* Hamburg: Mittler Verlag, pp. 623–635.

Huntley, James Robert (1998) *Pax Democratica: A Strategy for the Twenty-first Century.* Basingstoke, UK: Macmillan.

Huysmans, Jeff (1998) "Revisiting Copenhagen: Or on the Creative Development of a Security Studies Agenda in Europe." *European Journal of International Relations* 4, no. 4 (December): 479–505.

Hyde-Price, A. (1991) *European Security Beyond the Cold War: Four Scenarios for the Year 2010.* London: Sage.

———. (1996) *The International Politics of East Central Europe.* Manchester: Manchester University Press.

———. (1997) "The New Pattern of International Relations in Europe." In Alice Landau and Richard Whitman (eds.) *Rethinking the European Union: Institutions, Interests and Identities* (London: Macmillan), pp. 15–35.

IFSH (1997) *OSZE-Hochkommissar für Nationale Minderheiten van der Stoel im Haus Rissen* [OSCE High Commissioner van der Stoel at House Rissen], in: IFSH aktuell 26.

Ignatieff, Michael (1998) *The Warrior's Honour: Ethnic War and the Modern Conscience.* London: Chatto and Windus.

International Institute for Strategic Studies (1997) *The Military Balance, 1997/1998.* London: Oxford University Press.

———. (1999) *The Military Balance, 1999/2000.* Oxford: Oxford University Press.

Jablonsky, David, and James S. McCallum (1999) "Peace Implementation and the Concept of Induced Consent in Peace Operations." *Parameters* (Spring).

Jackson, Robert H. (1990) *Quasi-States: Sovereignty, International Relations, and the Third World.* Cambridge: Cambridge University Press.

Jahn, E., P. Lemaitre, and O. Wæver (1987) "European Security—Problems of Research on Non-Military Aspects." Copenhagen Papers 1. Copenhagen: Centre for Peace and Conflict Research.

James, Barry (1997) "French Face Off over Immigration." *International Herald Tribune*, February 18, 1997.

————. (1997) "Immigration to France Unchanged in 20 Years." *International Herald Tribune*, February 28, 1997.

————. (1997) "New Victory of Far Right Stirs Doubts in France." *International Herald Tribune*, February 11, 1997.

Jehl, Douglas (1993) "China Breaking Missile Pledge." *Washington Times*, May 6, 1993.

Jepperson, Ronald L., Alexander Wendt, and Peter J. Katzenstein (1996) "Norms, Identity, and Culture in National Security." In Peter J. Katzenstein (ed.) *The Culture of National Security: Norms and Identity in World Politics*. New York: Columbia University Press, pp. 33–75.

Jervis, Robert (1978) "Cooperation Under the Security Dilemma." *World Politics* 30, no. 1 (January): 167–214.

————. (1981) "The Spiral of International Insecurity." In M. Smith, M. Shackleton, and R. Little (eds.) *Perspectives on World Politics*. Milton Keynes: Open University Press.

————. (1997) *System Effects: Complexity in Political and Social Life*. Princeton: Princeton University Press.

Job, Brian L. (1997) "Matters of Multilateralism: Implications for Regional Conflict Management." In David A. Lake and Patrick M. Morgan (eds.) *Regional Orders: Building Security in a New World*, University Park: Pennsylvania State University Press.

Joenniemi, Pertti (ed.) (1999) *Confidence-Building and Arms Control: Challenges Around the Baltic Rim*. Mariehamn: The Åland Islands Peace Institute.

————. (ed.) (1997) *Neo-Nationalism or Regionality? The Restructuring of Political Space Around the Baltic Rim*. Stockholm: NordREFO.

Joenniemi, P., S. Dewar, and L. Fairlie (2000) *The Kaliningrad Puzzle—A Russian Region Within the European Union*. Karlskrona: The Baltic Institute and the Åland Islands Peace Institute.

Joffe, J. (1995) "Deutsche Aussenpolitik—Postmodern." *Internationale Politik* 50, no. 1 (January): 43–45.

Kahl, Colin H.(1998–1999) "Constructing a Separate Peace: Constructivism, Collective Liberal Identity, and Democratic Peace." *Security Studies* 8, nos. 2–3 (Winter-Spring): 94–144.

Kaiser, Karl, and Hans-Peter Schwarz (eds.) (1995) *Die neue Weltpolitik*. Baden-Baden: Nomos Verlagsgesellschaft.

Kanin, David (1997) "The State, Its Dysfunction, and Ours." *International Politics* 34, no. 4 (December): 355–370.

Kapstein, Ethan B. (1996) "Workers and the World Economy." *Foreign Affairs* 75, no. 3 (May-June): 16–37.

Katzenstein, Peter J. (ed.) (1996) *The Culture of National Security: Norms and Identity in World Politics*. New York: Columbia University Press.

Kauffman, Stuard (1995) *At Home in the Universe: The Search for Laws of Self-Organization and Complexity*. New York: Oxford University Press.

————. (1993) *The Origins of Order: Self-Organization and Selection in Evolution*. New York: Oxford University Press.

Keat, R., and J. Urry (1975) *Social Theory as Science*. London: Routledge.

Keck, Margeret E., and Kathryn Sikkink (1998) *Activists Beyond Borders: Advocacy Networks in International Politics*. Ithaca: Cornell University Press.

Keegan, John (1993) *A History of Warfare*. London: Hutchinson.

————. (1999) "So the Bomber Got Through After All." *London Daily Telegraph*, June 4, 1999.

Kegely, Charles Jr. (1993) "Cold War Myths and the New International Realities: Reconsidering Theoretical Premises." *Österreichische Zeitschrift für Politikwissenschaft* 22, no. 2 (1993): 149ff.

Kendall, E. Bailes (1990) *Science and Russian Culture in an Age of Revolutions: V. I. Vernadsky and His Scientific School, 1863–1945.* Bloomington: Indiana University Press.

Kennedy, Paul (1987) *The Rise and Fall of the Great Powers: Economic Change and Military Conflict from 1500 to 2000.* New York: Random House.

Keohane, Robert (1993) "Institutionalist Theory and the Realist Challenge After the Cold War." In D. Baldwin (ed.) *Neorealism and Neoliberalism: The Contemporary Debate.* New York: Columbia University Press, pp. 269–300.

Keohane, Robert O., and Lisa L. Martin (1995) "The Promise of Institutionalist Theory." *International Security* 20, no.1 (Summer): 39–51.

Keohane, Robert O., and Joseph S. Nye (1993) "Introduction: The End of the Cold War in Europe." In Robert O. Keohane, Joseph S. Nye, and Stanley Hoffmann (eds.) *After the Cold War: International Institutions and State Strategies in Europe, 1989–1991.* Cambridge: Harvard University Press.

Keohane, Robert, and Joseph Nye (eds.) (1977) *Power and Interdependence.* Boston: Little, Brown.

————. (eds.) (1989) *Power and Interdependence.* 2nd ed. New York: HarperCollins.

————. (eds.) (1972) *Transnational Relations and World Politics.* Cambridge: Harvard University Press.

Kerr, William A., and Ed MacKay (1997) "Is Mainland China Evolving into a Market Economy?" *Issues and Studies* (Taipei) 33, no. 9 (September): 31–45.

Kim, Samuel S. (1994) "China's International Organizational Behaviour." In Thomas W. Robinson and David Shambaugh (eds.) *Chinese Foreign Policy: Theory and Practice.* New York: Clarendon, pp. 401–434.

————. (1996) "China's Quest for Security in the Post–Cold War World." Carlisle, Pa.: Strategic Studies Institute Monograph, U.S. Army War College, July 29.

Kissinger, Henry (ed.) (1994) *A World Restored.* Boston: Houghton Mifflin.

Klare, Michael, and Thomas Daniel (eds.) (1994) *World Security: Challenges for a New Century.* 2nd ed. New York: St. Martin's.

Klare, Michael, and Chandrani Yogesh (eds.) (1998) *World Security: Challenges for a New Century.* New York: St. Martin's.

Klein, Jean (1998) "Interface Between NATO/WEU and UN/OSCE." In Michael Brenner (ed.) *NATO and Collective Security.* Basingstoke, UK: Macmillan, pp. 249–277.

Klein, Paul (1993) *Probleme in multinationalen militärischen Verbänden am Beispiel der deutsch-französischen Brigade.* München: Sozialwissenschaftliches Institut der Bundeswehr (SOWI-Arbeitspapier nr. 83).

Knutsen, T. (1999) *The Rise and Fall of World Orders.* Manchester, UK: Manchester University Press.

Kolodziej, Edward A. (1997) "Order, Welfare and Legitimacy." *International Politics* 34, no. 2 (June): 111–151.

Kolodziej, Edward A., and Roger E. Kanet (eds.) (1996) *Coping with Conflict After the Cold War.* Baltimore: Johns Hopkins University Press.

Koskenniemi, Martti (ed.) (1998) *International Law Aspects of the European Union.* The Hague: Kluwer Law International.

Kovalio, Jacob (1991) "The 1989 Tiananmen Square Incident: Retrospective and Prospective Considerations." *Asian Perspective* 15, no. 1 (Spring-Summer): 5–36.

Krause, K., and M. Williams (eds.) (1997) *Critical Security Studies: Concepts and Cases*. London: UCL.

Krauss, Clifford (1997) "U.S. Doubtful Japanese Will Join Plan for Missile Defense." *New York Times*, February 14, 1997.

Kristof, Nicolas (1993) "China Raises Military Budget." *New York Times*, March 17, 1993.

Kropotkin, Petr (1924) *Ethics, Origin, and Development*. New York: Dial.

———. (1955) *Mutual Aid: A Factor of Evolution*. Boston: Extending Horizons.

Kugler, Richard L. (1996) *Enlarging NATO: The Russia Factor*. Santa Monica, Calif.: Rand.

Kühne, Winrich (1999) "Peace Support Operations: How to Make Them Succeed." *International Politics and Society* 4: 368–379.

Kydd, Andrew (1997) "Sheep in Sheep's Clothing: Why Security Seekers Do Not Fight Each Other." *Security Studies* 7, no. 1 (Autumn): 114–155.

Lachowski, Zdzislaw (1999) "Prospects for Regional Arms Control in the Baltic Sea Area." In Pertti Joenniemi (ed.) *Confidence-Building and Arms Control: Challenges Around the Baltic Rim*. Mariehamn: The Åland Islands Peace Institute, pp. 9–32.

Lake, David A., and Patrick M. Morgan (1997) "The New Regionalism in Security Affairs." In David A. Lake and Patrick M. Morgan (eds.) *Regional Orders: Building Security in a New World*. University Park: Pennsylvania State University Press, pp. 3–19.

Lampton, David M. (1994) "America's China Policy in the Age of the Finance Minister: Clinton Ends Linkage." *The China Quarterly* 139 (September): 597–621.

Landay, Jonathan S. (1997) "Clinton Team Forges Foreign Policy Vision." *Christian Science Monitor*, April 2, 1997.

Larrabee, Stephen L. (1997) *NATO Enlargement and the Post-Madrid Agenda*. Santa Monica, Calif.: RAND; and Cambridge: Cambridge University Press.

Lax, David A., and James K. Sebenius (1986) *The Manager as Negotiator: Bargaining for Cooperation and Competitive Gain*. New York: Free.

Layder, D. (1993) *New Strategies in Social Research*. Cambridge: Polity.

Lerner, Daniel, and Morton Gorden (1969) *Euratlantica: Changing Perspectives of the European Elites*. Cambridge: MIT Press.

Levy, M. (1995) "Is the Environment a National Security Issue?" *International Security* 20, no. 2 (Fall): 35–62.

Lewin, Roger (1992) *Complexity: Life at the Edge of Chaos*. New York: Macmillan.

Lin, Chong-Pin (1994) "Chinese Military Modernization: Perceptions, Progress, and Prospects." *Security Studies* 3, no. 4 (Summer): 718–780.

Lindström, G. (1997) *Sweden's Security Policy: Enlargement—the Middle Way*. Occasional Paper 2, Institute for Security Studies, Western European Union, Paris.

Linz, Juan J., and Alfred Stepan (1996) *Problems of Democratic Transition and Consolidation: Southern Europe, South America, and Post-Communist Europe*. Baltimore: Johns Hopkins University Press.

Lipschutz, R. (ed.) (1995) *On Security*. New York: Columbia University Press.

Liska, George (1962) *Nations in Alliance*. Baltimore: Johns Hopkins University Press.

Long, David (1997) "The CFSP and Beyond: The EU's Territorial and Functional Conceptions of Security." In Michel Fortmann (ed.) *Multilateralism and Regional Security.* Clementsport: The Canadian Peacekeeping Press, pp. 166–183.

Lord, Winston (1995) "For China, Not Containment but True Integration." *International Herald Tribune,* October 13, 1995, p. 8.

Lumsden, Charles J., and Edward O. Wilson (1981) *Genes, Mind, and Culture: The Coevolutionary Process.* Cambridge: Harvard University Press.

Luttwark, Edward N. (1996) "A Post-Heroic Military Policy." *Foreign Affairs* 75, no. 4 (July-August): 33–44.

———. (1995) "Toward Post-Heroic Warfare." *Foreign Affairs* (May-June): 109–122.

Lynn-Jones, S., and S. Miller (eds.) (1995) *Global Dangers: Changing Dimensions of International Security.* London: MIT Press.

Lyons, Terrence, and Ahmed I. Samatar (1995) *Somalia: State Collapse, Multilateral Intervention, and Strategies for Political Reconstruction.* Washington, D.C.: Brookings Institution.

MacGregor, Burns (1997) *Leadership.* New York: Harper and Row.

Mahncke, Dieter (1999) "The Role of the USA in Europe: Successful Past but Uncertain Future?" *European Foreign Affairs Review* 4, no. 3 (Autumn): 353–370.

Mann, M. (1996) "Authoritarian and Liberal Militarism: A Contribution from Comparative and Historical Sociology." In S. Smith, K. Booth, and M. Zalewski (eds.) *International Theory: Positivism and Beyond.* Cambridge: Cambridge University Press, pp. 221–239.

Marantz, Paul (1997) "Russian Foreign Policy During Yeltsin's Second Term." *Communist and Post-Communist Studies* 30, no. 4 (December): 345–352.

March, J. G., and J. P. Olsen (1989) *Rediscovering Institutions.* New York: Free.

Marshall, Ian, and Danah Zohar (1997) *Who's Afraid of Schrödinger's Cat: All the Science Ideas You Need to Keep Up with the New Thinking.* New York: Morrow.

Marshall, Ray (1995) "The Global Job Crisis." *Foreign Policy,* no. 100 (Fall): 50–68.

Matthews, Jessica T. (1997) "Power Shift." *Foreign Affairs* 76, no. 1 (January-February): 50–66.

Mattli, Walter (1999) *The Logic of Regional Integration: Europe and Beyond.* Cambridge: Cambridge University Press.

McSweeney, B. (1996) "Identity and Security: Buzan and the Copenhagen School." *Review of International Studies* 22, no. 1 (January): 81–93.

———. (1998) "Durkheim and the Copenhagen School: A Response to Buzan and Wæver." *Review of International Studies* 24, no. 1 (January): 137–140.

———. (1999) *Security, Identity, and Interests: A Sociology of International Relations.* Cambridge: Cambridge University Press.

Mearsheimer, John J. (1990) "Back to the Future." *International Security* 15, no. 1 (Summer): 5–56.

———. (1991) *Back to the Future: Instability in Europe After the Cold War.* Reprinted in Sean M. Lynn-Jones and Steven E. Miller (eds.) *The Cold War and After: Prospects for Peace.* Cambridge: MIT Press.

Metz, Steven (1997) "Which Army After Next? The Strategic Implications of Alternative Futures." *Parameters* (Autumn): 15–26.

Meyer, John W. (1980) "The World Polity and the Authority of the Nation-State." In Albert Bergesen (ed.) *Studies in the Modern World System.* New York: Academic, pp. 109–137.

Milanovic, Branko (1996) *Nations, Conglomerates, and Empires: The Tradeoff Between Income and Sovereignty.* World Bank Policy Research Working Paper 1675, October.

Möller, Kay (1993) "China in Ostasien: Die Renaissance der Pax sinica." In Albrecht Zunker (ed.) *Weltordnung oder Chaos?* Baden-Baden: Nomos, pp. 317–327.

Moore, Molly, and John Ward Anderson (1997) "U.S. Officials Visit Mexico for Parlay on Drug Policy." *Washington Post,* March 6, 1997.

Moravcsik, Andrew (1998) *The Choice for Europe: Social Purpose and State Power from Messina to Maastricht.* Ithaca: Cornell University Press.

———. (1992) *Liberalism and International Relations Theory.* Centre for International Affairs Working Paper, no. 6, July 1992.

Morgenthau, Hans (1985) *Politics Among Nations.* 6th ed. New York: Alfred A. Knopf.

Möttölä, Kari (1998) "Collective and Co-Operative Security Arrangements in Europe." In Martti Koskenniemi (ed.) *International Law Aspects of the European Union.* The Hague: Kluwer Law International, pp. 87–98.

——— (1997) "The OSCE: Institutional and Functional Developments in an Evolving European Security Process." In Michael Bothe, Natalino Ronzitti, and Allan Rosas (eds.) *The OSCE in the Management of Peace and Security: Conflict Prevention, Crisis Management, and Peaceful Settlement of Disputes.* The Hague: Kluwer Law International, pp. 1–33.

———. (1998) "Security Around the Baltic Rim: Concepts, Actors and Processes." In Lars Hedegaard and Bjarne Lindström (eds.) *The NEBI Yearbook, 1998: North European and Baltic Sea Integration.* Berlin: Springer, pp. 363–404.

Mueller, John (1994) "The Catastrophe Quot." *Journal of Conflict Resolution* 38: 335–375.

———. (1995) "The Perfect Enemy: Assessing the Gulf War." *Security Studies* 5, no. 1 (Autumn): 77–117.

———. (1995) *Quiet Cataclysm: Reflections on the Recent Transformation of World Politics.* New York: HarperCollins.

Mufson, Steven (1997) "Ethnic Turmoil Roils Western China." *Washington Post,* February 23, 1997.

———. (1997) "Major Speech Puts Li Peng in Spotlight." *Washington Post,* March 2, 1997, p. A-22.

Myers, Norman (1993) *Ultimate Security: The Environmental Basis of Political Stability.* New York: W. W. Norton.

NATO (1995) *Study on NATO Enlargement.* Brussels: NATO.

Naumann, Klaus. "NATO's New Military Command Structure." *NATO Review,* no. 1 (Spring): 11.

Naumkin, Vitaly (1998) "The Russian-Iranian Relations: Present Status and Propsects for the Future." *Perceptions* 3, no. 1 (March-May): 67–85.

Nelson, Daniel N. (1994) "American and Collective Security in Europe." *Journal of Strategic Studies* 17, no. 4 (December): 105–124.

———. (1999) "Balkans Need More than Stability." *Los Angeles Times,* July 30, 1999.

———. (1996) "Civil Society Endangered." *Social Research* 63, no. 2 (Summer): 345–368.

———. (2000) "Dangerous Assumptions." *Bulletin of the Atomic Scientists* (July-August): 24–28.

———. (1997) "Germany and the Balance Between Threats and Capacities in Europe." *International Politics* 34, no. 1 (March): 63–78.

————. (1994) "Great Powers and World Peace." In Michael Klare and Thomas Daniel (eds.) *World Security: Challenges for a New Century*. 2nd ed. New York: St. Martin's.

————. (2000) "Kosovo One Year Later." *Boston Globe*, March 24, 2000.

————. (1999) "NATO Emerges with Blood on Its Hands." *Boston Globe*, June 14, 1999.

————. (1997) "Threats and Capacities, and Germany." *International Politics* 34, no. 1 (March): 63–78.

Newhouse, John (1997) "Europe's Rising Regionalism." *Foreign Affairs* 76, no. 1 (January-February): 67–84.

Nowak, Martin A., et al. (1995) "The Arithmetics of Mutual Help." *Scientific American* 272, no. 6 (June): 76–81.

Nye, Joseph (1990) *Bound to Lead: The Changing Nature of American Power*. New York: Basic.

————. (1997) "China and the Future of the Asia Pacific Region." Paper presented to IISS annual conference, Singapore, September 14, 1997.

————. (1997–1998) "China's Re-emergence and the Future of the Asia-Pacific." *Survival* 39, no. 4 (Winter): 65–79.

Nye, Joseph, and Sean Lynn-Jones (1988) "International Security Studies." *International Security* 12, no. 4 (Spring): 5–27.

Nye, Joseph S. Jr., and William A. Owens (1996) "America's Information Edge." *Foreign Affairs* 75, no. 2, (March-April): 20–36.

O'Neill, Michael (1996) *The Politics of European Integration: A Reader*. London and New York: Routledge.

Odom, William E. (1997) "Transforming the Military." *Foreign Affairs* 76, no. 4 (July-August): 54.

Offe, Claus (1994) *Der Tunnel am Ende des Lichts: Erkundigungen der politischen Transformationen im Nahen Osten* [The Tunnel at the End of the Light. Inquiries into the Political Transformations in the Near East]. Frankfurt/M.

Onuf, Nicolaus Greenwood (1997) *The Republican Legacy in International Thought*. Cambridge: Cambridge University Press.

Organization for Economic Cooperation and Development (OECD) (1997) *Final Report of the Ad Hoc Working Group on Participatory Development and Good Governance*. Paris: OECD.

Organization for Security and Cooperation in Europe (OSCE) (1996) *OSCE Handbook*. Vienna: OSCE Secretariat.

Overholt, William H. (1996) "China After Deng." *Foreign Affairs* 75, no. 3 (May-June): 63–78.

Ozolina, Zaneta (1998) "The Impact of EU and NATO Enlargement on Baltic-Nordic Cooperation." In Aivars Stranga (ed.) *The First Round Enlargements: Implications for Baltic Security*. Riga: The Latvian Institute of International Affairs, University of Latvia, pp. 41–101.

Paribatra, Sukhumband (1994) "From ASEAN Six to ASEAN Ten: Issues and Prospects." *Contemporary Southeast Asia* 16, no. 3 (December): 243–258.

Paris, Roland (1997) "Peacebuilding and the Limits of Liberal Internationalism." *International Security* 22, no. 2 (Fall): 54–89.

Pechstein, Matthias, and Christian Koenig (1998) *Die Europäische Union: Die Verträge von Maastricht und Amsterdam*. 2nd ed. Tübingen: Mohr Siebeck.

Pennock, J. Roland (1996) "Political Development, Political Systems, and Political Goods." *World Politics* 18, no. 2 (April).

Pentikäinen, Merja (1997) "The Human Dimension of the OSCE in the 1996 Vienna Review Meeting." *Helsinki Monitor* 8, no. 1: 1–18.

―――. (1998) "The 1997 Implementation Meeting on Human Dimension Issues of the OSCE." *Helsinki Monitor* 9, no. 2: 18–37.

Peters, B. Guy (1999) *Institutional Theory in Political Science. The "New Institutionalism."* London. New York: Pinter.

―――. (1996) "Political Institutions, Old and New." In Robert E. Goodin and Hans-Dieter Klingemann (eds.) *A New Handbook of Political Science.* Oxford: Oxford University Press, pp. 205–220.

Peters, Ingo (1996) "Die Beziehungen der OSZE zu anderen internationalen Organisationen." Iin Institut für Friedensforschung und Sicherheitspolitik an der Universität Hamburg (ed.) (1996) *OSZE-Jahrbuch, 1996.* Baden-Baden: Nomos Verlagsgesellschaft, pp. 417–434.

―――. (1994) "Normen—und Institutionenbildung der KSZE im Widerstreit politisch-er Interessen: Die Durchsetzung des Gewaltverzichts als Prüfstein für die KSZE." In Bernard von Plate (ed.) *Europa auf dem Wege zur kollektiven Sicherheit? Konzeptionelle und organisatorische Entwicklungen der sicherheitspolitischen Institutionen Europas.* Baden-Baden: Nomos Verlagsgesellschaft, pp. 155–186.

―――. (1997) "Von der KSZE zur OSZE: Überleben in der Nische kooperativer Sicherheit." In Helga Haftendorn and Otto Keck (eds.) *Kooperation jenseits von Hegemonie und Bedrohung. Sicherheitsinstitutionen in den internationalen Beziehungen.* Baden-Baden: Nomos Verlagsgesellschaft, pp. 57–100.

Porto, Giovanni (1999) "Albania's Path to Democracy—New Law on Civil Service." *OSCE Newsletter* 6, nos. 11–12 (November-December): 8–10.

Pöschl, Josef, et al. (2000) "Transition Countries Clamber Aboard the Business Boom in Western Europe. Upswing Masks Persistent Transition-Related Problems." Research Report 264 of the Vienna Institute for International Economic Studies (WIIW), February.

Powell, Colin (1996) *My American Journey.* New York: Ballantine.

Prins, G. (1998) "The Four-Stroke Cycle in Security Studies." *International Affairs* 74, no. 4 (October): 781–808.

Prins, Gwyn, and Robbie Stamp (1991) *Top Guns and Toxic Whales: The Enviroment and Global Security.* London: Earthscan.

Prunier, Gérard (1997) *The Rwanda Crisis: History of a Genocide.* London.

Putnam, Robert D. (1988) "Diplomacy and Domestic Politics: The Logic of Two-Level Games." *International Organization* 42, no. 3 (Summer): 427–460.

Pye, Lucian W. (1990) "China: Erratic State, Frustrated Society." *Foreign Affairs* 69, no. 4 (Fall): 56–74.

Ray, S. (1980) *Decline in World Power Trends and U.S. Foreign Policy.* Boulder: Westview.

Record, Jeffrey (1999–2000) "Operation Allied Force: Yet Another Wake-Up Call for the Army?" *Parameters* (Winter): 15–23.

Reinalda, Bob, and Bertjan Verbeek (1999) "Autonomous Policy Making by International Organizations: Purpose, Outline, and Results." In Bob Reinalda and Bertjan Verbeek (eds.) *Autonomous Policy Making by International Organizations.* London and New York: Routledge, pp. 1–8.

Reiter, Erich (ed.) (2000) *Der Krieg um das Kosovo 1998/1999.* Mainz: v. Hase and Koehler.

―――. (2000) *Jahrbuch für internationale Sicherheitspolitik, 2000.* Hamburg: Mittler Verlag.

Reschke, Brigitte (1997) "Der OSZE-Hochkommissar für nationale Minderheiten" [The OSCE's High Commissioner on National Minorities]. *Humanitäres Völkerrecht—Informationsschriften* 2: 101–103.

Richter, Andrew (1999) *The Revolution in Military Affairs and Its Impact on Canada: The Challenge and the Consequences.* Institute of International Relations, University of British Columbia Working Paper no. 28, March.

Risse-Kappen, T. (1994) "Ideas Do Not Float Freely: Transnational Relations, Domestic Structures, and the End of the Cold War." *International Organization* (Spring).

Robinson, Gwen (1997) "Targeted by Washington." *Financial Times,* April 29, 1997.

Rohde, Joachim (1997) *The Roles of Arms Industries in Supporting Military Operations.* Ebenhausen: Stiftung Wissenschaft und Politik (AP 3045).

Rosas, Allan, and Lahelma Timo (1997) "OSCE Long-Term Missions." In Michael Bothe, Natalino Ronzitti, and Allan Rosas (eds.) *The OSCE in the Maintenance of Peace and Security: Conflict Prevention, Crisis Management, and Peaceful Settlement of Disputes.* The Hague: Kluwer Law International.

Rosenau, James N. (1994) "New Dimensions of Security: The Interaction of Globalization and Localizing Dynamics." *Security Dialogue* 25, no. 3 (September): 255–281.

———. (1990) *Turbulence in World Politics: A Theory of Change and Continuity.* Princeton: Princeton University Press.

Rosenberg, Nathan, and I. E. Birdzell Jr. (1986) *How the West Became Rich: The Economic Transformation of the Industrial World.* New York: Basic Books.

Rosner, Jeremy D. (1995–1996) "The Know-Nothings Know Something." *Foreign Policy* 101 (Winter): 116–129.

Rotberg, Robert I. (1996) "Clinton Was Right." *Foreign Policy* 102 (Spring): 135–142.

Rousseau, David L., Christopher Gelpi, and Dan Reiter (1996) "Assessing the Dyadic Nature of the Democratic Peace, 1918–1988." *American Political Science Review* 90, no. 3 (September).

Ruggie, John G. (1998) *Constructing the World Polity: Essays on International Institutionalization.* London: Routledge.

———. (1993) "Multilateralism: The Anatomy of an Institution." In John Gerard Ruggie (ed.) *Multilateralism Matters: The Theory and Practice of an Institutional Form.* New York: Columbia University Press, pp. 3–47.

———. (1996) *Winning the Peace.* New York: Columbia University Press.

Rühle, Michael (2000) "Das neue strategische Konzept der NATO und die politische Realität." In Erich Reiter (ed.) *Jahrbuch für internationale Sicherheitspolitik, 2000.* Hamburg: Mittler Verlag, pp. 637–654.

Rusi, Alpo M. (1997) *Dangerous Peace: New Rivalry in World Politics.* New York: Westview.

Russell, Frederick H. (1975) *The Just War in the Middle Ages.* Cambridge: Cambridge University Press.

Russett, Bruce M. (1993) *Grasping the Democratic Peace: Principles for the Post–Cold War World.* Princeton: Princeton University Press.

Russett, Bruce, John Oneal, and David R. Davis (1998) "The Third Leg of the Kantian Tripod for Peace: International Organizations and Militarized Disputes, 1950–1985." *International Organization* 52, no. 3 (Summer): 441–467.

Sahnoun, Mohamed (1994) *Somalia: The Missed Opportunities.* Washington, D.C.: United States Institute of Peace.

Sakwa, Richard, and Mark Webber (1999) "The Commonwealth of Independent States, 1991–1998: Stagnation and Survival." *Europe-Asia Studies* 51, no. 3 (May): 379–415.

Schauble, Wolfgang (1994) *Und der Zukunft zugewandt.* Berlin: Siedler Verlag.

Schlotter, Peter (1996) "Von der KSZE zur OSZE: Marginalisierung oder neue Aufgaben?" [From CSCE to OSCE—Marginalization or New Responsibilities?]. In Hanne-Margret Birckenbach, Uli Jäger, and Christian Wellmann (eds.) *Jahrbuch Frieden, 1996,* Munich: C. B. Beck, pp. 111–124.

Schmidl, Erwin A. (1995) "The Austrian Medical Unit in the Congo, 1960–1963: Austria's First Participation in a UN Operation." Maintien de la Paix de 1815 à aujourd'hui, Actes 21 (Ottawa: Commission canadienne d'histoire militaire 1995), pp. 629–635.

———. (1995) *Blaue Helme, Rotes Kreuz: Das österreichische UN-Sanitätskontingent im Kongo, 1960 bis 1963, Innsbrucker Forschungen zur Zeitgeschichte 13.* Innsbruck—Wien: StudienVerlag.

———. (1997) "Im Land der Skipetaren: Die internationale Friedensoperation in Albanien 1913—1914." *Österreichische Militärische Zeitschrift* 35, no. 4 (July-August): 431–440.

———. (ed.) (2000) *Peace Operations Between Peace and War.* London: Frank Cass.

———. (1998) *Police in Peace Operations.* Vienna: Austrian Ministry of Defence (Studien zur Sicherheitspolitik, No. 11).

Schmidt, Peter (1996) "Security Challenges and Institutional Responses: A German Perspective." In Gunilla Herolf (ed.) *Europe—Creating Security Through International Organizations.* Stockholm: Swedish Institute of International Affairs, pp. 73–84.

———. (1997) "Stand und Perspektiven der NATO-Erweiterung." In Erich Reiter (ed.) *Österreichisches Jahrbuch für internationale Sicherheitspolitik, 1997.* Vienna: Styria, pp. 245–259.

———. (ed.) (1992) *In the Midst of Change: On the Development of West European Security and Defense Cooperation.* Baden-Baden: NOMOS.

Schmidt-Skipiol, Joachim (1997) *Die Militärreform in Rußland, Teil I: Sachstandsbericht.* Köln: Aktuelle Analysen des BIOst 48 (25.9.).

———. (1997) *Die Militärreform in Rußland, Teil II: Ausblick.* Köln: Aktuelle Analysen des BIOst 49 (25.9.).

Schneider, Heinrich (1997) "The Twelve/Fifteen's Conference Diplomacy: Has the CSCE/OSCE Remained a Successful Platform?" In Elfriede Regelsberger et al. (eds.) *Foreign Policy of the European Union: From EPC to CFSP and Beyond.* Boulder: Lynne Rienner Publishers, pp. 237–262.

Schröder, Hans-Henning (1997) *Die russischen Militärausgaben 1995–1997. Eine Auswertung der Haushaltsdaten.* Köln: Berichte des BIOst 23.

Schulz, John J. (1998) "China as a Strategic Threat: Myths and Verities." *Strategic Review* 26, no. 1 (Winter): 5–16.

Scott, W. Richard (1995) *Institutions and Organizations.* Thousand Oaks, Calif.: Sage.

Sergounin, Alexander (1998) *Russia: A Long Way to the National Security Doctrine.* Copenhagen Peace Research Institute, Working Papers no. 10.

Shambaugh, David (1996) "China's Military in Transition: Politics, Professionalism, Procurement, and Power Projection." *The China Quarterly* no. 146: 265–298.

———. (1998) "China's Security Policy in the Post–Cold War Era." *Survival* 34, no. 2 (Summer): 88–106.

———. (1996) "China in 1995: A Balance Sheet." *The Official Journal* (January): 34–38.

Sharp, Jane M. O. (1998) "CFE and the Baltic Rim." In Lars Hedegaard and Bjarne Lindström (eds.) *The NEBI Yearbook, 1998: North European and Baltic Sea Integration.* Berlin: Springer,: pp. 423–437.

Sheehan, Michael (1996) *The Balance of Power.* London: Routledge.

Sieff, Martin (1995) "U.S. Probes China on Missiles." *Washington Times,* July 9, 1995.

Siemienski, Guillaume, and John Packer (1997) "Integration Through Education: The Origin and Development of the Hague Recommendations." *International Journal on Minority and Group Rights* 4: 187–198.

Simon, Gerhard (1997) *Rußland auf der Suche nach seiner politischen Identität. Visionen und Wirklichkeiten.* Köln: Berichte des BIOst 33.

Smith, M. L. R. (1997) *Fighting for Ireland? The Military Strategy of the Irish Republican Movement.* London: Routledge.

Smith, M., M. Shackleton, and R. Little (eds.) (1981) *Perspectives on World Politics.* Milton Keynes: Open University Press.

Smith, S., K. Booth, and M. Zalewski, eds. (1996) *International Theory: Positivism and Beyond.* Cambridge: Cambridge University Press.

Snyder, Jack, and Robert Jervis (eds.) (1993) *Coping with Complexity in the International System.* Boulder: Westview.

Solana, Javier (1999) "NATO's Success in Kosovo." *Foreign Affairs* 78, no. 6 (November-December): 114–120.

Soros, George (1996) "Can Europe Work?" *Foreign Affairs* 75, no. 5 (September-October): 8–14.

Spence, Arnhild, and David Spence (1998) "The Common Foreign and Security Policy from Maastricht to Amsterdam." In Kjell A. Eliassen (ed.) *Foreign and Security Policy in the European Union.* Thousand Oaks, Calif.: Sage, pp. 48–58.

Steans, Jill (1998) *Gender and International Relations.* Cambridge: Polity.

Stein, Arthur A. (1990) *Why Nations Cooperate: Circumstance and Choice in International Relations.* Ithaca: Cornell University Press.

Stein, Torsten (1997) "Rechtsfragen des Eurokorps und der deutsch-französischen Brigade." In Christian Tomuschat (ed.) *Rechtsprobleme einer europäischen Sicherheits- und Verteidigungspolitik.* Heidelberg: C. F. Müller Verlag, pp. 53–68.

Stephens, J. C., et al. (1998) "Dating the Origin of the CCR5-Delta 32 AIDS-resistance Allele by the Coalescence of Haplotypes." *American Journal of Human Genetics* 62, no. 6 (June): 1507ff.

Stranga, Aivars (ed.) (1998) *The First Round Enlargements—Implications for Baltic Security.* Riga: The Latvian Institute of International Affairs, University of Latvia.

Sugawara, Sandra (1997) "Japanese Face Up to Need for Change." *International Herald Tribune,* March 10, 1997.

Sweeney, John (1996) "Stuck in Haiti." *Foreign Policy* 102 (Spring): 143–151.

Talbott, Strobe (1998) *Address to the Paasikivi-Society* (Helsinki). January 21. 1998.

Tao, Bingwei (1996) "Dongbeiya jushide fazhan bianhua" [Changes in the Development of the Northeast Asian Situation]. *Guoji wenti yanjiu* no. 2 (April): 13–16.

Terriff, T., et al. (1999) *Security Studies Today.* Cambridge: Polity.

Thomson, James (1997) "A New Command for NATO's New Mission." In David C. Gombert and F. Stephen Larrabee (eds.) *America and Europe: A Partnership for a New Era.* Cambridge: Cambridge University Press, pp. 79–103.

Thun-Hohenstein, Christoph (1998) *Der Vertrag von Amsterdam. Die neue Verfassung der EU.* Wien: Manz.

Thurow, Lester (1993) *Head to Head: The Coming Economic Battle Among Japan, Europe, and America.* New York: Warner Books.

Tickner, J. A. (1995) "Re-visioning Security." In K. Booth and S. Smith (eds.) *International Relations Theory Today.* Oxford: Polity, pp. 175–197.

Tilford, Earl H. Jr. (1999–2000) "Operation Allied Force and the Role of Air Power." *Parameters* (Winter): 24–38.

Tirpak, John A. (1999) "Lessons Learned and Re-learned." *Air Force Magazine* (August), p. 23.

Toynbee, Arnold J. (1934–1961) *A Study of History,* 12 vols. New York: Oxford University Press.

Trenin, Dmitri (2000) "Russian-Chinese Relations: A Study in Contemporary Geopolitics." In Erich Reiter (ed.) *Jahrbuch für Internationale Sicherheitspolitik, 2000.* Hamburg: E. S. Mittler, pp. 913–930.

Tsoukalis, Loukas (1997) "Why Europe's Global Record Is So Patch." In Philip Morris Institute for Public Policy Research, *What Global Role for the EU?* Brussels, September, pp. 65–73.

Ullman, R. (1983) "Redefining Security." *International Security* 8, no. 1 (Summer): 129–153.

United Nations Development Program (UNDP) (1996) *Human Development Report, 1995.* New York: Oxford University Press.

United Nations Economic Commission for Europe (1999) *Economic Survey of Europe, no. 3* (electronic version: http://www.unece.org/ead/ead_h.htm).

United States Information Agency (USIA) (1995) *The New European Security Architecture.* Washington, D.C.: USIA Office of Research and Media Reaction, September.

Van Creveld, Martin (1991) *On Future War.* London: Brassey's (published as *The Transformation of War* in the United States by Free Press).

Van den Broek, Hans (1996) "The Council of Europe and the European Union: Complementing Each Other." In *The Challenges of a Greater Europe and Democratic Security.* Strasbourg: Council of Europe, pp. 173–175.

Van der Meulen, J. S. (1997) "Post-Modern Societies and the Future Support of Military Missions." In G. C. De Nooy (ed.) *The Clausewitzian Dictum and the Future of Western Military Strategy.* The Hague: Kluwer Law International.

Van der Stoel, Max (1997) "Minorities in Transition." In *War Report* no. 48 (January-February): 16.

———. (1999) *Peace and Stability Through Human and Minority Rights, Speeches by the OSCE High Commissioner on National Minorities.* Ed. Wolfgang Zellner and Falk Lange. Baden-Baden.

———. (1998) "Report of Mr. Max van der Stoel, OSCE High Commissioner on National Minorities." Warsaw, November 12, 1997. *Helsinki Monitor* 9, no. 1: 68–76.

———. (1994) "The Role of the CSCE High Commissioner on National Minorities in CSCE Conflict Prevention." Address to the Seminar "The CSCE as a Security Tool in Europe: Which Role for the CSCE?." Brussels, June 4, 1994.

Van Eekelen, Willem (1998) *Debating European Security.* The Hague: Sdu Publishers.

Van Ham, Peter (forthcoming) *Testing Cooperative Security in Europe's North: American Perspectives and Policies* (forthcoming in a publication from the Finnish Institute of International Affairs).

Van Oudenaren, John (1996) "Die Transatlantische Agenda." *Internationale Politik* 51, no. 5 (May): 49–52.

Van Rensen, Peter (1997) *Informationsbedarf der Gemeinsamen Aussen- und Sicherheitspolitik der Europäischen Union: Ansatzpunkte für eine Bewertung.* Ebenhausen: Stiftung Wissenschaft und Politik (IP 3046).

Van Riper, Paul, and F. G. Hoffman (1998) "Pursuing the Real Revolution in Military Affairs: Exploiting Knowledge-based Warfare." *National Security Studies Quarterly* 4, no. 3 (Summer): 4.

Vasquez, J. (1998) *The Power of Power Politics: From Classical Realism to Neotraditionalism.* Cambridge: Cambridge University Press.

Wæver, Ole (1997) "The Baltic Sea: A Region After Post-Modernity?" In Pertti Joenniemi (ed.) *Neo-Nationalism or Regionality? The Restructuring of Political Space Around the Baltic Rim.* Stockholm: NordREFO, pp. 293–342.

————. (1996) "European Security Identities." *Journal of Common Market Studies* 1, no. 34 (March): 103–132.

————. (1995) "Securitization and Desecuritization." In R. Lipschutz (ed.) *On Security.* New York: Columbia University Press.

Wæver, O., et al. (1993) *Identity, Migration, and the New Security Agenda in Europe.* London: Pinter.

Wallace, W. (1999) "Europe After the Cold War: Interstate Order or Post-Sovereign Regional System?" *Review of International Studies* (Special Issue, "The Interregnum: Controversies in World Politics, 1989–1999") 25 (December): 201–224.

Wallander, Celeste (1999) *Mortal Friends, Best Enemies: German-Russian Cooperation After the Cold War.* Ithaca: Cornell University Press.

Wallander, Celeste A., and Robert O. Keohane (1999) "Risk, Threat, and Security Institutions." In Helga Haftendorn, Robert O. Keohane, and Celeste A. Wallander (eds.) *Imperfect Unions: Security Institutions over Time and Space.* Oxford: Oxford University Press, pp. 21–47.

Wallerstein, Immanuel (1979) *Capitalist World-Economy.* Cambridge: Cambridge University Press.

————. (1991) *Geopolitics and Geoculture.* Cambridge: Cambridge University Press.

Walt, Stephen M. (1987) *The Origins of Alliances.* Ithaca: Cornell University Press.

————. (1991) "The Renaissance of Security Studies." *International Studies Quarterly* 35, no. 2 (June): 211–239.

Waltz, Kenneth N. (1993) "The Emerging Structure of International Politics." *International Security* 18, no. 2 (Fall): 44–79.

————. (1979) *Theory of International Politics.* Reading, Mass.: Addison-Wesley.

Wan, Lingying (1993) "Mayue fengbo jiqi yingxiang" [Disputes About the Maastricht Treaties and Their Implications]. *Guoji wenti yanjiu* no. 3: 13–19.

Wang, Jisi (1996) "China-Politik der USA: Eindämmung oder Engagement?" *Beijing Rundschau,* October 22, 1996, pp. 6–9.

Wängeborg, Manne (1995) "The OSCE at 20: Breakthrough for 'Citizen Diplomacy'? Towards Closer OSCE-NGO Interaction?" *European Security* 4, no. 3 (Autumn): 393–399.

Wassenberg, Philipp (1999) *Das Eurokorps: Sicherheitsrechtliches Umfeld und völkerrechtliche Bedeutung eines multinationalen Grossverbands.* Baden-Baden: Nomos.

Weiss, Charles (1997) "A Marshall Plan We Can Afford." *Foreign Policy* 106 (Spring): 94–109.

Wendt, Alexander (1994) "Collective Identity Formation and the International State." *American Political Science Review* 88, no. 2 (June): 384–396.

Wessels, Gert, and Günter Winzen (1996) "Interoperabilität und Ausrüstung." In Ernst Martin (ed.) *Eurokorps und Europäische Einigung.* Bonn: Edition Zeitgeschichte, pp. 375–418.

Wheeler, N., and K. Booth (1992) "The Security Dilemma." In J. Baylis and N. Rengger (eds.) *Dilemmas of World Politics: International Issues in a Changing World.* Oxford: Clarendon.

The White House (1995) *A National Strategy of Engagement and Enlargement.* Washington, D.C.: The White House, February.

Wie, Yang (1995) "How China Views the World and How It Should Face It." *Liaowang* (official journal of the Communist Party of China), December 11.

Wieland, Joachim (1999) "Ausländische Vorgesetzte deutscher Soldaten in multinationalen Verbänden." *Neue Zeitschrift für Wehrrecht* 41, no. 4 (July-August): 133–142.

Wiener, Jarrod (1995a) "'Hegemonic' Leadership, Naked Emperor, or Worship of False Gods?" *European Journal of International Relations* 1, no. 2 (June): 219–243.

———. (1995b) "Leadership, the United Nations, and the New World Order." In Dimitri Bourantonis and Jarrod Wiener (eds.) *The United Nations in the New World Order: The World Organization at Fifty.* New York: St. Martin's, pp. 41–63.

———. (1995c) *Making Rules in the Uruguay Round of the GATT: A Study of International Leadership.* Aldershot, UK: Dartmouth.

Williams, M. (1998) "Modernity, Identity, and Security: A Comment on the 'Copenhagen Controversy.'" *Review of International Studies* 24, no. 3 (July): 435–439.

Williams, Michael C. (1998) *Civil-Military Relations and Peacekeeping.* Adelphi Paper 321. Oxford: Oxford University Press for IISS.

———. (1997) "The Institutions of Security: Elements of a Theory of Security Organizations." *Cooperation and Conflict* 32, no. 3 (September): 287–307.

Wilson, Edward O. (1998) *Consilience: The Unity of Knowledge.* New York: A. A. Knopf.

Woodward, Susan L. (1995) *Balkan Tragedy: Chaos and Dissolution After the Cold War.* Washington, D.C.: Brookings Institution.

World Bank (1994) *Governance: The World Bank's Experience.* Washington, D.C.: The World Bank.

Wright, Robert (2000) *Nonzero: The Logic of Human Destiny.* New York: Pantheon.

Young, Oran R. (1991) "Political Leadership and Regime Foundation: On the Development of Institutions in International Society." *International Organization* 45, no. 3 (Summer): 288–302.

Zaagman, Rob (1994) "The CSCE High Commissioner on National Minorities: An Analysis of the Mandate and the Institutional Context." In Arie Bloed (ed.) *The Challenges of Change: The Helsinki Summit of the CSCE and its Aftermath.* Dordrecht: Martinus Nijhoff, pp. 113–175.

Zacher, Mark W. (1992) "The Decaying Pillars of the Westphalian Temple: Implications for International Order and Governance." In James N. Rosenau and Ernst-Ottto Czempiel (eds.) *Governance Without Government: Order and Change in World Politics.* Cambridge: Cambridge University Press.

Zagorski, Andrei (1997) "Die Politik Rußlands gegenüber der GUS—zwischen Anspruch und Wirklichkeit." *Österreichische Zeitschrift für Politikwissenschaft* 3 (Special Issue, "Rußländische Transformationen. Räume, Akteure, Felder"): 319–329.

Zellner, Wolfgang (1999) *On the Effectiveness of the OSCE Minority Regime: Comparative Case Studies on Implementation of the Recommendations of the High Commissioner on National Minorities of the OSCE—A Research Project of IFSH*. Hamburg: Hamburger Beiträge zur Friedensforschung und Sicherheitspolitik (Heft 111).

Zellner, Wolfgang, and Pal Dunay (1998) *Ungarns Außenpolitik 1990—1997. Zwischen Westintegration, Nachbarschafts und Minderheitenpolitik* [Hungary's Foreign Policy 1990—1997: Between Western Integration, Neighborhood, and Minority Policy]. Baden-Baden.

Zimmermann, Tim (1987) "The American Bombing of Libya: A Success for Coercive Diplomacy?" *Survival* 29 (May-June): 195–214.

Zöckeler, Markus (1995) "Germany in Collective Security Systems—Anything Goes?" *European Journal of International Law* 6, no. 2 (Spring): 274–286.

Zürn, Michael (1995) "The Challenge of Globalisation and Individualisation: A View from Europe." In Hans-Henrik Holm and Georg Sørensen (eds.) *Whose World Order? Uneven Globalisation and the End of the Cold War*. Boulder: Westview, pp. 137–164.

Zydowics, Krzysztof (1997) "Nationality Versus Regionality: A Central–East European Perspective Pertaining to the Southern Baltic." In Pertti Joenniemi (ed.) *Neo-Nationalism or Regionality? The Restructuring of Political Space Around the Baltic Rim*. Stockholm: NordREFO, pp. 54–84.

The Contributors

Heiko Borchert, Consultant and Independent Researcher, Lucerne

Walter C. Clemens Jr., Professor of Political Science, Boston University; Associate Professor, Harvard University Belfer Center for Science and International Affairs and Davis Center for Russian Studies

Heinz Gärtner, Professor, Institute for Political Science, University of Vienna; Senior Researcher, Austrian Institute for International Affairs

Jan Willem Honig, Senior Lecturer, Department of War Studies, King's College, London; Visiting Fellow, Center of International Studies, Princeton University

P. Terrence Hopmann, Professor of Political Science and Research Director, Program on Global Security, Thomas J. Watson Institute for International Studies, Brown University

Adrian Hyde-Price, Professor, Institute for German Studies, University of Birmingham

Pertti Joenniemi, Senior Researcher, Copenhagen Peace Research Institute

Walter Kemp, OSCE Public Information Officer; Lecturer, London School of Economics

Gerhard Mangott, Research Fellow, Austrian Institute for International Affairs, Laxenburg

Kay Möller, Senior Research Fellow, Stiftung Wissenschaft und Politik, Ebenhausen

Kari Möttölä, Special Adviser, Security Policy, Finnish Ministry of Foreign Affairs, Helsinki

Daniel N. Nelson, Professor of Democratization and Civil-Military Relations, George C. Marshall Center for European Security Studies, Garmisch, Germany

Erich Reiter, Director General, Department of Strategic Studies, Austrian Ministry of Defense; Head of the Bureau for Military Scientific Studies, Vienna

David Robertson, Professor, St. Hugh's College, Oxford

Alpo M. Rusi, Adviser to the President of the Republic of Finland; Deputy Special Coordinator of the Stability Pact for Southeastern Europe, Brussels

Erwin A. Schmidl, Researcher, Institute for Military Science, Vienna

Peter Schmidt, Head of Department, Stiftung Wissenschaft und Politik, Ebenhausen

Wolfgang Zellner, Research Fellow, Institute for Peace Research and Security Policy, University of Hamburg

Index

457

Eurasia, 247–249, 332–333
Euro-Atlantic Partnership Council
(EAPC), 14, 127–130, 192, 326
European Bank for Reconstruction and
Development, 191
European Commission, 132, 188–190
European Council, 132–133, 181
European Court of Human Rights
(ECHR), 170
European Court of Justice (ECJ): crisis
management, 132; doctrine of direct
effect, 193; foreign and security
policy role, 195–196; human rights,
170; monitoring and enforcing
international norms, 173, 199
European Monetary Union (EMU),
362–363
European Rapid Deployment Force, 114
European Security and Defense Identity
(ESDI), 197, 339; cooperative
development of, 130; EU foreign
policy and, 362; strengthening of,
201–203; three criteria for mission-
oriented structure, 137
European Union (EU), 11, 13–15, 20,
165; admission criteria, 190–191;
Central Asia and, 336–338; crisis
management, 135(table), 143(table);
Dayton Accords implementation,
242–244; development of CFSP,
155–156; economic power and
security-political role, 113–114, 168;
enlargement of, 53(n71), 151–152,
161(n1), 176–177; ESDI
establishment, 202; EU-Russian
relations, 401–402; future policy
issues, 155–157; institutional
framework for conflict management,
305; institutional incentives for
defection, 181–182, 182(table);
institutions of, 209(n13);
interinstitutional relations, 137–139,
177–179; International Peacebuilding
Mission, 201(fig.); move toward
defense autonomy, 129–130;
multilateral cooperation, 45;
multilateralism, 363–365; norms for
international behavior, 169–171, 303;
passive institutional leadership,
188–189; potential global role,
115–120, 362–363; role in Kosovo

crisis, 121–122; security function
reform, 153; WEU merger, 157–158.
See also individual states
European Union/Western European
Union (EU/WEU), 14, 165, 300,
306–307. *See also* European Union;
Western European Union
Evolution, 56–57
Executive leadership, 188–189

Falkland Islands conflict, 80
Feminist perspective, on security, 35
Finland, 118, 323–326
Fitness, 56, 59–64
Foreign investment, in Russian
economy, 383–384
Foundation on Inter-Ethnic Relations,
273
Fragmegration, 8–9
France, 155–156; controlling EU, 117;
focus on crisis management, 132;
multilateralism, 363–364, 376(n50);
organizational and policy
compatibility, 150; OSCE Contact
Group, 233; role in global security,
362
Freedom of the Media Representative,
228, 256, 285
Front Nationale, 364
Frowick, Robert, 243

Gamsakhurdia, Zviad, 222–223
General Agreement on Tariffs and Trade
(GATT), 4–9, 120
Geopolitics, 332–333
Georgia, 331; conflict resolution, 238;
cooperation efforts, 391, 405(n38);
postconflict peacekeeping, 236; rise
of ethnopolitical conflict, 221–223;
territorial autonomy arrangements,
270
German Political Science Association,
263
Germany, 195; Chinese view of
unification, 409–410; controlling EU,
117; multilateralism, 363–365;
NATO's enlargement, 152; OSCE
Contact Group, 233; role in global
security, 362
Globalization, 8–10, 113, 115

NATO/EU/WEU consultation and cooperation, 136–139; organizational and policy compatibility, 149–150; OSCE relations, 250; peace operations in Kosovo, 344; political objectives of collective security, 307–308; post-conflict peacekeeping, 236; restructuring for modern needs, 126–130; selective engagement, 139–144; U.S. role in, 185
NATO-Russia Act, 195
NATO-Ukraine Charter, 195
Natural resources, 19; Caspian Sea area, 331–332; growing dependence on, 116; as justification for Iraqi invasion, 95–96
Natural selection, 56
Naval resources, 71
Neomedieval international system, 8
Neorealism, 41, 56, 63, 223–224
Neoutilitarianism, 31
Non–Article 5 operations. *See* Crisis management
Nongovernment institutions (NGOs), 262–263
Nonmilitary concerns, 32–34
Nonstate actors, 93, 183
Nordic Council, 310
Nordic regions, 323–325
Norms: and democratic peace, 169–171; as effective counter to interstate wars, 94–97; enforcing, 172–173; improving rule orientation, 199; monitoring the implementation of, 171–172
North Atlantic Treaty Organization. *See* NATO
North Korea, 97
Norway, 323
Nuclear weapons, 46, 253(n3); Chinese-Iranian cooperative security, 418–419; Chinese-U.S. cooperative security, 415–418; development of CFSP, 156–157; ESDI establishment, 202–203; Indian-Pakistani relations, 335; Japan-China-U.S. relations, 421–422; postmodern arms control, 317–318; Russia-China-U.S. relations, 418–420; Russia-Japan-China relations, 420–421; Russian

status, 388, 406(n65); theater missile defense, 367–368
Nye, Joseph, 35

Obuchi, Keizo, 367
Office for Democratic Institutions and Human Rights (ODIHR), 227, 243–245, 257, 262
Open Skies Treaty, 193
Operation Alba, 244
Operational capabilities concept (OCC), 129
Operation Allied Force, 121–122
Operation Desert Storm, 104
Organization for Security and Cooperation (OSCE), 11, 15–17, 59, 184, 253(n7), 326; admission criteria, 190–191; Assistance Group to Chechnya, 312(n12); binding effects of CFSP instruments, 193–195; collective security, 299–302; common policy, 191–192; conflict management and resolution, 225–226, 236–242; conflict resolution, 236–242; core competence, 186; decisionmaking, 175; democratic structures, 173–174; democratization as long-term conflict management, 226–230; employee exchange, 198; engaging NGOs and academics, 262–263; Eurasian security, 249–252; evolution and growing awareness of, 256–258; goals of peacekeeping operations, 344; implementation and enforcing of norms, 169–173; institutional framework for conflict management, 304–306; institutional incentives for defection, 181–182, 182(table); interinstitutional relations, 177–179, 198; International Peacebuilding Mission, 201(fig.); low profile of, 259–260; majority voting for integration, 192–193; norms for international behavior, 169–170, 303–304; passive institutional leadership, 188–189; political objectives of collective security, 307–308; political security, 168; political will and public awareness, 255–256; postconflict security building, 242–247; preventive

About the Book

A central point of controversy among both academics and policymakers is the nature and significance of security in the post–Cold War world. Engaging that discussion, this original collection explores the new security challenges facing Europe.

The authors assess the relevance and usefulness of various actors and various approaches for tackling those security challenges. Seeking to avoid dichotomous thinking, their nuanced efforts probe the areas of ambiguity and complexity between war and peace, conflict and cooperation, "hard" and "soft" security, and state and society.

Heinz Gärtner is senior researcher at the Austrian Institute for International Affairs and professor of political science at the University of Vienna. His *Models of European Security* was awarded the prestigious Bruno Kreisky Award. **Adrian Hyde-Price** is senior lecturer at the University of Birmingham, England, based jointly at the Institute for German Studies and the Centre for Russian and East European Studies. His publications include *European Security Beyond the Cold War: Four Scenarios for Europe in 2010* and *The International Politics of East Central Europe*. **Erich Reiter** is professor of international economic and social relations at the University of Graz, Austria; he has also served as commissioner for strategic studies and head of the Institute for Military Science at the Austrian Federal Ministry of Defense. He is author of numerous publications, including *Neutralität: Mythos und Wirklichkeit*.